# SAILING DRIFTERS
★

*By the same author*

SPRITSAIL BARGES OF THAMES AND MEDWAY
SAILING TRAWLERS

## "THE OLD ORDER CHANGETH"

L.T. 944 *I'LL TRY*, Early steam drifter 33 tons, built 1902 at Galmpton.

L.T. 724 *SWEET BUD*, 39 tons, built 1897 at Lowestoft.

# SAILING DRIFTERS

*by*

*Edgar J. March*
Associate of the Royal Institution of Naval Architects

★

THE STORY OF THE HERRING LUGGERS
OF ENGLAND, SCOTLAND
AND THE ISLE OF MAN

★

DAVID & CHARLES : NEWTON ABBOT
INTERNATIONAL MARINE PUBLISHING COMPANY, CAMDEN, MAINE, USA

ISBN: 0 7153 4679 2

© 1969 Edgar J. March

First published in 1952 by Percival Marshall & Company Limited
Reissued in this edition by David & Charles (Publishers) Ltd 1969
Second impression 1972
Third impression 1978

## INTRODUCTION 1969

It gave me great pleasure when David & Charles suggested a re-issue of this book as following its publication in 1952 I received so many letters telling of the interest roused in my story of the old sailing drifters and the enormous catches of herring made before the 1914-18 war. Alas! over-fishing by modern intensive methods and other causes have brought about a catastrophic decline in landings and near disaster to the once prosperous Yarmouth Fishery. The immense fleets of Scottish boats no longer come south as in the days of sail and the early steam drifters. It just does not pay. Year after year I have noted the fall in the number of crans landed, often scarcely the equivalent of a few days' hauls sixty or more years ago.

On the other hand pilchard catches in Cornish waters are almost too prolific. Fashions have changed, bulking ceased long ago, canning is hardly worthwhile owing to the big imports of tinned pilchards, and so huge landings remain unsold.

Recently I had a visit from Dr. Alexander Wood who told me that his grandfather designed and built the first Zulu *Nonsuch* for William Campbell and that his family were building boats and steam drifters at Lossiemouth until about 1918. He spoke of his first visit on board a Zulu at the age of four, his recollections of the magnificent sight a fleet made leaving or coming back to harbour and how ashore curers were busy salting and barrelling the herring for the Russian market. A few months back a Russian vessel landed herring at Yarmouth!

In a 21-page letter John Hall of Berwick-on-Tweed wrote of his memories of the past and how he "liked to dwell upon the period of 70 years ago when as a boy I spent the happiest years of my life amidst the scenes you describe."

Writing of the Sunday morning scene in the Tweed dock he goes on "the summer mornings were full of sunshine then, scores of fishing boats lying as if they, as well as their crews, were enjoying the weekend leisure, their brown sails stowed and galley chimneys smoking and the sound of the Church Bells ringing across the river, all was at peace.... To this day I always remember the names of the Scottish boats whose crews were made up of sturdy, quiet, independent men and never once can I remember any harsh or undesirable conduct among them. I often wondered who chose the names of the boats such as *Integrity, Concord, Fidelity, Dauntless, Kindly Light, Family's Pride, Good Tidings, Consolation.* No wonder that the names of the boats typified the class of men. I have yet to meet a more contented group of men who can equal them. These were men who never had luxuries of any kind. How different from the present affluent age... St. Ives' boats berthed side by side all along the beach... we could buy four freshly cured kippers at the price of one penny, and the best of fresh herring at three a penny."

My research into the old ways of fishing was only just in time. Many of the fine fishermen I knew found it surprising that I should find worth recording what was to them just a way of life, but here in these pages their story remains for all time.

Edgar J. March
Green Acre
Colwell Bay
Freshwater, Isle of Wight

*Printed in Great Britain by Lowe & Brydone Printers Limited, Thetford, Norfolk*
*Published by David & Charles (Publishers) Limited, Brunel House, Newton Abbot, Devon*

*To*

*The tens of thousands of fishermen, known unto God,*
*who sleep in the deep waters*
*or in churchyards hard by the sea.*

★

# PREFACE

For generations the cliffs around our coasts have seen the warm-coloured sails of fishing boats stealing out from little harbours bound for grounds which have yielded their silver harvest since Time was.

These fleets have now sailed beyond the horizon of man's sight, never to return, and seem likely to vanish into the gloaming of forgotten things unless some record be made whilst it is still possible to contact those who knew them.

The time this book should have been written was fifty years ago when sail rode the waters as a thing of life and beauty. In the interim two fierce storms of man-made violence have swept this country, the first saw the extinction of the sailing drifter, during the second priceless records have vanished, some to swell salvage drives, others burnt up on the funeral pyre of Nazi hate. Then the fatal propensity to clear away "Dad's old junk" has seen irreplaceable papers and photographs destroyed without any data having been recorded, while many an old salt has carried his hard-won knowledge with him to the grave.

Time has had a flying start, and now it is impossible to work to windward of him, but fortunately a few fishermen, who have long since passed man's allotted span, have seen my signals, borne down to my assistance, and in penmanship a joy to read have told me of days, fifty, sixty, nay seventy and more years ago. One and all, even those who at the end of a long and arduous life have sought refuge in the almshouse, speak with affection of the days of sail. Many a man has said to me "They were happy days."

Fortunes have been lost and won from the sea, but none can value the debt owed to those hardy pioneers, who in tiny craft faced the perils of the seas, and on whose efforts rose the great industry we know to-day. Some attained wealth, while others lost their all, for the sea is a cruel mistress who claims her toll of those wooing her favours. A fisherman's life has ever, and will always be a hazardous one. Though man has devised new and cunning inventions, the sea remains as of yore. Dynasties and civilisations have left their mark on the face of the earth, but the turbulent waters around our shores, swirling and contending as they have done since the dawn of history and will do until the end of time, show no trace of the tens of thousands of keels which have furrowed their surface. Great battles have their chronicles, and innumerable names of warriors are written on the scrolls of fame, but scarce indeed are the records of those who have waged ceaseless war to glean the harvest of the sea. Those splendid men matched their skill and puny strength against the forces of nature, that though the tempest raged yet should it not prevail, wresting a living from the cold, hungry sea, enduring hardships untold, that folk ashore might have fish.

None can measure the depth of the cup of bitterness, filled to overflowing with the tears of women and children, for be it remembered when grumbles are raised at the price of fish that it is bought, not only with gold, but with men's lives. To gather the fruits of the earth calls for toil and sweat, but to garner the harvest of the deep needs blood and tears as well.

In order to keep this volume to a reasonable size I have had to confine my research to the principal fishing stations, leaving the smaller ports, such as Hastings, etc., where beach boats were used, to a subsequent book. Throughout I have endeavoured to obtain my information first-hand from the few surviving old men who can recall the days of sail in its prime, and their names are mentioned in the text. I and everyone interested in the past owe a deep debt of gratitude to them, without their valued co-operation it would have been an almost impossible task to present an authentic picture of a way of life now gone for ever. In, alas, too many instances I only just caught the tide as to my knowledge at least three of my helpers have slipped their cables, Thos. Adams, R. W. Crome, and Wm. Peek, whilst others now in failing health told me their stories before it was too late.

As over half a century has passed since sailing drifters were built in any numbers, it will be realised how difficult it has proved to trace accurate data, so much was never committed to paper, but stored in wise old heads, having been handed down from father to son. Plans were not used save in one or two exceptional cases, fortunately some of the St. Ives designs remain after over eighty years. Few half models have survived the passing years, and I count myself fortunate in having had the privilege of taking off the lines of two from which Scots fifies were built, thanks to the courtesy of Mr. W. P. Miller, of St. Monance.

I also wish to record my sincere appreciation of the help given by others whom I mention, especially the splendid co-operation of Mr. H. Oliver Hill, a fellow member of the Society for Nautical Research, a painstaking and enthusiastic recorder of Cornish craft, and a photographer after my own heart. His unfailing assistance has proved invaluable in many ways.

Before the war the Coastal Craft sub-committee of the Society for Nautical

Research had made a start at taking off the lines of any boats still available, and the late Mr. P. J. Oke prepared excellent plans of several before the outbreak of hostilities put an end to such research. The late Sir Geoffrey Callender kindly placed them at my disposal, and I have been able to obtain photostats of many from the Science Museum at South Kensington. I am indebted to the Director for permission to reproduce photographs of some of the excellent models in that collection.

The Royal National Lifeboat Institution also assisted me with information, and my thanks are due to the Ministry of Agriculture and Fisheries for permission to quote from their voluminous statistics containing many an interesting item, of which I have made full use. The few back numbers of Olsen's Almanacks which I have been able to handle also yielded fruitful returns.

In Isle of Man waters I was held up for months waiting for a slant before I picked up a fair wind by contacting Mr. Basil Megaw, Director of the Manx Museum, whose efforts at trying to preserve the unwritten history of the past through the medium of the Manx Folk Life Survey provided the means to get into touch with old fishermen, sailmakers and others, who answered my questionnaires in a most gratifying manner. Mrs. Anne Barishnikov, of Port St. Mary, and Miss Z. M. Sayle, of Castletown, were assiduous in taking down all the material in shorthand.

In many waters I shot my nets and caught nothing, but in Scotland I had a rich haul when I wrote to Mr. Wm. McIntosh of Buckie, who not only sent data on construction, but gave me the names of Mr. Wm. Imlach and Mr. John Addison, who both made valuable contributions. Mr. McIntosh and Mr. Imlach most kindly took the trouble to check over the MS. of my chapters on Scottish luggers, thus ensuring accuracy.

For suitable photographs I searched high and low, finding in attic and cellar many a superb plate, neglected and forgotten these many years, but I did *not* explore the well down which a priceless collection of plates was flung some years ago. Once again my old friend Capt. F. C. Poyser, of the Nautical Photo Agency, supplied me with a large number of negatives.

The authentic plans, some available for the first time, should enable model makers to enlarge their scope of activity and build delightful replicas which would be a welcome breakaway from more conventional designs.

The threads that make up the warp and weft of my canvas have thus come from many sources, and if a few of the bolts are not so strong as I could have wished, I hope they will suffice to carry some record of the old sailing luggers and drifters into that future which seems destined to be purely mechanical; and if my efforts help to preserve the memory of the splendid men who manned them, my task will not have been in vain.

*Westgate-on-Sea, Kent.*                                                  EDGAR J. MARCH.

*PHOTOGRAPH ACKNOWLEDGMENTS*

Mr. A. Artis 18. Mr. E. Bowness 57, 188, 189. Mr. W. Bryant 99. Mr. Peter Cowie 150, 161. Mr. W. S. Cumming 151. Mr. F. C. Faragher 130, 138, 139. Mrs. Elsie Garden 183. Mr. C. J. Greene 74. Mr. R. H. Green 23.

Mr. H. Oliver Hill
    14, 32, 51, 59, 60, 61, 62, 63, 64, 65, 66, 67, 68, 69, 70, 71, 72, 73, 76, 77, 78, 79, 80, 81, 82, 84, 85, 88, 89, 90, 91, 92, 93, 95, 96, 97, 98, 101, 102, 103, 104, 105, 106, 107, 108, 109, 110, 111, 114, 115, 119, 120, 121, 122, 123, 124, 125, 126, 140, 141, 142, 143, 144, 145, 152, 170, 177, 186, 190.

The late Mr. James Hornell 127, 128.

Messrs. H. Jenkins
    Frontispiece, 4, 5, 7, 8, 9, 10, 11, 12, 13, 15, 16, 26, 27, 28, 34, 35, 36, 38, 39, 43, 44, 45, 46, 47, 48, 49, 52, 53, 117, 156, 168, 169, 171, 174, 175, 176, 181, 182, 184.

Mr. W. T. Kelly 146. City of Liverpool Museums 137. Margate Public Library 37. Mr. L. W. Moore 6.

National Maritime Museum
    86, 87, 112, 147, 155, 157, 158, 160, 162, 163, 164, 165, 166, 178, 179, 180, 185, 191.

Nautical Photo Agency
    19, 20, 21, 22, 24, 29, 30, 31, 33, 40, 50, 83, 94, 116, 118, 132, 133, 134, 135, 136, 153, 154, 167.

Mr. J. Phillips 100. Science Museum, South Kensington (Crown copyright) 1, 2, 17, 75, 113, 129, 131, 159, 187. Messrs. J. & W. Stuart 148. The Times 58. Messrs. A. & S. Yallop, Ltd. 25, 41, 42, 54, 55, 56, 172, 173.

# CONTENTS

PREFACE

PHOTOGRAPH ACKNOWLEDGMENTS

| Chapter One | HISTORICAL | 1 |
| --- | --- | --- |
| Chapter Two | DEVELOPMENT OF THE LUGSAIL | 15 |
| Chapter Three | DRIFT NET FISHING | 23 |
| Chapter Four | EAST COAST LUGGERS | 34 |
| Chapter Five | CONVERSION TO DANDY RIG | 55 |
| Chapter Six | THE GREAT AUTUMN FISHERY | 76 |
| Chapter Seven | CORNWALL | 97 |
| Chapter Eight | EAST CORNISH LUGGERS | 117 |
| Chapter Nine | WEST CORNISH LUGGERS | 138 |
| Chapter Ten | ISLE OF MAN | 179 |
| Chapter Eleven | SCOTLAND | 223 |
| Chapter Twelve | FIFIES AND ZULUS | 254 |
| Chapter Thirteen | YORKSHIRE COAST | 289 |

| GLOSSARY | 359 |
| --- | --- |
| LIST OF PLATES | 367 |
| LIST OF FIGURES | 373 |
| LIST OF SCALE PLANS | 375 |
| INDEX | 377 |

## CONTENTS

**Chapter One — HISTORICAL**
Early references to fishing—barrelled herring—Dutch competition—herring busses.

**Chapter Two — DEVELOPMENT OF LUGSAIL**
Early square sail rig—introduction of two and three masts—change over to dipping lug—3-masted luggers—methods of going about.

**Chapter Three — DRIFT NETS**
Herring shoals—drift net fishing—early twine nets—an old fisherman's story—cotton nets—trawling for herring.

**Chapter Four — EAST COAST LUGGERS**
3-masted Yarmouth lugger—construction—work in a shipyard—plans of 2-masted lugger *Gipsy Queen*—masting and rigging—crew's duties—shooting the nets—big hauls.

**Chapter Five — EAST COAST DRIFTERS**
Conversion to dandy rig—introduction of steam capstans—inventory of a drifter—Lowestoft and Yarmouth drifters—speed—plans of Lowestoft drifter *Strive*—masting and rigging—sailmaking—costs of building.

**Chapter Six — THE GREAT AUTUMN FISHERY**
Cracking on—entering port in bad weather—Caister lifeboat disaster—counting the catch—reminiscences of drifter skippers—French drifters—shares—early steam drifters and costs—barrel making—curing.

**Chapter Seven — CORNWALL**
Historical—3-masted luggers—improvements due to coming of railway—navigating instruments used—"yawlers"—mackerel and pilchard driving—storm damage and losses.

**Chapter Eight — EAST CORNISH LUGGERS**
Transom sterned boats—harbours—plans of Polperro "gaffer" *Gleaner*—plans of Mevagissey lugger—masting and rigging—sail plan—nets and fishing seasons.

**Chapter Nine — WEST CORNISH LUGGERS**
Early boats—plans of St. Ives boats—pilchard and mackerel drivers—plans of *Ebenezer*—construction—speed—nets used—differences between St. Ives and Mount's Bay boats—plans of counter-sterned *Colleen Bawn*—construction—launch—costs—sail plan—sailmaking—handling a lugger at sea—fishing seasons—plans of mackerel driver *Boy Willie*—masting and rigging—decline of the fishing.

Chapter Ten              ISLE OF MAN

Historical—cutters and luggers—nickeys and nobbies—Kinsale fishing—old fishermen's stories—Shetland fishing—plans of nickey *Expert*—masting, rigging and sailmaking—plans of nobby *Gladys*—decline of the fishing.

Chapter Eleven            SCOTLAND

Historical—1848 disaster to fishing fleet—inquiries into the disaster—plans of early open scaffies and fifies—method of fishing—introduction of decked boats—old fisherman's experiences in scaffies—plans of scaffie yawl *Gratitude*—fifies—introduction of zulus.

Chapter Twelve            FIFIES AND ZULUS

Improved hull designs—1881 disaster—life in a fishing village—notable record of a boat building firm—half models of fifies—plans of fifies—fishing seasons—earnings—handling the big luggers—building a fifie—plans of *True Vine*—masting, rigging and sailmaking—plans of skiff—building a zulu—plans of *Fidelity*—sailmaking—zulu skiffs—decline of sail.

Chapter Thirteen           YORKSHIRE COAST

3-masted luggers—yawls—construction of luggers—fishing—change over to dandy rig—Conclusion.

CHAPTER ONE

# *HISTORICAL*

FISHING must have been one of the first occupations to engage the attentions of primitive man, since the acquiring of food has ever been a paramount necessity for survival. The means employed to capture fish must be purely conjectural, but one can imagine that throwing pieces of rock at passing shoals may have been some tribesman's bright idea of obtaining a dinner, and as civilisation developed, by spearing or hooking with hardwood crooks sharpened with flints. While these methods would suffice to supply the needs of a man and his family, more wholesale means were required as populations increased, and obstructions made by interlacing branches of trees may well have been the forerunner of nets, the making of which was known in Ancient Egypt, to judge from wall paintings depicting seine nets.

Broadly speaking, edible fish are divided into two main groups: pelagic, which swim near the surface, and demersal, those found in the lower depths and on the seabed. Each demands an entirely different method of fishing. The first are meshed in a wall of nets submerged a few fathom below the surface, the second can only be caught on a baited hook or by means of a trawl net dragged along the bottom. Hooking is of time immemorial, but trawling is a comparatively recent innovation.

Man's ingenuity fashioned hooks from bones or sharpened pieces of hardwood twigs, and discoveries from excavations of Roman camps show that fishermen nearly 2,000 years ago had little to learn from the modern design of fish hooks. Constant reference to fishing is found in the Scriptures. Isaiah 19, viii: "the fishers also shall mourn, and all they that cast angle into the brooks shall lament, and they that spread nets upon the waters shall languish. Moreover, they that work in fine flax, and they that weave networks, shall be confounded." Frequent mention of the "Casting of nets into the sea" tells that this method of enmeshing fish was already well known.

The coming of Christianity and the ordinances of the Roman Catholic faith, calling for the eating of fish—fresh or salt—on certain days, must have given a tremendous impetus to the fisheries. The unwieldy coracles used by the Ancient

Britons could have been suitable only for inshore fishing in favourable weather, but the raids on the East Coast by the fierce Norse pirates left a lasting legacy, as their magnificent clench-built longships influenced the design of local craft right down to present times. On our South-west shores, however, carvel building—a Mediterranean practice—suggests a closer contact with Latin neighbours. Contemporary evidence, c. 1140, shows the fishing vessels to be small open boats, rowed by 14 to 26 oars, and setting a single square sail when the wind was fair. Such craft regularly went from Hastings to take part in the Yarmouth fisheries. Longshore fishermen have always favoured the open boat, propelled by sail and oar until the coming of the steam and motor engine revolutionised the type of vessel used.

The monks showed considerable astuteness in founding their abbeys near rivers and estuaries where fish were plentiful, witness Whitby Abbey, within sight of the immense shoals of herring passing in the summer, or the Priory on the Isle of May, amid the fisheries in the Firth of Forth, which were controlled by the Brethren, who alone had the authority to grant licences for fishing. Somehow that word has a familiar sound to-day! It is not unreasonable to suppose that they engaged in the herring fisheries themselves, and that their conventional dress of cowl and robe survived in the shape of the sou'wester and long duffle coat which was the common form of attire until mass-produced oilskins replaced home-made articles.

Salt fish and pickled herring were staple articles of diet in the Middle Ages, and cod fishing was pursued as far north as Iceland, a lengthy and hazardous voyage for the unwieldy vessels of those days. Just how long prior to 1415 it is impossible to discover, but in that year the King of Denmark, who had sovereignty over that bleak island in the Northern Seas, complained to Henry V about the conduct of English fishermen, who, no doubt, painted the town red when they went ashore for a spree after weary weeks of isolation from the pleasures of the land. The buying of salted fish from the local inhabitants of the Orkneys and Shetlands was an established trade, and in Henry VIII's reign about 150 vessels were engaged in the Icelandic fishery, that the sending of fishing craft to those distant waters is of considerable antiquity, and not a modern development by steam trawlers, as is sometimes supposed. These "coggs" sailed from ports all down the East Coast as far south as Ramsgate, whilst "barks" from Bristol went west about to Northern waters. So numerous were the complaints about the fishermen's behaviour that in 1585 Queen Elizabeth had to sit up and take notice to the extent of issuing an Order in Council "hauling them over the coals" for their excesses, and officers were appointed at various ports to take bonds from men sailing for Iceland to ensure their good behaviour. In spite of all these regulations, the trouble continued, and a few years later the Danes took the law into their own hands, seized several vessels, and would only permit fishing under licence from their own king.

The catching and barrelling of the herring has had a greater influence on the history of nations than is generally realised. Much of the wealth of the Hanseatic Towns was derived from the herring which frequented the Baltic until 1425, when they suddenly changed their habits and deserted those waters, never to return in vast numbers again. It will be recalled that these Hanse merchants—the Easterlings— came to this country and founded a steelyard in Cannon Street in London, probably the origin of the term "Sterling," and strange to say, I recently saw the name "Easterlings" on a lorry passing through Westgate-on-Sea. The importance of the fisheries to the inhabitants of our island had been recognised as far back as 1284, when on the 16th May the Fishmongers' Company was formed, one of the ancient guilds which still thrives to-day, and in 1357 was passed the famous "Statute of Herrings," which brought the industry under a certain amount of Government control. The Cinque Ports figure largely in the history of herring fishery. In 1067 the Barons appointed bailiffs to govern the great Herring Fair at Yarmouth, where Hastings men held the right of dene and strand, a situation which led to many bitter quarrels with the local fishermen, whose ancestors were catching herring when Yarmouth was but a sandbank gradually increasing in size as silt raised its level. During the long centuries of Roman occupation many nationalities resorted thereto, as the garrison afforded protection against pirates. The records of the Monastery at Evesham, founded c. 710, contain references to sums paid for salted herring, which were brought inland on the backs of packhorses. At Beccles a rental of thirty thousand herring was paid to the Abbey of St. Edmund, later increased to sixty thousand in Norman times. The Norfolk town was granted its first charter by King Henry I in 1108, and in return for many privileges, the Kentish and Sussex ports had to find so many vessels and men for the King's service when need arose. The fishing industry has always provided seamen to man the fleet, and the two recent wars have shown the splendid response of fishermen to the call of duty.

In 1209 King John granted a charter on condition that a payment of £55 was made for ever, and 57 ships were provided for 40 days at the town's charge as often as the wars gave him occasion to demand them. During these frequent clashes of arms many a barrel of salted herring was shipped to France for consumption by the English armies who must have found the French wines welcome after meals of such thirst-provoking food. On the 12th February, 1429, Sir John Fastolfe, who owned land and a castle at Caister, was convoying salted herring for the troops besieging Orleans when he met the French under the Duc de Bourbon, and defeated them in a battle which has come down in history as "The Battle of Herrings."

When the herring forsook the Baltic and teemed in the North Sea, the thrifty Dutch were quick to see the wealth to be had for the trouble of taking, and after van Beukels of Biervliet perfected the method of preserving herring c. 1386, they held the key of a treasure-house whose riches made the fabled wealth of the Incas fade into insignificance. Whilst other nations pursued the chimera of easily-obtained gold and silver, the burghers of Holland amassed riches from the humble herring, built fine towns and beautiful homes, the admiration of the civilised world until the Hun wreaked his vengeance upon them in 1940, urged on by yet another who sought easy money. But the true source of a nation's prosperity is trade and commerce, which is not produced by the issue of edicts and regulations, or by the creation of scrip, as many a theorist has discovered sooner or later.

The Flemings, who had built up their fisheries, saw them wither away before Dutch competition, and by the middle of the 16th century their trade diminished until they scarcely caught sufficient to supply their own needs, whilst the Dutch fleets increased in numbers from about 1,000 in 1560 to 1,500 fifty years later, and by 1620 over two thousand vessels were engaged, and their barrelled herring were exported all over the civilised world.

The Scottish kings were always rather touchy about foreigners fishing in their waters, and sought by licence and otherwise to restrict fishing liberties. Access to firths and bays was prohibited, prompted more by a desire to obtain revenue easily for the replenishment of depleted exchequers than concern for their nationals, since there was plenty of fish for all. The Dutch were not allowed to fish within a "land-kenning" of the coast, or no nearer than where they could discern the land from the masthead. This distance was about fourteen miles, but at times the authorities insisted on greater distances. On the other hand, in English waters French, Dutch, Fleming and Swede fished without let or hindrance, and each made use of the other's ports in case of need. This fraternisation was of mutual benefit, fishermen were quick to see advantages in another's methods, and such an interchange of ideas improved craft and gear.

In 1532 war broke out following the refusal of King James V to allow the Dutch to fish for herring off the Scottish coast, and it was not until 1545 that a truce was concluded. These restrictive policies were introduced into English waters soon after James VI of Scotland became James I of England, and united the crowns of the two countries. In 1610 Parliament prohibited any foreign vessel fishing off our coasts unless a heavy duty was paid. Here was a pretty kettle of fish. Ambassadors and lesser lights sped between The Hague and London, the Dutch claimed immunity by reason of ancient custom and from the fact that they had been instrumental in establishing the great Herring Fair at Yarmouth, where, from Michaelmas, September 29, to Martinmas, November 11, French, Norman, Fleming and Hollander attended to barter their produce.

The immediate result of this government interference with trade was the complete failure of the herring fishing off the East Coast. Prices rose steeply for the few fish landed by the small craft then used by our fishermen, and a last of herring fetched over £15 against £10 in the money of those days, which was about five times the value of the sovereign in pre-1914 days, and only a political mathematician can work out what it was worth in to-day's paper currency. No doubt the spectacle of thousands of Dutch vessels fishing off our shores was a mortifying sight, but the fish were there, free for all, and it was up to our men to use the same ingenuity as that displayed by other seafaring nations. Three years later the price of a barrel of red herring was 20s., an unheard-of sum.

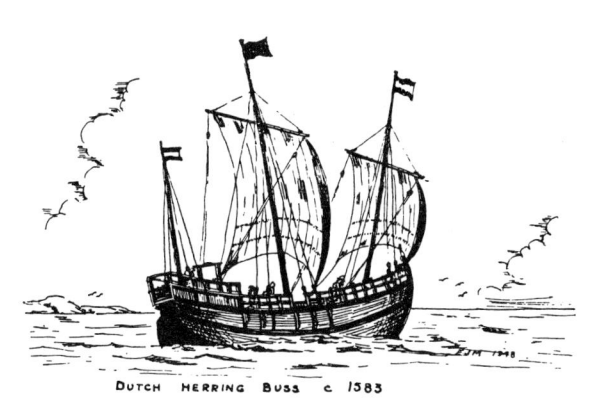

FIGURE 1

DUTCH HERRING BUSS c. 1583

The Dutch had brought drifting to a fine art—the first drift nets were made at Hoorne early in the 15th century—and they were supreme in every method of preserving the fish. Year after year an enormous fleet of busses, schuits, jagers, pinks, doggers, and other picturesquely named craft sailed from Holland for Northern waters, assembling at Bressay Sound in the Shetlands during early June, then they left in fleets under the direction of a commodore and were guarded by men-of-war. They were not permitted to start fishing until St. John's Day, the 24th June. The period when the fishing might begin was fixed at five minutes past twelve o'clock on that night, and skippers and pilots of every vessel leaving Holland for the fishery were obliged to make oath that they would respect the rules.

As anything up to two thousand vessels were at sea, they must have presented a magnificent sight, for the fashion of those days was a wealth of carved and gilded decoration, bright paintwork and a lavish display of bunting.

A Dutch map of the North Sea, c. 1583, has some interesting little pictures of herring busses as decorations, from these I have drawn a three-master running before the wind, with square sails set on fore and main only (Fig. 1). In front of the mizzen mast are the gallows on which the fore and main masts rested when the buss was lying to her nets (Fig. 2). Here the warp, with the barrels supporting it, is seen coming in over the bows, below hangs the cork rope to which the nets are attached by short lines—the "orzels." They are hauling in over the starboard side, and a man with a large lade-net is picking up the herring which fall out of the meshes. The hulls have a well-curved stem and high stern, with two heavy rubbing strakes, but the busses working their nets have no sail set on the mizzen, surely a strange omission. In accordance with mediaeval practice, reefing was accomplished by first removing the drabbler, then the bonnet laced to the foot of the sail, a method seen down to the last days of sail in Yarmouth and Lowestoft drifters. The two aftermasts are stepped upright, but the foremast rakes well for'ard, all are supported by

FIGURE 2

DUTCH HERRING BUSS c 1583    HAULING NETS

shrouds, those on fore and main apparently being unhooked when the masts were lowered. I have not included any rigging not shown in the originals, but from other sources it is known that stays supported the masts fore and aft.

The whole scene is very similar to one in the North Sea 300 years later, when gallows were still to be seen in the three-masted Yarmouth luggers, c. 1829 (Plate 3). In essentials the hull has changed but little in size or build during the centuries between as can be noted in examining Fig. 3, which I have sketched from a contemporary Dutch painting of the mid-17th century. Here the mainmast is lowered back on to the high taffrail, and the foremast is held at an angle of some 45 degrees by the forestay. The square sail on the mizzen is aback, and the crew are hauling in the nets over the port side.

A typical Dutch herring buss of the late 16th and early 17th centuries had a heavy, bluff-bowed hull with a keel length of about 50 ft., beam 15 to 17 ft., and was capable of carrying some 35 last of herring, although the largest were reputed to have a capacity of 100 lasts. Each of the three masts carried a square sail, while the mainmast had a topsail set on a short topmast scarphed into the lower mast. The crew numbered 14 to 15 men, including skilled coopers and picklers, who were paid a weekly wage. The hull cost about £260 with another £45 for masts, spars and sails. A fleet of nets numbered 50, each 30 yards long and 14 yards deep, and cost some £170 tanned ready for sea. Rope was an expensive item, with four cables and anchors costing £100. Seven hundred and fifty fathom of warp, then called "war-ropes," made from the best hemp, cost £45. War-ropes was an abbreviation of wearing-away ropes. Barrels were cheap, as £75 purchased 1,200; 30 weys of salt cost £60, and corks and bowls needed another £20. The total cost of fitting out a buss, ready for sea, was about £800, and she was reckoned as useless after three voyages, as all her gear was worn out. The fact that the hull was somewhat clumsy

FIGURE 3

17ᵀᴴ CENTURY DUTCH HERRING BUSS

mattered little in a vessel in which seaworthiness and ability to ride to her nets in all weathers counted for more than speed and handiness.

On arrival at the fishing grounds the nets were shot at dusk, then the fore and main masts were lowered back on to the gallows near the stern and under mizzen only the buss lay to her train of nets, which were about a mile in length. The huge fleet of drifters covered hundreds of square miles, and numerous guard ships prevented any interloper from shooting his nets anywhere in the vicinity. At dawn hauling commenced. Immediately after being shaken out of the nets, the herring were gutted and evenly sprinkled with salt by well "rousing" them. They were then sorted according to size and quality, packed in layers, head to tail alternately, salt sprinkled over them, the barrels headed up, and marked with the date of capture.

The greatest care was exercised in all operations, elaborate regulations were drawn up and rigidly enforced. No boat was permitted to sell any herring at sea, and steps were taken to prevent pollution of the sea by disposal of dead fish, as the Hollanders realised that the herring is a delicate feeder, and shuns waters which are contaminated, especially with its own kind. All herring brought in by the jagers had to be re-cured within three weeks of landing, and only the best Portuguese and Spanish salt was used. This was imported free of duty. Herring lay in pickle for ten days before being packed in barrels, whose quality was examined and then marked with a brand. The number and size of staves in each was specified, and not more than three pieces were allowed in the bottom, only dry, heavy wood could be used, and any faulty barrels were broken up. This scrupulous care was well worth while, as it ensured the excellence of the cure, and resulted in the Dutch having the pick of the world's markets. For two centuries their pickled herring were supreme, fetching as much as two and a half times the price of other nations' curing. About 1580 Yarmouth cured herring realised £10 a last against £25 for Dutch-cured.

Some idea of the extent of this trade can be realised from the fact that over a million barrels of fish were cured annually, and employment given to some forty thousand men afloat, not to mention the tens of thousands engaged ashore in ancillary trades. Distribution inland was by packhorse and wagon, and when one thinks of the magnitude of such operations in those far-off days, present-day restrictions and faulty handling with every means of speedy transport do not show up to advantage.

The herring, a seasonal fish, frequented certain waters at times practically identical with those fished to-day, and the immense Dutch fleet drifted slowly southwards, catching, barrelling and despatching, day after day. They re-provisioned from the jagers, which brought out fresh supplies and took back the full barrels. Until St. James' Day, the 25th July, the busses fished in the neighbourhood of the Shetlands, then they gradually worked down the coast, and early September saw them off Yarmouth. Here many of the smaller craft made use of facilities ashore, and the Sunday before the 21st September was known as "Dutch Sunday." Booths were erected on Yarmouth quays, and the famous Fair was held, ending with the ceremony of "Wetting the Nets," a custom which prevailed until modern times with the "Blessing of the nets" in the magnificent church of St. Nicholas, one of the largest parish churches in England, alas, almost totally destroyed in the Nazi raids on the town in the 1940's, when so many priceless records of the past were lost for ever. Fishing continued in the vicinity of Yarmouth until St. Catherine's Day, the 25th November. Many of the Dutchmen sold their fish to local curers with whom they "hosted," and these pickled herring were exported to the Continent, realising about £15 a last. Christmas saw the fleet working the fishery off the Thames Estuary, and then they returned to Holland to re-fit.

To enforce his new regulations, King James I employed warships, which approached the Dutch vessels when they neared English waters. A few paid the tax demanded, but the majority refused, encouraged, no doubt, by the presence of their own men-of-war, who far outnumbered the English vessels, which retired with honours in favour of the Dutch. In 1652 Blake's capture of some 100 herring busses off Buchan Ness, in an endeavour to enforce King Charles I's demand for £30,000 for licences to fish, was one of the prime causes of the first Anglo-Dutch wars. In 1653 not one of the fleet of over 2,000 sail was permitted to leave for the usual fishing owing to fear of capture or molestation. Again in 1663 and 1666 all fishing was prohibited. The Peace of Nymegen in 1678 brought a slight return to prosperity, but it was fleeting, as 1702 saw the outbreak of the War of the Spanish Succession, which was not concluded until the Peace of Utrecht in 1713. By that time a mortal blow had been struck at the fisheries, trade never recovered, and in 1736 only 300 vessels sailed; by 1779 this remnant had fallen to 162, and in spite of bounties, trade continued to decline, Denmark and Norway having taken advantage of the continual wars to capture almost the whole of the lucrative Russian trade.

Early in the 19th century complaints were again made about Dutch busses fishing close to the Scottish coasts, and in 1824 the King of the Netherlands issued a Royal Decree prohibiting any of his subjects approaching within six miles of the shore, and right down to the outbreak of the 1914 war the Dutch fished from twelve to fifty miles out.

The heavy three-masted buss was gradually replaced by a more barge-like hull fitted with leeboards, and a high mast, stepped well aft, carried a square mainsail and topsail, a stay foresail and a jib set on a running bowsprit. Aft was a small mizzen with a triangular sail which was most useful for keeping the hoeker to the wind when riding to her nets. Being heavy vessels to work, a large crew was needed, numbering fourteen to fifteen men and boys. About the middle of the 19th century the hand-made hemp nets were superseded by lighter factory-made cotton nets, purchased in Scotland, and the old-fashioned hoeker gave way to craft known as bom-schuits with a similar hull. A shorter mainmast carried a fore and aft mainsail with a short gaff, a hand capstan reduced the heavy work, and only eight men were needed; many retained the small mizzen on account of its usefulness when fishing. Each vessel caught, cured and barrelled about 660 barrels a year. Later in the century the Dutch paid us the compliment of copying the design of our East Coast drifters, and steam capstans still further reduced the labour of hauling in the nets (Plate 48).

I was deeply touched one day to receive from Mr. A. Artis, of Grimsby, a page or two from a *Graphic* of 1876, one of the few treasures which survived the bombing of his home, and it contained some interesting data concerning the Dutch herring trade. The fleet that year consisted of 250 vessels called Loggers and Hookers, two-masted schooner rigged craft of about 80 tons, carrying a crew of fifteen, and costing, fully equipped for fishing, about 25,000 guilders, or £2,000. The nets were about 90 ft. long, and each craft was furnished with forty to fifty. On the last day of May the boats sailed for the best ground for summer herring, which lay between 53 deg. and 59 deg. North. The fleet was accompanied by five fast sailing yachts, called jagers, and on given days one received what each fishing boat had caught, pickled and barrelled. She then crowded on all sail for Vlaardingen, where watchmen in the church steeple looked for her approach. The cargo was at once auctioned to the highest bidder. The first arrivals, about the last week in June, fetched a high price, 450 guilders or £37 10s. a barrel being realised. The big fish dealers bought up the catch, repickled the fish according to their own private trade brand, which secret was jealously guarded. They were despatched to special customers, packed in small barrels of six, twelve, eighteen or twenty-four fish, and the choicest herring sold at a guilder apiece, and a barrel containing a dozen would cost the equivalent of a sovereign. Each successive cargo was disposed of in the same way, the fishmongers announcing a new arrival by hanging over their shop doors a basket decorated with evergreens, ears of corn, and bits of silk and tinsel. In July the price fell to six guilders a dozen, and by the beginning of August it dropped to three. After being skinned, cleaned out and cut in slices, the fish were put together again in shape on a dish with a flower stuck in each gill, and were eaten raw, forming a side-dish for breakfast, luncheon or dinner. The first herrings were the best, being young, short in length and fleshy. The season was over in September, when the price fell to 2d. each for the best quality. The eating was an acquired taste, and the epicure extolled the exquisite gout, which had the exact saltness of oyster water, giving the fish a very delicate flavour.

I am afraid I have tacked a long way to the S.E., and must get back to more Northern waters and Stuart times. Most of the English boats were small and poorly equipped, and the "fivemen" cobles, which came from Yorkshire and Durham to the Yarmouth fishery, were but light open boats, ill able to keep at sea in heavy weather, and capable of carrying at the most only three lasts of herring. Various suggestions were put forward at different times as to how best to combat the Dutch monopoly of herring fishing and curing. Experts worked out schemes with alluring estimates of the profits to be made and the employment given to "strong and lustie beggars," but they soon found that there is a great difference between plans on paper and stern reality. In 1632 the first company was founded, but could do little against the long-established Dutch trade, and they suffered considerably from the ravages of armed privateers. To build and equip vessels equal to the Dutch busses meant the importation of many materials from abroad, masts, spars and deal boards had to come from Norway, pitch and tar from the Baltic, hemp from Prussia, salt from Lisbon, barrels and willow hoops from Hamburg. Then some means had to be found to tempt Dutch curers to teach their secrets. A 70 ton herring buss with 50 ft. keel, 17 ft. beam, and carrying 35 lasts cost £260 for hull, cockboat, and oars. Mainsail and bonnet were 11 yds. deep and 16 cloths wide, the foresail 10 yds. deep, 12 cloths wide, mizzen 5 yds. deep, 4 cloths wide. The total for a buss fully equipped with nets, gear, and one year's charges for salt, casks, wages and victuals for crew was nearly £935. Russian hemp lasted only one year, but when home-made, another six months' wear could be expected.

In 1641 Simon Smith thus describes the English herring fishery. The nets were shot in the evening and the vessel drove all night. In the morning the crew hauled in the nets, gipped, salted and packed the herring away before they set on kettle. When the fish were inboard a man took them out of the well with a ladenet and filled the gippers' baskets. Nine gippers cut the herrings' throats, gutted them, and flung the full into one basket, the shotten into another. Another man took the full baskets to the "rower backe wherein is salt," and a boy roused the fish up and down in the salt, then the rowed herring were taken in baskets to the packers. Four men put the herring into barrels and a fifth took the full ones from the packer. The casks stood open for a day so that the salt could dissolve in pickle, then they were filled and headed up. "Deepings" or quarter nets were always in readiness to renew the nets, which were made from all the twine that can be got of a summer spinning, and tanned with the bark of ash trees.

In October, 1666, herring were so abundant that the nets were full as soon as they were in the water, but salt was scarce until the capture of a prize, laden with the precious commodity, eased the situation for a time. Even so, the price of salt rose to £13 a wey—40 bushels—and hundreds of lasts of herring had to be thrown back into the sea.

On his return from exile, King Charles II granted to the citizens of Bruges a charter allowing them to send fifty vessels to British waters, to use East and South Coast ports, with the privilege of drying their nets ashore. This charter continued for some two hundred years, and its withdrawal aroused much bitterness, as the three-mile limit was now rigidly enforced.

Early in the 18th century a typical three-masted Scottish herring buss averaged about 50 tons, and carried a master and crew of 14. The method of fishing was to sail out to deep water and then fish from small boats. The expenses of fitting out amounted to about £950, the hull accounting for £366, spars, blocks and three boats £74, blacksmith's work £22, sails and rope £160, 32 lasts of barrels £80, 462 bushels of salt £45, 1,500 yards of nets £78, buoys £8, victuals for crew for three months £42, with an extra £5 for spirits. Wages for 13 men at 27s. a month came to £52 13s. with £10 for the master and 15s. for clearance by the Customs.

A gradual evolution was taking place in the rig of the English herring buss. It was soon found that a foremast, spreading only a small square sail, was a disadvantage, as, together with the mainmast, it had to be lowered whilst fishing was in progress. A boltsprit, on which a jib could be set, took its place, and the mainstay carried a large staysail, while the square sail on the mizzen was replaced by a jibheaded sail. This change coincided with the development of the fore and aft rig.

In 1749 another attempt was made by Parliament to encourage the herring fishery, and a number of influential people met at the King's Arms Tavern in Exchange Alley; £214,900 was subscribed, and contracts placed at £6 10s. to £7 a ton. Crews were to be paid £3 10s. a month, and each man was to have one gallon of beer a day.

The price of barrels seems high compared with the Dutch accounts of a century before as £63 6s. 8d. was spent on 400. Four hundred bushels of salt cost £22 10s., one barrel being allowed for 3½ barrels of herrings, with two extra bushels if the fish was repacked. Stores, wages and victuals for a two-month voyage came to £165; a fleet of nets, each 16 fathoms long, cost £237, and it was reckoned they would catch about 160 to 200 barrels per haul, or 150 crans.

At the second meeting on April 9th, 1750, at the Queen's Arms, the promoters evidently decided on getting things done. Three busses were to be built before the 26th May, with all necessary nets, and envoys were sent to Holland to engage experts in gipping, curing and barrelling herring. But the wily Dutch were not having any, and did not see why they should divulge their hard-won secrets to upstarts. The promoters had to make do with an instruction to their masters to avoid all friction with any Dutch vessels fishing nearby, and to endeavour, by the judicious use of bribes of a gallon or two of brandy, to learn the secrets.

The first buss to be launched was *Pelham*, built by Whetstone and Greville at Limehouse Bridge; the second was *Cartaret*, launched on the 25th. Two others, *Argyll* and *Bedford*, were built at Southampton. A bounty of 30s. a ton was offered to the owner of any decked vessel of from 20 to 80 tons, built in any port of Great Britain, which assembled in Bressay Sound by June 11th.

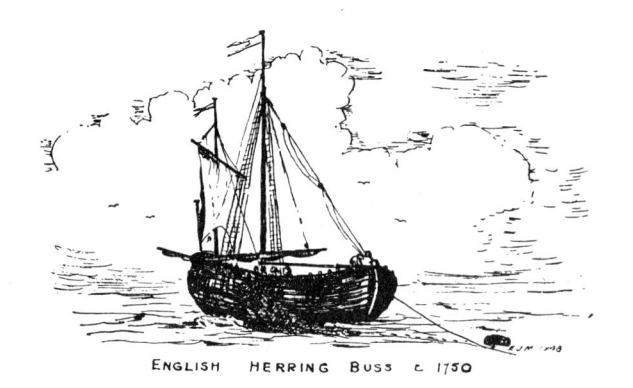

FIGURE 4

ENGLISH HERRING BUSS c. 1750

In accordance with a custom of the time, this first visit of a British deep-water herring fishery to Brassa in Shetland was considered auspicious enough to warrant commemoration by special prints, and a reproduction of an engraving by A. Walker from a drawing by T. Craskell, which I have before me, depicts *Pelham* and *Cartaret* hauling in their nets on 14th July, 1750, and Figs. 4 and 5 have been sketched by me from the prints. The design has obviously been copied from the bomb ketch with mainmast stepped amidships and mizzen a very short distance aft. This rig was certainly known a century earlier, and was similar to that used in the Dutch "doggers."

The square topsail has been lowered and stowed aft, where the yard projects over the taffrail, and the mainsail has been lowered almost a-port-last, or on to the rails, but the mast itself is left standing. The single square sail on the mizzen is aback, whilst the nets are being hauled. In this picture the mast has four shrouds a side, other prints show only three. The bowsprit, set to starboard of the stem, is run in, and has the jib stowed on top.

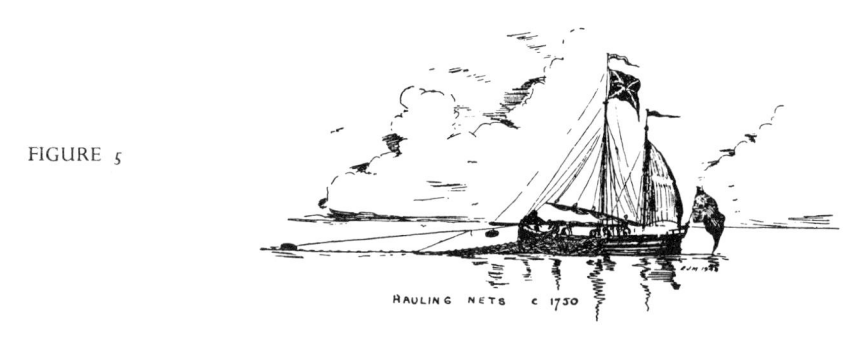

FIGURE 5

HAULING NETS c 1750

Fig. 5 shows that they hauled the nets in a similar manner to that seen down to the last days of sail. The warp, with its barrels attached, is being led in over the bows to a capstan aft, and three or four men are bringing in the nets over the port rail. The hull measures about 66 ft. from stem to stern, with a keel length of 56.6 ft., beam 16.2 ft., and depth in hold 8.7 ft. The bowsprit, with jib stowed on top, has been run in, and the heel lashed to the mainmast, which is stepped well amidships, and has three shrouds a side, set up with deadeyes and lanyards. The square yard, with sail furled, is lowered, and a small triangular sail is hooped to the mizzen mast, which is supported by a stay running to foot of mainmast and two shrouds a side. A short main topmast carries an enormous union flag, and vane flags flutter from the trucks of both masts. Low bulwarks are fitted, with open rails extending aft from the mizzen shrouds to a stern which bears a marked likeness to that found in the later Yarmouth and Lowestoft luggers. Efforts were being made to get away from the square tuck or transom stern, and the deck now projected over the sternpost, which was subsequently given more rake aft. The resulting stern—known as a "lute stern"—gave increased lift in a following sea, and was the forerunner of the counter stern.

In the print another buss is shown hauling her nets in the vicinity of a Dutchman making sail, whose hull, fitted with leeboards, has the clench-built, tumble-home form so typical of Holland. The fishery is guarded by warships of both nations, and two interesting little cutter-rigged craft show the type of vessel used to take the catch to market, the forerunners of the carriers. A French two-masted square-rigged vessel, with tacks boarded and yards sharply braced up, clearly shows what a slight alteration was necessary to convert the rig to that of a lugger. The whole scene is an animated one, and if the busses shot their nets so close to one another as shown, there must have been angry scenes when fouling occurred, and with heated words in various languages leading to blows, perhaps the presence of warships was not so unnecessary after all.

Even in the staid Victorian times the authorities found it necessary to issue an Order in Council, dated April 6th, 1889, with regulations forbidding any person on board of or belonging to any British or foreign fishing boat from discharging or presenting any firearm, or discharging or throwing any stone, ballast, coal, bottle, missile, or thing at any other sea fishing boat or boats, or at any person or persons on board of or belonging to any fishing boat or boats, or use any threatening, abusive, or obscene language to, or attack, intimidate, or molest any other person on board of or belonging to any sea fishing boat or boats, or do any act likely to provoke a breach of the peace, or make any person or persons to do any of the aforesaid things, under a penalty of £10. Phew!!

In 1755 70,000 barrels were cured at Yarmouth, and Lowestoft of which about 52,000 were exported, the remainder being for home consumption. But the affairs of the company did not prosper. Nasty things were said about certain officials, hinting at falsification of accounts, and the burning of certain cashbooks. In spite of Government assistance, it was impossible to compete against free enterprise, and the company failed in 1772 and the vessels and gear were sold at Southwold for £6,391 12s. 2½d. I like this careful accountancy down to the last halfpenny!

Many years ago when I was lecturing in Liverpool I had the pleasure of handling a mint copy of Chapman's *Architectura Navalis Mercatoria*, published in 1768. This treasure was, and I hope still is, in the City Library, and it was through the courtesy of the then librarian, Mr. Shaw, who knew my interest in ships, that I was able to study the various draughts so beautifully delineated by this English naval architect, who found his talents best appreciated in Sweden. He shows detailed draughts of English and Dutch herring busses, and the difference between them is striking. The wall-sided English hull contrasted with the tumble-home so beloved by the Dutch, to my mind shows that we were quite capable of designing vessels to our own ideas, and did not copy everything from Holland, as some schools of thought would have us believe.

CHAPTER TWO

## DEVELOPMENT OF THE LUGSAIL

From the dawn of sailing history a single square sail, set on a mast stepped amidships, has been a favourite rig for an open boat in Northern waters. The head of the loose-footed sail was bent to a yard which was attached to the mast by a parrel, the two vertical sides—the "leeches"—were of equal length, with ropes to control the sail attached to the lower corners—the clews. Corresponding with later deep-sea practice, the windward rope was always called the "tack," the leeward the "sheet," and every time the boat went about the name of the rope was altered—no doubt the origin of the term "tacking," or the art of going to windward.

Such a rig was simple in the extreme. The yard was square to the mast when the boat was running before the wind, and braced up more or less sharply when reaching or close-hauled, although it was not a very efficient sail on a wind. It was then desirable to keep the weather leech taut by means of a bowline led for'ard to the bowsprit, the only use for that spar after the abandonment of the Roman artemon, or by a spar known as a "vargord," which did away with the need for a bowsprit. This square sail was seen in the boats of Ancient Egypt and Phoenicia, the Viking Longships, mediaeval craft, and down to present times in the Fair Isle skiff.

About the middle of the 15th century, when two or three masts were introduced, the same square sail was set on each mast, often with the addition of a square topsail —the rig of a herring buss, and unchanged in essentials for the next 300 years. By the 1750's it was a moot point whether many a fisherman on the South Coast was a smuggler in odd moments, or a smuggler who went fishing in his spare time, and I think it is quite likely that the need for speed for this nefarious occupation influenced the change-over from the clumsy square-rigged buss to the fine-lined three-masted lugger. The sails of the old bluff-bowed craft were tall and narrow, with the rigging not widely spaced at the masthead. Hence the yards, which in square rig are always *outside* the rigging and *before* the mast, could be braced up quite sharp. On a wind, with the tacks well bowsed down and the yards peaked up, these square sails somewhat resembled lugs. It did not require much alteration of gear to convert from square to lug rig. All that was necessary was to bring the yards *inside* between the rigging, and sling them in a fore and aft position at a distance of about one-third from the fore end instead of in the middle, as experience soon showed that the sail set better with the halyard nearer the throat. This resulted in a quadrilateral sail, with the luff shorter than the leech.

Standing rigging was simplified, and shrouds soon disappeared in favour of a burton, which, with the halyard, had to be shifted over to the opposite side of the deck every time the vessel tacked, as the lugsail had to be lowered—dipped—and reset on the leeside of the mast. The alteration in rig thus brought in an entirely new method of going about when working to windward. The fore-end—the tack —of a lugsail always remains for'ard, instead of changing places every time the yards are swung round, as in square rig, where the tack is always the weather side. The lugsail, being loose-footed, could easily be let fly if the vessel was in danger of being overpowered, and there was no risk of the foot of the sail getting full of water, as when laced to a boom.

Its merits having been proved by smugglers, the lug sail was speedily adopted by fishermen in many of our East and South Coast harbours, although Brixham never used the rig, and it remained popular in the West Country to the last.

The French brought the three-masted lugger to a high state of perfection about 1770, using such craft for privateering, smuggling, and trading, and no doubt visits to French ports by South Coast fishermen led to their adopting the rig. So adept did they become at designing swift sailing vessels that a smuggling lugger could show her stern to any Revenue ship afloat, being unrivalled in her ability to eat into the wind. Soon laws had to be passed regulating beam, and making it a serious offence to build a boat too narrow, and any such craft found were seized by the Preventive-men and sawn in two.

The advantage of the three-masted rig was the facility with which sail could be shortened. In fine weather three lugsails, a jib, and a topsail could be set; in heavy she would handle under one or two only, selected from the smaller sails; the lightness of the spars and the ease with which one or more could be struck relieved the boat of the heavy pressure of too much top hamper. The masts were small and light in proportion to the large area of canvas spread, so that the boat rode easily with less labouring in a seaway than when a single heavy mast was stepped.

Fortunately a very fine contemporary model, *c.* 1820, exists of one of the South Coast luggers, and is now in the Science Museum (Plate 1). She bears a strong resemblance to the craft depicted in some of E. W. Cooke's meticulous etchings, and is to all intents and purposes an open boat, as there is only a short foredeck to give meagre shelter below, where the crew could cook and sleep. The length B.P.

1 MODEL OF SOUTH COAST LUGGER, c. 1820
  Open boat with fore deck.

2 MODEL OF YORKSHIRE 3m LUGGER, c. 1800

3 YARMOUTH 3m LUGGER, *c.* 1830

4 CARTING NETS, LOWESTOFT

5 NET DRYING GROUND, NORTH DENES, LOWESTOFT
Note left-hand lay in warps, corks in cork-rope.

6 3m LUGGER OFF GORLESTON

7 LOWESTOFT LUGGER, c. 1870
Note chain bobstay and halyard tye, iron spider, timber heads.

8 YARMOUTH LUGGER *DEW DROP*, c. 1871
40 tons, built at Surlingham, 1871, for W. Brighton.

9 LOWESTOFT DANDY *PRINCEPS*, 1884
Note main horse, lumber irons, light stanchions, bilge keel.

is 40 ft., beam 13.2 ft., and depth about 6.4 ft. The hull is clench-built with a wash-strake above the gunwale running for'ard to form a low rail round the foredeck, at the after end of which is a coaming to keep any water coming in over the bows from entering the open section. A reeving bowsprit, set to port of the stem, has its heel stepped between two bitts. Immediately aft is the foremast, stepped on the floors, and supported by two shrouds and a backstay on either side. On the aft side of the main thwart is a three-sided tabernacle in which the main mast is stepped, lowering back between two carlings extending to the after thwart. It is supported similar to the foremast, and the pole topmast is stayed by two light shrouds set up to short channels outside the washstrake. The mizzen, stepped close to the transom, is likewise supported by two shrouds a side, hooking into similar channels. The sail plan consists of a jib hooked to an iron traveller on the bowsprit, a dipping lug on the foremast with its tack to the stemhead and sheet belaying by after mainmast shroud. On the mainmast is a standing lug, set to port, with tack to port side of mast and sheet led well aft; above is a square topsail with halyards leading through sheave set athwartships near truck. It is seen stowed on its yard along the thwarts; at the foot of the mast is a small barrel winch. On the mizzen mast is a smaller standing lug, set to starboard, with tack to aft side of mast and sheet to sheave at outer end of an outrigger set on starboard side of transom. Running gear is belayed to timber heads or pins inside gunwale, and three lines of reef points are on fore and main lugs, but none on mizzen.

On the East Coast the early years of the 19th century saw the three-masted lugger a fine, able vessel, fully decked, with hull and masting showing an ancestry dating back to the first herring busses, as fore and main masts were lowered back when fishing was in progress. A contemporary model, c. 1800, can be seen at the Science Museum (Plate 2), and comparison with the lugger drawn by E. W. Cooke (Plate 3) shows how like they are in essentials. Fore and main lugs are only slightly peaked up, and clearly depict their development from the earlier square rig, but the mizzen is peaked more sharply and is the forerunner of the later shape of lugsail. The clench-built hull is 61 ft. B.P., but a stem curving aft and a raking sternpost make a keel length of 44 ft. Beam is 19 ft. 6 in., depth 7 ft. 6 in., and tonnage about 90. A peculiarity of fore and main masts is that the topmast is stepped abaft the masthead to enable the lug topsail to set better. No bowsprit is fitted in model, but one was usually found in the Yarmouth luggers. There are no rails to the bulwarks other than short ones fore and aft, extending as far as the timberheads. Short bilge keels are fitted, as there is a considerable deadrise to floors. The foremast, stepped into a tabernacle below the deck, is lowered back into an opening in deck—known as the "scuttle"—by the forestay, which is set up by a tackle consisting of two double blocks—a twofold purchase—with fall leading from lower block. In contrast to the South Coast lugger, no standing shrouds are fitted, but a burton, consisting of a runner and a luff purchase, is set up on one side of the deck, and the lug halyards go to the other. They have a luff purchase with the single block hooked to eye in covering board and fall leading from upper double block to a cleat on stanchion for'ard of eye. The dipping lug has a long tack pendant hooked to eye in deck at foot of stemhead, and the sheet has its standing end hooked to eye in covering board well aft and reeves through single block at clew, back to a single block hooked in covering board and fall leads for'ard along deck to belay on cleat opposite the mainmast. The topsail halyards are single, and reeve through a thwartship sheave in topmast head. Three reef cringles are in luff and leech boltropes, no reef points are shown in the sails, but, no doubt, were fitted.

The mainmast, raking slightly aft, is stayed for'ard by a heavy stay set up with a two-fold purchase, with the lower double block hooked to eye in deck aft of fore hatch grating, and has a burton a side set up with a gun-tackle purchase, the lower single block hooking to eye in covering board. The square-headed dipping lug has a long tack pendant hooking to eye in deck amidships, the sheet has its standing end hooked to eyebolt outside bulwarks right aft, the fall reeves through a single block at clew, back through single block hooked to a second eyebolt for'ard of standing end, and leads in over rail to belay round aft timberhead. The halyards have a luff purchase led aft to eyebolt in starboard covering board with fall belaying to cleat on stanchion. The topsail, set flying, has the halyards hooked to eye on top of yard; after reeving through a fore and aft sheave, they lead down to single block hooked in eyebolt in covering board, and for'ard to belay round cleat on stanchion. The sheets reeve through small single blocks on upper side of each yard arm, on through separate sheaves in a double block slung under yard, for'ard of mast, and down foreside to belay round a horizontal bar-cleat, where also belays the downhaul from the weather topsail yardarm.

The mizzen mast, stepped to port in a thwart, also rakes aft, on it is set a standing lug to port, with its tack to a hook aft of mast. The halyard goes to starboard, the stay to port, and both belay to cleats on thwart. The sheet reeves through a sheave at end of outrigger, and belays to cleat on stanchion. The topmast is stepped for'ard of the masthead and no sail is set on it. A heavy crutch, on which the mainmast rests when lowered, is stepped in a recess cut in the starboard side of thwart, and secured by an iron bar.

On deck the anchor is lashed to the port timberheads, which have eyebolts on lower faces, with three eyebolts in the covering board. Aft of the scuttle is the fore hatch grating, then the hatch to the warp room with the main hatch for'ard of the main mast. The main scuttle, slewed slightly to starboard, is longer than that at foremast; next comes a high conical capstan, and the companion leading down to the cabin. The tiller goes outboard under the thwart, and short stern timbers carry up to the taffrail, with two carlings on the deck taking the thrust of mast and crutch.

The hull is clench-built up to the heavy wale under the covering board, but the bulwarks are carvel-built, the whole of the model is bright varnished, with the exception of the yards and the whelps of the capstan, which are painted pale blue.

These luggers had a loaded displacement of about 56 tons, and cost £550 with sawn oak frames made fast by trenails to every plank. On the Yorkshire coast they were known as "Fivemen boats," and at Scarborough as a "Farm," local names no doubt due to the make-up of the crew, which consisted of five men who were partners in the fishing and three paid hands, largely recruited from among the agricultural community. One or two cobles were carried on deck, and their brightly-painted strakes made a vivid splash of colour amidst the prosaic neutral tints.

Eventually about 1840 the mainmast was discarded, and the fore and mizzen masts only retained, larger sails were set, and the mizzen mast was stepped farther inboard. The chief reason vouchsafed for this change was that the mainmast got in the way of the nets. It is rather curious that this discovery was only made after some seventy years' use, and coincides with the decline of smuggling and the need for getting the utmost speed out of a boat.

The next development, which increased weatherly properties, was the higher peaking up of the yard, bringing a further shortening of the luff, and the resulting dipping lug—always a quadrilateral shape—was one of the most efficient sails ever devised, and the choice of fishermen, pilots and beachmen, men whose experience and knowledge of local waters made them excellent judges of the most useful rig for their calling. But there is nothing new under the sun, as the lugsail was known to the Chinese in the days of Confucius.

With the foremast stepped as far for'ard as possible, there was no need for a bowsprit, always a nuisance in a crowded harbour. The dipping lug, the most powerful sail known, is a lifting sail, making for safety and weatherliness in a seaway. By letting go the single halyard, the sail fell by its own weight, folding up on itself, and when the yard was unhooked from its parrel, the whole was easily laid on one side whilst the boat rode to her nets.

A lugsail requires fewer ropes than any other rig. In its simplest form in a small boat, the single halyard serves as a stay, with the main sheet the only other rope. The fore lower clew still retained its old name of tack, and was hooked to the weather bow or the stemhead, making a mainsail and foresail in one. The only drawback is the fact that the sail must be lowered—dipped—and rehoisted on the lee side of the mast *every* time the boat goes about. It was considered lubberly to see yard and sail pressing against the mast, where it was far less efficient, although the practice was countenanced when short boards were the order of the day. In Scotland and on the

East Coast a dipping lug was sometimes set with the tack to an eyebolt close to the foremast, a practice known as "a'monk," which obviated the need to dip. Was this word a survival of the days when the Brethren went to sea after herring, and monks, not being so proficient as professional fishermen, were perhaps prone to adopt the easiest way of going to windward? Although a large crew was needed, that mattered little when labour was cheap and many hands were wanted to handle the nets.

There were three methods of dipping the lug, each calling for smart handling. The first was to lower the sail right down, release the tack, unhook the yard from the traveller, shift it round aft of the mast, rehook on leeward side, then secure the tack, hoist sail again and trim the sheet. This was the usual East Coast practice.

The second—one of the crew slacked the halyards a little, whilst another attended to the tack and gathered in the foot, a third eased off the foresheet. At the instant the boat was in stays, as shown by the mizzen shaking, one hand swung the forepart of the yard round the after side of the mast, then the tack was secured, the halyards sweated up, and as soon as the sheet was hauled in, the lugger was on the fresh tack. This method was favoured by East Cornish fishermen.

The third method was that adopted by West Cornishmen and the Royal Navy for boat work. The foresheet was unhooked as the helm was put down, the halyards were eased up, and some of the crew stood on the lee side close abaft the mast and hauled down the leech and gathered in the foot, working towards the after yardarm until the peak of the sail could be shifted round the foreside of the mast, a proven mark, consisting of a length of yarn stuck through the strands of the halyards, prevented any unnecessary lowering of the yard. The tack was *never* started, and this kept the fore part of the sail acting as a jib aback, and so helped to pay the head off. Should the boat miss stays, the yard was kept into the mast to allow only the forepart of the sail to fill and the mizzen sheet was let fly. When the boat was round, the yardarm was let go, the halyards set up, and if the tack was not hooked to the stemhead it was shifted over from the lee to the weather bow. All these operations had to be done whilst the boat was in stays. I have sketched this method of going about in Fig. 56.

A lugsail hooked to the stemhead enabled a boat to sail closer to the wind, and if the sail was smartly handled, it was more convenient when going about, as the tack did not have to be shifted. On the other hand, hooking the tack to the weather bow ensured the boat going about, as the forepart of the sail formed a better back sail than when hooked to stem, and in this position the sail was also more efficient when the wind was free. Hooking the tack to the weather bow was customary in the Yorkshire herring cobles.

When taking in sail the sheet was checked and the luff hauled down; this took the wind out of the sail and allowed it to come down easily. If the leech was hauled upon it kept the sail filled and brought so much strain on the traveller that the yard would not come down. It was to facilitate lowering that many fishermen used a split traveller instead of a solid ring, two half-hoops jointed together by eyes (Fig. 6). Such a traveller was said never to jam. Keeping the sail close to the mast so as to avoid loss of power was always a problem.

To take in a reef the halyards were lowered, tack and sheet shifted, the former to eyebolt at varying distance between stem and mast, while the iron nearer the mast was used for the sheet. The foot of the sail was hauled taut, the reef points quickly tied up, and sail hoisted again. If the foot was rolled up, it made the neatest reef, but formed a bucket to hold a sea. When the wind took off, the reef was shaken out while the sail was set, then the halyards were lowered, tack and sheet shifted to original positions, and sail made again.

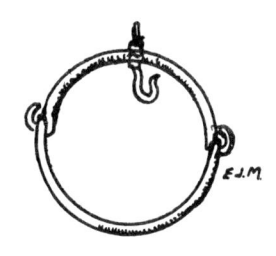

FIGURE 6

In the smaller boats in moderate squalls the sheet was eased sufficiently to relieve the boat, and enough steerage way maintained to ensure that a touch of lee helm and a pull on the mizzen sheet would bring the lugger into the wind should the squall increase. When caught in a hard squall, the helm was put down immediately and the foresheet let fly, and if there was a chance of a sudden veer in the wind the sail was lowered, for should it be caught aback, great difficulty would be experienced in getting it down, not to mention the danger from sternway.

The need to dip is obviated in the standing lug, where the tack is taken to the foot of the mast and never shifted, and such a lug is invariably set on the mizzen mast.

The opening years of the 19th century saw the end of the Napoleonic Wars, and men turned from the arts of war to those of peace. The wealthy were able to cruise in the Channel and visit ports denied to them for many a year. Yachting developed, and sailing matches brought the necessity for better hull design to obtain an increase in speed. The heavy scantlings required when guns had to be mounted gave place to lighter timbers, while the fact that men were prepared to pay for speed, instead of carrying capacity, induced shipbuilders to improve design. Then the coming of the railways offered wider markets for fish, and speed was of prime importance if the catch was to be in time for the London train. But speed has to be paid for. The magnificent sea-keeping abilities of the old rounded hulls had to be sacrificed to a certain extent, flat floors and generous beam were replaced by more deadrise and narrower hulls. Sailmakers were shaken up when the famous schooner yacht *America* sailed in our waters and brought home the fact that a well-cut and setting suit of sails was necessary if full advantage was to be taken of finer underwater lines.

Many fishermen, sailing as yacht hands during the summer months, had the opportunity of seeing improvements which could be introduced into their own craft, without too much sacrifice of their special requirements. Regattas at various ports encouraged attention to speed, many a new idea was adopted as a result of a rival centre sending a boat which sailed away with the local cup. Commercialism had not yet swept away all pride in the appearance of a fishing smack; owners and skippers insisted on a high standard of smartness, while the mediaeval love of colour still prevailing on many parts of the coast made a delight for the eye.

Although in the main alike in design, luggers from each port had local characteristics essential to the conditions of the vicinity. Thus, East Anglian boats, using deep-water harbours, were larger and had sharper floors than those from Hastings, which had to be beached frequently. Yarmouth and Lowestoft drifters carried their mizzen outriggers to port, but Scarborough and Hastings had theirs to starboard. East Cornish luggers had square transoms, but those from the West had sharp sterns, as had practically all the Scottish boats, where similar conditions prevailed. Both had their outriggers to port. (Plan 28)

By many minor points, such as rake of masts, cut of sails, line of sheer, or shape of stern, a fisherman could instantly spot the port to which a lugger belonged, and where she was built. Thus, a Porthleven round stern differed from one built at Lowestoft, while Cornish outriggers steeved more sharply than those on the East Coast, and the cut and set of sails was totally different. East Angliamen carried their sweeps in lumber irons on both quarters, Cornishmen in crutches on port quarter, but Hastings fishermen slung theirs over the port side in raft ropes.

Hence there was always a wide diversity of rigs amongst the fishing fleet. As may be supposed, changes did not take place in a day, and, no doubt, many an old salt clung to the ways of his youth, and declined to follow in his son's footsteps.

CHAPTER THREE

## *DRIFT NET FISHING*

DRIFT net fishing, as carried out in our waters since early times, is the method most suitable for catching some out of the vast shoals of pelagic fish—the herring, mackerel, pilchard, and sprat—which at certain times swim at or near the surface. Even to-day very little is known of their habits and what causes these movements at appointed seasons, but no doubt the quest for food and reproduction of their kind are the principal influences.

Herring swim in immense shoals, closely-packed together and covering an area of many square miles, and each shoal is largely composed of fish of the same age and characteristics. Thus, one drifter may catch full-roed herring, another a short distance away finds only spent fish in the nets. Shoals have been measured up to eight or nine miles in length and three to four in breadth, and of unknown depth. Yet what a small proportion they are compared with the hundreds of thousands of square miles in the North Sea and Channel. In August 1877, Captain Macdonald of H.M.S. *Vigilant* found at a depth of 108 feet a solid mass of fish, which extended some four miles in length, and two in breadth.

Herring are divided into three main classes—maties, full and shotten. Maties, a corruption of the Dutch word *maatjes*, or fat, are in the finest condition, as the roe being undeveloped, the whole of nutriment is taken by the fish. As the breeding season advances, this fat is gradually absorbed and when the roe or milt is fully developed the herring is known as full. Spawning having taken place near the seabed, the exhausted fish is called "spent" or "shotten," and has little food value.

The herring is a prolific fish, a female laying anything from 30,000 to upwards of 75,000 eggs at a time, the only fish ova which sinks to the bottom, where they adhere by a viscous substance to shingle, stone or shell, always on clean ground, never muddy. The fish spawn at all times of the year, but most of those caught in British waters do so in September and the autumn, and each local group spawns at a constant time of the year, varying according to the locality, and has marked characteristics which differ as regards appearance and quality. The largest and finest fish are caught off the Isle of Barra, those taken further south off Blyth and Shields are very rich and fat, but having a big distended gut are difficult to clean, and are, therefore, not so suitable for curing as those caught later in the year off Yarmouth, where the herring are firm and hard, with a small gut and in excellent condition for curing. The nearer the herring are to spawning time the better the market.

Herring have keen sight and smell, and shun polluted water; instances have been known of shoals forsaking an area where nets full of dying fish have got adrift in bad weather. The shoals are accompanied by immense hordes of predatory fish, chief of which are the cod and dogfish, in whose stomachs as many as twelve to fifteen herring are often found. Dogfish are the pest of fishermen, as they kill for the sake of killing, while their rough spiky skins play havoc with the nets. Running from 2 ft. 6 in. up to 6 ft. in length, they are unpleasant customers to deal with on a slippery deck. Their powerful jaws can grip a handspike so fiercely that the fish can be dragged about; the usual fate was for the belly to be ripped up and the fish thrown overboard, but now-a-days the flesh is to be found on fishmongers' slabs masquerading under some fancy name.

These fish and the enormous numbers of seabirds must account for millions of victims, and to consider the countless trillions caught over a period of years is to stand awed at the bounty of nature, which has provided such a rich harvest for man's food.

During the hours of daylight herring swim close to the bottom, but at dusk they rise near the surface; the milder the night the better the fishing is likely to be, but the season will not open while summer lingers late into autumn. Larger catches are made during S.S.E. winds, smaller in calm or during a spell of northerly winds, while a green sea will yield a greater harvest than a blue one. Drift fishing is carried on only at night and just after sunset, at moonrise, and before sunrise the fish are on the move, and especially likely to strike the nets, while the period of full moon generally sees very heavy catches. In some localities herring swim within a mile or two of the shore, in others they are only to be found at distances up to sixty or seventy miles from land. Their whereabouts is indicated by various signs—the slight trace of oil on the surface from the glands exuding the lubricating mucus which reduces friction between fish and water—the presence of abnormal numbers of seabirds, grampus, or cod near the surface. At times, especially in fine calm weather, certain minute marine life produces a phosphorescent light, very beautiful and uncanny, and every movement of fish is betrayed by flashes of light. This phenomenon is known by the names of marfire, waterburn, or brimming, but, as a rule, its presence augers ill for a successful night's fishing. An experienced eye can judge from the colour of the water if the shoals are about, and some exceptionally gifted men seem to have a sixth sense which unerringly tells them where the nets should be shot. Naturally, such skippers are always in great demand, and one was my friend Harry George, now living in retirement at Caister, where I had the pleasure of meeting him in October 1946. In his young days, so high was his reputation that he never had any difficulty in obtaining a command. He told me that many firms would build and equip a drifter, a matter of a couple of thousand pounds or more, if he would take charge, and he never had an unsuccessful season. As mentioned elsewhere, he was the youngest skipper ever to take a steam drifter across Yarmouth bar. I cannot do better than quote from one of his many interesting letters to me.

"In order of nutrition the herring comes first, the salmon second and the brill third. With the crusties—the shellfish—the shrimp first, the lobster second, and the prawn third. The herring is rich in phosphorus, calcium and vitamin D; when ripe for spawning they congregate on the seabed, mostly on rough ground, and they get together in astronomical numbers, almost in one solid mass, with their noses on the bottom, their tails up about halfway between the horizontal and the perpendicular, giving forth just enough energy to keep in position and head on to the tide. The female deposits her spawn, which is fertilised by the male, and if all the eggs come to perfection, anything between thirty and fifty thousand young come forth. Almost everything which lives and moves in the sea will eat a herring or its spawn, such is the mortality that only five per cent. live to grow to a marketable size. I have seen haddocks caught near the Dogger Bank chock full of herring spawn; were it not so and the herrings left to grow undisturbed, the North Sea would become one mass. The cod, haddock, ling, tusk, conger eel, coalfish, whale, porpoise, and many other fish eat until they have filled themselves with herring; gulls also take terrific toll.

Herring live on plankton, animal, minute organisms which swim, vegetable, microscopic plants which float, both invisible to the naked eye. The plankton arrive on the fishing grounds at the beginning of the herring season in such immense quantities that they turn the sea from its natural colour to a light milky-looking brown, but if you dipped up a bucketful the water would appear crystal clear. When a drifter skipper is steaming about looking for herrings, this is what he is really looking for. On reaching water which by its colour he can see is full of plankton, he stops his engines and lays until it is time to shoot his nets, and more often than not he will get a good haul, but not always, for some nights the herring "skulp," that is, they stick to the sea bottom and do not rise to swim near the surface, and as a result the fishermen draw a blank, but the wise skipper will keep amongst that plankton water, and sooner or later he will get a good haul. If you catch a herring and wish to know its age, take a scale and put it under a microscope, and you will see one ring around the scale for each year of its age just as when you saw through the trunk of a tree, a ring will be seen for each year of growth; on the south side the rings are furthest apart, on the north side they are closer together. That, when you come to think about it, is very wonderful, for each time the earth completes its orbit around the sun it leaves a ring on the scale of a herring, a ring in the trunk of a growing tree, and it leaves its mark on you and me, and on every living creature which lives and moves on the crust or in the waters of this lovely old planet called Earth.

The herring has its habits, its likes and dislikes, one of the habits is that when it rises to swim near the surface to feed on the plankton, 999 times out of 1,000 it swims from the north towards the south. We know that by the way it is meshed in the nets. If one drifter has his nets in the sea and another chap comes along and shoots his nets close along the north side, the language of the skipper whose nets are blanketed is anything but parliamentary, and when he meets the other chap ashore, he tells him in no uncertain terms just what he thinks of him. The herring likes a fine night with the wind blowing steadily from one point of the compass, and what we call a "crack" on the water, that is a gentle breeze, just enough to make the sea murmur, but when the wind keeps backing and veering, sometimes west, sometimes sou'west, veering again to nor'west, as a general rule few herrings are caught on a night like that. The fish will always swim towards a light, that is one reason why more are caught on a moonlight night. On a dark night when a drifter is hanging to her nets, the watch will sometimes put a spare net overboard and keep it within the range of the regulation lights, and will often get two or perhaps more baskets of herring. The fishermen will then know that they are amongst the shoals, and will heave the drifter up to the main fleet of nets to see what's doing. When the first net comes alongside it is like a blue sheet of flame, caused by the phosphorus in the sea, but that only happens on a "dark," never when it is moonlight. The skipper, if he is wise, will now hang on until daylight starts to penetrate the waters, then the herring will rise to meet it, and the result is a good catch, which the fishermen call "daylight swimmers," and for some reason or another they are nearly always fish of the very best quality. Herring do not like a calm, and when there is a great calm, especially off the Scottish coast, for all that you catch one might as well keep the nets aboard, except when they are shot on the inshore spawning grounds, then heavy catches are sometimes taken, but calm or not, the nets are shot, as there is always a chance of a breeze springing up, which stirs up the herring and causes them to rise. Fishermen know when a particular shoal is about finished; they may have been getting good hauls night after night, perhaps for weeks on end, one night they will find about ten or twenty per cent. of spent herring amongst the catch. That is the beginning of the end of that particular shoal, and in two or three nights they are gone. One of the big mistakes is fishing on the spawning grounds. A drifter will sometimes get a haul of 200 crans of fish about to spawn—200 crans means about two hundred thousand herrings. Assuming that half are males and half females, it means that forty or fifty thousand young herring, multiplied by one hundred thousand, have been destroyed, but if a law was made to prohibit fishing on spawning grounds, it would have to be international to make it effective.

We know much about the herring, how to determine their age, what they feed on, where and when to fish, but where they come from and whither they go after the season still remains a mystery. One theory is that they swim down from the Arctic Circle, encircle the British Isles, and then return to whence they came. Another is that after the season they bury themselves in the sand or mud, and remain there until the next season. The fact is, nobody knows, for they are a mysterious fish. In so far as the herring is concerned, the harvest of the sea, unlike that of the land, comes ripe for reaping up north first. A very prolific ground is situate 55 miles

N.N.E. from Baltasound, the most northern port in the Shetlands, where the finest quality can be caught early in the summer, but the fishing does not start at Great Yarmouth until about October 10th. One would think that this upholds the theory that the herring encircle the British Isles, but a fisherman can tell at a glance that the fish caught off Yarmouth or Lowestoft are not the same class as those which he caught to the norrard of the Shetlands. The East Anglian herring fishery is the greatest in the world, it begins about October 10th and lasts until about December 20th. Towards the end of December there often comes a strong gale from the north, and the fishermen, who up till then have been getting good hauls, will make for shelter and remain in port until after the storm has blown itself out. When they put to sea again, the chances are that they will draw a blank. A night or two after, they will hear of a big haul caught off the French coast; one would think that also upholds the theory, but again they are not the same herrings which have been swimming about off Yarmouth, for they are not nearly such good quality. When first caught the herring is a very beautiful fish, much more so than when you see it on a fishmonger's slab, for in the process of hauling aboard the scales get disturbed and come off, and it is generally mucked about.

In the year 1896 or thereabouts there were 1,050 vessels on the register at Great Yarmouth; I think I am correct in saying the bulk of that great fleet were herring drifters. Last autumn, 1947, all that were in commission fishing for herring out of Yarmouth were thirty-five steam and two motor drifters. Most of the steam drifters were anything from thirty to forty years old; some were brought back to port leaky, but all survived the autumn storms. The port is now but a shadow of its former self, in spite of all the thousands of millions of herrings which have been landed there.

The steam drifter is a little ship of 86 ft. keel, 18 ft. 6 in. beam, and $9\frac{1}{4}$ ft. depth of hold. She bunkers about 15 tons of coal, if she is fitted with a cross bunker about 35 tons. Fitted with triple expansion engines, cylinders $9\frac{1}{2}$ in., $15\frac{1}{2}$ in., and 26 in., 18 in. stroke. Working pressure 180 lb. Speed about $9\frac{1}{2}$ knots. She shoots sometimes 70, sometimes 100 nets, each 32 yd. long and 48 ft. deep, carries a crew of ten, and will easily bring 250 crans to market, a quarter of a million fish. A cran is four baskets, each basket weighing about six stone. The crew are paid by a share of the catch. The running expenses are deducted from the gross earnings, the rest is divided into sixteen shares, nine for the owner, seven for the crew. The crew's share is again divided into shares, and paid to the men according to their rating aboard the drifter. Skipper one and three-quarter shares, mate one share and one eighth, engine-driver one share and one-eighth, waleman one share, and so down to the boy, who gets half a share. Since the war the crew's share has been adjusted so that they get slightly more; the owner also takes one and a quarter shares for the use of capstan. A few years before the war a drifter could be built for £4,000, now she would cost about £20,000. When there is a glut of herring and they fail to make control price, they are bought cheap for margarine. It takes 54 cran to make a ton of margarine, or 216 baskets, in other words 54,000 herrings. Weight for weight, there is 34 times more nutrition in a pound of herrings than in a pound of oysters. That is a scientific fact."

This account, coming from so eminent a fisherman as Mr. Harry George, is invaluable evidence of the unerring accuracy of these old-time skippers in locating shoals. To-day I heard on the wireless that radar, rather than a skipper's instinct, is to be used to trace the presence of the fish!!

Down to the middle of the last century the nets were made of hemp, hand-spun and twisted into twine, which the women knitted into narrow lengths called "lints," the diamond-shaped meshes being 30 to 34 to the yard, and just over 1 in. square. The lengths varied from 15 to 21 yards to suit the size of the boat. The lints were laced together, one below the other, the upper was the "hoddy," the lower the "deepyne," and depth was three to four lints according to the fisherman's choice. The upper edge of a length of net was called the "back," the lower the "foot" or "sole," and the two ends were the "heads." The back was roped to a small line about two-thirds of the length of the net so that the lint set slack and bellied to the tide like a sail to the wind, and being flexible gave a little when the fish struck, and held them better than if it had been fully stretched. The back and heads were roped, but the foot was usually left free so as to be less liable to catch up in anything when used in shallow water.

Two nets laced together by the heads made a "dole," and in the 1790's a Yarmouth net was 21 yards long, and four lints deep, each lint having 52 meshes measuring 34 to the yard. A dole, barked ready for sea, was worth about £3 3s.

To preserve the twine from the harmful effects of constant immersion in salt water, which quickly rots the fibres, the nets were tanned in a solution made from the bark of oak or ash trees, later superseded by catechu or cutch, as it is generally known, a liquid obtained from the bark of a Spanish or East Indian tree. This solidifies as hard as pitch, and has to be heated up in huge coppers to dissolve it ready for use. The nets were barked once or twice in the season, but never tarred, and 27 bushels of bark were required for tanning 80 to 90 nets, one-fourth of which were renewed annually.

The back of the net was fastened at intervals of a few inches by short lines variously called norsolls, norsals, nossles, nozels, or orzels, to the cork-rope, a small double rope threaded through pieces of cork, some 70 to 80 at equal distances, which gave the necessary buoyancy to keep the back of the net uppermost; if the net was to be held at the surface more corks were required. The number of nets carried varied according to the size of the vessel; English drifters always shot odd numbers, Scottish even. Each net was fastened together head to head, seven to a warp, coupled to form a train, fleet or drift of nets, which might extend for a distance of upwards of a mile. This immense wall of netting was attached by lines called "seizings" to a 7 to $7\frac{1}{2}$ in. hemp warp which in turn was supported by barrels, small kegs, or canvas buoys, known as "bowls," secured by strops at 15 fathom intervals. The length of these strops determined the depth at which the nets floated. The foot of the net hung free, and when a shoal struck, the nets were forced up, and the noses of the herring could be seen sticking through the meshes.

Some years ago my friend, the late Mr. Kerbey Cleveland, of Margate, loaned me an old book written by the Rev. John Lewis, Vicar of Minster, and published in 1723. I made notes of items throwing some light on the fisheries in the Isle of Thanet. The men seem to have been "pretty hard workers" and were equally skilful as fishermen or husbandmen, able to put their hands to helm or plough, and steer a straight course. Farm labourers bargained with their employers to be allowed to go "shot-fare" and "herring-fare." The first was the mackerel fishing in May, when barley sowing was finished, the second, after the harvest was embarned, they could fish for herring until November, when wheat had to be sown. In other words, after plough and mow, to reef and stow.

Poor people ashore were engaged in spinning, twisting and knitting nets, for which work, done at home, the following prices were paid:

| | |
|---|---|
| Spinning by the pound | Two pence |
| Twisting | One penny |
| Knitting a shot net, which is but two deeping by the awlne | Three farthings |
| Knitting a herring net of three deepings by the awlne | One penny |
| Beating or mending nets | One shilling a day with victuals, or 1s. 3d. with breakfast only |

The awlne was a French measure, equivalent to 5 ft. 7 in. Sixty awlnes made a "dole" or parcel of shot nets, while thirty awlne made a "dole" of herring nets.

Thanks to another old book, the *Brighton Costumal*, c. 1580, it is known that a "fare" was the period during which certain kinds of fishing took place. "Shotters" were boats of from 6 to 26 tons burden used in the mackerel fishery. A "mox," from the Anglo-Saxon word *max*, was the mesh of a net, called at Hastings a "moak." A "rann" was a division of a net, as "in deepness two ranns, each 50 moxes deep."

Many of these old names still survive, although perhaps in slightly altered form, as in "ransackers," the name given at Yarmouth to the men who overhaul the nets, or "beasters," those who mend them. These words, to my mind, show the once close association of the Norfolk town with the Cinque Ports.

Until the passing of the Sea Fisheries Act in 1868 an inch mesh was the minimum allowed by law, and nets were frequently measured as the size continually diminished through the contraction of the twine.

In the Middle Ages these laws were stringently enforced, as witness the case of some Barking fishermen who in 1320 were caught using small mesh nets, which were seized and burnt by order of the Mayor. Again, early in 1406 there was the making of a fine old riot when certain nets were seized. The irate fishermen chased no less a dignitary than the Sub-Conservator of the Thames, and recaptured the nets. But, alas, the culprits were arrested and tried at Westminster, and seemed likely to be "for it" when special pleas were put in on behalf of the fishermen—poverty, nay, ruin of families if their means of livelihood was taken away. So justice graciously permitted the use of the offending nets until Easter, when they had to comply with the regulations or be burnt.

In the 19th century Yorkshire yawls used nets 60 yards long, and 12 yards deep, with $7\frac{1}{2}$ in. hemp warps, totalling 2,200 yards in length. Each net weighed about

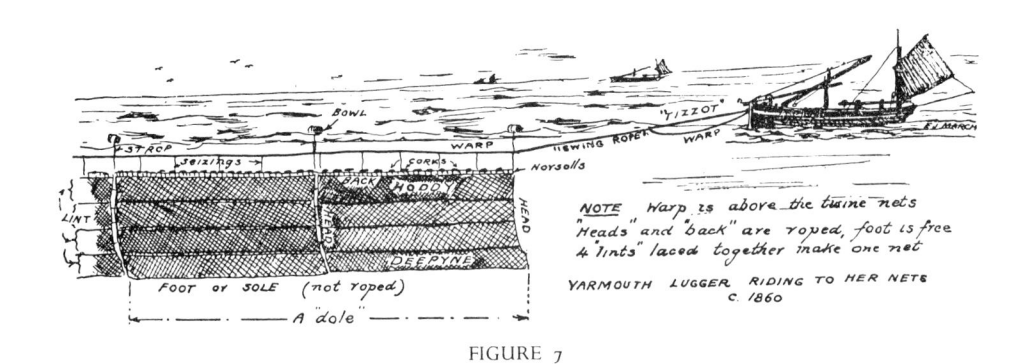

FIGURE 7

28 lb. In Scotland the nets were of 1 in. mesh, 50 yards long, and 32 feet deep, and measured by barrel bulk, each barrel holding two nets. The "drifts," always an even number, were fastened together by the back rope, and the warp was known as the trail rope, baulch, or bush line, while the short ropes to the nets were called "daffins." The bowls were made of inflated sheep, goat or dogskins—Buckie men breeding special dogs for this purpose. In Cornwall the warp was called the "foot line," and the connecting ropes the "lanyards." The length of each net varied considerably according to locality, fierceness of tides, and fisherman's choice.

Fig. 7 shows a Yarmouth lugger riding to her fleet of nets with the warp uppermost.

The invention by James Patterson, a working man, of a loom to weave nets of American cotton completely revolutionised drift net fishing. Patterson was in the Army and had fought at Waterloo; all the time he was developing the idea, and eventually he tried to make a machine, but found great difficulty in making a knot which would not slip. He was never completely successful himself, but Walter Richie, a plasterer of Leith, achieved this aim. Using a Swedish machine, one girl could make a million knots a day, and Hellyer's machine enabled one operator to make fifty yards of net a day. Plate 148 shows an early 19th century loom.

Cotton nets were lighter, more flexible and far more destructive in catching power than twine, and soon hand-made gave place to factory-produced, chiefly at Musselburgh, Patterson's home town, and Bridport in Dorset. The machines turned out "pieces" 60 yards long and 9 to 10 yards deep, the depth of net containing two hundred meshes. Each piece was divided into two nets 30 yards long, which were rigged with ropes in the same way as for twine. The nozles were manilla, generally spun up by the boys, and well barked before being put to the nets. At first the nets were saturated with linseed oil, and then boiled for two or three days in bark liquor, later they were dressed with linseed, and pine oil in the proportion of one part pine oil to two of linseed, and it took about one gallon to dress a net. After dressing, the nets were spread out to dry in a field for about a fortnight. Next they were tanned three times with cutch before being bent to the rope, after which they received yet another dressing of cutch before being put on board and used for a fortnight. Then they were taken ashore, dried and barked again twice, used for three weeks, dried and barked again, worked for six weeks before being barked again. The cost in the 1880's was £1 for cartage, and £3 to £4 for every barking. (Plates 4 and 5).

If the nets were not used for two or three days they had to be brought up from the net room and wetted to prevent overheating, as there is always a serious risk of fire with cotton. On the 11th July 1888, the 39 ton yawl *Countess of Fleetwood*, built 1879 at Whitehaven, was some nine miles west of Barrow, Lancs., when smoke was seen coming from the netroom hatch, and in spite of all efforts the fire, started by spontaneous combustion of a new net, completely destroyed the vessel.

In the 1830's the number of twine nets aboard a lugger varied from 61 to 91, but by the 80's 80 to 130 of the lighter cotton nets were frequently carried. Each net in the fleet was supported by a buoy, and certain divisions were marked by bowls of different colours. The first net had a small white bowl called the "puppy," and at the end of four nets was a dan with a staff and flag. The rest of the fleet was marked in four divisions, at the first quarter from the dan was a bowl painted one-quarter red and three-quarters white, the second half-red and half-white, and the third was three-quarters red and one-quarter white. The intermediate bowls were tarred black and had to be marked with the owner's name and boat registration number. The bowl strops were $1\frac{1}{2}$ in. manilla, one to three fathoms long.

As cotton is far lighter than hemp, there was not so much weight to keep the nets down, and the position of the warp was reversed, being suspended below the fleet by "seizings" of $1\frac{1}{2}$ in. manilla, five to six fathoms long, one to each net. The warp, $3\frac{1}{2}$ to 4 in. manilla, was dressed with Stockholm or coal tar, and the ropes were worked all the season, then taken on shore, dried and stored away until wanted again. The weight helped to keep the nets extended, and more or less upright in the water, and the warp was the backbone of the whole fleet, taking the direct strain off the nets when hauling, and should any be cut away by a vessel running through them, it prevented their being lost. In modern times the bowls are called "buffs" or "pallets," the seizings are "stoppers," and the drifter rides to the "tizzot," a length of rope attached to the warp to take the chafe.

Fig. 8 shows a Scottish fifie shooting her nets over the starboard quarter with the warp below the nets.

Although drifting was the age-old method of catching herring which swim near the surface, at times sailing trawlers landed fish scraped off the seabed. In the autumn

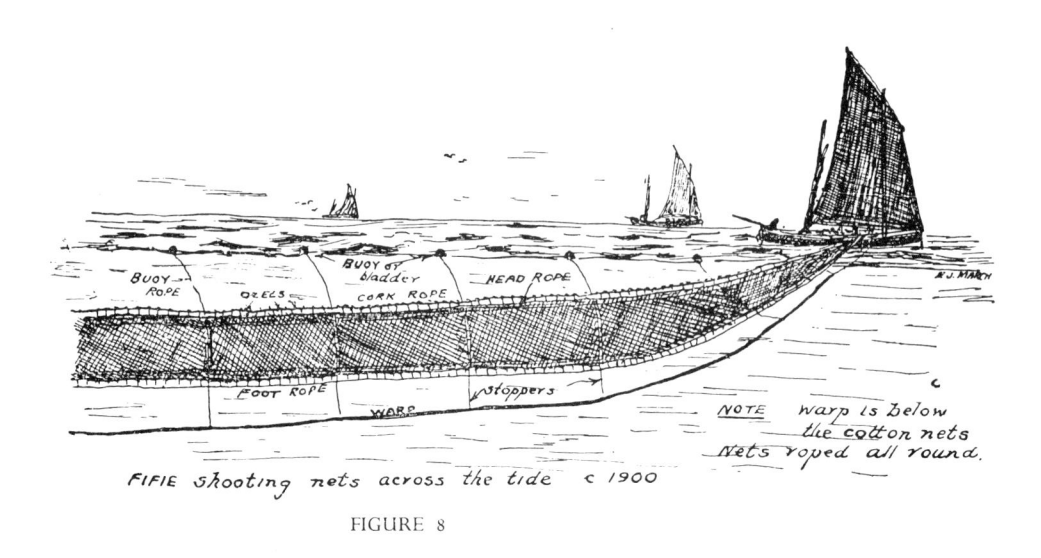

FIGURE 8

of 1859 the smack *Andrew Marvel*, owned by Davis of Great Yarmouth, caught over a thousand large full herring in her trawl, and in the spring of 1870 over five thousand shotten herring were found in the net of *John and Edmund*, owned by J. Becket, Yarmouth.

These were but isolated instances, and no serious efforts were made to trawl over the herring grounds, as the fish are generally on the seabed at spawning time. When intensive steam trawling came in it was another story, for with the continuous scraping over the best grounds, the catches of demersal fish became less and less, and eventually owners and skippers began to think of trawling for herring. In 1902 the first catch was landed at Wick by the steam trawler *Strathnaver*, and so incensed were the local drift fishermen that they stoned the skipper responsible for this break with tradition. Great was the outcry up and down the coast, but the hard fact was that both trawlers and drifters had a right to fish unrestricted in open waters, and the antiquity of drift fishing gave no special privileges when a newer method came along. It was alleged that the small meshed trawl net caught immature fish, whereas a drift net only meshed

10 LOWESTOFT DANDY *PRINCEPS*, 1884
Note ringbolt for tizzot, gammon iron, bullseyes for jib sheets, chain plates and mitchboard.

11 A LOWESTOFT SHIPYARD, c. 1877
*Eclipse*, 25 tons, built Lowestoft, 1870, note lute stern; *Gem*, 26 tons, built 1877, note elliptical stern.

12 JOHN CHAMBERS' SHIPYARD, LOWESTOFT
*Lottie*, Y.H. 434, ready for launching.

13 DRESSING SAILS, NORTH DENES, LOWESTOFT
Note method of working cringles in boltrope.

14 LOWESTOFT LUGGER *YOUNG JOHN*, c. 1895
Note wooden batten under slings of fore-yard.

15 *LIZZIE* LEAVING LOWESTOFT
Sails set for "two mizzen breeze."

16 HAULING HERRING NETS
Note cork rope, orzels, buoy in background.

17 MODEL OF YARMOUTH LUGGER *FISHERMAN*, BUILT AT YARMOUTH, 1852
Note didlenet in use, seizings, warp, buoy and buoy rope, Scudding pole between foremast and mitchboard.

18 YARMOUTH DANDY *BREADWINNER*, 37 TONS, BUILT AT YARMOUTH, 1896
Note size of bowsprit, and mast of zulu astern.

good-sized herring, the smaller ones wriggling through. Then the trawl, scraping along the bottom, destroyed the eggs on the spawning grounds, while to fish intensively where herring were in the act of breeding was wasteful in the extreme. The catch, usually damaged in the rough handling received, fetched only a low price, as the fish were not so suitable for curing. The huge drifter hauls made in 1913 realised 42s. a cran at Grimsby, but trawled fish only fetched 5s., and the previous decade had seen a decline of nearly 40 per cent. in tonnage landed, but, strange to say, drifter catches had increased by over 60 per cent.

On the other hand, many of the trawled fish were caught in deep water on the West Coast, where the drifters could not work, and the champions of trawling claimed this as a virtue by adding fish to the food supply which would not otherwise have been landed. Such was the state of affairs when the outbreak of the 1914 war gave everyone something else to think about.

CHAPTER FOUR

## EAST COAST LUGGERS

OWING to the simplicity of the lugsail, the lugger was always a favourite with fishermen. The three-masted Yarmouth luggers were reputed to be faster than any other East Coast craft, but unfortunately very little information is available about them. For an authentic illustration, it is well to turn to E. W. Cooke's beautiful etchings, and study his delightful drawing of a Yarmouth lugger unloading her catch at the quay (Plate 3). Her bows and general build are very reminiscent of the old herring busses seen in Fig. 3, with the arched gallows aft on which fore and main masts rested when fishing was in progress. The bowsprit, carried to port, is run in and hoisted clear of the deck by the jib halyards. The foremast, stepped close to the stem, has its lugsail stowed up and down the mast and burton and halyards hook to chain plates. The mainmast, supported by a burton on either side, has the topmast abaft the masthead. The main yard is resting on the gallows, while the mizzen lug is up and down the mast. The conical capstan, timberheads above the rails, and sweeps stowed to port in lumber irons are typical lugger practice. The catch, landed in double pannier baskets known as "swills," is being loaded on to a curious low cart, which is also to be seen in another etching showing cobles on the beach. Here the luggers are cruising off-shore, and the catch is being landed in ferry boats, and although but a minor feature of the drawing, the detail is perfect when studied under a glass. Swills —peculiar to the port—are still in use to-day.

On page 297 are plans of a 3m. lugger built by W. Teasdel, of Great Yarmouth, length overall 52 ft., moulded beam 14 ft. 8 in., depth 7 ft., burthen O.M. $49\frac{35}{94}$ tons. The hull, costing £300, was clench-built and copper-fastened, with $1\frac{1}{2}$ in. plank up to the binns, then 3 in. carvel. Draught light was 3 ft. for'ard, and 4 ft. 6 in. aft, loaded 5 ft. 6 in. for'ard, and 7 ft. aft. The hull weighed 18 tons with a load displacement of 48 tons, and 7 tons of ballast was carried. The sailplan consisted of three lugsails, a main topsail, and a jib set on a reeving bowsprit. The crew numbered eleven, and ready for sea the lugger cost £500. Some had a round stern, others a "lute," known locally as a "chopped-off stern." The bilge was fuller and the lines finer than the Lowestoft boats built by Samuel Sparham, with a length of 46 ft. 9 in. overall, keel 36 ft. 2 in., beam moulded 14 ft. 6 in., and depth 6 ft. 6 in. Loaded draught was 5 ft. 6 in. for'ard, 7 ft. 6 in. aft, hull weight 12.34 tons, load displacement 43.4 tons. The hull alone cost £325, and 10 tons of ballast was carried. They were rigged similar to the Yarmouth boats, and manned by a crew of ten.

Thanks to my friend Mr. L. W. Moore, I have a photograph of one of these three-masters, taken off Gorleston, the only one I have ever seen. The jib has been taken in, but a main topsail is set. Such a picture—and it is a picture—is invaluable evidence as to the appearance of these old luggers; I only wish it were possible to state her name and when the photograph was taken (Plate 6). The fore-end of mainyard is braced aft.

Many of these luggers were long-lived, considering the arduous usage to which they were subjected, and often they met their end through the forces of nature or marine disaster rather than old age. Take the 31-ton *Ebenezer*, built in 1835 and afloat until 1880, when she stranded on Yarmouth beach in an easterly gale during the exceptionally stormy October of that year. Or the 16-ton *Queen*, built 1843, which ran on the Scroby Sands in a strong N.N.W. wind on the 27th August, 1880, while the 22-ton *Samaritan*, built 1838, survived until the 8th May, 1886, when she was run down by an unknown steamer 22 miles E. by S. of Lowestoft, and sank with her crew of six.

When the mainmast was discarded about the 1840's, a "mitchboard" was stepped in its partners, and while the foremast was lowered, it rested in the crutch on top. The heavy gallows were removed, but the position of the fore and mizzen masts remained the same, and their old names were retained.

It is known, however, that two-masted decked boats, *c.* 1791, carried a crew of twelve and stayed at sea for periods up to six days. The herring, well-salted and stowed away as soon as possible after "scudding," were in suitable condition for curing "red," the time at sea being equivalent to a similar time steeping ashore.

By the 1860's the two-masted lugger, with jib set on a reeving bowsprit, was well established, the largest running up to 60 ft. L.B.P., with a keel of 52 ft., beam 17 ft., and 7 ft. depth of hold. Fully decked, they registered from 50 to 80 tons, costing up to £1,000 equipped ready for sea. They did not return to port every morning, but remained at sea from three to six days, salting the catch after every haul. Stowage was for 50 lasts of herring, and five to six tons of salt were carried, worth about 29s. a ton *c.* 1870.

The hull, a splendid example of boat-building as distinct from ship construction, was built on stocks, heavy baulks of timber at least a foot square, fixed upright in the ground in a line a few feet apart. Notches were cut in the top to receive the keel, which had to be firmly held in place to withstand the force used in bending and fitting the planking of the bottom. The stem and sternpost were tenoned into mortices in the keel, then the apron and a heavy oak knee were bolted to the inside of the stem, and the deadwood set up aft. The holes for the long through-bolts were bored with an auger slightly less in diameter than the bolts to be used. Considerable skill was needed for this job, which was long and laborious, especially when the bolts were

FIGURE 9

several feet long. Bolts had to be driven through tight holes, otherwise there would always be a chance of a leak. On the afterside of the stem, and the foreside of the sternpost, a V-shaped groove—the "rabbet"—was cut, into which the ends of the planks—the "hooding ends"—butted, while the rabbet in the keel took the edge of the garboard strake. The transom, some 4 in. thick, was cut to the required mould and the edges bevelled; it was then bolted to the outside of the sternpost. After being erected on the keel, these timbers were plumbed and secured by wooden struts.

Next the garboard strake was fitted, and its shape determined the lines of the

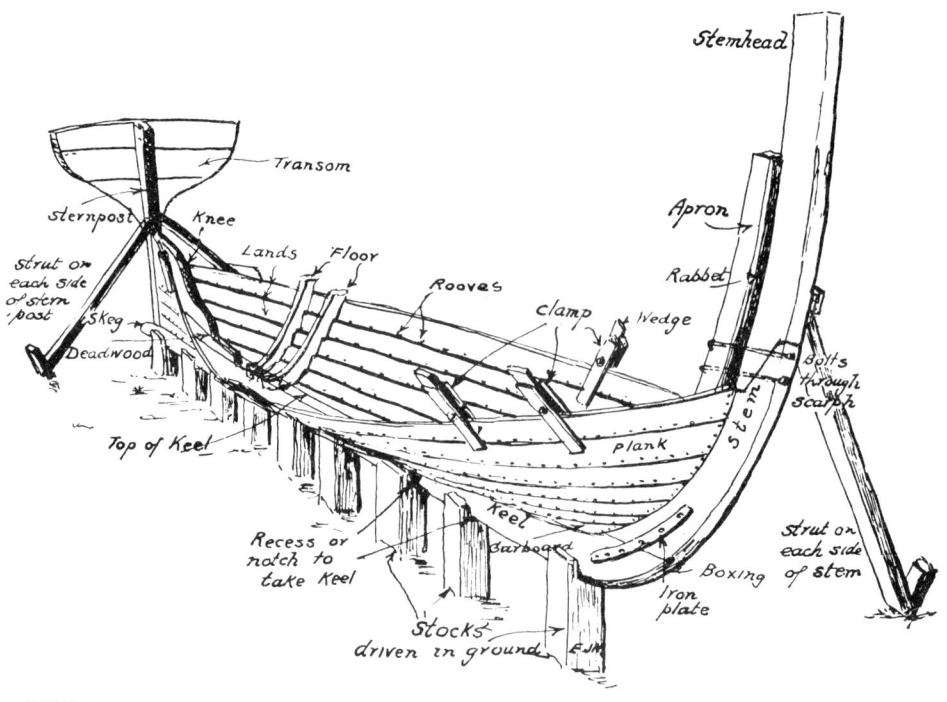

FIGURE 10

hull. It was straight on its upper edge before being bent round from stem to sternpost, and the under-edge was cut to fit the rabbet. After careful fitting, it was nailed to the keel every few inches (Fig. 9). The next plank, usually 1½ in. oak, was held as closely as possible outside the upper edge of the garboard strake, and a line marked along to correspond with the edge. This line was more or less curved, and as the same number of planks had to be fitted at stem and stern as at the broadest part amidships, it was necessary to mark the taper on each plank before sawing it out, after making allowance for the overlap, usually about one inch, which formed the "lands."

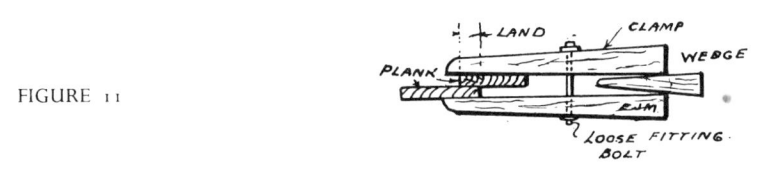

FIGURE 11

(Fig. 10). Whilst the planks were being nailed, they had to be held at intervals of about three feet by clamps, called "gripes" at Hastings, made from two pieces of hardwood loosely connected by a screw-bolt which allowed plenty of play, so that when the clamp gripped the strakes, a wedge could be driven in to hold them tightly (Fig. 11). The planks were nailed together at distances of a few inches with copper nails clenched inside over copper washers, known as "rooves," hence the name clench-built—variously known as clencher, clincher, clinker, or lapstrake, in which the strakes overlap, in contrast to carvel-built, where the edges butt against each other, so presenting a smooth surface.

An experienced builder never used moulds, save possibly one amidships; the lines depended for their sweetness entirely on his eye, and every plank was unbroken from stem to stern.

In order to get the strakes round the bilge in a fair curve, the upper outer edge of each strake was bevelled off—"browed"—and sometimes it was necessary to bevel the inner lower edge of the overlapping strake as well. The strakes were worked in alternately to port and starboard, and when the turn of the bilge was reached, some builders fitted in the floors, others carried on up to the binns—"bends"—before doing so.

The floors were hand-sawn out of suitable sized and shaped timber and joggled —a piece cut out—to fit in the lands of the plank (Fig. 12). These joggles tended to weaken the floors which crossed the keel and extended into the turn of the bilge. Copper nails, trenails or bolts were driven through every overlap of plank, the former being clenched on top of the floors, which were through-bolted to the keel. Above the binns the 1½ in. lapstrake gave place to 3 in. carvel build up to the covering board. Then the oak frames were sawn out, joggled in, and fastened similar to the floors.

37

An oak shelf, fitted low enough to allow the beams which rested on it to come flush with the top strake of planking, was now through-bolted to every timber. The beams, cut out of suitable curved timber, were bolted to the shelf, breasthooks for'ard tied shelf, top-strake, stem and apron together; aft, knees performed the same function with the transom, to which the stern timbers were fitted to form the counter. The oak covering board was cut to fit the curve of the deck, and through it at the bows were morticed five or six heavy timbers, about 4 in. square, which were carried up six to nine inches above the rail, and usually went right down to the floors. To them

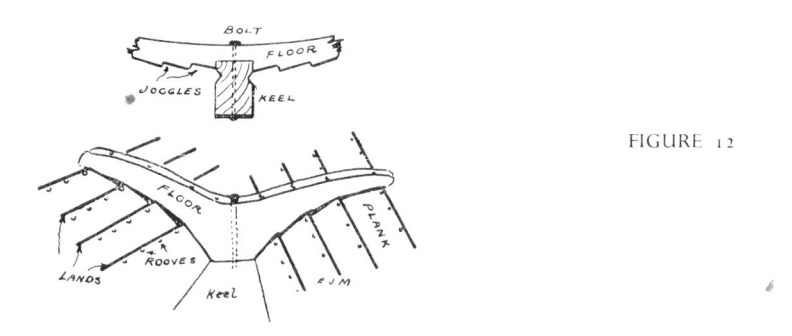

FIGURE 12

were belayed various halyards, the anchor cable, warps, mooring ropes, etc., as no winch, bitts, or windlass were fitted. Stanchions were morticed through the covering board and bolted to the frames, or else the timber heads were carried up and the bulwark planking nailed to them. Through the covering board, slightly aft of the mast, were two heavy eyebolts to take the lower blocks of the halyards and burton.

In essentials this method of construction was identical with that used by the Vikings hundreds of years before.

The foremast, almost upright, stood close to the bows in a heavy wooden tabernacle, open on the aft side except for an iron strap which kept the mast in position when upright. The three sides of the tabernacle stepped on the floors or the keelson, if one was fitted, which was not always the case with luggers. The lower half was filled with deadwood so that the heel of the mast rested about four feet from the floors. At Hastings the mast heel was on deck, with a heavy samson post below to take the thrust, and the mast lowered back between two curved timbers—the "feathers"—extending from the deck up to heavy knees for'ard of the mast. In the famous Yarmouth yawls these timbers were called the "lears."

Aft of the foremast was an opening in the deck called the "scuttle," into which the mast was lowered by the forestay or burton. In the Yorkshire yawls this was known as the "gauntry" or "gantry," in the Cornish boats as the "scottle." It was cased inside to prevent water getting into the net room, and covered with a hatch, which was removed when the mast was to be lowered. This was done by easing away on the purchase from masthead to stem until the mast, pivoting on its rounded heel, came to rest in the crutch of the mitchboard, a broad timber some twelve feet high, which was stepped in the partners of the old mainmast in luggers which had converted from three-masters, or into a hardwood case in a similar position in the newer craft. The port arm of the crutch was longer than the starboard, as prior to 1868 it was used as a standard on which the regulation light was fixed when the lugger was lying to her nets. If the mast was left standing, the boat lay very uneasy, and would drift too fast if any wind.

The mizzen mast was stepped in a tabernacle just for'ard of the rudder head, and a little to port so as to allow sufficient play for the tiller. At Hastings and Scarborough it was the custom to step the mizzen to starboard. The mizzen, always kept standing, was supported by shrouds and carried a fidded topmast which was housed when the fugger was fishing. At Yarmouth it was upright, but at Lowestoft it raked sharply lor'ard so that the topmast truck was within a few feet of the peak of the fore yard (Plate 14).

I was fearfully bucked when I found amongst the treasures stacked away in Mr. Jenkins' cellar at Lowestoft four magnificent plates of clench-built luggers, taken well over seventy years ago. For detail they are unsurpassed, even a failure to hit a nail on the head sees the bruising on the wood faithfully recorded. Fishermen favoured "bright work," because varnishing the planks showed up the slightest defect in workmanship or material, there was no chance of hiding up either with putty and paint. Varnish preserves wood from water absorption better than paint.

Plate 7 shows L.T.500 lying on the hard at low water, and the toggery worn by the men is worth more than a passing glance; those thigh-high seaboots, made of beautifully supple leather, the barked canvas jumpers with no buttons to catch up in the nets, and the extraordinary shaped headgear, were they possibly a survival of those high-crowned hats beloved by the Dutch in Stuart days? Plate 8 of Y.H.483 *Dew Drop*, also taken in Lowestoft harbour, clearly shows the copper sheathing at the bows to prevent the flukes of the anchor from catching in the lands of the planking. In each lugger the change from clench to carvel build at the binns will be noted, also the bilge keels. *Dew Drop* is a "converter" smack, to judge from the berthing to protect the planking where the trawl head came inboard. It was customary to fit out for trawling after the herring season, and at Yarmouth they fished on either side, not always on the port side, as was the usual practice, except occasionally when it was handy to tow over the starboard quarter. It would appear that the same father and son were photographed in each picture, but who they were I have no idea. Mr. Harry George recalls an interesting incident about Y.H.483. Through some oversight, sufficient heed was not taken of the build of her skipper, Walter Nobbs, who, like so many of the fishermen of that day, was of herculean stature. When well out to sea he went to go below, found that his girth prevented him from squeezing down the hoodway, and had to make do under some sort of a shack in the boat until the lugger returned to port, when the hoodway was enlarged. Mr. Woodhouse tells me that this particular lugger was built under a tree, from which the dew dropped on to the hull, hence the name.

Plates 9 and 10 of L.T.272, *Princeps*, are most interesting as the beautiful underwater lines can be admired. She was dandy-rigged, as evidenced by the presence of the iron horse on which the mainsheet traversed, and there are five timberheads, against the six in the other luggers. Note also the eye at stemhead to take the forestay, the gammon iron and the ring-bolt on stemplate to take the swivelhook of the tizzot. The four shaped iron standards aft are to take the light boards, and the mitchboard, stepped amidships, gives a good idea of the angle taken by the foremast when lowered, as the tabernacle head can just be seen. Altogether, *Princeps* is a very fine example of the boatbuilder's art. It will also be noticed that she carries her bowsprit to starboard, while the others have theirs to port. I have many photographs which show that there was no hard and fast rule as to the position of this spar. Usually the nets were hauled on the starboard side, which necessitated bowsprit, capstan, etc., being to port, and I think it is possible that this custom originated among the more deeply religious fishermen from the incident described in John xxi, where Simon Peter complains that they had toiled all night and caught nothing. Our Lord replies, "Cast the net on the right side of the ship and ye shall find. They cast therefore, and now they were not able to draw it for the multitude of fishes." In Cornwall and Scotland the nets were always hauled on the starboard side, and some fishermen held that it was exceedingly unlucky to shoot the nets over the port side.

*Princeps* was built at Lowestoft in 1881 and registered 32 tons. She had a very short life, as on the 21st March 1884, the lugger was in collision with the German barquentine *Joaquin* eighteen miles S.S.W. of the Eddystone, when fishing out of Plymouth. There was a fresh easterly breeze blowing, and the fishing vessel was a total loss. Her owner was J. E. Burrage, of Lowestoft, the master H. Breed, and the crew numbered eight.

To give some idea of a shipyard over seventy years ago, I cannot do better than quote from a letter I received in June 1946 from Mr. Thomas Adams, then the oldest surviving shipwright in Lowestoft:

"I was apprenticed to shipwrighting in the year 1876 to Messrs. Capps and Crisp of Lowestoft. The hours of work were 6 a.m. to 6 p.m. Monday to Friday, and 6 a.m. to 4 p.m. on Saturday, with half-an-hour for breakfast, one hour for dinner. We had to serve seven years' apprenticeship, starting at 2s. 6d. per week and 1s. raise every year. When we came out of our time we got 30s. per week, which was considered good wages then. We built a sailing lugger called the *Start* in the year 1876. She was 44 ft. long on the keel and was clinker-built, that is, one plank overlapping the other, and fastened with copper nails and washers. The timbers were cut by hand and fitted inside. We used to cut our timbers on the pit saw, which means that the timber was laid over a pit. One man stood in the bottom of the pit and another was on top, and the saw was pushed up and down; it was very hard work. The ribs were chopped out with an adze.

We used blearing hair on the seams, that means we put hot pitch and tar mixed on with a stick and then put hair on. We built a sailing smack in 1886 for Mr. Saunders, which was named *Renown*. We then built what is known as a carvel-built boat, that is the timbers were all erected into position on the keel first and then the planks were fastened to them with $\frac{5}{8}$-in. galvanised bolts, the trunnel or trenail had passed out by then. All shaping of timbers had to be done by hand with an axe or adze. We would take the rough tree big enough to make the opposite sides and then it would be put over the pit saw and sawn down the centre, one being for starboard and one for port side. All planking would be cut on the pit saw, which was six to eight feet long."

To my lasting regret I did not have the pleasure of meeting Mr. Adams, because when I called at his house in the October I learned that he had passed away two months before, and that he spoke to the day of his death of his pleasure at my interest in recording something of the old days and ways.

Mr. L. W. Moore and I unearthed some exceedingly fine photographs of shipyards in Mr. Jenkins' cellar. Plate 11 shows an old type lugger, *Eclipse*, hauled up on the hard, perhaps for conversion, as it is just possible to discern the iron horse for the main sheet, and the foremast, resting on the mitchboard, has standing shrouds. Ahead of her is one of the then new-fashioned elliptical-sterned dandies, L.T. 502, *Gem*, a clue to the date as my records show she was a 26-tonner built in 1877, and still afloat in 1898. The primitive hand capstan, the hauling-up cradles on rollers, and the timberheads in the foreground are of great interest.

*Mary Louisa*, built by Fuller in 1877, was the first round-sterned carvel-built drifter launched. She finished up in Jersey.

Mr. Wm. S. Parker, who was a designer at Hervey Reynold's Lake Lothing Yard, and now well over eighty years old, writes me concerning this picture:

"This was Henry Reynold's South-side shipyard, Lowestoft, till about 1898, the site now taken up by the Co-operative Co. Works and the East Anglian Ice Co. Many a smart sailing drifter and smack was turned out from this yard whilst in the hands of Henry Reynolds and his practical shipbuilding foreman, Daniel Fuller. On the other side of Kirkly Herm was the boat-building yard of Samuel Richards, who also turned out a number of smart sailing drifters during his time."

Mr. Parker says of Plate 12:

"John Chamber's Shipyard, Lowestoft, situate on the north side of Lake Lothing near the railway engine sheds, as shown in the left-hand corner of the photo. It was formerly in the hands of Messrs. Fuller, shipbuilders, about 1870-75 or thereabouts. Fullers were undoubtedly the forerunners of the round-stern type of smack. Many a smart one was turned out from this yard whilst in their hands, and also when the yard was run by Page and Chambers, Chambers and Colby, and later John Chambers, when it was fitted with two hauling-up slipways for steam drifters, etc."

One drifter is being planked, the other, nearly ready for launching, I have identified as *Lottie*, Y.H.434, built in 1899, so that fixes the date as some fifty years ago. She was a wooden steam drifter registering 32 N.T.51 G.T. on dimensions 73.5 by 17.2 by 7.7. Her 15 h.p. engine would not give much reserve of power. In 1920 this drifter was owned by S. J. W. George, of Yarmouth, and J. W. George, of Winterton.

In October 1946 I wandered round the site of this once busy yard; the shed in the foreground was tumbling into ruin, and rank grass grew everywhere. Down at the water's edge were the half-submerged rotting hulks of several smacks, their gaunt timbers a vantage point for gulls.

Amongst other prints rescued from oblivion in our treasure hunt, for such it was to me, were two views of the North Denes, with well-wooded slopes almost hiding the 53 ft. tower of the lighthouse. In the foreground of Plate 5, nets and warps are laid out to dry after barking, while Plate 13 shows sails being dressed with that mixture of horse grease, red and yellow ochre, and sea-water, which gave them such pleasing tints. The heavy red pantiles are typical of old dwellings and sheds in Suffolk and Norfolk.

Photographs of East Coast luggers under sail appear to be exceedingly rare; I have only two in my collection. One, Plate 14, is L.T.526, *Young John*, of 27 tons, built 1877 at Penzance and photographed in Mount's Bay about 1895. Note the pronounced rake to the mizzen mast. The other, Plate 15, is L.T.757 *Lizzie* of 28 tons, built 1891. Here again the hull appears to have been built in the West Country, no timberheads show above the rail as in L.T.526, instead mooring cleats are fixed to stanchions, typical Cornish practice, and the mizzen is stepped more upright than was usual at Lowestoft.

Up to the time of writing I have been unable to discover any photographs of Yarmouth luggers under sail, and should be pleased to hear if any exist. I was therefore the more delighted when visiting my friend, Mr. C. J. Greene, to find in his magnificent collection of models a contemporary one of a Yarmouth lugger hauling in her nets, a perfect gem, and obviously the work of a master craftsman. It is signed C. J. Saunders, Great Yarmouth, a rather unusual feature, and I am inclined to think he was also responsible for a similar model of Y.H.256 *Fisherman*, which was on loan to the Science Museum until 1946, as both show similar craftsmanship. Mr. Greene readily agreed to my suggestion that I should take off the lines, and in June and July, 1947, I spent many interesting hours at this pleasant task, and the resulting plans will be found on pages 298-301. The lugger is Y.H.56 *Gipsy Queen*, and further research has found that she was built in 1859 and registered 20 tons. Thanks to Mr. H. Oliver Hill's painstaking work in recording casualties to fishing craft, I find that she was still afloat in 1882, as on October 24th of that year she lost sails, mizzen mast, boat, etc., and one of her crew of ten in a heavy W.S.W. gale just outside the Haisborough Sands, Norfolk, when fishing out of Great Yarmouth. At the time she was owned by R. Warner, of Gorleston, and S. Morris was master.

The hull is beautifully built to a scale of ¼ in. to 1 ft., with the distinctive clench building clearly detailed. Although a waterline model, the hull has been sunk in a recess made in a ⅜ in. board, well carved to represent the sea, and it was therefore possible to take off the underwater lines, which faired perfectly when set out on the drawing-board.

Apart from the exquisite workmanship, the first thing that strikes one is the bright paintwork. Below the bends or binns, the hull is dark green, with varnished strakes between black wales, while a gold line sets off the beauty of the sheer. The transom is green with white stern boards, and the name *Gipsy Queen* emblazoned in gold on a black ground, with a touch of red on rudder post where it enters the helm-port. Masts and spars are varnished, hatch coamings red inside, black out, bulwarks and stanchions are green, the tiller is green with a bright red grip, companion, called in Norfolk the "hoodway," is green with red inside, the lantern box red, capstan black spindle and green whelps, fore tabernacle red inside, green out, mizzen tabernacle black and green. The three capstan men are wearing red caps of a curious mediaeval design, short blue jackets and buff trousers. The crew of nine, mostly in yellow barked jumpers and sou-westers, are at the stations to be described presently.

*Gipsy Queen* was one of the big luggers, measuring 66 ft. L.O.A., 60 ft. L.B.P., keel 53 ft. 6 in., extreme beam 17 ft., depth 8 ft. Draught 5 ft. for'ard, 6 ft. 9 in. aft.

The stem is sided 8 in., moulded 12 in., with an iron stemplate carried up to form an eye at head to take forestay tackle hook. To starboard is an iron bumpkin for the tack of the forelug, and 2 ft. 6 in. down is a ringbolt for the swivel hook of the tizzot. To port is the gammon iron through which the bowsprit reeves. Immediately inboard is the anchor lashed to eyebolts in deck, then comes the tabernacle standing 18 in. above deck, with a heavy iron bar on the open aft side to keep mast in position. To port are the iron bitts for the heel of the bowsprit. Aft of the foremast is the scuttle, then a companion with the usual sliding hatch. On either bow are six timberheads, 4 in. square and 9 in. above the rail, which is on the heavy side, measuring nearly 9 in. wide against the more usual 6 in. On their faces are heavy thumb cleats and eyebolts in the covering board for the various purchases. Next comes the net room hatch, on its aft coaming are the thwartship boards, 4 in. thick, 1 ft. 6 in. high, with a 9 in. dia. roller over which the nets pass when being drawn into or out of the hold. Nearly amidships is the fish hatch, 9 ft. by 5 ft. 6 in., with 9 in. wide bankboards, seven a side, extending to the bulwarks. These boards prevented any possibility of the nets catching up as they passed over the deck and rails. Aft are the partners, painted green, holding the "mitchboard," a stout timber, 12 in. wide and 6 in. thick, with the crutch about 12 ft. from deck level, and a wooden step on either side. On the port step the heel of the bowsprit rests and is lashed to the fore mast when the spar is run in. About three feet above the deck is the scudding pole, the fore end bevelled to suit the angle of the lowered mast to which the 6 in. diam. pole is lashed. A tenon on the after end slips into a corresponding mortice in the mitchboard. Aft is the chain locker hatch and the fish pounds, divided up by the dog kid boards about a foot high. To port is an eyebolt in the deck to take the mizzen jump stay and the belaying pin in the rail is for the topmast stay. Two low bollards were probably used when stoppers were put on warp or cable. Then comes the hatch over the rope room, with a roller on aft coaming so placed that the warp passes under before reaching capstan, and over after. The high conical capstan stands in the centre of the 14 ft. dia. walk, which has oak battens nailed to deck to give a grip for the men tramping round and round. The companion, or hoodway, has an octagonal box to starboard, where the lantern is stowed when not in use, and thus within easy reach of shelter when lighting the candle or oil lamp. On either quarter the fore sheet hooks to an eyebolt outside the bulwarks, with the single block for'ard, ready to hook in the clew of the fore lug. This arrangement allows the fall to be led along the deck from the second sheave of the double block, then a number of men could tail on, for those big lugs took a deal of sheeting home in a strong breeze. On the quarter rails are the lumber irons, here 1 ft. dia. rings, usually the aft iron was open like a rowlock, in them are stowed the spare sails, sweeps, etc. To port is the big mizzen lug made up on its 24 ft. yard, the sweeps are 24 ft. long, with 8 ft. blades, the hitcher is 30 ft., boathook 22 ft., and another with a pitchfork head is 26 ft. long. The light boards are shipped on iron stanchions stepped through the rail into a socket in the covering board.

The mizzen mast is stepped in a tabernacle open on the fore side, with an iron bar across, at foot is an eyebolt in deck to take the lower block of the lug halyards. Abaft is a heavy thwart, painted black, carrying various eyebolts and belaying pins, and morticing into a stout post 9 in. square and 2 ft. high above each rail. Amidships is a small hatch giving access to the sail locker, and to port is the outrigger heel, held in position by a fid through a timber to port. Outside the hull on the port side is an iron spider to give sufficient spread to the shroud, and here also the topmast backstay is set up. The oak tiller is held amidships by relieving tackles to eyebolts in either rail. The planking extends halfway up the stern timbers, above is open to the taffrail, a fashion common to smacks and drifters at this period. An iron collar on the port side of the taffrail secures the outrigger in position.

FIGURE 13

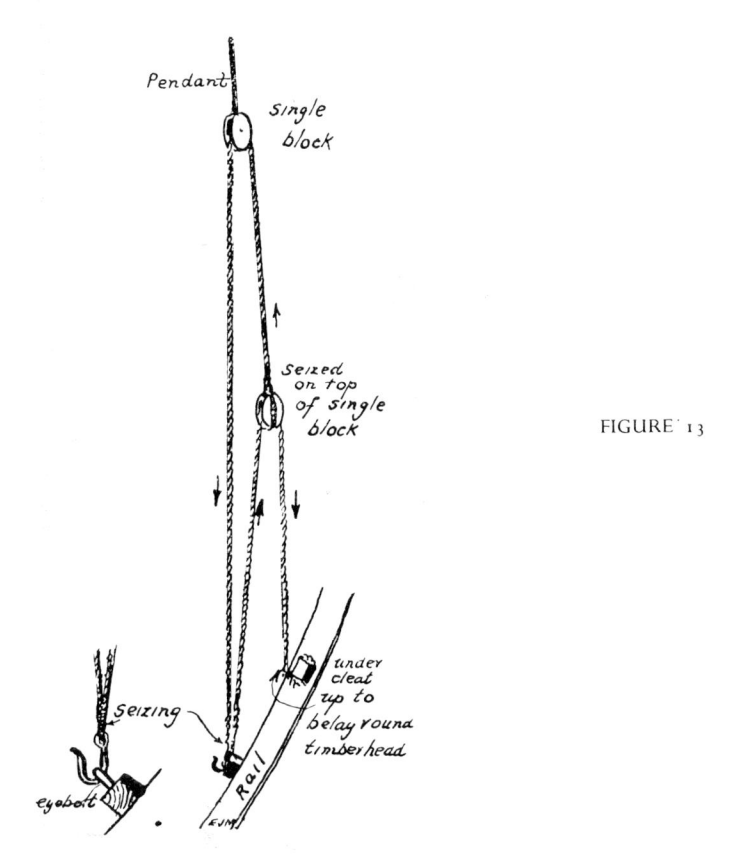

Water was carried in four large barrels lashed to eyebolts in deck and stanchions, the spar buoy and bowls to support the warp are stowed on deck for'ard.

Below deck the hull is divided up by bulkheads. Aft is the cabin, with a sail locker extending into the counter, then comes the warp room, where the salt was stored in the wings. The chain cable coils down into a locker amidships immediately below the hatch. Next is the fish hold—in the smaller luggers the nets were stowed amidships, and the fish packed in the wings, for'ard is the net room, and forehold, where spare gear was kept.

Masts and spars are on the heavy side, as is the rigging, which, being of hemp, necessitates the use of large blocks. The foremast, 40 ft. from deck to head, is 12 in. square at deck, where it steps into the tabernacle, and has no standing rigging. The forestay, or burton, used for lowering the mast, consists of a heavy pendant with eye resting on the shoulder at the masthead, and an 18 in. single block stropped to lower end. The purchase is a runner and tackle with the standing end of the runner hooked to the eye at stemhead, then reeving through the upper single block with an 18 in. double block stropped to lower end. The 12 in. single block of the luff purchase also hooks into eye at stemhead and has the standing end of the fall fast to its head. The fall leads up through one sheave in the double block, down through sheave in single block, up to second sheave, and then it reeves through another 10 in. single block at stem before belaying round first timberhead on the starboard rail.

A single Spanish burton is to port, consisting of a pendant with eye round masthead and a single block stropped to lower end. The fall is fast to the head of a second single block, reeves up through sheave in first block, down to deck, where the bight is fast to a hook which goes to eye in face of timberhead; the fall leads on up through second single block, down under a thumb cleat, and up to belay round fifth timberhead (Fig. 13).

Only the big luggers had forestays, which either hooked to foot of mast when not in use, or could be set up on the lee side as an additional support. In the smaller boats the burton was taken for'ard to the stemhead when the mast had to be lowered. While the mast rested on the mitchboard it was steadied by taking the lug halyards to starboard, the burton to port, and the forestay to stemhead, the falls belaying round the timber heads, but as soon as the mast was raised and the lug hoisted, both halyards and burton were *always* set up on the weather side, and so had to be shifted over every time the boat went about, the burton hooking to an eyebolt about 2 ft. aft of the halyard.

On the foremast was set a large dipping lug, 12 to 14 cloths at the head, and 18 to 24 at the foot, with three lines of reef points. The yard was moderately peaked, and the tack hooked to a short iron bumpkin projecting out some 2 ft. from the stem, or to a hook at stemhead, the sail sheeting home well aft on the mizzen thwart. It was bent to a 30 ft. yard with rovings, short lengths of line at each eyelet instead of a continuous lacing, the long ends serving as tyers. These rovings were usually called "knittles" by fishermen.

The yard has a rope grommet secured between two chocks about one-third of the distance from the throat, or some 10 ft. Round the mast was a parrel of beads or an iron traveller with a large hook which went into the grommet. To this traveller the tye of the halyards was bent, and was of rope kept well greased, or chain in the later boats, reeving through a dumb sheave about 18 in. from the top of the mast, with a large double block stropped on lower end. The single block of the luff purchase, hooked into eye in covering board, has the standing end of the fall fast to its head. The fall reeves through one sheave of upper block, down through sheave in lower block, up through second sheave, then down under a thumb cleat and up to belay round fifth timberhead. If not in use, the traveller was secured by a rope lashing near the foot of mast, and when the bowsprit was run in, the lug was lashed on top or else stowed along the bulwarks on the port side of deck. Six inches above the dumb sheave is a shoulder on which the eyes of rigging rest, and above is a sheave for the jib halyards; no truck is fitted, the head tapers up to 6 in. dia.

The bowsprit measures 38 ft. overall, with 24 ft. outboard, and is 1 ft. square at heel for first 11 ft., then tapers to 9 in. dia. at outer end. In the heel is a score to take the heelrope and three fidholes, 3 ft. apart, allow the spar to be reefed to suit the jib set. When run in, the bowsprit heel rested on the deck, except when the mast was lowered, then it was lashed to step on port side of the mitchboard, some 8 ft. clear of deck. The bowsprit, stepped between an iron bitt and the tabernacle, reeves through a gammon iron to port of stem, and is stayed by a bobstay of chain or rope, with its standing end fast to eyebolt in stem near waterline, and a single block at outer end. Fall is fast to tail of single block at bowsprit end, reeves through first block, back to second block, and leads inboard through a bullseye in bulwarks, or over rail, before belaying to timberhead. The jib traveller outhaul reeves through sheave at outer end of bowsprit and back over rail to belay round timberhead. The jib halyards had a luff purchase hooked to eye in port covering board and fall belayed to timberhead above; when not in use they hooked to eyebolt near foot of mast.

The mizzen mast, 34 ft. long, is 10 in. square at heel, where it steps into a tabernacle off centred 2 ft. 6 in. to port of midship line. Six feet from masthead is a dumb sheave for the lug halyards, 2 ft. above is a shoulder on which eyes of the shrouds rest, 18 in. higher is the sheave for mastrope, and the iron caps for the topmast heel. As a standing lug is always set to port, the mizzen mast could be supported by shrouds, consisting of a hemp pendant with double block stropped to lower end. The single block of the luff purchase hooked in an eyebolt on a stanchion to starboard, and fall belays round pin on thwart, to port it hooks in an eye on the spider, and fall belays round its own lower end with two half hitches.

The mast is stayed for'ard by a jump stay with a thimble at lower end, and sets up with a lanyard to an eyebolt in port side of deck, one foot from covering board. The masthead, tapering to 6 in. dia., has no truck, but the 16 ft. topmast has one; this spar is stepped through two light iron rings on masthead, and is supported by a stay for'ard, belaying to pin in port rail, and backstays with bullseyes at lower ends. A lanyard, fast to an eyebolt on stanchion on either side, reeves through the bullseye and belays to pin in rail. When the topmast was housed, the backstays were shortened by making a sheepshank in the lower end of each pendant. The mastrope leads up through sheave in masthead and belays to pin on thwart.

The outrigger, 31 ft. long, is 12 in. square at heel for 7 ft., with a score for heelrope, and three fid holes allow for reefing. It tapers to 9 in. dia. at outer end, where a single block is lashed. The spar is stepped below the thwart between a timber bitt to port and the tabernacle, and secured to taffrail in an iron collar.

The big lug, made up on its 24 ft. yard, is stowed in the port lumber irons, and the small "drift" mizzen, with a 16 ft. 6 in. yard and two lines of reef points, is set. The halyards have the single block of the luff purchase hooked to eye in deck, and fall belays round pin in thwart. The tack cringle goes to a hook on aft side of thwart, and the clew is hooked to a long S-shaped hook on the pendant, which reeves through the single block on end of outrigger and has another single block stropped to its inner end. The fall of the sheet is fast to an eyebolt on aft side of thwart, reeves through this single block and belays to pin on thwart. When the lugger was lying to her nets the sail was sheeted home amidships.

The topsail was bent to a 20 ft. yard, the halyards belayed to starboard, and sheet led through a bullseye or single block at peak of lugyard, rove through another block at slings, and down mast to belay on tack hook; the tack had a whip purchase hooked to eyebolt in deck. I have so far been unable to find out if the topsail was always to leeward, or left standing to port when the lugger was on a wind.

East Coast luggers did not shift lugs as was the Cornish practice; they always reefed down.

Plan 2 page 300 shows that the underwater lines are pleasing, the floors are sharp, and the curved stem is similar to that of the herring buss 300 years before.

The crew numbered eight to twelve, the big luggers carrying a master and mate, a netrope scudder who assisted the mate in scudding the fish, hauled the warp from below, and was capable of mending the nets. The netrope man shot and hauled the nets with the waleman, who also kept the nets in the proper order for fishing, in addition he had to be able to keep a watch, steer, reef, and splice. The hawseman put on and cast off buoys and seizings when shooting and hauling the nets, salted the fish, was able to work ship and keep the lights in order. The four capstanmen, or three capstanmen and a netstower, known in Norfolk as "Joskins," were not fishermen, but the farm labourer type of man, whose strength was the principal consideration, as it was back-breaking work, especially in strong winds. Each haul meant a tramp in a rotary direction of from seven to thirteen miles, according to the length of warp out, and that often in pitch darkness, pouring rain, sleet, or snow, when an icy deck called for a shoulder pin at the end of each 7 ft. bar to prevent a man flying overboard if he slipped on the capstan walk. These men helped to salt the fish and keep ship clean.

The boy, or "younker," was at everyone's beck and call. Poor little devil! The twelfth hand was the cook, whose knowledge of the culinary art was often exceedingly elementary; he was also supposed to keep the cabin clean and obey all lawful commands.

The men usually wore a canvas jumper reaching nearly to the knees, with no buttons to catch up in the nets. To make them waterproof these serviceable garments were barked like the sails. The master often wore a longer version, reaching to the ankles, which made him look as if he had come on deck in his nightshirt! Sometimes a sheepskin was turned inside out and well dressed with linseed oil, making a wonderfully warm jacket, forerunner of the fleecy-lined waistcoats of our airmen! Thick, home-knitted woollen stockings were thrust into thigh-length seaboots in dirty weather

19 *DUKE OF CONNAUGHT*,
   c. 1895
   Note lug mizzen sheeting to
   outrigger, length of gaff.

21 *TWILIGHT*, c. 1895
   Note vertical set of topsail, set-up of bobstay, bonnet on mainsail.

20 *JAMES*, c. 1895
   Note lute stern, flywheel capstan, clench
   build.

22 *YOUNG LINNETT* ENTERING LOWESTOFT Note curved gaff. Was lugger rigged in 1885.

23 *SUSIE* LEAVING YARMOUTH Note lute stern.

24 CAISTER OWNED DRIFTER ENTERING YARMOUTH Note m board stepped amidsh

25 *MAUD* ENTERING YARMOUTH. 32 tons, built Southtown, 1883. Note clench build.

26 *FLORENCE MAY*, 1883
Note jacky topsail on mainmast, jigger one on mizzen.

27 *FREDA*, 1884
Note bonnets on foresail, mainsail and mizzen.

28 *LITTLE PET*, 1884
Note bankboards amidships under rail.

but clumpers or short boots were worn in fair. Caps, varnished bowlers, and tophats, or sou'westers, were favourite headgear. Many of the families were descended from Hastings men who had settled in East Anglia.

A lugger's best point of sailing was reaching—"ratching" in fisherman's parlance—with the sheets just started. Very weatherly they would sail to within four points of the wind, or five when a jib was set and being very fast could outpoint and outsail most fore and afters.

How homely and appropriate were the names the fishermen gave to their boats: *Gleaner*, *Harvest of the Sea*, *Breadwinner*, *Thankful*, *Provider*, *Our Boys*, *Thrift*, *Shades of Evening*, not to mention those named after loved ones.

What a lovely sight it must have been to see the herring fleet standing out to sea in the golden haze of an autumn day, the red, brown, and tan sails of the Low'stermen eclipsed by the lofty dark brown or black lugsails of the Scottish fifies and zulus. Here the smaller Cornish luggers, there the brilliantly-coloured "splashers"—the Yorkshire cobles with bold bows and squat sterns. The setting sun, touching the tops of the waves, burnishes the white wakes with a golden light, and brings out all the glowing colours of hulls and sails. The distant shore grows indistinct as the sky darkens and night falls.

One and all are steering for that spot where, in the experience of the master, herring are likely to be found. Extending seaward off the Norfolk coast for a distance of some fifty miles lie long, narrow, parallel banks of sand where in patches the water shoals rapidly to barely $2\frac{1}{2}$ fathom. In the deeps between, soundings range from 12 to upwards of 20 fathom, and the bottom is fine sand. Strong tides run N.W. and S.E., the ebb to the north, the flood towards the south, at varying speeds according to the quarter of the moon. Here the nets can drift up and down between the banks for a distance of some seventy miles from the Knoll to the Dowsing, where in the autumn months the herring assemble in numbers which stagger the imagination, and literally thousands of miles of drift nets are shot in the deep water to mesh this harvest of nature, which is free to all comers, with none to say them nay until these days of controls and licences. Away up north in the long days of June there is plenty of sea room, but off Norfolk conditions are often very crowded, with perhaps one thousand miles of nets shot in a single night. This wall of netting drives with the tide, and because the nets do not normally move in the water they can be shot side by side quite close to one another, a couple of hundred yards or so apart.

If on arriving on the ground where he thinks the shoals are likely to be, a skipper finds other drifters, not only has he to look for a berth with sufficient space to shoot his nets, but he must judge if his train will drive during the night clear of shallows, buoys, lightships and especially wrecks on the seabed, for should any nets become "fast," all those upstream will pile up into a most glorious tangle, and the odds are that they will have to be cut away—a loss perhaps amounting to hundreds of pounds.

This was especially the case after the two 20th century wars, when hundreds of vessels were deliberately sunk by mine and torpedo on the fishing grounds, but at the time of which I write such insensate doings were undreamed of. Again, huge areas of drifting seaweed may hamper the shooting of the nets.

A decision made, the skipper put his craft before the wind, and as much across the tide as possible, and shooting began about sunset. The netrope scudder hauled the warp up from below to be paid out aft over the quarter. The nets, all stowed in regular order in the net room, were brought up over the roller, thus easing the strain on them, while the bankboards, placed between the coamings and rail, prevented any danger of their hitching up whilst passing over the deck. Two hands, the netrope man and the waleman, shot the nets, one being in charge of the lint, the other the corks and bowls; a capstan man had the job of looking out for the seizings as the nets came on deck, and ran aft with them to the mate, who made them fast to the warp, his judgment as to whether the fish were swimming deep or shallow deciding the length of the strops. After four nets were out, the dan buoy with its flag went overboard, then followed fathom after fathom of net and warp. When all the nets were clear 15 to 20 fathom more warp was paid out as a swing rope, the lugger was brought round head to wind, sail was taken in, the foremast lowered on to the mitchboard and either a small mizzen —the drift mizzen—was set, or the bonnet taken off the larger lug, the regulation lights hoisted, and the watch set. Prior to 1868 a lantern was fixed on the port crutch of the mitchboard, although an Act of 1843 ordered that two lights, one over the other and three feet apart, were to be hoisted on one of the masts. This Act was honoured more in the breach than the observance, no one took very much notice of its provisions, and drifters carried just what lights they pleased, and placed them where they liked. As might be supposed, this happy-go-lucky state of affairs led to endless confusion, especially when intensive trawling developed, and it was no use blaming a smack for cutting through a fleet of nets when the skipper had not the faintest idea that a drifter was working in the vicinity; trawling was not supposed to be carried on within three miles of any boat drift fishing. In point of fact, many of the men had never bothered to read the regulations, and were in blissful ignorance of what lights they had to carry, or where they were not supposed to trawl. Perhaps one could hardly blame the drift fishermen for not hoisting the regulation lights and proclaiming to all and sundry that their nets were out, since it was not unknown for crews of vessels to drift down quietly, pick up a few nets, help themselves to what fish were meshed therein, and then cut or throw the nets overboard. This mean practice was prevalent in Tudor times, and an Act of 1571 prohibited any vessel anchoring in the tide stream used by fishermen between sunset and sunrise during the period 14th September to 14th November, old time. The Sea Fisheries Act 1868 was drawn up to enforce the regulations more strictly, and later the position of the lights was altered, and two white lights had to be so placed that the vertical distance between them was not less than six or more than fifteen feet, with a horizontal distance not less than five or more than ten feet. The lower of these two lights has to be in the direction of the nets, both must show all round the horizon, and be visible for at least two miles.

Steadied by the mizzen, the boat now drifted under the influence of wind and tide, and a strain was placed on her fleet of nets, whose bowls bobbed about in the tideway in a long zig-zag line. Should the wind be light, a drifter exerts little pull on the nets, but in half a gale the drag must be lessened by paying out more swing rope, and at times up to 100 fathom may be necessary. If the boat starts to tow her nets there is the risk that they will coil round the warp and tangle, whilst any undue movement may scare the fish. Should the wind shift, luggers and nets will get crossed over each other. It may be possible to sort this out in the morning, but a loss of nets must be expected.

All around is the plaintive cry of the herring gulls, the slap and gurgle of the tide, the plop as a porpoise heaves itself out of the water and falls back again. A thin chilly wind moans in the rigging, and the hundreds of twinkling lights all around are not unlike those of a great city. Overhead is the domed vault of the sky, with fitful glimpses of stars as the clouds move slowly across, and perhaps a sickle moon low on the horizon. A thousand boats and more may be out, each riding to upwards of a mile of nets, one man remains on deck whilst the rest turn in for a short spell.

Meanwhile, all the boats are driving with the tide, and during the night a lugger might cover fifteen miles with a spring tide under her, but only about five if a neap, the nets hanging in a wall fifty to seventy feet deep. Occasionally the warp is hauled in till the first net—the look-on net—is reached, to see whether herring are about or dogfish numerous, for these hated fish can do great damage if the nets are left too long in the water.

Drifting is a chancy business, a lugger may have a full strike almost as soon as the nets are in the water, or hours may pass before the shoals rise, and some of the fish become entangled by their gills in the fine meshes. On one occasion a Yarmouth lugger shot her nets for three weeks without getting a herring, until one day the master saw a gull swoop on the nets and seize a fish; within a few minutes there was a tremendous strike which yielded 12 lasts.

When the swim comes, a drifter may catch from ten thousand to upwards of a quarter of a million herring in an hour or so. This may happen in a comparatively small patch, and only a few lucky ones benefit, or it may come to the whole fleet of luggers, in which case there will certainly be a glut on the market, and prices will tumble down. If the nets become overloaded with fish, their weight will take the nets to the bottom, since being unable to work their gills, the herring drown and become so much deadweight. If the catch is got on board it may be necessary to throw thousands overboard because of the danger of the lugger sinking beneath the weight.

In 1853 *Perseverance* of Great Yarmouth caught 126 last, or some 1½ million fish, many of which had to be sacrificed; four years later *Racehorse*, with 91 nets, caught so many herring that the master had to throw overboard about a quarter of the catch. Again, in 1870 three luggers meshed 137, 138 and 142 lasts, or 5½ million fish. On the 21st October 1865 Robert George, master of *Bluejacket*, of Yarmouth, was fishing with 121 nets when the strike was so heavy that the warp broke and all went to the bottom, a loss of £400 for gear alone. By dint of perseverance, he managed to recover five nets, in each of which half a last of herring were meshed.

A last, nominally ten thousand fish, actually numbers 13,200, and weighs about two tons, the wholesale value then averaged about £20, but might be as much as £40 to £56, or as low as £10, or even £5 if a glut.

In 1881 the French drifter *Gabrielle* of Boulogne succeeded in taking 35 lasts on board, which was as many as she could carry. The master gave 10 lasts to two Penzance luggers fishing near by, which had not benefited by the phenomenal swim, then the French crew were more than eight hours scudding overboard the fish in the remainder of the nets.

Normally, some time after midnight the long task of hauling began. The warp was led in through a snatch block near the fore mast, and under the roller just in front of the capstan so as to keep the first turn low down, the conical shape of the capstan then preventing any overlapping turns. Slowly the men tramp round and round, hour after hour the heavy warp comes in, foot by foot, with occasional spells to give the men a breather, and is coiled down in the rope room by the boy, who ran round and round flaking down the wet rope in almost pitch darkness, except for what feeble light filtered down through the small hatch. A giddy, unpleasant job.

The hawseman, standing near the bows, cast off the buoys and seizings, so disconnecting the warp from the nets as they came on board. The mate and the netropeman got the nets over the side, one at the corks, the other at the lint, while the netrope scudder and the master shook the nets over the scudding pole fixed fore and aft between the mitchboard and the lowered mast. As breadth after breadth emerges from the water, they flash with iridescent hues, blue and gold, green, silver and purple, lit up by the soft rays of the newly-risen sun, for the herring is a beautiful fish when alive, but the colours soon dim as the fish are shaken from the nets and fall in slimy masses, which slat about as the drifter rolls and pitches, before being shovelled down with wooden shovels into the well below. Those that fall on deck are dropped through the scudding holes, openings in the planking nine to ten inches long, and the full width of the plank. These are normally closed by blocks of wood tightly wedged in. Meanwhile the nets are stowed away below by the net stower in regular order, ready for shooting again. Such was the scene on a fine night. In the best of weather hauling the nets was, and is, a long, laborious job. In a bitter nor'easter with sleet and hail squalls driving down, lashing the face like a flail, it could be absolute hell, with the boat rolling viciously, and a false step often meant a man overboard. This, not for a few minutes, but maybe ten or fifteen hours at a stretch if the haul was a good one. Even to-day, when power has lightened the task of hauling in the warp, the nets, with their weighty burden, have still to be man-handled over the side out of the icy water (Plate 16).

The fish were sprinkled with salt—roused or roosed—before being stowed away in the wings of the hold. Should the haul be a heavy one, only part of the fleet of nets was got in, and the fish salted and stowed away before the remainder was brought inboard. Sometimes a haul would be made early in the night and if a light one, a second shooting was made before sunrise. The fishing over, the foremast was raised, sail made, and if unlucky, the lugger continued fishing night after night until she had a full hold, then she returned to port. No easy job in the rain-lashed blackness of a winter's night to find the channel through the numerous shoals and sandbanks off the Norfolk coast. The slightest error of judgment and the drifter was in broken water, struck, a few wild cries carried away on the howling gale, and next morning scraps of driftwood were all that remained of a fine lugger, while wives and sweethearts waited for loved ones who never returned from sea.

Yarmouth Haven is not easy to enter under certain conditions, especially when a strong ebb of three to four knots is running out against a freshening on-shore wind. Then a heavy sea breaks on the bar, and in such weather the luggers often anchored off the beach in front of the town and landed their catch in ferry boats, large open craft with a good carrying capacity and manned by the famous beach men. These boats came off loaded with empty baskets—swills—which held about 500 herring, and returned deep-laden and were beached broadside on for ease in unloading. The full baskets were raised on the gunwale and then carried up the beach by two boatmen, who linked arms and held the swills against their shoulders. As soon as the catch was ashore it was auctioned and sold by the last, mostly for curing. The system of Government branding, popular in Scotland, found little favour on the East Coast, where the local firms preferred to stand or fall on their reputation, and their stencil marks on the barrels were a sufficient hall-mark to satisfy any Continental buyer.

Plate 17 shows the fine contemporary model of the Yarmouth lugger *Fisherman*, c. 1860, which was on loan to the Science Museum until 1946, and is very similar to the one in Mr. C. J. Greene's collection. The crew are in the positions described when hauling in the nets, and evidently they were more careful in those days over fish which slipped out of the meshes, judging by the man using the long-handled didlenet. A contrast to the hundreds of excellent fish we saw wasted during a visit to Lowestoft in 1946 when they lay trodden underfoot on the quays or floated away out of the harbour. The gulls sat idly by, no doubt too gorged to eat any more—a strange sight indeed, as they are voracious feeders, and on my part of the coast one has only to make the motion of flinging scraps into the air for flocks to fly in from seaward to seize the morsels.

In January 1951, after this book had gone to press, I purchased yet another model practically identical with *Fisherman* and *Gipsy Queen*, except for the colouring of the hull which is dark green up to the binns, then black to the rails, with no varnished strakes between. It is of *Everest*, Y.H. 172, and at one time had been in a case as marks show where the hull had been recessed into a carved sea. As it had hung unprotected in the hall of a house which was badly bombed in 1940, everything was covered with a thick layer of grime, but hours of careful cleaning with tiny mops soaked in water and O'Cedar oil worked wonders. It is certainly remarkable that three perfect models, undoubtedly the work of the same craftsman, C. J. Saunders, should have survived the vicissitudes of a century.

Mr. A. Artis, of Grimsby, who kindly sent me the photograph of Y.H.856 *Breadwinner* (Plate 18), writes very graphically of his experiences in one of these old luggers, known colloquially as "salt-carts":

"They used to be away for two or three nights, but when we had the full moon they used to go out in the morning and be back the next full up and out again the same day. I was in one of the old salt-carts. We used to go on the Dogger Bank and had some rough times, blowing and snowing and wet through. When we had a gale of wind we could not get our nets, and had to ride by them, sometimes we used to cut from them, because there were too many ships there, also French and Dutchmen. We used to salt our herring, which were big, and when smoked made the best Yarmouth Reds. The old salt-carts used to go trawling as well, we only went herring fishing for three months. The old Dutch "boms" were built both ends alike, and they used to say they put chains to keep them from falling to pieces, but they had some fine big ships. We had some very bad times, still we got used to them, when the drifters like the photo were built they sold the salt-carts to farmers to break up, after taking the masts and boilers out of them. You could buy one for £2, but they took a lot of breaking up. They towed them up the river out of the way, and that was the finish of the old salt-carts. Some of the best were made into houseboats on the Broads."

These are the words of an old man who in his youth fished for herring exactly as had his ancestors hundreds of years before.

Huge hauls are still being taken, but in a somewhat different manner. As I write, I have before me an account of Norwegian purse-seine fishing 120 miles from Bergen in 1948 when from a circle of 160 fathoms long net, thirty to forty crans a minute were loaded into the hold by means of huge bailers, each holding ten crans. An average haul yields five hundred to a thousand crans, with three thousand crans from one shoot as nothing unusual, while sometimes the nets break with the vast weight of fish.

Truly the harvest of the sea is plenteous.

CHAPTER FIVE

## CONVERSION TO DANDY RIG

In the early seventies there was a revolutionary change over from the lug to the dandy rig on the East Coast, due, I think, to the following reasons. About 1854 Samuel Hewett, owner of the famous Short Blue fleet of sailing trawlers, began the transfer of his business from Barking to Gorleston, thereby introducing an entirely different method of fishing to East Anglia. With the opening of the railway, opportunity offered to dispose of hitherto unsaleable catches by sending fish to inland markets, especially London, and when the herring season was over, many of the drifters went trawling, but it was soon found that the lug rig was very inefficient for the new technique. For heaving-to, fore and aft sails were far more suitable, as the main tack could be triced up and the foresail laid aback. The many shoals and sandbanks off the coast necessitated innumerable short tacks, then the gaff rig showed to advantage, being quicker and handier, as constant dipping of the lug was obviated. With the increase in size of sails and weight of yards, handling them was becoming a more and more dangerous job in hard winds, especially with a clumsy or inexperienced crew. In the dandy or ketch rig, the sail area was more cut up, and could be managed by a smaller crew, an item well worth consideration as costs were constantly mounting, but conversion reduced speed by about a knot.

At first some of the luggers changed over to a gaff mainsail on the foremast, and retained the old mizzen with its standing lug. For'ard the new rig practically amounted to a split lug, as the sail area before the mast became a high, narrow staysail, and the boomless mainsail was about the shape of the old lugsail abaft the mast, with the foot cut so that the sail sheeted to an iron horse just for'ard of the mizzen mast. It was fitted with lines of reef points or a bonnet, sometimes both. The pole mast was retained, giving the boats a squat appearance compared with the lofty rig of the true trawler. A large gaff topsail was set above the mainsail, called a "jacky" at Lowestoft, a "jubilee" at Yarmouth.

This rig is clearly seen in L.T.98, the 27-ton *Duke of Connaught* built at Penzance in 1879, photographed c. 1895 making for Newlyn harbour (Plate 19). All the sails are reefed, and it would seem that the gaff was about the same length as the old lug yard, as the mainsail is twelve cloths by the head, and cut with a vertical leech. No boom is fitted. The standing lug on the mizzen sheets home to the end of a long outrigger, well steeved up, and the length of the pole topmast will be noted. The bowsprit is run in and the jib halyards have been hooked into the upper reef cringle of the foresail, which is sheeted to the after timberhead. Wire is beginning to take the place of hemp for standing rigging, and the foremast is supported by a wire stay, set up with a twofold purchase to the stemhead, a Spanish burton a side and standing shrouds, set up to chain plates outside the hull, and a little further aft than is usual practice, so that when the mast was lowered they could be unhooked and stowed up under the mast. The hull is now carvel-built, but the square stern is retained. She was probably originally rigged with a fore lug. On the 11th March, 1888, *Duke of Connaught* was fishing out of Plymouth and lost one of the crew of ten, binnacle and compass in a whole gale from west'ard, two miles west of Start Point.

It was soon found that the gaff rig was quite as suitable for drift fishing as for trawling, and the old lugsails rapidly disappeared, but amongst fishermen the boats were still known as luggers. There being no alteration in the position of the masts, the long space aft was still available for handling nets and fish. When the mast was lowered, the gaff, with its sail and gear stowed underneath, topped up reasonably well out of the way, although perhaps not quite so conveniently as the lug yard, which could be unhooked, and with its sail stowed, laid up along the opposite side of the deck to the one used for working the nets, or else lashed on top of the bowsprit.

The conical capstan, turned by men tramping round and round, was being replaced in many drifters by a patent capstan worked by two handles acting on a rack and pinion fitted either to the top of the spindle or to an iron standard alongside.

It was not long before the standing lug on the mizzen was superseded by a gaff sail, hooped to the mast and easily stowed under the gaff; the boom could be topped up in port, getting rid of the long unwieldy outrigger. When the bonnet laced to the foot was taken off, the mizzen sail was a convenient size to keep the boat head to wind when riding to the nets. A conversion to this rig can be seen in Plate 20, *James* L.T.503, a 29-ton clench-built lugger, built at Lowestoft in 1870, and fitted with the old-fashioned lute stern, held by many fishermen to give increased lift in a seaway, and reduce the volume of water coming aboard. Note the flywheel capstan, a further development, the sweeps, etc., stowed in the lumber irons, the bowsprit run in with jib halyards hooked to the upper block of the forestay tackle, the copper sheathing at bow, and the bonnet on the mizzen, with a line of reef points above and below. A very small jacky topsail is set, with its leech almost horizontal. Compare this with the jigger topsail carried by L.T.178 *Twilight* (Plate 21). Her long straight yard is vertical to the mast, with a short jigger yard at clew of sail, the big jib, or spinnaker as it was usually called, is cut diagonally with a vertical leech; generally this sail sheeted home well aft. The mainsail has a bonnet at the foot with a line of eyelets for a lacing, the mizzen also has a bonnet and two lines of eyelets instead of reef points. One of the early steam capstans is fitted, and three of the crew are working one of the heavy sweeps. Both these photographs were taken in Mount's Bay about 1895.

Plate 22 of L.T.270 *Young Linnett*, a 25-tonner built 1868, is interesting because of the pronounced curve to the gaff. In the eighties the fashion was to have curved heads to sails as a means of making them sit flat, and it can also be seen in Plates 27, 28 and 34. In 1885 *Young Linnett* was owned by C. T. Day, and lug-rigged.

A typical Yarmouth drifter of the transition period was Y.H.308 *Susie* (Plate 23), a photograph kindly loaned me by Mr. R. H. Green, of Gorleston. Here is a real old-timer with her lute stern and open stern-boards. Note that she has set her topsail to windward, not on the port side, as was the custom, while the white paint under the counter must have made it a little easier for an overtaking vessel to avoid running her down, as it would show up at night.

Plate 24 of Y.H.1063 was identified by Mr. J. J. Haylett as being Caister-owned, but the name had slipped his memory. Note how the big jib is pulling her along. It is rather unusual for the mitchboard to be still standing, being generally unshipped as soon as sail was made, otherwise it fouled the mainsail when the boat went about, but she has evidently had a broad reach from the fishing grounds, and is about to enter Yarmouth Haven, as the St. Nicholas light vessel, the leading mark for the Hewett Channel, can just be seen on the horizon, between the leech of the foresail and the bunt of the main. Do look at the men at the heel of the bowsprit; one is wearing the little round sealskin cap so favoured by fishermen in those days, while the other sports nothing less than a tophat, a real old "beaver," as its shagginess can clearly be seen under a magnifying glass. I also like the nonchalant attitude of the man standing with folded arms in the boat astern. They seem to have taken the Sea Fisheries Act of 1868 to heart, as the regulation lights can be hoisted on the halyards to the short arm on the port side of the mizzen mast.

Plate 25 shows Y.H.872 *Maud* entering Yarmouth Haven, standing well over to the south side to avoid being set by the tide on to the North pier. The entrance is but 200 feet wide, and the tide stream runs at full strength by the shore at high and low water, and if there is a lot of flood water coming down, the ebb will run out fiercely at some six knots, causing a wicked sea to break on the bar outside. The easiest time to enter is near low water, and it is most hazardous to run for the entrance when there is a heavy sea and a N.N.W. wind, as the flood tide, running to the south, sweeps through the open timber piling of the North pier, strikes against the South pier, and causes a fearful backwash (Plate 41).

Mr. Harry George, now living in retirement at Caister, went to sea in 1887 in one of these "converter" smacks, skippered by his father, whose pay was one penny an hour for a twenty-four hour day, or 14s. a week, and 1s. in the £ on the boat's earnings. This was then the rate of pay for a master either in a smack or a drifter-trawler, yet many a man brought up a large healthy family and saved enough to buy a part share in his craft, eventually owning her, and perhaps a fleet as well. He writes me that at that time all the Yarmouth drifters were clench-built to the waterline, with carvel upper works, the reason being to strengthen the hull, as the planks were twice the thickness of the clench work. Then there were so many smacks and drifters in Yarmouth harbour that they could not be moored broadside to the quays, but had to be made fast stem on. Owing to the strong tides, the pressure on their sides was very great, and much knocking about resulted. Another advantage was that a clench-built craft did not roll so much as a carvel one, as the overlap of the planks acted as a rolling chock.

When I was chatting with this fine old fisherman in October 1946, he gave me some interesting facts regarding the introduction of steam capstans by the firm of Elliott and Garrood. Mr. William Elliott, an agricultural engineer, had made an engine to stand on the top of a hay cutter. A fisherman happened to see this machine at work and said it was just what was wanted to drive a capstan. Mr. Elliott put his fertile mind to work, but was defeated by the problem of getting power to the engine without the steampipe getting in the way of the warp, until he had the brain-wave of making the spindle hollow on which the capstan rotated.

I wrote to Messrs. Elliott & Garrood, of Beccles, who most courteously placed plans and information at my disposal, and replied:

"We have a record of most of the capstans made and installed by us since the first one was fitted in the *Beaconsfield* at Lowestoft in 1884, and it is surprising at times to be asked for spare parts for capstans known to have been supplied early in this century. We regret that we have insufficient data regarding the very earliest capstans to pass on to you anything worth recording. Wm. Garrood, the grandfather of the undersigned, and his partner, Wm. Elliott, were at the start of their partnership in 1884 when they made their first capstan, and very little record remains. We do know that these were the first capstans to have the engine mounted on the bedplate (as they are to-day) and that the principle of the hollow steel post, taking the steam and exhaust pipes, was in 1884 an innovation and patented. The small boilers which we made and supplied to provide steam for the capstans were, no doubt, constructed for a working pressure of 100 lbs. per sq. in. Regarding the working, both steam and exhaust pipes are carried up to the engine through a hollow steel post, on which the barrel rotates. The engine has two horizontal cylinders, and the barrel is rotated by a bevel pinion driving a horizontal bevel wheel. A pulley used for discharging fish can be operated separately when required. We hope that this meagre information we have been able to give you will be of interest."

Later capstans weigh from $11\frac{1}{2}$ to $17\frac{1}{2}$ cwt., according to type of base, and have a winding speed at 100 r.p.m. of 3½ fathom a minute, at 400 r.p.m. 14 fathom, with considerable increases if size of pulley is altered.

It was good to hear of a firm still carrying on with a design which has stood the test of time, and in passing, I might mention that Elliott & Garrood are numbered amongst the very few firms who have taken any interest in my efforts to preserve the history of fishing craft and gear.

Most of the drifters built after the early eighties had carvel planking with short elliptical sterns, clean bows just full enough to give lifting power in a seaway, and finer lines below water. The new steam capstans reduced the time of hauling in the nets, but in some instances their introduction led to trouble, as a share of the catch had to be taken to pay for their cost, and use; and disorders, known as the capstan riots, occurred in many ports.

To bring the catch to market in the shortest possible time, "cracking on" was indulged in. Well-cut cotton sails and huge jackyard topsails were carried on both masts. On the bowsprit was a colossal jib—the spinnaker—with its head almost touching the mast head, and the clew well aft of the fore shrouds. Sometimes when making a passage, a staysail was set on the "Tommy Hunter," the local name given to the tackle used to stay the mizzen mast for'ard. East Coast drifters were among the hardest driven of all sailing craft, as their skippers clung to their jackyarders even when the lower sails were reefed by taking off the bonnets. This reduced size and weight of sails at the same time and so avoided the heavy sodden mass of canvas at the foot when reef points were used, while the gaff being much in the same position, there was little chance of a sea breaking into the foot of the sail, a serious danger with the mast stepped so far for'ard (Plate 40).

An early example of the new type of hull is seen in L.T.318 *Florence May* of 23 tons, built at Lowestoft in 1883 (Plate 26). A small jacky topsail is set on the foremast and a jigger one on the mizzen, the foresail is high, and although it has only six cloths in the foot, two lines of reef points are fitted. The second jib of nine cloths is set on a reeving bowsprit; there are no bonnets, but three lines of reef points on main and mizzen. Evidently economy has been practised in the sail loft, as foresail and mizzen are second-hand, the one has an L in third cloth, the other a T80, so probably an old mainsail was cut up to make two new sails, both are barked, but not the rest of the suit. The two men with fine bearded faces have sealskin caps, the others wear high-crowned hats or bowlers.

Many of these drifters had a yacht-like appearance, with their suits of cream-coloured sails, it being customary to leave the canvas unbarked for the first season.

Plate 27 is L.T.347 *Freda*, registering 34 tons and built in 1884. Sealskin caps have gone out of fashion, bowlers predominate, but the three men with light-coloured jumpers sport new ideas, the one aft of the foremast has a flat "cheese-cutter" cap, number two has the forerunner of a trilby, while the chap in the bows has a cross between a crash helmet and a sou'wester. Beards are definitely out, except for the little group amidships; were they owners and friends? The man at the back might well be from the backwoods, while the two old gents favour a white fringe. The lad aft wearing trousers and a white jumper could easily be a modern young lady going for a yachting trip! I think this priceless array as interesting as anything in the photo. Look at the crowd on the quay, two and three deep, with five kiddies perched up on the struts of the shed.

The sailplan calls for some attention, as both topsails have curved yards, with a very light jigger yard on the mizzen whipped like a fishing-rod. The mainsail has a bonnet with a line of reef points below and three lines of eyelets for lacings above, and note how the upper line will make the sail almost a trysail, if the wind is blowing hard enough to call for such drastic reefing. Even the comparatively small foresail has a bonnet with a line of eyelets above, while the mizzen has a bonnet and reef points above and below. Evidently they expected to have some reefing to do, and I wonder if the unprecedented gales of the previous year had anything to do with it. Note also the fine run aft, and how prettily she sits in the water; the twenty-two cloth spinnaker would be a powerful sail with such a hull.

Now turn to Plate 28. L.T.397 *Little Pet*, 39 tons, and built in the same year, has quite a different sail plan. The bonnet on the mainsail is much deeper, with two lines of eyelets below and only one above; the mizzen has also eyelets for a lacing, instead of reef points, both above and below the bonnet. The big foresail is set, the spinnaker is diagonal cut, a staysail is set on the Tommy Hunter, and both topsails have their yards standing almost vertical.

Considering their age, these plates were in excellent condition, and so clear that it is possible to read the name of the sailmaker, "W. Jeckells, maker, Lowestoft," on the second leech cloth of the mainsail in L.T.397, while the other shows a placard on the dockshed which it is almost possible to read! Although one plate was rather badly scratched and affected by damp, the blemishes were luckily not where it mattered.

A typical herring "lugger" of this period was about 50 ft. overall, with a length of keel 46 ft. 7 in., breadth 15 ft. 4 in., and depth 6 ft. 10 in. With the dandy rig, it became customary to call the masts the main and the mizzen, and thus I shall refer to them in future.

The mainmast, 40 ft. from deck to truck, with a 25 ft. gaff, and a 29 ft. topsail yard, was rigged with a pair of 4 in. rope shrouds, and a burton a side, with a $2\frac{1}{2}$ in. wire forestay set up with 12 in. double and treble blocks. The bowsprit, 36 ft. long, was fidded into iron bitts and bowsed down with a 10 ft. chain bobstay set up with a luff tackle. The mizzenmast, 28 ft. long, with a 9 ft. topmast, was stepped about 12 ft. inboard, and supported by a pair of 3 in. rope shrouds and $2\frac{1}{2}$ in. backstays;

the gaff measured 16 ft., topsail yard 14 ft., and boom 18 ft.

A full suit of sails, dressed with horse grease and red or yellow ochre, consisted of a mainsail, one large topsail, one jacky topsail, one stay foresail, four jibs, two mizzen sails, and one mizzen topsail. Fourteen tons of ballast and four tons of salt were carried. The deck stores included a mitchboard, capstan and handles, two stoppers, devil's claw with chain, two sets of bank boards, two thwartship boards, four dog kid boards, eight salt wing boards, two sets of pump gear, one large ring for drifting purposes, one lead line about 50 fathoms, two leads, two cork fenders, two hand spikes, one didlenet staff, one beef and one pork cask, spare rope, one boat with two pairs of oars.

The ground tackle was one best bower $2\frac{1}{2}$ cwt., one second bower $1\frac{3}{4}$ cwt., one kedge 1 cwt., one grappling iron 28 lbs., and 60 fathoms of $\frac{3}{4}$ in. chain cable. In addition, there were 70 fathom of 7 in. warp, 80 fathoms of 6 in. tow-rope, and two mooring ropes, each 20 fathom long.

The running gear was as follows:

| | | |
|---|---|---|
| Main halyards | 19 fathoms | $2\frac{1}{2}$ or $2\frac{3}{4}$ in. |
| Peak halyards | 13 ,, | $2\frac{1}{2}$ or $2\frac{3}{4}$ in. |
| Topsail halyards | 13 ,, | $1\frac{1}{4}$ in. |
| Topsail tye | 7 ,, | $2\frac{1}{2}$ in. |
| Staysail halyards | 13 ,, | 1 in. |
| Main sheet | 8 ,, | $2\frac{1}{2}$ in. |
| Staysail sheet | 6 ,, | $1\frac{1}{2}$ in. |
| Main tack tackle | 3 ,, | $\frac{3}{4}$ in. |
| Truss line | 10 ,, | $\frac{3}{4}$ in. |

Two fore-burtons each about 22 ft. long, $3\frac{3}{4}$ in.

### BLOCKS

| | |
|---|---|
| Two main halyard double blocks | 8 in. patent |
| Four peak halyard, Single | 7 in. |
| Two staysail, Single | 5 in. |
| One topsail, Single | 5 in. |
| Four fore-burton 2 single, 2 treble | 7 in. |
| Two runner blocks, iron-bound, double and treble | 12 in. |
| Two mainsheet blocks, one iron-bound | 12 in. |
| One topsail sheet block | 7 in. |
| Two staysail sheet blocks and two bullseye | 6 in. |
| One truss line block | 4 in. |
| Light main sheet or reef tackle double and single | 8 in. |

Handy Billy

### BOWSPRIT GEAR

A traveller with hook.
Outhaul chain $\frac{3}{8}$ in., inhaul rope $\frac{3}{4}$ in.
One bobstay chain 10 ft., two blocks, double and single, 8 in.
One outhaul block, single, 7 in.

## CONVERSION TO DANDY RIG

Two jib sheet single blocks, 7 in.
One pair jib sheet pendants, 2¾ in. rope.
Bowsprit iron with three eyes, gammon iron, inner iron, tripping line, and belaying pins.

### MIZZEN MAST GEAR

| | |
|---|---|
| Two pairs backstays | 2½ in. rope |
| Two burtons | 3 in. ,, |
| Two stays | 3 in. ,, |
| One halyard | 2 in. ,, |
| One peak halyard | 2 in. ,, |
| Three iron-bound blocks for peak halyards | 6 in. |

### CABIN UTENSILS

One shovel  Two masthead lights. Two side lights. One fog horn. One fog bell. Two compasses. One clock. One telescope. One burgee. One club flag. One small flag for mizzen mast. Patent log and line. Flare-up. Oil tins. Turps tin. Serving mallet. Marline spikes. Sewing twine. Four beating needles. Palms and sail needles. Hammer and nails. Gimblets. Axe and chisels. Drawing knife. Different shackles. Small lanterns. Two pricking candle-sticks. Two stoves. Two kettles. Two boilers. Two saucepans. Four tin dishes. One water dipper. One mop. Two shovels. Two sweeping brushes. Two sugar tins. One coffee tin. One tea caddy. Cabin lamp. Oil feeder. Baskets. Spunyarn. Forecastle lamp. Binnacle lamp. Salt bag and pepper-box. Mugs and plates. Butter jar. Master's box.

### FISHING GEAR

13 warps, 120 fathoms long. 3¾ in. to 4 in.
120 nets, each 24 yards on the rope.
120 bowls.
120 seizings.

The nets were of American cotton, ordered 32 or 33 meshes to the yard, 18 and 15 ply, depth 200 to 240 meshes, and length 32 yards. For mackerel the same length but 25 to 26 meshes to the yard, 120 to 140 meshes deep.

Sails were set to suit the weather. If blowing up, the small mizzen, third jib, foresail and mainsail were carried. If this was too much, the foresail would be hauled down and a reef put in, or the bonnet unlaced. On the gale still freshening, mainsail and mizzen were reefed and a small jib hauled out.

To lay to, the foresail was taken in and the jib half-horsed. If caught in a gale while lying to the train, the nets were got in as quickly as possible if it could be done, if not, cut away, then after casting the boat, the mast was heaved up and stay foresail set, then the small jib was run out, and mainsail hoisted. Some skippers preferred to set the mainsail before the jib.

In heavy weather much damage was done by boats driving down on one another, and such collisions frequently resulted in the loss of one or both. To avoid a crash, it was usual to drop a grapnel into the other man's nets, get in as many of your own as possible, then heave up the mast, make sail, pick up grapnel, and slip the other nets clear. Even such drastic methods might not save a loss of £250 to £300 worth of gear.

In that awful E.S.E. gale on the 24th October 1882, three luggers were lost with all hands, and thirty-one men were washed overboard from other boats. Those lost were the 27-ton *Children's Friend*, built 1866, the 21-ton *Edward and Ellen*, built 1865, both with a crew of ten, and the 32-ton *Silver Streak*, built 1872, with twelve hands aboard.

Men thought nothing of crossing the North Sea in these comparatively small craft, although not always with impunity. On the 16th July 1894, the 27-ton *Two Brothers*, built 1876, foundered, with her crew of two, four miles E. by N. of Winterton Lighthouse, when bound for Mandel in Norway. While the *William and Alice* was damaged by ice on the 6th February 1891 and foundered nine miles above Cuxhaven with her crew of three when bound for Hamburg with salted herring. She was a 25-tonner, built in 1876.

When the drifters went trawling, the narrow stay foresail was replaced by a balloon or tow foresail, but as the early boats only averaged 25 to 30 tons, they were really not powerful enough to haul a heavy beam trawl in deep water.

Mr. R. W. Crome writes me in a beautiful copper-plate hand that the Yarmouth "converter" smacks were so called because about September the whole foremast, together with topmast and crosstrees, was removed, and the vessel fitted with a pole-mast and boomless mainsail. He first went to sea in 1886 as a boy guest in the converter smack *Fern*, Y.H.511, and later in the year his first rating at sea was half-boy in the drifter *Zealous*. *Fern* was of 32 tons, built 1871, and owned by W. H. Crome. On the 12th October 1894, she caught fire and became a total loss in Botney Gut. At that time she was owned by J. Wright, with W. Wyatt master. Plate 29 shows Y.H.782 *Zealous* hoisting her jacky topsail preparatory to slipping the tow. Note how the mizzen boom is topped up in the smack to leeward. Y.H.840 is *Content*.

Mr. William Freeman, of Gorleston, who first went to sea in the early eighties, writes me in a beautiful hand:

"These small half-and-half boats started fishing in early spring fifty or sixty miles off the land in deep water for what were called spring herring, which were small, tasteless and dry, realising a few pence a hundred, being mostly used only as bait for the liners. The nets used were of smaller mesh than those for later fishing, and ran 39 or 40 meshes to the yard. The spring fishing continued until early May, when the boats were fitted out for summer herring, with nets of larger mesh, and these fish, found only a few miles out, were fatter, but still without roes. Some of the boats went mackerel fishing instead, using nets 25 to 26 meshes to the yard with cotton, 22 to 23 if twine was used. This midsummer fishery, as it was called, continued until mid-July, when the boats went down the North Sea and fished out of Shields, Scarborough and Grimsby, as the small half-and-half boats could not carry enough to make it profitable to bring the catch to Yarmouth, but they returned to their home port in time for the Great Autumn fishery from September to the end of November. Then they converted for trawling."

Mr. Freeman relates a jolly good yarn about a lugger which came into port with such a large catch of herring that the skipper had been forced to throw some of the shingle ballast overboard in order to stow the fish. Having discharged his catch, he went to sea again and returned with yet another big haul, and told his owner that when he thought he had reached the spot where he caught the first lot, he stopped the boat and dropped the lead into the shingle ballast he had dumped on the previous trip! How's that for rule of thumb navigation, or is it too fishy a yarn? But it was remarkable how those illiterate old fellows could find their way about the North Sea, the nature of whose bed they knew from long experience perhaps better than their own, especially in the case of smacksmen, who were only in their home port one week in every eight.

Not all the drifters engaged in the Spring fishery in the North Sea, many went down Channel and fished out of Plymouth and Penzance in early March, remaining in the West until the latter part of June, when they returned to their home ports for the mackerel voyages, before fitting out for the Autumn herring fishery.

This long passage was not without hazards, as on the 21st February 1889, when *Verbena* of 30 tons, built 1879, ran on the Goodwins and became a total loss, while on the 20th February 1885, in spite of being in charge of a pilot, the 25-ton *Witch of the Wave*, built 1873, managed to get stranded at Walden near Calais, and was lost with all hands.

Mr. Harry George mentions that for speed the Yarmouth drifter *Paradox*, Y.H.951 (Plate 30), carvel-built at Lowestoft in 1884 for Walter Haylett of Caister, was in a class by herself, and would go like a train. Even now after sixty years, the old fellows still talk about her, as I can bear witness from my visit to Norfolk in 1946. At one time *Paradox* was skippered by Harry Brown, who at the age of ninety-two was taken to Norwich by the Rector of Caister, the Rev. Henry Felix, to be confirmed by the Lord Bishop of Norwich, who afterwards sent the aged skipper the text "When thou passeth through the waters I will be with thee." The old fisherman died at the great age of ninety-six. It is remarkable how hale and hearty these men were, in spite of the hard life.

The best looked-after drifter was *Nell*, Y.H. 868, owned by Harry Horn. She had a lovely suit of brown sails, the black bulwarks had a gold sheer line, and her name was emblazoned in letters of gold on each bow. When I was in Caister I had the pleasure of meeting Mr. J. J. Haylett, now well on in his seventies, and grandson of the famous James Haylett, whose immortal words "Caister men never turn back" will ring through the ages as a tribute to the indomitable courage of those splendid fishermen who manned the lifeboat at the call of humanity. I had with me a number of photo-

29 DRIFTERS LEAVING YARMOUTH IN TOW
Y.H. 782 *Zealous*, Y.H. 840 *Content*. 29 tons, built Lowestoft, 1876. Note length of mizzen gaffs.

30 *PARADOX* ENTERING YARMOUTH
The fastest Yarmouth drifter. 36 tons, built at Lowestoft, 1884, for Walter Haylett. Note crew running in bowsprit.

31 TOWING DOWN THE YARE
Y.H.868 *Nell*, 37 tons, built Southtown 1883 for J. J. C. Sutton of Caister. L.T. 87 *Primrose*, 33 tons built 1886.
Tug *Reaper* clench built of wood at North Shields 1867, 82.5 x 17.3 x 9.3. 5 N.T. 75 G.T. 30 h.p., paddle.

32 *MIZPAH* L.T. 607, c. 1895
Note man sheeting home the mizzen.

33 *HILDEGARDE*, L.T. 465, c. 1895
Note Tommy Hunter set up to starboard side of deck.

34 *BESSIE* LEAVING LOWESTOFT
Note huge jigger topsail, bonnets on main and mizzen.

35 *PARAGON*
Note jacky topsail and bonnets.

36 *EXPRESS* LEAVING LOWESTOFT
Note mizzen deadeyes set up on short length of chain to clear sweeps, etc., in lumber irons.

37 SAILMAKER AT WORK, NEPTUNE SQUARE, MARGATE
Note sailmaker's hook in use on left of bench.

38  *CONSOLATION* UNDER CONSTRUCTION, LOWESTOFT
Note garboard strakes in position, stern timbers at counter, harping mould to ensure fairness of frames, long skeg to keel.

39  *CONSOLATION* READY FOR LAUNCHING
The first steam drifter built and owned at Lowestoft. 27 N.T. Built 1897, by S. Richards. 40 h.p. engine. Note bankboards amidships and head of tabernacle.

40 *ACTIVE*, Y.H. 979 ENTERING YARMOUTH
37 tons, built at Lowestoft, 1896.
Note bonnets off all sails.

41 *DAISY* Y.H. 260 ENTERING YARMOUTH
52 tons, built at Southtown, 1878.

42 JAMES HAYLETT OF CAISTER
　　Assistant Coxswain Caister Lifeboat, 59 years a lifeboatman, assisting in the saving of 1,300 lives.

43 COUNTING HERRING CATCH, LOWESTOFT
*Monitor* L.T. 703, 40 tons, built 1896. Note drift between deadeyes, Spanish burton, tumbler in jaws of gaff, men with two herring in each hand.

44 A BIG CATCH OF MACKEREL, LOWESTOFT

graphs, and while glancing through them, Mr. Haylett instantly spotted one as being of *Nell*, and he told me he had sailed in her in his youth, but had never before seen a picture of the drifter. By a stroke of luck, this was the only print of which I had a duplicate, and his delight when I gave it to him was worth going miles to see. She is towing down the Yare with other drifters, L.T.87 is *Primrose*, built 1886, in the centre is Y.H.1053, a trawler, and the ancient clench-built paddle-wheel tug *Reaper* is well worth attention, while *Sweetheart*, lying alongside the quay, was one of the first steam trawlers to be owned by Hewett & Co., of the Short Blue Fleet (Plate 31).

During the last decade of the 19th century the sailing drifter reached its zenith with the magnificent craft working out of Lowestoft, many running up to 40 tons net register, larger than some of the trawlers, but terribly heavy to row in a sultry calm with a big catch aboard. Mizzen sails were now enormous, with very long gaffs and booms, and lines of reef points above and below the latchets of the bonnets on both main and mizzen sails.

In spite of the ports being less than ten miles apart, there were noticeable differences in the drifters from Lowestoft and Yarmouth. At the Suffolk harbour the preference was for lofty mizzen masts, raked well for'ard and capped with ornamental trucks, while Norfolkmen stuck to the shorter and more upright mast, usually with a flat truck. Raking the mast allowed the boom to be steeved up higher without spoiling the flat set of the sail, saved the helmsman ducking his head every time the heavy spar swung across the deck, and bringing the sail area more inboard was held to increase speed.

With their immense sail plans, many of these latest drifters had a surprising turn of speed, considering their short water-lines. Mr. Peek, who went to sea in 1893, told me that in 1898 he was in L.T.607 *Mizpah*, a 39-tonner built 1894, when they hauled their nets the Longships bore 80 miles N. by E. The wind was abaft the beam and under two jacky topsails, the big jib and tow foresail, she made the 77 miles to Newlyn in seven hours (Plate 32). The photograph, taken in Mount's Bay, c. 1895, shows her putting to sea, the mizzen is being sheeted home and the "Tommy Hunter" is set up to foot of starboard shroud, she is still carrying her untanned mizzen and main topsail, and her mainsail, once belonging to L.T.488, has three lines of reef points, likewise the mizzen, which also has a bonnet.

Plate 33 shows L.T.465 *Hildegarde*, 31 tons, built 1884, leaving Penzance, her mainsail has four lines of eyelets and the mizzen has a bonnet in addition to three lines of eyelets above, and one below. Note the pronounced forward rake to the mast and the vertical setting of the topsail yards. On the 22nd November 1884, this drifter was unlucky enough to sink the dandy *Wave*, 24 tons, built 1863, in a collision off Pakefield.

A typical drifter of this decade was L.T.519 *Bessie*, 34 tons, built 1892, and very smartly kept (Plate 34). Compare her huge jigger topsail with the smaller jacky set on L.T.610 *Paragon*, 39 tons, built 1894. In the background is a trawling smack, with lofty topmast and crosstrees (Plate 35).

Plate 36 is a very fine view of L.T.173 *Express*, 32 tons, built 1890. A jigger topsail is set on the mainmast, and a jacky on the mizzen, the bowsprit is about to be run out, the tiller is hard-a-weather, and one of the crew is sheeting home the mizzen sail. The small transom-sterned 665 L.T. *Boy Charles* is an interesting craft, with her mizzen mast stepped to port.

It was indeed my lucky day when I got into touch with Mr. J. Breach, and thanks to the wonderful amount of data he kindly sent, it has been possible for me to draw up a set of plans of L.T.766 *Strive*. Mr. Breach writes:

"I am pleased you met Mr. H. Summers, of Ramsgate, he was my brother-in-law, having married my eldest sister, that is how I become apprenticed to his father. Our sail loft was directly beneath the Tidal Ball on the West Cliff on the top floor of the building. Three men and another apprentice used to enter from the top of the cliff, down some steps. After my apprenticeship, I came home to Lowestoft and did my father's work. In 1898, the year I started on my own, he had two new sailing drifters built, *Fame* and *Strive*, sister ships, and it is one I have roughed out enclosed. They had, as you will see, plenty of canvas and were very fast."

It has been a great pleasure for me corresponding with one so willing to co-operate, and future sail lovers will owe a debt of gratitude to Mr. J. Breach for his assistance in helping to preserve the records of the past.

*Strive*, registering 39 tons, was built at Lowestoft in 1898 by H. Reynolds. Two years later, when Mr. Breach's father disposed of his fleet of sailers, she was sold for £620, and was still registered in 1930. Length from stem to taffrail was 64 ft., L.B.P. 59 ft., extreme beam 18 ft., depth 8 ft. Plans 3 pages 302-5.

The straight stem is sided 8 in., moulded 12 in.; the usual iron stem plate has eyebolt at L.W.L. for the standing end of the bobstay, six feet up is another for the tizzot, and a third at the head is for the forestay tackle. To starboard is the gammon iron for bowsprit. Then comes fore hatch, giving access to sail locker, the heavy 6 in. tabernacle and its scuttle, with iron bitts to starboard for the heel of the bowsprit. Six timberheads with thumb cleats on faces are morticed through each covering board. Aft of the mainmast is the net room hatch with roller on after coaming, then the fish hold. On either side of the deck are the bank boards and thwartship boards, then comes the warp room hatch with roller on aft coaming, and fish pounds on either side. An Elliott & Garrood capstan supplies the power to haul in the warp. Aft is the companion giving access to the cabin, which is fitted up with the usual bunks and skylight. To port is the stove and amidships the boiler, so no lack of warmth below in the summer months. Across the deck is a 4 in. wrought iron horse, securely bolted to the stanchions, next the mizzen mast, raking well for'ard. On the quarter rails are the lumber irons in which sweeps, spare spars, etc., are carried, and the cavil rail extends from port stanchion for'ard of main horse, round the stern to the starboard side, and has eyebolts, belaying pins, and cleats for running gear, with a fairlead and eyebolt on taffrail for the mizzen sheet. I have broken the deck planking aft so as to show the method of framing up the stern timbers in an elliptical stern.

The keel is moulded 12 in., sided 8 in., keelson 9 in. moulded, 7 in. sided, room and space 1 ft. 8 in., floors and first futtocks 8 in. moulded, 4 in. sided, erected in pairs, beams 5 or 6 in. square, planking 2 in. thick.

Mainmast is 32 ft. deck to shoulder, 18 ft. shoulder to top, and stepped in a three-sided tabernacle with heel four feet up from floors. Mizzen mast 26 ft. deck to shoulder, 16 ft. shoulder to top. Main gaff 30 ft. Mizzen gaff 25 ft. Mizzen boom 26 ft. Bowsprit 42 ft. overall, 25 ft. outboard. Square heel is stepped in iron bitts alongside tabernacle and has five 2 in. holes, 2 ft. 3 in. apart to take the iron fid, some 3 ft. long, which goes through the hole appropriate to the jib set and sets hard up against the foreside of the tabernacle to prevent the spar coming aft.

The tabernacle is stepped on the keelson and filled in with deadwood for about four or five feet, with a thick iron band round it where heel of mast rests. This band not only strengthened the tabernacle, but also served as a preventer of the mast tripping or skidding when upright. The scuttle was as previously described, and when the mast was lowered it touched the mizzen mast midway between cheeks and sheave-hole, being held steady by the burtons and forestay. No mitchboard was fitted.

The fore jacky yard is 24 ft. Mizzen jacky 21 ft. Big fore topsail yard 36 ft., jigger 24 ft. Mizzen big topsail yard 30 ft. Jigger 20 ft.

The topsail yards were slung in the thirds, *i.e.*, two-thirds above the masthead, and one-third below, nearly upright with the lower end touching the port side of the mast. The jigger yards were slung in the centres.

I asked Mr. Breach about the cutting out of sails, and he replied:

"Now regarding the allowance for stretching of the canvas. There were different ideas with sail-makers, some used to put their ropes on tight, that is put a lot of slack canvas in, which used to make the sails baggy. I did not believe in that. I used to allow as much slack canvas as I thought the rope would stretch, and made the following allowances. Take the length of the spars:

Gaffs, 30 ft. Allowance, 1 ft. 9 in. 25 ft. allowance, 1 ft. 6 in.
Boom, 26 ft., allowance 2 ft., extra allowance for traveller and hook.
Topsail yards. Jacky's. 1 ft. Big topsail yard. 1 ft. 6 in. Jigger, 1 ft.
Spinnaker, 6 ft. on stay.
Big jib, 6 ft. on stay.

When you start on the plans of *Strive*, if you are putting in the seams of the sails, they are parallel with the leech in mainsail, mizzen, stay foresail and the two jigger topsails. The others are diagonal cut, that is, parallel with both leech and foot.

The clew of mainsail is approximately 7 to 7 ft. 6 in. from deck, and 3 ft. 6 in.

## CONVERSION TO DANDY RIG

from mizzen mast. Sailing drifters did not have booms to their mainsails, instead there is a very heavy main sheet horse about 4 in. dia., wrought iron, running from port to starboard, bolted to stanchions, over which is a large shackle, large enough to travel easily over the horse. This is attached to the lower sheet block on which is also an iron cleat to make the sheet fast.

I should have liked to have been able to get an old plan from the boat builder, but it is very remote as you see it is now about fifty years since there were any boats built. No doubt the plans have all been destroyed, and steam drifters came and poor old sail was forgotten."

In other letters Mr. Breach sent a vast amount of invaluable data, such as yardage of sails, ropes, costs, etc., which I give below.

### SAILS

The yardage includes linings, bands, strengthening pieces, etc.    1,307 yards.

| Sail | Dimensions | | | Canvas / Yards |
|---|---|---|---|---|
| Spinnaker | Stay 54 ft. | Leech 45 ft. | Foot 45 ft. | 24 in. 8 oz. cotton canvas — 192 yards |
| Big jib | Stay 48 ft. | Leech 34 ft. | Foot 23 ft. | 24 in. No. 6 flax canvas — 76 yards |
| Second jib | Stay 44 ft. | Leech 30 ft. | Foot 18 ft. | 24 in. No. 4 flax canvas — 54 yards |
| Third jib | Stay 32 ft. | Leech 25 ft. | Foot 14 ft. | 24 in. No. 3 flax canvas — 36 yards |
| Storm jib | Stay 20 ft. | Leech 15 ft. | Foot 10 ft. | 24 in. No. 1 flax canvas — 14 yards |
| Foresail | Stay 28 ft. | Leech 24 ft. | Foot 16 ft. | 24 in. No. 2 flax canvas — 48 yards |
| Mainsail | Luff 24 ft. Head 29 ft. | Leech 46 ft. | Foot 28 ft. | No. 2 canvas — 220 yards |
| Mizzen | Luff 20 ft. Head 24 ft. | Leech 37 ft. | Foot 25 ft. | No. 3 flax canvas — 165 yards |
| Fore jacky topsail | Head 23 ft. Foot 30 ft. | Leech 20 ft. | Luff 16 ft. | No. 4 canvas — 65 yards |
| Fore jigger topsail | Head 35 ft. Foot 44 ft. | Leech 22 ft. | Luff 16 ft. | 24 in. 8 oz. cotton — 127 yards |
| Mizzen jacky topsail | Head 20 ft. Foot 26 ft. | Leech 21 ft. | Luff 14 ft. | No. 4 canvas — 54 yards |
| Mizzen jigger topsail | Head 29 ft. Foot 34 ft. | Leech 22 ft. | Luff 13 ft. | 24 in. 8 oz. cotton — 112 yards |
| Staysail | Leech 30 ft. | Stay 30 ft. | Foot 25 ft. | 24 in. 10 oz. cotton — 64 yards |
| Big foresail | Leech 31 ft. | Stay 28 ft. | Foot 21 ft. | 24 in. 10 oz. cotton — 80 yards |

### ROPE

Four-strand yacht manilla.

Spinnaker halyards — — — — — — — — — — — 16 fm. 2½ in.

Spinnaker sheets - - - - - - - - - - 20 fm. 2¼ in.
Jib halyards - - - - - - - - - - - 14 fm. 2¾ in.
  sheets - - - - - - - - - - - 14 fm. 2¼ in.
Topsail halyards - - - 8 fm. flexible wire 17 fm. 2¼ in. rope. 1½ fm. chain
  sheets - - - - - - - - - - - 17 fm. 2¼ in.
  tack - - - - - - - - - - - 16 fm. 2 in.
Foresail sheets - - - - - - - - - - 8 fm. 2¼ in.
  halyards - - - - - - - - - - 16 fm. 2 in.
Main halyards - - - - - - - - - - 24 fm. 2¾ in.
Peak halyards - - - - - - - - - - 36 fm. 3 in.
Main sheet - - - - - - - - - - - 20 fm. 2¾ in.
Big foresail sheet - - - - - - - - - 20 fm. 2¼ in.
Staysail halyards - - - - - - - - - - 11 fm. 2¼ in.
Mizzen topsail halyards - 7 fm. chain, 1¼ in. 6 ft. small chain
                                           20 fm. 2¼ in. rope
  sheet - - - - - - - - - - - 15 fm. 2¼ in.
Mizzen main halyards - - - - - - - - - 18 fm. 2½ in.
  peak halyards - - - - - - - - - 27 fm. 2½ in.
  sheet - - - - - - - - - - - 24 fm. 3½ in.

The foremast is fitted for lowering with two 3-sheave blocks, which take about 40 fathoms 3 in. best manilla rope.

Two Burton falls to steady mast and act as guys - 7 fm. each side or 14 fm. 2¼ in. rope
Approx. two cwt. various sizes.

## ROPE AND TWINE FOR SUIT OF SAILS

Best hemp boltrope at 8d. - - - - - - - - £7  9  4
Seaming and roping twine - - - - - - - -  3  0  0
Allowing one hour's labour per yard of all sails—1,307 hours at 6d. per hour  32 13  6
Cost of canvas - - - - - - - - - - 48  3 11
                                                    ─────────
Total approx. cost - - - - - - - - - £91  6  9

You can to-day multiply this by 4½ or 5 for present costs. Wages are now 2s. 3d. to 2s. 6d. per hour, and materials have gone up to ridiculous prices, and not obtainable except by Government permit.

## RUNNING RIGGING

Including extras to that already quoted: tackles, outhaulers, boom guys, etc.
About 4 cwt. 4-strand best yacht manilla - - - - - £18 13  4
To-day's price not less than £500 for suit of sails.
Cringles are passed first through two holes worked in the edge of the canvas and made to fit thimbles, the ends are passed through rope at the finish.

## COST OF MATERIALS AND LABOUR IN 1898

Haywards flax canvas, No. 1: 12½d. 24 in. bolts, falling ½d. per no.
American cotton, 8 oz., 5d., 10 oz., 7d. 24 in. bolts.
White yacht manilla, 10d. a lb.
Best hemp rope, 8d. a lb.

Labour, 6d. per hour, 57 hours a week.
All materials are 24 in. width.

| | | | |
|---|---|---|---|
| No. 1 flax | 14 yds. at 12½d. | | £0 14 7 |
| No. 2 ,, | 268 yds. at 12d. | | 13 8 0 |
| No. 3 ,, | 201 yds. at 11½d. | | 9 12 8 |
| No. 4 ,, | 173 yds. at 11d. | | 7 18 7 |
| No. 6 ,, | 76 yds. at 10½d. | | 3 6 6 |
| 8 oz. American cotton | 431 yds. at 5d. | | 8 19 7 |
| 10 oz. ,, ,, | 144 yds. at 7d. | | 4 4 0 |
| Total cost of material | | | £48 3 11 |

With this information I was able to get to work on the drawing-board, and roughed out a set of plans, lines, etc., which I forwarded to Mr. Breach for his inspection, and his reply was most encouraging:

"I have inspected the sail plan and taken the liberty of correcting a few things, and hope I have not damaged it too much. It is a very smart plan, and the extra peak is an improvement to my rough sketch, as it is years since I have had an occasion to draw one. The following are the alterations:

Third Jib: little shorter on the foot.
Stay foresail sheet to come aft to mast.
Big foresail enlarged—it looks small.
Topsails—put the sheet in line from end of gaff to masthead.
Foresail—another reef in bonnet and sail.
Mainsail—another reef.
Mizzen—another reef.

I notice that the sails are full size, if you prefer to allow for stretching allow 1 ft. 9 in. on main gaff, 1 ft. 6 in. on mizzen gaff. Foot of mizzen 2 ft. shorter on boom, the sheet hooks to traveller and chain. The outhauler rope belayed to a cleat starboard side of boom about five feet from gooseneck hook at mast end. Other sheets of sails are flying, and no need to make any change to them.

I have added a staysail. *Strive* did not have one, but I leave it to you whether you like to include one or not. Not many of the latest did have one, they were not used, only on long runs " off the wind." Made of about 60 yds. same material as big topsails. In most cases they were below long enough to go rotten owing to this infrequent use, and so owners would not order them. When set, the tack rope spliced in to allow it to be about six feet above deck, positioned centre of deck between main and net room. Single part of Tommy Hunter halyards used to hoist. Sheet as far aft on the transom as possible."

Then to my joy, Mr. Breach replied in great detail to various queries I made regarding eyebolts, belaying of ropes, and those many items which crop up when trying to set out a complete plan of a vessel, as distinct from a bare outline. I give his answers verbatim.

The Spanish Runner Fall for "burtons," that is the title the fishermen call it

FIGURE 14

SPANISH RUNNER FALL FOR BURTONS

1. Rope spliced round single block, leads UP, reeves through outer sheave first.
2. Leads DOWN, to seizing on head of single block hooked to eyebolt in rail.
3. Leads UP through inner sheave.
4. Leads DOWN through sheave in lower block.
5. Leads UP through sheave in single block.
6. Leads DOWN under cleat on stanchion and UP to belay round timberhead on rail.

NOTE.—Fall is seized AFTER passing through the upper block so that middle block hangs about midway between upper and lower blocks.

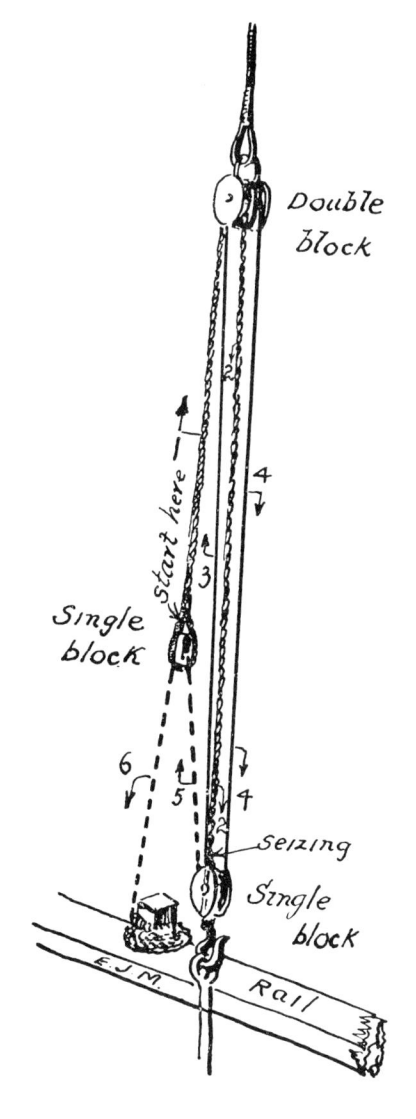

by, like most things, it is easy when you know, but I have seen many ponder over it when rigging out (Fig. 14). Fall is spliced round single block, reeves through outer sheave, then down to seizing, up through inner sheave, down to lower block, up

## CONVERSION TO DANDY RIG

through single block and finish. The fall is seized *after* passing through upper block, so that the middle block hangs midway between upper and lower block.

### RUNNING GEAR

1. Spinnaker halyards near starboard after shroud. No purchase fitted.
2. Jib halyards to port. Luff purchase.
3. Foresail halyards. Down foreside of mast to cleat. No purchase.
4. Main halyards to port.
5. Peak halyards to starboard.
6. Topsail halyards to starboard. Eyebolt in deck near side of fore shroud, belayed to cleat on stanchion. Purchase to wire runner or whip.
7. Mizzen main halyards to port. Peak halyards to starboard.
8. Mizzen topping lift to starboard. Single wire served and purchase. The topsail being set on the port side, the topping lift would be in the way in hoisting and lowering and in tacking down to eyebolt in deck close to mast, if to port.
9. Tommy Hunter hooked in eyebolts in stanchion near after shroud.
10. Mizzen topsail halyards to starboard near fore shroud. No purchase, eyebolt and pin in cavil rail.
11. Mainsail tack eyebolt in deck. Two single blocks.
12. Main truss. Small block on under-jaws starboard. No purchase. Single rope spliced in lower hoop, up through block and back to hoop again with enough slack to fasten.
13. The mast is stepped about midway between keelson and deck. From keelson to step is filled in with deadwood and iron band fitted round at this point. When mast is lowered it touches mizzen mast midway of cheek and sheave hole.
14. Mizzen clew hooked on traveller, as already stated.
15. Tommy Hunter is hooked to eyebolt in stanchion near after shroud. No wire. It is one long runner of manilla rope, the end is passed through thimble in lower block strop and belayed on its own parts.
16. Eyes are in deck. Forward for topsail halyards, starboard side. Jib halyards, port side. Topsail tack, port side, to cleat on tabernacle.
    Eyes aft. On cavil for topsail halyards, topping lift, peak halyards, starboard.
    Main halyards port on cavil and pins for belaying.
    Halyards for main and peak of mainsail on timberhead and cleat, also for belaying jib halyards.
    Mizzen sheet. Double block with bullseye for fairlead, then to cleat on transom.
    Boom guys each side, belayed on transom.

### BELAYING OF ROPES

1. Bobstay fall: led through hawsepipe and belayed on fore timber head.
2. Forestay runner fall: starboard on a large cleat on hawser box.
3. Foresail sheets: two single blocks on sheets cringle. The rope shackled to

deck near after shroud, led up through block and back to cleat on stanchion.
4. Jib sheets: through deadeye in bulwarks to cleat on stanchion.
5. Topsail sheets: to cleat on starboard side of mast. Main and mizzen the same.
6. Topsail tacks: to eyes in deck on port side, to cleat on tabernacle for main topsail. To cleat on port side of mast for mizzen topsail. There is usually about a fathom of 3 in. manilla spliced in the tack cringle with loop to take the tackle.
7. Spinnaker sheets: under the horse as shown, to cleat.
8. Eyebolt on stem is to hook on a spring rope or "tizzot," to use fisherman's language. There are two of these, one for fine weather, one for heavy weather, comprised of 10 fathom of 5 in. and 10 fathom of 8 in. Bass rope made *left*-handed lay same as the herring warps, with large swivel hook in one end and shroud knot in the other, with a length of line attached. When adrift at their nets, this tizzot is hooked on the stem eyebolt, the other end is fastened to the warp. It tends to keep the boat in the " wind's eye," aided also by the mizzen set in the middle with the aid of a tackle hooked in the mizzen sheet band and belayed on either side of the transom.
9. Cleats on mainmast. Topsail tack, port side, sheet starboard side. Foresail sheet, fore side.
  On mizzen mast. Topsail tack on port side, sheet on starboard side.
10. No mitchboard was used; the forestay, the fore shroud being exact in line with the mast athwartships and the two burtons kept the mast in position.
11. The *Strive* was built at Lowestoft by Mr. H. Reynolds. I cannot say what she actually cost, but was sold two years old for £620 when father sold off his sailers in 1900.
12. The dandy rigged sailing drifters did not have a cavil forward, but they did aft, from the stanchion fore-end of mizzen rigging, aft to the transom, round aft.
  The stanchions forward with large thumb cleats on the face, the tops of same stanchions being above the rail about 6 in., acting for belaying halyards, etc.

Fortunately there is in the Rowe Collection in the Margate Public Library a splendid photograph of a local sail loft in Neptune Square, which shows a sailmaker working at his bench and chatting to an old fisherman who has a marlinspike through the strands of a boltrope (Plate 37). The date 1889 on the beam above suggests the year when the photo might have been taken, and certainly those old photographers had little to learn about indoor studies. The general paraphernalia of a sail-loft is well worth studying, the rope-stropped block is about as big as a man's head, and once again, what hats! What yarns those old boys must have been able to spin; our friend in the priest's hat could certainly recall smuggling days after the Napoleonic wars. Such grand old characters are sadly missed to-day in our world of mass production.

Mr. E. J. Crews, of Lowestoft, whose father, the late Capt. J. Crews, was the most successful skipper in the local regatta, winning thirteen races out of fourteen,

## CONVERSION TO DANDY RIG

and never sailing one of his own vessels, saw my appeal, and most kindly loaned me a copy of a booklet giving details of the Lowestoft fleet on the 31st December 1898, and reports of the regattas—which will appear in my book "Sailing Trawlers." It was so interesting that I copied out the entire contents and analysed the result. I find that 483 fishing vessels were on the register, made up of: 233 sailing drifters, 247 sailing trawlers, one line fishing smack, one crabber, and only one steam drifter, *Consolation* of 27 tons. The oldest drifter was the 25-ton *Fanny*, built 1859, then came *Surprize*, 19 tons, *Reform* and *George and Thomas*, 31 tons, built 1867. The smallest were *Fawn*, 8 tons, and *Mystery*, 13 tons, built 1897, the majority were fine drifters of from 36 to 40 tons, less than ten years old.

In 1913 there were *only* 192 sailing drifters in English ports.

By the turn of the century sail was doomed, for three years previously the first steam drifter, *Consolation*, L.T.718, had been built at Lowestoft, so named because the consolation was if steam failed it was still possible to sail, as she carried a full suit. Plate 38 of her in frame gives an excellent idea of the strength of the timbers used in a sailing drifter, for the addition of an engine and the necessary alterations in the sternpost to take the propeller shafting were the only differences. Plate 39 shows her ready for launching.

The last two sailing drifters built at Chamber's yard, Oulton Broad, were laid down in April 1900 and named *Content* and *Pretoria*. Through the courtesy of Mr. Wm. S. Parker, I am able to give the nett costs of hulls and spars, which added to the costs of sails, etc., given by Mr. J. Breach, enables one to know the exact cost of a typical herring drifter.

Nett Costs. *Content.*

| | £ | s. | d. |
|---|---|---|---|
| Wages | 151 | 19 | 9 |
| Timber and materials | 158 | 8 | 3½ |
| Fastenings, stores, etc. | 25 | 1 | 9 |
| Spars and blocks, etc. | 45 | 4 | 5½ |
| Smith's shop work | 55 | 0 | 0 |
| Castings, Brook's account | 2 | 12 | 0 |
| Stove stones | 0 | 14 | 7 |
| Cartage, etc. | 6 | 2 | 6 |
| Small boat | 9 | 11 | 11 |
| | £454 | 15 | 3 |

The stove stones were the flag-stones placed round the galley stove to prevent adjacent woodwork from catching fire.

The contract price for each was £575. *Pretoria's* nett costs amounted to £493 13s. 5d., as £189 10s. 3½d. was expended on wages, and stores and fastenings came to £34 6s. 1½d., with various slight differences to make up the remainder. To these costs must be added sawmill labour and indirect expenses, so that it will be seen there was not much margin for profit; but in those days a master builder, who often worked on the job himself, was satisfied if the return showed a slight increase over costs.

*Content* was later sold to Scottish owners, and in 1920 I find she was sailing out of Lerwick, rigged as a ketch, but I have been unable to trace anything about *Pretoria*.

At Lowestoft the success of the first steam drifters was phenomenal, and by 1903 no less than one hundred and one were registered. Owners who could not afford to go in for steam or were prejudiced against it, saw their sailing fleets rapidly becoming obsolete; 1909 saw 139 steamers at Yarmouth and 243 at Lowestoft; at the outbreak of the 1914-18 war over 300 were registered at the Suffolk port, while the 622 sailing drifters afloat in 1906 were reduced to 152 in eight years. Not one survived the first World War, during which only a few went fishing; most were broken up, as their oak timbers and copper fastenings were far more valuable for war purposes.

I am happy to have done something towards preserving the memory of those magnificent sailing drifters, and my thanks go to all who contributed towards this aim.

CHAPTER SIX

## THE GREAT AUTUMN FISHERY

FIFTY years and more ago, what glorious sights there must have been when all the wonderful variety of sail assembled for the Great Autumn Fishery off Yarmouth. Those brisk days with a kick on the water, the big Scottish zulus hoisting their towering lugs as soon as they had hauled their nets, then heeling to the freshening breeze, and smoking through the water at ten knots and more; the local dandies cracking on, big jackies aloft, spars whipping like fishing-rods and the huge spinnakers, billowing white clouds, standing out in hard curves. Then was seen the art of handling hard-pressed vessels racing for market, with skippers scorning to take in sail until the seas swirled round the hatch coamings, hanging on come hell or high water.

Those quiet October mornings when in the haze of dawn the fleet begins to make for port, the gay colours of the Scottish luggers reflected in the translucent water. Their lofty peaks seem to stab the sky, but the brown sails hang limp and the heavy sweeps are out, the men toiling with an easy rhythm. Presently one of the clench-built paddle tugs—*Reaper*, *Gleaner*, or some such rustic name—surges through the fleet, as picturesque as steam can ever hope to be, and from the starboard sponson the tug master bawls stentoriously across to a Banff fifie "D'ye want a tow?" The crew, sweating at the oars as ever a galley-slave did in the days of old, anxiously await the skipper's decision which will relieve them from their back-breaking labours, for a fifie with some thirty to forty tons of fish aboard is not exactly a racing eight. But the canny old man is weighing up whether it is worth the "siller" for a tow. Does yon darkening patch betoken the coming of a breeze?

The little Cornish luggers are sombre craft with black hulls relieved only by touches of white, and their dark tanned sails still seem to cling to the blackness of night, some relic, perchance, of smuggling days, when a light-coloured sail could easily be seen against the horizon. The ruddy sails of the East Coasters, catching the rays of the newly-risen sun, glow with a more intense flame. As far as the eye can see is the panoply of sail—a thousand or more—all steering for one point, the harbour entrance.

Then those days when the boats were caught in a black nor'easter, the men hang on to the nets as long as they dare—herring are generally about in blowing weather—then maybe they have to cut away their precious gear and run for it. As they close the land the dangers increase, low-lying sandbanks bar the way, seething breakers marking their line. To enter such broken water is to court disaster, and the safe channels are not easy to find. Both Lowestoft and Yarmouth are difficult ports to enter in bad weather, the Suffolk harbour entrance is barely 130 ft. wide, with 8 to 13 ft. of water at low tide, while the narrow entrance to the Yare, between two long wooden piers, is but 200 ft. across, and if the ebb is running out at six knots, as when flood water is coming down, there will be a tremendous sea breaking on the harbour bar (Plates 40 and 41).

On comes the hard-pressed drifter, close-reefed with bonnets off, yawing slightly as she lifts to the seas hurling her on, then her bows bury themselves to the hawse pipes and white water foams along the deck. The crowd on the pierhead scarcely dare to breathe as the lugger, picked up on a terrific scend, flies straight as an arrow towards the narrow entrance. Will she make it? The slightest error of judgment, or just bad luck, and she is set by the stream foul of the north pier, her hull is crushed like an eggshell against the heavy piles, and stout timbers splinter like match-sticks.

Maybe the tide sweeps the unfortunate boat past the haven, then no skill of master or crew can avail to enable her to beat back, she is carried remorsely on to be flung up on the north sand and battered to pieces, leaving the men struggling in the icy water, the undertow carrying even the strongest swimmer out to sea unless help be at hand, as well it may be, and men form a human chain, the foremost waist deep or more, regardless of their own lives if they can aid a fellow in distress.

Meanwhile perhaps another lugger has swept in to safety, bringing news of a vessel ashore on the sands, and instantly comes the call for volunteers to man the life-boat. By what yardstick can we measure those valiant fishermen? Rough and uneducated by the standards of our time maybe, but lion-hearted and courageous, never hesitating to go to the help of anyone in greater danger than themselves. Any medals and rewards gained by their splendid efforts are earned by the saving of life, not its taking.

Such was James Haylett, whose deathless words "Caister men *never* turn back" should ever stir the hearts of men, urging them on to nobler deeds than mere self-interest. How can one compare those men with the Greenock tug men who, in February 1946 by 78 votes to 11, refused to go to the assistance of the grain ship *Ponce de Lion*, aground on the Gantock rocks, in the Firth of Clyde, during heavy weather after the American ship had passed safely through one of the worst of her Atlantic crossings. The reason? Because forsooth they were on strike over some petty grievance or other. Such despicable actions tarnish the glorious traditions of the sea.

Glasgow tugmen came to the same ignominious decision, and as no assistance was forthcoming from any tugmen, the British destroyer *Brilliant* went to the aid of the vessel in distress, while a Dutch tug raced down the Clyde from Glasgow and stood by the steamer.

Perhaps it is not to be wondered at when mealy-mouthed humbugs, posing as oracles, whose voices can be heard in every home over the wireless, tell lies, utter platitudes, decry traditions, and sneer at voluntary public services, while themselves guilty of taking the opportunity of defrauding their fellows—the brothers or comrades, as they are pleased to call them, and make use of nationalised undertakings and fail to pay for the same.

In the crown of earthly achievements few jewels scintillate with greater brilliance than those connected with the saving of life at sea by humble fishermen and smacksmen. Services ofttimes unrewarded, and glossed over by the heroes themselves as being nothing out of the ordinary.

Think of that wild night of the 13th November 1901 when it was blowing a whole gale from the N.N.E., with deluges of icy rain and a terrific sea rolling in on that open beach at Caister. Soon after 11 p.m., when folk ashore were snuggling down in the blankets and commenting on how the wind shook the houses, the Cockle Lightship began firing signals of distress. A Lowestoft smack was being driven on to the Barber Sands. Without a moment's hesitation, the lifeboat crew assembled and the No. 2 lifeboat *Beauchamp* was launched, but the tremendous seas washed her off the skids and flung the boat, weighing five tons without gear, up on to the shore, so that she had to be hauled up the beach to be made ready for another launch. It was intensely dark and perishing cold, yet foremost amongst the launchers was the veteran assistant coxswain, James Haylett, sen., carrying his seventy-eight years lightly. For nearly three hours these splendid fellows, soaked to the skin and with faces flayed by the icy downpour, struggled to refloat the heavy 36 ft. boat. About 2 a.m., with the aid of a warp and tackle, they succeeded in their efforts. Sail was set and the lifeboat stood out to sea. Most of the helpers went home to change their wet clothing, not so the grand old man—he had two sons, a son-in-law, and two grandsons in the boat—five out of her crew of twelve, and without food or rest he remained on watch.

Closehauled on the port tack, the *Beauchamp*, which had gone to the assistance of 81 vessels since placed on the station in 1892, and saved 146 lives, flew towards the distant sands, which lay dead to wind'ard. On nearing the sands the cox'n wore his boat, stood ashore, and tacked just outside the surf. After making another board, he went about and came towards the shore, but on tacking again near the surf, the boat missed stays. He filled again and renewed the attempt, but she failed a second time to come round, and was now in the breakers close to the beach. The cox'n, seeing that it was impossible to avoid going on shore, ordered the mizzen to be lowered and put his helm up, but had only just time to get the boat straight before the seas when her bow struck the sand about fifty yards north of the place of launching. Almost simultaneously a very heavy sea caught the lifeboat on the starboard quarter, and she was keel up in an instant. The masts broke off short and the crew, all entangled in ropes and sails, was pinned under the boat.

It was about 3 a.m. and blowing as hard as ever when Frederick Henry Haylett came back to the lifeboat house after changing his wet clothes and heard cries coming from the water's edge. He called to his grandfather and both ran down the beach, and to their surprise and horror discovered, not a shipwrecked sailor washed ashore, but the *Beauchamp*, bottom up in the surf. The sight might well have unnerved the strongest man, for mortal hands could not upright that massive hull. There was a tremendous sea and sweep on the beach, but James Haylett dashed at once into the surf and succeeded in catching hold of his son-in-law, Charles Knights, who was struggling to get clear of the boat. Fred Haylett managed to seize John Hubbard, skipper of the drifter *Lily*. Having assisted Knights ashore, the gallant old man went in a second time and found one of his grandsons, Walter Haylett, who, seeing through the rowlock holes that they were on the beach, dived under the gunwale and was helped by his grandfather to reach safety.

It needs little imagination to realise the great danger incurred by those two rescuers, had it not been for their efforts it is almost certain no one would have been saved.

At intervals eight dead bodies were washed from under the boat and recovered, the last being at 11.30 a.m., when a large number of men succeeded in righting the lifeboat. One body was carried out to sea and never seen again.

James Haylett lost two sons, Aaron Walter Haylett, the cox'n, and James Haylett, jun., as well as a grandson, Harry Knights, a lad only nineteen years old, making his first and, as it unhappily turned out, his last trip on service in the lifeboat. William Brown, the assistant cox'n, whose head was practically severed by the fall of the gunwale, was owner of the *Alpha*, of which his brother Charles was master. Both lost their lives. Charles George, master of *Queen Alexandra*, John Smith, master of *Snowdrop*, William Wilson, and George King also gave their lives in this brave attempt to rescue strangers to whom they owed no allegiance save the call of humanity. These splendid fellows, many of whom sailed in herring drifters, were at home because the weather was too bad for them to be at sea fishing, but there was no holding back in answering the lifeboat bell.

Two men left ten children each; one nine, one eight, in all forty-four youngsters were left fatherless, with six widows and four other dependant relatives to mourn their losses. The smack drove over the sands into deep water, anchored, and sailed at daylight unaware of the catastrophe ashore.

Such a disaster naturally raised national, even world-wide interest, and the sum of £12,000, collected by a fund started by the Mayor of Yarmouth, included £2,000 from the Committee of Management of the R.N.L.I., which also defrayed the cost of the funerals and provided compensation for the survivors. To James Haylett, sen., came the Gold Medal, a copy of the vote inscribed on vellum and framed, and twenty-five guineas for his gallantry in remaining on the open beach for twelve hours, wet through and without food. These awards were handed to him by King Edward VII on the 6th January 1902. For fifty-nine years that noble fisherman had been a member of a lifeboat crew, assisting in the saving of 1,300 lives (Plate 42).

At the inquest the Coroner suggested that possibly the lifeboatmen had given up their errand as a bad job, James Haylett retorted "Caister lifeboatmen never turn back, and would have kept there till now if necessary to save men in distress."

Certainly it was not remuneration which sent such men to the rescue—ten shillings by day or a sovereign by night.

Undeterred by the loss of so many able-bodied men in a tiny village, a new crew was formed on the 21st December, and a few hours later towards midnight flares were seen burning on those same Barber Sands. With Jack Haylett as coxswain, the No. 1 lifeboat *Covent Garden* put to sea, assisted at the launch by that indomitable veteran, James Haylett, and the survivors, Haylett, Hubbard and Knights. Again it was a fruitless errand, as the stranded steamer refloated without assistance.

What a noble story to add to a record unsurpassed by any other lifeboat station in the United Kingdom—1,381 lives saved in the forty-three years a lifeboat had been stationed in that little fishing village hard by Yarmouth, with a foundation dating back to Roman times as evidenced by its name, Caister, a camp.

When I stood on that same beach on an exhilarating October day in 1946 and gazed out to sea, where a keen easterly wind was whipping up a line of breakers on the dreaded sands, I thought of that black winter night forty-five years before—of that sad procession winding its way to the churchyard near by, to be met by the self-same words which kings receive at their burial, "I am the Resurrection and the Life," where not only relatives, but a nation mourned sons it could ill afford to lose. There the poor battered bodies sleep peacefully within sound of the sea which gave them their living and took away their lives. I like to think that their spirits still hover over the scenes they knew and loved so well, for Caister can have changed but little since their day, inspiring their descendants who still hear the same call, feel the same urge to man the lifeboat, now no longer dependant on sail and oar. Even though a powerful motor drives her seaward into the very teeth of a gale, there is still the same work to do.

My wife and I walked over the dunes and I went into the lifeboat house to have a yarn with Mr. J. Woodhouse, cox'n, and his son, who is the motor mechanic, and inspect the boat, which is beautifully kept. It was good to think that though the boats

45 HERRING DOCK, LOWESTOFT
   L.T. 27 *Earl of Rosebery*, 25 tons, built 1878. L.T. 318 *Florence May*, 23 tons, built 1883. L.T. 150 *General Buller*, steam drifter, built of iron at Beverley, 1900, 39 tons, 17 h.p. engine.

46 ASHORE IN ENTRANCE TO LOWESTOFT HARBOUR
   L.T. 468 *Girls Own*, 35 tons, built 1892, drifter. L.T. 517 *Prairie Flower*, 59 tons, built 1892, trawler.

47 A CLOSE FIT, LOWESTOFT HARBOUR
Big trawler leaving with a drifter on either beam.

48 A LOWESTOFT AND A DUTCH DRIFTER LEAVING PORT
L.T. 561 *Thankful*, 35 tons, built 1892. A Scheveningen drifter, note tiller working in a port in sternboards.

49 **DRIFTERS LEAVING LOWESTOFT**
L.T. 319 *Comfort*, 35 tons, built 1896. L.T. 572 *Lily*, 37 tons, built 1893. W.K. 672 *Southern Cross*. N.N. 18 *Free Will*, 31 N. tons, built of wood at Shoreham in 1888, 7 h.p. engine, but fully dandy rigged.

50 **FRENCH LUGGER AT RAMSGATE**
Note standing lug on mainmast sheeting to iron horse on taffrail, and the curious peak halyard on foreyard.

51 **BOULOGNE DRIFTER ENTERING NEWLYN, 1920**
Note length of gaffs, elliptical stern, ornamental mizzen truck, bonnet off mizzen, all typical Lowestoft practice.

52 FRENCH DRIFTER ON LAUNCHING WAYS
Built by S. Richards at Lowestoft. Note wheel steering and heavy wooden fairleads for'ard.

53 AN EARLY STEAM DRIFTER, LOWESTOFT
*Lowestoft*, H. 492, 36 tons, built by Chambers & Colby, 1900, 15 h.p. engine.

have changed, the spirit of the crew remains the same, and a similar story could be told of many another station, but to-day the lack of men following the calling of their fathers means a difficulty in finding crews, and boats have had to be withdrawn.

We talked of those awful war years when the foul Nazi rained down fire on the ancient town of Yarmouth, destroying homes, the old church of St. Nicholas, and many another landmark. Mr. Woodhouse spoke in moving tones of the sight of the town in flames, of calls to go to the assistance of vessels sunk by mine, torpedo, or bomb, as well as ordinary marine disasters, of the difficulties of rescue work in the black-out conditions of wartime, and we unanimously agreed that there was much to be said for the old days and ways.

It was a privilege to meet these men. Theirs not the hot valour capable of doing an heroic deed on the spur of the moment when there is little chance of counting the cost, but that cool, calculating courage which, aware of all the risks entailed, takes men quietly out, not once but hundreds of times, to face hidden dangers and known perils to succour others unknown to them.

It was men like these who manned the sailing drifters of which I have written. Both were heart of oak.

Now to deal with the hauls they made. In the old days when the luggers returned to port the herring were ladled up from the well amidships, carefully sorted and counted by two men into a basket. Both men picked up two fish in each hand, the first counted one and put his into the basket, the second counted two, and so on, four herring made one "warp," thirty-three warps or 132 fish made a buyer's "hundred," and ten such hundreds made a thousand, and ten thousand—a "last"—actually numbered 13,200. The extra fish were "overtail" and belonged to the dealer as his commission, so that the salesman had nearly one-third of the profits of the catch just for handling the fish ashore.

This method of counting can be seen aboard L.T.703 *Monitor* of 40 tons, built 1896 (Plate 43). Note the square kettle standing on the scuttle hatch, made to fit in the top of the stove to prevent its being dislodged when the boat was rolling. The heavy spar with three fid holes is the bowsprit, with its heel hoisted up by the "Tommy Hunter"—the tackle on the fore side of the mizzen—and the drift between the deadeyes is unusually long. Beards are just beginning to give place to clean-shaven cheeks, with long drooping moustaches. In 1899 the tellers received some £2,000 for counting the fish, and cartage amounted to £3,600.

When the Scots fishermen came South with their fine cotton nets and light $3\frac{1}{2}$ in. warps, they introduced a new method of fishing and computation. They never scudded their nets at sea, everything was bundled into the hold together—warp, buoys, nets, herrings and all, then sail was made immediately and the luggers were racing for market long before the rest of the fleet had hauled their heavy twine nets and hemp warps.

The Scotsmen cleared their nets in the calm waters of the harbour, and the fish was shovelled into two-handled round baskets, holding a quarter of a cran, made of willow of specified sizes and numbers, hoop-iron, hardwood and cane. The bottom diameter was $14\frac{1}{2}$ in., the mouth $17\frac{1}{2}$ in., height $14\frac{1}{2}$ in., all inside measurements. The catch was sold by the cran, nominally a thousand herring, but naturally varying with their size and packing.

Soon the old ways gave place to the new, and the cran is still the standard measure.

During the long watch whilst the drifter was lying to her nets some of the men passed the time fishing with hook and line, especially for cod. All fish so caught were free from auction charges, and made a small addition to the earnings.

Mackerel generally swim near the surface, and the nets have to be well corked to float close to the top of the water. A fleet or train often numbered eleven or twelve score of nets, extending two to two and a half miles, or about double that of a herring fleet. The meshes were 22 to 23 to the yard, and the nets were originally of twine, but later cotton was used. Mackerel "voyages" were chancy, in some years very profitable, in others the reverse.

Plate 44 shows a big haul of mackerel being landed at Lowestoft from the drifters L.T.330 *Emblem*, 27 tons, built 1890, L.T.561 *Thankful* 35 tons, built 1893, and L.T.730 *Spring Flower*, 40 tons. Note the huge pile of nets on the deck of *Thankful*.

Writing to me of such scenes, Mr. J. Breach says:

"In the year 1913 Autumn mackerel voyage there were plenty of mackerel. I had one boat with three last (30,000) large fish as big as your arm, so to speak. Could not sell them, as so many boats had good catches, and they had to be put into the G.E.R. barges and dumped back in the sea. One sailer had caught six last, which was about the highest I know for a sailing drifter to catch and carry. Luckily the weather was very fine at the time, I can tell you there was not much freeboard."

So much for the ups and downs of fishing. One day a catch so big that most of it had to be thrown away, and another so small that its sale did not pay expenses.

A hundred of mackerel is thirty warps, or 120 fish.

What scenes there were in the Herring Dock on those October mornings in the closing years of the 19th century, especially about the time of the full moon. Power had not yet swept sail off the waters, although the portent was there when the first steam drifters showed to the discerning the shape of things to come. Save in hard winds, they were always the first of the fleet in port, but as the morning wore on the dozens of sailers grew to scores, then to hundreds, packing every inch of space, with crews doing their utmost to land catches on to the quay to be auctioned before prices began to tumble (Plate 45).

Everywhere is the sight and smell of fish, decks glisten with scales as if covered with crushed diamonds, and the men's jumpers sparkle like the sequins on a dowager's dress. Baskets and barrels full of fish, swimming but a few hours before, are being hurried off to the curers, while boxes in thousands are being packed for the London market. Still the boats come in until it seems that such a haul can never be cleared before the next morning witnesses similar scenes, which will continue until the end of the season.

Mr. J. Breach writes of those days:

"Regarding the catching power, in former days there were some big catches of herring, but the prices were not so big, £10 a last—20s. a cran—was a good price, more often than not they were £5. Our nets then were smaller and made of stouter cotton, usually 30 yds. long, 12 score meshes deep, and 18-ply cotton, the large sailers shooting or casting about 160 to 200 nets of this sort. Now the nets are finer meshed, 55 yds. long, 18 score meshes deep, and of 9-ply cotton, shooting 100 to 120 nets each.

When the local buyers had got all they wanted, and there was good fishing, the rest of the herrings would fall to very small prices, to say £3 a last, or anything you could get. I remember one year when the herring fell to £3 a last, my father put 60 last in the pickling vats, that is, salting them, and letting them remain there, and after the New Year came in would, through an agent, sell them to the Dutchmen, and they would bring one or two of their sailing luggers (boms) and take the herring to Holland.

Speaking of records, I remember one sailing boat having caught 24 last, that is 240 crans; of course, she was one of the latest type."

At times fog would hold up the entire fleet, and salesmen, buyers and porters would hang about for hours in the clammy mist. When it lifted with the coming of a breeze a race ensued to get alongside, and perhaps five hundred drifters would be unloading, with prices fluctuating wildly.

During my stay at Lowestoft, I had the pleasure of meeting Mr. W. Peek, who told me he first went to sea in 1893, and claimed with pride that he sailed with the same skipper for the first eight and a half years of his life at sea. He was the late Charley Brittain, a man of 18 stone, and known as "Suet" Brittain. Mr. Peek went one voyage in L.T.51 *Hearts of Oak*, then four years in L.T. *Boy Ernest*, followed by four years in L.T.607 *Mizpah*, and one voyage in L.T.307 *Prosperity*. At the end of the voyage in *Prosperity*, "Suet" said to Mr. Peek, "Bill, how would you like to go Master?" (Aside, "We didn't have tickets in those days and I hadn't even been mate.") I told him that I didn't think I'd like to go skipper, but after we'd been up in the town for a drink, I thought about it again and I asked him what he thought. He said, "You'll learn more in a year as Master than you will in ten as man," so I decided to go. I took the *Reward*, L.T.574 of 32 tons, built 1895, for the mackerel voyage round to the Westward, and then had the *Welcome Home*, L.T.749, of 40 tons, built 1898, for one voyage. After that I went over to Yarmouth in steam for a year or two, first into *Bera* S.N.353, then *Pearl*, L.T.461. In 1906 a week's fishing off Lerwick brought in

£628, the first night we landed 120 cran, which sold for £214 10s., the next only brought 25 cran, the third 80, with only 20 and 50 the following nights, shooting 140 nets, each 20 yds. long and 12 score meshes deep. In 1907 I took a quarter share in L.T.1034 *Silver King*, just built at a cost of £2,400 ready for sea, but with no fishing gear. In three years I cleared my share, then missed a year, took up another quarter share, and cleared that in two years, and in 1914 I took her on my own."

On my asking for his best catch in sail, Mr. Peek said:

"One morning we were off Lowestoft in *Mizpah*—that would be about 1900 or 1901. When we finished hauling in the morning we had about 9½ last. The wind was about S.S.E., and it was a bit mucky. 'Suet' said 'Them owd Scotties can't be out while the wind hold like this. We'll salt this lot down and have another shot!' We got the sail up and turned away to wind'ard a bit and then we got the nets over again. Then we went below and salted the whole of the first night's catch. We didn't have any food or rest—just a biscuit and a mug of tea—and by the time we finished it was time to haul again. This time we'd got another nine last. That's about 180 crans in a little boat like the old *Mizpah*! We got the sail on her again—two Jackie topsails and a spinnaker—and we turned away for home. There was a nice breeze, everything drawing nicely, but as soon as we got away I had to put the tiller up. If I hadn't she would have sailed right under. However, we took some of the sail off her and got home in nice time. When we lay alongside the quay we had a little list to port, and the water was just up to the deck. As soon as we got alongside we started to get the fish out, and don't forget that in those days there wer'n't any crans, and we had to pick 'em all up. (He demonstrated how they were picked up—four at a time, two in each hand.) Then when they were all ashore we went below to get a meal and I well remember we all fell asleep with a platter on our knees. That 'Home' voyage was only nine weeks, but we took the record of £1,450 and drew a share of £68 2s. 4d. for each of nine men. The previous record of £61 a share was held by old John Breach, and when we beat him he gave the skipper a gold ring."

Mr. Peek went on to speak of the fantastic rise in costs to-day (1946), saying that in 1914 a net cost £2 12s. 6d., fully rigged ready to go in the water; by 1939 the price had risen to £4, but in 1946 £10 was freely offered for a new net, or £7 for a second-hand one. In 1914 a cran of herring averaged about 48s., in 1946 90s.

I happened to mention this incident to Mr. J. Breach, and his reply makes an interesting sequel:

"It seems a coincidence that you should mention the *Mizpah* making the record share of £68 2s. 4d. She was owned then by Mr. Brittain, who was one of father's fortunate skippers, and he had the *Mizpah* built for him and gave him a start in life on his own, although as he told me, he had not the price of a boiler then, but he made good and retired comfortably off. I might say he was one of several who were helped in the same way; if they were good skippers, as my father would help those who tried to earn a living, but he had *no* time for slackers. It was my father who held the record of £61 a share in 1876, when he was skipper of his boat, and first *Brothers* L.T.216."

In another letter Mr. Breach gave a list of sailing drifters his father had built:

| | | | | | |
|---|---|---|---|---|---|
| *Brothers I* | L.T.216, | blt. 1875 | *Five Sisters* | L.T.231, | blt. 1877 |
| *Brothers II* | L.T. 88, | blt. 1879 | *Never Can Tell* | L.T.283, | blt. 1881 |
| *Boy Willie* | L.T.331, | blt. 1884 | *Band of Hope* | L.T.175, | blt. 1887 |
| *Boy Jack* | L.T.199, | blt. 1888 | *Girl's Own* | L.T.468, | blt. 1892 |
| *Jockey* | L.T.534, | blt. 1893 | *Mizpah* | L.T.607, | blt. 1894 |
| *Constance I* | L.T.642, | blt. 1894 | *Happy Return* | L.T.137, | blt. 1895 |
| *Enterprise* | L.T. 77, | blt. 1896 | *Perseverance* | L.T.710, | blt. 1896 |
| *Constance II* | | | *Fame* | L.T.754, | blt. 1898 |
| *Strive* | L.T.766, | blt. 1898 | | | |

He adds: "This is as far back as I can go according to history, as I was not born until 1877. Father sold out all his sailing drifters in 1899, had two years' rest, then went in for steam, but first bought five sailers for the home mackerel fishing. They were *Verbena, Nugget, Nil Desperandum, Shades of Evening, Good Hope*.

From 1901 to 1912 he had the following steam drifters built: *John and Sarah* (my parents' names), *Reliance, Searcher, Energy, Girl's Friend, Boy Jack II, Phillis Annie, Enterprise II, Sarah Marion, John Alfred, Pevensey Castle, Hastings Castle, Two Boys, Nil Desperandum, Emily, Brothers II, Qui Sait, United Boys, Never Can Tell II, Boy Roy, Boy Nat, Boy Philip, Margaret Hide,* and *Sarah Hide* (my mother's maiden name)."

I give these lists in full, seventeen sailing and twenty-four steam drifters, as showing what could be done by an energetic and persevering skipper, a story which could be repeated in many instances.

I have in my collection a photo of L.T.468 *Girl's Own*, taken when she ran aground alongside the trawler L.T.517 *Prairie Flower*, at the entrance to Lowestoft Harbour in a southerly gale with driving rain (Plate 46). I sent this to Mr. Breach, who informed me that the drifter was his father's boat, but he could not remember the incident.

The many differences between a drifter and a smack can clearly be seen—the pole mast instead of a fidded topmast with crosstrees, no boom, and the sheet traversing over an iron horse, against the smack's heavy boom with lower block working in a sheet box, while the two shrouds and a burton a side with no ratlines, the Tommy Hunter, the bowsprit to port, timber heads in the rails, sweeps in lumber irons, fish pounds on deck, the forestay tackle, and companion abaft the mizzen are other features peculiar to the drifter.

As mentioned previously, the 130 feet between the piers does not allow any too much room for running in, especially after easterly gales, when the sand is liable to be washed in, but it was amazing how many sailing craft managed to enter or leave together. Plate 47 shows a big trawler leaving with a drifter on either beam, even four or five was nothing unusual. L.T.561 *Thankful* and a Scheveningen drifter are seen in Plate 48.

It must have been a splendid sight to see the hundreds of drifters sailing out of the harbour at tide time, and Plate 49 gives some idea of the spectacle. Here dandies, fifies, zulus, and the usurper, the steam drifter, with a "cigarette" funnel and full suit of sails, are all getting under way, while the offing is dotted with scores of sail. The rig of the boat on the port side of N.N.18 *Free Will* is worthy of study, as is the huge lug of the boat ahead. Never shall we see the like again.

Even more crowded conditions were to be found at the neighbouring Norfolk port, as well over a thousand drifters were often based on Yarmouth during the autumn.

The most famous of the Yarmouth sailing drifter skippers was William Larner, nicknamed Wilks, who was master of Y.H.1065 *Concordia*, owned by Wm. Crome. Year after year Wilks would earn more money with *Concordia* than any other drifter afloat. Very often his earnings were more than double that of many of his rivals. He said that if ever he was beaten he would give up, and he kept his word when, after many years, George Dyball, in the *G. and E.* just managed to top him, and Wilks went herring drifting no more. My informant, Mr. Harry George, tells me that in his boyhood the lads would look at Wilks in much the same way as a young A.B. would look at an admiral. *G. and E.* was a 49-tonner, built in 1879, on the 17th November 1890 she stranded between the Cross and Scroby Sands in a light W.N.W. wind, and became a total loss.

The big French drifters working in the North Sea carried very large crews, as the Government subsidised the industry to ensure having a reserve of seamen for any naval emergency, and they fished with anything up to 280 nets, extending upwards of three miles.

In the old *chasse-marée*, literally a vessel which works the tides, the hands numbered from fifteen to thirty, and if the sail plan looked crazy, with masts and yards at every angle, those luggers could sail, for their underwater lines were fine. Down to a few years before the second world war, two-masters were quite a common sight from my windows at certain seasons, when luggers from Boulogne and Gravelines worked at the back of the sands, until bad weather sent them round to Ramsgate harbour for shelter (Plate 50). The Frenchmen were not above poaching inside the three-mile limit if there was no Fishery cruiser about, and through my big telescope I have watched them with trawls down, less than a mile out.

Some of the French fishermen working off Yarmouth appreciated the advantages of the ketch rig, and ordered similar vessels, many being built in East Anglia. When I had the good luck to meet Mr. Wm. S. Parker at Lowestoft, he very kindly loaned me the original sail plan, from which I set out the drawing on page 306. I sent my plan to Mr. Parker for his approval, and his signature thereon marks its authenticity. He told me that this drifter was the largest ever built at Lowestoft, as she measured 84 ft. overall, and carried a crew of twenty. When he was asked to design her, he sent over to France for a copy of the regulations regarding crew accommodation, as every man had to have so many cubic feet of space. He purchased an English-French dictionary and puzzled out the requirements, then worked out a fo'c'sle which would pass the authorities. Then he designed the hull round the fo'c'sle, and a sail plan to match! Many of these drifters had a crew of twenty-five, as the laws compelled the carrying of a certain complement according to tonnage. Some followed the fishing down Channel, and Plate 51 shows one, close-reefed, entering Newlyn Harbour at Easter 1920. Judging from certain features, she might well have been Lowestoft-built, although she is registered at Boulogne.

It is interesting to compare the sail plan of the French drifter designed by Mr. Parker with that of *Strive*, since both were built at the same yard.

## MASTS AND SPARS

| | | |
|---|---|---|
| Foremast | Deck to shoulder | 39 ft. |
| | Pole extreme | 17 ft. |
| | Gaff, bolt to hole | 33 ft. 6 in. |
| | Topsail yard, hole to hole | 27 ft. |
| Centre of foremast to foreside of stem at deck | | 24 ft. |
| Bowsprit : Outside stem to pin of sheave | | 24 ft. |
| Mizzenmast | Deck to shoulder | 34 ft. 6 in. |
| | Pole extreme | 16 ft. 6 in. |
| | Gaff, bolt to hole | 26 ft. 6 in. |
| | Boom, mast to pin of sheave | 29 ft. 3 in. |
| | Topsail yard, hole to hole | 20 ft. 6 in. |

## SAILS

| Jibs | Weather | Lee | Foot | |
|---|---|---|---|---|
| Storm | 35 ft. | 24 ft. | 15 ft. | |
| Second | 45 ft. | 30 ft. | 22 ft. | |
| Third | 53 ft. | 33 ft. 6 in. | 30 ft. 6 in. | |
| Spinnaker | 63 ft. | 50 ft. | 57 ft. 6 in. | |

| Sail | Weather | Lee | Foot | Head |
|---|---|---|---|---|
| Working foresail | 34 ft. | 27 ft. 6 in. | 20 ft. | |
| Big foresail | 35 ft. | 32 ft. | 30 ft. | |
| Mainsail | 23 ft. 6 in. | 50 ft. 6 in. | 35 ft. 6 in. | 22 ft. |
| Mizzen | 20 ft. | 41 ft. | 27 ft. | 26 ft. |
| Main topsail | 12 ft. 6 in. | 20 ft. | 30 ft. | 26 ft. |
| Mizzen topsail | 13 ft. 6 in. | 17 ft. 3 in. | 24 ft. 6 in. | 20 ft. |
| Main trysail | 26 ft. 6 in. | 43 ft. | 33 ft. | |
| Mizzen trysail | 22 ft. | 23 ft. 6 in. | 25 ft. | |

A similar drifter, but with wheel-steering is seen ready for launching at Richards' Yard, Lowestoft (Plate 52).

## SHARES

The proportions into which the shares were divided varied at different ports.

## THE GREAT AUTUMN FISHERY

In the 1840's the doles for herring fishing at Lowestoft were: Nets 55, boat 28, master 16, mate 11, hawseman 10, netrope man 7, nets owner 6, 1 capsternman 6, the other 6, boy $4\frac{1}{2}$, vicar (tithe) $\frac{1}{2}$, a total of 150.

In the mid-eighties for the large Yarmouth boats the nett account was divided into 17 shares, the owner taking 10, the crew 7. These seven were divided by $85\frac{1}{2}$, a relic of the time when the men were paid by the last at £4 5s.6d. a last some twelve years previously. Then the skipper took 16, mate 10, hawseman $8\frac{1}{2}$, waleman $8\frac{1}{2}$, netrope man 7, net stower 7, five capstan men 5 each, and the boy $3\frac{1}{2}$, a total of $85\frac{1}{2}$.

Settling was at end of voyage or season, and the crew was made up of half fishermen, half yokels, or joskins.

At Gorleston the nett earnings were divided into 16 shares, the owner taking 9, the crew 7. The skipper had $1\frac{1}{2}$, mate $1\frac{1}{8}$, hawseman 1, waleman 1, netrope man $\frac{7}{8}$, net stower $\frac{7}{8}$, four capstan men $\frac{3}{4}$ each, and the boy $\frac{1}{2}$.

At Grimsby the settling ran from 12 to 20 weeks. Out of the gross earnings the following expenses were deducted: Provisions, salt, oils, tanning, carting, towing, commission, etc., then the nett earnings were divided into two parts, the owner of the boat took one-half, the remainder was divided into 9 or 10 shares among the whole crew. The master took $1\frac{1}{2}$, mate $1\frac{1}{4}$, five men 1 share each, three boys $\frac{3}{4}$ each, the youngster $\frac{3}{8}$.

Compared with Yarmouth and its charters relating to herring fishing dating back to the early 12th century, the fisheries at Lowestoft are of comparatively recent growth. During the decade 1772-81 there were only 33 craft, catching a yearly average of 714 last, sold for about £12 10s. a last. In 1790 24 boats earned £2,475 19s. $3\frac{1}{2}$d., or £103 3s. $3\frac{1}{2}$d. a boat, and the nets cast by the Yarmouth and Lowestoft boats would have stretched over 200 miles if in a direct line. In 1797 a gigantic king herring $15\frac{1}{2}$ in. long and $3\frac{1}{8}$ in. breadth was caught by John Ferret, in the lugger *Daniel and Mary*. In 1821 one catch of 16 boats realised £5,252 15s. $1\frac{1}{4}$d., or an average of £328 5s. $11\frac{1}{4}$d. a boat. These meticulous accounts were taken from an old book belonging to a rector, who, being entitled to tithe, took good care that the catches were accurately recorded.

In 1853 there were about 200 luggers at Yarmouth, and ten thousand lasts of herring were cured, requiring a ton of salt per last. Ten years later fifteen thousand lasts were cured. In 1844 there were only 65 craft working out of Lowestoft, and the number fell to 32 a decade later, but the following ten years saw an increase to 166, besides eight trawlers, as the opening of the railway gave a tremendous impetus to both drifting and trawling. The last year of the 19th century saw 18,000 lasts landed at Lowestoft against 26,000 at the rival port, valued at £300,000. The luckiest steam drifter earned £3,400, of which the skipper's share was £200, the mate £140, six of the crew £124 each, and the boy £31.

The 22nd October 1907 saw all records broken when sixty million herring were landed at Yarmouth in one day; actually the fleet caught about one hundred million, but owing to lack of quay space, some of the drifters had to discharge their catch at Grimsby. At Yarmouth one vessel landed a quarter of a million herring, 25 lasts. The price opened at 12s. a cran, or 3 lbs. of herring for one penny, but as the silver torrent cascaded on to the quays, the market was glutted, and the price fell to 3s. a cran, nominally a thousand fish, weighing about $3\frac{1}{2}$ cwt.

In 1910 the highest earning by a sailing drifter was £310 against the £1,100 of a steam drifter, while the lowest was £75 against £140, and the average for sail was only £162.

The 1913 fishery, the last before war upset everything, was the most prosperous ever known, and the mind is bewildered at the vast quantities landed—536,400 crans at Lowestoft, 823,600 at Yarmouth, and sold at an average price of 20s. a cran, over one thousand vessels fishing from Yarmouth against 600 from the Suffolk port; 1,163 Scottish boats came to the English fishing, consisting of 854 steam, 100 motor and 209 sail, and their average earnings were £794 for steam, £365 for motor, and £235 for sail. In fourteen weeks 825 million herring, weighing 157,000 tons, were landed, and prices ranged from 91s. a cran to 7s., and the total value amounted to over £1,350,000.

The average price for the year for all herring landed in the United Kingdom was 8s. a cwt., or some 32 fish for 10d., and the retail price averaged 4d. a lb. The previous decade had seen nearly 62 per cent. more fish landed, rising from 2,913,671 cwt. to 6,935,413 cwt.

The outbreak of war completely disorganised the fishery. Many of the steam drifters were taken over by the Admiralty for war service, and in 1915 some 120 million herring were landed. Prices had quadrupled in two years, ranging from 40s. to 146s. a cran, or an average of 80s. In September 1917, fresh herring at Yarmouth made 40s. a long hundred, 132 fish, or $3\frac{1}{2}$d. each in the wholesale market. I can remember as a boy seeing the local luggers coming into Margate Harbour, laden down to the gunwale with the silvery freight, delicious herring which were hawked round the neighbouring towns at 24 a 1s. During the war bloaters cost 10d. each in London against the pre-war 1d. to $1\frac{1}{2}$d.; 1917 season saw only 5,700 tons landed in England, and prices averaged 87s. a cran.

One or two sailing drifters carried on during hostilities, but the Armistice saw the death of sail.

It is not my intention to go "into steam," but I cannot refrain from including two photographs of early wooden drifters, fitted out with a full suit of sails, as many were hopelessly under-powered. In a chat with Mr. Harry George, he told me that Mr. Wm. Elliott was seriously perturbed at the loss of power in the Yarmouth drifter *Cicero*. "If you blew the whistle the steam pressure fell." After hearing Mr. George's suggestions as to how matters could be improved, including increasing the size of the boiler, Mr. Elliott exclaimed, "Has't got £100, bor? If so, I'll build 'ee a drifter." So much for character and reputation. Mr. George was the youngest skipper to take a steam drifter across Yarmouth Bar, being master, at the age of 19, of Y.H.414 *Puffin*, the second drifter to be registered at the port. The first was *Salamander*.

Plate 53 is of *Lowestoft*, a 15-h.p. 36 N.T. drifter built in 1900 by Chambers and Colby for Hull owners. In those spartan days a wheelhouse was considered an unnecessary luxury, although some boats had canvas dodgers. I have no doubt the ancients looking on had plenty to say about going to sea in a steam kettle, and that the urchins passed a few pointed remarks about the lad in an Inverness cape!

Plate 54 shows Y.H.547 *Grace Darling*, with a slender "cigarette" funnel, safely entering Yarmouth Haven in weather which has flung a Scottish zulu on to the North beach, and put a barque ashore. A wheelhouse now gives the helmsman some protection against the elements.

Thanks to my friend Mr. Wm. Parker, I am able to give some invaluable details of the nett costs of the wooden hulls of these early steam drifters. In 1900 Chambers built the *Glengairn*. The contract price was £1,190 and the nett costs £980 15s. 8½d., made up as follows:

May, 1900. *Glengairn* for Steam Herring Fleet, Aberdeen.

| | £ | s. | d. |
|---|---|---|---|
| Shipwrights' wages | 252 | 11 | 4½ |
| Joiners' wages | 59 | 11 | 0 |
| Timber | 189 | 7 | 2 |
| Galvanised bolts, 12 cwt. 1 qr. | 14 | 7 | 11 |
| Black bolts, 3 cwt. 0 qr. 23 lb. | 3 | 3 | 10 |
| Two steel beams | 4 | 10 | 4 |
| Ballast, 5 tons pig iron | 14 | 11 | 3 |
| Steering wheel | 4 | 8 | 8 |
| Anchors and chain cable | 29 | 10 | 10 |
| Wire rigging | 2 | 17 | 2 |
| Steering gear | 6 | 0 | 0 |
| Sails, etc. | 20 | 10 | 5 |
| Water tank | 3 | 15 | 0 |
| Spars and blocks, "blockshop" | 38 | 12 | 8 |
| Ironwork, "smithshop" | 42 | 13 | 9 |
| Rope outfit | 16 | 9 | 2 |
| Small boat | 10 | 17 | 0 |
| Navigating stores | 33 | 18 | 0 |
| Brass screws | 1 | 2 | 3 |
| Brass work, fittings to cabin, etc. | 7 | 5 | 6 |
| Paint, etc. | 1 | 17 | 6 |
| Sundry stores | 2 | 1 | 8 |
| Cement | 1 | 12 | 0 |

| Sundries | - | - | - | - | - | - | - | - | - | - | 7 | 7 | 5 |
| Direct expenses | - | - | - | - | - | - | - | - | - | - | 14 | 19 | 3 |
| | | | | | | | | | | | | | |
| Nett costs | - | - | - | - | - | - | - | - | - | - | £784 | 1 | 1½ |

| Sawmill wages, etc. | - | - | - | - | - | £66 | 6 | 7 | | | |
| Indirect wages | - | - | - | - | - | 85 | 10 | 0 | | | |
| Sawmill and indirect expenses | - | - | - | | | | | | |
| Coals, oil, general expenses sawmill | - | - | 44 | 18 | 0 | | | |
| | | | | | | | | | 196 | 14 | 7 |
| | | | | | | | | | £980 | 15 | 8½ |

The following year the contract price for a similar drifter, *Diamond*, 79.4 by 18.2 by 8, 40 N.T. 64 G.T., and 15 h.p. engine, had fallen to £880, with the nett costs £697 11s. 3½d., and similar boats averaged about the same figures. In July 1901 the motor drifter *Pioneer* was built for F. Miller, contract price £680, nett costs £463 15s. 10½d.

There was certainly not a large profit made on the building of drifter hulls, as these figures do not include sawmill expenses and indirect wages, which were in the region of £200, to judge from the figures relating to *Glengairn*.

Generally speaking, the price for timber seems to have ranged from about £190 to £280 per hull, but that used in *Pioneer* was only £177 8s. 3½d. The cost of building the small boat was very low, £7 16s. 10½d. for *Diamond's*, only two shillings less for another, and a few pence more for others. The expenses for delivery to Aberdeen were £11, with another £2 for towage at the Scottish port, nearly one-fifth of the cost of taking the drifter north. A Walker's taffrail log was £3 8s. 6d., and £6 seems to have been the charge for the mast tabernacles.

Before the drifter was ready for sea the engine and boiler had to be fitted by a specialist firm, and then a complete outfit of nets, warps, bowls, etc., was required.

After Chambers' yard came into the hands of H. Reynolds, an average of twenty-four to twenty-five smacks and drifters were built per year, the highest number being twenty-six. In 1902 a record was made when a drifter was framed in three days, launched in seven weeks, and finished off in another, eight weeks in all for building the hull. The word "prefabrication" was unknown in those days, but they got results!

Another fortnight's work saw the engines fitted, and she was ready for sea. In 1904 it cost £3,400 to build and fit out a drifter for the fishing, with nets at 50s. each, all roped complete, and buffs 2s. 6d. each. After the 1914-18 war the cost of a net was £9. In 1904 the price per cubic foot for pitch pine was 2s. to 2s. 3d., c. 1946 29s.

When the Autumn fishery was at its height, the drifters lay in the Yare as tightly packed as the herring in the shoals outside (Plate 55). By now steam predominates, but here and there can be seen the huge masts of the fifies and zulus, and the lofty spars of square-riggers—probably bringing timber from the Baltic—can be discerned in the smoky haze.

This was but one side of the many ramifications of the herring industry. Further down the river, on the South Denes, were the vast curing yards with thousands of barrels waiting to be filled with pickled herring, with the Nelson Monument looking down on the activity (Plate 56).

It may be of interest to devote a few lines to the art of a cooper, a highly-skilled craftsman of an ancient trade, which is yet another where the eye, rather than any measuring instrument, is the arbiter, for a competent man reckons to construct a barrel or cask from start to finish without using gauge or rule. The finished job has to be capable of keeping the pickle in and the weather out, and withstand the rough usage to which a full barrel must necessarily be subjected.

The staves, made from imported billets, are chopped at the ends to a rough taper, rounded on the outside and hollowed on the inside. The edges are run over a "jointer," a large plane 5 to 6 ft. long, and 4 to 5 in. wide, fitted sole up, and the wood is run over the plane, not *vice versa* as in ordinary carpenter's work. This is to ensure that the edges of the staves are dead straight, and will make a close joint when brought together. During this operation the cooper constantly holds the stave to his eye to gauge size and shape. The finished staves are about $\frac{1}{2}$ in. thick and so exactly cut that they just fit round the same sized "head" at each end, and in the finest work the joints will be so close as to be almost imperceptible. The staves, held together by wooden hoops, are moistened inside with water and held over a fire made from wood chips. The cooper judges by the feel of the outside the exact moment when they are sufficiently heated for bending. The chimes or rims are cut with an adze and grooves made for the heads with a special tool known as a "croze." The heads are of oak boards dowelled together with a strip of flag—dried reed, placed between each for packing—the willow hoops are fastened on, the iron bands driven down, and the bung-hole bored. When the barrel is filled with pickle, this will be closed with a wooden shive driven well home. When assembling the staves into a finished barrel, the cooper uses a curious arched-handled hammer (Plate 57).

Now for a few words on the disposal of the immense catches. The drifters come in from sea and tie up at the wharf, where the catch is unloaded in round baskets holding a quarter cran, and measured off into swills, the peculiar pannier-shaped double baskets made from unpeeled willow and taking about 500 herring, or half a cran. Large numbers of these are arranged on the wharf in front of each boat. The catch is auctioned, loaded on lorries—low wagons without sides, drawn by one or a pair of horses, often the proud Suffolk Punches, and taken from the market to the curing yards. Here the contents are shot into long, shallow wooden troughs about four feet wide, and a sprinkling of salt enables the gippers the more easily to seize and hold the slippery fish. This work is done by the Scottish lassies, working in crews of three, who stand in a row, pick up a fish, gut it by inserting a small sharp knife just below and behind the gills, a quick upward cut brings away the gut, which is dropped into small tubs in front of each girl, and sold for manure. Behind each lass are three shallow tubs, into which the gutted fish are thrown according to size and quality.

These girls, paid so much subsistence plus so much a barrel, earn their money, standing hour after hour in all weathers—pitiless downpour, bitter east wind, or autumn sunshine all alike to them. Some are bare-headed, others wear bright coloured shawls as turbans, all have their sleeves rolled up, with dresses covered with scales, blood and slime. Back-chat flies all the time. Many have followed the fishing all their lives, and the title of girl scarcely applies to these dexterous women, yet so are they called. Their speed is amazing. Knives flash in and out of the fish at the rate of about one a second (Plate 58).

The barrels are stacked in long rows parallel to and some distance from the gutting troughs. The full tubs of gutted fish are taken and emptied into the rousing tubs, where the herring is again sprinkled with salt and kept well roused—stirred up. Then the packer takes an armful, drops the herring into the barrel and packs them in layers, bellies up, and again sprinkles with salt. Each layer is separated by a layer of salt, just coarse enough to keep the fish from touching each other, but hard enough to withstand pressure. On an average each girl will pack about three barrels an hour. The salt should dissolve slowly and extract the water from the fish, about 1 cwt. being allowed for each barrel, which is now headed and allowed to stand, being frequently examined to see that no leakage is taking place. After some eight days the barrels are opened and the pickle drained off. The fish have shrunk and so more are added until the barrel is full. Then it is headed up once more, turned over on its side, filled with brine pickle, and bunged up.

Naturally the number of fish in a barrel varies, according to size and quality, from 750 to 1,000. If the weather is warm the fish must be more heavily salted by using seven to eight tons of salt per 100 cran against five or six. This method of curing herring has changed but little since the Middle Ages. The secret is that the fish should be gutted, cured and packed within 24 hours of being in the sea. To-day motor lorries have supplanted the horse to a great extent, and concrete is replacing the old wooden troughs.

Before the 1914-18 war these barrels of pickled herring were in great demand for the German and Russian markets, millions being exported annually. But history repeated itself as it did with the Dutch 250 years and more before, and the end of hostilities brought changed conditions and fashions so that sales dwindled away to an alarming extent, bringing depression to a once thriving industry.

Not all the herring landed are pickled, some are sold fresh, but many more are cured locally in smoke houses tucked away in the Rows—later in more up-to-date fish houses—by methods handed down from father to son for generations. For centuries the Yarmouth Red herring, cured by smoking, has been esteemed abroad, especially in Italy and the Mediterranean countries.

Fashions changed. Sometimes the demand was for heavily-salted fish, smoked for many days; at others for less highly-flavoured herring. After a preliminary washing, the fish are dry-salted very carefully, for on that depends the quality of the finished product. The mixing is done with wooden shovels, using about one ton of Liverpool salt to a last—10 cran. Then the herrings are placed in tanks full of brine pickle and left for a number of days, varying according to the grading of the fish and the cure required. If trade is bad they may be left for weeks.

To meet varying tastes fish have lain in brine for two days, then smoked for fourteen, or five days in pickle to ten in the smoke-houses, or fourteen days in each. For palates liking a less pungent taste, pickled for eight days, smoked for one night, a favourite cure for Italian buyers; others pickled for five, smoked for five. Whatever the cure, the fish are taken out of the pickle, washed and sent to the smoke-houses. Here they are "rived" or "speeted" through one gill-cover and out at the mouth on thin sticks about 3 ft. 6 in. to 4 ft. 6 in. long, pointed at one end, and taking a score or thirty on each. A quick woman worker can handle about a last a day. The old-fashioned smoke-houses were lofty buildings about 16 ft. square, within were a series of wooden frames reaching from floor to ceiling, with small transverse racks called "loves," probably a corruption of the French word "louvres." The speets, some six inches apart and a foot above each other, are placed in position by men straddling the span, each chamber holding about a last, or three to a house.

The roof was covered with heavy tiles, left uncemented to allow for a good draught and the escape of the smoke. On the stone floor about sixteen fires were made, usually of oak shavings, sawdust and billets, which burn quickly with a heavy resinous smoke, giving the fish a high colour. Sometimes ash would be used if a special colour was required for certain markets. The fires were lit and allowed to burn for two days, then the fish dripped for a day, and the process repeated for a fortnight, or the fires would be lit every day for ten days, all depended on the cure desired. In cold weather, when it is more difficult to keep the inside temperature up, curing takes longer, and the fish is hard-cured; in very warm spells it may be difficult to keep the temperature down, and half-cooked fish result, quite unsuitable for packing.

Whichever cure is adopted, the conclusion sees the fish packed in barrels by two men; one holds the speet and slides the fish in four at a time, which for convenience count as two; the other, the teller, calls out 2, 4, 6, etc., up to 12, which thus represents 24 fish. When the barrel is filled it is put under a screw press, which flattens down the fish and allows an extra number to be packed. A full barrel usually takes 650 full-sized fish, but more if a smaller size is being cured. The curer's name and the number of fish were then marked on each barrel.

Compared with the Red herring and its centuries of history, the bloater is a comparatively modern innovation, reputed to have been accidentally discovered by a curer named Bishop about a century ago. He lightly dry-salted a number of full-roed prime herring which he had left on his hands one day, and hung them in a smoke-house where fires were already burning. The next day he was surprised at the appearance and flavour of the fish, and so a new delicacy was launched on the market, to become the famous Yarmouth bloater, so called because the fish has just begun to bloat. Its fame was spread abroad by the summer visitors now beginning to make the ancient fishing town a popular resort. Landladies were quick to find out the merits of a tasty breakfast dish which had the advantage of being very cheap. But, alas, in many a seaside town where curing was done, the fussy visitors objected to the sight and smell of the smoke-houses, and the local curer was forced out of business when bye-laws were introduced dealing with noxious trades! To be at its best, a bloater should be eaten as soon as possible after curing.

About the same time one John Woodger, of Newcastle and later Yarmouth, tried the experiment of splitting the fish before curing, the result being that once so tasty morsel, the kipper. At this process the women could work outdoors, throwing the fish into baskets holding about fifty fish, or indoors in sheds. Here the herring, fresh from the sea, are emptied on to long tables, the women plunge a short-bladed knife into the middle of the back, slip it forward, and then back to the tail, so laying the fish open. The gut is removed to become manure, the roes or milt are made into a delicacy. The fish is well washed to remove blood and slime, then thrown into brine tanks and left for half an hour or so. Next the herring is opened out, impaled on hooks and hung on kipper speets, one inch square bars of wood about four feet long, and smoked overnight. They are ready for packing in boxes the next day.

At one time only the very finest fish were used for this process, then came in the practice of using "overdays," fish 24 or more hours old.

The oak tree was extremely valuable to the old-world fisherman. His boat was built from its timber, the crooks made knees to tie frames and beams together, the bark tanned his nets and sails, while a fire made from twigs, small billets or sawdust provided the most suitable smoke in which to cure his catch. Would that such simple methods prevailed to-day. Some experts have discovered that long "overday" fish, soaked in brine and *dyed*, will satisfy the majority of the public, many of whom have never known the delicacy of a properly-cured and smoked herring or haddock.

I have mentioned but a few of those who look to the herring for their prosperity. Many are the ancillary trades connected with the fishing—the spar and block makers, sail and rope makers, the ransackers and beasters, the salt and coal miners, the makers of baskets and swills, the buyers and salesmen, the clerks and principals, the carters and vanmen, not to mention the hosts indirectly employed. Since before the days of Cedric the Saxon the shoals have visited our waters, millions of millions of millions have been meshed, yet still they come, a harvest free for all, provided by nature's bounteous hand.

The years between the two wars brought many changes. The tremendous drop in drifter catches can be realised from the fact that in 1913 7,785,000 cwt. of pelagic fish were landed against 4,221,000 in 1930. In the year before the 1914 war some two and a half million barrels were exported, but only 727,000 in 1933. In 1913 about 1,500 steam drifters grossed £2,400 a year; twenty years later some 1,000 earned £1,100 gross, which worked out at less than £1 a week per man, against £6 in pre-war days, when money had a greater purchasing power. In the palmy days of the fishing sixty years ago about fifty thousand men found employment, by 1913 these figures had fallen to half, and another twenty years saw barely fifteen thousand employed.

In the old days practically every boat sailed on its own keel, the only capital needed being a boat and nets. If a man was trustworthy, tradesmen would freely allow credit for fitting out, and it was the ambition of every lad who went to sea to one day own his own boat. The taxpayer had no financial interest. Often carpenter, netmaker, sailmaker, and fisherman pooled their labours and shared alike in profits and losses, in which that indefinable something called luck frequently played its part—the weather, damage to boat and gear, good or bad season.

Then began the practice of Government loans to fishermen for the installation of motors. In 1919 it was £33,566, but each year saw an increase, until in 1933 the amount topped £100,000, and averaged about the same for subsequent years.

When the economic blizzard struck this country in the early thirties, ruin came to many a fisherman who had by thrift and hard work built up a profitable way of life. An owner told me that one day he went into his bank to see how he stood, and learned that he had £26,000 to his credit, and in addition he had his fleet of drifters. The slump came and he lost practically everything.

Then followed Herring Boards. Numerous restrictions as to the number of nets each man could shoot, the number of drifters allowed to sail, catches not to exceed so many crans, penalties inflicted for any breach of the many regulations makes one wonder if the days of sail were not the golden years in more senses than one.

54 *GRACE DARLING* ENTERING YARMOUTH
37 tons, built at Lowestoft, 1900, 15 h.p. engine. Note zulu ashore on North beach.

55 DRIFTERS PACKED IN THE YARE
Note huge masts of Scottish luggers, transom sterned ketch barge alongside a brigantine with foreyard cock-billed and fitted with bentinck boom. Tug ahead has twin funnels side by side.

56  A CURING YARD AT YARMOUTH

57  A COOPER AT WORK.

58  GIRLS ROUSING HERRING, YARMOUTH

59 MACKEREL DRIVERS LEAVING PENZANCE, c. 1886

60 SETTING OUT FOR THE FISHING GROUNDS, c. 1880 Note small mizzen set on foremast and watch mizzen aft.

61 LANDING MACKEREL AT HUGH TOWN, c. 1880

62 MEVAGISSEY HARBOUR
Brigantine *John Pearce*, with luggers alongside.

63 LUGGERS LEAVING MEVAGISSEY
Note wide hatches, scottles, bowsprit bitts, crutch, thwart with four bolts for capstan, lantern and sweeps on lugger in foreground.

CHAPTER SEVEN

# *CORNWALL*

THE Cornish fisheries came next in importance, and the men from the Duchy have always been renowned as fishermen and builders of able craft. The Cornish luggers were of two distinct types, instantly recognisable on account of the shape of their sterns. Boats from the East Cornish ports of Fowey, Polperro, Looe, and Mevagissey —all registered at Fowey and distinguished by the letters F.Y.—invariably had transom sterns, while those west of the Lizard from the harbours in Mount's Bay, Porthleven, Penzance, Newlyn and Mousehole—registered at Penzance, letters P.Z.—or from St. Ives—S.S.—were generally pointed sterned, or "two-bowed," to use a local name, although a few transom and counter sterns were to be found. Both types were alike in being carvel-built, instead of the clench work popular on the East Coast, and were either fully or partly decked, the latter known as hatched boats.

The reason for this distinction in sterns was the harbour accommodation available. To the eastward lay plenty of good natural harbours, where the luggers could lie afloat or dry out in excellent shelter, but to the west were only tiny rocky coves or small artificial harbours, drying out at low water, and fully exposed to certain winds. This meant that berthing facilities were far more limited and a greater number of sharp-sterned craft can be packed into a small space than with the wider variety. A lugger running into a crowded basin could nose her way into a narrow space between two others in a manner impossible for square sterns. Carvel planking, hooding on stem and stern-post, made for greater strength to withstand the pounding received as the keel struck bottom when the tide was ebbing or making, and a pointed sterned vessel is held to run better before a heavy breaking sea than a square-sterned one, but on this thorny subject are two schools of thought.

To what influence can be attributed this difference in construction on East and West Coasts? Can it be traced back as far as the days of Tyre and Sidon, when it is known that Cornwall was visited by the Phoenicians in search of tin? Like all Mediterranean craft, their boats were carvel-built, and reference to this form of construction can be found in the Old Testament. In Ezekiel xxvii, we read that the ships were built of fir trees of Senit, cedars from Lebanon for masts, oaks of Bashan for oars, while the sails were made of linen from Egypt. Prophesying the fall of Tyre, the seer foretells that the site of that beautiful city "shall be a place for the spreading of nets in the midst of the sea." The belief that these boats were carvel-built is strengthened by the verse, "The ancients of Gebal and the wise men thereof were in thee thy caulkers," and in another verse is a reference to "thy mariners, thy pilots, thy calkers." Only carvel-built vessels are caulked.

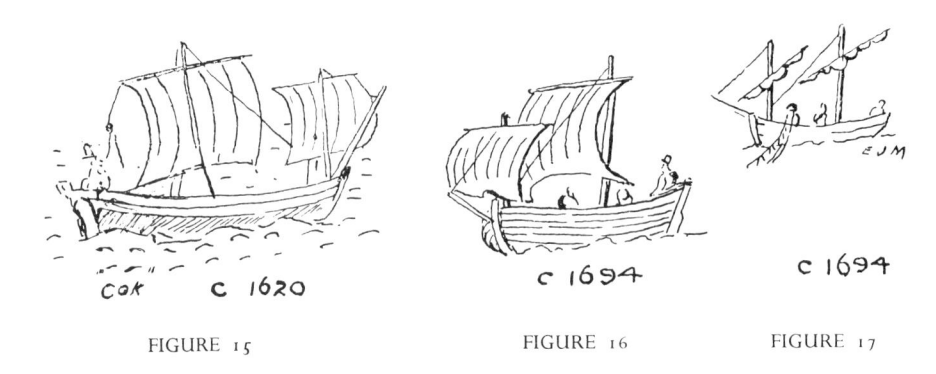

FIGURE 15            FIGURE 16            FIGURE 17

Again, the Cornish harbours are opposite the French ports in Brittany, where Latin, rather than Viking, influence is found, and no doubt constant communication between the two countries influenced design and build. It is probable that the first boats were open, with the usual single square mainsail, but any evidence on this point is lacking, which is not surprising considering how cut off Cornwall was in those days of poor communications, even retaining its own language. We have to wait until 1620 for the first picture of a "cok" or pilchard boat ornamenting a terrier map of the Church lands of St. Just-in-Roseland (Fig. 15). A two-masted double-ended boat is depicted, with the foremast stepped well for'ard, and a sharply steeving bowsprit, presumably used only as a lead for the bowlines. The square sails are braced up sharply, and the mainmast has a stay leading to the foot of the foremast. The hull bears a striking resemblance to the boats of the early 19th century.

Another estate map drawn by G. Withiel and dated 1694 shows a similar boat under sail, with a bowsprit reeving through a hole in the topstrake. The tiller, shipped over the rudder head, is similar in shape to that seen down to the last days of sail (Fig. 16). Another sketch (Fig. 17) shows the sails furled to their yards, which are hoisted half-way up the masts and cockbilled. This suggests that the custom of lowering the sails and stowing them on one side of the deck came in after the introduction of the lugsail. The net is being hauled in over the port side, contrary to later Cornish practice. Although crudely drawn, the vignettes do give some idea of the type of boat used in the

17th century, and one similar to that found on other parts of our coast. In spite of the fact that elsewhere by the beginning of the 18th century a spar bowline had taken the place of rope ones, there is nothing to tell us when it was first used in Cornish craft, where it was known as a "vargord." As early as 1720 mention is made that a crew consisted of six men and one boy.

A drawing by Joshua Cristall in 1790 shows two-masted boats, very like those of

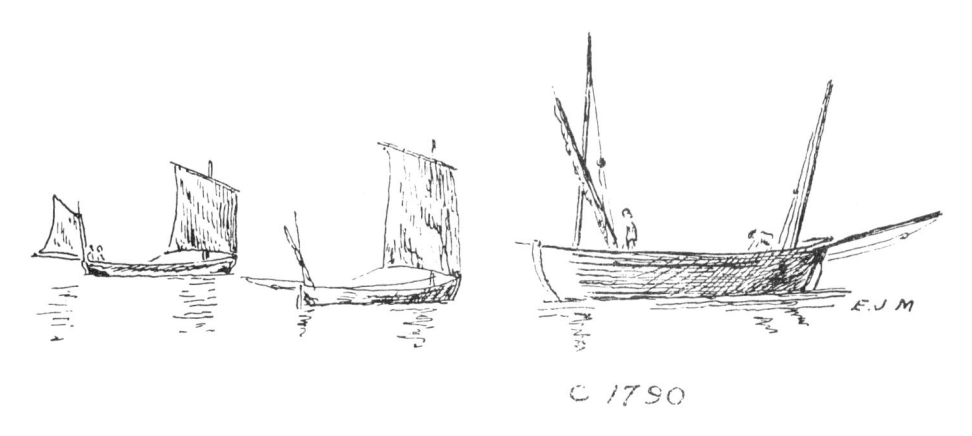

FIGURE 18

half a century later, with curved stems, full bows, and pointed sterns (Fig. 18). It is possible that they are three-masted luggers with the mainmast lowered, the fore lugs are still very square-headed, and the shape of the mizzen suggests either a spritsail or a standing lug.

The Mousehole fisherman poet, Richard Trewavas, describes how his first boat, *Minerva*, was carvel-built of oak, with tarred planking, at St. Michael's Mount about 1785. At the launch the assembled company drank to her success, and the builder dashed as much as he thought fit of a glassful over the bows. The poet goes on to mention how, when fishing, the foremast was lowered, the tye smeared with slush, and the "raft," a bundle of sails rolled up with their spars, oars, etc., was tied up and laid in the "crutches." These were two irons fixed about fifteen feet apart on the port side, the fore crutch being a closed ring, the after one open, like a rowlock. The watch, set by casting lots, was kept by one man, and the remaining six turned in beneath the foredeck and slept in warm hooded boat capes. Trewavas speaks of the use of a slate as a temporary chart, barked nets, aprons made from tough, broad rams' hides, and how, to ride out a gale, they slung the mainmast for a floating raft by making a sea anchor of spars with nets wound round them. A close-reefed mizzen was set, and the crew toiled at the pumps and buckets, while "the washstrakes cry," for these boats were open, save for a short foredeck. When the gale began to blow itself out, the foremast hand unbent the goose-winged jib, which had served as a riding sail, and hoisted the three-reefed mizzen.

Here is a contemporary description of life aboard a lugger at the end of the 18th century which might well apply to a hundred years later, so little did customs change.

Smuggling was rife in the latter part of the 18th century, and it is probable that the design of the local craft was much influenced by contact with France. Mevagissey-built luggers were renowned for swift sailing, and could cross the Channel in some eight hours. There a cargo of brandy could be purchased for about £1,500, and if all went well from the smugglers' point of view, these precious kegs would fetch double the money and more on our side of the water. Little wonder that men in every walk of life were mixed up in this illicit traffic. Then, as now, hoodwinking the Customs was not considered the most heinous of crimes. If the risk of capture was slight, the smugglers threw caution to the winds, ran the lugger into a cove in broad daylight, and practically every man, woman and child in the neighbourhood helped to carry the golden liquid to hides where even the keenest-eyed Preventive man could never find it. Should a Revenue cutter try to intercept her at sea, the odds were on the lugger, which could sail two feet to the other's one, while if need be, she was armed heavily enough to put up a good fight, so much so that it often paid the King's men to turn a blind eye to the seemingly innocent fishing lugger, for these Cornishmen were tough, merciless fighters. Truly the King's writ was difficult to enforce in those most westerly of his domains.

In common with other fishing ports, the three-masted lugger appears to have been adopted about the 1770's. Mr. Morton Nance, who kindly gave me permission to use his notes on the early Cornish luggers which appeared in the *Mariner's Mirror*, writes:

"To the custom of taking small supplies of butter to sea in a section of a cow horn, fitted with an oak bottom and a cork lid, we owe the best portrait I have been able to find of one of the old three-masted luggers. It was usual to scratch with a knife point on these butter horns their owner's initials, and any such scrimshaw additions as they fancied. One so decorated at St. Ives is dated 1814, and shows, cut with great precision, a contemporary lugger in addition to initials and a mackerel. She is shown under fine weather canvas, but without the lash-up jib which was sometimes carried." (Fig. 19.)

The hull was apple-bowed, flat-floored and round-sterned, with a keel length of about 35 ft., but a considerable rake to stem and sternpost increased the overall length. Beam was 11 to 12 ft., and draught for'ard was 2 ft. 6 in., aft 5 ft. The sides were raised with a washstrake, and a rubbing strake extended from just abaft the foremast nearly to the mizzen mast. She was to all intents and purposes an open boat except for a small decked forepeak which provided some sort of shelter for the crew.

The foremast, stepped close to the stem, was almost vertical and carried a square-headed dipping lug with its tack hooked to a short iron bumpkin, and the luff extended by a vargord, a light spar used instead of a bowline, and a necessity until the introduction of better cut sails rendered it obsolete. The mainmast, raking slightly aft, had a mainstay leading to the foot of the foremast, and carried a dipping lug with a bowline on the luff. A topmast, stepped abaft the masthead, had a rather square-headed topsail whose luff also had a bowline leading to the middle of the foremast. The short mizzen mast, stepped well aft, just clear of the tiller, raked so as to bring its head abaft the rudder post, and carried a standing lug, set to starboard, sheeting to the outer end of an

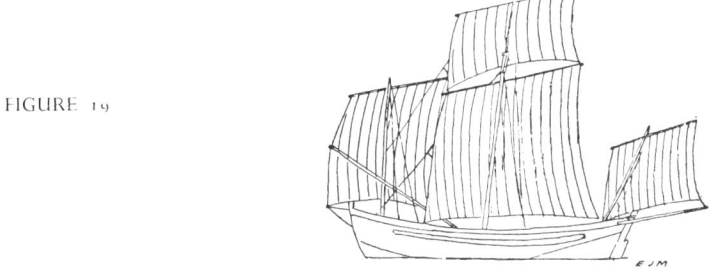

FIGURE 19

CORNISH 3m LUGGER C 1814

outrigger set to port of the sternpost. To judge from such contemporary evidence as is available, it would appear that the mizzen lug was set to leeward of the mast, as were the fore and main sails, and that setting it always to port was a later practice.

Cloths are indicated on all sails, but no reefs; from other sources it is known that there were four reefs on the foresail, one or two on the main, and three on the mizzen sail.

So far as is known, no contemporary model of a three-masted Cornish lugger exists, but the late Mr. Wm. Pezzack, whose father was a boat builder, made a very fine model of *Emily*, built c. 1830, which is now in the possession of Mr. Morton Nance, who from time to time has added further details gleaned from old fishermen who sailed in similar boats as boys (Fig. 20).

The stem is curved with a rounded forefoot, the bows are full, and the run hollow. Short bilge keels keep the hull almost upright when stranded, the older boats were too flat-bottomed to require them. For'ard is the foredeck, under which the men slept, entering through a sliding hatch in the bulkhead. In this deck is the long opening with a hatch, known as the "trunk," at St. Ives as the "locker," which allows the foremast to be lowered. At the after end of the deck is a coaming to keep back the water coming in over the bows, and guide it to a scupper on either side. Next comes the fore room, extending aft to the main thwart, on whose after side is a recess to receive the mainmast, which is held by an iron "claps." The beam or fish room comes next, then the "sheet," net room or mesh room, separated from the fish room and aft locker by bulkheads beneath the thwarts. The pump is fixed amidships to the thwart abaft

FIGURE 20

"EMILY"
CORNISH 3 MASTED LUGGER
EARLY 19TH CENTURY
MIZZEN MORE VERTICAL

the sheet, the well room being beneath the boards at the bottom of the net room, here also is the clamp for the heel of the outrigger—the mizzen boom at St. Ives—which runs out aft through a hole cut in the washstrake. The aft locker is terminated by another thwart, before which the mizzen mast is held. The stern sheets are open. The breasthook has a horseshoe nailed to it for luck, according to an old custom.

Owing to the mizzen mast raking so far aft, it was impossible to use a tackle from its masthead to raise the head of the lowered foremast sufficiently high for its halyard, hooked in an eyebolt right for'ard, to purchase. A short spar, called in Mount's Bay a "gijolter" or "gudgawlter," was passed beneath the foremast so that two men, one on either side, could lift the mast to the required height, when the fore halyards could be used.

The tabernacle, or mast case, in which the foremast stepped, is formed of three upright timbers—the "brudges"—and a moveable chock, fitting into slots in the side timbers, keeps the mast in position. The heel of the bowsprit is lashed to the foot of the foremast, and another lashing holds it down to an eyebolt for'ard, so that the spar rests close beside the stem head, there was no gammon iron as at Yarmouth. In the outer end of the bowsprit a hole is bored or an eyebolt fitted for the jib tack, which also serves as a bobstay, leading down under a small iron crook or wooden half-cleat—at St. Ives known as the "may-bob"—before coming in over the bulwarks to be made fast to the heel of the bowsprit. Here also belays the fall of the jib halyard, after reeving through a single block with a long eye strop, temporarily fitted over the masthead when the jib was set.

The tack of the fore lug sets up to an iron "bunkin," and the luff is stiffened by a vargord. This spar had at its outer end a nailed-on horn cleat—the "prong"—which was thrust into one of the two or three cringles—the "war-eyes"—worked on the luff above the highest reef cringle. The squared foot of the vargord rested in one of five or six notches—the "snatches"—cut in a timber called the "comb" at St. Ives, at Mount's Bay the "nabob" or the "timmynoggy." This notched timber lay along the top of the gunwale against the washstrake, fitting between the two stanchions just for'ard of the main beam. Usually the one to port was fixed, while that to starboard could be moved out of the way while fishing. The boys had the job of seeing that the prong was set properly in the war-eye whilst the men struggled to get the foot of the 23 ft. spar into the correct snatch. As a wet sail dried and slackened, or when hauling the wind, the vargord had to be set up another snatch to tauten the luff of the sail. The use of this spar dispensed with a bowsprit, hitherto only used to extend the bowlines of the foresail, when a lugger did not set a jib.

Another link with mediaeval days, nay earlier, for a Greek vase 500 B.C., shows circular oar holes, were the round oar-ports, known locally as "hurrels" or "hurl-holes," cut through the washstrakes. When not in use, the oars were lashed together and carried in the crutches. Here also stowed the "raft" or bundle of spare sails rolled up on their yards. The tiller was curved, and the slot was a loose fit fore and aft on the rudder head—local name "rother," a term I have seen used in old Admiralty specifications, in Stuart days a "ruther." This slight play allowed for lowering the tiller to clear the mizzen mast, and when pushed hard over, raising it gave sufficient clearance to pass over the washstrake on the quarter. Then it could be lowered again and would stay held; this feature clearly shows in several photographs c. 1880 now in my possession. Although this gave extra room aft when the lugger was not under way, there was a considerable danger from a jammed tiller, as the pressure of water on the rudder would ofttimes prevent any shifting it, the cause of several fatal accidents.

In the St. Ives boats a short pole—the lantern spear—lashed to one side of the pump, had at its head a flat crutch-piece into which were inserted two iron prongs to form with it the "forkle." These prongs passed up through two holes bored in the bottom of the wooden lantern near its back, and so held it projecting forward from the forkle. The lantern consisted of a wooden box with an up-sliding glass front, and sometimes a fixed glass back as well. Here the candle, or in more modern times the oil lamp, was carried. Immediately over the flame was a hole covered by a plate of copper or tin, punched full of holes. In Mount's Bay the lantern stand was usually a cranked iron fixed to the mizzen mast. The binnacle consisted of an oblong box with two compartments, one for the compass, the other for the candle. Over the flame hole was a copper disc, usually perforated in a geometric pattern. A sliding door on the sloping front gave access to the candle. When the mainmast was removed in bad weather, the appearance of the boat with a fore and mizzen only was similar to the later two-masted craft.

By 1813 Mount's Bay luggers had well-peaked sails, but those at Mevagissey were still very square-headed. The following twenty years brought various improvements in hulls. A slight rise in floors saw the need for short bilge keels to keep the boats upright when stranded in cove or harbour; bows were made finer, stems more upright, and hollow runs were introduced, but by 1838 these were giving place to more elliptical waterlines. But the old boats died hard, and many still went to sea that were built one hundred years before. The mainmast, carried only in summer, was now dispensed with, spars and masts were made larger, and a mizzen topsail introduced, always carried on the lee side so that on the port tack the mizzen standing lug was to port, and the topsail to starboard of the mast. The bowline was retained in many boats, and a bridle—the loop of the bowline—spliced in the luff rope of the sail, passed through a cringle in the upper end of the bowline, whose lower end was made fast by a couple of half-hitches round the foremast as high as possible. This bowline kept the luff of the topsail taut when the lugger was close-hauled.

About this time, *c.* 1850, St. Ives men can be given the credit of being the first in adopting a higher peaked sail, with a heavier boltrope on the luff, which made a vargord needless. They sent a lugger thus rigged round to a Mount's Bay regatta, and she swept the board; Newlyn and Mousehole saw the advantage of the new cut, *Harmony* being the first boat from Mousehole so fitted, but they went one better and a higher peak distinguished a Mount's Bay from a St. Ives boat to the last.

Sails were now cut to one pattern, but in different sizes, so that all except the largest foresail could be set on either mast, thus saving reefing. The mizzen, being given more forward rake and the outrigger steeved well up, called for a standing lug cut high in the clew, which, when moved for'ard, set equally well as a dipping lug with its tack to an eyebolt in the deck, and the sheet to the foremost iron.

Manned by bold, hardy fishermen, who thought nothing of going to fishing grounds seventy or eighty miles off shore, these splendid luggers rode the seas beautifully, and were capable of facing any weather, as is evidenced by the fact that in the 15-ton half-decked Mount's Bay boat *Mystery*, Joseph Hocking set out from Newlyn in 1846 bound for Australia, with five others as adventurous as himself. He put into Cape Town for stores, and the sight of this tiny craft, no bigger than a ship's boat, caused the greatest astonishment amongst the locals, especially when they heard she was from home. After the hull had been scrubbed, the skipper was ready to run his easting down, and as the regular mail boat had not turned up, he agreed to take letters to Melbourne, where in due course he arrived safely without serious incident, other than having to ride to a sea anchor for several days in the worst of the westerly gales.

Aids to navigation were primitive. A chart was seldom, if ever, carried, and had the "Old Man" appeared on deck to shoot the sun with a sextant and consult a chronometer, the crew would have had the surprise of their lives, and said the skipper wasn't the man his dad was! Yet he was seldom at a loss as to his position, relying on a traverse board, often consisting of no more than a homely pair of bellows, which could also do duty as a fire raiser if the stove was sulky! The thirty-two points of the compass were marked by lines radiating from the centre, each with eight holes into which pegs could be inserted to mark how many half-hours the lugger had sailed on a particular course. Equidistantly spaced at the bottom were short vertical lines, numbered 1 to 12, with four holes in each. These were to record the speed for any hour of the watch. At the extreme right were three vertical lines with holes marked

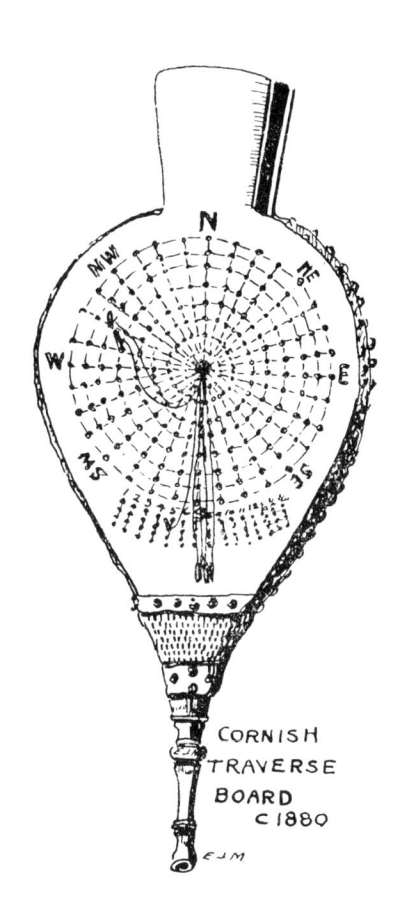

FIGURE 21

CORNISH
TRAVERSE
BOARD
C 1880

$\frac{1}{4}$, $\frac{1}{2}$, $\frac{3}{4}$, to enable fractions of a knot to be recorded. The pegs were fastened to the board by lengths of twine, hanging down when not in use (Fig. 21).

Thus the helmsman kept a score of how many glasses—the old-fashioned sand hour-glass, not those for liquid refreshment—the lugger had sailed on any point during his watch, and at what speed. Occasionally the master took a squint at the board and conjectured the boat's position, and could take her from Cornwall to the North Sea and find his way home again, whilst it is on record that one ancient reached Australia with only a traverse board to aid his navigation. The courses were sometimes marked up in chalk on a slate.

The late Mr. William Pezzack is my authority for much of this information, which he wrote to my excellent correspondent, Mr. H. Oliver Hill, who most generously placed all the letters at my disposal. Would there had been more like him, recording before it was too late these facts about a bygone age.

The old fisherman, who was a boy in the early sixties, tells how his father, who was born in 1819, went to the North Sea herring fishing when about twenty years old, in *Betsey*, the last three-master to sail out of Mousehole, as somewhere about the 1830's the rig fell from favour, many hulls being re-rigged as two-masters, others went to rot in their last berths. A few retained the mainmast and sail as a spare, fitting it at the beam thwart when taking a cargo of mackerel to Plymouth, as in the days before the railway came to Penzance it was impossible to sell surplus fish. The mast was also used for going over to the Irish coast for the summer herring fishing. Mr. P. K. Hosking writes: "The idea of the mainsail was told me by an old friend, Charley Pearce, about thirty years ago (c. 1902), and he died at 88 years of age. He owned several boats at different times, and was never tired of talking about the *Mary Bone*, called after his wife."

The early foghorns were made from conch shells brought from warmer climes, and Mr. Pezzack used one until well into the nineties, and by its use could feel his way into Mount's Bay in thick fog by listening for the echo thrown back from the high granite cliffs. Then bullock horns superseded the conch shell, sometimes being lowered overboard to allow the water to run through them, thus making a harder sound. These primitive horns in turn gave way to tin trumpets fitted with a reed.

Cooking arrangements were crude, often consisting of no more than a hearth made from a hollowed-out piece of granite, or a small box filled with clay and stones. Those old fishermen must have been as hard as their native granite, for luxuries like a fire were non-existent unless a bucket brazier was used, and that was a constant source of danger.

Yes, life was hard in those days, but it bred *men*, who lived to a ripe old age, were self-reliant, fearless and staunch as the oak from which their boats were built. As Mr. Pezzack says:

"Men were tough in those days, and could walk or pull all day. My great-grandmother would take half a cowal of fish, etc., on her back, 20 lb. of salt each side in large pockets (40 lbs. slung round her waist on her under-clothes), about a hundredweight in all, and visit farms in nine parishes between dark and dawn on a misty or moonless night, as her usual market round. My father never pulled in a race, but on one occasion in Plymouth winter fishing some argument arose about pulling, by opposing pilots when at home. They favoured beer, father belonged to the Mousehole teetotalers. The beery ones were going to pull from Mutton Cove, Devonport, to Morwellham, the weir head of the Tamar, in record time. Father's party let them choose their six-oared gig at Peter's yard, and as soon as they were out of sight, took the next best gig and were off on a stern chase. They let the first gig land and the crew get at their beer. Then they landed, stretched their legs after their 29 miles pull, jumped into the gig again without bite or sup, and started on the return 29 miles. The others swallowed their beer on being told that the teetotalers had landed and were off again and started to chase, but never caught the tt's. I have also known the rival gigs at Mousehole start in the dark from Mousehole to meet the London steamer then calling at Penzance for casked pilchards and pull around the Lizard in hopes to intercept her, sometimes to miss her altogether, or if one got her, the other would pull back, practically never leaving the oar out of their hand, except that each in turn would have a spell at steering and baling. Wet, cold, hungry, but took it as part of the day's work."

The mackerel and pilchard were to Cornwall what the herring was to Yarmouth and the haddock to Scotland, but of all the fish caught in British waters, none deteriorates so rapidly in value as the mackerel, as it should be eaten immediately it is out of the water. Stale fish go limp and dark, and may even be poisonous to persons allergic to them.

From as far back as Tudor times drifting or "driving" for mackerel was always one of the most important branches of the Cornish fishing, but prior to the opening of the railway into Cornwall in 1859, its sale was of necessity purely local. The boats were beamy, with flat floors to allow them to lie upright in coves and harbours when the tide receded. Speed was of little account, there was no market to catch, and seagoing abilities were the prime consideration in waters exposed to the full force of gales from the Atlantic. Design changed but little from decade to decade, if not century to century. The catch was sold by fishwives who hawked it from door to door in "cowals," large square wicker baskets supported by a broad plaited band worn round the forehead over the hat. The younger Newlyn women generally wore bright scarlet cloaks and large black beaver hats, but many of the "jousters" were old grey-haired women, with toothless gums and wrinkled skins, who wore long tasselled shawls over crumpled white aprons reaching to the ankles. There must have been a considerable trade, as in 1838 120 boats were fishing out of Newlyn, Mousehole and Porthleven.

The completion by Brunel of the Saltash Bridge over the Tamar completely revolutionised the industry. If time and tide wait for no man, the fisherman who thought the 2 p.m. market train would delay its departure until he had landed his catch certainly had another guess coming to him. It no longer paid to land fish in any convenient harbour when Newlyn offered facilities for despatch to London, and soon practically the whole of the Mount's Bay catch came to that port. In the 70's and 80's there were over one hundred big boats at Newlyn, including six or eight counter-sterned ones, but none at Mousehole, where the crowded state of the harbour, with 66 mackerel drivers and the frequent times of great surf with much crashing together of craft, made counters unsafe.

At that time Newlyn boats had permanent anchorages off the old harbour, known as "Loja," and when bad weather set in, they went to Penzance, where they had another set of moorings in tiers, off Jennings Street and the gasworks, as the wharfs were not then built. To lay these chain moorings cost about £3. At Newlyn each lugger kept a four-oared boat at anchor, but at Mousehole three-oared jolly boats were preferred. These boats were left in charge of a "yawler," a lad of from ten to fourteen years, who was paid 1s. 6d. a week. Mr. Pezzack writes:

"Whilst the season lasted the yawler was the slave of the lugger by which he was employed. Early in the morning, often before daybreak, he would shoulder the two long oars required by the crew for pulling ashore, and his own short paddle with which he sculled the jolly boat, and went down to the harbour, where he would find some fifty other yawlers. If it was low tide, each helped the other to get afloat. When the fleet was sighted in the offing, all sculled away to the best position for bearing down before the wind to 'take' the lugger and the greatest rivalry resulted from each lad's efforts to be first alongside his special lugger, perhaps his father's boat. It was no easy job to take station to pick up a lugger smoking along, but one likely to teach the handling of an open boat in a seaway, while the ability to recognise a lugger when but a speck on the horizon was an accomplishment of no mean order. As she approached the yawler would get right ahead of his lugger as it bore down under full sail. The faster the greater the boy's joy. With jolly-boat pointing the same way as the big boat, the yawler waited with the coiled painter in his hand, ready for the critical moment when, with foam piled up at her bows, the lugger rushed by. As she did so, the painter was thrown to those on board, and the lad crouched down in expectation of the jerk when the rope became taut, then the jolly-boat sat up almost on end, with water boiling up behind the stern. To be towed to Newlyn market in this style was a supreme joy. To miss this feat, a disgrace too deep to contemplate, in practice it very rarely occurred, owing to the skill and judgment in manoeuvring their craft which the boys attained. If the fleet was becalmed, it might mean a scull of many miles to meet the lugger and take off the fish, which was rowed in to Newlyn by one or two of the younger members of the crew. Very often the yawlers had a strenuous time sculling out against wind and tide, and the jolly-boats were always equipped with a kedge rope with a stone attached to one end. When exhausted sculling out, the boys would drop anchor for a time and rest, then press on. When the fleet was at sea the lads amused themselves as they liked, and there was no prank with wind or wave they would not try, and knowing every trick of the boat, would go into nooks and crannies round the rocks, in and out of breaking seas, rejoicing in the dangers evaded by their skill. They were not all boys, a few were aged fishermen with no strength for the strenuous life at sea, who returned to their boyhood's job and did it well. Some of the old fellows wore tall 'stove-pipe' hats tilted on the back of their venerable heads, and these weather-beaten men could tell of days long past, of being hunted by the press gang, of smugglers, and wrecking, and other incidents of their venturous youth.

The employment of a yawler produced a class of men supremely expert in handling small craft, and so most suitable for yachts, where many found employment."

Whilst the jollyboat was under tow, as much of the catch as could be transferred in baskets was taken on board so that little or no time was lost when moorings were reached. Then some of the crew tumbled into the boat and with lusty strokes sent the deeply-laden craft fairly flying across the water, since much depended on early arrival, especially if the market was likely to be glutted should the fleet have made a good haul. Early in the season catches might not exceed a thousand fish a lugger, and many a one would come back "clean." Accordingly prices ruled high, up to 50s. a long hundred. A hundred of mackerel is 30 warps, or 120 fish. The movements of the fish were affected by the temperature of the water, a cold snap or the prevalence of easterly winds would send the shoals down deep, and few would be meshed. Sometimes they would be found inshore within a line from the Lizard to the Wolf, at others far out to sea, in which case it might be difficult to get the catch ashore in marketable condition. A good night's haul was reckoned to be four to five thousand fish a boat, and a successful season from March to June might give a share of £40 a man. When Newlyn Harbour was completed, the day of the yawler came to an end, as the fleet was able to enter port and discharge catches direct on to the quays.

The sixties saw vast improvements in the design of the luggers, floors rose sharper and sharper, until legs were necessary to keep the hulls upright in harbour, and apple-bows gave place to finer entrances, but speed has to be paid for, and these wedge-shaped boats were apt to be very wet in a seaway. Hand-in-hand went greater attention to the cut and set of sails, and the next twenty years brought hulls with yacht-like lines, easily driven by beautifully cut lugs and the final development of the West Country lugger was at hand.

What pictures can be conjured up from the past. In the noonday sunshine the harbour sleeps peacefully, with tiers of luggers nestling against the stone quays, masts and spars making fascinating patterns in the still green water, and deep shadows lurk below the black hulls. A couple of old men watch with critical eye a lad splicing a rope as they yarn over their pipes, in those far-off days tobacco was not a viciously taxed luxury. Gulls swim idly in the centre of the harbour, stand motionless along the walls or perch on mastheads, looking with baleful eye and screeching defiance at any bird venturing to come near. The distant shore is hidden in a soft blue haze, and the stifling heat brings out all the rich aroma of fish and cordage, mud and tar, that nostalgic mixture one always associates with harbours. A gull rises from the water, leaving behind a tiny pool of ripples, circles round, and alights on the truck of a trawler moored to a buoy, silvery wavelets lap gently against the weed-covered steps, and recede with a slop and a suck, wisps of blue smoke rise from galley chimneys, the bark of a dog and the shrill cries of children shatter the silence. As the sun westers and the shadows lengthen, life aboard awakens, men in big seaboots come clumping along the setts, the boats are rowed away from the shelter of the harbour walls, and slowly creep out of the entrance—the creak and cheep of blocks carries across the water, the evening breeze fills the brown sails, and the luggers stand boldly out to sea. Long rays of light shoot up from behind the cloudbanks to the west'ard, edging them with gold. The darkness gathers and a myriad twinkling lights dancing on the waters mark where the skippers are shooting their nets "in the name of the Lord" (Plates 59 and 60).

In the early decades of the 19th century living conditions in Cornwall were very low. A skilled farm labourer earned 9s. a week with a cottage, or 12s. without, and up to the '40's the standard wage for surface workers in the mines was 35s. to 40s. a month. Rents for a cottage with a garden ranged from 50s. to £5 a year. With fish a staple article of diet, it can readily be seen how much depended on successful hauls when seining was possible during the short time the shoals of pilchards were close inshore. Every cottage usually laid in about one thousand fish for winter use, each housewife curing her own supply in a large earthenware pot known as a "bussa." A usual price was from eight to ten fish for a penny, but if a glut they were often as low as 6d. for 120 fish. The great trouble was often lack of salt, which carried a tax of £35 a ton during the Napoleonic Wars; 7 lb. was required to cure 100 fish, and in 1809, when its price was 1½d. a lb., it cost about 8s. 9d. to salt down a winter's supply, but the increase to 4d. meant a rise to £1 3s. 4d., which made a serious inroad into a man's wages. Farmers also laid in large stocks, and frequently the fish were split open and hung in the sun to dry, being then known as "scroulers." Salt purchased wholesale for curing in bulk was exempt from tax, so every opportunity was given for extensive smuggling, and the illegal use of tax-free salt, which was stored in the cellars, and this state of affairs continued until the repeal of the tax in 1825 removed the incentive to outwit the Customs.

Before "bulking" pilchards was introduced, the fish were smoked and the resulting delicacy was a "furmadoe," later corrupted into "fairmaids," a name by which cured pilchards are still called. What a task it was to bulk a huge haul of pilchards, as in November 1834, when thirty million fish were caught in one hour at St. Ives. Day and night the silvery catch was carried up into the cellars in hand barrows, called "gurries," and dumped on the floors to be seized by the children, who carried the contents to the women who stood in front of an enormous and ever-growing heap of fish. Every type of head-dress was to be seen—shawls, straw hats, little flat bonnets, weird and ancient millinery, finery of days long past. Most of the women wore long aprons, called "soggets," once spotless, but soon covered with scales. The white-bearded owner, gorgeously attired in frock coat and glossy silk hat, and carrying a malacca cane, walked around supervising and making notes in his little book, while the children dodged to and fro. As dusk fell candles threw flickering shadows over the stone walls, and the hum of conversation rose and fell.

The cost of curing a hogshead was from 21s. to 23s., including 6s. for salt, and they were sold at 35s. to 42s.

The pilchards usually swept round the coast in immense shoals, their presence heralded by clouds of screaming gulls, and the colour of the sea, which took on a dark, almost blood-red tinge. The drifters worked in mid-channel, well clear of the seine nets ashore. The nets, corked on the edge and with no leads, were invariably shot to the accompaniment of a prayer: "Lord spare our labour and send them in with a blessing, Amen." Sometimes a silver coin was placed as an offering in the first cork float, and whilst the boat lay to her nets the men sang hymns or read the Bible, for many of them were devout Methodists.

At times millions of fish were meshed, landed, washed, heavily salted, and stacked away in cellars under heavy stones. When all the oil had been pressed out, the fish were packed in barrels for export to Mediterranean countries, especially Italy, where they were highly esteemed. Prices averaged about £3 a hogshead, and in 1847 upwards of forty thousand barrels were exported, or some 120 million fish. Thirty to forty fast sailing vessels, employed as carriers, brought back fruit and olive oil. A good or bad season made all the difference to the living conditions of the fishermen, whose primitive cottages were lit with the oil pressed out from the fish. I wonder what it smelt like!

Some years saw such a glut that the fish were scarcely worth curing, and tons went for manure, as in 1801 when, owing to the French wars, ten thousand hogsheads were sold at St. Ives at 10d. a cartload for manure. Then might follow lean times, for the fish were fickle, and would desert grounds for no apparent reason, to reappear perhaps elsewhere. Strange to say, when the old-fashioned method of curing the fish in cellars a practice frowned on by the authorities in latter days on hygienic grounds, and curing in brine tanks was adopted, whereby hundreds of men were thrown out of employment, the old men said it was the end, and so it was, for the fish forsook the waters some forty years ago, and the vast hauls of more primitive days were no more. Make of it what you will!

After the pilchard season, the herring nets were put on board, and the boats fished out of Plymouth until January, but many went after the mackerel, which were returning down Channel to warmer waters, working out of Newlyn until the shoals were too far away for the boats to stand a chance of landing their catches in time for the train. Then the whole paraphernalia of the industry moved over to the Scilly Isles—lock, stock and barrel, salesmen, buyers and packers. The fish were now miles away to the west'ard, and the problem confronting the fishermen was to find the shoals and return in time to load the catch on the next morning's steamer. Then, if their luck was in, their haul would realise from 10s. to £1 a long hundred; if too late, well they had to take what offered, 6s., 3s., 2s. a hundred—a poor return for a hard night's toil.

What an animated scene it was in those now distant 1870's, the grey waters of the Sound foam-flecked, with lines of breakers on the low-lying reefs, and against the ironbound cliffs. Good navigation and local knowledge of tides and currents in the Sounds were needed to avoid disaster amid a thousand and one hidden dangers. Under a lead-coloured sky, the deep-laden luggers run in before a howling sou'-wester to gain the shelter of the harbour at Hugh Town. Bows are hidden in flying spray, and astern lies a seething wake. As soon as she comes in sight, each lugger hoists as a signal a string of pads at the masthead, a pad meaning a thousand fish. This enabled the salesmen and stevedores to get a rough estimate of what was needed in the way of packing and stowing, for every moment is precious. Soon the boat joins the scores clustered round the tiny steamer, whilst the early arrivals beat out to sea again. The fish are sold by auction and packed in "pads," boxes containing fifty to sixty fish.

Within the inner bay lies a big French *chasse-maree*, partly dried out, her huge masts towering above those of the local craft, which are so thickly massed that they resemble a forest. Big cutters from Plymouth lie alongside East Coast dandies. Everywhere is seething yet orderly activity. A few late arrivals, despairing of ever getting alongside the quay, have run in on the sandy beach, and the silver harvest is transhipped in baskets to waiting carts, or to women, some of whom have tucked up their skirts and waded out to meet a jolly-boat, whose gunwales are level with the water. Even the staid Victorian buyers, complete with stove-pipe hats, have been caught up in the excitement, and have put to sea in their carts to haggle over prices, or see that their consignments catch the steamer, whose warning siren scares the gulls into sudden flight, and redoubles the activity. Carts clatter along the rough stone setts, drivers hoping against hope that the mate supervising the loading will accept the baskets at the last moment. Meanwhile, the hawkers stand nonchalantly by their light carts, well knowing that they will come into their own when the steamer leaves, and the unlucky ones will be glad enough to dispose of the remainder of their catch at almost any price (Plate 61).

Perhaps 150,000 fish have been auctioned at an average price of 10s. a long hundred, 1d. apiece, or over £600 for one night's fishing, yet by the time the mackerel are on the slabs of the West End fishmongers the next day, the price will have risen to

64  POLPERRO HARBOUR, 1931

66  DRYING SAILS, LOOE, c. 1908

65  POLPERRO HARBOUR, 1931

67  TOSHERS AT MEVAGISSEY, 1936

68 TOSHERS AT MEVAGISSEY, 1935
Note platforms below thwarts, straight tiller and short foredeck.

69 *GLEANER*, LOOKING FOR'ARD, 1935
Note bulkheads below thwarts, tabernacle and iron collar.

70 *GLEANER*, LOOKING AFT, 1935

71 *MAGGIE*. DECK VIEW
Note lantern, pump aft of thwart, iron horse on transom, cork "cobles" and wide hatches.

72 *GLEANER*. BOW VIEW
Note rise of floors and rounded bilges.

73 TRURO RIVER OYSTER BOAT
Note pole mast, carvel build, yards on topsail.

74 F.Y. 205 UNDER ALL SAIL
Note mizzen topsail, flywheel capstan, lantern spear.

75 MODEL OF MEVAGISSEY LUGGER, c. 1883
Note fine run aft, round bilges, crutch, small hand capstan and short foredeck.

76 FOAM, c. 1894
Note crutch, channel for legs.

6d. each or more, for steamer and rail charges were high. At first £6 a ton was the transit cost, but as a result of many protests, it was reduced to £5, and then £4 a ton, but even at that price it worked out at about 2s. a pad, or 4s. per hundred fish, nearly half the prime cost when an average price was paid, but leaving little margin if there was a glut and prices ruled low.

A good season saw upwards of thirty thousand pads despatched, each weighing half a hundredweight, or forty to the ton, but a bad year might mean less than seven thousand. For many years this harvest of the sea averaged about 500 tons, or some £10,000 for the Scilly Isles fishing alone, and in those days a pound was a golden sovereign, not the depreciated paper currency of to-day. But now all have gone for ever.

Any violent fluctuations in the prices realised might mean starvation, if not ruin, to the fishermen. Fishing will ever be a precarious living at the best of times, especially when all are co-partners in the boat and nets. No fish means no wages.

Paradoxically enough, the opening of the new harbour at Newlyn spelt the beginning of the end of the Cornish fisheries, the rapid decline of mackerel driving and finally the disappearance of the picturesque sailing lugger. Hitherto the trawlers had worked out of Plymouth, but when the new facilities were offered, they began working in Cornish waters. Long and bitter were the disputes between the drift-net fishermen and the trawlermen. Frequently upwards of one hundred vessels, mostly from the East Coast, trawled day and night over the best mackerel grounds, many a train of nets was cut through—sometimes it was said, deliberately. The Cornishmen, who never fished on a Sunday, saw strangers with no such scruples landing their catches in what, after all, was the local men's own harbour. So high did feelings run that in May 1896 a free fight led to such disorders that troops had to be called in from Plymouth to quell the riots. But worse was in store. The steam drifter was looming on the horizon, and its coming meant the doom of sail. In 1907 there was a wonderful harvest, but no one would buy. The East Coast steam drifters had glutted the market. In one week alone they landed over four million mackerel and threw tens of thousands overboard. The local men, arriving too late, found their bountiful hauls valueless, the final blow to an age-old industry.

Like the Scottish and Devon men, these Cornish fishermen were in the main a God-fearing class, never going fishing on a Sunday and always endeavouring to be in port over the weekend. As far back as 1622 Sunday fishing was prohibited at St. Ives, and breaking the Sabbath meant a 10s. fine for the owner and 3s. 6d. for each man, a very substantial amount in the currency of those days. So firm were the men in their beliefs that shoals could pass inshore without a man putting to sea, even though the previous week's fishing had brought nothing.

Who could doubt the presence of a Supreme Being at whose command the stormy waves arose and whose Voice said "Peace, be still." Those long nights of watching in open boats far out at sea gave time for meditation. "They that go down to the sea in ships see the wonders of the Lord"—the first soft flush of dawn—the majestic rising of the golden orb to run its appointed course—the gathering of the storm clouds—the vivid flash—the crash of thunder—the rain hissing down on the waters. The calm of summer nights with a moon riding low in the sky—those beautiful sunsets over an ocean stretching away to Newfoundland, when a hush descends over the sea—those lovely coves where the crystal-clear tide plays with the rocks—the gentle ripple and swirl of lacy foam, whilst overhead gulls wheel and cry, the reincarnation of sailors lost at sea—the wonderful colours of the sea, deep blue changing to emerald green where golden sand replaced the rocky bottom—perfect autumn days when not a leaf stirred, and the distant shore stood clear and near, a "weather brooder" if ever there was one. That heaving restlessness of the sea as shingle ground to each receding wave—the slow clouding over of the sky and catspaws ruffling the glassy calm—soon white horses are prancing in from the Atlantic, and huge seas come rolling on in all their majesty, urged by winds that have the distant ocean from which to draw their power. Their crash against an iron-bound coast fills the air with noise and flying spray—soon the Wolf lighthouse is swept as high as the lantern—then the tiny luggers run for port, while anxious wives and sweethearts struggle down to the harbour to pray, their menfolk crouch at the tillers to pick up the leading marks—a touch of helm and a boat shoots into safety, and the seas, robbed for once of their prey, hurl themselves against the man-made defences and drench the waiting women again and again.

Even now perils are not over, for many of the harbours, open to winds from certain quarters, provided very uneasy anchorages on those days when a heavy southeaster howled over the bay, and a big spring tide came flooding in. Then two anchors might not be enough to hold those plunging craft, sheering wildly and tugging at their moorings. The men could do no more than watch the precious boats on which their livelihood depended, the drenching spray would gradually seep below—now one would sink—then another parts her cables and comes hurtling before the gale, to crash against the quay and splinter to firewood, or be flung like a child's toy far up the beach.

On a wild January day in 1895 when it was blowing a living gale from the southeast, the 17-ton Penzance lugger *Swan*, built in 1865, was torn from her moorings in Newlyn harbour and flung up on the strand. On the 12th November 1891 a whole gale from the south, driving into Newlyn, lashed the seas to fury, and filled the 19-ton lugger *Mayflower*, built 1880, until she sank. A few days later she was raised, but had sustained such damage that she had to be broken up. Think what that meant to her master and owner, W. Mitchell, and his crew of six. Boat and gear gone, over £600 worth, and families to feed and clothe.

Then the damage sustained when boats broke adrift and collided with nearby craft, as on the 9th March 1886, when a 60 m.p.h. south-easter smashed the *Susan Ann* into the *Rival* and *Saucy Jack* in Mevagissey harbour, damaging her so that she became a total loss.

Such losses were grievous enough, but what of those harrowing scenes when no power on earth could save men fighting for their lives in the seething cauldron of the ocean's wrath, within sight of home and loved ones. Some were overwhelmed by the seas, as was the 15-ton lugger *Jane*, built 1878, which foundered with all hands only half a mile S.E. of Penzance pier on the 7th October 1880. Others missed the entrance, as *Boy Tom*, 10 tons, built 1886, and *Kite*, 16 tons, which stranded near their home port of Mousehole in a fresh N.E. gale on the 28th January 1890. Both were total losses, one with a crew of four, the other six.

April is usually a smiling month, but not so that day in 1882 when a W.N.W. storm of 70 m.p.h. arose and caught the 16-ton *Grace Darling*, built 1874, at sea. Running for home, she stranded in St. Ives Bay and was lost.

Perhaps even worse for relatives ashore was to know a lugger was overdue; their men had set out with high hopes and courage, but the weary days dragged into weeks, the weeks into months, and never a word as to the fate of loved ones. Missing with all hands.

Think of the *Louie*, a 15-ton lugger, brand-new and not yet registered, which sailed out from Plymouth, owned and skippered by R. Barrow of Mevagissey. On the 19th November 1887 she was in collision with the German barquentine *Frederica Hietundler* 12 miles S.E. of the Eddystone, and sank.

Yes, the danger of being run down was very real in those small luggers, mere specks on the tumbling waste of waters. *Gideon*, a 17-ton St. Ives lugger, built 1876, was fishing about 15 miles W. by N. of Gurnards Head on the 2nd April 1892. A moderate E.N.E. wind was blowing when death came silently in a collision with the schooner *Earnest* of Preston, for a sailing vessel makes but little noise save the swishing sound as the seas part before her bows.

Again, on a June day in 1909 the French steamer *Orne* ran down the 15-ton St. Ives lugger *Family* built 1881, some five miles N.W. by W. of St. Ives Head.

What of those men and boats who, after facing the hazards of the long passage from Cornwall, sank beneath the cold waters of the North Sea? How dangerous were those hazy September days when the sailing craft lay helplessly becalmed, but steam swept remorselessly on. On the 17th September 1879, the 15-ton lugger *Primitive*, of Mousehole, master J. T. Harvey, was fishing out of Scarborough when she was sunk in collision with the Dutch S.S. *Talisman*, eight miles west of Robin Hood's Bay. The following day the 18-ton Penzance boat *Malakoff*, built 1868, met a similar fate in the same place from the sharp prow of S.S. *Erith* of London, sinking with three out of her crew of seven. Only five days later the Fowey lugger *Mary* was in collision with the lugger *John and Ann*, of Flamborough, five miles N.E. of Whitby Lights, in a moderate S.S.W. breeze, and the local craft was a total loss.

These few instances, picked at random, vividly show the many dangers of a fisherman's calling. Even a simple accident might result in loss of life, a slip on deck, a wild cry and the sea claimed another victim, for those low bulwarks were death-traps. Gear carrying away brought disaster to the 14-ton Fowey lugger *Garland*, built 1905, on the 28th September 1908, while coming in from the fishing grounds the mast went by the board, and knocked the master overboard, three miles east of Blackhead, St. Austell Bay.

But this mistress who calls men to her bosom is not always the most dangerous when angry; her softest caresses may lure men to their doom, as witness that sunlit April day in 1872 when William Munday, cox'n of the lifeboat, his two sons and another young man left Mullion Cove for Porthleven to fetch some nets. True, it was a Friday, but what of that? The sea was smooth and the wind light from the N.N.E. Within a mile of the pier, when standing in on her last tack the lugger lost way and disappeared in a moment, the crew lowering the sail as she sank. Boats from the shore raced to the spot, arriving in under ten minutes, but no trace could be found of boat or men. The sparkling waters had claimed their toll.

Even a big haul of fish could bring disaster, as was the case when *Lily and John* was fishing in St. Ives Bay on the 20th November 1910. A tremendous shoal of herring struck the nets and the lugger became overweighted and sank. The owner, John Perkin, and two hands, John Broad and Joseph James, were drowned, and the fourth man was picked up in an exhausted condition.

Truly, harvesting the shoals is a costly venture.

CHAPTER EIGHT

## EAST CORNISH LUGGERS

East of the Lizard the principal fishing ports are Mevagissey, Polperro, and Looe, where in the days of sail the transom, rather than the pointed stern, predominated. In the main, the early fleets were open boats, then came the decking-in of the forepeak, with the remainder of the hull divided into open compartments by bulkheads beneath the thwarts; next some of the rooms were covered with hatches, and finally the boats were decked fore and aft, with hatched net and fish rooms.

The smaller boats averaged about 25 ft. overall, and most of the Polperro craft, known locally as "gaffers," were cutter-rigged with a boomless mainsail. At Mevagissey they were called "toshers," ran up to 19 ft. 11 in. overall, in order to avoid the increased harbour dues paid on boats 20 ft. and over, and were mostly rigged with a single lugsail. The larger boats, from 30 ft. to 40 ft. overall, were lug-rigged, and practically all were alike in design, a slight difference being that sternposts were well raked at Mevagissey and more upright at Looe and Fowey.

Mevagissey has an outer harbour where there is a depth of two fathoms at L.W.S., shallowing towards the inner harbour, which dries out. Here picturesque old stone sheds and cottages cling to the natural rock, with a shipyard at the eastern end, and a rope walk on the cliffs above, with green fields beyond. Schooners, brigantines, and other coasting vessels lay here to discharge their cargoes, surrounded by the fishing boats, whose mastheads scarcely topped their bulwark rails at low tide (Plates 62 and 63).

Polperro is guarded by a rocky cliff, weathered by time into a distinctive appearance, and white where gulls congregate before sweeping out with effortless flight to meet the incoming fleet (Plate 64). Behind the shelter of a stone arm, the boats lie in a quaint little harbour where cottage walls rise sheer out of the water, or stand on the steep hillside amidst trees and shrubs (Plate 65).

The third port, divided by the river into East and West Looe, is a lovely spot with warm brick and stone dwellings nestling by wooded slopes, with an old arched bridge connecting the two villages. Here the luggers lay alongside the long quay to unload their silvery catches, whilst sails dried in sun and air (Plate 66).

The toshers at Mevagissey were either pole-masted cutters or rigged with a single lug, and Plate 67 shows one-time sailing boats *Minnie* F.Y. 264, *Snowdrop* F.Y. 360, *Doris* F.Y. 268, *Mona* F.Y. 140, and *Willie* lying at anchor in August 1936. All are fitted with the ubiquitous motor. A study of hulls reveals practically every variety possible. *Doris* is an open boat, *Minnie* has a small foredeck, whilst *Snowdrop* has quite a good-sized cuddy. Note how the mainsails are stowed up and down the mast with the gaff jaws uppermost, for use only in an emergency. Ahead lie the larger boats, all with motors and cut-down sail plans. The fastest tosher under sail was F.Y. 53, seen in Plate 68, when fitted with an engine; except for a very short foredeck, she is an open boat, divided off by bulkheads beneath the thwarts.

The lines of a typical Polperro gaffer F.Y. 8 *Gleaner*, built by T. Pearce at Looe in 1898, were taken off by the late P. J. Oke in 1935 on behalf of the Coastal Craft Sub-committee of the Society for Nautical Research. Plans 5 pages 307-9. Length overall is 25 ft., beam 9 ft., keel length 20 ft. 9 in. The scantlings are: keel 8 in. by 4 in., floors 7 in. by 4 in., thwarts 5 in. wide, 3 in. deep, planks 1½ in. thick, covering board 4½ in. wide by 1½ in. deep, bulwarks 1 ft. high.

The cuddy under the foredeck is 6 ft. 6 in. long with a maximum width of 6 ft. 3 in., height amidships 4 ft., and is fitted with locker bunks, stove, etc. The foredeck is 6 ft. 8 in. long, to starboard of the stem is the bowsprit with its heel stepped in wooden bitts morticed into thwart, having lodging knees on its aft side. On either bow is a long cleat bolted to the stanchions. Now I come up against a slight discrepancy between the plans and the photographs. The drafts show hatches and coaming extending 1 ft. 9 in. for'ard of the beam thwart, but the photographs of *Gleaner*, in common with other gaffers, show the coaming against the foreside of the thwart. On the aft side is the foremast, with its heel resting in a step on the floors and a three-sided trunk extending up to the thwart, where the mast is secured by an iron collar. Below is the bulkhead with two square hatches giving access to the cuddy (Plate 69). Across the open fish room is a roller winch, as no capstan was fitted; in the waterways 6 in. aft of the beam thwart are eyebolts for the shrouds. The net room, 3 ft. 9 in. long and the full width of the boat, is hatched over and divided from the fish room by a bulkhead below the net room thwart. In the waterways 4 ft. 6 in. aft of the shrouds are eyebolts for the backstays. Off-centred 1 ft. 3 in. on the aft side of the after thwart is the pump; 1 ft. 6 in. below the waterways are the hatches over the sternsheets, the 4 in. coaming extends to within 1 ft. of the transom, through which passes the wooden tiller, a 6 in. thwart below providing a seat for the helmsman. On either quarter are cleats extending from the after stanchions and round the stern; above is the iron horse on which the main sheet works; to port is the rowlock used when sculling. A lantern was usually carried on a wooden standard. In harbour the boat was kept upright by legs secured by a bolt through a stanchion. All these features can clearly be seen either in Plate 70, taken on board *Gleaner* on the 21st September 1935, or in Plate 71 of F.Y.22 *Maggie*, where can also be seen the four or five pound of cork discs strung on a becket and doubled up into a bundle known locally as a "coble," the lantern and its standard, the pump, fish baskets, and the loose covers over the net room. Plate 72 shows the sharp deadrise of the floors in *Gleaner*, the legs and the bowsprit reeving through a hole in the starboard bulwarks.

To my eye the sailplan has a marked resemblance to that of a Thames bawley, except that the Polperro boat is pole-masted, but the long topsail yard makes up for the absence of a topmast. The 6 in. dia. mainmast, 30 ft. overall, with a 5 ft. dia. $3\frac{1}{2}$ in. masthead, is supported by a forestay, one shroud a side, and a backstay set up with a guntackle purchase—two single blocks. The bowsprit, 22 ft. overall, 15 ft. outboard, is 4 in. dia., tapering to $3\frac{1}{2}$ in. The gaff is 16 ft. dia. 3 in. Topmast pole 22 ft., dia. $2\frac{1}{2}$ in. to 2 in.

The foresail, fitted with two lines of reef points, has a luff of 20 ft., leech 19 ft., and foot 11 ft. The jib has a luff 27 ft., leech 18 ft. 6 in., foot 12 ft. In fine weather a jib topsail, with a luff of 37 ft., leech of 20 ft., and foot 19 ft. 6 in., was set with the halyards to the head of the topsail pole.

The loose-footed mainsail has two lines of reef points, and a luff 17 ft., leech 27 ft. 6 in., head 15 ft., and foot 14 ft. The 20 ft. luff of the topsail is laced to a 22 ft. yard and has a leech 14 ft. and foot 18 ft., with an 8 ft. jackyard at the clew. It was usually set to port.

Unfortunately I have been unable to discover any photographs of these gaffers under sail, but Plate 73 is a Truro River oyster boat with a similar rig, except that the mainsail is fitted with a boom.

The larger boats ran about the same size as the West Cornish pilchard drivers, and all carried a dipping lug on the foremast and a standing one on the mizzen. Originally they were only decked for'ard, then the fore and fish rooms were hatched over, but the net room was open, and aft were hatches just below the waterline over the open stern sheets. From these boats were developed the fore and aft decked craft with 12 in. waterways and hatches over the various rooms.

Between 1860-70 about half-a-dozen decked counter-sterned boats were built at Mevagissey, running up to 45 ft. keel, 55 ft. overall, but they were not a success, and were eventually sold to East Coast owners. They were followed by smaller decked boats, about 36-40 ft. on keel, carrying a mizzen pole topmast on which was set a jackyard topsail, but the local fishermen considered this sail was more trouble than it was worth, and the type only survived about a decade. Plate 74 shows F.Y.205 with a mizzen topsail set, but she appears to be a typical Mount's Bay lugger with a flywheel capstan and companion to starboard of the mizzen mast.

To the hardy Cornishmen a trip to the North Sea was a summer outing when in 1863 the first Mevagissey lugger *Band of Hope* went to the East Coast fishing. Her length overall was only 32 ft., with a 28 ft. keel and she was completely open except for a 9 ft. cuddy for'ard, extending from the inside of the stem to a bulkhead. In this tiny space, barely 3 ft. 6 in. high, were 5 ft. lockers on which four men took their rest, wrapped in warm hooded capes big enough to shelter two or three men at a pinch. In winter a boy coiled up to sleep right for'ard, and the heel of the foremast still further reduced the available space. When thinking of these cramped quarters, it is as well to remember that in the so-called highly civilised years of the 1940's, thousands of families crept into Morrison or Anderson shelters, scarcely as commodious, and had to sleep, not to the murmur of the sea, but the wailing of sirens and the crash of bombs.

The net room was open, but the rest of the rooms were hatched. In the early seventies *Rival* was only 4 ft. longer on the keel, but she had 9 in. waterways, and a low deck aft. The freeboard was 2 ft. 10 in., and the low bulwarks were made up of a 10 in. fixed strake and a 6 in. movable one.

In the Science Museum, South Kensington, there is a very fine contemporary model of a Mevagissey lugger which was exhibited at the Fisheries Exhibition in 1883 (Plate 75). Her dimensions are 38 by 11.1 by 6.2, registered tonnage 11, and the scale of 1 in. to a foot allows for plenty of detail. The foredeck, covering about one-third of the boat's length, has the foremast stepped in a tabernacle, with a scuttle aft, into which it can be lowered; at the aft end is a coaming with a thwart below. To port is the bowsprit reeving through a hole in the bulwarks, and fidded into the tabernacle; across the deck are three eyebolts to take the tack hook of the fore lug, an unusual feature being the timberheads round which the jib sheets belay. The remainder of the boat is open, except for narrow waterways, and has four thwarts across—the beam thwart carrying a small hand capstan, with a bulkhead on its foreside, the three sets of hatches over the fish room rest aft on the net room thwart, the after thwart has a crutch on its foreside, into which the foremast was lowered, and a pump to port. This thwart has lodging knees on its aft side. The mizzen thwart has a recess on its fore side in which the mast rests, held by an iron strap; to port are two wooden chocks between which the heel of the outrigger is fidded; on either side are eyebolts for the stays, and belaying pins, with lodging knees on the foreside of the thwart. The fore room is open with a platform on to which the crew dropped when entering the cuddy through the square hatches cut in the bulkhead, the fish room is hatched over, the net room is open to the floors, the space between after and mizzen thwarts is hatched over about 1 ft. below the waterways, with an opening just for'ard of the mast to give access to the sail locker below; the stern sheets have floor boards on which the helmsman stands. Two long sweeps lie to port for use in the iron rowlocks in the rail opposite the fore room. At the stern the fashion timbers carry up to form timberheads on either side of the transom.

A wide iron strap on each side of the stem carries a hoop athwartships on which is the tack hook for the fore lug, and aft of the mizzen mast is a similar hook for the tack cringle of the standing lug. The jib tack hooks to an iron traveller with its outhaul

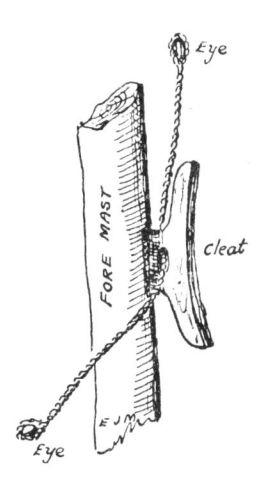

FIGURE 22

reeving through a sheave at the outer end of the bowsprit, then leading back through a bullseye in the starboard bulwarks to belay round a cleat inside.

The jib halyards have a single block shackled to a lug eye on the iron band round masthead, the fall is fast to its tail, reeves down through single block hooked to head cringle of sail, back through upper sheave, down foreside of mast to belay round cleat at foot. Double sheets reeve through bullseyes on short pendants before belaying round the timberheads.

The fore lug halyards have the thimble of the rope tye fast to the eye of the hook on the iron traveller, which goes through a rope grommet or eyebolt on the yard, then tye reeves through a dumb sheave at masthead down to a luff purchase, with its single block hooked to eyebolt in covering board, the fall goes under a thumb cleat on stanchion and belays round cleat just aft.

When not in use, both jib and lug halyards hook to thimbles at either end of a short mastrope which reeves through a hole in the cleat at foot of mast (Fig. 22). Tightening up one fall prevents undue slatting of the halyards against the mast.

The burton, or "fore stay," as it was known locally, is of wire, shackled to aft lug on mastband, and sets up with a guntackle purchase to eyebolt aft of halyard. The double sheets of the fore lug have single blocks hooked on the outside of transom with the falls fast to their tails. At clew of sail two single blocks hook into cringle, the fall reeves through the appropriate block, back through first block, and belays round cleat on stanchion inside bulwarks.

The mizzen stay, also of wire with an eye over the masthead, goes to port and is set up with a gun-tackle purchase with the lower single block hooked to eyebolt in mizzen thwart, and the fall belayed to pin just for'ard. The jump stay has a single block on a strop over masthead, with the rope fall, fast to its tail, reeving through a lower single block hooked in a thwart amidships, when used as a stay; at times it served as the staysail halyard. When not set up, the tackle was up and down the mast, or hooked to port alongside the stay. The lug halyards have a luff purchase with lower single block hooked to the eyebolt to starboard.

It would appear from the photograph that at some time the halyard and stay in this model have been reversed—they were when I inspected the model. To take the halyards to port gives a crossed lead, as the lug was always set to port of the mast.

The outrigger, fitted with three fid holes for reefing, has its heel stepped in a chock on the mizzen thwart, and a single block shackled to eye on a band at its outer end. The mizzen sheet is fast to the tail of this block, reeves up through a single block hooked in clew cringle, back through first block, and inboard to belay round fid iron. The spar rests in a notch cut in the transom, and is secured by a half-collar of iron, and a pin which can easily be removed.

When in harbour the legs to keep the hull upright were held by a bolt passing through a stanchion with a butterfly nut on the inside, or by an eye in the head of the leg passed through an oval hole in a small channel outside bulwarks, with a pin to secure it. This channel can be seen in Plate 76, 62 F.Y. *Foam* in the outer harbour at Mevagissey, *c.* 1894. Note how sharply the outrigger steeves, the short yard arms, and the two lines of reef points, with the crutch standing up amidships.

In 1872 there were 16 first-class luggers of over 15 tons, and 324 second class boats registered at Fowey.

The more modern boats were fully decked fore and aft with 12 in. waterways and hatches amidships, but to the last the average size was 33-34 ft. on keel, beam 11 ft. 9 in., to 12 ft., draught for'ard 4 ft. 3 in., aft 6 ft. 9 in.

I have drawn up a set of plans from contemporary data of a lugger built in the early years of the 20th century (pages 310-12). The frames were of oak, about 4 in. square, centred 16 in. with the first futtocks bolted on the for'ard side of the floors, and the second futtocks again on the for'ard side of the first, so that the 12 in. space between frames was practically filled in if a third piece had to be used to obtain the necessary length (Fig. 23). Keel, garboard strake and bilges were of elm, the planking was Riga or pitch pine, but the two upper strakes were oak. Stringers were of pitch pine and beams, knees, stanchions and covering board of oak. It is interesting to note that the beams were still known locally as thwarts, a relic of the days of open boats.

They were 3 in. deep and 6 to 10 in. wide. All fastenings were galvanised iron.

The fine underwater lines can be seen in Plate 77 of F.Y.42 *Jane* on the hard at Mevagissey for a scrub down. Note that the lugger to starboard has her mast stepped in a tabernacle on deck, and does not lower back into a scuttle. This feature was to be found in several luggers. When the photograph was taken in August 1936 *Jane* was fitted with a motor.

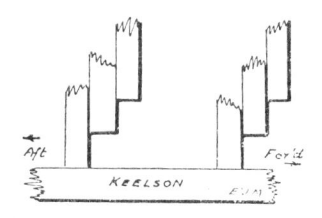

FIGURE 23

The older boats carried from five to ten tons of stone and old iron as ballast, but those built towards the end of the 19th century had from ten to fourteen tons. This was usually stowed under the floor of the fish room, but sometimes a little was placed under the net room or fore hatches, according to how the boat trimmed. From 7 to 15 cwt. was stowed in the wings of the fish room, mainly for trimming purposes. The cost of a hull c. 1900 was about £80.

My plans show a typical Mevagissey lugger with a length overall of 40 ft., length of keel 33 ft., beam 12 ft., depth 6 ft.

## CUDDY

In the larger boats accommodation was provided for six men in the cuddy, which had two berths a side, one above the other, whilst right for'ard was a wide athwartship bunk where two men could sleep side by side. Lockers under lower bunks provided stowage for domestic gear, coal, etc., and a small stove was fixed to the bulkhead. Water was stored in a wooden breaker carried chocked-off on the fore hatches, or on the aft deck in a cradle on the starboard side.

## FORE HATCHES

Aft of the cuddy were the fore hatches, covering a narrow 2 ft. space the full width of the boat at about water-line level, by which the crew entered their quarters through square openings cut on each side of the bulkhead, and fitted with a sliding hatch. Below was a space where the foot line was usually stowed. The hatch planks either ran the full width between the coamings or were in three divisions as shown, and they were not close-fitting, but space enough was left for a man to slip his fingers between any two planks.

## FISH ROOM

A bulkhead below the beam thwart divided the fore hatches from the fish room, which was about 4 ft. long, divided into three compartments fore and aft, the capacity of the centre one being about equal to the other two combined. When waterways were introduced, scudding holes, 10-12 in. long and the full width of the planking, were made in the deck, through which fish could be swept down into the fish room, which had a fixed floor, and in some boats there was a platform consisting of two or three planks supported on the stringers about 18 in. below deck level. When the boats were open, a man stood on this platform to haul in the nets, but it was no longer needed when the size of hull was increased, and decks and waterways added. It was retained in some luggers, as the men found it handy to stand on when striking fish below. The hatches were also a loose fit, but over the net room, immediately aft, they were a close fit. The coamings were 3 in. high.

## NET ROOM

The net room, about 6 ft. long, was the full width of the boat, and the platform consisted of planks laid on top of the ballast and lower stringers, the plank next the after bulkhead being made a good fit round the pump to prevent any risk of the suction pipe getting choked by the nets.

## AFTER DECK

The after deck extended from the net room bulkhead right to the stern, and the space below was used for spare sails, gear, etc., entrance being by a small opening just for'ard of the mizzen mast, and covered with a flat hatch, not a companion.

## FORE DECK

Immediately inside the stem was a breasthook to strengthen the angle between the bulwarks; amidships in the deck, about 3 ft. aft of stem, was an eyebolt to take the tack hook when one of the smaller lugs was set; on either bulwark were cleats bolted to the stanchions (Fig. 24). To port were the bowsprit bitts, usually of iron, sometimes only the outer one was fitted, and the heel of the spar fidded into the tabernacle on the inner side.

## FORE MAST

The foremast, about 9 in. dia. at the partners, 6 in. at sheave, was 36-37 ft. overall, with its heel rounded to facilitate lowering. The mast was stepped about 5-6 ft. inboard in a three-sided trunk, which went from the mast step up to an oak frame running fore and aft in the deck, and supported from the sides of the hull—in some boats it was carried about 18 in. above the deck—and this trunk formed the tabernacle, which was always kept well greased. When erect, the mast was kept in position by a chock on the aft side fitting into slots on each side of the deck casing.

## SCOTTLE

Immediately abaft the mast was a slot in the deck, known locally as the "scottle," about 5-6 ft. long, 8 in. deep, and 10-11 in. wide, and off-centred $\frac{7}{8}$ in. out on the starboard side aft to allow the foremast to clear the mizzen mast when lowered. The coaming, some 3 in. above the deck, was rabetted to take the hatch cover about 2 in. thick, called the "mast covering board," which was placed over the opening when the mast was upright. A collar of painted canvas round the mast prevented any water getting below (Fig. 25).

## EYEBOLTS

On either side of the deck in the covering board under the bulwarks were eyebolts with eyes athwartships. The foremost one, about 2 ft. aft of the mast, was for the lug halyards, 3 ft. further aft was one for the fore stay or burton.

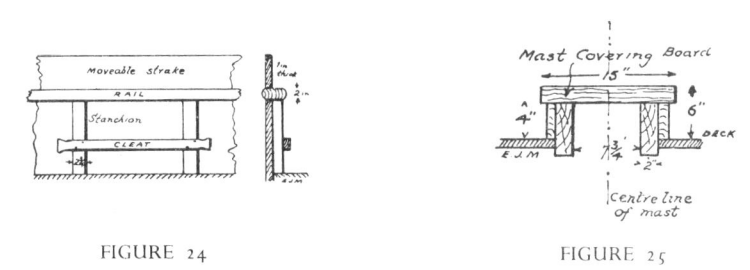

FIGURE 24

FIGURE 25

## LEG CLEATS

Outside the hull were the leg cleats, pieces of timber bolted on to either side, to carry the legs which supported the boat when dried out in harbour. An oval hole took the eye or U-shaped iron driven into the top of the leg, and a bolt passed through kept the strut in place, with chains or ropes attached to the foot of the leg and carried fore and aft to cleats inboard to steady it in position. Some boats had the legs held by a bolt passing through an iron plate in bulwarks and secured by a butterfly nut inside the stanchion. This bolt could be easily withdrawn and the leg hauled inboard.

## PUMP AND CRUTCH

On the fore side of the after thwart was the pump and a little to starboard was the 5 ft. high crutch in which the foremast rested when lowered. Amidships on the net room thwart was an eye to take the jump stay.

## MIZZEN MAST

The mizzen mast was generally stepped as far inboard from the sternpost as the foremast was from the stem. Its length was 26-27 ft., $4\frac{1}{2}$ in. dia. at sheave hole, 7 in. dia. at deck, worked down to 7 in. by 4 in. where the heel was stepped in a chock on the deadwood. The mast was further supported by the mizzen thwart, which went over the deck in the early boats, but underneath after the turn of the century. On the fore side a half-circle was cut out to take the mast, which was held secure by an iron collar. On either end of the thwart were eyes, or in the deck in the later boats, the one to port took the stay, to starboard the halyard.

## OUTRIGGER

Aft of the thwart on the port side of the deck was a chock to take the heel of the outrigger used to stretch out the mizzen lug, which was not fitted with a long boom, only a short "jinny" or "jenny" boom at the clew. The spar projected outboard some 20 ft., with an overall length of 26 ft., was 4 in. dia. at sheave, 6 in. at butt, which was squared for about 3 ft. The heel was flattened on one side to rest on the deck, where it was held down by a clamp or iron collar, which could be easily opened by withdrawing a pin when the spar had to be brought inboard. A similar strap was fitted on the transom, which was notched to carry the outrigger, thus keeping it well steeved up.

## BULWARKS

In the later boats the standing bulwarks were about 12 in. high, increased to 18-20 in. by the addition of a movable strake kept in place by pins on the under side fitting into corresponding holes in the standing bulwarks. These extra strakes were in two lengths, and the after one was always removed on the working side of the boat when hauling the nets, and so was a looser fit than the for'ard one. Cleats, 2 ft. 6 in. long, 2 in. wide, and $1\frac{1}{2}$ in. thick, were fitted inside bulwarks on each side opposite the masts to take the various halyards. Pin rails were never fitted in Cornish boats (Fig. 24).

## TILLER

The tiller, which went through the transom, was of iron, 5-6 ft. long, with a wooden handhold about 18 in. above the deck. It fitted through a slot in the rudder head, which was here strengthened by an iron band, and was easily removable as the rudder often had to be unshipped if the nets fouled it. The tiller was either jammed into the slot or held by a pin put through the part aft of the rudder. The iron band was about $1\frac{1}{2}$ in. thick and 4 in. deep, put on 6 in. below the head. When both rudder pintles were set point upward, a piece of chain was usually secured by a staple to rudder heel and sternpost. An upward curve was worked in the tiller to allow free passage over the outrigger when the helm was put hard-a-port.

## CAPSTAN

East Cornish luggers never had steam capstans, but used a small portable capstan placed a little to port of amidships on the beam thwart.

## LANTERN

The lantern used to light up the deck was either fixed to the top of the crutch or to a wooden standard alongside the pump.

## SIDE LIGHTS

The side lights were carried on the usual boards placed on T-shaped iron standards stepped through holes in the stanchions just for'ard of the mizzen mast, and raised about 5 ft. above the deck. When not in use the lamps were stowed on their respective sides in the cuddy in the corners formed by the top bunk and the bulkhead.

## ANCHORS

The two anchors—known locally as "grapers"—were of the grapnel type, with four or six arms. The usual size was 4-5 ft. in the shank, with a spread of 2-3 ft. across from fluke to fluke for the large anchor, and about a foot smaller for the other. Some were made so that the arms could be moved for stowing purposes, when the anchor became like the usual pattern, but without a stock. The end of the shank, for about 4 in. from the crown, was squared and the movable arms, which had a square hole, were kept in place by a key put through a slot in the shank. When the anchor was to be stowed, the key was withdrawn, and the movable arms slipped over the squared part until they could be turned round to lie under the fixed arm on being pushed back on to the squared part again. They were sold by weight, a usual price being 6d. a lb., about 1 lb. per foot length of boat giving an average weight.

## BINNACLE

The binnacle was a box with a sliding door and two compartments, one for the lamp, the other for the compass, and was about 12 in. long, 9 in. high, and 10 in. deep. It stood on deck at the foot of the mizzen mast, to which it was lashed in heavy weather; when not in use it was slewed round against the hatch just for'ard of the mast.

All these items can be seen in Plates 78 and 79. Plate 78, taken on board F.Y.151 and looking for'ard, shows the entrance to the cuddy by way of the fore hatches; the sails made up on their yards and stowed on the port side of the deck, the graper on top of the mast covering board, the iron bitt for the bowsprit heel, the hole in bulwarks through which the spar reeves, anchor cable, cleats, eyebolts in covering board for halyards and fore stay, coaming round waterways, the beam thwart and the net room hatches, divided into three sets of covers. The halyards are hooked to stemhead out of the way. Plate 79 is the view looking aft, with the net room hatches in foreground, the lantern standard with pump alongside, the raised companion giving access to the motor, the binnacle alongside, the mizzen mast with the lug traveller secured by the hook passed through the thimble of the mast rope, the cleats on bulwarks with eyebolt for mizzen stay, the movable strake above the fixed bulwark, the curved tiller, and the hole in rail to take the standard for the side lights. The outrigger is run in, and the jump stay is set up to eyebolt at foot of lantern standard. Both photos were taken in August 1934, when the lugger was fitted with a motor.

## SAILS

For a 40 ft. boat the foresail took 130 yards of canvas, the big mizzen one-third less, and the second mizzen one-quarter less. A full suit of sails for a Mevagissey lugger consisted of a big foresail with an area of 80-83 sq. yds., a large mizzen of

50-55 sq. yds., a mizzen of 35-40 sq. yds., and a "kicker" of 25-30 sq. yds. Three jibs were carried, set according to the weather, a storm jib known as a "smiter," of 17 sq. yds., a working jib of 20 sq. yds., and a balloon jib of 40 sq. yds.

A typical sail plan *c.* 1906 is seen on page 312.

Originally the lug sails had three lines of reef points, later only two, but actually the custom was to reef once; if the wind came away still stronger, the foresail was taken in, and the large mizzen set in its place, while the second mizzen was used aft,

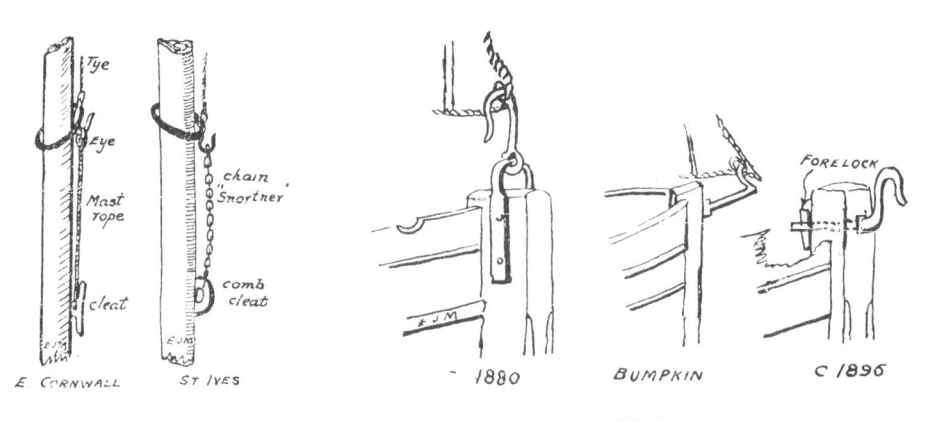

FIGURE 26

FIGURE 27

and so on until only the kicker was set in the heaviest weather. This sail was principally used as a riding sail when fishing. Each sail had its own yard, to which it was kept made up, and those not in use were stowed up for'ard on the port side of deck, seldom in raft irons as was West Cornish practice. Spare sails with no yards were kept in the space under the after deck.

Up to the eighties the foresail was cut much squarer, with a long foot which sheeted home at the stern, as the sail became higher peaked, so the foot shortened until finally the sail sheeted just for'ard of the mizzen mast.

## FORE YARD

The foreyard was 22-24 ft. in length, 6-7 in. dia. at slings, tapering to 4 in. for'ard and 3 in. aft, with an iron strop round the yard about one-third from the fore end, the eye went over the hook on the iron traveller on the mast, to which the tye was attached. Originally of chain or well-greased rope, in the later boats of wire, the tye rove through a dumb sheave cut in a fore and aft direction at the masthead. The tackle was a luff purchase with the single block hooking into eyebolt in covering board about 2 ft. aft of mast. When not in use, the traveller was kept in position by the "mastrope," about 3 ft. long, with an eye at one end, the other spliced round the stem of the cleat on the foreside of the mast (Fig. 26).

77 *JANE* ON THE HARD, 1936
Note rise of floors, fine run.

78 F.Y. 151 *EMILY*, LOOKING FOR'ARD
Note graper, mast covering board, eyes for halyards, etc., sails stowed in bundle, hatches in bulkhead.

79 F.Y. 151, *EMILY*, LOOKING AFT
Note curved iron tiller, pump, lantern, traveller and mast rope, hatches over net room.

80 *IDA*, SEPT., 1908
Note fore tack to weather bow, sweeps being placed in raft irons.

81 LUGGERS LEAVING MEVAGISSEY
190 F.Y. *Nellie*, note jenny boom on mizzen, base of capstan aft of thwart, curved iron tiller.

82 MEVAGISSEY LUGGER UNDER ALL SAIL
Note fore lug to bumpkin, jenny boom to mizzen and big balloon jib. May be F.Y. 46 *Smiling Morn*.

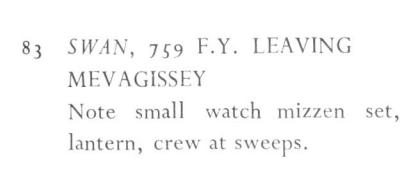

83  SWAN, 759 F.Y. LEAVING MEVAGISSEY
Note small watch mizzen set, lantern, crew at sweeps.

84  UNLOADING MACKEREL, MEVAGISSEY
F.Y. 729 Britannia, F.Y. 26 Undine. Note legs, sails stowed up for'ard, wide hatches in Britannia.

85  EDITH AND ANNIE AT MEVAGISSEY, 1936
Note foremast in scottle in Annie, but in tabernacle above deck in Edith, iron collars on transom to take outriggers.

86 LOOE LUGGERS AT BRIXHAM, c. 1880

87 PLYMOUTH LUGGER LEAVING BRIXHAM, c. 1880
Note curved iron tiller, sheet through sheave in bulwarks, roller on starboard rail and bumpkin in stemhead. Boat was probably built at Portleven.

## FORE STAY

The fore stay or burton, shackled to the aft lug eye on the iron band at the masthead and led to an eye, 2-3 ft. aft of the halyard, where it set up with a luff purchase. In the older boats it was of hemp with an eye over the masthead, in the later craft it was frequently of wire. Halyards and stay were *always* on the weather side of the mast, and when the sail was dipped, they were unhooked and taken across to the eyes on the

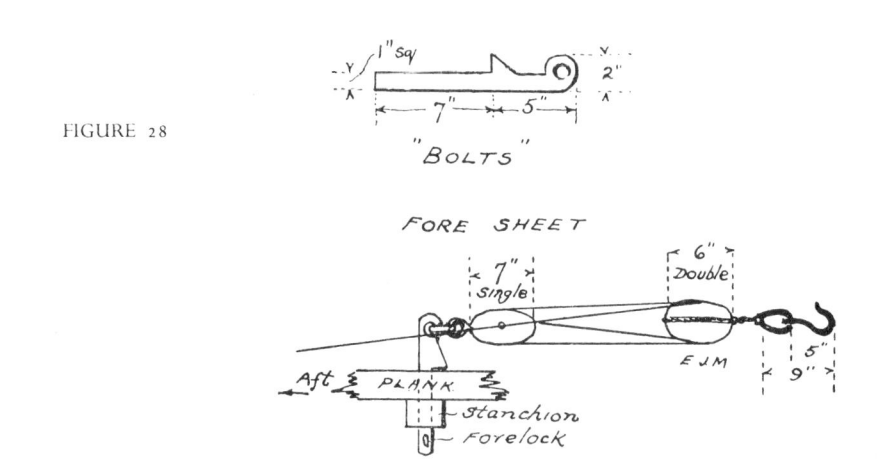

FIGURE 28

opposite side of the deck. When the foremast was lowered, this stay was taken for'ard, hooked to the stemhead and the fall eased away until the mast rested in the crutch.

## TACK

The fore lug was cut with an almost vertical luff, and the tack was made fast in a variety of ways. In the eighties by an iron hoop fixed over the top of the stem, then came the tack hook on a short iron bumpkin extending out about 1 ft. beyond the stem, finally the hook was brought right up to the stem, passing through midway between deck and stem head, and kept secure by a pin on the inside (Fig. 27). When the small lugs were used in bad weather, the tack was made fast by an S-shaped hook to an eye half-way between stem and mast, or in the case of the smallest sail, to an eyebolt at foot of mast, then the triangular watch mizzen was set aft. The tack was always taken as far for'ard of the mast as was necessary to allow sail to sheet fair, otherwise the lug would be pulled out of shape. When running before the wind, the tack would sometimes be carried on the bulwark, abreast the mast (Plate 80).

## SHEET

The fore sheet—a luff purchase—had a 6 in. double block fitted with a swivel, and a long hook which went into the clew cringle, the 7 in. single block hooked on to a small iron bumpkin—the "fore sheet iron"—which projected outside the bulwark for about 5-7 in. This iron had a shoulder outside to prevent it going right through the hole in the bulwark and stanchion, and was held in position by a pin (Fig. 28). The fall of the sheet led in over the top of the rail to a cleat. Two sheets were fitted in the closing years of sail, one on each side, to avoid the inconvenience of changing over every time they tacked ship. With the big lug the aftermost iron was used, but when sails were shifted and the mizzen lug set on the fore mast, the hole 2-3 ft. further for'ard had the iron in it.

FIGURE 29

### MIZZEN LUG

The sail on the mizzen mast was always a standing lug, set to port, so that the halyards went to the starboard eyebolt, the stay to port, and were never shifted over. The yard for the big mizzen was 17-18 ft. long, 4½-5 in. dia. at slings, the small mizzen 14-15 ft., and the kicker 12-13 ft. All were hoisted by halyards similar to those on the fore mast.

### TACK

The tack cringle went to a hook on the aft side of the foot of the mast. An iron collar, made in two pieces, clamped round the mast, each piece having a projection left on it at right angles to the fore and aft line of the boat, between these projections a bolt was passed, which carried the hook (Fig. 29).

### SHEET

The large mizzen had a light spar known as a "jenny" or "jinny" boom attached to the clew, and extending about a quarter of the way along the foot. In the middle a rope strop was seized into which the runner of the sheet hooked; a single block was shackled to the iron band at outer end of the outrigger, and the runner rove through this block, and at its inner end another single block was stropped. From its tail the sheet rove through yet another single block hooked on the heel of the spar, or else to an eyebolt on the transom, went back to the block at end of runner, and the fall belayed round a cleat on the outrigger. Plate 81 of *Nellie* 190 F.Y. shows the jenny boom and big mizzen, but when a smaller sail was set the runner hooked in the clew cringle, as can be clearly seen in Plate 83.

## JUMP STAY

The mast was stayed for'ard by the jump stay—a luff purchase—with the double block hooked to eye in fore-lug of the iron band at masthead, the lower single block hooked into an eyebolt in deck near after end of net room. The fore and mizzen lugsails comprised the working sails of the boat, but when making a passage, one of the jibs was often set as a s aysail, the jump stay being used for the halyards, then the tack of the sail hooked to an eyebolt at the break of the cuddy.

## BOWSPRIT

Not all the East Cornish luggers had a bowsprit—local name "bospard"—but when one was carried it was a reeving spar, the same size as the outrigger, and was always run in when not in use. The heel set in bitts to port of the foremast, and the spar rove through a hole in the bulwarks. It could be reefed to suit the size of jib set, there being three holes, 2-3 ft. apart, to take the fid—"heel bolt."

## JIBS

In the palmy days three jibs were in use. The working jib had an area of about 20 sq. yd., with its foot stretching from the stem to the sheave hole. In fine weather a balloon sail of 40 sq. yd. was set, with the foot reaching to the break of the foredeck; the storm jib—or "smiter"—was a small sail of only 17 sq. yd. Latterly only one jib was carried, or at the most two, one of which could be used as a staysail, or a watersail set under the bowsprit when occasion demanded. The jib was run out on a traveller whose outhaul at times served as a bobstay by being led under a cleat on the starboard side of the stem, just clear of the water, and brought in through a bullseye or hawse hole and belayed round the bowsprit bitts.

## HALYARDS

The halyards were a gun-tackle purchase with a single block hooked into an eye on the front of the iron band at masthead. The fall was fast to the tail of this block, rove down through a single block hooked in head cringle, led back through top block and belayed to a cleat on foreside of mast near the deck. When not in use, the halyards were kept in place by a lanyard which went round the mast under the cleat. This lanyard had a loop at one end and a thimble at the other. It was passed round the mast, the thimble put through the loop and the halyard block hooked to the thimble.

## SHEETS

Double sheets led in through bullseyes at the bottom of the bulwarks just aft of the foremast, positioned according to the jib used.

Plate 82 shows a Mevagissey lugger under a press of sail, and the large number of men aboard, nine, suggests the photo may have been taken at a regatta. The balloon jib is set, the tack of the fore lug goes to an iron bumpkin, and the big mizzen has a jenny boom at the foot. The bowsprit has a short bobstay set up with a gun-tackle purchase.

The late Wm. Pezzack writes that in many of the Mevagissey boats it was the custom to haul the nets in over the stern, not the bows.

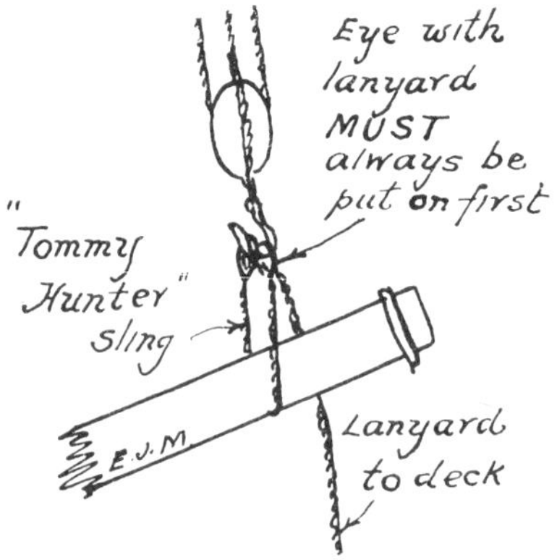

FIGURE 30

When the lugger was riding to her nets the foremast was lowered into the crutch just aft of the net room. In very fine weather the mast was sometimes only lowered as far as the "saddle," *i.e.*, on the beam at the aft end of foredeck, and the head was lashed to the mizzen mast. In this position the heel was not raised at all.

In really bad weather the foremast could be lifted right out of its casing and laid down in the boat with its heel on the breasthook and head lashed to the mizzen mast. As can be supposed, this was no easy job with the lugger rolling madly and plunging like a frightened horse. First the mast was lowered on to the crutch by the fore stay; this raised the heel about half-way up the trunk. The jump stay on the mizzen now took the weight by means of a special rope strop known as a "Tommy Hunter" (Fig. 30). This had a loop at each end and a rope lanyard attached to one of the loops, which was always put first on the hook on the tail of the block. The strop passed round under the foremast and the second loop was slipped on the hook. With the weight now on the jump stay, the mast was lowered until its head projected over the stern, thus bringing the heel up to deck level. The mast was then launched forward to rest on the breast-hook, where in the older boats it was secured by a pin.

When the wind fined off, the mast was run back to its casing, and the head raised as high as possible by the jump stay, then the fore stay took the weight, and the jump stay was cast off by pulling on the lanyard. This depressed the hook, and the two loops slipped off and the Tommy Hunter remained in the hands of the man who pulled it off.

The mast was then raised in the normal manner. In the later luggers the stays were wire and the running gear manilla.

Speed was surprisingly good for such small boats, eight knots was common, but a really fast vessel would do ten comfortably, and could sail within five points of the wind with a jib set, or four without. The best point of sailing was with the wind abeam and the sheets just started. For use in calms and for getting into and out of harbour, two or three sweeps or oars were used—at Mevagissey oars were preferred, not sweeps. The starboard oar was shipped 1 ft. abaft the break of the cuddy, and the port one 2 ft. abaft the beam thwart, in crutches or rowlocks which fitted in holes cut between the bulwarks and two stanchions specially fitted for this. When not in use the oars were kept for'ard with the spare sails, seldom in raft irons, although Plate 80 shows the sweeps of a Looe lugger being stowed in irons on the port side. Plate 83 shows 759 F.Y. *Swan* with others of the fleet putting to sea, the man for'ard is sitting on the fore hatches, and the oars are shipped in crutches. The small watch mizzens are set in readiness for the night's fishing.

At night it was the custom to shorten down and set the smaller sails, whatever the weather, "just in case." When going about, the man steering gave the necessary orders, which were brief and to the point, the preparatory "ready about" being followed by the active order, "lower away." The lug was lowered right down and brought round aft of the mast, never forward, as was West Cornish practice.

## NETS

For herring and pilchard, Mevagissey luggers fished with nets 120 yds. long on an 80 yd. head-line, but at Looe they used a 180 yd. net on a 120 yd. head-rope. The number of nets carried depended on the size of the boat and the financial means at the disposal of the crew, but twelve to fifteen was the usual complement. For mackerel the nets were 60 yds. long, set on a 40-yd. head-rope, and sixty to eighty would be used.

Instead of corks in the head-rope, the herring nets had 4 to 5 lb. of cork discs strung on a becket, doubled into a lump known as a "coble." The cobles were made fast to the head-rope by means of a "dropper," or "coble strap," four fathoms long, and $5\frac{1}{2}$ fathoms apart; these were used to regulate the depth at which the net should fish.

The mackerel nets had no cobles or straps, the corks were in the head-rope, which consisted of two small manilla or hemp ropes fastened together by "norsells," short lengths of spun yarn or twine that also attached the net to the head-rope, which floated on the surface.

Plate 84 depicts mackerel being landed at Mevagissey from F.Y.729 *Britannia*, which has a transom stern, but F.Y.26 alongside has a pointed one. Note the sails stowed up in the port bows.

A primitive flare—the "flambow"—was used to warn off shipping when the lugger was lying to her nets, and consisted of a round tin half-full of oil, with a lid from which an iron rod, wrapped in old rags or tow, projected into the oil. When the lid was taken off by a handle outside and a match applied to the oil-soaked bundle, a serviceable flare could be held aloft, the tin lid protecting the hand from any burning pieces of rag or drops of oil (Fig. 31).

FIGURE 31

FIGURE 32

A bullock's horn or conch shell was used as a fog-horn. The hulls were usually tarred outside, but in some of the smartest luggers a mixture of graphite with the tar resulted in a dark grey colour. Inside of bulwarks and top of rail were painted white, spars and masts greased or oiled, and decks dressed with varnish or pilchard oil.

I, in common with all sail-lovers and those interested in trying to preserve the records of the past, owe a deep debt of gratitude to my friend and fellow S.N.R. member, Mr. H. Oliver Hill, who most generously allowed me to make full use of his invaluable notes. Otherwise I fear my information would have been somewhat scanty, as none of my appeals in the local papers, etc., met with the slightest response from fishermen or boat-builders.

Sail did not survive the first war, when the motor came into its own, and Plate 85 shows two typical present-day boats at Mevagissey in August 1936. In *Annie* the foremast is stepped in the usual scottle, while in *Edith* it rests in a tabernacle on deck, a companion aft giving access to the engine-room.

Mr. R. Pearce, writing in the magazine, *Old Cornwall*, of the changes in the fishing at Looe, states that prior to the seventies the local pilchard drivers were about 25 to 26 ft. long, and carried a sprit mainsail, foresail, jib and topsail, with a small standing lug on a mizzen mast stepped against the transom stern (Fig. 32). Then came the change-over to a lug rig similar to that in the Mount's Bay craft, with many of the boats counter-sterned, but the small crabbers retained the spritsail rig. In the early days the nets were hand-made of hemp, and steeped in oak bark collected from nearby woods. The bark was chopped into pieces about one inch square, and put into a large copper, which the women filled with water and kept boiling for hours to get the full strength out of the bark. The nets had to be dried before and after barking, which was done frequently, every week if possible. When cotton nets were introduced, they were tanned in cutch, imported from Burma, and drying was unnecessary, as the wetter cotton nets are, the better, both for working and durability.

The fishing year was in four seasons, first for crabs, then mackerel, next pilchard, and lastly herring. Many owners of pilchard and mackerel boats went crabbing, others used their small boats to collect seaweed, taking it up the river and selling it to farmers as manure. A few of the big luggers went long lining, using six to seven hundred hooks. In early April the mackerel fleet was fitted out, the men going crabbing in the mornings and in the afternoons they cleaned and painted the boats. The shoals were generally caught in seine nets, worked from the shore, but a few of the bigger boats went "driving" with drift nets. The catch was landed and counted into a "gurry," an open box some 4 ft. long, 2 ft. wide, and 2 ft. deep, standing on short legs, and fitted with handles projecting from the two ends. These hand barrows were carried away by the women, who again counted the fish out into the jowter's carts, to be hawked around the neighbourhood. For every mackerel taken home, a penny was deducted from the crew's share. Mackerel seining went on until the end of June or the beginning of July, when the boats were got ready for pilchard driving. At the start of the season, the drifters would have to go a little outside of the Eddystone to fish, shooting their nets at dusk out straight for about five hundred fathom. Cork buoys were attached to the head lines at intervals of five to six fathom by ropes three fathoms long, which allowed the nets to sink deep enough to permit vessels to pass over them without doing any damage. When hauling in began, the fleet would be surrounded by thousands of screaming gulls and many a gannet, lured by the shimmering mass of fish, dived down into the nets to become entangled in the meshes and drowned. Big hauls were sometimes taken; in August 1812 one man at East Looe received £400 for fresh fish caught during one week.

It was only as the season advanced that the shoals came towards the land into shallower water—under ten fathoms—and could be caught in seine nets owned by a large company. The old men had a saying "Corn up in shock, fish in to rock," and it was only in harvest time that the seines were worked. Everybody took part in this fishing, and when the last haul was made in 1866 the master seiner was a tailor, and the catch was about 200 hogsheads. When catches were good and the price down to about 1s. or 1s. 3d. a hundred, every Looe household began to take in its winter stock of pilchards, some families storing from 1,500 to 2,000 fish. Captains of local trading smacks and schooners took in enough to feed their crews during the winter months, and the needs of people living inland were supplied by the jowters. All day long the women were cleaning pilchards, and putting them down in casks; as many fish as possible were sold fresh, the remainder was "bulked," from three to four tons of salt always being kept in store. First the women put a layer of salt on the stone floor of the cellar, then a layer of fish, then a layer of salt, and another of fish, until the bulk had reached a height of five to six feet, a haul of, say, 200 hogsheads taking about a day and a night to stack. After lying in bulk for 28 days, the fish were taken out and washed before being packed in barrels by the women, being laid heads outwards with a rosette of fish in the centre. Men put the hogsheads under press, using a "buckler"—a false barrel head—and a pole set into a hole in the cellar wall, with a large stone slung upon its free end, which acted as a lever in pressing down the buckler on the fish. To extract all the oil would take from nine to ten days; first they would press the fish down to the quarter hoop, then the women refilled the hogshead, which was again pressed down. Finally the fish were "back laid," so that they looked the same, whichever end the barrel was opened. Ready for sale, a hogshead weighed $4\frac{1}{4}$ cwt., and contained about 2,500 fish, the women being paid 2s. 6d. each for every one packed. Most of the men had a small weekly wage and a share in the profits. All the oil extracted from bulk and barrel drained away into cisterns, the quantity depending on the season, but at least two gallons a hogshead was expected, the early fish caught in drift nets producing the most. This oil was much used by leather dressers and as an illuminant in Cornish cottages.

Seining on the South Coast was never on so large a scale as in North Cornwall, where at one time enormous hauls were made in St. Ives Bay, as in 1868, when 5,600 hogsheads, or some sixteen and a half million fish, were taken in one seine.

The catch of a drifter was divided into eight shares, one went to the boat, three to the nets, and four to the men; the master getting the same as his crew, but the boy was only allowed the fish which fell in the sea when the nets were being hauled and were picked up in a bag net at the end of a long pole, and called a "keep" net. In the early part of the 19th century a fair week's share came to 18s. per man. At Newquay the men were paid 7s. a week and one-quarter the net proceeds of fish and oil, which amounted to £15 to £25 each for the season.

Seining has now gone the way of many another old industry, finishing up at St. Ives in 1924, although the last big haul was away back in 1907, when 8,000 hogsheads, or 24 million fish, were taken in the Bay, but drift net fishing is still carried on well away from land.

To return to the fishing at Looe. In October some of the pilchard nets were taken out of the boats for the winter, and after shooting the remainder, the men would fish for hake with a hook and line, while the boat drove all night, a good catch being 10 to 30 dozen fish, which would realise 6d. to 8d. each.

The following month some of the boats went herring fishing out of Torquay and Brixham for a time, before coming down to Plymouth to fish in Bigbury Bay. Others went after hake and pilchard all the winter, fishing from their home port.

Plate 86 shows part of the Looe fleet lying in Brixham harbour in 1880, their spars making squiggly patterns in the still green waters, and Plate 87 depicts a Plymouth lugger leaving Brixham with various Looe boats lying alongside the quay.

In the 1905 *Olsen's* appear the names of 89 first-class boats of 15 tons and over, with Fowey registration; in 1923 58, made up of one sail and 57 motor, the power craft including 31 one-time sailing luggers. By 1936 the total fleet of first-class fishing boats had fallen to 36, all motor.

CHAPTER NINE

## WEST CORNISH LUGGERS

THE luggers sailing from harbours west of the Lizard were divided into two classes—the small half-decked hatched boats used for pilchard driving, and the larger fully-decked mackerel drivers which set a jackyard mizzen topsail. Both types were developed from the older open boat, with fore deck only, by the addition of a short after-deck and hatching over the fish and net rooms, or in the largest boats by fitting a full deck with smaller hatches.

Owing to the fact that the hulls were built by eye or occasionally from a half-model, few of which have survived, very little authentic information is available until the middle of the 19th century, when the lines of typical luggers from Penzance and St. Ives were given in the Washington Report of 1849. The Penzance boat, built by M. Mathews, was half-decked with hatches, and would appear to be very similar to the St. Ives three-masted lugger described in Chapter Seven. The curved stem and straight sternpost were both well raked, so that the keel length of 34 ft. was increased to an overall length of 40 ft. 6 in. Beam was 12 ft., and depth of hold 6 ft. The floors were flat with well-rounded bilges, the bows bluff, and the lines full. The hull, carvel-built and copper-fastened, weighed 10 tons, draught for'ard was 4 ft., aft 6 ft. 6 in., ballast carried amounted to 7 tons, crew numbered seven, and ready for sea the lugger cost £200. The sail plan was simple, consisting of a lug foresail and mizzen.

The St. Ives lugger, built by Wm. Paynter, was of improved build, with finer lines and a straighter and more vertical stem and sternpost. Keel length was 37 ft., overall length 40 ft. 9 in., beam 12 ft. 3 in., and depth 6 ft. The hull weighed 11 tons, draught was the same as the Penzance boat, but two more tons of ballast were carried, and crew numbered seven. The hull was only decked for'ard, with hatches fore and aft, except for the open net room. Ready for sea she cost £200.

Unquestionably the most valuable evidence which has come down to us is a book of drafts by the St. Ives boat-builder, Wm. Paynter, and now preserved in the National Maritime Museum. His boats, built in the late sixties, show a strong resemblance to the earlier type, having the same flat floors and well-rounded bilges. As the originals were unsuitable for reproduction, the plans were redrawn by the late P. J. Oke, and on page 313 are the drafts of two pilchard boats.

The one built for Wm. Rowe had a 28 ft. length of keel, moulded breadth 9 ft. 6 in., depth amidships 5 ft. 3 in., height for'ard 5 ft. 10 in., aft 6 ft. 8 in. The greatest beam was 12 ft. 6 in. from forepart of stem, or 6 in. more than three-sevenths the length of keel. Room and space $14\frac{1}{2}$ in., keel 8 in. deep, ought to be 7 in., or $6\frac{1}{2}$ in. by 4 in. Huck post 5 in. wide at top, after apron 6 in. wide, 4 in. huck on top, fore apron 4 in. thick, $5\frac{3}{4}$ in. wide on top. Gunwales 3 in. by $2\frac{1}{2}$ in., stringers 3 in. by $2\frac{1}{2}$ in., thwarts 5 in. by $3\frac{1}{2}$ in., top of thwarts 9 in. from top of gunwale, bends 6 in. wide, leader 7 in., wash strakes 5 in. wide, upper strake 7 in.

The foremast was $6\frac{3}{4}$ in. dia., mizzen $5\frac{3}{4}$ in. The afterpart of foremast thwart 4 ft. 11 in. from after-part of apron, length between fore thwart and the next one 3 ft. 8 in., forepart of mizzen thwart from apron 4 ft. $1\frac{1}{2}$ in. From forepart of mizzen thwart to the afterpart of after net room thwart 2 ft. 7 in.

With the exception of the bilges, which were of 2 in. oak, the boat was planked with 1 in. Norway balk below the leaders. Hull alone cost £45, and an average price for a pilchard boat with nets, etc., ready for sea was £120, c. 1870.

The interweaving of the lines makes the draft more difficult to read than the conventional form, also the position of fore and after body lines is reversed to normal practice in naval architecture.

The second boat had a keel length of 30 ft., breadth moulded 10 ft., depth amidships 6 ft., depth for'ard 6 ft. 6 in., aft 7 ft. 7 in., with midship section 13 ft. 4 in. from stem, 16 ft. 8 in. from post. Room and space, 16 in.

The foremast, $7\frac{1}{4}$ in. dia., was 5 ft. $1\frac{1}{2}$ in. from the apron, space between two fore beams 4 ft., mast beam from fore apron 14 ft. $9\frac{1}{2}$ in., mizzen mast $6\frac{1}{4}$ in. dia., and 4 ft. 5 in. from apron, forepart of after net room beam from apron 7 ft. 7 in., length of net room 5 ft. 4 in., top of stringers 9 in. from top of gunwale.

The 2 ft. increase in length of keel brought the hull price up to £50.

The plans of *Godrevy*, built at Porthleven c. 1898, show the final development of the St. Ives pilchard driver (Plate 88). The lines were taken off by the late P. J. Oke in 1935.

Length of keel is 31 ft., length overall 34 ft. 10 in.; beam 11 ft., depth of hold 3 ft. 8 in. The plans are on pages 314-16.

The fore side of the foremast is 6 ft. from the outside of stem, and the aft side of mizzen mast is a similar distance from sternpost. The floors have more deadrise than in the earlier boats, and bilge keels are fitted. The cuddy, entered from a companion on port side of deck, has barely 4 ft. headroom between beams, and is fitted with locker bunks, while a small stove provides warmth and comfort unknown half a century before. Fore room and net room are hatched over, with an 18 in. waterway on either side; aft is sail locker and store, entered by a small hatch amidships, to port is the outrigger, its heel resting in clamp against aft coaming of net room.

The foremast, 38 ft. overall, 9 in. dia., tapering to 6 in., is stepped upright on the floors, and lowers back into the usual scuttle; the mizzen, 32 ft. overall, is raked slightly for'ard. The foresail is a dipping lug, bent to a 22 ft. yard, and fitted with a single line of reef points, and the tack cringle going to a hook outside stemhead. The mizzen, a standing lug, is bent to a 16 ft. yard and sheets to a 30 ft. mizzen boom or outrigger.

Plate 89 shows a typical St. Ives pilchard boat, *Agnes*, under sail. Plate 90 depicts 579 S.S. *Delhi* having a new stem fitted in August 1921. She has a 32 ft. keel, a length overall of 35 ft., and well-rounded bilges. *Delhi*, built by R. Bryant, was afterwards sold for a houseboat.

The year 1920 saw the last sailing pilchard driver, P.Z.278, fitted out at Newlyn (Plate 91), and the contrast between her lines and those of *Delhi* (Plate 92) can be clearly seen, her deadrise being such that legs are required to keep her upright when dried out. She is seen under sail in Mount's Bay (Plate 93). The fore lug is being hoisted, one of the crew is at the pump, and a third has the tiller between his legs. The low bulwarks will be noted, also the scuttle hatch and the square openings in the bulkhead giving access to the cuddy.

The lines of a transom-sterned pilchard boat, taken off by the late P. J. Oke *c.* 1936, are seen in plans 9 pages 317-19.

She is P.Z.111, *Veracity*, ex *Boy's Own*, built by J. Blewett at Newlyn in 1902, and owned by Paul Humphreys of Mousehole. She is somewhat smaller than *Godrevy*, having a keel length of 26 ft. 4½ in., length overall 32 ft., beam 10 ft. 3 in., depth 4 ft. 7½ in. The deck arrangements are reminiscent of the earlier days, with stem raking aft and sternpost raking sharply for'ard, and hatches extending over the after room, leaving only a short deck at the stern. Headroom in cuddy is 3 ft. 9 in. between beams, the net room has a second platform resting on the stringers in addition to the one over the ballast, thus allowing fish to be stowed below the nets. A pump is fixed amidships against the after thwart.

The foremast, 32 ft. overall, and 7-5 in. dia., is stepped so as to lower back in the usual manner, on it is set a dipping lug with two lines of reef points, bent to a 19 ft. yard, with tack cringle to a hook on stemhead, and sheets to an iron some 8 ft. for'ard of transom. The mizzen mast, stepped a foot from the transom, rakes aft and measures 16 ft. overall, dia. 4½-3 in. The standing lug, always to port, has a 12 ft. yard, with the tack to the foot of the mast and sheet to end of a 16 ft.—11 ft. outboard—outrigger. The foresail has an area of 417.875 sq. ft., and the mizzen 113.9 sq. ft., a total sail area of 531.775 sq. ft.

## SAILING DRIFTERS

A photograph of a similar boat, P.Z.492, is seen in Plate 94. The small drift mizzen is set, and the big sail is lying along the port side of deck.

When the lines were taken off, *Veracity* was fitted with a motor, and a certain amount of reconstruction was necessary to make her conform to her appearance under sail alone. Plate 95 is a bow view taken at Mousehole in February 1936.

The mackerel drivers varied in size from about 35 ft. in the keel, 40 to 44 ft. being an average size, with a few built at the turn of the century running up to 47 ft. The type was first evolved about 1865, when the need arose for boats capable of

FIGURE 33

greater speed and carrying capacity, the opening of the railway into Cornwall, and the desire to visit the North Sea fishing grounds being the principal reasons for the change. Up to that date bows had been rounded—apple-bowed—and the luggers were practically open boats with a small cuddy for'ard where the crew lived hard. The old stem had a considerable rake, but the new sharp-bowed craft had a straight stem from the waterline when afloat, and only a slightly rounded forefoot. It was a gradual evolution, boat after boat being built sharper in every way. Richard Warren and James Wills at Newlyn were the prime builders, but Wm. Williams, father and son, at Mousehole were not far behind; Porthleven followed suit. St. Ives men had a difficulty; they had a terrible harbour, with frightful side surf, and legs were impossible. This problem was solved by building a peculiar boat with a small bottom to obviate the leg necessity, the midship section being as Fig. 33; bow and stern were wedge-shaped, but it was impossible to use a keel iron, as the sand would get under and force it off. Old Wm. Williams at Mousehole used to build by rule of thumb, set up three frames, midship, bow and quarter, put on his ribands, and mould the other frames by the ribands, but his son, who built the *Ganges*, had her properly laid out on a moulding floor, and the other builders designed their boats on paper, and finally on a floor. Mr. Pezzack says that in his boyhood Warren of Newlyn excelled in the great beauty of the " tucks."

St. Ives adopted a narrow flat bottom with shallow, strong bilges and heavy bends for bumping one against the other, and very strong stem and sternposts, as instead of mooring to ring bolts in the fore thwart, they moored to their strongly breast-hooked stem and sternpost, which were often pulled out, before the west pier was built. At first the boats were half-decked, with narrow waterways, but as size increased they were fully decked, and the crew of six men and a boy lived aft in more comfort in the cabin, which was fitted with three bunks on each side, and one aft of the mizzen mast for the boy.

*Martha*, built by Wm. Paynter at St. Ives, *c.* 1869, had a length of keel of 35 ft., moulded beam 11 ft. 6 in., depth amidships 6 ft. 6 in., depth for'ard 7 ft. 6 in., aft 8 ft. 9 in. Room and space of timbers was 16½ in., with a maximum breadth two-fifths from the forepart of the stem, or 14 ft. The thwarts were 5½ in. wide by 5 in. deep, forepart of mizzen thwart 5 ft. 3 in. from forepart of apron. After net room thwart 3 ft. 9 in. from forepart of mizzen thwart. Length of net room 6 ft. 2 in. within, mast beam from afterpart of F.N.T., 4 ft. 2 in. Foremast 5 ft. 6 in. from apron, from fore beam to second beam 4 ft. 11 in., length of deck 12 ft. 9 in., post 6 in. wide, stem 6½ in. wide on top, fore apron 5½ in. deep, 7½ in. wide, after apron 5 in. by 7 in., gunwale 3½ in. by 3 in., top of stringer 6¾ in. from top of gunwale, strakes 7 in. deep, mast carlings 5 ft. 6 in. long, 8 in. deep, 4 in. thick, and 9¼ in. apart, keel 10 in. deep and 5 in. wide.

Here is a mackerel driver but little bigger than a pilchard boat, with similar lines and the crew still living in a cuddy under the fore-deck.

The following hull scantlings are taken from a manuscript book by Wm. Paynter:

Hull planking - - 6 in. strakes, next to keel 6 in. by 1½ in.
Bilge strakes - - 7 in. to 8 in. by 3 in.
Above waterline - 6 in. by 1½ in. thick
Bend planks - - 6 in. by 2 in. thick, with iron outside
Deck planking - - 5 in. by 1½ in.
Forehold beam - - 5½ in. deep by 4½ in.
Frames - - - 2¾ in. by 4 in. wide (thwartship)
2nd futtocks, or lower frames: 4 in. by 3 in. wide
Floors, approx. 6 in. deep: spacing about 1 ft. 6 in. centres
Bulwarks: 1 ft. 6½ in. deep inside. Toprail: 2½ in. by 4 in. wide

The draft of *Barnabas* shows a 36 ft. keel, a 5 in. increase in depth amidships, and bulwarks 14 in. deep. Length of foredeck is 13 ft. 6 in., after deck 9 ft. 5 in., net room 5 ft. 4 in. within, fish room 4 ft. 4 in., with platform boards about 12 in. from deck, a foot line room 2 ft. 11 in. fore and aft amidships in fore room, which is 3 ft. 4 in. within. The foremast had a 8⅝ in. dia. and the mizzen mast 7½ in., the foreside of foremast and aftside of mizzen being 6 ft. from inside of stem and aft apron respectively.

These two drafts appear in plan 10 page 320.

Such a boat is seen in Plate 96 of P.Z.131, *Edgar*, *c.* 1880. The nets are being hauled out of the net room over a roller on the starboard bulwark, to be laid out on the beach to dry. One of the crew, taking advantage of the boat being high and dry, is tarring the hull; the fore yard, hooked to a bead parrel, has no yard arms, and the mizzen is more upright than in the later boats. A primitive winch helps to ease the labour of hauling in the nets. The length of the oars will be noticed, also how little the boat lists, owing to her flat floors, but the lugger in the background, of the later type, has legs to keep her upright. Fitted with a motor, *Edgar* was still about in 1923.

The boats shown in Plates 118 and 61 of P.Z. 49 at Whitby, and 190 P.Z. at Hugh Town are also of similar type.

Other drafts by Wm. Paynter show boats with keels of 38 ft. and 40 ft. Each owner had his own individual ideas. The 38 ft. lugger has a moulded breadth of 12 ft. 8 in., and a depth of 7 ft., but the 40-footer for Daniel Freeman has 2 in. less beam and a depth of 6 ft. 8 in., although she was actually built 1 in. deeper, while John Care, who also ordered a 40 ft. keel boat, preferred her to be 2½ in. narrower on the quarter, with the timbers cleaner and not so round. By such trial and error was the lugger finally brought to perfection.

In John Care's boat, the foremast was 6 ft. 10 in. from the apron, the length of foredeck 14 ft. 8 in., second beam 12 ft. 10 in. from apron, forepart of A.N.B. 11 ft. 2 in. from apron, third beam 18 ft. 4 in. from apron. Length of net room 6 ft. 8 in., afterpart of fore N.R.B. 23 ft. 9 in. from fore apron, and the top of the stringers 10 in. from top of gunwale. Room and space of timbers was 17½ in., with midship section 18 ft. 6 in. from forepart of stem.

To my mind the most interesting draft is of S.S. 340, *Ebenezer*, built 1867 for John Stevens, and still fishing in 1930, according to Olsen's Almanack, which gives the following particulars: 17 net tons, built at St. Ives 1867. Owner, J. Stevens, Jun. The lugger no longer relied on sail, but had a 26 h.p. motor. The original draft, dated 1868, gives the length of keel as 44 ft., breadth moulded 13 ft. 6 in., depth amidships 7 ft., depth for'ard 7 ft. 10 in., aft 8 ft. 9 in. The lines, taken off by the late P. J. Oke, c. 1936, are given in plans 11 pages 321-2, and the date of building is there given as 1869.

Length overall was 48 ft. 9 in., beam 14 ft., depth inside 6 ft. 6 in., and the plans were reconstructed in certain details owing to the boat having auxiliary power. *Ebenezer* represents a typical fully-decked mackerel driver of the mid-19th century, with smaller hatches amidships and scudding holes in the deck. The foremast, stepped in a tabernacle some 8 ft. from the outside of the stem, lowers back into a 7 ft. long scuttle, the aft side of the mizzen mast is 10 ft. from after side of sternpost, the outrigger, or mizzen boom, to use the St. Ives name, is stepped in a chock to port of the skylight, the companion is to starboard, with a pump amidships against after coaming of net room and the lantern spear alongside. When built, *Ebenezer* would have had a hand capstan, but a steam one was fitted in later years.

Below deck is the fore peak, where spare sails and gear were stowed, then came the footline room, fish room, and net room, all with fixed platforms over the ballast. Aft is the cabin fitted with bunks and lockers, a stove for cooking, and the boiler supplying steam to the capstan. Headroom is 5 ft. between beams.

The foremast, 40 ft. from deck to head, is 10 in. dia. at deck, 6 in. at sheave, the mizzen mast 32 ft., with a 12 ft. pole, or 44 ft. from deck to head, and 8·5 in. dia. The outrigger measures 30 ft. overall, 20 ft. being outboard, with a dia. 10·5 in.

Fortunately, Mr. John Stevens was good enough to give every possible assistance to Mr. Oke, who noted anything of the slightest interest. As a general rule, the following timbers were used in the construction of the hull:

| | |
|---|---|
| Keel | Elm |
| Stem and sternpost | Oak or elm |
| Frames and beams | Oak, sawn or grown |
| Knees | Oak |
| Planking, Hull | White, yellow or pitch pine, or oak 2 in. thick |
| Planking, Deck | Yellow pine, 2½ in. thick |
| Spars | Fir, spruce or yellow pine |

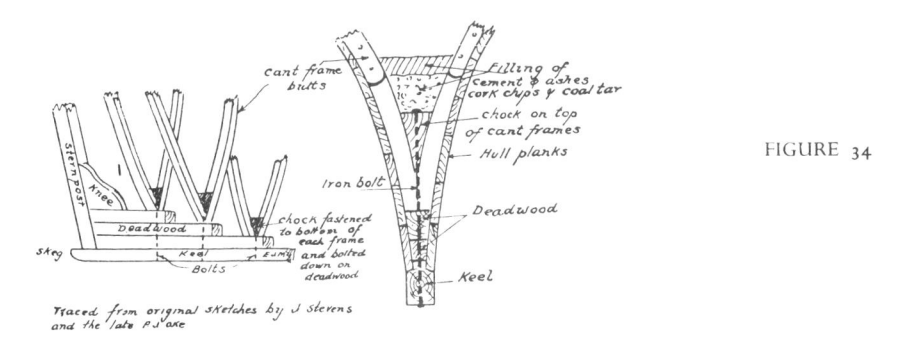

FIGURE 34

Construction varied in different boats, some had double frames, others long scarphed ones, when the floor was the first piece on the keel, then the first futtock about two or three feet from the keel, the second futtock fitted close against the end of the floor, so that when the boat lay on the ground on her bilge, the futtocks supported the floors from rising. The tops fitted on the second futtocks and all St. Ives' boats had them, not stanchions, on every frame. Some had double floors and futtocks with single tops, two stringers, and fore and aft knees on each beam.

The first piece of deadwood aft was about 8 ft. long, the second 6 ft., and the third 4 ft., and all were 1 ft. deep. The frames on the deadwood had a cross chock fastened to the bottom of each frame and bolted down through the keel. All the boats were filled in above the cross chocks to within about six inches of the cabin floor, not with the usual cement, but cork chips, ashes and coal tar, with a thin layer of cement on top to run the water off. The idea was for less weight, all ballast was in the middle of the boat, none in the ends fore and aft, to be like a pair of scales with a little more on the aft side, so that when the lugger fell in a sea she picked herself up quickly for'ard (Fig. 34).

The planking was fastened to the apron, so that it was possible to take off the stem without interfering with the "wood ends." Mr. Stevens stated that the rudder

88 *GODREVY* AT ANCHOR, ST. IVES

89 *AGNES* UNDER SAIL

90 *DELHI*, FITTING NEW STEM, 1921

91 THE LAST PILCHARD DRIVER AT NEWLYN
Fitting out for the last time at Newlyn, 1920.

93 THE LAST PILCHARD DRIVER AT SEA, 1920
Hoisting forelug which is aback as boat will soon fill on starboard tack.

92 *DELHI*, ST. IVES PILCHARD DRIVER. STERN VIEW

94  P.Z. 492 TRANSOM STERNED PILCHARD BOAT
Note small mizzen set, larger one is stowed on port rail.

96  DRYING NETS, MOUNT'S BAY, c. 1880
131 P.Z. *Edgar*. Note winch instead of capstan, the wide hatches, pump, bead parrel, net roller on starboard bulwark, short yardarms.

95  *VERACITY*, BOW VIEW, MOUSE-HOLE, 1936
Note legs, round bilges and sharp rise to floors.

97 *WATER LILY*, S.S. 635, c. 1895
The fastest lugger ever built in Cornwall. Note inhaul to mizzen, topsail sheet, topsail halyards twisted round jump stay, and men sheeting home forelug.

98 *MORNING STAR*, S.S. 589
Note bumpkin with iron bobstay, topsail tack to foot of jumpstay, topsail sheet down to tack hook on port side.

99 MODEL OF *MORNING STAR*, S.S. 589
Made by her builder, R. Bryant, at the age of 78. Note topsail is to starboard, mizzen lug to port as boat is on port tack.

100 ST. IVES HARBOUR
94 luggers lying strake to strake.

101 *TEMPERANCE STAR*, 59 P.Z.
Note jenny boom at foot of mizzen lug, short iron bumpkin, no yardarms.

102 TRANSOM STERNED MACKEREL DRIVER ENTERING NEWLYN
L.T. 689 *Minnie*, 38 tons, built 1896.

103 THE FLEET PUTTING TO SEA, c. 1885
 P.Z. 147 *Favourite* has a warp to bows of *Branch*, most of the East Coast drifters have lute sterns. Note sweeps in crutches on port rail of *Branch*.

104 MACKEREL DRIVERS IN MOUNT'S BAY, c. 1895
Note sheet hooks into clew of mizzen.

105 *ST. MICHAEL* LEAVING PENZANCE, *c.* 1895
Sheeting home forelug, note counter stern, iron bumpkin trhough stemhead.

106 *MARY & EMILY*, P.Z. 533
Note foremast lowered back into scottle, capstan, small hatch over fish room, large ones over net room.

107 BREAKING UP A LUGGER, NEWHAVEN, 1945
Note beams, knees, scottle, covering board, stringer, mast step, floors with footicks bolted on fore side, top timbers on aft side of footicks.

108 MAST COVERING BOARD. JULY, 1943

109 SCUD HOOK AND STEMHEAD

was unshipped every time a boat came into St. Ives Harbour, owing to the bad conditions there. The tiller was of wood and fitted over the rudder head with a wedge at the back. Wheel steering was never adopted until a motor was installed.

The colour of the hull was usually black, the toprail white, with white inside the bulwarks. One of the features of the St. Ives craft was the method of painting the upper part of the mizzen mast like a barber's pole, with red and white rings alternately or half red and half white, so that different boats could be more easily distinguished when in port among the maze of masts.

The small boat was known locally as a "punt," and from Wm. Paynter's draught book the following particulars were taken of various punts built for luggers then in existence:

1864. *Margaret's* punt, 15 ft. 6 in. long, £7.
1864. Capt. Anthony's boat *Palace*, 15 ft. 6 in., £9.
1864. Punt 12 ft. long to the *Kate Roach*, £6 10s.
1864. Punt 12 ft. long to the *Emu*, £6 10s.
1864. July 14. Boat 16 ft. long, to the *C.H.S.*, Capt. C. Hodge, £11.
1865. Punt to *Charles*, 12 ft. long, £6 10s.
April, 1865. to *Majestic*, *Boomerang* and *Queen*, each 12 ft. long, £6 10s.
July, 1865. New 17 ft. boat to *Queen of the Sea*, £12.

At sea the punt was kept in chocks on the starboard side of the deck.

*Ebenezer* carried six tons of stone ballast, and one ton iron shifting, and Mr. Stevens mentions that their boats used about forty to sixty ½-cwts. to shift to wind'ard according to the wind. He has seen them all up to wind'ard with the punt filled with water to keep the lugger upright for speed. He goes on to say: "The fastest boat ever built in Cornwall was *Water Lily*, S.S.635 (Plate 97), built by Henery Trevorrow, 47 ft. keel, with 14 ft. 6 in. beam and still afloat in the thirties, when she was owned by Thomas Chambers of Kilkeel, Co. Down. She was an all-round boat, fast in light or hard winds. Another was *Lloyd*, S.S.5, sold to Annalong, Co. Down, and since lost, she held the record from Scarborough to St. Ives, 50 hours, in 1902, and landed fresh herring on the quays, caught in the North Sea two days before. More depended on the man than the boat for making these fast passages. Her skipper was a hard man, who would keep up his big sails, in strong winds, pitch-dark nights, or foggy weather, when a more careful man would have shortened down. A lot depended on how you met the tides; if you had the first of the tide with or against you." (Scarborough to St. Ives, about 600 miles.)

The luggers *Leading Star*, S.S.615, and *Johanna*, S.S.601, came from Scarborough to St. Ives in 55 hours; *British Workman*, S.S.494, and *T.R.C.*, S.S.539, came from Peterhead to St. Ives, about 850 miles, in less than 100 hours, while *James*, S.S.638, went from her home port to Howth in 19 hours. *Nelly Jane*, S.S.503, built 1897 by

Kitto at Porthleven, Master B. Thomas, sailed from Scarborough home in 56 hours in 1905, with only two nights at sea. The conditions were plenty of wind from the N.E.; he carried the small foresail of 137 yards and an 80-yd. mizzen for the first 24 hours, which was done at an average of eleven miles per hour; the weather moderating, the rest of the journey was done with full canvas, a 200-yd. foresail and 137-yd. mizzen. The boat was sold for conversion into a yacht in 1938, after laying up at Lelant.

The best point of sailing for most of the boats was on a wind, when speeds up to ten knots were frequently obtained. Passages from St. Ives to Whitby or Scarborough

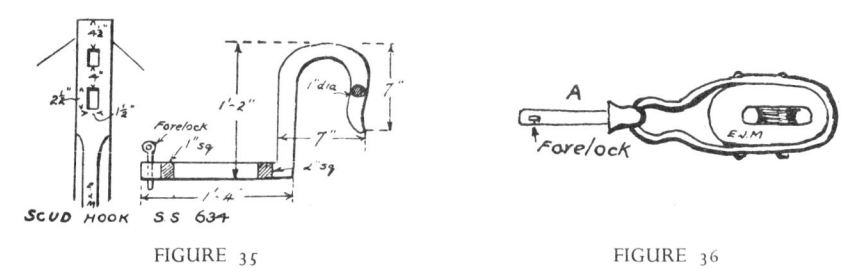

FIGURE 35

FIGURE 36

varied from three days to three weeks, to Kinsale from 19 to 40 hours. About the turn of the century when there was not a good market for herring at St. Ives, large quantities were salted down in the cellars under the houses. Later they were loaded for Kinsale or Milford; on the return journey a customs permit would be obtained, and the lugger loaded up a cargo of potatoes, which were brought over and stored for the winter, when in the Bristol Channel a cargo of coal was taken aboard.

*Ebenezer* first went to the Irish fishing in 1870; later, after fishing at Howth, Co. Dublin, they would go through the Firth and Forth Canal, to fish on the east coast of Scotland, finishing up at Berwick and Scarborough, returning home in September or October, all under sail.

The 160-yd. foresail, bent to a 26-ft. yard, 5 in. dia. at slings, has an area of 789.5 sq. ft., with a weather of 26 ft., leech 42 ft., head 24 ft., and foot 29 ft. 6 in. The tack cringle of the large foresail goes to an iron "bunkin" about 1 ft. from the foreside of the stem, the smaller sail to the "scud" hook (Fig. 35). These were fitted through holes in the stem, never over it. The foresheet consists of a "fiddle" block, single for the small boats, double for the large, about 12 in. long (Fig. 36). The bar A is equivalent to the boomkin in the Penzance and East Cornish types, the block being attached by an iron fiddle-shaped ring, hence the name fiddle-block, although the block itself is not strictly fiddle-shaped. The bar A is placed through the bulwarks and locked by a pin or "forelock" inside the bulwarks. There are two fiddle blocks, one each side. When going about, the tackle is unhooked when the sail is lowered, and the new lee sheet is hooked into the clew cringle. The sizes of the blocks vary with the size of the boat, being from 8 in. to 1 ft. in length. The bar is not through a stanchion, but the bulwarks, which are strengthened on the inside by an extra chock about 2 in. thick, which is placed between two stanchions beneath the rail (Fig. 37). Usually there were three positions for the sheets, according to the size of sails used, and each chock B is about 3 to 4 ft. apart. In *Ebenezer* the chock is about 2 ft. for'ard of the mizzen mast, she may have had others in her early days, but there was only one a side in 1936.

There were two sheaves in the masthead, one live for the lug halyards, the other a half or dead sheave for the jib halyards. Chain tyes were usually fitted at St. Ives,

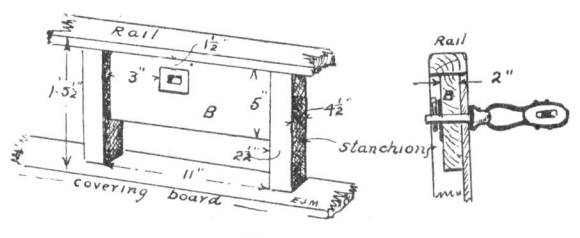

FIGURE 37

wire at Newlyn and Penzance (Fig. 38). Eyebolts to take the halyards and burton are set athwartships in the covering boards, and all boats had eyebolts for squaring the foresail when the wind was abaft the beam. When the sail was taken in to the mast for making short tacks, it was known locally as "trysailed," and corresponded to the "set a'monk" on the East Coast and in Scotland. All the eyebolts were taken down through deck and beam, and secured with a stout forelock underneath.

FIGURE 38

FIGURE 39

The 120 yd. mizzen, bent to a 20 to 21 ft. yard, $4\frac{1}{2}$ in. dia. at the slings, has an area of 504.4 sq. ft., with a weather of 22 ft. 6 in., leech 32 ft. 6 in., head 19 ft., foot 24 ft., with two lines of reef points. The 80-yd. mizzen has a weather of 18 ft., leech 28 ft., head 17 ft. 6 in., and foot 20 ft. The tack went to a hook on a clamp round the foot of the mast (Fig. 39), and the sheet rove through single block on end of outrigger. The halyards went to starboard, the shroud to port of the mast. When the small mizzens were set on the foremast, the tack went to the hook at the foot of the mast, or the one 3 ft. further for'ard. The 45-yd. quadrilateral topsail has an area of 123 sq. ft., with a head of 19 ft. 6 in. bent to a 21-ft. yard, 3 in. dia., a foot of 24 ft. has a 12 to 12 ft. 6 in. jackyard, 2½ to 3 in. dia., at the clew, a weather of 9 ft., and a leech of 7 ft. The total sail area is 1,420.9 sq. ft.

Mr. Stevens thus describes the setting of the topsail:

"It was always at the head of the mast, hauled up tight, then a 'handy billy' put on it and set up as tight as possible, then pull down the tack with two single blocks and haul out the lee sheet. Our boats never did carry a jib, only when the wind was aft side of the beam, then the boom was out over the luff of the bow. Ours was not really a jib, it was a 'spinker,' the boltrope or luff rope was tight and the sail would go out like a balloon. It was no use by the wind, and was made of very light canvas, about 80 yards. A jib foreside of a lugsail was not much good. The staysail was not set very often, it was hoisted up with the burton and the jump stay was always set up. The staysail was most used when shooting the nets, being hoisted up with the jib halyards with the tack to the stem, when in the middle we used the burton, that is a double block on the mizzen mast at the hounds and a double block below. We used this mostly to get in the punt and get up our heavy moorings in the harbour. Our sails were stowed away every time we came in harbour, and every night our nets were 'shut,' the sails were stowed, the bolt rope hauled half tight, then the sails rolled in snug. The name for the sails when stowed at the side was the 'raft,' the oars were put upon them and lashed down with ropes through the rail. They were never kept in crutches as in Mount's Bay. The sweeps were about 22 ft. long, two in number, and the oar crutches were kept below in the cabin; we did very little rowing, you could get no speed out of man power. We only carried one spare small mizzen, called the jigger, which was kept below unbent. When not in use the topsail, staysail and jib were also kept dry below on a rack fore side of the foremast. The big lug had one reef, the rest two, about 3 ft. deep. On deck all sails were stowed away on the port side of the deck on a wood grating with two watertight coverings over them.

When dipping the lug the foresheet was first unhooked, the halyards lowered, tack unhooked, sail pulled into the mast, lee end of the yard on the deck; the tack would be about 4 ft. off the deck, then the lee end of the yard was passed around the mast (Fig. 40) At St. Ives the yard was hooked into a 'traveller,' at Newlyn this was called a 'parrel.' The mast box was called the tabernacle and the long cleat the 'Kebble.' When the yard had been dipped, the tack was again hooked on, the other sheet tackle hooked in the clew, and the sheet trimmed. This dipping was an elaborate process, requiring intimate knowledge, thus each man had a regular station when going about, with one man always at the tiller, which was placed midships during the operation, but it was imperative to have sufficient headway on the boat before changing tacks. When the foresail was not set, the traveller was kept in position at the foot of the mast by a short length of chain, the 'snortner,' the lower end was fast to a comb cleat, and the upper link went over the hook on the ring." (Fig. 26.)

In another letter Mr. Stevens describes the nets used:

"For pilchard drifting, 36 rows to the yard, 18 score deep, for mackerel driving,

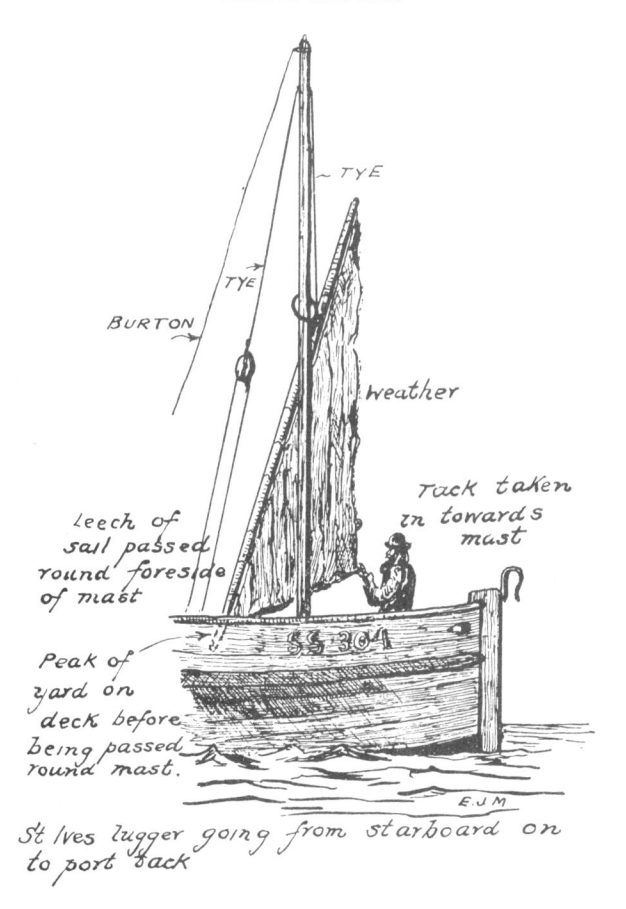

*FIGURE 40 — St Ives lugger going from starboard on to port tack. Labels: TYE, TYE, BURTON, weather, Tack taken in towards mast, Leech of sail passed round foreside of mast, Peak of yard on deck before being passed round mast.*

26 rows to the yard, 8 score deep, for herring 30 rows to yard, 18 score deep. A row means knots or half mesh. A pilchard fleet was about twenty 100-yard nets, a mackerel one sixty-four 80-yard nets, and a herring fleet about thirteen 100-yard nets, but an Irish fleet was twenty-four in number. The pilchard net was four fathom under the surface, with a small cork in the head rope every four feet, with four cork buoys to keep it up on each net. The mackerel net is on the surface, the herring net we work in the Bay or inshore is one fathom down, but those worked in Plymouth waters are four fathom down, so that large steamers can pass over them without doing any damage. In the Irish Sea we used footrope nets, that is, a rope at the bottom of the net, then the net is one fathom under surface. When lying to the nets, two riding lights were set 12 ft. apart, the after one 9 ft. above the deck, and the fore light 5 ft.

The ground gear consisted of a working anchor of about 35 to 40 lbs., 4 ft. in the shank and 3 ft. across the palms; a second one of 40 to 50 lbs., 5 ft. in the shank and 4 ft. across the palms; and the big one, about the same size as No. 2, but weighing 50 to 60 lbs. The anchor cable was a 3 in. hawser, and 100 fathom of 4 in. towrope was used when towing out of harbour during calms. Boat-hooks were carried, and a spare topsail yard and jenny boom for the foot of the mizzen topsail.

The method of reefing was by shifting the big 120 yd. mizzen to the foremast and setting the small mizzen aft. When shifting again, the 80 yd. mizzen was set on the foremast and the 45 yd. jigger aft. This was the storm rig. St. Ives men never used a triangular mizzen as did the Mount's Bayers, the jigger was the same quadrilateral shape, similar to the big mizzen. On the big foresail the length of the weather is approximately the same length as that of the yard. The overall length of the foremast was generally about the length of the keel, and the mizzen approximately the length of the boat."

Regarding cost of building, there is a note in the manuscript book of Wm. Paynter that Thomas Paynter's boat was sold on December 11th 1862 for £140 complete.

In winter it was customary to step a stump mizzen mast and a smaller foresail was set. A typical St. Ives mackerel driver is seen under sail in Plate 98. The tack of the foresail is hooked to a short iron bumpkin, and one of the crew is trimming the fore sheet; the tack of the topsail goes to the foot of the jump stay, and the sheet straight down and round the fore-side of the mast to belay round the tack hook. The topsail bowline is not set, but is hanging down to the foot of the jump stay.

One of the few who responded to my appeals published in Cornish newspapers was Mr. W. Bryant, of Launceston, who kindly sent me two excellent photographs of a model of the St. Ives lugger *Morning Star*, S.S.589, and it was not until I was finally choosing illustrations that I noticed I had a photograph of the actual boat, and decided to include it rather than others from my collection.

Mr. Bryant wrote me in January 1947 concerning this model:

"The original was built by my father, the late Wm. Bryant, a shipwright at St. Ives, when he was nineteen years old, in the year 1879. He made the model when he was seventy-eight years old. Unfortunately I cannot get the dimensions of the *Morning Star*, but I enclose some measurements of the model—maybe it will be of some help in your quest."

These figures gave a length overall of 25 in., a beam $7\frac{3}{4}$ in., depth for'ard $5\frac{1}{2}$ in., amidships $5\frac{1}{8}$ in., aft 6 in., so evidently the model is to a scale of $\frac{1}{2}$ in. to 1 ft. In another letter Mr. Bryant said:

"I have made enquiries at St. Ives, but the replies are negative. For what it is worth, I will tell you all I know of my father's activities in boat-building. He was apprenticed to his uncle Robert Bryant, when he was fourteen years old; his father, also an old shipwright, died at that time. He served six years, commencing at 1s. per week, and built several fishing boats on his own during that time, the two I have heard him mention being the *Morning Star* and *Louisa Jane*. The demand for fishing boats fell away, and he went into the merchant service, with Messrs. Hain Steamship Co., and did several voyages in the S.S. *Trewellan*. He then went to Portsmouth, and later to

Devonport Dockyard, where he remained until sixty years old. He returned to St. Ives and the old urge to build sailing craft came back. His first effort was to build a sailing yacht for himself, the *Ivor*, with this boat he won several prizes."

It will be noticed in Plate 99 that the mizzen topsail is to leeward of the mast, while the standing lug is to port, for, as might be supposed, every detail is faithfully depicted, chain for the pendants and where the nip comes in the halyards, and a cover over the chain pipe leading down into the footline room. A beautiful piece of model-making. Thank you, Mr. Bryant.

The only photograph I have of St. Ives Harbour in the golden years of sail was sent me by Mr. J. Phillips, and about 94 luggers lie strake to strake (Plate 100). Those were the days!

Although in the main alike in appearance there were slight differences between the St. Ives and the Mount's Bay luggers. The former, although not quite so big as the Penzance boats, were far heavier tonnage for tonnage, with a rounder midship section, being built to withstand the open harbour conditions, where there was a very sweeping side surf as well as a tremendous surge fore and aft from the swell, whereas Newlyn was far more sheltered. The Penzance luggers had a more graceful and yachty appearance, with finer lines, and they continued their beautifully-round bilges in a "tuck" tapering more or less finely to the deck line at the sternpost, which gave them great beauty. Then the tyes were generally of chain at St. Ives, or wire at Penzance and Newlyn, where the use of patent blocks gave a good set to the sails. An iron traveller was more generally in use on the north coast, while a bead parrel was frequently found in Mount's Bay craft. Again, there was a considerable difference in draught, at St. Ives the ballast, consisting of iron pigs and boulders, was placed in the centre of the hull, so that the ends were entirely free, with the draught for'ard light and much deeper aft, whereas at Newlyn they tended to be deeper for'ard. This was due to the build of the boats, St. Ives having a very round body so that legs were not needed at low water, owing to the run of the tide, etc.; if any legs had been fitted they would have been broken off through the surging of the boats one against the other.

St. Ives stepped the foremast much further for'ard, as much as 5 ft. in some cases; this gave the foresail a straighter luff and a squarer head. At Newlyn, stepping further aft, the luff was more raked, this governed the peak of the sail. To use a sailmaker's expression, their forelug could almost be described as a jib-headed lug, whereas St. Ives was a square sail, cut much narrower and higher in the mast; the foot was much shorter, and the foresheet did not come so far aft. Again, St. Ives used a longer outrigger and no jenny boom on the foot of the big mizzen. The tack of their topsail was made fast by a tackle to the foot of the mizzen, or to the jump stay. Mount's Bay made the end of the tack fast through an eye about 2 ft. down the mizzen luff, led it up through an eye at the topsail tack, and down to the top reef cringle on the mizzen, where it was made fast with two half-hitches. St. Ives never used a triangular "watch" mizzen, and in dipping the forelug, their men usually started the tack, while in Mount's Bay they seldom did so, although towards the end of sail they sometimes handed the tack. Again, raft irons were seldom seen in St. Ives boats, and the name "punt" was given to the small boat, against the name "jolly boat" used at Newlyn and Mousehole. The net room was often called the "sheat" or sheet room at Newlyn and at St. Ives the term "street boards" was given to the cabin floor boards.

As elsewhere, the design of the Mount's Bay luggers originated in the open boat, with its hull divided as follows. First came the "foredeck," below which the crew lived, then the "fore room," in which the footline was coiled down beneath the boards, this extended to the middle of the boat, where the main beam was situated, on which the winch for heaving in the footline was fixed. Abaft the beam, the "mast room," a name remaining from the former main mast, was the main fish room, where fish could be stowed below the boards or above. Mr. Pezzack mentions that in his boyhood days, in the pilchard season when hakes were numerous, they would be put below the boards as they were caught by hand lines, and the pilchards meshed in the nets left above the boards. The fourth room was the "sheat," in which the nets were carried; this came to within a short distance of the mizzen mast; in the older boats it was boarded low and open, but about the sixties "after decks" replaced this open part. Here the big anchor and newest anchor rope, fenders, etc., were stowed. Each side of the fore room was a shifting ballast wing. When sailing to wind'ard, the lee wing of ballast would be piled on the weather ballast, so that great pressure of canvas could be carried on an upright keel. In fact, everything movable would be got to windward. In the old fisherman's own words, "If you had any pride (and we mostly had), a regatta started at leaving port and ended at the return, and no shift of ballast, sail or stores, was too much to gain a point on a rival."

The old open boats were built with gunwale and washstrake, but with the deck came the bulwarks and rail. The gunwale was bolted down to the timberheads, chocks were let in between the timbers to finish the deck up to the sides for'ard. Opposite the net room there was a piece to unship, and in that opening the roller, over which the nets were worked, was fixed when fishing. It was the only roller in the boat, so was known as *the* roller. There was a V-shaped groove in the stanchion each end, into which the loose washstrake was dropped when sailing. When decked boats came in, the gunwale and washstrakes ceased, and covering boards went right round on top of the timberheads in line with the deck. Stanchions were fitted down through the covering board and on the top of them a continuous rail was fixed with tenons on the tops of the stanchions and mortices about half-way up in the rail, then bolted askew (Fig. 41). The last boat Mr. Pezzack could remember with a notch in the beam for the mainmast was the *Sanders Hill* of Mousehole. Newlyn boats were the first to depart

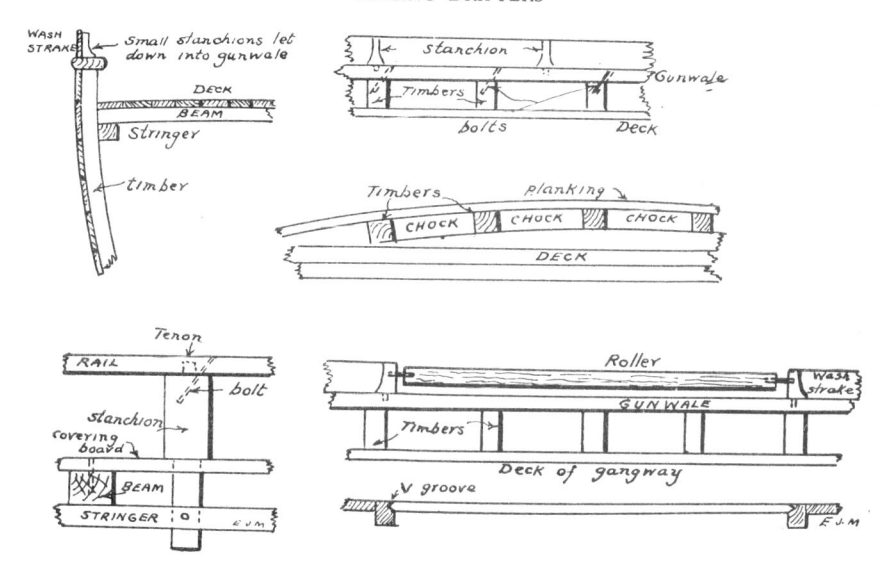

FIGURE 41

from the old round-bowed boats, somewhere about 1865, and to produce the yacht-like model. Mousehole and Porthleven soon followed, and a year or so later came the first of the fully-decked boats. At the International Fisheries Exhibition in London in 1883, the Committee held the Mount's Bay fleet to be the finest in the world, racing daily to land, and serve a fresh fish market.

The mackerel drivers were never dandy or cutter-rigged in Mount's Bay, but occasionally the dandy rig was used for the small pilchard boats. When the wholly-decked boat with cabin aft came into use, this shifted the net room, fish room, etc., rather more forward than in the open boats, and in some cases the shifting ballast wings were removed to the sides of the fish room, next the sheat or net room. There was practically no difference in rig, and only a slight increase in size from the time of the first decked boats in the early seventies to the coming of the motor. A few had square transom sterns, and one or two counter or elliptical sterns were introduced in the eighties.

Plate 101 is of a typical Mount's Bay lugger, 59 P.Z., *Temperance Star*. Note the short jenny boom at the foot of the mizzen, the topsail bowline, tack and sheet, whilst in Plate 104 the luggers have the mizzen sheet hooked to the clew.

Plate 102 shows a transom-sterned mackerel driver entering harbour; she also has a jenny boom. The big drifter L.T.689 is the 38-ton *Minnie*, built 1896. Plate 103 gives some idea of the picturesque scene when the herring fleet was putting to sea, c. 1885. The lugger 147 P.Z., *Favourite* has a bowler-hatted crew hauling on a warp to the bows of *Branch*, which is also seen in Plate 117 when she was registered at Lowestoft. A big Plymouth cutter is in the background, two lute-sterned Lowestoft dandies are ahead with sweeps out, with one of the elliptical-sterned drifters to starboard.

Plate 104 shows two mackerel drivers standing out to sea, with St. Michael's Mount almost hidden in the mist.

About the eighties a few luggers were built with elliptical sterns, and P.Z.55 *St. Michael* is seen coming out of Penzance harbour with some of the crew tailing on the fore sheet; the tack of the foresail goes to a short iron bumpkin, but P.Z.167 astern has hers hooked to the stemhead (Plate 105).

Thanks to Mr. L. J. B. Corin, of Penzance, who loaned me his copy of Dixon Kemp's sixth edition, *c.* 1888, I have been able to draw up from the tables of offsets, etc., contained therein a set of plans of one of these rather rare counter-sterned luggers. The boat P.Z.104 *Colleen Bawn*, built by J. R. Wills at Penzance, is described as one of the fastest luggers yet built in the West. Plans 12 pages 323-6.

Length overall, 51 ft. Keel, 48 ft., rake of sternpost 1 ft. 4 in.; extreme breadth 14 ft. 10 in.; mid-section 1 ft. 8 in. ahead of centre to waterline; C.B. abaft centre L.W.L. 4 in. Displacement 36 tons, displacement per inch at load line, 1 ton 2 cwt. Tonnage B.M. 41, ballast 14 tons, draught for'ard 4 ft., aft 6 ft. Siding of keel, stem and sternpost, $6\frac{1}{4}$ in., moulding (depth) of keel, 9 in. Siding of frames, 4 in. Room and space, 1 ft. 5 in. Planking, $1\frac{1}{2}$ in.

The first bulkhead, A, of the footline room is 13 ft. 9 in. abaft the fore perpendicular; bulkhead B of the fish room is 6 ft. from A, C of the net room is 6 ft. from B, and D of the cabin is 7 ft. from C.

Foreside of foremast is 10 ft. 6 in. from outside of stem and aft side of mizzen mast is a similar distance from taffrail. The midship section is sharper than in *Ebenezer*, but there is not quite so much deadrise as in *Boy Willie* a decade later. Foremast, deck to sheave, 37 ft. 6 in., dia. at deck 11 in., at sheave $6\frac{1}{2}$ in.

Mizzen mast, deck to sheave 29 ft., dia. at deck $10\frac{1}{2}$ in., at sheave $6\frac{1}{2}$ in., mizzen pole to halyard sheave 8 ft. 6 in.

Outrigger 30 ft., 20 ft. outboard.

Fore lug: Head, 28 ft.; foot, 34 ft.; luff, 26 ft.; leech, 46 ft. Area, 980 sq. ft. Clew to weather earing, 36 ft.

Mizzen lug: Head, 24 ft.; foot, 29 ft.; luff, 20 ft.; leech, 41 ft. Clew to weather earing, 36 ft. Area: 730 sq. ft.

A sail cut to the dimensions given has the clew only 1 ft. from outrigger sheave, and when moved on to the foremast it will not sheet fair. I have drawn one which will, by shortening the leech to 35 ft., and the foot to 28 ft.

Mizzen topsail yard, 31 ft.; jackyard, 8 ft.

Sails were usually made of cotton and tanned with oak bark and catechu.

## CONSTRUCTION OF A MACKEREL DRIVER

'The keel, usually of American elm, was laid horizontally on the blocks, then stem

FIGURE 42

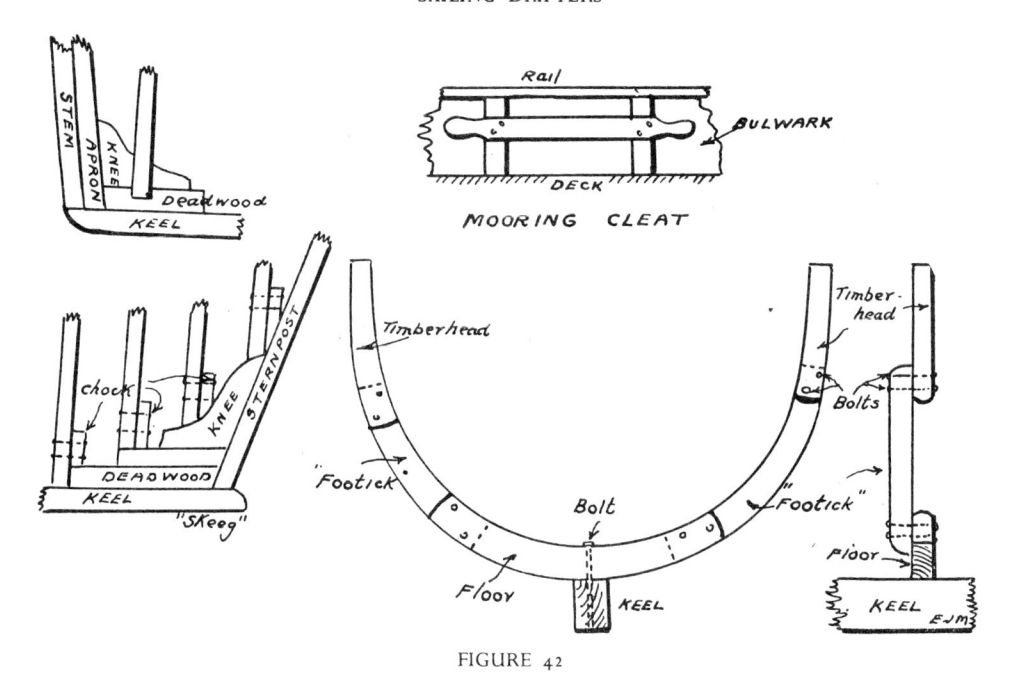

and sternposts of oak were erected at either end, and the deadwood built up aft and for'ard. The oak frames were set up vertically at right angles to the keel, so that when the boat was launched and trimmed to her correct waterline, the frames raked aft.

The first frame for'ard was close to the bottom of the stem and tapered to a wedge point which was bolted to the deadwood, as did the next two frames. The frames aft butted on the deadwood, and were bolted to chocks aft of the foot of each. The continuous frames were usually made in five pieces—the floors were 4 in. sided, 12 in. moulded over the keel, 6-7 in. at the bilges. For'ard of amidships on the fore side of the floors were bolted the "footicks"—futtocks—which extended round the turn of the bilge to the topsides, where the timber heads were bolted on the after side. Aft of amidships the footicks were bolted on the after side of the floors, and the top timbers on the fore side of the footicks. Thus bolted, the top timbers or second footicks were always in line with the floors. On a 42-ft. keel there were usually 33 timbers, but room and space varied with different builders (Fig. 42).

In some of the later boats stanchions were bolted to second footicks, which extended to the covering board.

Beams were of oak, the garboard strakes, middle part of bilge, stringers, and all large bendable work of American elm. When funds ran to it, oak planking was preferred, if not, Norway deal or pitchpine was used. Decks were of yellow pine. The old boats had wash strakes, but in the later luggers the bulwarks were 20 in. high to capping.

## WEST CORNISH LUGGERS

The size of the hatches was to fisherman's choice, and often the net and fish room hatches were not quite central, but nearer the starboard side. Coamings were 6 in. high. Fore and aft were cleats from stanchion to stanchion (Fig. 42).

Between the floors was cemented and all ballast was inside, the main weight along the bottom under the fish and net rooms. At the sides were wings which also contained ballast, always moved over to wind'ard side when sailing. When at anchor these wings had ballast filled up to the waterline (Fig. 43).

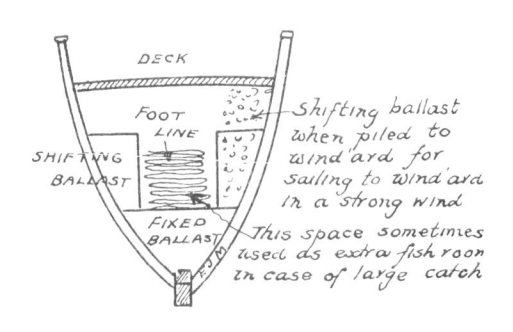

FIGURE 43

FIGURE 44

The fishermen who were to sail the boat frequently helped to build her, as did the late William Pezzack, from whom much of this information was obtained.

To allow the foremast to be lowered when the lugger was lying to her nets, it was stepped in a mast case or tabernacle inside a long narrow slot in deck, known as the "scottle" (Plate 106) which had grooves cut in the sides into which a very strong chock was dropped to prevent the mast coming aft. When the mast was upright, the scottle was covered by a hatch—the "mast covering board," the coaming being about 3 in. high.

These details of construction can be seen in Plate 107 of a Mount's Bay lugger being broken up at Newhaven in October 1945. The peculiar bolting of the frame timbers, the mast step on the floors, stringers, beams with knees on aft side in the way of mast, the tabernacle or trunk with side bridges, and the carlings of the scottle, the covering board with eyebolts for halyards and burton, stanchions and bulwarks with breasthook inside stemhead, and hawse timbers below, can all be identified.

Plate 108 is a close-up of the mast, etc., before demolition was as far advanced as in previous plate. The squared heel of the foremast rests in the trunk, with chock in sides of carlings, abaft is the mast covering board or hatch, which covers the open scottle.

Plate 109 shows the stemhead with the tack hook passing in through a square hole in the stem plate. Note shoulder worked to prevent it going too far home, the breasthook on inside of stem, and the roller to starboard over which the foot line was drawn inboard, the eyes in covering board, and cleat above.

The heel of the foremast was well rounded to facilitate lowering, which was done by slacking away the forestay or burton. When lowered, the foremast rested on the "mast thwart," with its head between the mizzen mast and its backstay. In order to permit this, the scottle was slewed slightly to port. The most important thing after raising the mast was to put the chock in place, otherwise the first plunge the boat took would have been disastrous. Note the following differences to East Cornish practice—no crutch is used, and the mast lowers to port, not to starboard, and no wire was used in the rigging. The early boats had hemp, the later manilla rope, coir was only used for warps and buoy ropes, where its elasticity was an advantage. All blocks were rope-stropped and running gear was made fast to cleats, as there were no pin rails (Figs. 42 and 44).

The late Mr. William Pezzack writes:

"In the days of my youth the launch was a great time. There was a tea for the crew and builders, with a launching cake. In the drinking days there was a jar of beer alongside the boat for the drinkers (before my time). Just about my birth James Teare came from the Isle of Man with his teetotalism, and my father was one of the first society formed at Mousehole. Before that every boat had a bottle of wine or brandy tied to her stem top. The christener, usually the owner's daughter or wife, stood with the bottle in her hand, with the ribbon from its neck to the stem, waiting for the first start. As soon as the boat moved, she aimed at the stem, and to smash the bottle with a direct hit on the iron was the successful christening. In my days the teetotallers used a bottle of spring water, the drinkers wine.

The words were few, just 'Success to the *Wasp*,' or whatever name was given, usually kept secret until that moment. I think since the gusto has gone out of the fishing, it has all become very tame. At Mousehole it was a straight launch from the bank down to the beach, with plenty of greased blocks, spars under the bilge, with the short ends of spars as rollers on them, and a check rope to the stem to prevent her taking charge, and a man at the stem easing her away. Uncle Henry was hired for a shilling the launch to 'holla.' Shouting 'Alaw boat haul, alaw boat haul, haul, haul,' as they got her to go, and when she began to run, 'Stump and go, stump and go' until it was 'two blocks,' then fleet out your tackles and begin again."

From Mr. R. Hosking, better known by his nickname "Billy Bosen," and now (1949) aged 84, I have obtained further information concerning the building of luggers, which he was good enough to send to Mr. H. Oliver Hill.

It was the usual practice for the owner to purchase the timber for the hull, including that for all masts and spars, from Southampton, and this cost about £140. A local boat-builder would then build from this material for £1 per foot length of hull. Masts and spars were included in this price, but spares cost, fore or mizzen mast £2, 140 yd.

foresail yard 15s., 100 yard 15s., a spare mizzen yard also 15s., a jigger spar 5s., bowsprit boom 10s.

The hull was built in the open, there being a saw-pit at Newlyn about where the site of the Seamen's Mission is now, and was ready for launching in six weeks, and for sea within ten weeks from the start. The fastenings were one trenail and one galvanised nail per plank, at Porthleven two galvanised nails. It was customary to make all the trenails before building commenced, and put them in the local bakehouse to season before being very carefully fitted quite dry.

A hand capstan cost £10, made locally in the Newlyn Foundry in Foundry Lane, which closed down about seventy years ago. A compass and binnacle cost £4 to £5, net roller 10s., the iron for same and all ironwork, which was not a lot, was included in the cost of building the boat. A masthead lamp and lower light cost 30s. each, navigation lights of zinc £1 each, if copper 30s. each, and paraffin oil was 5d. a gallon.

Manilla anchor hawser, 30 fathoms, £3; iron anchor 30s. A boat could be rigged for £2, but the fore halyard blocks cost £3.

Paying up, generally once a year before the boat went to the North Sea fishing, was done by the crew for nothing, with paint costing 5d. per lb., some 20 lbs. being required, while the patent paint for the bottom cost another ten shillings.

Canvas for the sails cost 10d. yard, cotton 7d. a yard, and to make a suit would cost for materials and making about 1s. 1d. a yard. A 140-yard foresail costing about £6, and 100-yard one, £5. A 90-yard mizzen about £4 10s., a 40-yard jigger £2, and a 35-yard mizzen topsail £2 5s., with a 30-yard jib costing 32s. 6d.

A tarpaulin to cover the spare sails carried on deck, 30s. A fleet of nets numbered 42, of 87 yards each, costing with ropes and corks, but not footline, £1 each. Each member of the crew was responsible for providing the footline for four nets, and this came to 14s. per length for one net. Cork for buoys was 12s. a cwt. The men usually made their own oilskins, which came to about 10s., but a sou'wester would cost 3s. 6d. for a good one. Fifty-six mackerel nets were shot, no pole buoy being used, and the corked headrope kept the nets at the surface, but wooden buoys were used for herring nets, secured by buoy ropes. A good night's haul of mackerel would be four to five thousand, worth £1 to 5s. 100; herring, three last; pilchards three last, at 7s. 1,000. The fish were counted and sold by the hundred, but at St. Ives a gurry was sometimes used as a measure, holding about 800 large herring. For mackerel the grounds lay sixty miles W.N.W. of the Scillies, or about a hundred miles from Newlyn. In winter they would fish in the bay or off the Lizard. Somewhere about the time of Queen Victoria's Jubilee, Mr. Hosking was down off Ushant when the lugger was blown away in a south-easter, and they had great difficulty in getting into Plymouth. It was usual to ride to their nets in a hard blow, a "raft" was never used locally. The faithful work put in by these skilled boatbuilders can be judged by these words of Mr. Pezzack's:

"I can just remember the original of that old *Gleaner* whose model is in Penzance Museum. When she was building, after being planked but not caulked, heavy rain set in while she lay over on one side. She was so well built that she filled up so much with water that the old builder—that I knew well—gave a boy a big gimlet to bore a hole to let the water out. I think she was about 35 to 36 feet keel, so the scale of the model would be about ½ in. Old Captain Cary, who built the model, was the owner."

Speaking of breaming he says: "When I was a boy they used to 'brim' or 'brem,' as it was pronounced, the boats. They had a pitchfork on which was fastened a wad of

FIGURE 45

FIGURE 46

old net dipped in tar. They set fire to it, and one man held it against the side of the boat and melted the tar and pitch to bubbling point. Another man had a three-brushed tar brush and swept her down to the wood, filling up the seams and leaving her with practically one coat of pitchy tar. They had a bucket of water to dip the brush in when it took fire. It was a very blazy business, much enjoyed by small boys! It also killed all life, mussels and barnacles, that sometimes fastened in the seams." This operation can be seen in progress in Plate 96, and Fig. 45 shows the tools used.

He thus describes the making of the masts for a typical lugger with a foremast 10 in. diameter at deck line, and 5 in. at the head, usually made with a quarter sweep, sometimes a half sweep (Fig. 46): "The mast maker drew a diagram similar to one of these and marked the mast in six places, and according to the difference in the six places made a fat or lean mast, but never a straight-sided one. The 'half sweep' carried the roundness farther up the mast. The mizzen was 9 in. at deck line and about 5 in. at the head to allow for the live hounds of iron in its iron box for carrying the chain tye, also for strength to the mizzen pole for the topsail, which had very little stay, only the topsail halyards, and if there was much wind and the mast bending above the mizzen backstay, at the mast head and foot of the pole, the halyards would almost lie parallel to the pole for its whole length.

The rudder was an inch and a quarter oak plank with the feather bolted on two planks of about 9 in., and no taper. There was a 'ding rope' or 'ding chain' fastened to the top of the rudder and having a hook to go in an eye in the sternpost. The boats would often jump so quickly after a plunge as to raise the rudder, or in passing over a taut rope the rudder might lift, being so light and free in its gudgeons. The long straps of the pintles were extra strength to assist the bolts. The tiller was curved downwards without any ball at the steering end, and an iron strap at the after end to prevent it from splitting, with a wedge at the back to raise or lower the inner end (Fig. 47). In rough weather the helmsman had a low stool, but he often sat on the anchor cable, which was invariably coiled abaft the mizzen mast. This was known as the "cuddy rope," as it was stowed in the cuddy, as that end of the boat was called, in opposition to the "peak" for'ard. This rope was 60 fathom of hawser-laid hemp rope, tarred, and used for anchoring in stress of weather, towing, mooring, etc.

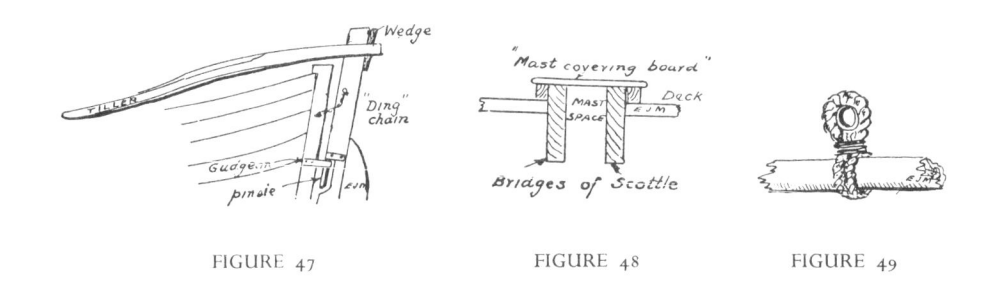

FIGURE 47          FIGURE 48          FIGURE 49

There were usually twelve hatches on the net room, in three rows resting on two carlings fore and aft. In the early boats the hatches over fish room and net room were separate, but in the later craft were in one continuous coaming, and the division was only apparent when the hatches were removed. There was no fixed rule, almost every boat had some difference in the placing of the hatches.

The jolly boat was usually 12 ft. long, of no regulation shape, but a good fat boat, capable of carrying a couple of crews off to an anchored big lugger, and fitted with a good transom for putting off with an anchor in an emergency. It was stowed on the net room hatches when sailing, but when getting in the nets it was between the mizzen mast and its backstay on the port side of the deck, as the nets were always worked over the starboard rail.

To get down into the peak, either the fish room hatch or the scottle was used; the latter, being some 10 in. wide would take an average man down easily. There was no companion for'ard. The scottle was just long enough to allow the mast, when resting on what was called the "mast thwart," to touch the mizzen mast head under the fastening of the mizzen backstay, and lie between the mast and the backstay. To allow this, the scottle was pointed slightly to port on the after end. The side bridges were strong to take the strain of rolling when the mast was being lowered, and the scottle cover would thus be about twice the diameter of the mast in width (Fig. 48).

If the foremast was lowered back, the jumpstay raised it to the limit of its pull, then the forestay was used to get the mast right up. When not in use, the forestay was made fast to a loop on the foremast and lay up and down the mast."

111 *MARY & EMILY*, P.Z. 533. OUT-RIGGER
Note ding chain, play on tiller head, traveller with double block for sheets, pinnate leading through single block end of outrigger.

112 TACKING IN A LIGHT WIND
Note peak of yard is on deck, leech of sail being worked round foreside of mast, tack not started.

110 MACKEREL DRIVER UNDER ALL SAIL
Note tack of forelug to weather bow, bowsprit lashed to stem and mast.

113  *EMULATOR*, 265 P.Z. c. 18
Note bowline from luff of t
sail, chocks between stan
ions with holes for "bolt
pump, rowing crutches, d
chain, chain tye for miz
halyards.

114  LUGGERS LEAVING
PENZANCE
Note step at foot of mizze
11 P.Z., big mizzen for
watch mizzen aft.

115  A TWO MIZZEN BREEZE, c. 1890
     *Fiona*, 207 P.Z. with big mizzen for'ard, small one aft.


116  BOAT GRAVEYARD, GALWAY, 1932
     Note flat floors in boat to left, sharp floors in centre lugger, clinker build of boat to right.

117  BRANCH, L.T. 580, AT LOWESTOFT

118  49 P.Z. AT WHITBY, c. 1860
Fore and aft decks with narrow waterways, typical of early boats.

Lighting when Mr. Pezzack first went to sea was a single candle in a lamp, used both for the cabin and on deck.

In the larger boats the fore side of the foremast was usually about 7 ft. from outside of stem, its height 40 ft. above deck, and dia. 10 in. at deck, 5 in. at head.

The mizzen mast was placed so that its after side was some 7 ft. from after side of sternpost, its height 44 ft. above deck, dia. 9 in. at deck, 5 in. at head. Both masts had travellers for the lugs, in the early boats bead parrels were often used, but later a solid or split iron ring was preferred (Fig. 6).

When a bowsprit was carried, it was about 25 ft. long, with heel lashed to the foremast and another lashing at stemhead, the spar was never stepped in bitts. When not in use, it was stowed in the "raft" or crutches on the port side.

I have only one photograph of a Mount's Bay lugger with a jib set (Plate 110). Note the tack of the fore lug has been taken to the weather beam opposite the foremast, the head of the capstan can just be seen above the bulwarks, the sweeps in the crutches, the mizzen topsail set to leeward, and the sharp steeve to the outrigger. The original is not very distinct, but her number appears to be 247 P.Z.

The outrigger was always to port, its heel being sufficiently far from the centre line of the deck to allow the spar to pass out over the quarter, where it rested in a wooden chock, and give the rudder head room to come over to port when the helm was starboarded. In some luggers it went straight out, in others the outer end came in to align with the centre of the masts. This spar was always sharply steeved up so that it would not dip too far when the lugger rose to a steep sea. If it was broken, it usually went just outside the stern and could be brought inboard fairly easily; a few minutes' work with an axe and a new heel was shaped to fit in the iron clamp, and a smaller mizzen was then set. The position of the heel depended on the height of the bulwarks, but it was generally a little for'ard of the mizzen mast. In the open boats it fitted into a clamp on the after net room thwart, in decked boats close to the coaming. The heel clamp was a metal strap, and there was a similar one on the chock on the quarter.

Plate 111 shows the outrigger of *Mary and Emily*, P.Z.533, with the single block for "pinnate" at outer end, traveller with double block for "sheets," and ding chain on rudder head.

At the slings the foreyard measured about 6 in. dia., the big mizzen yard 5 in., the second 4 in., and the jiggers about 4 in. All yards were fitted with oak battens under the slings to take the chafe. They extended for about a third of the length of the yards, to which they were lightly nailed, and then bound with three or four seizings of spunyarn. The slings were rope grommets just long enough to allow one complete round turn on the yard in addition to the bight into which the thimble was seized, bringing it snugly on top of the yard. This eye went over the hook of the iron traveller on the mast (Fig. 49).

## SAILS

The working sails were a fore lug containing about 145 linear yards of canvas, each cloth being 21 in. wide when made up, one large mizzen of 110 yards, second mizzen of 70 yards and the small mizzen or "jigger" of 35 yards. Two jiggers were always carried, so that in heavy weather one was set on the foremast, the other on the mizzen. There were usually two rows of reef points in all sails, except the big foresail, which had only one. When reefed right down, the jiggers were about 20 yards, and these sails were always of the newest canvas.

The procedure in reducing sail was always to set the mizzen then in use, as a foresail, and put the next size on the mizzen mast, and so on until the two jiggers were in use. Mount's Bay luggers generally had jenny booms fitted to the foot of the big mizzen and the topsail, extending from the clew about a quarter of the length of the foot, with the sheet hooked to the centre of the spar. All sails were bent to their yards by means of rovings at each eyelet, instead of a continuous lacing.

In summer a 70-yard jib and a 35-yard mizzen topsail were set. The jib was only used when sailing free or before the wind, never close-hauled. If boomed out, spinnaker fashion, the second lashing of the bowsprit was to a cleat or eyebolt instead of to the stemhead. The jib was seldom used except on a passage and few West Cornishmen set a staysail on the jump stay, as did the Manx and East Cornish fishermen.

Thanks to Mr. H. Oliver Hill, who wrote to his friend, Mr. Peter Hosking, a Newlyn sailmaker, it is possible for me to give an accurate account of the making of a suit of sails. He states:

"My method of cutting out sails I took from my father, instead of to-day's method, which is to draft out by scale. All lug sails from say a 180-yard to a 40-yard jigger mizzen were worked out as follows.

Foresail for *Albania*, afterwards called *Orion*, built 1897, 160 yards. The first cloth cut nearest the weather, called the 'mast cloth,' was 24 ft. 2 in. in length. The foreyard was 25 ft. The 'mast cloth' for her next sail (mizzen) was cut 20 ft. 8 in. Mizzen yard 23 ft. We never did measure it all round, but I have tried to give them to you in modern measurements (Fig. 50). Foresail, 160 yards. Head, 25 ft. Foot, 33 ft. Weather, 23 ft., lee, 41 ft. Diagonal, 39 ft.

First mizzen, 127 yards. Head, 23 ft. Lee, 36 ft. Weather, 21 ft. Foot, 31 ft.

Second mizzen would be 90 yards. Jigger, 50 yards. Topsail, 40 yards. Spinnaker, 70 to 80 yards. Staysail, 40 yards.

*Young John*, of St. Ives, S.S.18, still working from the port (1938) and about 50 years old, must be about 52 ft. on keel. Her foresail, 180 yards, was cut out, first cloth 25 ft. 2 in., and fore yard was 25 ft., so you can see the difference in cut of the two ports by comparing the two foresails.

St. Ives sails all narrower and higher in the mast. An 80-yard mizzen would work out about as follows: Lee, 28 ft., head 18 ft., weather 16 ft. 3 in., foot 24 ft., and diagonal 27 ft. 6 in.

There are measurements of sails in book which I think you had one time. Boat

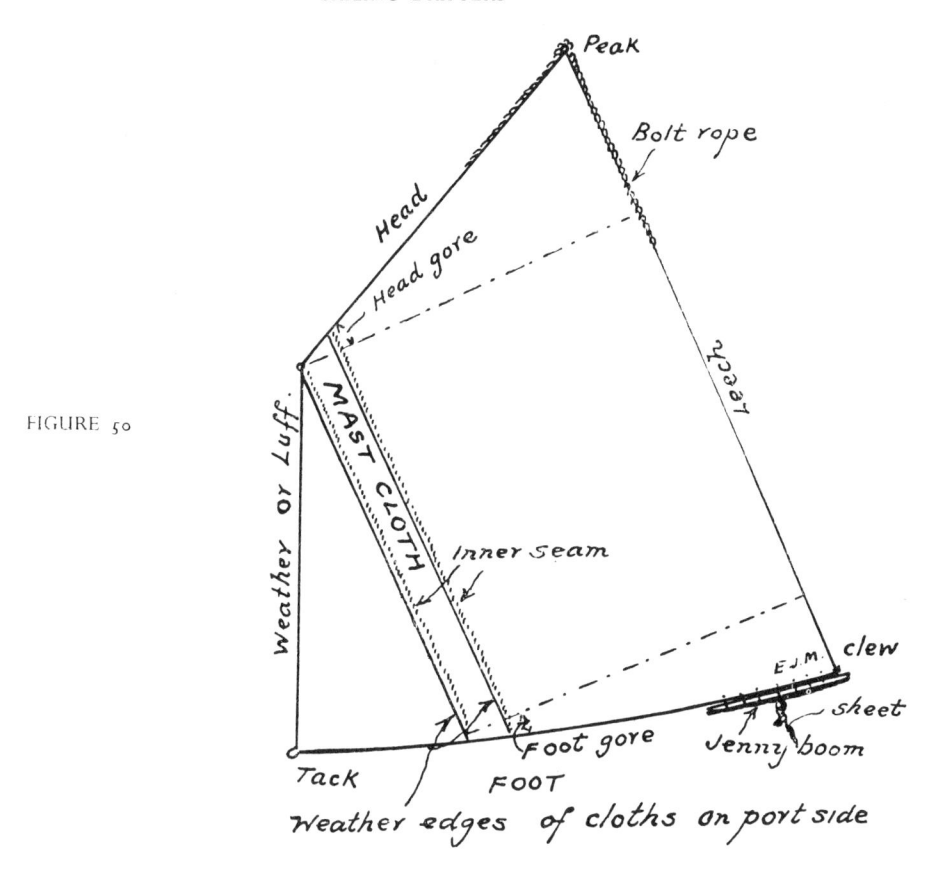

*FIGURE 50* — labels: Peak, Bolt rope, Head, Head gore, Leech, Weather or Luff, Mast Cloth, Inner seam, Clew, Sheet, Jenny boom, Foot gore, Foot, Tack. Weather edges of cloths on port side.

built by James Wills, name *Colleen Bawn*. I will put down the measurement of the foresail. Weather 26 ft., lee 46 ft., foot 34 ft., head 28 ft., diagonal 36 ft. In drawing it to scale I was not satisfied that measurements were correct.

St. Ives boats' sails I have mentioned were narrower, and their big mizzens would be sheeted out on a fixed boom or outrigger but Mount's Bay sails big mizzen would all have a jackyard on the foot, about 10 ft. long, and could do with less outrigger over the stern. The sail would set better when hoisted on the foremast in heavy weather.

Porthleven boats mostly had their foremast leaning aft a little. Their foresail had more peak, and they generally carried a smaller mizzen than Newlyn or Mousehole, owing to the difference in the build of the boats.

The shape of the St. Ives foresail was better for dipping, as they had rather shorter foreyard and longer weather. I may say that many of our foresails had a short end of rope kept in the tack, so that the bos'en would always hold on to it when dipping sail to go about ship, weather of sail being shorter. The wide-made sail, taking less mast, could be kept up longer in a breeze."

In January 1949 a further letter was sent to Mr. Hosking, who replied:

"As regards speed, there was always contention between Mount's Bay and St. Ives whose was the fastest boat. St. Ives masts were taller and used to carry more lofty sails. You could always recognise a St. Ives boat through this. Mount's Bay sails carried shorter masts and sails were longer on foot and head, foresail used to come aft further in the boat. My general opinion, and others as well, that a Mount's Bay boat could carry the sail longer in increasing wind. In making sails I had always to keep the difference of shape in view. I made the sails for the model of *Morning Star*, S.S.589, which was built by a shipwright, Wm. Bryant, who died recently (Plate 99).

The large jib and staysail were mostly for April, May and June, in the old sailing days when going beyond the Bishop, or to get to St. Mary, Isle of Scilly, to put their catches on the steamer trading daily to Penzance. This would be fifty or sixty years ago. The sails were made from light material. Question about time taken in making a suit of sails, may be just under two months. Foresail 200 yds., mizzen 120 yds., second mizzen 80 or 90 yds., jigger about 50 yds., staysail and topsail about 40 yds., and some jibs for light weather 80 to 100 yds. A 200-yd. foresail would take, maybe, eight days to make. The bowsprit I have heard called a ' bosperd.' "

The weather boltrope was 4 in. circumference, the others somewhat lighter.

The rigging was simple. In the big boats there was a fore stay on the foremast as well as a burton and the halyards. The fore stay led to a luff tackle, with the double block hooked on the tack hook at the stem. This was only used when one of the mizzen sails was set with its tack to an eyebolt halfway between stem and mast. When not in use, the fore stay went to a cleat at the foot of the mast, or it could be set up to leeward to give additional support to the mast. The halyard tye of chain or well-greased rope rove through a fore and aft dumb sheave about 18 in. below masthead and had a double block spliced into the lower end. The purchase was either a luff tackle, or two double blocks, with the lower block hooking into an eyebolt in the covering board abreast or just aft of mast and the fall belayed to cleat on stanchion.

The burton—or "fore backstay," as it was called—had a luff purchase, with single lower block hooked to an eyebolt some 2 ft. abaft the halyards, and the fall belayed to the backstay cleat. The jib halyards—two single blocks—belayed to cleat at foot of mast, when not in use they were twisted round the fore stay.

The fore sheets were two in number, one on either side, with the lower block hooking into a short iron bumpkin, usually called "bolts," about 5-9 in. long, projecting out from the bulwarks. (Fig. 28). The fore sheet consisted of two single blocks, with the upper one long and narrow, and fitted with a swivel hook (Fig. 44). The sheet was spliced to the tail of this block, led through lower block, up to first block at clew, and fall belayed to cleat on bulwarks. Some boats had a lower double block and fall rove through second sheave, and several men could tail on when sheeting home. The very big luggers often had two double blocks.

When dipping the fore lug, the sheet was unhooked from the clew of the sail, and as it came round the mast, the other sheet was hooked on. Originally only one sheet was fitted, and the lower block had to be unhooked, taken across the deck, and re-hooked in the "bolt" on the opposite side.

Plate 112 shows a lugger going about in a light wind, the tack has not been started and the peak of yard and leech of sail are about to be passed round the foreside of the mast.

The late Mr. William Pezzack thus describes the method of going about as practised in his youth:

"In working sails at night, if each man did not know his job all would be confusion, as there was no sort of light except in the binnacle on rare occasions. The smartest man managed the tack, another stood by the sheet, unhooked the clew as soon as the sail began to flap, and then ran round the mast with the clew, caught hold of the leech of the sail and hauled in on it until he had got the lee yardarm, which he landed in front of the foremast, at the same time giving a word to the halyard man to hoist or lower a bit. As soon as the yard arm was landed, the clew was hauled aft and hooked to the other foresheet. The halyard man passed the halyards the other side and hooked them, the boy passed over the backstay and set it up. The tack man, holding on to the tack, helped to pass the sail round the mast. When clew was hooked, halyards and backstay over, the captain would gather in on the foresheet, the clew man would run to the yard arm, say to the halyardman 'hoist away,' and as soon as the yard was off the deck, the clew man would pass the yard arm clear of the sail and let go. Down came the tack with the swing of the yard, the tackman hooked it to the stem, and as soon as there was no danger of its unhooking went to help the halyardman. The boy passed the end of the halyards aft to the captain, and all hands were at the halyards, which were finally put under the cleat, with two men to 'swig off' a little bow in the halyards and let them fall back quickly before the blocks could take it back, the other men and the boy behind jerking in that inch or two until when another inch was impossible. Possibly the tackman nearest the cleat, with the two halyardmen hanging on above, at the word 'belay' would catch a round turn round the head of the cleat in a flash, and not lose more than an inch if those behind were smart to let go at the word 'blay.' All sails with yards had their own yards to which they were kept bent, when not in use they were stowed under a tarpaulin on port side of deck; there was a wooden grating underneath to keep the sails above the water, so frequent and abundant on deck. There were three lashings to keep the sails to the side when stowed. The rings on port rail in which the four oars and the bowsprit were kept were known as 'raft crutches,' those for rowing, 'oar crutches' " (Fig. 51).

The mizzen mast, having a standing lug, was supported by the halyards going to starboard, the backstay to port, and the jump stay leading for'ard. The jump stay had a short pendant from the mast with a double block of a luff purchase stropped in the end. The lower single block hooked into an eyebolt in deck amidships, and the fall passed through the eye of the hook and belayed above with two half hitches.

The mizzen halyard tye, reeving through sheave set askew to port on the aft side, was usually of chain with the double block of a luff purchase at the lower end, the single block hooked into eyebolt in gunwale to starboard, abreast the mast, and the fall belayed to cleat on stanchions. Some boats had the halyards up and down the mast, and then a backstay was set up to starboard as well as to port. The backstay purchase was usually two single blocks.

The mizzen tack went to a hook bolted through the mast, or to a piece of chain round the foot of the mast, which jammed as soon as the strain of the sail came on it. The sheet consisted of a single part—the "pinnate"—sometimes of chain, which had

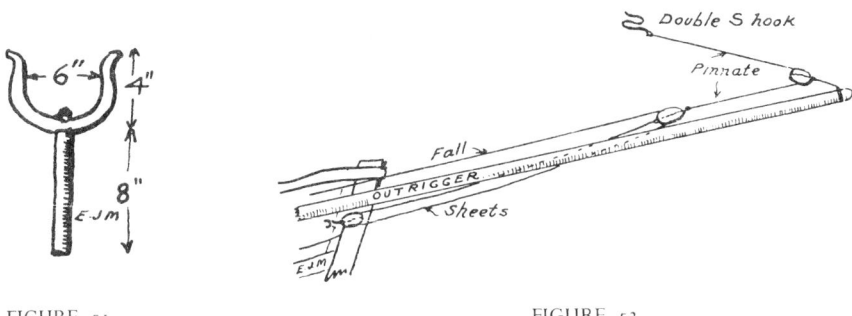

FIGURE 51              FIGURE 52

a curious form of double S hook (Fig. 52). This went into the clew cringle of the mizzen lug or to the thimble seized in the centre of the jenny boom. The pinnate rove through a sheave or a single block at outer end of outrigger, and had a single block spliced into its inner end. The "sheets," as they were known, led from the tail of this block through a single block hooked outside bulwarks, back to the outer block, and fall led inboard along top of spar to belay round a cleat fixed on it. In the small boats the standing end of the sheet was inboard and rove out through single block and back to belay inboard. Sometimes the pinnate had an iron traveller sliding freely on the outrigger, and the sheets were a luff purchase (Plate 111).

Unlike the forelug, which was dipped, the mizzen was always set on the port side of the mast, but the topsail on the lee side, so that frequently the mizzen was to port and the topsail to starboard of the mast. Immediately before tacking, the topsail was taken in and the halyards and sheet unbent. After the boat was about, the sail was re-bent on the leeward side of the mast, and hoisted to the pole head, chock-a-block, and the halyards set up. It was then sheeted home and finally the tack was hauled down.

Halyards and sheet were made fast to yard, and jenny boom respectively by an anchor bend (Fig. 53), a round turn and two half hitches, the first of which was carried round the standing part and under the round turn also, the second round the standing part only. The slinging of the yard would have to be shifted according to whether the sail was wet or dry, quite a small difference in the position altering the entire set of the sail.

The topsail halyards consisted of a long double-ended rope rove through a thwartship sheave in the masthead, and reaching to either bulwark, thus allowing the sail to be hoisted on either side of the mast. One end of the rope was bent to the yard, the other belayed to a cleat on the stanchions. When not in use, the halyards were twisted round the mizzen backstay or jumpstay, as can be seen in S.S.635 *Water Lily* (Plate 97),

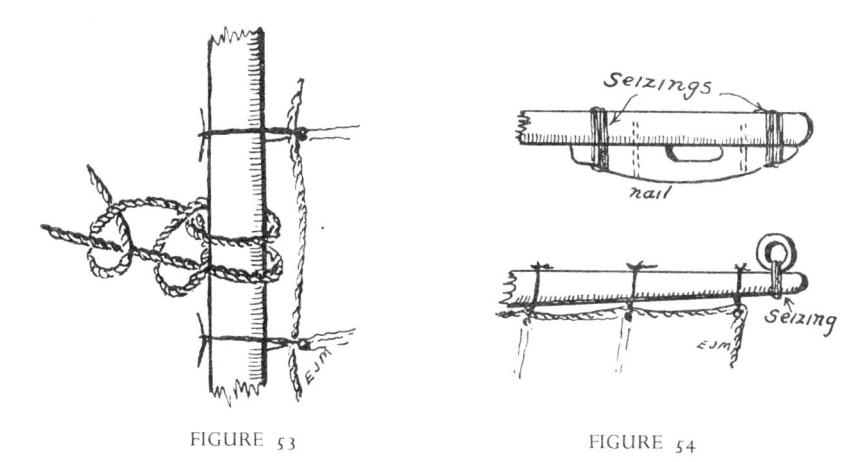

FIGURE 53   FIGURE 54

which also has an inhaul to the mizzen lug; the topsail sheet rove up and down to deck on starboard side of the mizzen, and the traveller on the pinnate will also be noted.

The topsail sheet led either through a thimble eye seized on top of the peak of the mizzen yard, or to a cleat seized or nailed on to the side of the spar (Fig. 54). It belayed to the tack hook on the port side of the mast.

The tack went in a variety of ways. In some boats it led up from lower end of mizzen lug yard, through a single block at clew of topsail and belayed at foot of jump stay; in others it was exact length to belay to the reef cringle in the bolt rope of mizzen lug, being fastened with a round turn and two half hitches (Fig. 55). A third way was to have an eye or a single block at the end of a pendant and reeve a whip purchase through it from the deck.

When on a wind the luff of the topsail was often set taut by a bowline. It consisted of a rope with a cringle spliced in the upper end working freely on a bridle spliced into the luff bolt rope. The lower end was made fast round the foremast as high as possible with a couple of half hitches.

The bowline can be clearly seen in Plate 113, a very fine contemporary model of 265 P.Z. *Emulator*, c. 1880, exhibited at the Fisheries Exhibition in 1883, and now in the Science Museum. Her keel length is 43 ft., overall length 47 ft., breadth 13 ft.6 in., depth of hold 7 ft.

The lug sails are more square-headed than in the boats to be built at the turn of the century, and the proportions are that the luff equals the length of the head and is two-thirds the length of the leech. The foresail is twelve cloths in the head, seventeen in

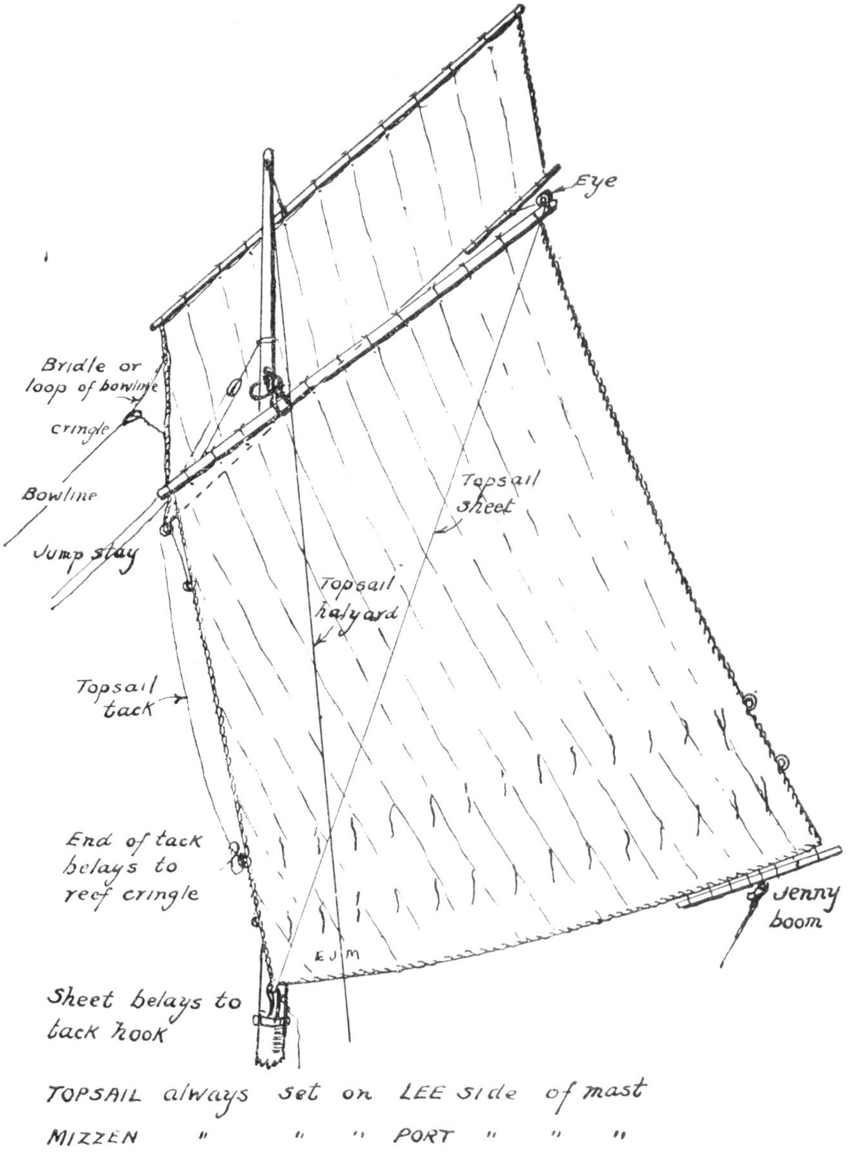
Eye
Bridle or
loop of bowline
cringle
Bowline
Jump stay
Topsail
sheet
Topsail
halyard
Topsail
tack
End of tack
belays to
reef cringle
Jenny
boom
EJM
Sheet belays to
tack hook
TOPSAIL always set on LEE side of mast
MIZZEN " " " PORT " " "

FIGURE 55

the foot, the mizzen eleven cloths in the head, fifteen in the foot. The burton has a runner purchase set up with two single blocks, and the mizzen halyards are chain. The fore sheet is single and shifted over every time the boat went about, the two holes for the "bolts" can be seen, also the one amidships for the bolt holding the leg in position. The topsail sheet leads through a small single block under the slings, and, as in many Mounts' Bay luggers, no bowsprit is fitted. Note the position of the rowlocks, one is to starboard just abaft the foremast, a second to port 5 ft. further aft, and another pair still further towards the beam.

A similar lugger, 11 P.Z. is seen leaving Penzance, c. 1882 (Plate 114). She is snugged down for the night as the large mizzen is set on the foremast, but not yet sheeted home, and the watch mizzen, or "jigger" is set aft. Other boats are being rowed out of the harbour. Note the step on the starboard side at the foot of the mizzen mast, on which the head of the foremast rested when lowered in harbour, as can be seen in Plate 122.

FIGURE 56

"Going about" c 1880
Penzance lugger, working sail round foreside of mast to pass from being on starboard tack on to the port tack.

The favourite amount of wind was known as a "two mizzen breeze," when the big mizzen was set on the foremast and the small one aft. Then the tack of the forelug went to the bumpkin or the tack hook on the stemhead, but when the smaller sails were set, the tack went either to the eyebolt halfway between stem and mast, or to the one at foot of mast, which was now stayed for'ard by the fore stay, the only occasion it was set up, except perhaps when it was used instead of the burton for lowering the mast.

Plate 115 shows *Fiona*, 207 P.Z., with other mackerel drivers, leaving Penzance, c. 1890, prepared for a two-mizzen breeze.

Luggers could not very well be hove-to, they had to be kept "trying" by the wind or scudding before it. In the '80's when a boat was going about, the fore sheet was unhooked from the sail as the helm was put down; as the boat came head to wind, the halyards were eased up and the leech of the sail hauled down until the peak of the yard could be shifted round the foreside of the mast (Fig. 56). The tack was *never* started. The sail was gathered in by the foot and leech and passed round the foreside of the mast, the upper block of the other sheet was now hooked in the clew cringle, the halyards sweated up, and the sail trimmed.

In contrast to the gay colours of the Scottish and East Coast luggers, the Cornish boats were very sombrely painted. Hulls were nearly always black, tar being the chief preservative used, with bulwark rail occasionally white. Some boats used a mixture of blacklead, which gave a dark grey colour. Inboard the bulwarks were generally white, with stanchions sometimes picked out in blue. The stemhead, rudder-head, end of outrigger and its chock, mastheads, and the band round the mizzen, or the entire pole mast, blocks, tiller and companion were white. In some boats hatch coamings, companion and scottle were blue, others had a blue diamond painted on the roof of a white companion, and scottle hatch. In accordance with the fashion of the day, when an owner died, the white was changed to blue as a sign of mourning for about a twelvemonth. The hatch covers were painted black, masts and spars varnished or dressed with pilchard oil.

Cornish boats were generally kept beautifully clean, with sails neatly stowed and ropes coiled down when in port. The fishermen took the greatest pride in the cut and set of their sails, and it was a rare sight to see a lug pulled out of shape by careless stretching. Their ideal was a full leech, straight luff and rounded foot, and a smart, well-handled lugger could outpoint most fore-and-afters. For speed and seaworthiness, considering their size, the West Cornish "drivers" were unexcelled, although perhaps rather lively in a seaway.

In 1885 one of the Newlyn luggers came home from Scarborough in 72 hours, while in 1910 three Penzance boats, *Emblem*, P.Z.117, *Nellie Jane*, P.Z.130, and *Children's Friend*, P.Z.619, set out from Mount's Bay for the North Sea fishing. For a time they were becalmed in the Bay, then the wind came away fine and strong, and sheet and tack were hardly touched until the boats were off the Yorkshire coast, when a heavy squall forced them to lower away. Even so the luggers were only 70 hours on the passage to Scarborough, a distance of nearly 600 miles.

Cornishmen nearly always dipped their lugs even for short boards, and seldom set their foresails a'monk or against the mast.

The local boat-builders were fine craftsmen, hull lines were sweet and above water the decks had bold curves fore and aft, giving the boats a very distinctive appearance when heeling to a fresh wind. Some idea of the honest work put in can be judged from the fact that *Freeman*, built at St. Ives in 1861, was still fishing out of Co. Down in 1930, where she was registered as B.77, although then fitted with a motor, and many a Porthleven boat, built in the eighties, was still at work in Ireland.

Mr. Corin kindly sent me a cutting dated May 8th 1947 stating that the counter-sterned *Elizabeth*, once owned by the late Abner Williams of Newlyn, and the *Ibex*, late of Mousehole, were still fishing out of Arklow, Ireland, although probably 70-80 years old, the only Mount's Bay craft left out of the many purchased from Cornwall when the local fishing declined.

Plate 116 is of the boat graveyard in Galway, 31st May 1932, with two ex-Cornish luggers rotting in their last berths. One is an old round-bilged craft, lying almost upright; the other, G.132, a later, fine-lined lugger, and a more striking contrast in hulls would be hard to find.

The West Country luggers also found favour amongst East Anglian fishermen, and many a fine drifter was built for them, especially at Porthleven, a port once noted for the quality of its work. I more than regret that all my efforts to find anyone in the town interested in its past glories have been ignored or unavailing.

Plate 117 shows L.T.580, *Branch* in Lowestoft harbour, and to judge by the reception committee on the quay, it would appear to have been a special occasion. A study of beards and head-gear is well worth while—I like the gent with a quilted waistcoat, a pointed beard, and, of all things, a pith helmet! Perhaps he had heard of Hocking's exploit, and was seeking passage to the colonies. If still living, the boys in the picture are now old men, and all is forgotten as to the reason for this splendid photograph. What was the solitary female doing in this masculine line-up descending in order of grandeur and social scale? On the foreyard will be noticed an iron handgrip, probably used for swinging the yard round the mast when dipping, the fore stay is made up on the foreside of the mast, note also the bead parrel with its hook into the rope grommet, and the chain halyard tye shackled to the eye of the hook.

The jump stay, or "Tommy Hunter," as it was called on the East Coast, is hooked to the peak of the fore yard, which is steadied by guys to either beam. It will be remembered that "Tommy Hunter" was the name given to the special rope strop used in conjunction with the jump stay when lowering the foremast to deck level in East Cornish luggers. When the West Country boats came to the North Sea fishing, no doubt they used it, and the name intrigued the East Angliamen, but they gave it to the jump stay. Was Tommy Hunter a contemporary of the Mathew Walker and the Burton whose names are immortalised in rigging?

The mizzen yard is topped up, the outrigger run in, and the spare sails stowed on the port side, bowsprit and sweeps are laid up in the lumber irons to starboard, and several other features show local, rather than Cornish, practice. The low bulwarks call for special attention, also the heavy rubbing strakes and the small wooden capstan.

*Branch* is also seen in Plate 103 alongside the quay at Penzance. To judge by the dark wale round the boat, on the starboard side of deck, she was Lowestoft-owned when the photograph was taken, c. 1885.

The West Cornish luggers fished all the year round, and were supplied with three fleets of nets. The mackerel season commenced in January and lasted until June or July. A fleet of nets numbered from 42 to 50, each net, roped and ready for sea, measured from 50 to 55 yards, with meshes $1\frac{1}{5}$ in., or about 30 to a yard, and were the property of the crew in the following proportions.

The master, if also owner, had fifteen to eighteen, but if only the skipper he had eight to ten, and the owner had an additional eight to ten nets on board. The second, third, fourth and fifth hands had six or seven nets, if they possessed them, the sixth hand, called the half-share man, and the boy, had none, and were both paid alike. In addition to the nets, each man owned as many lengths of line—the "foot line"—as nets, and these were fastened to the nets by ropes about six fathoms long, called "lanyards."

An interesting point is that in certain parts of West Cornwall, a short fathom of 5 ft., not 6, was frequently used, so much so that the 1868 Fisheries Act had to specify that all mention of fathoms meant one of 6 ft.

While the nets were being shot, the master took the helm, the second hand fastened the lanyards to the foot line, the third and fourth hands threw the nets overboard, one taking hold of the head—or back—rope, the other the foot. The fifth hand passed the lanyards from the net room to the second hand, the sixth tended the foot line as it went overboard to prevent it from getting foul, while the boy was at anyone's beck and call.

When all the nets were out, the foremast was lowered and boat and nets "drove" with the tide, hence the name, mackerel "driver." It was of vital importance to know just where to shoot the nets, as the shoals took one course at certain times of the year. A warm-water fish, mackerel frequent southern seas, but come up Channel as spring raises the temperature of the water, and their mottled marking resembles rippled water. The shoals swim high, so that it is essential that the head rope floats on the surface. Mackerel are not a delicate feeding fish like the herring, and do not shun polluted waters.

The fearless Cornish fishermen would go more than a hundred miles out into the stormy wintry seas to meet the shoals as they came northward, and it needs little imagination to think what conditions they faced, ofttimes riding to a sea anchor made from spare spars and canvas, and as soon as the weather moderated, beginning fishing again. An added danger came from the Atlantic record-breakers, driving at full speed through rain and fog—a sudden huge form looming out of the mist, a crash, and splintering of timbers, and six or seven men left to struggle for a few minutes before the cold waters closed over them for ever, with those on board the liner often heedless of the fate of men suddenly sent to face their Maker.

The fishing grounds frequently lay across the track of shipping making a landfall or taking a departure from the Bishop Rock or Lizard Lighthouses, and a tramp steamer, with a poor look-out, cutting through a fleet of nets, could do untold damage, difficult to replace if fishing was bad and money scarce. Then the agonised suspense of a man overboard with the lugger perhaps running at ten knots before a fierce sou-wester—a quarter of a mile or more before all hands could flatten in the sheets and bring the boat to the wind for the long, heart-breaking beat back to where they thought their comrade was. This, maybe, in the rain-soaked blackness of a winter night, with only a faint cry to guide them if the unfortunate fellow had not sunk immediately, handicapped as he was with oilskins and sea-boots, not to mention the icy water.

Yes, money is not the only price paid for fish.

The procedure when bringing in the nets was for the skipper and second hand to be in the net room, with the latter hauling in the backrope or headline of the net. Two hands were for'ard at the bows drawing the nets towards the boat and casting off the seizings, two more were at the capstan, and the boy was below in the foot line box, coiling down the warp.

When the mackerel season was over the boat was fitted out with another fleet of nets for herring, numbering 20 to 25, with meshes of about one inch, or 36 to the yard. The crew at this season was usually five men and a boy, but sometimes a sixth hand was carried. Fifth and sixth hands had no nets, and the boy was on a weekly wage. The nets were proportioned, ten to the master if also owner, if only skipper five, and the owner five or six, second, third and fourth hands had four nets each.

The summer herring fishing commenced about the end of June or early July, and the boats went round to fish off Ireland, or else in the North Sea, either east or west about. From early in the 17th century Cornish fishermen went to the waters round the Isle of Man and then on to Ireland, where the fishing lasted until the end of August or the beginning of September, although a few luggers sometimes remained for the winter fishing. In 1832 over 250 St. Ives and Mount's Bay boats were engaged in Irish waters, but the season was disastrous owing to a price combination among the buyers. In the 1880's and '90's many luggers went up as far north as the Shetlands.

The Cornishmen made the ports of Whitby and Scarborough their rendezvous for the North Sea summer fishing, and Plate 118 of 49 P.Z. heeled over on the mud within sight of the historic Abbey, gives an excellent view of deck arrangements in the luggers of the sixties. Note the scottle slewed to port with the mast covering board in position, the galley chimney, low bulwarks, and the coamings round the hatches. One of the crew is standing in the fore room, here a sliding hatch in the bulkhead gave access to the cuddy where the crew lived, slept and had their meals. The fish room is open, but the close-fitting hatches are over the net room, on the after coaming of which is the pump. The mizzen mast is against the fore side of the mizzen thwart, with the outrigger to port. Aft is a small flat hatch giving access to the sail locker. The bowsprit is laid up in the raft irons on the port side, and amidships the starboard movable topstrake is unshipped.

Whitby was noted for the excellence of its kippers; only the finest, hand-picked herring were cured, and smoked over fires made from oak shavings and billets—"bavins." The resulting kipper was a delicacy as different from the average salted and dyed abomination now passing under that name as day is from night. If the dye stains the water when the fish is steeped before cooking, what does it do to one's inside?

The smoke from the many curing houses, however, was scarcely likely to improve the colour of the washing hanging out to dry in numerous backyards, and even on the foreshore!

The North Sea fishing lasted until early October, the shooting and hauling of the nets being similar to the procedure in the mackerel fishing.

After arrival in their home ports, some of the luggers were fitted out with a third class of net—the pilchard net—which had a smaller mesh of $\frac{3}{4}$ in., or 45 to the yard, often shrunk herring nets were used. The fleet numbered fourteen to sixteen, belonging to owner, master and crew in similar proportions to the other nets. Each man had his own hand-line, about 50-60 fathom in length, with which he fished for hake, always plentiful in October and November, when they preyed on the pilchard shoals. In 1812 one Newlyn boat landed 600 hake, which sold for 2s. 9d. a "burn" of 21 fish, and as many as 40,000 were landed at Newlyn and Penzance within twelve hours after a successful night in the Bay.

When the pilchard season was over, herring or mackerel nets were put on board again and the boats fished out of Plymouth until January, or else went mackerel driving off the Scillies.

In the 1870's the cost of a big lugger, properly fitted out with nets, was about £600.

By the nineties the insistent call for speed and yet more speed saw hulls reach their extreme form, if seaworthiness was not to be sacrificed altogether. It is possible to form some idea of underwater lines by studying the three photographs of P.Z. 505 *Lizzie Tonkin*, 29 net tons, built 1892 at Porthleven and still fishing in 1930, fitted with a 26-h.p. motor, and owned by S. D. & J. H. Tonkin, Newlyn.

Plate 119 shows the broadside view, the deep draught aft, short bilge keels and one of the legs bolted through the bulwarks. Plate 120 gives an excellent view of the fine entry and sharp deadrise, the stem iron with the hole which took the tack hook in the days of sail, and the higher bulwarks fitted after a motor was installed, while Plate 121 shows the clean run, position of light boards, the wide rubbing strake, and the well-rounded quarters. A stump foremast and a gaff mizzen with boom have replaced the spars and sails of other days.

The old-fashioned Cornish fishermen never took to trawling or the ketch rig, and the lug remained popular to the last. An odd boat or two converted to dandy rig, but it never caught on. One is seen in the foreground of Plate 122. She is fitted with a transom stern, the others have sharp sterns, and many have lowered their foremasts back on to the step on the mizzen mast, a usual practice when a boat was in harbour. *Veracity* was originally dandy-rigged, but soon changed to lug sails.

Strange to say, the Manxmen were so impressed with the Cornish drivers which came to fish in their waters that they abandoned their cutter and dandy rig in favour of the lug, a complete reversal of the practice on the East Coast in the seventies. The probable explanation is that deep water prevails around both coasts, and long boards could be worked when the boats were close-hauled, and with no shoals or sandbanks to worry about, the handiness of the fore and aft rig was not an essential.

Towards the end of the 19th century some very fine luggers were built, and as they represent the final development of the West Cornish mackerel driver, it is fortunate that the lines of one, P.Z.602 *Boy Willie* were taken off by a fellow S.N.R. member, the late Philip J. Oke, whose efforts on behalf of the Coastal Craft Sub-Committee of the Society have done much to preserve the memory of the old sailing craft. Plans 13 pages 327-9.

In the more modern luggers the steam capstan has replaced the flywheel capstan, which in turn had superseded the earlier hand-worked one, but as the boiler and the cooking stove were both in the cabin, which provided living and sleeping accommodation for six men, not to mention the unfortunate boy, who was cook, steward, cleaner-up, stoker, etc., the atmosphere below in the hot summer months must have approached that of Dante's Inferno.

*Boy Willie* was built at Newlyn in 1897 by Henry Peake for James Pender of Mousehole, and measured 52 ft. 5 in. L.O.A. Beam 14 ft. 10½ in., depth inside 7 ft. 3 in. Length B.P. 51 ft. 5 in., length of keel 47 ft.

The scantlings were:
Keel, 6 in. sided, 12 in. moulded.
Stem, 6 in. sided, 8 in. moulded at heel, 6 in. at head.
Fore apron, 6 in. sided, 6 in. moulded at heel, 4 in. at head.
Sternpost, 6 in. sided, 9 in. moulded at heel, 6 in. at head.
Aft apron, 6 in. sided, 6 in. moulded at heel, 5 in. at head.
Floors, 4 in. sided, 12 in. moulded over keel, 6 in. at head.
First futtocks, 4 in. sided, 6 in. moulded at heel, 5 in. at head, bolted on fore side of floors.
Second futtocks, 4 in. sided, 5 in. moulded at heel, 4 in. at head, bolted on aft side of first futtocks.
Beams, 5 in. sq. Carlings, 5 in. sq. Stringers, 6 in. by 4 in.
Coamings, 12 in. by 3 in., 10 in. high from deck.
Bulwarks, 21 in. high. Rail, 4 in. by 2 in. Platform bearers, 4 in. by 3½ in.
Planking: Deck, 5 in. by 2 in. Bulwarks, 1 in. thick.
Side planking: Top strake, 9 in. by 3 in. Bilge strake, 8 in. by 3 in.
Planks amidships, 6 in. by 2 in. Covering board, 7 in. by 2 in.

Accommodation below was a store for'ard for sails and gear, next the foot line room, fish hold and net room, on after bulkhead of which was the pump. Access to the cabin aft was by a companion, headroom between beams 5 ft. 3 in., the usual bunks and locker seats were on either side, and across the stern, the boiler and stove were against the fore bulkhead.

On deck the foremast was stepped in the usual tabernacle or trunk with side bridges 2½ in. thick, aft of mast was the scottle. To starboard was the capstan, next the hatches with covers 1 ft. wide and 2 in. thick, scudding holes about 20 in. long and 5 in. wide, were cut in deck planking to allow fish falling on deck to be swept down into the wings below. Covers were dropped in when fishing was over. Coamings were some 10 in. above deck and on after one was the pump and lantern spear. Then came the chimneys for boiler and stove, the companion with sliding roof just for'ard of mizzen mast, to port was the chock to take the heel of the outrigger, and another on the quarter where the spar went outboard.

The boat was steered with a long wooden tiller, on the port rail were the raft irons, about 1 ft. 3 in. dia., and below the rail were sockets to take the iron "bolts" for the fore sheets. For'ard of the foremast and aft of the mizzen were mooring cleats bolted across two stanchions, with cleats on the faces of suitable stanchions where the running gear belayed. The 6 in. by 5 in. bends were faced with $\frac{1}{2}$ in. iron rubbing strakes, and there were two irons on top of the rail.

The foremast was 40 ft. from deck to head, 11 in. dia. at deck, 6 in. at sheave, with an iron band at head with lug eyes for the jib halyards for'ard and the backstay aft.

The mizzen mast was 37 ft. 6 in. deck to hounds, dia. $10\frac{1}{2}$ in. at deck, with a 10 ft. 6 in. pole topmast, 6 in. dia. tapering to 4 in.

The bowsprit was 28 ft. overall, with 15 ft. outboard and 6 in.-4 in. dia. When not in use it was always carried in the raft irons. Outrigger was 30 ft. overall, with 20 ft. outboard, 10 in. dia. tapering to 6 in.

The fore lug, made from 165 linear yards of canvas, had an area of 993.3 sq. ft., and was bent to a 32 ft. yard, 6 in. dia. at slings, tapering to 3 in. The small fore yard was 21 ft. long.

The large mizzen was made from 125 yards of canvas, had an area of 568 sq. ft., and was bent to a 26 ft. 6 in. yard, 6 in. dia. at slings, tapering to 3 in. Along the foot from the clew was a 7 ft. $2\frac{1}{2}$ in. dia. jenny boom. The small mizzen had 90 yards, and the jiggers 45 yards of canvas.

The mizzen topsail took 40 yards, was 92.125 sq. ft. in area, and was bent to a 26 ft. 4 in. yard, 3 in. dia., with a 9 ft. 8 in. jenny yard of $2\frac{1}{2}$ in. dia.

The area of the working sails was 1,653.425 sq. ft.

For passage making in fine weather, a jib made from 60-100 yards of canvas and a 40-yd. staysail were set. The lugs were peaked higher than was the custom in the eighties.

*Boy Willie* was still fishing up to the war, fitted with a motor. Plate 123 of her at Mousehole in February 1936 shows the fine run aft, bilge keel, leg, wheelhouse, etc. Plate 124 shows the sharp deadrise of floors and the fine entry, an interesting comparison with Plate 125 of *Ebenezer*, built 30 years before.

What the fisheries meant in terms of local employment can be realised from the following figures. In 1832 Newlyn had 100 drift boats, Mousehole 20, and St. Ives 25.

119  *LIZZIE TONKIN, c. 1920*
   Note deep draught aft, leg, bilge keel.

120  *LIZZIE TONKIN, c. 1920*
   Note rise of floors, scud hook hole in stemhead, legs on either beam.

121  *LIZZIE TONKIN, c. 1920*. STERN VIEW
   Note clean run, round bilges, top of rudder head cut to take tiller.

122 NEWLYN HARBOUR
   Note transom sterned boat is dandy rigged, others have foremast lowered on to mizzen step.

123 *BOY WILLIE*, MOUSEHOLE, 1936

124 *BOY WILLIE*. BOW VIEW
   Note sharp floors, round bilges, face of stem chamfered between stemhead and forefoot.

125 *EBENEZER*, 1936. BOW VIEW
Note contrast in rise of floors to *Boy Willie*, typical of difference between St. Ives and Mount's Bay boats.

126 OLD HARBOUR, NEWLYN
283 P.Z. *Breadwinner*

S.S. 26 LAID UP AT LELANT, *c.* 1936
Note mast is stepped in tabernacle on deck.

128 LUGGERS LAID UP AT LELANT, c. 1936
S.S. 99, S.S. 626 *Gratitude*, S.S. 18 *Young John*, built 1888, S.S. 340 *Ebenezer*, built 1867, S.S. 65 *Freeman*, S.S. 89 *Gleaner*.

129 MANX DANDY, COMMONLY CALLED A "LUGGER", c. 1883
Note pole mast, gaff topsail, standing lug on mizzen, lead of main sheet, single bowsprit bitt, fine run.

In 1849 Penzance had 300 large boats, employing about 2,000 hands. In 1859 St. Ives had 50 first-class boats, average crew five men and one boy, 60 second class, four men and a boy, and 290 seine boats, 30 tow boats, and ten followers.

| | | | | | | |
|---|---|---|---|---|---|---|
| In 1870 St. Ives | 86 first-class | 100 second-class | - | - | 602 persons | |
| Mousehole | 55 ,, | 40 ,, | - | - | 385 | ,, |
| Newlyn | 90 ,, | 40 ,, | - | - | 730 | ,, |
| In 1872 Penzance | 41 ,, | 466 ,, | - | - | | |

One thousand, three hundred and eighty-nine hogsheads of pilchards were caught in Mount's Bay, Penzance sending away 3,300 tons of fish, while St. Ives took 3,759 hogsheads. Two years before a record had been set up when 5,600 hogsheads, or 16½ million fish were taken in *one* seine.

In 1877 all told there were 538 boats and 2,241 men. In 1884 2,700 men. In 1885 Newlyn had 110 big mackerel drivers and Mousehole 66. Plate 126 shows the old harbour at Newlyn at low water with many luggers clustered together inside, while others lie on the strand, propped up on legs.

In the 1905 *Olsen's* I can trace 134 first-class boats registered at Penzance, and 81 at St. Ives. In 1910 numbers had fallen to 98 and 66 respectively, but by 1923 only 15 sailing luggers survived at Penzance, all with motors, with nine similarly fitted in the St. Ives register. A newspaper cutting I have, dated 17th May 1913, vividly proves the tremendous decline of the Cornish fisheries in the opening years of the 20th century.

"On a grey Sunday afternoon, near about sundown, we walked to Lelant, where the St. Ives boats are laid up. There, on one side of the broad sand and mud flats of Hayle harbour, we saw a fleet of seventy or eighty boats, mostly luggers, moored up with old chains and rotting ropes to the rusty railway lines of the old broad gauge along a grass-grown quay. In local phrase, they were the St. Ives boats that have died. The unpainted hulls of many were ripe and rotten. On their still standing masts, the running gear, left as it returned from sea for another season that never came, had flapped in the wind till it parted. Only one boat of all that laid-up fleet was being repaired, perhaps not for the St. Ives fishing. The picture of that silent dead boats' graveyard remains vividly in our minds. It impressed upon us, more than all the sometimes contradicting representations we have heard, far more than angry protests, the decline of the West Cornish fisheries."

Plate 127, of S.S.26, a St. Ives boat, shows the mournful spectacle of a boat, once her owner's pride, falling into decay.

I think the following factors may well have contributed to this tragic state of affairs:

(1) The penny-wise, pound-foolish intensive inshore trawling over local feeding grounds, and the catching of immature fish.
(2) The dumping of tens of thousands of unsaleable fish, causing their kind to desert the waters.

(3) The enormous increase in costs when wooden luggers, with simple gear, made locally, gave place to craft fitted with expensive engines, probably burning costly foreign fuel, and every item many times the price which satisfied men years before.

In the 1930's history repeated itself when, following the economic blizzard which struck our island, dozens of boats, fitted with motors, were laid up at Lelant, among them our old friend *Ebenezer*, built 1867 (Plate 128).

Since then generations of stalwart fishermen have walked her decks, and slept in those cramped bunks. Boys have grown to be fathers, and lived to see grandsons take their place. Yet still the grand old lugger had carried on—*Ebenezer*, of St. Ives, designed by one Wm. Paynter, who was building boats when Victoria was but a young Queen, a mute testimony to the honest toil of now unknown craftsmen, long gone to their rest. Those timbers, bleached with sun and rain, snow and frost, tell of days when proud clippers, loveliest of Ocean's queens, laden with the precious teas from the Orient, made their numbers at the Lizard—of wool ships storming up Channel in wintry gales to be in time for the January sales in London—of days when upwards of 400 sail sheltered in Mount's Bay—of steamers, then the world's finest, now long forgotten, whose ribs rest amongst the rocks the fishing boat has avoided—of the turn of the century, when a great Queen died, and her son, married at the time the boat's keel was laid, took the crown—of the awful days when U-boats sank millions of tons of shipping in the Chops of the Channel—of great convoys escorted by seaplane and airship—of the years of hope and depression following one war, ere the beginning of another—the old hull has seen them all. Now, with open seams, she lies in that quiet backwater alongside other craft which, too, have passed their day.

In the 1930 *Olsen* I find the names of 34 motor boats registered at Penzance, and 25 at St. Ives, *but no sail*.

*Sic transit gloria.*

CHAPTER TEN

## ISLE OF MAN

THE history of the Isle of Man is bound up in the fortunes of the herring fisheries. Is not a Deemster, on taking office, sworn in by the following ancient oath:

"By this book and by the holy contents thereof, and by the wonderful works that God hath miraculously wrought in heaven above and in the earth beneath in six days and seven nights, I do swear that I will without respect of favour or friendship, love or gain, consanguinity or affinity, envy or malice, execute the laws of this Isle justly betwixt our sovereign Lord the King and his subjects within this Isle, and betwixt party and party, as indifferently as the herring backbone doeth lie in the midst of the fish—so help me God and by the contents of this book."

I cannot help thinking that if politicians of every party took and adhered faithfully to such an oath, the world would be a happier place in which to live.

I am indebted to Mr. and Mrs. B. Megaw for permission to make use of their notes on early Manx fishing craft which appeared in the *Mariner's Mirror*. Until 1265 the island owned allegiance to the Kings of Norway, hence the Viking influence is very strong in the design and build of the open boats—the herring scowtes—used in the fishing until well into the 18th century. One of the earliest references to herring fishing is during the episcopate of Bishop Thomas (1334-48), and the Church claimed tithe on all fish until the end of the 18th century, but in the old days the Lords of Man regarded only the herring as their perquisite, claiming one in five, and they considered it was the duty of their subjects to assist annually in the equipment of the herring fleet and the successful prosecution of the fishing. Bishops, abbots, priors and archdeacons held permission to have and use herring scowtes, and fishing boats without payment of "tythes." A statute of 1613 states that small boats engaged in the herring fishing during the season were obliged to pay to the Lord of the Island "two Maze of the best fish," and the scowtes "fower Mazes for all their Custome during the Tyme of Fisshinge." These boats were obviously very small, as in 1677 the cost is given as 30s. to 40s. each, a low price even in the currency of those days.

By an order in 1610 all farmers in the Island had to have in readiness eight fathoms of nets, furnished with corks and buoys, containing three deepings of nine score meshes upon the rope. This was undoubtedly an inheritance from the ancient Norse institution of ship levy, known as "leidang." Nobody was permitted to fish from Saturday morning till Sunday at night after sundown upon pain of forfeiture of boat and nets. As there was a Friday superstition against fishing for herring, this left only four days, so evidently our ancestors were "one up" on the five-day week! The Water Bailiff, or Admiral, was to take care to have all boats where the fish were, and to see they "drive for same." No man was permitted to shoot his nets until the Admiral or Vice-admiral had first taken in their flags, or given a watchword "if the night be dark, so that the men may know when to shoot the nets." Any offences meant a fine of 10s. to the Lord, and 20 days' imprisonment. If anyone met with a "scul" of fish and failed to reveal the fact to the next boat, so that information might spread to the fleet, that all could be "partakers of that blessing," he suffered a fine of 40s. and imprisonment. The first boat to discover herring was ordered to sound a horn.

In 1650 the catch was divided into eight shares, three went to the owner of the nets, one to the owner of the boat, and one share to each of four men, the usual crew. The Admiral and Vice-admiral were elected annually, and the Government allowed the former £5 and the latter £3 for the season, their boats carried a small flag at the topmast and their job was to conduct the fleet to the herring grounds. The offices are still maintained, but have lost much of their ancient importance. The late Mr. P. J. Oke mentions in one of his notebooks, now before me, that *Zephyr*, P.L.29, which he measured in 1935, was formerly owned by Levi Greggor of Peel, who was Admiral of the Fleet. Latterly the Admiral was attached to Peel, the Vice-admiral to Port St. Mary.

Evidently slackness and neglect to observe these orders resulted in the impoverishment of the inhabitants, as well as depriving the Lord of his customs and dues, as in 1687 an order was confirmed by the Tynwald Court that all masters and owners of boats and nets were to have them in good order by the 1st July, and to attend where fish were discovered, with a penalty of a fine of £3 on any master or owner neglecting to attend the fishing. I like the wording at the end, "shall attend with their Boates and netts at such place as the fish is found and discovered, when notice shall be given them thereof, either by the Coroner or Lockmen of the Sheading, and use all possible means to further and keep up the fishing according as it pleaseth God to offer the same."

The herring "scowte" was an open boat of pronounced Viking appearance, having a sharp bow and stern, with a curved stem and straight sternpost, a considerable sheer fore and aft, with a low freeboard amidships, only about two strakes deep. A single mast, stepped amidships, was supported by standing rigging and carried a yard slung symmetrically, which suggests a true square sail rather than a dipping lug. For rowing, four sweeps were provided, and no doubt the same number of thwarts. Such a boat is seen in an engraving by J. Goldar from a painting by Richard Wright, c. 1760 (Fig. 57).

The word scowte, or scoute, is generally considered to derive from the Old Icelandic *skúta*, a fast vessel carrying both sail and oars, as the Norse dialect was spoken in Man until the 13th century. A Celtic variant gives the word "skiff," a term used on the Scottish coast for an open boat similar in design to the Manx scowte.

Unfortunately, very little is known of the scowte, other than a reference in 1610 to the need for them to be "of the Burthen of ffour tunns," but boats of only two tons made up the herring fleet of the early 18th century, according to Bishop Wilson. By 1774 it is known they were from 20 to 24 ft. length in the keel, with a crew of eight

FIGURE 57

men, and the word "squaresail" superseded the old word scowte, in order to distinguish their rig from the fore and aft sails then coming into favour.

Between 1780 and 1830 the boats were mostly cutter-rigged, many converting from squaresails after the disaster to the herring boats, wrecked in Douglas Bay in 1787. The new boats were larger, running from ten to twelve tons, having a forecastle, and pumps were fitted to take the place of the "spoocher" or bucket previously used for baling. No stove was provided, the crew brought down their own food in provision wallets, or "murlins," ozier baskets carried on the back containing a bannock, oat cake or barley bread, some cheese, and the butter box. The mast could not be struck, and no rollers were fitted for handling the nets. A contemporary account says they were from 23 to 33 ft. on the keel, 13 ft. beam with 6 ft. depth of hold, cutter-rigged, and costing, when new, 70 to 80 guineas with nets. The smacks were larger, and cruised round the fleet as "fresh buyers," taking the catch into port; they also traded red herring to Liverpool, and to Leghorn, Naples and Genoa. The builders are mentioned as being uncommonly clever, and adroit in their business, constructing entirely by eye, never making use of line or rule, unless in laying down the keel. The boats were held in high repute, being handy, fast, and riding like ducks in a rough sea. They were mostly clench-built.

The smack *Maria*, registered in 1789, was of 46 tons burthen, and Fig. 58 is based on a design on a contemporary china dish. Her master was Richard Karran, and she hailed from Port St. Mary. Another smack launched from Crellin's yard, Peel, in 1793

*The Maria of Port St. Mary*

*Richard Karran Master.*

*1797*
*A "buyer" smack engaged in the herring fishery, after the design on a contemporary china dish*

FIGURE 58

was of 60 tons burthen. It is possible that the fishermen copied the cutter rig of these "fresh buyers" when they abandoned the squaresail in the old scowte.

The boats were seldom the sole property of the fishermen, and the produce of every night's fishing was now divided into nine shares. Two went to the owner of the boat, one to the owner of the nets, the remainder to six fishermen, two of whom were generally skilled seamen, the rest came at the beginning of the fishing season from the interior of the Island, leaving their womenfolk to cultivate the potatoes, and they returned well content if they earned sufficient fish to maintain their families until the next fishing. A pernicious custom was the pronounced dram drinking, a "fresh buyer," if in keen competition with a rival, would frequently expend twelve to twenty gallons of spirits in a morning, ere a cargo could be made up, presenting an "earnest" bottle to each lugger, with perhaps only a few hundred herring to sell. By the '40's this custom was slowly dying out, and a "fresh buyer" seldom distributed more than two to four gallons.

Like the Scottish and Cornish fishermen, with whom they had considerable contact, the Manxmen were very superstitious, having certain lucky words, but reference to the elements, various animals and people, was rigorously avoided. Men were known by nicknames, or a slight alteration to the surname would suffice, mention of a bishop or priest meant that a skipper might prefer to return to port rather than risk the consequence of such rashness on the open sea. Unsuccessful boats had the witches exorcised by carrying lighted brands into every corner; this custom is still remembered by a few of the oldest men. Until the 1890's only Manx was spoken at sea; English words were never used, and down to the last days of sail it was considered unlucky to be the third boat out of harbour, and several would bunch together as they passed between the pierheads, a single boat waiting until she could go out in the company of others.

This concludes my brief analysis of Mr. and Mrs. Megaw's article, and I now turn to the influence of the St. Ives craft on the local design. Prior to the coming of the Cornish boats to the summer fishing in the early 1820's, the cutter or smack rig was the favourite of the Manx fishermen, who were quick to notice the advantages of a lowered foremast with a sail set on the mizzen when the lugger was riding to her nets. The local men therefore shortened the main boom and stepped a jigger mast well aft, with a small standing lugsail sheeting to the end of a steeved-up outrigger, thereby converting to a "dandy" rig, but on the strength of the lugsail they curiously enough called their boats "luggers," although they still retained a gaff and boom mainsail. The hulls were somewhat similar to those from the south, being sharp-sterned, but with rather fuller lines above water and little sheer.

After considerable search, I was able to obtain the loan of the original Report by Captain John Washington, R.N., on the Fishing Boats on the East Coast of Scotland, which was ordered by the House of Commons to be printed, 28th July 1849. Through the courtesy of the present Librarian, who told me of its whereabouts after being among the archives of the House, I was able to have the loan for a short while, thanks to the good offices of the Librarian of the London School of Economics. I took the opportunity of copying out practically the entire Report, and traced the numerous plans contained therein, so that I can now give the comments of the experts of the day on these Isle of Man fishing vessels.

Mr. James Peake, naval architect to H.M. Dockyard, Woolwich, wrote of the plans reproduced on page 330:

"The lines of the bow are long and good, but the after lines are full, the form of the midship section is such as would do well in a seaway, and the boat is, no doubt, found in practice to be an efficient one."

Mr. James Mackenzie, Officer of the Fishery, stationed at Douglas, Isle of Man, wrote on the 7th November 1848: "I have to inform you that I went yesterday to Peel, where the best part of the Isle of Man boats are built, and I find that the following are the dimensions of one of the medium size of the Peel boats. She is half-decked and of the burthen of 16 162/3500 tons, length from the inner part of the main stem to the forepart of the sternpost aloft is 37 ft. 6 in. Length of keel 32 ft., breadth in midships 11 ft. 6 in., depth in hold at midships 6 ft. 6 in. Rig, smack with mizzen lug, carvel-built, draught when light 3 ft., loaded 5 ft. 6 in. Quantity of ballast, eight tons; number of crew in summer from six to seven men, in September and October from seven to nine men.

Cost, with spars, oars, sails, etc., £155, but many of the boats cost £200. They will last from thirty to forty years, with repairs. At the Isle of Man, during the fishing season, there are always vessels termed 'fresh buyers,' which take the fish in the bay. The herrings are generally sold here by 'tale,' and the fish are removed from the boat into the vessel in baskets that contain 100 herrings each, but if the fish are sold to the curers on shore, the boats have to wait in the bay until there is sufficient water in the harbour to float them in, which is a very great inconvenience, both to fishermen and curers. The fish is removed in baskets, carried by women, from the boats into the curing house, and often the boats are left dry before the fish is delivered to the curers, which, of course, prevents them from going to sea that night."

Mr. H. W. Burns, writing from Peel on the 10th November 1848, says:

"I have the pleasure to forward the lines and dimensions of the most approved model of a Manx herring boat, as recently built by Mr. Henry Graves, timber merchant, at Peel. This boat is 40 ft. 8 in. overall in length, with 11 ft. 9 in. breadth of beam, and 7 ft. 6 in. depth. She has a forecastle deck, extending 14 ft. from the stem, which affords sleeping berths and shelter for her crew. The name of the boat is the *Dove* of Peel. Hugh Crellin, master, and her fishing performance this last season has been highly satisfactory to the crew and owners. She is essentially a poor man's boat, doing the greatest service at the least cost, light in her materials, sails, spars, and nets, and indeed may be classed as one of the best boats in the entire Manx herring fleet."

Further particulars given in the Report show that her length of keel for tonnage was 33 ft. 9 in., moulded breadth 11 ft. 6 in., which gives a thickness of planking of $1\frac{1}{2}$ in. Displacement to light draught, or weight of hull, was 7.5 tons, displacement to load draught 24.8 tons. Weight of ballast 7 tons. Cost complete for sea, £200, carvel-built and copper-fastened. Her draught was: light, for'ard 2 ft. aft 4 ft. 6 in.; loaded, for'ard, 5 ft. 6 in., aft 7 ft. 6 in. She carried a crew of six men, and her burthen in tons, O.M. was 23 69/94, with a carrying capacity of 17.3 tons. Another improvement was that the mainmast was now stepped in a tabernacle and lowered back into a slot in the deck, which was covered with a hatch—the "mastslide"—when the mast was erect. This allowed the boat to lie more quietly to her nets, while a small jigger lugsail aft kept her head to wind.

The following copy of a memorandum gives the cost of building in the sixties:

MEMORANDUM OF AGREEMENT between Henry Graves and John Quayle & Co., on the part of the former agreeing to build a boat for the latter 38 ft. by $12\frac{1}{2}$ ft., frame oak, floors elm, ash or oak, for the sum of £212, half when launched, balance at end of herring season 1865. Interest allowed for money paid before it becomes due and interest charged if not paid when it becomes due.

Crew to assist in launching and rigging boat as usual.
We agree to these terms and bind ourselves in the penalty of £20.
As witness our names this 10th day of September 1864.

HENRY GRAVES
JOHN QUAYLE, $\frac{1}{4}$

| | |
|---|---|
| Witnessed by David Dodd. | Wm. Dodd, ⅛ |
| | Jas. Clinton, ⅛ |
| | John Shimmin, ¼ |
| | Thos. Caine, ¼ |

By the seventies size had increased to a length overall of 50 to 51 ft., beam from 12 to 16 ft., with a keel length of 38 to 47 ft., and a tonnage of about 50. The name "Lugger" was still retained, although actually dandy-rigged, and many had counter sterns. The smaller boats were frequently open, with a short forecastle deck, but the majority of the bigger ones were fully decked. A large gaff topsail was set on a pole topmast above a gaff and boom mainsail, a survival of the original cutter rig, for'ard was a foresail set on a stay, and a jib hooked to a traveller on a reeving bowsprit set to starboard of the stem. On the mizzen mast was a standing lugsail.

In the Science Museum at South Kensington is a contemporary model of one of these luggers, built for the Fisheries Exhibition in 1883, so that its accuracy can be assumed (Plate 129). The bowsprit, stepped in a single bitt, reeves through a hole in the starboard bulwark and is run out with a heelrope. The mainmast, resting in a wooden tabernacle with a barrel winch on its foreside, is supported by a single fore shroud a side set up with a luff purchase, with the lower single block on a short length of chain hooking into an eye in the channel outside hull, and the fall of the tackle belaying round the timberhead projecting above the rail. A burton has its runner hooked to the third eye in the channel, and leads up through a single block on the pendant, down to a luff purchase hooked in middle eye, the fall belaying round second timberhead. The forestay, set up with two treble blocks, has its fall leading from the lower block, and is slacked away when the mast is lowered back into the trunk.

The mizzen mast has the lug halyard set up to starboard with a luff purchase, the lower single block hooking to eye in covering board, and the fall belaying round cleat on stanchion for'ard of eye. The backstay, to port, is set up with a gun-tackle purchase —two single blocks—and fall belays to cleat aft of eye. When not in use, the jump stay hooks into the same eye as the backstay. The outrigger is stepped into an iron clamp on deck to port of the mizzen mast, and passes outboard over the taffrail, where it is secured by an iron collar.

The long hatch over fish and net rooms has rounded corners to the coamings, and the covers are marked S.I to VI, M.I to VI, and L.I to VI, the L. being for larboard, the old name for port. Aft is a skylight, then the eye for the main sheet, and a companion giving access to the cabin below. An iron tiller is fitted to the rudder head, which is inboard, as the vessel has a counter stern, with a sharp stern the wooden tiller came in over the rail aft. The boathook and two long sweeps are carried in ring-shaped irons on the port rail, evidently adopted from Cornish practice. The anchor cable comes in through the port hawsehole, and goes down a chainpipe for'ard of the mast to stow in a locker below.

The stem is straight, with a slightly-rounded forefoot, the floors are sharp, and the run long and fine.

The loose-footed mainsail has six bead parrel hoops on the upper part of the luff, then is laced to the mast as far as the tack cringle, evidently for ease in casting off when the sail is scandalised or triced up. The main halyards have two double blocks with the fall leading to port, and the peak halyards reeve from the tail of a single block hooked

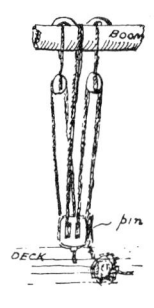

FIGURE 59

to an eye on a band round the masthead, just above the thumb cleat which takes the rope strop for the jib halyard blocks. Then the halyards reeve through a single block on gaff, back through first single block at masthead, then through second single block on gaff, and back to single block on mast above the first, and lead down to starboard to a stanchion between the timberheads.

The gooseneck of the boom goes into an eye in aft side of mast, which is here squared to fit in the tabernacle, and the tack of the mainsail is secured in a curious way —a short rope strop, hooking into eyes on each side of the tabernacle, has a bullseye working on it with a hook which goes into the tack cringle of the sail. Two lines of reef points are fitted, with the usual reefing tackle hooked to the boom. The main sheet has its standing end fast round the boom between two small comb cleats, and reeves down through the aft sheave of a double block hooked to an eye in the deck, up to a single block on a rope strop passing through after comb cleat, then down to the second sheave in double block, up to a single block on a strop passing through for'ard comb cleat, and finally the fall belays round the pin on side of double block. This peculiar lead can be seen in Plate 129, and I have sketched it in Fig. 59.

The gaff topsail, set on a pole topmast, has its halyard set up to starboard with two single blocks, the lower one being hooked to the same eye in the covering board that takes the fore sheet block. Then the fall belays round the hook, which seems odd to me, as round a cleat would surely be more secure. The tack goes to a luff purchase, with the lower single block hooking to an eye in deck aft of the mast, and fall belaying round cleat on aft side of tabernacle. The sheet reeves through a hole in the peak of the gaff, and leads down through a single block under jaws on starboard side, and fall belays round for'ard timberhead.

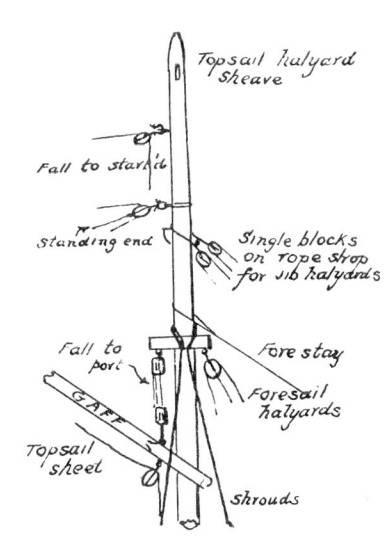

FIGURE 60

The foresail tack lashing hooks into eye on the starboard side of stemhead, and the sail is laced, not hanked, to the forestay. The halyards have a single block hooked to eye under the hounds, and the fall, fast to the tail of this block, leads down through single block hooked to head cringle of sail, back to upper block and down to cleat on port side of tabernacle. The sheets lead through single blocks hooked into eyes in the covering board either side, and belay round cleats on stanchions. The jib outhaul leads through sheave at end of bowsprit, and in over the port rail to belay round the head of the single bitt at heel of bowsprit. The halyards have their standing end fast to starboard timberhead, lead up through single block on rope strop round masthead, down through single block hooked into head cringle of sail, back to a second single block on strop, and down to luff purchase with lower single block hooked into eye in port covering board, and fall belays to cleat. The single sheets reeve through holes in bulwarks to belay round long cleat between two stanchions. Most of these details of gear can be seen in Fig. 60.

The standing mizzen lugsail has one row of reef points, with the tack to a hook on port side of mast and the sheet, hooked to clew cringle, leads through sheave at end of outrigger and is fast to an iron traveller on spar with a double block spliced in. A single block, hooked to eye outside counter, has the fall fast to its tail, then it reeves through one sheave in double block, back through single block to second sheave to lead in over taffrail to belay round pin in transit rail round stern. The hook on the iron traveller on the mast goes into eye on yard, and halyards go to starboard.

The usual crew consisted of seven men, and the proceeds of a week's fishing were divided into 21 shares, ten went to the nets, each man providing his due proportion so all shared accordingly; the boat took two and a half shares, food and cartage for the nets absorbed one and a half shares, then each man had one share. The boats were generally the property of the fishermen, now a thrifty, industrious race who banked their surplus money, or built better boats.

Prior to the passing of the Sea Fisheries Act 1868, the statistics of the Manx fisheries were included among the returns made by the Scottish Fishery Board, but since that date the Isle of Man has been an independent division, although the many local regulations, such as an old Act of Tynwald whereby herring fishing was prohibited between January 1st and July 5th within nine miles of the island, were repealed, and the fisheries became subject to English laws as exemplified in the above Act.

The herring season now commenced early in June north of Peel on the western side of the island, and the boats worked southwards to the Calf of Man as the season advanced, finishing up about the end of September, when the fish were said to spawn on the rough ground in the neighbourhood.

The coast scenery was, and still is, magnificent. North of Peel lie beaches of golden sand, with green hills rising in the background, but sandstone cliffs flank the ancient harbour, where the ruins of castle and cathedral dominate the landscape. Shafts of sunlight, striking through gaunt open windows, touch the grim ramparts with flaming gold and red, but at times the stone quays and houses lie dripping under weeping skies as fierce squalls drive across the sea. The ever-restless gulls sweep out in swirling clouds from the high rocky cliffs around which their mournful cries echo and re-echo, and gannets dive like plummets into the opalescent blue sea. The brown-sailed luggers make for harbour over the shimmering waters in which the piled-up masses of snowy clouds are reflected. Everywhere the scents of the land blend with the tang of the sea, and the golden glory of the gorse perfumes the air with its heady, haunting fragrance. Little white-thatched cottages stand amidst fields of emerald green, many the homes of the fishermen, who in the months between the fishing seasons tilled their tiny crofts or worked on the farms. To the south lie desolate cliffs, grey-black, awe-inspiring, rent with narrow clefts or wooded glens down which streams sparkle and tumble. The tops are purple with heather, and below are rock-strewn beaches where the seas break in ceaseless confusion, crashing into caves and leaping up to kiss the unyielding face of the cliffs. The south-west corner is beautiful with coloured rock flowers, and between the mainland and the Calf of Man runs a furious tidal race, a few hundred yards wide, with the Chickens Rock Lighthouse sending out its warning rays from sunset to sunrise. The gigantic cliffs at Spanish Head are streaked with veins of crimson, purple and brown, which give gorgeous rainbow effects, while the Chasms, gaunt 300 ft. bastions, are split and rent with great fissures. But what a wicked coastline with a gale from the south-west.

The screaming seabirds are protected by an Act of 1867 as being "considered of great importance to persons engaged in herring fishing, inasmuch as they indicate localities where bodies of fish may be, also of much use for sanitary purpose by reason that they remove offal of fish from harbours and shores." Hence they fly unmolested behind the slow-moving ploughs, or stalk majestically along beach and strand.

The nets were shot at dusk and as the summer night slowly darkened, a long, sparkling necklace of lights, low on the horizon, marked the presence of the ever-growing holiday resorts, which were absorbing many a young man who would have gone to the fishing in earlier days. The first rays of dawn, striking the top of the mountain Cronk ny Irree Lhaa—Hill of the Rising Day—was the signal for hauling the nets, which came in silvery-green with herring and brown and red with clinging seaweeds. All were piled in the net hold until after breakfast, then the men cleaned the nets, throwing the fish into the next room, while the lugger foamed along towards the harbour.

In October herring were in Douglas Bay, but they were entirely different to those caught off the Calf during the summer, and were believed to come from the north-east. When the local fishing was over, many of the boats went to the Irish coast to fish for herring during November and December, favourite ports being Ardglass and Annalong in Co. Down.

There was at that time very little curing done in the Island; almost all the local herrings were sent to Liverpool or Wales, being lightly sprinkled with salt, just sufficient to preserve them until they reached market, to which they were generally shipped in sailing vessels from Castletown.

The nets were hand-made of flax, which had a short life, and required more barking than the cotton nets introduced about the middle of the 19th century, and made locally with beautiful machinery. In the sixties the cost of cotton or flax nets was much the same, but the extra cartage and barking for the latter added more to the expense of upkeep, and it was not long before the old industry gave place to the new, as the cotton thread nets caught more herrings than the flax.

From notes compiled by Mr. William Dodd of Peel, I find the following:

"Mr. Thomas Arthur Quayle, M.H.K., informed me in 1935 that his father and grandfather always grew flax in Ballaquayle, Patrick, in meadows near the river Neb and at the top part of Ballaquayle towards the mountains. After being prepared in the flaxpond, it was given out the following winter to women in Peel who spun the flax into thread on spinning wheels."

John Cowell, aged ninety years, in 1936, goes on to say that the nets were made at home by the fishermen during the winter and spring evenings, each mesh in turn being worked round a square piece of wood with grooved edges. The gauge for a herring net was $1\frac{5}{8}$ in. by $\frac{1}{4}$ in. thick, for mackerel $3\frac{1}{4}$ in. by $\frac{1}{4}$, and a man could make a fathom of net a day—a fathom was seven fathom deep and one wide. Each net was usually made of ten or fourteen pieces, afterwards joined together by meshed stitching to make a complete net. Each fisherman generally had two nets, and a boy one.

About the 1850's Robert Corrin, of Knockaloe-beg, set up a factory in Peel for making cotton thread nets, and two others were built and equipped a few years later by J. Joughin and Thos. C. S. Moore. The first nets were 100 yards long and six jebbins, or 600 meshes deep, and mounted on 80-yard ropes, the "topbacks," to which they were attached by short lines called "hossels" or "hauslas," the openings where the nets joined were known as "baneys," and a lot of fish fell through them when hauling. The nets were hung on a warp, known locally as the "springback," usually of three or four thicknesses, the heaviest, $3\frac{1}{2}$ in. to 4 in., being nearest the boat, the lightest, $2\frac{1}{2}$ in., towards the tail of the train, which was marked by a "mollag" carrying the boat's number. "In case the springback burst with the swell," to quote Mr. John Gawne's own words, the boat rode to a rope called the "swing," secured to the nets.

The net floats, or "mollags," were made of sheep or dog skins, the four legs being warped up tight, the inside was coated with Stockholm tar, the outside with coal tar. A small wooden spool was put in one leg, and the skin was blown up through a hole which was afterwards plugged with a wad of oakum, called locally a "spithag," sometimes cork or wood was used instead of oakum. Between each mollag was a ring of corks—the "headcorks"—and there were about thirty mollags and fifty headcorks on a herring train, each secured to the nets and springback by the "stoppers" or "thows," but none on a mackerel train as the topbacks were floating, having corks fixed every 12 inches. It took about three hours to haul a herring train, usually 22 to 24 nets, each 100 yards long and 14 yards deep, extending for about a mile, but a mackerel train numbered 54 to 56 nets, each 100 yards by 7 yards deep, mounted as a herring net, and taking four to four and a half hours to haul in favourable weather.

Fig. 61 drawn from a sketch by Mr. John Gawne shows the mounting, etc., of the nets; later many boats fished with the springback below the nets.

In the early days, when the men supplied the nets, their share of the catch would vary according to the number they owned, but later it was often the custom for the owner of the boat to supply the nets, and the shares were altered in proportion. After the introduction of the steam capstan, a man's share went to the boiler.

The herrings were counted three to a "warp," forty warps plus "cast" equalled three plus tally, which equalled one, and this was called a "hundred," but was actually 124, and five hundred—620—was a "mease," an old Irish measure roughly equal to half a cran. A good fishing would be from forty to eighty mease of herring, and from six to ten thousand mackerel.

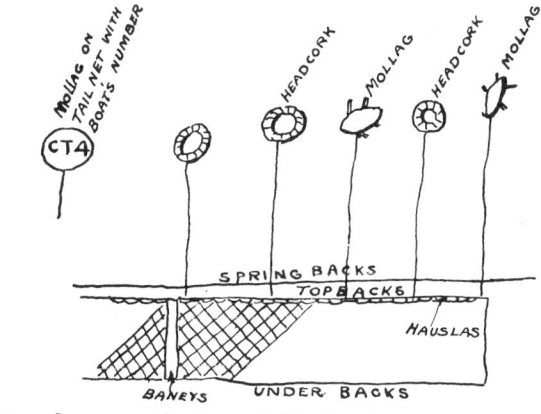

*Manx herring net from sketch by J. B. Gawne.*

FIGURE 61

Although there was no regular mackerel fishing on the Manx coasts in the middle of the 19th century, a few of these fish were sometimes taken with the herring on the west side during June, July and August.

Prior to 1864 or thereabouts, there was no recognised fishing for mackerel in spring and early summer off the south-west of Ireland, except for casual fishing by local men using coracles and small yawls. Robert Corrin, of Knockaloe-beg, an astute man, who was reputed to have made a fortune later by being far-seeing enough to buy up cotton just before the Civil War in America, formed a theory that the mackerel shoals, which turned regularly at Peel grounds in July and August, came in from the Atlantic by the south-west of Ireland and up the Irish Sea. He equipped one or two boats with his own new make of mackerel nets and sent them south, and this pioneer effort was immediately successful, and within a few years some 800 vessels from the Isle of Man, Cornwall, Scotland, France and Ireland, were at the fishing, giving employment to over 6,000 fishermen, and causing a boom in shipbuilding.

Mr. William Dodd, of Peel, recalls that about 1913 he interviewed Robert Corkill of Marown, then over seventy years of age, nicknamed "Corrin Lucy," who was one of the crew of the first or second vessel which initiated the Kinsale fishing, as it was afterwards known, and Mr. Gawne says Jack Carine was one of the first to go from Port St. Mary about 1864.

The fishing grounds lay thirty to forty miles from land, and the speed and weatherly abilities of the Cornish luggers excited general admiration amongst the Manx fishermen, whose dandies and smacks were outpaced, and soon the well-known St. Ives builder, William Paynter, was inundated with orders, so much so that he opened a yard in Kilkeel, Ireland. The first boat for the Isle of Man was *Zenith*, C.T.65, built by him to the order of Dick Duke, who later owned or part-owned several boats whose names began with the letter Z, such as *Zebra*, C.T.10, *Zetetic*, C.T.35, and *Zetland*, C.T.97. *Zebra* and *Zetland* were still in the 1905 register, and *Zebra* is given in the 1923 one as being fitted with a motor.

These new boats carried a fore and mizzen lug only, and as the name "lugger" had already been given—rather misleadingly—to the dandy-rigged boats, it became the custom to call the newcomers "nickeys," possibly because so many Cornish men answered to the name of Nicholas, but an alternative is that one of the first boats to be brought to the Island was *Nicholas*.

Soon the local builders were turning out similar craft, the first from Port St. Mary being *Alpha*, C.T.19, in 1869, and from that year until about 1882 the whole fleets of Peel and Port St. Mary were built, so the local carpenters must have been smart at their job.

Mr. William Dodd writes that W. Cannan, superintendent for Henry Graves of Peel, had never seen a nickey, but said if he was given her length and beam, and the distance from stem to foremast, he would design and build a boat to hold her own with the best. Mr. Dodd's father, carpenter of Peel, obtained this information for Cannan, and soon two to four nickeys were being built side by side in the yard on the quay, and launched within a month, the prototype having proved her ability, being a good sea boat, with fast sailing qualities.

Joshua Dodd tells that when he went to work as an apprentice joiner in Graves' Yard in 1876, they launched nine nickeys that year, and again in 1877, increasing to thirteen to fourteen for subsequent years, but the numbers declined after 1880, when the round-sterned "nobby" was introduced. Tom Watson built three in 1876, and five or six in the following years.

Other well-known builders were Kneale and Watterson, William Cowell, who built a nobby in his garden, had the hull cradled on an axle with high wheels, and hauled by horses down to the slipway in Peel Harbour at low water, the boat floating off at high tide.

Alan Radcliffe, over eighty in 1939, said that when he was in business as a blacksmith with his father, William Radcliffe, they did the ironwork of 21 nickeys in a twelvemonth—six from Kermeen & Graves of Ramsey, three from Qualtrough of Douglas, three from John Holmes of Peel, six from Tom Watson, two from William Cowell, and one from Meyrick. Graves had their own smithy with James Watterson in charge of three forges, while Henry Maddrell Graves, a cousin of Henry Graves, often had as many as six nickeys building at one time, two on each launching way.

Boats built in Corris's yard were pulled on skids along Athol Street and down Bridge Street to the shore, and then left for the tide to rise and bring them into harbour. There were always plenty of helpers as a barrel of beer was often emptied before starting

130 *GLEE MAIDEN* LEAVING PEEL

131 MODEL OF NICKEY, c. 1883
Note standing shrouds on foremast, staysail, rounded corners to hatch covers, water barrel, iron tiller, length of lee yardarms.

132 NICKEYS IN PEEL HARBOUR
Note trading smack on left.

133 NICKEYS AT PORT ERIN
C.T. 22 *Elate*, C.T. 58 *Alert*, C.T. 91 *Sunbeam*, C.T. 29 *May Queen*, C.T. 52 *Dancing Waver*. Note bladders or "mollags".

134 PORT ST. MARY HARBOUR
C.T. 9 *Cedar*, C.T. 73 *Mystic*, C.T. 105 *Isabella*, Peel schooner *Kate*, built 1872.

135 FITTING OUT, PORT ST. MARY
C.T. 53 *Elizabeth*, C.T. 64 *Ben my Chree* are nickeys. C.T. 25 *Confidence*, C.T. 54 *Alice* are dandy rigged trawlers.

136 NICKEYS AND DANDIES AT PORT ERIN
C.T. 1 *Shah* and C.T. 7 *Puffin* are dandies. C.T. 55 *Expert*, C.T. *Stephen*, C.T. 27 and 110 C.T. 59 are nickeys.

137 MODEL OF NICKEY *EXPERT*, C.T. 55

138 *LILY*, P.L. 172
   Built as a nickey, later re-rigged as a nobby. Note foresail at foot of fore stay, jib traveller run in with sail hanging from masthead.

139 *XEMA*, P.L. 37
   Note counter stern, iron tiller, tack of fore lug to horse at foot of mast, fore stay tackle for lowering mast.

and another when the boat was safely launched, this being the only payment made for casual help.

At Port St. Mary the change-over was not so rapid, only a few nickeys fishing in 1872, then a great increase in building took place. Mr. John Gawne says the Manxmen improved many of the boats built in Cornwall by raising the decks, first taking off bulwarks and stanchions, and then scarphing pieces on to the timberheads. This old fisherman, who first went to sea in 1895, tells how his wife's grandfather served his time with Neddy Nelson, born 1799, who started building boats in the cave at Perwick as far back as 1824, launching them over the beach. The men used to go home at five o'clock so that the "little people" could come after and carry on! It would be interesting to know how much work was found done next day. His wife's father worked in Castletown in the early sixties, building on the Claddagh and launching the boats on a high tide. Boyd, and Cooil & Qualtrough were well-known builders there at that time. Tommy Gale was building at Port St. Mary in the eighties, Josie Qualtrough started building in that port in 1845, but most of the old carpenters were blown up when the brig *Lily* was wrecked in 1852. The Wattersons were all carpenters, and Mr. Gawne says, "Old Tom could sail a boat and drink a pint of ale as well as any man. He built the 'lugger' *Jenny* upon the Howe, the only boat to be laid down there, and then rolled her down to the water. Her hull was carvel-built below, and clinker-built above the waterline. Old Tommy's father was in her, and in those days they all wore top-hats. One night the *Jenny* was out fishing to the nor'ard of the Calf and they had an awful good shot of fish, and was that deep that old Joe's swallow-tails were down in the water as he sat steering."

It is strange, but interesting to note that at about the same time the East Anglian fishermen were abandoning the lug in favour of the fore-and-aft rig, on the other side of England the Manxmen were converting to the dipping lugsail instead of the dandy rig with a gaff and boom mainsail, a rig of which they were the pioneers. One reason may be that with deep water right close inshore, they were able to work long boards when going to wind'ard, and it is a well-known fact that a lugger can outsail any fore-and-after.

The new sail plan consisted of an enormous dipping lug on the foremast and a large standing lug on the mizzen, later a high-peaked topsail, cut somewhat differently to the Cornish one, was set on the mizzen pole and a big staysail was hoisted between the masts with a beam wind, or boomed out for'ard when the breeze was right aft. Reef points were seldom used, as the Manxmen adopted the Cornish custom of shifting sails, often carrying three sets of lugs, with a fourth storm suit. The local names were second foresail, trysail, seventy, rider, staysail, and mizzen topsail, the storm rig being the seventy on the foremast and the rider on the mizzen.

When set, the sails had little natural belly, and as a result, a nickey could lie closer to the wind than one of the old-fashioned "luggers," easily within four points, while she could make rings round a "nobby," a rig which came into favour in the late eighties, and believed to be a copy of that used in skiffs on the West Coast of Scotland, where they were known as "nabbies," a name also given to the Irish craft which had the same rig. Most of the hulls had sharp sterns, but later the round or elliptical counter stern was added to increase deck space and generally speaking, the Manx nickeys ran somewhat larger in size than the Cornish craft, and they followed their practice of carrying oars, topsail, etc., in "lumber irons," rings about 1 ft. dia., set in the port rail, and the spare sails were stowed on a grating about 4 in. above the deck on the port side.

For speed the nickeys were unsurpassed, to quote Mr. Gawne's own words, "My word, them nickeys could sail! They could do ten knots in favourable conditions, there was no rig ever created that would beat the lugsail. They used to have two lugs on them, and one lug on the deck, and the other aforeset, and when racing they would up with the lug before dropping the other one. You would be racing another boat to shoot the nets and while she would be dropping one lug before putting the other up, we would be putting one up before dropping the other."

Fred Corris, aged eighty-four in 1939, told Mr. Dodd that when he was skipper of *Glee Maiden*, P.L.139, 20 tons built 1879, and afloat until 1926—on one occasion she made the run from the Copelands at the entrance to Belfast Lough to Peel, a distance of forty miles, in four hours, the wind being on the beam. Plate 130 shows her leaving Peel Harbour. When first registered, *Glee Maiden* was owned by Robert Corrin, pioneer of the Kinsale fishing.

A typical nickey was about 48 ft. long, 15 ft. beam, and 8 to 10 ft. deep. Draught for'ard was 5 ft., aft 7 ft., and when the boat was aground the deck had a very steep angle, running from the stern down to the bow, and iron or wooden legs were needed to keep her upright. The foremast was about the same length as the boat, 48 ft., with its heel in a step on the floors, and lowered back into the mastcase, resting against the "kicking beam." It was stepped upright on the keel and so raked slightly aft when the boat was afloat, but the mizzen raked for'ard on the keel, and so was approximately upright at sea.

The foremast was held in position by wedges, with two single shrouds looped over the masthead, each set up with a luff purchase. There was no forestay, the tack of the lugsail acting in lieu. Many of the nickeys set up their big lugs to a short iron bumpkin, others to a heavy tack hook passed through the stemhead and held by a forelock.

The foreyard hooked to an iron traveller, the halyard tye was a single well-greased rope or wire rove through a sheave in the masthead with a double block at lower end, the tackle usually being a luff one with the single block hooked in the covering board aft of the mast, but some of the biggest boats had a treble block aloft and a double block on deck. When going about the lug was dipped, not lowered right down, the yard being up-ended on deck to take the weight and the sail worked for'ard round the mast, as was St. Ives practice, and the halyards taken over to the weather side. With a good crew this could be done in about five minutes. The foresheets were a luff purchase, with the single block hooked to an eye opposite, or just aft of the mizzen mast.

Plate 131 is of C.T.122, a very fine contemporary model exhibited at the Fisheries Exhibition in 1883, and now in the Science Museum. She has a round counter stern, with the rudder head inboard and an iron tiller with wooden handgrip. The binnacle is just aft of and the skylight companion for'ard of the mizzen mast. Note the rounded hatch covers, the hand capstan, and the water barrel, holding about four gallons. The quadrilateral topsail is similar in design to that used at St. Ives, but the sheet leads down through a small single block under the slings of the yard to belay round a cleat under the starboard rail.

Nickeys usually carried a small boat on the starboard side of the deck, 12 ft. long, 5 ft. beam, and 2 ft. deep, costing £5 10s. to build. Many were fitted with sails, only used if it was a long way to go for water.

The hulls were built out in the open, and the average time taken by four men was three to four months. Generally the yard provided all the timber required, local-grown elm being used for the keel, but owing to the scarcity of oak in the Island, much had to be imported from Ireland. Henry Graves used to send his cousin, H. Maddrell Graves, or William Cannan or John Kermode across to select oak trees while standing, paying the owner about 2s. a cubic foot, the timber being brought over in schooners or smacks.

Clench-built hulls were copper-fastened, but when carvel-build was introduced about 1830, trenails of lance wood were used, then iron bolts and nails, which necessitated renailing the planking to the oak ribs after a number of years, an expense obviated when galvanising was brought into use. Up to the middle of the 19th century, it was often the custom for a carpenter to build a lugger for a stone mason if he would build a house for the shipwright, whose wages were 24s. for a week of sixty hours. All frames were doubled with stanchions bolted to the timberheads, and a covering board fitted round and well caulked.

Hand capstains were fitted prior to 1881, and the crew numbered seven men and a boy, but only six men were required when steam power was used, most of the engines being supplied by John Knox, of Douglas Bridge.

The cost of a nickey ready for sea was about £700, including two trains of nets, one of 54 for mackerel and another of 22 for herring. A boat frequently belonged to a number of men, who shared the expenses and the profits, with the skipper getting an extra £3 a year for all his responsibilities.

Mr. William Clucas, sailmaker of Port St. Mary, informs me that four men took three weeks to make a suit of eight sails, and were paid £1 a week each. The first cloth cut was the one nearest the weather—known as the "tack cloth," tablings and linings were on the starboard side, boltropes on the port, in the following sizes: luff $4\frac{1}{2}$ in. and 5 in., clew $2\frac{1}{2}$ in. and 3 in., leech 2 in. and $1\frac{3}{4}$ in., head 2 in. and $1\frac{3}{4}$ in., foot $1\frac{3}{4}$ in.

In the early boats with short yards, it was possible to dip the lugs as was St. Ives practice, but as the length increased, the sail had to be lowered right down, unhooked and reset on the opposite side of the mast.

From his own and his father's ledgers, Mr. Clucas gives quantities and prices, 1870-80.

### NICKEY'S SUIT OF SAILS

|  | £ | s. | d. |
|---|---|---|---|
| Big foresail, 195 yards No. 6 cotton, 24 in. | 15 | 8 | 9 |
| Second foresail, 155 yards, No. 3 cotton, 24 in. | 13 | 11 | 3 |
| Trysail, 115 yards, No. 3 cotton, 24 in. | 10 | 1 | 3 |
| Big mizzen, 80 yards No. 2 cotton, 24 in. | 6 | 6 | 8 |
| Small mizzen, $46\frac{1}{2}$ yards No. 2 cotton, 24 in. | 3 | 13 | $7\frac{1}{2}$ |
| Staysail, 55 yards No. 6 cotton, 24 in. | 3 | 6 | $5\frac{1}{2}$ |
| Topsail, 32 yards No. 7 cotton, 24 in. | 1 | 17 | 4 |
| Big jib, 69 yards No. 7 cotton, 24 in. | 4 | 0 | 6 |
|  | £58 | 5 | 10 |

Mr. John Gawne tells how the men wore smocks going right down over the knee-high leather seaboots, and that all the work available in winter-time was in fixing the nets.

"I remember young Dick Crebbin and me would be making a thousand hau'sls a night and doing our home lessons after that. A hau'sl was made of thicker stuff than string. When they were making them they had in every house what was called a 'forrum,' and the old men would stick their knife in it, and he would be holding his thumb so, and putting the string round, and then giving the knife a snick and cutting it. He would cut thousands a night and hand them to the boys. We would be putting these braces on the nets. It was a proper treat to be a proper fisherman in those days, there is no fishermen about now. An old skipper I was with first at Kinsale was a rigger, and he would rig for them. I was down a whole winter passing the ball for him. The first time I ever went to work was down here in Edward Qualtrough's Net Factory making rigging. You would have to watch you didn't go wrong twisting, or there would be a row. He was a good hand at splicing wire rope, we made lots of rigging for the schooners in here. I was getting 6s. a week, and thought I was a millionaire. I was only thirteen at the time."

The principal herring fishing ports were on the west and south sides of the island. Peel on the west had a fine natural harbour facing north, with two entrances prior to the building of the stone causeway connecting St. Patrick's Isle with the mainland.

Jack Kelly, aged ninety in 1939, stated that when he first went to the fishing, it was the custom of practically every member of the crew of each vessel to bare their heads when passing Peel Castle on their way to the fishing grounds. It is possible that this was originally a mark of respect to the Bishop who had his cathedral and residence on the isle. Lying at the mouth of the river Neb, the harbour has a fine sand and gravel bottom and is sheltered in all winds from N.W. through S. to East.

Plate 132 shows the forest of masts when the fishing fleet was in port, with one of the old trading smacks in the foreground; on the right is the causeway under construction.

A little further to the south lies Port Erin, facing west, with its half-mile wide bay sheltered by the towering mass of Bradda Head, and affording a safe anchorage in all winds from north through east to S.S.W. Jutting out from the south shore was a stone quay, now partially destroyed and covered at high-water spring tides. Plate 133 shows five of the Port St. Mary fleet of nickeys lying against this pier, with mollags hanging up to dry. The inner boat is *Dancing Wave*, C.T.52, with an elliptical stern; the others with sharp sterns are *May Queen*, C.T.29, *Sunbeam*, C.T.91, *Alert*, C.T.58, and *Elate*, C.T.22, all owned at one time by J. Qualtrough. Plate 136 gives another view of the bay.

On the south side of the Island, to the east'ard of The Chasms, lies Port St. Mary, tucked away in a bay of the same name, with its harbour made by building up a stone causeway on a reef of rocks running out into the bay. The port faces east, looking across Bay ny Carrickey to Poyllvaish—the Pool of Death—where many a fine sailing ship crashed to her doom. Plate 134 shows the fleet in the harbour, which is sheltered in all winds from N.W. through west to S.W. The schooner is *Kate*, built by Graves in 1872, and whose relatives had shares in the vessel. Registered A1 at Lloyd's, she was engaged in the South American trade, carrying a royal and t'gan's'l above her topsail on the foremast. Later she was cut down for the coal trade between Peel and Whitehaven, loading from 230 to 250 tons. Sold to English owners about 1910, she was in the coasting trade and on one occasion drove ashore on the Welsh coast, and it was a grand testimonial to the work put in her by Peel shipwrights that she was found fit to be repaired and strong enough to carry china clay from Cornwall to Runcorn for many years, and was in this trade over sixty years after her launch when she was accidentally destroyed by fire and sank in Moelfre Bay on the 1st February 1933. *Mystic*, C.T.73, *Cedar*, C.T.9, and *Isabella*, C.T.105, can be recognised amongst the crowd of nickeys. The elbow with the white lighthouse was built on to the original quay about 1829.

Between Scarlet Point and Langness Point is Castletown Bay, about one and a half miles wide and long, with a sandy beach and flat shore giving shelter in all winds from N.W. through N. to S.E. Round Langness Point, guarded by a lighthouse since 1880, is Derby Haven, one of the best natural harbours in the island, but never developed as a fishing port, although many boats, crowded out of their own harbours, used to lie up there for the winter; boats would often run round for shelter in west and sou'west gales when Castletown Bay was untenable.

Douglas and Ramsey on the east side of the island were seldom used by the herring fleets, although at one time a few trawlers were based on them. Of all these ports, by far the most important were Peel and Port St. Mary, and with such a number of harbours, each facing a different point of the compass, it was always possible in stress of weather for the fishing fleets to find a sheltered anchorage, even though all the harbours dried out at low water.

Concerning sea-marks, Mr. John Gawne, of Port St. Mary, says: "The Bollagh on the Folly and Port Erin shut on the nor'ard, and the two lights on the Calf was a great mark too, you would get the two lights in one, and so be N.N.W. of the Calf, then you judged the distance you were off the land, five or six miles N.N.W. And five or six miles W.S.W. of the Chickens in the first of the season you would be up in the big bay, Bay Mooar.

Another good mark, you know, early on the season, was the Bollagh on the Folly and Port St. Erin shut to the nor'ard. That was Bradda Head shutting Port Erin from you. You would be out off Cronk ny Iree Lhaa, maybe a little bit to the south. The road coming up the Folly you would be seeing.

Another mark down there would be Greeba and the Gut on the mountains. (Greeba Mountain 1,383 ft., Cronk ny Iree Lhaa 1,449 ft.). They would be looking at that about the last week in August till the last week in September. The herring was moving round, you see, from Dalby to Laxey Bay was the spawning ground. All the fishing was mostly down there from Clay Head to Peel; as a rule they never went further north than that."

With the coming of the nickeys and their splendid sea-keeping abilities, it was possible for the Manx fishermen to venture further afield in search of the shoals. Preparations to get ready for the Kinsale mackerel fishing started about the 1st March. First to appear was the boy, usually aged thirteen to fourteen, although in the early days many went to sea at the age of twelve, and even earlier. He began by cleaning out the cabin, which was pretty dirty after the boat had been laid up on the beach during the winter, the galley funnel had to be swept, the lockers washed out, and the floor well scrubbed, as all meals were eaten off the floor, no table being provided. Then the men turned up and scraped the spars, set up the rigging, and raised the foremast if it had been lowered; next they painted the bulwarks, etc., and tarred the outside, only a few boats being painted lead colour, although some had a band of red to the waterline. Then the sails were got on board. If the boats were lying at Derby Haven, the men took the sails from the lofts in Port St. Mary and carried them across in carts, then they sailed back to collect the nets from the warehouses. Fifty nets or more went to a mackerel train, and the heavy springback had to be coiled down below deck. Water and provisions were put aboard, two sacks of potatoes, two stone barley, a box of raisins, three dozen boxes of condensed milk, two sacks of sea biscuits, a sack of bread, about twenty pounds of beef and half a pig, one pound of tobacco for each man, some tea and a few cabbages, two stone of rice, and some butter and cheese.

These preparations completed, it was usual to await a fair N.E. wind before shaping course for the Tuskar Rock, some 120 miles away, then they made for Kinsale, another 94 miles, a total of about 214 miles; if going to Crookhaven, it was another 166 miles from the Tuskar. Twenty-eight hours for the passage to Kinsale was good going. The record run from Port St. Mary was made by the old "lugger" *Swift*, Jimmy Kinley skipper. She carried a strong nor'easter all the way, arriving in 21 to 22 hours.

Tommy Quine, fisherman, states that *Bee*, P.L.173, 25 tons, built at Penzance in 1871 for J. Teare and others, did the run from Peel to Kinsale within 24 hours. As it was a two hours' sail to the Chickens Light, this passage compares very favourably with the Port St. Mary record of 22 hours from the Chickens to Kinsale, but Willie Jones says he once left Peel at 5 p.m. and arrived at Castletown, Berehaven, 55 miles beyond Kinsale, at 7 p.m. the following evening, a faster time than any other, but he did not give the name of the boat.

Henry Leece confirms the fast run by the *Bee*, but gives the time as 26 hours, and that the passage was made in company with *Kate*, a nickey skippered by Thomas Kaye and built by Graves. She was launched from the same yard and on the same day as *Blue Jacket*, P.L.158, 19 tons, also owned by John Teare and others, and first registered in 1871, skipper Michael Newman. Leece, who was eighty years of age, says both boats were caught in Peel Bay by a gale of wind with the tide out, and the skippers decided to take advantage of a fair wind to make the run to Kinsale.

Ports used by the Manxmen were Kinsale, Crookhaven, Castletown Berehaven, Baltimore, Fenit, Tralee, and Valencia. The fishermen taught the Irish the handling of boats and the making and shooting of nets, but the local men took little interest in the harvest of the sea almost on their doorsteps, many preferring to drink away the takings of a trip while their boats lay idle in the harbour, and men of other nationalities were bringing in big catches.

From Crookhaven the boats would go down off the Fastnet Rock and shoot the nets about 8 p.m., then fix the watches, one man always being on deck, but the cook, the boy, kept no watch at sea. Hauling started about 11.30 p.m. to midnight, taking until 4 to 4.30 a.m. under favourable conditions. The boy had to go down below and coil all the heavy springback before his breakfast, pulling the rope down through a hole in the deck, all dripping with wet. When the nets were in, he had to go on deck, clean about a dozen mackerel and boil or fry them for breakfast, then wash up. If there was a fresh wind, the boat would now be nearing harbour, and here is where the nickeys scored, as their fine sailing abilities usually enabled them to be in before noon. Arriving in port at Crookhaven, she went alongside a hulk, a big condemned sailing ship, and counted her catch over the side into her, the skipper keeping tally and obtaining a receipt for the total.

The hulk always had a plentiful supply of ice on board, brought over from Norway in sailing ships, and as the Manx carpenters were not building boats when the fleet was away fishing, they went to Crookhaven to box fish. There was only one hulk anchored in the lough, so every boat had to go alongside, but those with few or no fish would anchor further away and send in the punt. The Manx fish-curers owned the hulk. An average good fishing would be two to three thousand mackerel, but Mr. Gawne once saw a catch of 16,000 landed by *Maria Jane*, P.L.58, an 18-ton dandy built in 1886 for W. Moore and others, skipper Charles Christian; she was not in the 1902 register.

At Kinsale the catch was landed on the quays, the fish were not cleaned, but packed in ice, a "hundred" in each box, and sent away to Milford by carrier. Sailing cutters were used prior to the coming of steamers in the late sixties. In 1872 about 60,000 boxes, equal to some 6,000 tons, were sold at Kinsale, a smaller quantity than in the two preceding years, being the catches of local boats and strangers, but not the numerous French ketches which cured their fish on board, Kinsale not being one of the Irish ports at which, by the Declaration annexed to the Convention of November 11th, 1867, French fishermen were allowed to land their fish.

In 1877 and '78 when the fishing was at its zenith, there were 180 Peel and about 100 Port St. Mary boats at Kinsale, and Charles Morrison, who owned a large fleet, mentions that in 1887 170 Peel boats averaged over £300 each, bringing in more than £50,000 to their home town for three months' fishing. There were no boats from Ramsey, and only four or five from Douglas.

Arthur Carran says his father, William Carran, held the record for the highest earnings, making £48 per man for 10-11 weeks' fishing. The boat was probably *Louise*, an old type "lugger," but he is hazy as to the exact name, as his father was skipper of several boats at different times.

On the other hand, Henry Leece, aged eighty years in 1938, recalls that he was at Kinsale in 1876 and '77 in *Bonita*, one of the old "luggers," skippered by his grandfather, and they were unlucky, averaging only £14 a season.

An average good season would yield £20 to £25 a man, but in some years when the fishing began to decline, it was as low as £9 to £10, the steam drifters and trawlers finally ruining this harvest, which must have yielded millions of pounds during its short life of under forty years. The last trip to Kinsale by a Port St. Mary nickey was about 1916, when *Expert*, C.T.55, about which I shall have more to say later, went to the fishing. The previous year the late Mr. Charles' nickey *Wanderer*, P.L.11, 21 tons, built 1881, for H. T. Graves, T. Moore and others, with a crew of Peel men, mostly former skippers, was shooting her nets some ten miles south of Kinsale Head under the command of William Ball, of Jurby. The date was the 7th May 1915, when unrestricted U-Boat warfare was at its height. The sea was smooth, the breeze light and visibility excellent when they saw a big four-funnel Cunarder coming up at about 18 knots. She was the ill-fated *Lusitania*, a world record-breaker, only eight years old, and carrying 1,959 people, including 440 women and children, and 702 crew under Captain W. T. Turner. At 1.40 p.m. those on board sighted the Old Head of Kinsale ten miles on the port bow, and observations were taken on the bridge before altering course. The crew of the nickey were idly watching this magnificent liner, and probably joking about the contrast between her and their craft, when to their horror they heard a loud explosion and saw the vessel begin to heel over. She had been torpedoed without warning by U20, commanded by Kapitan-Leutnant Schwieger, and was struck in one of the engine-rooms, which instantly flooded, making it impossible to take way off the ship, and rendering it most difficult to launch the lifeboats; a second torpedo also found its target some 100 feet aft of the first. Within twenty minutes *Lusitania* sank to the bottom, taking with her 1,198 lives, one of the foulest of the many crimes committed by the Germans in the 1914-18 war, and repeated again and again in the recent conflict. The whole civilised world was horrified at this example of German Kultur, but in the Fatherland it was hailed with jubilation, special medals being struck and high awards given to all concerned.

The only vessel in sight at the time of sinking was the tiny Peel drifter *Wanderer* close inshore under the lighthouse. Making all possible sail, she slowly came up to the scene of the disaster, and was able to pick up 160 survivors, taking 110 on board, and towing the remainder in a lifeboat and a raft until she was able to transfer them to other vessels, which came hurrying up as soon as the wireless S.O.S. from the stricken liner was received. Renamed *Erin's Hope* and fitted with a motor, *Wanderer* was still fishing in Irish waters in 1930.

In September, 1917, the callous, brutal Schwieger met his deserts, when in command of U88 he left a German port in company with another submarine. After the escort left, the two U-boats dived and ran submerged into a British minefield, the other boat fouled a mooring chain and was about to try and come to the surface when the commander heard a heavy explosion. Nothing more was ever heard of the U88, so it can be supposed she sank with all hands; her companion escaped.

At the turn of the century the glory of the Kinsale fishing had departed, with the exception of a few isolated voyages by individual boats. When Mr. John Quirk, of Peel Quay, who went to the S.W. Irish fishing in his youth, revisited the scene in 1936, he found Kinsale harbour empty, except for a few small yawls and one old nickey which he recognised as *Hannah*, of which he and his father had once been skipper. She was originally P.L.21, 20 tons, built 1877 for Thomas Quirk, and out of the Customs register in 1917 when she was probably sold "foreign." He tells how the barracks of the former British garrison were burnt during the 1917 rising, as were all the residences of the English families, and grass grew between the stones of the once busy streets.

To return to the more prosperous days. The Manxmen aimed to be home by Tynwald Fair Day, so the mackerel season ended about the middle of June, when a watchman, usually a local Irishman, was left in charge of the hulk. The fishermen thought nothing of bringing back in the fish holds live geese, donkeys, goats, and young cattle to replenish the farm stocks in the homeland. If they had a good passage, the fleets arrived home about the 25th June, were refitted and the herring nets put aboard. Only some 25 nets were carried, but they were twice as deep as the mackerel ones, and a smaller mesh. The majority of the boats went away to the Shetlands, but the old men stayed and fished round the coast, selling locally, as had been the general custom before the first boats went to Lerwick in the '70's. There was then much curing and kippering done at Derbyhaven and elsewhere.

The boats left about the second or third week in July on the long trip of over 500 miles, up the North Channel to the Mull of Kintyre, through the Sound of Jura, round Ardnamurchan Point, and away up the West Coast of Scotland through The Minch, round Cape Wrath, through the stormy Pentland Firth, and away for the Orkneys, then the Shetlands, arriving at Lerwick in about a week and a half. To quote Mr. Gawne:

"It was a lovely sight coming through the Highlands in the summertime in the month of July, but Pentland Firth was a wicked place. It is surprising the few accidents there was. Them old fellows would go up to Lerwick and they couldn't read or write, and all they would have would be Jefferson's Almanack, and they couldn't read it! They would give it to the boy and say 'What course is that?' and they would be getting there all right. I suppose about fifty Peel boats and about twenty to thirty from Port St. Mary would be going up, sixty or seventy altogether perhaps. They were a grand type of fishermen, the old ones, grand sailors, could handle a boat. When I was in *Eleanor* I would look at them old boys—they would be 115 years old now if alive—all were talking Manx and I couldn't understand them. I have seen them coming down after nets had been shot, on a watch night I would be sitting at the stove looking at the old fellows with their sou'westers on, and thinking they would only want two sheep's horns to make them into real Vikings.

The Shetland fishing, you know, they didn't go quite so far off the land to fish, only about ten or twelve miles, it was all creeks and big gullies running in. When the nets were shot, the men could fish for big fish if they liked. My gracious, it was a busy place, Lerwick, at that time. Whaling ships and Dutch coming in, fishing for ling and cod. They would come in with piles of ling on their decks, higher than the mantelpiece here. At the end of August and the beginning of September they would be making away for Rotterdam. There would be 1,000 boats in Lerwick. We used to leave there in the third week in September, and the corn would be as green as grass, and when we would get home the harvest would be all over. It was time to get out then, and you would have an awful path to get home, the prevailing wind was S.W. Sometimes there would be a lot of us together, the Peel fellows and the Port St. Mary and Arklow (Irish) as well. Sometimes you would lose sight of each other, you know, it was a good way from the Shetlands to the Orkneys, some of us would be gone a week before the others, but as a rule there would be five or six together, but some would be putting in to Long Hope, others to St. Margaret's Hope, others would carry on to get round the Cape to Larkerecool. When round the Cape there were lots of harbours. It was only 'fill and set,' tacking all the time, coming through the Highlands of Scotland, there was currents all the way down, but the worse part of it coming home was Sumburgh Head. Then down to Ardnamurchan Point, that was nearly as bad as the Cape, then it was more sheltered when you got to Jura. Sometimes they would be four or five weeks coming home. It was all sail then, I remember seeing steam trawlers going across and the old fishermen used to jaw about them and call them 'the invention of the devil.' Once the steam trawlers came in they ruined the drift net fishing. That was about sixty years ago. I remember the last year I was up in the Shetlands there wouldn't be a steam drifter there. Everyone had the same chance, you see, and they were doing far better."

An average trip home was about a fortnight, the worst might be six weeks. Mr. Radcliffe Quilliam, of Peel, aged seventy-six in 1945, states that the record passage home from Lerwick was made by the nickey *Elvira*, P.L. 44, 20 tons, first registered 1876 for Charles Morrison, and in service until 1919. She made the trip of almost 600 miles in 57 hours. She must have held a strong nor'easter all the way down, a fair wind which would give smooth water for much of the distance.

Of the Port St. Mary fleet, Mr. Gawne says *Annie Jane*, C.T.21, took 3 days, 16 hours for the passage, and that the last boat to go to the Shetland fishing was *Milky Way* about 1906.

Further proof of the surprising speed of these nickeys is given in a note in the *Mariner's Mirror*, written by Mr. R. Stuart Bruce, which he kindly permits me to quote: "In the summer of 1892 or '93, I was coming north from Lerwick to Whalsey, a distance of a little more than eleven miles, in our local mail steamer, *Earl of Zetland*, 232 G.T., speed eight knots when clean. It was a fine morning, with a full sailing westerly breeze off the land and smooth sea. We had cleared the north entrance to Bressay Sound when I saw a Manx lugger coming up astern, sailing very fast. She was *Honey Guide*, C.T.96, carrying her big lug and mizzen, but no mizzen topsail. When we got to the Mull of Eswick, roughly halfway between Lerwick and Whalsey, the boat had drawn ahead of us, and by the time we had reached our anchorage in Symbister Voe, Whalsey, she was through Whalsey Sound and well to the north of Wether Holm, say some three miles ahead. She was certainly sailing splendidly. These Manx luggers were small in comparison with the large Scots luggers of later days."

A good season of twelve weeks would give an average of £20 a man, and after refitting, it was the custom for some of the fishermen to go across to Northern Ireland to fish, staying until about Christmas, then the boats were laid up for the winter.

Plate 135 shows Port St. Mary nickeys fitting out. C.T. 53 was *Elizabeth*, one of the three painted lead colour, C.T.64 was *Ben my Chree*. Nearly all the boats have their gear on deck and lying against the quay are a few of the very largest of the dandy-rigged "luggers," used mainly for trawling. C.T.25 is *Confidence*, C.T.54 *Alice*, both launched about 1886.

What were the rewards for the extensive fishing then carried out? *Jefferson's Almanack* for 1882 quotes "the produce of herrings caught on the Manx coast this season is estimated at £100,000." Golden sovereigns, not paper currency!

But these earnings were not taken without loss. Think of the wild, rugged coasts off which the fishing was carried on, and the weather and tides with which the men had to contend, pitting their faith and skill against the elemental forces of Nature. The Mull of Kintyre has a bold, steep-to, lofty coast-line, with baffling tides as the waters of the North Atlantic and Irish Sea pour through the narrow fifteen-mile channel between Scotland and Ireland. Ardnamurchan Point is fully exposed to the fury of the Atlantic and frequently wicked seas are encountered. In the Sound of Sleat run eight knot currents at spring tides; overfalls and eddies are numerous, as soon as the distant shelter of the Hebrides is lost, the Minch is open to the Atlantic; Cape Wrath, with its gaunt, forbidding cliffs, seldom belies its name, and wind against tide kicks up an ugly sea. If the scenery is magnificent, the perils are many, even in summer, and safe harbours lie considerable distances apart. Pentland Firth is notorious for its tides, eight knots and more, not to mention races, whirlpools and eddies. One has only to recall the terrific damage done during the 1914-18 war to many of H.M. ships—battleships and cruisers as well as smaller craft—to realise that the tiny luggers of the hardy Manx and Scots fishermen faced risks few landsmen would care to encounter, least of all take as part of the day's work to earn a frugal living at the best of times, at the worst, another smashed boat and drowned crew all that remained of high endeavour. Those splendid men, descendants of the fierce Vikings, knew the dangers, yet at the most all you would probably get out of them would be "Aye, but it's a wicked place with wind at sou' west."

The West of Ireland offers similar conditions, being open to every wind from the wide Atlantic, even in the rare calms a heavy swell breaks on the ironbound cliffs, soon to be whipped up into angry seas as the wind gathers. Gales and mists add to the dangers but as compensation there was the beauty of many of the anchorages, set against a background of mountains, wooded glens, waterfalls, and green slopes covered with gorse, a turquoise sea reflecting every colour and beauty as the luggers rocked to the gentle tide.

As to losses, let us hear what Mr. Gawne has to say:

"I was just going to say that for all the fishing that was done here for a hundred years there were very few disasters, but on the coast from Liverpool to Fleetwood there has been more than a hundred wrecks. Of all the Peel and Port St. Mary fleets only two foundered, *Dart*, C.T.17, in November 1872, and *Sonnet*, P.L.45, in 1878, but there has been a lot lost. The *Dart* was lost coming from Skerrish, and I heard my father say he was in *Pet*, C.T.38, coming with her. They left Skerrish at daybreak, about eight o'clock on the 6th November. The wind was fair and they put the topsail over a reefed mainsail, although it was that fine there wasn't enough wind to have a reef. As they went the wind was gathering, and soon they had three reefs down, and had to run for it, they couldn't go back. By the time they got three or four miles off the Chickens lighthouse the storm was terrible. A shower came out, and they lost sight of the *Dart*, and when it was over they couldn't see her, and knew she was lost. She was the only open boat that crossed that day, they were going to deck her when she got home. She was swamped. It was breaking on the others too, but they had hatches on and that saved them. Eight men were lost and before that she had lost five men behind Langness. She was unlucky, a brute of a boat.

*Pearl*, C.T.102, was lost in 1883 coming home from the Shetlands, and *Willie*, C.T.43, went ashore on Sheep Island, but they got her off. *Maggie Maddrell*, P.L.48, drowned all but one man in the Sound of Jura. *Lydia*, P.L.70, was run down by the Cunarder *Pavonia*, thirty miles off Kinsale. *Olive*, C.T.13, was run down in April 1874 by *Oakworth*, a big ship on her maiden voyage. They didn't know what had happened to her until three months later, when *Oakworth* got to Australia and the passengers split on the skipper, who hadn't stopped for any survivors. He had run in close to show the passengers the men shooting the nets, and cut the boat through. The Mayor of Melbourne was Manx, and he wrote home to see if any Manxmen were missing, and the skipper got ten years and lost his ticket. *Monarch* was missing with all hands out of Douglas, being sunk through loading her with too many herring. In 1894 another went down, but it was a very small percentage that were lost. *May Lily*, C.T.47, was lost with four men coming out of Kinsale. *Cedar*, C.T.9, lost her skipper and one man on her first passage to Kinsale 11th March 1875. On the 20th March 1895 *Quickstep*, P.L.205 was going to Finet. A sea swept her and washed the crew overboard and only the cook and one man were left, and they took her into Berehaven. (*Quickstep*, P.L.205, 30 tons, built 1874, for John Teare and others, out of Customs Register 1907.)

*Rose Ann* grounded after she had been swinging to an anchor, but the cowl of the funnel was down, and in the night the wind shifted, the fumes came down and suffocated all of them. *Fear Not* with two men was lost in Port Erin, dashed to pieces on Bradda Head."

*Fear Not* was P.L.94, 23 tons, built 1877 for James Moore and others, out of Customs Register 1910. Mr. William Dodd says at one time this nickey had an outboard propeller fitted, power being supplied from the boiler ordinarily used to drive the capstan when hauling in the nets. The experiment was only partly successful, owing to the impossibility of keeping up steam for any length of time.

She was evidently not the first craft on which an inventive Manxman tried to experiment, as Willie Mylrea, aged eighty-seven in 1938, says one of the first nickeys to be built at Peel was the *Sea King*, owner George Faragher. She was later fitted with paddles, but was not a success as a fishing boat, and was sold to Douglas, being the first steam ferry to ply between the Victoria Pier and Douglas Head. Evidently the indomitable George had succumbed to the lure of steam, as he went to Liverpool, where he became a successful steam trawler skipper.

In weather which wrecked the schooner *Orion*, the nickey *Jane*, P.L.145, 20 tons, built 1870 for Robert Corrin, came into Peel Harbour in perfect trim with dry decks, as many a witness could testify.

As to the life on board, who better to describe it than a man who went to sea in 1895, John Gawne, of Fistard.

"The cook was the drudge. All the sleep he was getting was when he would have tea made and the dishes washed and they would be shooting the nets about half-past seven or eight o'clock, then he would be getting into bed. They always prayed after the nets were shot, and we all had to go down on our knees, the greatest sinners and all. There was one boat I was in and it was Manx they were talking all the time, but they always sung a hymn in English, for my benefit I always thought! I have been many and many a time, the old fellows there praying, and my head on the locker fast asleep, not knowing what they were saying and caring less. It's the finest sleeps I ever had in my life was in those nickeys, we wanted no rocking there, we were dead to the world. At midnight the cook was up again to coil that confounded rope, the springback, as thick as my wrist. You pulled that through a hole in the deck and coiled it down, good work if it was done in four hours. I have seen me down here for seven hours to get it in and tight against the deck. I don't know how fellows that were seasick did it. When shooting you had to watch the rope going out, and I would rather coil than watch. I remember a young Peel fellow got it caught round his leg and nearly went overboard; lots had their legs badly hurt. For five nights a week the cook coiled down the rope every night, the only light a little swinging lamp with no glass on it, and the smell of the lamp and the anchor chain! Jelly fish—barmoos we called them —made the rope slip out of your hands, and if you got them near your eyes, look out! They were awful, octopuses too, squids we used to call them, we would be hanging on, boat rolling, rope slipping! The poor old cook used to go through it when mackerel fishing, the nets then had a rope over a mile long. I could do with coiling the rope, but not the anchor chain. It was an awful job, coming down all covered with mud; you could wash your hands over fifty times and the smell would still be on them, the most horrible smell I've ever smelled. Terrible!

It's a fine life in the fishing boats, some terrible cooking going down, of course. All eyes of fat on the broth, and nine to ten pounds of beef going into the pot on Sunday, cabbage and barley too. I don't remember having much leeks or turnips. Any amount of cabbage in Kinsale, none in Lerwick, they wouldn't grow there, too windswept. We used to get duffs with raisins in, boiled in the broth and guaranteed to sink like a stone. We had a rice pudding on Sundays, made with condensed milk, a tin and a half, and two big handfulls of raisins too. The cooks would always be keeping the bottoms for themselves, where the raisins were! The boys always used to hide the rice pudding and have a good beano after tea on Sundays.

Every man had his mug, they would sit on a locker, there was no chairs, you see, and the seven mugs would be round about and the cook would take the kettle, the tea, water and milk would all be going in the kettle; he would pour out and then sugar would be added if you wanted it. A table would have been no use at all, even if bolted down, because when she was pitching the cups would be coming off. Sometimes you would see herring or mackerel all over the floor. They were wonderful at juggling with their old plate and pint mug, but a fellow that wasn't used to it wouldn't be getting much to eat, at all. There wasn't much sympathy with anybody, but I never got with a bad skipper, I was lucky.

The sugar was kept in a big stone jar, holding about a stone, with a big spoon stuck in it. Ordinary men could get their hand down in the jar, but one big fellow I knew couldn't, his hands were too big, and he had to shout for the cook to come and get the sugar for him. The water casks held three or four gallons, and there was a tank holding twenty to thirty. We never ran out of water, and always had plenty to eat too. If you were a long way off the land, you might have to heave-to all the week-end, but we never ran out of anything. After our tobacco was gone, you could go to a Dutch boat loaded with it, and whisky and all, or if you put a bag up, or an old cap, oilskin or anything, he would be at you in a minute.

The boys used to have a good time in Kinsale and Lerwick, we would go or steal ashore every Saturday night. Cooks had it clear after dishes were washed till supper-time; you could come aboard for tea or stay ashore. Given sixpence to go ashore with, they were millionaires, but when home had a real blowout; the boy got half a share and it was a lot of money to them. You never had a cook after he was fifteen at all, he then counted a man. On Sunday the men always went to church or chapel; there was a Protestant chapel in Kinsale, none in other ports as the Irish were mostly Roman Catholics, but there was a mission ship at Crookhaven and we used to go aboard to a service, you could get tobacco and home comforts there too. The Irish never seemed to mind us, I never saw any trouble, all sorts of boats would be in—Cornish, Manx, Irish, French, for the seas are open to all. The Frenchies would be down there, young fellows they were, hauling nets with a handspike and a capstan, walking round something like a treadmill.

The men liked the mackerel fishing, it was cleaner than the herring, but worse for the cooks, because they had double the amount of springbacks to coil. It was warm work herring fishing, the nets being three times as big. Mackerel was taken out of the nets as they were hauled in, but herring had to be sorted. Sometimes the men would do very well, at other times earn little, but money went a lot further in those days. Oh, my gracious, yes. A pound was then worth about three now. You could go and buy three dozen eggs for 1s., and a pound of butter for 7d. An eight-quarter tin of milk cost 1s., and potatoes were about two or three pence a stone.

Everybody had his fill of herring. I remember when I was a boy every man would have five hundred salted for the winter, some six or seven hundred. The Manx fishermen used to be superstitious, too. Used to have a stone on the nets called the "clish stone," never a white one on at all. They would never turn a boat's head when going away to the fishing, never turn her round against the sun. Used to lash two boats together so as there wouldn't be a third boat. Never give salt away, it was always from one boat to another. I knew one cook that gave a mugful to another, and the captain called him and said 'Did you give salt to the cook of the *Harvest Home*?' 'Yes,' he said. 'Well, we might as well go home, our fishing is finished.' It was the fault of one of the crew who told on the little cook. They went out that night and got sixty cran, and the cook said to the captain: 'My gracious, I never prayed for them herring to come to the nets before, but I prayed for them now. We had luck for all.' But the captain wouldn't agree, he still believed in the bad luck of the salt.

I remember one May night, thirty miles off the land at Kinsale, they were going round with torches 'burning witches off the boat,' going in every corner. You weren't allowed to mention a rat, cat or rabbit. I remember one time they had the nets ashore at Skull, near Crookhaven, and a little rabbit got in one, and the skipper, an awful superstitious fellow, said 'Our season's finished now, when that's got in.' If you stuck a knife in the mast, look out for wind; you weren't to whistle either, that was wind again. You were reminded of it all right if you forgot! They were always taking care of the first fish of the season—the 'eriey'—cooking him specially in the boiler and all taking a nip of him. You were not allowed to throw ashes overboard after sunset, they had to be done before or left in overnight. The old fishermen used to leave a bottle of rum when going out fishing on Mondays at Kione Dhoo (Black Head) for the beast of Kione Dhoo, and a very enlightened fisherman was reputed to collect the bottles when home at the week-end for his own use!"

Beyond rearranging some of his remarks to preserve continuity, I have throughout used Mr. Gawne's own words.

The fishermen evidently liked their fun, as the following story, related by Jack Kelly, aged eighty-nine, shows. After the Peel herring fishing, he took his boat to the balk fishing at Douglas, but had no luck at all. Week after week he had to lend money to his two men to enable them to get home to Kirk Michael. Jack planned to go to the Howth fishing, but the men refused and left the boat one Saturday morning. An hour or so later Jack went up the big street—Castle Street—and into Tom Kewin's pub to see if he could pick up a crew, and the first men he saw were the two Kirk Michael men, one on each side of Chalse the herbalist, drinking ale. They told Jack they had changed their minds and would go with him. The Howth fishing turned out very well, bringing some £11 to each man for six or seven weeks' work. When Jack was paying them off, the Kirk Michael men told him they knew the reason for the luck, pulled out their purses and pointed to a small piece of cloth that each possessed, cut off the tails of poor old Chalse's coat.

On another occasion some Peel fishermen heard that an insult had been offered to one of them in an old pub, "The Thatch," near Douglas Quay. They went along hot-foot, grabbed hold of the rafters and pulled the roof off to avenge the real or fancied insult! Most of the men followed the fishing all their lives, as did Jack Cashin of Dalby, who went to sea at the age of eleven, in his youth fished for cod off Rockall in the stormy North Atlantic in a half-decked "lugger," and at eighty-one was still fishing in home waters.

For much of this information I am indebted to the Manx Museum and its team of volunteer collectors, who are engaged in a survey of the folk-life and traditions of the

140 NOBBY *GLADYS*. BOW VIEW       141 *GLADYS*. STERN VIEW

142 *CUSHAG*. P.L. 41, 1935

143  *LILIAN*.  DECK VIEW
Note long cleat amidships, rounded corners to hatch coamings.

144  *BONNIE JANE* AND *ADA*.  1935
Note old Peel shipyard in background.

145  *ADA*.  BOW VIEW
Note rounded heel of foremast over starboard bow, flat floors and hollow garboards.

146 DOUGLAS HARBOUR
P.L. 42 counter sterned nickey *Ann*.


147 CURING SHED, BURNMOUTH c. 1882

148 EARLY 19TH CENTURY LOOM FOR NET MAKING

149 SCAFFIE *SEVEN BROTHERS*, B.F. 941
   Original sketch by Mr. John Addison, aged 84.

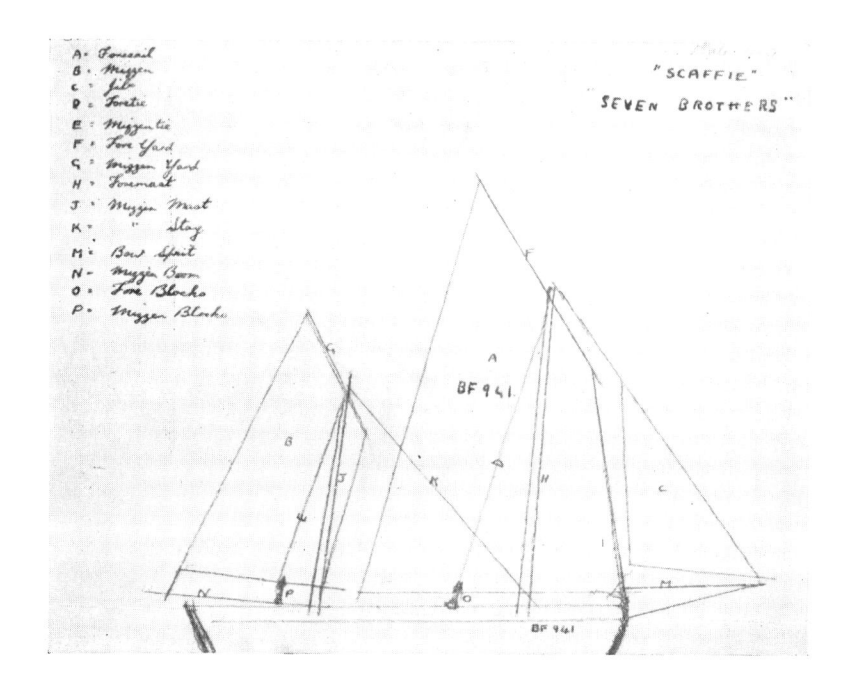

Island. Mr. Dodd, of Peel, has been gathering information on the Peel fishermen and boatbuilders for the Museum during the past twenty years, and from Mr. John Gawne, of Fistard, the collectors, Mrs. Anne Barishnikov and Miss Z. M. Sayle, have taken down enough material to make a book about the Port St. Mary fleets. Besides putting this original material at my disposal, the Museum collectors kindly offered to submit to certain people known to them any questions I cared to send. Needless to say, I took full advantage of this courtesy, and I, and all interested in the sea and ships, am deeply indebted to the band of helpers who gave their time to interview fishermen, shipwrights, sailmakers and others, taking down their remarks in full and sending the notes on to me, thus enabling me to deal more fully with the Manx fisheries than at one time seemed possible.

Plate 136 shows some of the Port St. Mary fleet lying in Port Erin about fifty years ago. C.T.7, *Puffin* was the last of the old "luggers," her mainsail is furled, but an interesting triangular watch mizzen is set, a typical Cornish practice. C.T.1, *Shah*, once a nickey, was one of several converted back to dandy rig in the 1890's, her gaff topsail is set, and note the high peaking of the yard. The other boats are sharp-sterned nickeys. C.T.110 is *Stephen*; C.T.59 has the typical Manx mizzen topsail with its yard standing almost vertical and set entirely aft of the mast. C.T.27 has her oars laid up in lumber irons on the port rail, but C.T.55, *Expert* is worthy of special notice. Built at Port St. Mary in 1881 by Qualtrough for W. S. Qualtrough, her length overall is 52 ft. 2 in., keel 47 ft. 3 in., beam 15 ft. 2 in., depth of hold 6 ft. 5 in., G.T. 23.36 tons, N.T. 15.45 tons.

Thanks to the work done by the late P. J. Oke in 1935 on behalf of the Coastal Craft Sub-Committee of the Society for Nautical Research, her lines and sail plan have been preserved for all time. Plans 15, pages 331-2.

Another photograph in my possession, taken at the same time as Plate 136, shows more of the fleet, with an interesting clench-built cutter, C.T.56, with a sharp stern, which Mr. Gawne says was *James and Mary*, a boat purchased in the Shetlands. The mizzen lugs were generally left standing when the boats lay to their anchors.

As in many respects *Expert* follows St. Ives practice, I propose to draw attention only to features in which they differ. A striking likeness will be seen to the lines of *Ebenezer* (page 321), but the foremast is stepped further aft, its foreside being 11 ft. from for'ard of stem, against 8 ft. in the Cornish boat. The bowsprit heel rests in a 1 ft. by $10\frac{1}{2}$ in. iron, 3 in. by $\frac{5}{8}$ in., fitted on the port side of the $6\frac{7}{8}$ in. square bitt, placed 5 ft. 9 in. from stem, 2 ft. 4 in. above deck, with a wooden cleat on the starboard side, and stepped down into the deadwood. Frames are doubled, not long scarphed, hatch coamings have rounded corners, while companion and skylight are in one.

There is a fine constructional model of *Expert* in the Liverpool Museum, and I had

## ISLE OF MAN

a photograph specially taken to show framing, deadwood, planking, etc. (Plate 137).

### SCANTLINGS

| | | |
|---|---|---|
| Keel | - | 6 in. sided, 10½ in. moulded, is of elm, stemhead 11 in. by 5¾ in. |
| Floors | - | 6 in. deep by 4¼ in. Oak. |
| Frames | - | Doubled. 3 in. by 4⅜, centred 1 ft. 7 in. Oak. |
| Mast beams | - | 5 in. by 6 in., small beams 5 in. by 4 in. Three short beams in forepeak 4 in. by 7½ in. spaced 2 ft. 2 in., with knee at foremast, 7 in. wide by 3 in. thick. Camber 5 in., at 20 ft. from stem 3¾ in. Oak. |
| Bulkheads | - | 1 in. thick. |
| Bulwarks | - | 1 ft. 7¼ in. high, with 18 stanchions 4 in. sq., spacing 2 ft. 3 in. to 3 ft., with rail 4 in. by 2 in. Elm. |
| Stringers | - | 4¾ in. below deck. 4 in. sq. |
| Floor stringers | - | 3 ft. 3 in. below deck, 2 in. by 4 in. deep. |

### PLANKING

| | | |
|---|---|---|
| Deck | - | 5 in. to 6 in., 2 in. to 2¼ in. thick. Pine. |
| Rubbing plank | - | 2½ in. below covering board, 2½ in. thick by 9 in. |
| Sheer strake | - | 2½ in. thick by 11 in. deep. |
| Hull planks | - | 1¾ in. thick, seventeen strakes. |
| Top plank | - | 6 in. deep, lower 7 in. deep, bilge 9½ in. deep. |
| Garboard (up) | - | 10½ in. and 11 in. |

### SPARS

| | | |
|---|---|---|
| Foremast | - | Pine. 48 ft. overall, 10½ in. to 6 in. dia., top 5 in. dia., 5 ft. 3 in. below deck, 9½ in. square for lower 5 ft. 10 in., stepped in tabernacle with 11 in. by 3 in. thick bridges, heel rounded and rests in step 3 ft. above keel, 2 ft. 6 in. long, 10 in. wide, 1 ft. 6 in. deep. |
| Foreyard | - | Larch. 33 ft. long, 6 in. to 3 in. dia., iron traveller 1 ft. 4 in. dia. by 1¼ in. |
| Mizzen mast | - | Spruce. 40 ft. 9 in. overall, dia. 9 in. to 5½ in., below deck length 5 ft. 9 in. |
| Mizzen yard | - | Larch. 22 ft. 6 in., dia. 4½ in. to 3 in. Shroud blocks: Single, 6 in. by 2½ in. Double: 5 in. by 7 in. |
| Mizzen boom | - | 20 ft. outboard, 30 ft. overall, dia. 8 in. to 4½ in., heel rests in ¾ in. thick iron step on a wooden base 2 ft. 3 in. long by 6 in. by 2¾ in. |
| Mizzen topsail yard | | Larch. 19 ft. 6 in., dia. 3 in. to 2½ in. |
| Yard on foot | - | Larch 15 ft. 3 in. |
| Pole topmast | - | Spruce. 9 ft. long, dia. 4 in. to 3 in. |
| Jibboom, or bowsprit | | 15 to 16 ft. |

### DECK DETAILS

| | | |
|---|---|---|
| Tiller | - | 10 ft. 6 in. overall, 2 in. dia. at inboard end. |
| Skylight | - | 7 ft. 10 in. long, 3 ft. 4 in. wide, 1 ft. 7 in. high, is 1 ft. 9 in. from foreside of mast, long window in sides. |
| Cleat | - | On third and fourth stanchions from sternpost is a 3 ft. 5 in. by 2½ in. wide by 3½ in. deep cleat, with a seat 8½ in. wide by 1½ in. thick, athwartships, on upper edge. |

| | | |
|---|---|---|
| Rail | - - | Deep rail on port side, notched for outrigger, extends to fifth stanchion, starboard side is $3\frac{1}{2}$ in. by $4\frac{1}{2}$ in. tapering to 2 in. deep. |
| Raft irons | - | Two on port rail, 1 ft. 6 in. wide by $\frac{3}{4}$ in. thick. |
| Long cleat | - | On stanchions eight to eleven from aft, 3 in. by 2 in., 8 in. from deck. |
| Vertical cleat | - | 3 in. sq., on sixth stanchion aft, extends $3\frac{1}{2}$ in. above rail. |
| Pump | - - | At after end of hatch on starboard side of skylight, 7 in. dia. by 1 in. |
| Coamings | - | $6\frac{1}{2}$ in. deep inside, 4 in. by 3 in. outside, slightly curved fore end, long knee fore and aft at aft end, 4 in. thick, 4 ft. 9 in. long. |
| Mast trunk | - | For'ard. 1 ft. 5 in. wide by 6 ft. long, sides 10 in. deep by $3\frac{1}{4}$ in., aft end 8 in. thick by 10 in. deep by 1 ft. 7 in. wide. |
| Cleats | - - | Small cleats on fourth stanchion for'ard, $7\frac{1}{2}$ in. dia. lead on fifth stanchion, post on sixth, and small cleat on seventh stanchion. |
| Ring bolts | - | In covering boards, $4\frac{1}{2}$ in. from bulwarks for shrouds, etc., between fourth, fifth, and sixth stanchions. |
| Long cleat | - | On first and second stanchions for'ard. 3 ft. 8 in. long by $2\frac{1}{2}$ in. by 4 in. deep. |
| Capstan | - | To starboard, just for'ard of hatch coaming. |
| Fairleads | - | On rails for'ard, iron fairleads for use when hauling nets. Below on port side hole for bowsprit to reeve through, to starboard hawsehole. |

## BELOW DECKS

| | | |
|---|---|---|
| Forepeak - | - | Or Bos'en's store for spare rope, barrels, salt, gear, potatoes, etc. Access either by way of mast trunk or through fish hold. |
| Fish hold | - | Amidships, divided into two rooms, one for fish, the other for nets. Ballast was stowed below the platform. |
| Cabin - | - | 5 ft. 6 in. to 5 ft. 8 in. high, with bunks 2 ft. 6 in. wide, and locker seats, contains stove, boiler, with deckhouse above large enough to allow boiler to be removed through it if necessary. |

In some nickeys the deckhouse extended aft, so that the mizzen mast went down through it. In her latter days *Expert* was re-rigged as a nobby, before an engine was installed.

## SAIL PLAN

There are marked differences in the cut of the sails to Cornish practice, especially in the set of the mizzen topsail.

| | | |
|---|---|---|
| Foresail - | - | Head 31 ft. 3 in., slings 10 ft. 3 in. from weather yardarm. |
| | | Leech: 46 ft. 3 in., with 6 in. round. |
| | | Weather or luff: 24 ft. 10 in. |
| | | Foot: 37 ft. 6 in. with 12 in. round. |
| | | Diagonals: 52 ft. 6 in. and 41 ft. 4 in. |
| | | Two reefs, 3 ft. 6 in. deep. Area, 1,104.25 sq. ft. |
| Mizzen lug | - | Head: 20 ft. Slings: 5 ft. from weather yardarm. |
| | | Leech: 31 ft. with 3 in. round. |
| | | Weather or luff: 17 ft. 6 in. |
| | | Foot: 21 ft. with 6 in. round. |
| | | Diagonals: 34 ft. 9 in. and 26 ft. |
| | | Two reefs, 3 ft. 6 in. deep. Area, 502.5 sq. ft. |

| | |
|---|---|
| *Mizzen topsail* - | Head of luff: 18 ft. 6 in.—for yard, lower luff 11 ft. 9 in. |
| | Leech: 11 ft. |
| | Foot: 27 ft., with a 15 ft. 3 in. jenny boom. |
| | Area: 252.25 sq. ft. |
| *Staysail* - | Luff: 33 ft. 6 in. |
| | Leech: 27 ft., with a 2 in. roach. |
| | Foot: 20 ft. 6 in., with a 6 in. roach. |
| | Area: 348 sq. ft. |
| *Total sail area* - | 2,207 sq. ft., without a jib, which was seldom carried. |

The disadvantages of the nickey were the necessity for dipping the fore lug when going about, and having to change the suits of sails according to the vagaries of the weather. As a result of the gradual difficulty of finding good crews, the "nobby" rig was introduced in the eighties, and from 1889 in the Peel fleet was the only rig fitted in boats built in the last days of sail, with the exception of the 28-ton nickey *Shamrock*, P.L.249, built in 1894 for Teare and Sons.

The chief difference between a nickey and a nobby was one of rig, the former used a dipping foresail and seldom had a bowsprit or headsails, the latter had a standing lug on the foremast, which raked aft considerably to allow a foresail to be set on the forestay, while a jib was set flying on a spar known locally as a jibboom, although actually a reeving bowsprit. On the mizzen was a smaller standing lug, all sails, except the jibs, had reef points and no changing of sails was done, thus making conditions somewhat easier for the crews, now mostly old men. Consequently many nickeys were converted to nobbies, but a true nobby was smaller, with a keel length of 30 to 35 ft. Many Port St. Mary boats reverted to the old dandy rig, but it is difficult to lay down hard and fast distinctions, for nobbies converted to nickeys, and *vice versa* according to the ideas held by the owner, who was often the skipper, and many hybrids were to be seen.

Plate 138 is of *Lily*, P.L.172, registered in 1871 as a nickey of 25 tons, owned by J. Teare and others, but later converted to a nobby. She is sharp-sterned, both lugs are set to port of the masts, the foremast being supported by shrouds, set up with luff tackles, and a forestay set up with two treble or double blocks. The foresail has been dropped and jib run in, the outhaul can clearly be seen below the bowsprit. The long sweeps are out for the weary row home with a heavy catch. *Lily* was not in the 1918 register.

Plate 139 is P.L.37, *Xema*, named after the genus of fork-tailed gull, she is of 25 tons, built 1877 for T. C. S. Moore and others as a nickey, and was not in the 1915 register. Note the counter stern, bowsprit with tack of jib hooked to its traveller, the standing lug with its tack to a hook on a short horse at foot of foremast, and the big sail sheeting home well aft. The jump stay is set up from mizzen masthead to an eye on port rail, and true nobbies never set a topsail.

It is thanks to Mr. Oke's work that it is possible to have accurate plans of a nobby,

## SAILING DRIFTERS

*Gladys*, P.L.61, built in 1901 for Mr. Watterson of Peel, by Neakle & Watson at Peel. Registering 12.17 tons, she is not in the 1936 register. Plans 16, pages 333-5.

The stem, raking aft with a well-rounded forefoot, measures 9 ft. 10 in. on the rake, while the sternpost is 12 ft. Length of keel 32 ft., length overall 40 ft. 9 in. Beam 11 ft. 11 in., depth of hold 6 ft. 2 in.

### SCANTLINGS

| | | |
|---|---|---|
| Keel | - | 9 in. by 6 in., with $\frac{1}{2}$ in. iron. |
| Stem | - | $10\frac{1}{2}$ in. moulded, 6 in. sided at head, 12 in. moulded at heel. |
| Sternpost | - | 6 in. by 6 in. at heel, 6 in. by $4\frac{1}{2}$ in. at head. |
| Stern apron | - | 13 in. by 6 in. at heel, tapering to 3 in. by $4\frac{1}{2}$ in. |
| Floors | - | 10 in. by 3 in. at throat, tapering to 5 in. by 3 in. Spaced 1 ft. apart. |
| Frames | - | Where doubled, $4\frac{1}{2}$ in. wide, single $2\frac{1}{4}$ in. by 4 in. |
| Beams | - | 6 in. by $5\frac{1}{4}$ in. Camber 3 in. Short beams, $2\frac{3}{4}$ in. by $3\frac{1}{4}$ in. |
| Platform | - | In hold, 7 in. by 1 in., resting on $1\frac{3}{4}$ in. "strongbacks." |
| Stringers | - | $4\frac{1}{2}$ in. by $3\frac{1}{2}$ in., 3 in. below deck, with knees and fillings. |
| Bulwarks | - | 1 ft. $5\frac{1}{2}$ in. high, stanchions 3 in. sq., spacing 2 ft., rail 4 in. by $1\frac{1}{2}$ in. Some nobbies had short and long stanchions alternating. |
| Mast trunk | - | 5 ft. 8 in. long, 1 ft. $2\frac{1}{2}$ in. wide, sides $3\frac{1}{2}$ in. thick by 9 in. deep. Aft end 4 in. by 8 in. |
| Tabernacle | - | Side bridges 10 in. by $2\frac{3}{4}$ in., $7\frac{1}{2}$ in. apart. |

### PLANKING

| | | |
|---|---|---|
| Deck | - | 4 in. wide by $1\frac{1}{2}$ in. |
| Hull planks | - | $1\frac{1}{4}$ in. thick, sixteen strakes to rubber. |
| Sheer strake | - | 7 in. deep, $1\frac{1}{2}$ in. thick. |
| Garboards | - | $8\frac{1}{2}$ and 8 in. |
| Bilge | - | $6\frac{1}{2}$ in. wide. |
| Covering board | - | $7\frac{1}{2}$ in. by $1\frac{1}{2}$ in. |
| Rubber | - | 4 in. thick by 7 in. deep, with 3 in. by $5\frac{1}{2}$ in. round iron. |
| Bulwarks | - | 1 in. thick. |

### SPARS

| | | |
|---|---|---|
| Foremast | - | L.O.A. 41 ft., below deck 6 ft. 6 in. Dia., 8 in. to 5 in. Heel rests in step on level of hold floor. Step, 2 ft. 2 in. long by 9 in. wide by 10 in. deep (Fig. 62). |
| Foreyard | - | 29 ft. Dia., 6 in. to 3 in. Has two eyes for slings (Fig. 63). |
| Mizzen mast | - | L.O.A. 24 ft. 8 in., below deck 3 ft. Dia., 5 in. to 3 in. Heel rests in step on deadwood in cabin. |
| Mizzen yard | - | 19 ft. Dia., 5 in. to 3 in. |
| Mizzen boom | - | 21 ft., of which 11 ft. is outboard. Dia., 5 in. to $4\frac{1}{2}$ in. |
| Bowsprit | - | 20 ft. L.O.A., 14 ft. outboard. Dia., 6 in. to $4\frac{1}{2}$ in. Heel rests in iron strap on $4\frac{3}{4}$ in. sq. post, 1 ft. 11 in. above deck, 4 ft. 6 in. from stem, and stepped into deadwood. |

### DECK DETAILS

At the stern on the starboard side is a long rail extending for'ard about 34 ft. 8 in., on the port side to the thirteenth stanchion, notched on the quarter to take the mizzen boom or outrigger.

| | |
|---|---|
| *Skylight* - | 6 ft. long by 4 ft. 1 in. wide, 1 ft. 1½ in. high. |
| *Hatch* - - | 10 ft. 4½ in. long, 6 ft. wide, coamings 2 in. thick, 8 in. high on deck. |
| *Pump* - - | 6 in. dia., 1¼ in. thick, 7 in. above hatch coamings with wooden handle 2 ft. 5 in. long, socketed into 1 ft. 10 in. by 1 in. iron head. |
| *Sockets* - - | For oar crutches at sixth and eleventh stanchions. |
| *Oars* - - | 17 ft. 6 in. to 17 ft. 10 in. long. |
| *Lead post* - | 2 ft. 1½ in. from fore end of trunk on starboard side, with cleat aft on side of casing. |
| *Leads* - - | Jib sheet leads on starboard side of deck, 1 ft. 9 in. from hatch coaming. |
| *Chain pipe* - | To starboard of fore end of mast trunk. |
| *Horse* - - | 1 ft. 2 in. long, 5 in. from deck, with freely travelling hook, 8½ in. long, 4 in. wide, to take tack cringle of fore lug. Just for'ard of mast (Fig. 62). |
| *Roller* - - | To port of stem. |
| *Breasthook* - | Inside angle of stem to strengthen same, has iron belaying pin to starboard to take fall of forestay tackle. |
| *Fairleads* - | Iron fairleads on either bow for use when hauling nets. |
| *Binnacle* - | 2 ft. wide, 1 ft. 1½ in. long, 1 ft. 6 in. high on aft end. 6 in. for'ard side, where box is ⅝ in. thick. |
| *Cleats* - - | Across second and third stanchions for'ard. Long cleat amidships from sixth to tenth stanchions. Cleat across last two stanchions aft. All about 2¼ in. wide, 2¾ in. deep. |
| *Tiller* - - | 6 ft. 9 in. overall. |
| *Ringbolts* - | Between third, and fourth and at fifth stanchions. |
| *Vertical cleat* - | On fourth stanchion, with iron ring just aft and another ring aft of fifth stanchion. Rings 2½in. by ½ in. |
| *Boomkin* - | On stemhead, 1½ in. by 1½ in., 1 ft. 5 in. outboard, with 2¼ in. eye set athwartships on outer end. |

It was a common custom to have one or two horseshoes nailed to the inside of the apron, under the breasthook aft.

### *BELOW DECKS*

| | |
|---|---|
| *Forepeak* - - | With chain locker to starboard, racks for sails and spare gear, nets kept in after end, where bulkhead was nailed to beam at end of trunk. |
| *Fish hold* - | Amidships, with three to four tons of pig iron ballast stowed below platform. Pump set on for'ard side of bulkhead aft, with pipe going through the platform to below level of floors. |
| *Cabin* - - | Height about 4 ft. 6 in., with 2 ft. 6 in. wide bunks, locker seats, stove, with lockers on either side, stood against for'ard bulkhead. |

The colour of the hull was a black bottom, white waterline with green above, topsides black with letters P.L.61, 10 in. wide by 1 ft. 2 in. high, spaced 3 in. apart.

Plate 140 shows the bow view of *Gladys* 6th November 1935, with the sharp rise of floors, white waterline, roller to port of stem and hawse hole to starboard. Plate 141 is a stern view, clearly showing how the strakes of planking sweep up into the sternpost, the three-bladed propeller was fitted in the latter days, when an auxiliary was installed.

Plate 142 is of P.L.41, *Cushag*, laid up in November 1935 and the beautiful underwater lines with the long, clean run will be noticed, also the great rake of the sternpost. Plate 143 is a deck view of C.T.4, *Lilian*, one of the last nobbies to fish out of Peel, and the last boat to go to the Kinsale fishing. The various deck fittings mentioned above can be seen, with the pump going down into the fish hold, and the reel on starboard bow used when line fishing. *Lilian* was built by Millar at Port St. Mary in 1900, and her L.O.A. was 38 ft. Her hull was blue, with black topsides and white line, with white inside bulwarks. A seat, on which the helmsman sat, was fitted athwartships on the after cleats, and can be seen under the baulks on which the foremast is resting.

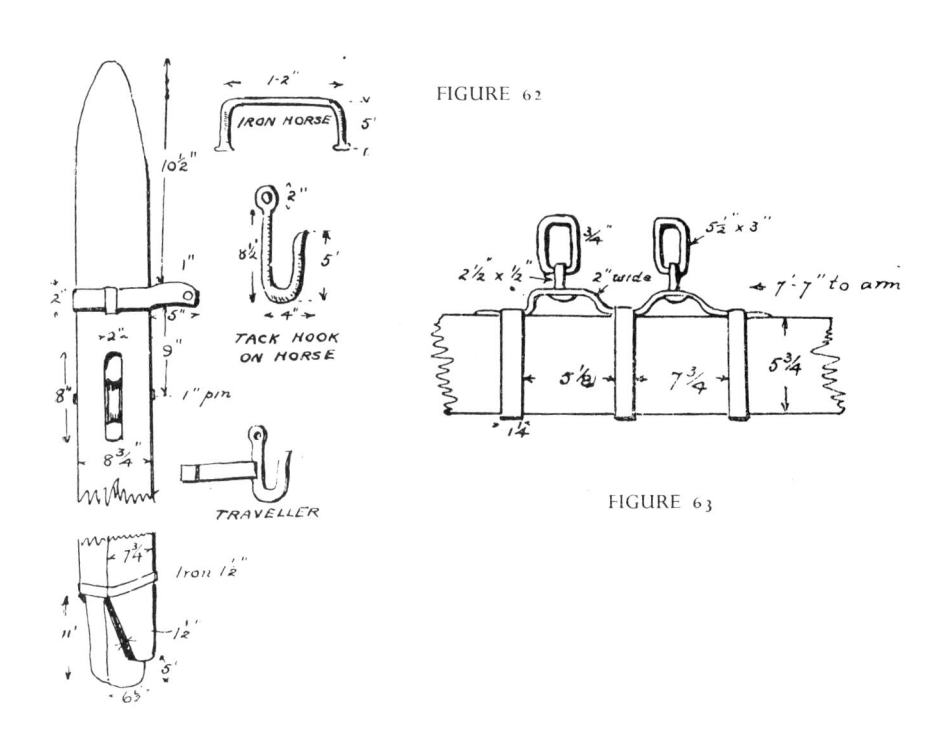

FIGURE 62

FIGURE 63

## SAIL PLAN AND RIGGING

The sail plan of *Gladys* was traced from the original sailmaker's plans, but unfortunately I have no information as to his name.

The rigging was simple, two shrouds a side on the foremast, set up with luff tackles, the blocks being rope stropped with the lower single one hooked in deck rings.

The forestay was set up with two double blocks, with end of fall made fast to belaying pin in stem breasthook.

Fore lug halyards: The tye went from hook on iron traveller and rove through sheave in masthead (Fig 62), and went down on starboard side to a two double block purchase.

The foresail halyards had a single block at masthead, and another of head on sail, which was hanked to forestay, fall belayed to cleat at foot of mast.

The mizzen mast shrouds were set up with gun-tackle purchase, and the lug halyards went to starboard.

| | | |
|---|---|---|
| *Fore lugsail* | - | Head, 27 ft. 3 in., with slings at 9 ft. from weather. |
| | | Luff or weather: 18 ft. |
| | | Leech: 43 ft. with 6 in. round. |
| | | Foot: 21 ft. 8 in. with 12 in. round. |
| | | Diagonals: 44 ft. and 27 ft. 9 in. |
| | | Area: 658 sq. ft. |
| | | Four reefs, 3 ft. deep, upper one being eyelet and lacing. |
| *Mizzen lugsail* | - | Head, 17 ft., with slings 5 ft. from weather. |
| | | Luff or weather: 9 ft. |
| | | Leech: 22 ft. 6 in., with 3 in. round. |
| | | Foot: 14 ft. with 6 in. round. |
| | | Diagonals: 24 ft. 8 in. and 16 ft. 4 in. |
| | | Area: 138.2 sq. ft. |
| | | Two reefs, each 3 ft. deep. |
| *Foresail* - | - | Luff or weather: 19 ft. 6 in. |
| | | Leech: 19 ft. 6 in. |
| | | Foot: 9 ft. 6 in. with 6 in. round. |
| | | Area: 90.25 sq. ft. |
| | | One reef 3 ft. deep. |
| *Balloon foresail or big jib* | | Luff or weather: 32 ft. 9 in. |
| | | Leech: 27 ft. |
| | | Foot: 24 ft., with 12-14 in. round. |
| | | Area: 316.25 sq. ft. |
| *Jib* | - | Luff or weather: 30 ft. |
| | | Leech: 23 ft. |
| | | Foot: 12 ft. 3 in., with 18-21 in. round. |
| | | Area: 135 sq. ft. |
| *Storm jib* | - | Luff or weather, 23 ft. 6 in. |
| | | Leech: 19 ft. 6 in. |
| | | Foot: 8 ft. 6 in. |

Total sail area without balloon jib: 1,097.825 sq. ft.

The fore lugsail tack went to a hook travelling freely on a short iron horse just for'ard of the mast (Fig. 62), the mizzen tack to a hook on a plate bolted to aft side of mast. In some nobbies the mizzen lug halyards were chain.

Mr. Faragher tells me in one Peel quayside warehouse the whole floor is shored up with massive iron pump shafts, 7 ft. to 8 ft. long, taken from broken-up nickeys and nobbies. I first heard of Mr. Faragher's interest in sailing craft through my friends Mr. and Mrs. Hubert Gregg, who made enquiries on my behalf in the Isle of Man during the summer of 1948. Although a busy bank manager, he was good enough to go to the trouble of making out specially for me a complete list of all fishing vessels registered at Peel from 1870, the first year registration was compulsory, until 1917, when the last sailing boat was built, a monumental piece of work involving extensive enquiries in addition to the searching of registers, and truly appreciated by me.

I am greatly indebted to Mr. F. C. Faragher and Mr. Basil Megaw for the interest they took in my efforts to record the activities of the once flourishing fishing industry.

An analysis of Mr. Faragher's lists yielded the following interesting facts. The first ten years saw 113 nickeys registered, with only five boats under 12 tons, and up to 1888 143 in all were listed, with fifteen under 10 tons. The largest nickey appears to have been P.L.132 *Mary Grace* of 36 tons, built 1888, owned and skippered by T. Comaish.

The year 1889 sees a great change, five boats were registered, all nobby-rigged and down to 1917 only one nickey was built, P.L.249, *Shamrock* of 28 tons, owned by Teare & Sons, and skippered by W. Christian. Only seven of the nobbies were given first-class registration, i.e., being 15 tons and over, the highest being P.L.5, *White Heather*, built 1913, owned and skippered by G. Gaskill, and only nineteen were added to the fleet after the turn of the century. In all 193 boats were registered, 144 being nickeys and 49 nobbies.

Many were given such poetic names as *Guiding Star*, *Sunshine*, *Golden Fleece*, *New Moon*, *Ripple*, *Full Moon*, *Flying Scud*, *Golden Stream*, *Flying Queen*, *Roving Swan*, *Silver Spray* to name but a few, a striking contrast to the more homely names popular in East Anglia, or the Biblical names beloved by Cornishmen, also given in a few instances by Manx fishermen, who chose names of loved ones as well.

The wave of teetotalism which swept the island about the middle of the 19th century is brought to mind by such names as *Blue Ribbon*, *Jonadab* and *Rechabite*, one of the descendants of Jonadab, the son of Rechab, who abstained from drinking wine (Jer. xxxv, 6), but what was *Can-Can* doing in such company?

Many of these sturdy boats gave long years of useful service to their owners, as P.L.149, *Guiding Star*, 20 tons, built 1870 for J. Teare and others, and fishing until 1918, as was *Lily*, P.L.172, of 25 tons, built 1871 for the same owners. *Dreadnought*, P.L.207, 22 tons, built 1875 for Robert Corrin, survived until 1925, but the majority seem to have disappeared from the register about the turn of the century, and during the first decade of the new.

One of the long-lived nobbies was *Bonnie Jane*, P.L.206, 10 tons, built 1889 for John Hall, of whom Mr. Faragher writes:

"I knew Hall and *Bonnie Jane* well. He died a year or two before 1939. I went after his foghorn—a large twisted ox horn blown with the mouth—now in the Manx Museum. Hall was one of the greatest characters ever born here, as straight as a die."

What finer epitaph could be written of any man, humble or wealthy?

Plate 144 is of *Bonnie Jane*, P.L.206, and *Ada*, P.L.270, lying up with other nobbies on the 6th November 1935, and it gives some idea of the rugged, wooded charm of the neighbourhood, with the old shipyard where so many of the boats were built and now,

1949, a garage. *Bonnie Jane* was sold just prior to 1939, and is out of the 1940 Customs register.

The lines of the old boats can be seen in Plate 145 of *Ada*, P.L.270, 11 tons, built 1896, owned and skippered by E. Quayle. She is lying dried out alongside *Bonnie Jane*, and the photograph was taken by the late P. J. Oke at the same time as Plate 144. Note the boomkin over the stemhead, and the rounded heel of the foremast lying over the starboard bow.

Thomas Watson, who served his time as a carpenter with Graves, set up on his own account and built many nobbies, a number being to the order of the Irish Fisheries Board, which inaugurated a scheme to equip South and West of Ireland fishermen with new and up-to-date fishing vessels. Kneale and Watterson were also well-known builders of these craft.

Mr. Gawne never thought much of the rig:

"The nobbies! The fishermen don't want to hear about them, they finished the fishing, converted nickeys into them, and spoilt them. The nickeys were hard to handle, the men got old and couldn't do the handling of the sails, and the young men weren't coming into the fishing. The first nobbies were built in Port St. Mary about 1899. It knocked the sailing off the nickeys when the sail were taken off them. James Kinley's *Mary Jane* was converted about 1903, about the only boat that was any success for speed after conversion, but she had a bigger sail plan than the others. The nobbies at least went by sails, that was better than steam. Once the steam trawler came in fishing was finished. Nature couldn't stand before that."

The only response I had to an appeal in every newspaper published in the Isle of Man came from far-away U.S.A. Miss Margaret J. Kelly writing me by air mail:

"Upon reading your request in the *Ramsey Courier* of August 6th for information about the boats of the Manx herring fleets, I looked for pictures, but found only a few very old ones. Enclosed also is a list of the names, numbers and masters of the Peel herring fleet as it existed about 1875 to 1890. I think that not all these were 'luggers' except those on the page so entitled. This list was made by a former fisherman, Mr. Fred Gorry, of Orrisdale, who lived in Cleveland, U.S.A., many years, and died there about four years ago. He sent the list to my father, who went to the fishing at the age of twelve as cook's assistant in 1875, and stayed in that calling (the fishing business—not cooking) until about 1888. I'm sorry that now at 85 years of age he cannot talk about the fishing boats, because he lies in the hospital suffering pain. He has told us numerous stories of the zestful, adventurous life on the sea, and from these accounts I came to understand the men that manned the boats, rather than the boats themselves. I am glad that you have undertaken the task of helping preserve the history of sailing drifters, because soon all memory of them is likely to be gone, yet they are highly worthy of being remembered. From the little I know about the men who sailed the Manx luggers, it seems to me they made great contributions to the life of their time, the influence of which is felt to-day.

Since their work took them among various nationalities, they came to understand other peoples, the basis of international relations. They carried out the Manx traditions of democracy in the management of their business. They developed fine business acumen and were straightforward in their public relationships. They learned to take failure on the chin as well as to stand prosperity. They had an intense loyalty to the crew, the ship, and the homeland. Thus, for the most part, the men of the herring fleets were of high and sturdy character. Even though they were far from home much of the time, and away from centres of world affairs, they did not lose contact. Much of their spare time in the forecastle was spent in discussion and debate on questions of public interest. In those days there were no such public centres of recreation as we have, but they did not lack recreation or entertainment. They used their own resources —mostly singing, instrumental music like the old fiddle or accordion, step-dancing, speech-making, readings, athletic sports when on shore, such as running races, quoit throwing, or jumping. But the zest, adventure and chance of the work itself gave enjoyment. Every venture with the fleet was really a sailing race from point to point. Then, too, the skill, originality and ingenuity often needed to overcome obstacles gave them that feeling of power from victory over seeming failure.

I am sorry that I have not the ability to express the feelings of those who took part in the events as they ought to be set forth. I like the account my father gives of how he started out in the fishing. In the early 1870's there was not much work a young person could get in the Isle of Man, except in farming or fishing. Farm hands were paid far less than a living wage. Since my father felt it was absolutely necessary for him to add to the family income, he determined at twelve years of age to go to the fishing. So one Sunday after the vesper service was over, during which he had sung in the choir, his mother walked with him for about a mile on the way to Peel, about eight miles away. When the time came that they must part, his mother tearfully exclaimed 'O Willie, I don't see how I can let you go, you are so small!' But courageously kissing him goodbye, she turned homeward, and the lad went on toward the centre of the fishing industry, to do a man's work in the world. The little boy, for he was small for his age, was refused work at every turn, until he could give his qualifications as a cook to one who needed a helper for the ship's cook. From then on, for twelve seasons of calm and storm, profit and loss, disappointment and reward, he grew to manhood.

He experienced the greatest anxiety of his career during a storm that hit the fleet of fifty luggers anchored in Smerwick Bay on the Irish coast. The gale, sweeping in from straight across the Atlantic, threatened to toss the ships on to the rocks near shore. As always, every boat was in ballast trim. The 'eighty' sail (80 sq. yds. of No. 1 canvas) stretched as stiff as a board on the 40-ft. boom, kept each boat headed into the sea. During the four days and nights of the storm, the men took their turns on watch, but no one slept. Their main anxiety was whether or not the anchors would hold. But hold they did, perhaps too well, for when the time came to leave the bay, the small kedge anchors came up, but the large ones stuck fast in blue clay bottom. Try as they would, the men could not raise those anchors. Finally they broke. Now the question was how to get more anchors. Some of the men walked the four and a half miles overland to Dingle, but could get only two. Others had to be brought from Cork. This meant a delay of several more days, but at least they had all weathered the storm.

In his second season at the fishing my father experienced a gale that blew the ships 200 miles out into the Atlantic. During this storm they sighted the White Star liner

*Germanic* hove to so as to keep her head into the sea. The fishing boats got back to their grounds by following charts and by frequently taking soundings, lowering the greased lead to the bottom and examining the kind of soil stuck to it.

When the fishing season was over, the fishermen usually did some other kind of work. My father often worked on farms or in gardens, and, when old enough, took berths on Atlantic freighters plying between Liverpool and the United States. As the fishing industry became less and less profitable, many left it for other work. Among others my father felt the lure of America, and sought his fortune there. But always he loved the sea and ships. I've thought that is why, subconsciously perhaps, he finally settled on the shore of the biggest of our chain of inland seas—Lake Superior. He sailed on Lake Michigan for a while before coming to Superior, a booming town of the wild west in those late 1890's. Here, too, he worked on boats, loading and unloading, building and repairing the 15,000-ton ore freighters. But I don't think that to him any of his later adventures equal those of the fishing.

Sincerely,

(signed) MARGARET JANE KELLY.

daughter of William Teare Kelly, of Orrisdale, I.O.M., who went to the fishing from Peel and loved that life and the memories of it during his whole life."

Thank you very much, Miss Kelly, for an extremely human story.

Plate 146 is one of the photographs sent, and shows *Ann*, P.L.42, skipper W. Gorry, leaving Douglas, with other nickeys and a sailing trawler in the background. The original is a postcard sent to Mr. Kelly from Douglas as far back as the 25th February 1908, but obviously treasured by one far from his homeland.

What a thrill it must have been for any passengers on *Germanic*, able to sit up and take notice, to see those tiny fishing luggers, probably not as big as the lifeboats up on the boat deck of the liner, driving past before a howling gale, half-hidden in flying spume and spray, out into the wastes of the North Atlantic, in weather that had forced their huge steamer to heave to.

They were prime seamen as well as fishermen who manned the herring fleets, and Miss Kelly confirms the remarks of the late William Pezzack, who tells how Cornishmen also took a pride in their job and made a regatta of it every time they put to sea. They were "true blue," and I count it a privilege to be able to record a little of their lives. I only wish more had been able to write me of their experiences; nothing can come up to first-hand data, written or spoken by the men themselves, now, alas, well into the evening of their days, if not already "safe anchored with the fleet, awaiting orders, Skipper Christ to meet," words I remember reading on the headstone of an old fisherman's grave.

The importance of the once thriving herring fishing can be realised by an examination of the numbers of boats and men then engaged in it.

In 1636 222 Manx boats were at the fishing, in which 48 British and Irish vessels also took part; in 1785 the local craft had risen to 313, but many were probably still the open boat or scowte. The drop to 250 boats, employing 2,500 in 1826, undoubtedly is due to the increase in size and better sea-keeping abilities of the cutters then coming into favour. In addition some 300 strangers visited Manx waters during the season. By 1845 the number of local craft had risen to 283, needing the services of about 2,800 men, and some 400 visitors took their share of the shoals. Twenty years later saw an increase to 300 boats, and in 1872 compulsory registration gives an indication of the sizes of the fishing vessels, there being 227 first-class, of over 15 tons, 82 second-class, and 66 third-class boats owned in the ports of Castletown, Douglas and Ramsey, Douglas then including the town of Peel. The eighties saw the fleets at their zenith, there being no less than 125 boats at Port St. Mary and 249 at Peel in the first year of the decade, while the last saw a total of 334, mostly fine nickeys of 20 tons and over.

The 20th century saw a rapid decline; in the 1905 *Olsen's* I can trace the following first-class boats: at Castletown 64, Ramsey 9, Douglas 15 sail and 3 steam, and at Peel 75, a total of only 163 sailing luggers. By 1910 there was a further drop to 130, with an increase of one in the number of steamers, and at the outbreak of war in 1914 but 57 survived, made up of 35 nickeys and 22 nobbies. After the war the fall was catastrophic. In 1923 Castletown had 2 sail and 12 motor, 14 in all; Douglas had half that number, made up of 1 sail, 4 steam, and 2 motor; Peel only 4, 1 sail, 1 steam, and 2 motor, with Ramsey owning the same number, half sail, half motor. This gives a total of 29 vessels registered in the whole island, with only 6 sail against 5 steam and 18 motor, among the latter many one-time sailing craft, but 1936 tells the melancholy collapse of a centuries old industry, *only six* vessels over 15 tons, 4 motor at Castletown and one each at Douglas and Peel.

Throughout the whole history of the herring fishing the majority of the craft belonged to Peel, followed by Port St. Mary. It would certainly seem as if the industry has now passed into other hands, as Mr. F. C. Faragher tells me that in 1939 no fewer than 163 vessels came to the fishing from other parts, principally Scotland. This fleet was comprised of 67 motor drifters, 64 steam drifters, and 32 ring net boats, Manx vessels landing a little more than 10 per cent. of the catch. In 1948 there were only about a dozen craft in local ownership, but all were modern diesel-engined boats. The Scottish 50-footers, with enclosed wheelhouses, electric light, power winches with interchangeable accessories, worked in pairs, using ring nets. Until 1947 these ring net boats towed a weighted piano wire when working. If the wire was struck by a shoal it vibrated and a skilled man could tell the density of the shoal. This method is now out-moded, for all the up-to-date craft are fitted with echo sounders, radio telephony, and even hot and cold wash-bowls for the crew.

As used in fishing, the echo sounder has a revolving band of paper, the edges of which are scaled as the edges of a chart in small divisions, each representing one minute's steaming, and in fact, is so calibrated that it takes one minute for the paper to move this tiny distance. The electrical impulses sent out strike the bottom, or any intervening obstruction such as a shoal of herring, and return, and the result shows on the paper in the form of shadows. If the shadows were to last, say, three minutes, i.e., over a distance of three of the graduations on the edge of the paper roll, then the fisherman would know that he was over a large shoal.

By means of two-way radio telephony the boats are in constant touch with each other, and moreover can be called up from shore and told which port to make for to obtain the best market. These radio sets have a range up to at least 20 miles, and are supplied to the boats on a rental basis. The echo sounders are purchased outright and cost several hundred pounds.

Old Manxmen aver that ring net herring are useless for salting down because they have lost their scales in the cod end of the ring net, and as a result go bad after being in salt for some time.

This form of fishing is not a new departure, as a similar method was practised by the West of Scotland fishermen eighty years and more ago.

A new fish meal and oil plant has been erected to deal with offal and the extraction of oil. Despite the passing of the Manx fishing fleet there are now more kipper processing yards in Peel than in the past, and there is a tremendous demand from the mainland for the succulent kipper. As the Manx Government prohibits the dyeing of the fish, the natural flavour is preserved, resulting in the excellence of the local kipper in comparison with some of the brands prepared elsewhere.

The great decline in the fishing in the early years of the present century coincided with the same state of affairs in Cornwall, and many fine, able boats were sold to Irish fishermen, who made a living in them until well into the thirties, fitting many with motors.

The pride which went into the building of the Manx craft and the excellence of materials and workmanship can be seen by a glance through the 1930 *Olsen's Almanack*. *Almas*, S.709, of 32 tons, fitted with a 24-h.p. motor, was built at Peel away back in 1878, yet was still fishing out of Cork, as was *Ebenezer*, S.156, 17 tons, built 1880, later owned in Bantry and fitted with a 13-h.p. motor. *Island Lass*, S.432, was an 18-tonner with an 18-h.p. engine, she took the water at Peel in 1879, while *Manx Queen*, S.481, came from a yard at Port St. Mary in 1885. Other Peel boats built were *Maria Jane*, D.293, dating back to 1885, *Rosebud*, D.600, from 1884, *St. Teresa*, D.42, 1883, *Sarah Jane*, S.7, 1875, and *Stella*, D.186, launched in 1884.

It is sad to have to record the collapse of a once prosperous industry, which gave employment to thousands of fishermen, shipwrights, sailmakers, and others, and enriched by millions of pounds the ports where fishing was carried on.

CHAPTER ELEVEN

# *SCOTLAND*

Drift net fishing for herring has long been an important economic factor in the lives of fishermen on the East Coast of Scotland, and the curing and barrelling of the catch a speciality. It will be remembered that in Stuart times the Dutch led the way in the development of the fishery, and their apple-bowed busses were a common sight off the shores and in certain harbours. During the reign of George I an Act was passed in 1718 for the granting of bounties for various kinds of fish and fishing vessels, in order to encourage the Scots to emulate the example of the Hollanders. Two shillings and eight-pence was paid on every barrel containing 32 gals of white herring; 1s. 9d. for "full" red herrings, and 1s. a barrel for "empty" reds. This system of subsidies was maintained for 112 years, the details varying with later legislation. As to the success of this scheme, I quote an extract from a letter from Hon. B. F. Primrose, Secretary to the Board of Fisheries in Scotland and dated 14th November 1848:

"An erroneous estimate of the Dutch fishing and the rash assumption that because the Dutch cure was the best, their system throughout, without reference to the forced circumstances under which it was carried on, must be the best too, led to our Government granting a bounty on open sea and deep-sea decked vessels, which proved a total failure, as will be seen by the following return:

| 1817 | Number Vessels | Tonnage | Men | Barrels of Herring | Tonnage and Barrel Bounty |
|---|---|---|---|---|---|
| Open sea | 19 | 464½ | 139 | 946½ | £1,497 |
| Deep sea | 3 | 145 | 33 | 398½ | 566 |
| 1818 | | | | | |
| Open sea | 23 | 587½ | 170 | 924½ | £1,829 |
| Deep sea | 6 | 296 | 67 | 327½ | 953 |

Whereas the returns of the three stations of Wick, Fraserburgh and Peterhead have been for this season with the open boats and no Government bounties:

| | Boats | Men | Barrels of herring |
|---|---|---|---|
| Wick | 822 | 4,110 | 131,520 |
| Fraserburgh | 395 | 1,975 | 43,911 |
| Peterhead | 438 | 2,190 | 81,906 |

A comparison of the averages derived from these returns exhibits the following results:

|  | Barrels per boat | Barrels per ton |
|---|---|---|
| Decked boats |  |  |
| 1817 for whole coast - | 61 | $2\frac{1}{3}$ |
| 1818 for whole coast | 43 | $1\frac{1}{2}$ |
| Open boats |  |  |
| 1848 for Wick only - - | 160 | $12\frac{1}{2}$ |
| Fraserburgh - - - | 111 | $8\frac{1}{2}$ |
| Peterhead - - - | 186 | $14\frac{1}{2}$ |

The bounties were abolished in 1830."

The size and type of the early boats had been restricted by reason of the lack of harbours and the need to save all possible weight, as they had to be hauled up shelving beaches. Again, the poverty of the men handicapped the building of larger craft, even where harbours were available.

Prior to 1767, Wick fishermen used herring only as bait for white fish, which were caught on crude iron hooks. I am indebted to Mr. Alexander Miller of Wick for the following information regarding the fishery from that port.

"It was not until 1767 and '68 that any organised efforts were made to catch the vast shoals of herring in these waters. In 1767 John Sutherland, John Anderson and Alexander Miller fitted out two sloops, they made an effort to secure the bounty paid by the Government, but failed in that year. For the following season they fitted out one sloop and secured the bounty of 50s. a ton. In 1795 200 boats were fishing at Wick, but a harbour was badly needed. In 1808 the British Fisheries Society, a body of patriotic men, commenced their establishment of Pulteney Town by building a harbour and granting feus for building, on liberal terms. The ground on which the town is situated was purchased from the laird and called Pulteney, in honour of Sir William Pulteney, who was Chief Director of the Society at the time of purchase. In 1810 the inner harbour was completed at a cost of £16,000, of which £7,500 was defrayed by the Government. Owing to the great increase in trade, an outer harbour was planned in 1824, and completed in 1831 at a cost of £22,000. The engineer was James Bremmer —a famous man in his day—who learned shipbuilding at Glasgow, and in his yard in Lower Pulteney built upwards of 56 vessels, ranging from 45 to 600 tons.

About this time small, open yawls, some 20 ft. long, were employed in inshore fishing in northern creeks. They were built chiefly at Pulteney Town, but also at some of the villages round the coast, the timber being brought from Scandinavia in sailing ships. The sails were made locally in the ropewalk and barked brown, and Wick eventually became the chief seat of the Northern herring fishery, with a fleet of from 800 to 1,000 vessels.

The nets were made by the women, who worked at home during the long winter nights, a fleet of 25 costing 30s. each net. On Mondays during the fishing season the

150 SCAFFIE ENTERING BUCKIE, c. 1870
Fore lug being lowered.

151 SCAFFIES AND FIFIE HAULED UP AT BUCKIE
B.F. 869 *Margaret*.

152 *GRATITUDE*, LOOKING FOR'ARD
Note baulk, skegs, thwarts below deck.

153 A SMACK-RIGGED FIFIE LEAVING YARMOUTH

154 EARLY CLINKER BUILT ZULU *TWINS* B.F. 915
Note "iron man" or flywheel capstan, length of sweeps.

155 *IONA* B.K. 265. CLINKER BUILT FIFIE, *c.* 1882
Note bladders drying across scudding pole.

156 CLINKER BUILT FIFIE LEAVING LOWESTOFT
Note bonnet at foot of forelug and bowsprit run in.

157 FIFIE DRIED OUT AT BURNMOUTH, c. 1882
Note carvel build, crutch aft of mizzen, and bladders.

nets were lifted from off the grounds where they had been drying since the previous Saturday, taken down to the boat, and "laid" in the hold in such a way as to allow them to be "set" without any hitch, buoys and sinkers were also placed in position.

Except at Wick and Lybster there were no harbours in Caithness, but in every little creek there were a few boats. The men often rowed a good distance to the fishing grounds, where the nets were set or shot. After a short interval the nets were tried, and if any herring were in the meshes the nets were shot again, and the fishermen lay on a little longer before looking at them a second time. If no fish, the nets were hauled and the men went to another place. If there was a fair catch, unless the weather was rough, the herring were shaken out of the nets as they were being hauled in. As soon as the boats came ashore, the nets were sent to the net ground and spread out to dry. This was done every day. After the men had hauled their boats up the beach above high-water mark, they went home and got some sleep whilst their womenfolk gutted and packed the catch. This went on every weekday. The boats did not go far to sea, had no decks, not even half-decks, or "dens," as they were called. The men had to lie on a kind of platform in the bows, with no shelter from rain or cold when they lay down to take some rest while the nets were in the sea.

Provisions were carried for one night only, the allowance being a bannock of oat-bread for each man and a small cask or jar of water. There was neither grate, stove nor fire aboard, and a flint and tinder took the place of matches.

There were few hired men in the earliest days, several men fitted out a boat as a joint adventure and shared equally in the expense and the profits or losses.

A feature connected with the fishing in those far-off days was that as soon as the nets were set, some food was partaken of, and immediately after part of one of the grand old Hebrew psalms was sung, and the skipper or one of the crew engaged in prayer. On a calm day the effect of this melodious strain of psalm singing, carried along the surface of the water, might truly be described as solemn and heart-stirring, especially when several boats were simultaneously engaged.

There was little trade in herrings with the Continent in the early days. Sailing packets or sloops took some of the output to Leith, and the passage was often a protracted one. The first steamer, the *Velocity*, began to run between Wick and Leith in 1833, but for long afterwards the smacks continued on the sea route. In 1833 women got 4d. a barrel for gutting and packing herring, coopers earned 9s. a week barrel-making. The timber came chiefly from Norway, and the staves were made in the local saw-mills which had by then come into existence."

In 1815 the first consignment of Scottish barrelled herring was exported to the Continent, in 1826 seven French luggers came to the Wick fishing, in which English boats took part for the first time the following year. Salt for curing came from Liverpool, and fleets of smacks and schooners brought in the timber, etc., required ashore, and returned with barrels of herring, hundreds being exported to Ireland and the West Indies, providing a cheap food for the slaves, but the abolition of slavery brought an end to this trade, and new markets had to be sought on the Continent.

The system of putting a Government brand on barrels to ensure the quality of the catch had been introduced in 1718, and in 1808 the Scottish Fisheries Act specified that all barrels had to be full legal size, with staves $\frac{1}{2}$ in. thick, the number of hoops and fastenings was fixed, and tightness secured by inserting "flags" at the seams of head and bottom. Fish had to be packed within 24 hours of capture, the minimum weight was fixed, and each barrel was marked with the day the fish was cured, name and address of curer, and the name of the officer branding.

It was not until 1843 that export rose to over one hundred thousand barrels, but the subsequent repeal of timber duty brought a reduction in the cost of barrels, and in 1850 some quarter of a million barrels were despatched from the Scottish fisheries. About 1837 the average price per cran was 11s.

The Great Summer Fishing at Wick was a remarkable sight in the first decades of the 19th century, between five and six hundred open boats taking part, in some years as many as eighty to ninety coming from harbours in the Firth of Forth, no inconsiderable journey as it was often the custom to row the entire distance. Catches varied from an average of 91 crans per boat to 148, and a man could easily carry his portion of nets in a creel on his back, each boat shooting about 25 nets. In thirteen years' fishing, a total of 10,202 boats averaged catches of 941 crans, and 735,318 barrels of herring were cured.

The introduction of machine-made cotton nets gave a tremendous impetus to the fishing, and the number of nets carried by each boat increased to from 30 to 35, but strangely enough, during the next thirteen years, although the number of boats had gone up to 13,522, their average catch had dropped to 519 crans, and only 539,719 barrels were cured, each containing about 700 fish. There was little, if any, fishing in the winter months, the frequent storms and dangerous coast making any attempts hazardous in the extreme with the frail, open boats then in use.

These old Scots fishermen held the belief that fish, like men, were better for a day's rest on the Sabbath, and even if a few did not think so, by the Scottish Fisheries Act of 1815, all nets, set or hauled within two leagues of the coast on a Sunday, were forfeited. The men were of superb physique, also the women, who had a hard life, frequently wading up to their waists in icy water to launch the boats and carry out the men so that they could go to the night's fishing dryshod. They cleaned and cured the fish, baited the lines when it was the white fish season, and in general did most of the work ashore. The men married young, as without a good wife a fisherman could hardly be expected to ply his calling.

And what a coastline! Gaunt, rocky cliffs, torn and jagged as they were at the

Creation and will be until the end of time. Unchanged, save for the slow erosion of centuries, where the fury of the seas has fretted into the softer places in those unyielding domains, so that isolated stacks stand like sentinels, the haunt of seabirds. Ashore, desolate, grim, heather-covered moorland, scarcely affording grazing for a few sheep, let alone the cultivation found in the more favoured lands of the south. Little wonder that such conditions bred a race inured to hardship, masters of their fate, yielding to none in endurance and courage. Wherever a "goe" or creek afforded some sort of shelter, there would be found a fishing village, with low, thatched cabins straggling up the braes, open to every wind that blows. Clannish and fiercely independent, these fisherfolk were distrustful of assistance not gained by their own efforts.

The shoals coming within a few miles of the shore meant that the use of open boats was no great drawback, but the danger lay when summer gales sprang up suddenly and the men had to run for shelter, being unable to face the seas in their frail craft. Many a boat was lost and its crew drowned within sight of home, and if a fleet was caught out at sea with the harbours dried out, disaster was sure to follow, while the shelter afforded by some of the creeks was so negligible that in certain winds boats lying at anchor would be wrecked, unless prompt steps were taken to haul them up to safety.

Such disasters were of no rare occurrence. To name but two, one night in 1839 twenty boats were lying inside Sarclet harbour, a tiny shelter of less than half an acre in extent, when a sudden storm came on and all were dashed to pieces before any could be hauled up the beach to safety. On 21st August 1845 thirty boats were almost completely destroyed at Forse, seven at Clyth, and as many damaged, two men were drowned here, and another two at Whaligoe. No estimate can ever be given of the number of boats which foundered during those sudden gales, or the lives lost when others were wrecked. In such isolated communities events like these were seldom heard of outside the immediate locality, communications being poor, and disasters to such humble craft had no "news value."

The great August gale of 1848 first drew public attention to the losses sustained by poor fishermen, although I can find no reference to this disaster in the *Illustrated London News*.

At Wick a large proportion of the 800 boats from the port left Pulteney harbour shortly after H.W. on the afternoon of Friday, 18th August 1848 and remained in the bay. Towards evening they stood out to sea, and shot their nets as usual about ten miles off the land. The afternoon had been fine, the evening was rather threatening, but not so much so as to deter a fisherman from pursuing his calling, although the barometer had fallen considerably. Few of the men, however, troubled to consult this instrument, preferring to trust to their own judgment.

About midnight the wind began to get up and many of the fishermen, not liking the look of the weather, rapidly hauled their nets and ran for the harbour, getting in safely about 1.30 a.m., the time of H.W. By 3 a.m. it was blowing a howling south-easter, with deluges of rain and the remainder of the fleet bore up for the bay. Ashore houses shook, windows rattled, awakening relatives, who hurried down to the harbour between four and five o'clock, and gazed anxiously out to sea. At one moment the boats could be seen on the top of the foaming billows, the next they were lost in the hollows between the crests of the waves. Every disappearance was greeted with groans of anguish and feared to be the final one, but the men struggled bravely on until the haven was reached, but alas, it was now half-tide with only about 5 ft. of water at the harbour entrance and a tremendous sea was running. No deep-loaded boat could possibly enter under such conditions, and those which tried were either swamped on the bar, thrown up on the back of the north quay, or wrecked on the south pier. Forty-one boats were lost and twenty-five men drowned before the eyes of their loved ones, and twelve others were lost at sea when their boats were swamped. Seventeen widows and sixty children were left destitute, and the loss of boats and nets amounted to over £1,600.

Thirty-four open boats were fishing out of Forse, nine were total losses with all their nets and eleven were badly damaged; three of the crew in a Lybster boat were drowned while trying to run for safety to Dunbeath, where eighteen boats were washed *out* of the harbour by the spate suddenly coming down after the heavy rain, and all were smashed to pieces on the beach by the surge.

At Helmsdale 130 boats put to sea on the evening of the 18th, and the following morning two were upset on the bar and four men drowned, two more were run down or foundered at sea with the loss of five men, and one man was lost overboard when hauling the nets, a total of ten lives lost. Another boat was driven by the force of the river flood among the rocks at the entrance to the harbour and wrecked, but many boats rode out the gale at anchor in the bay. So fierce were the spates at times that often with a strong fair wind all command of a boat was lost, even in ordinary weather it would be carried away by the "fresh."

Twelve Buckie boats were wrecked at Peterhead, eight severely damaged, and nets carried away, eleven men were drowned and the material loss amounted to £1,900. Three Port Gordon boats were lost with five men, one from Portessie, one from Findochty with five lives, a total of seventeen boats and twenty-one men from the Port Gordon district to add to the twenty-four boats and thirteen men from the Helmsdale district.

Banff, lying on the weather shore in a S.E. gale, escaped disaster, and of the 138 boats fishing, not one was lost, and no material damage was caused; Macduff was also lucky. At Fraserburgh the gale fortunately came on at about half-flood, and the fishermen were prudent enough to run at once for harbour, which all reached safely, but at

Peterhead it was disaster unparalleled. The boats began to run for harbour about 11 p.m., and continued to come in until 3.30 a.m., when it was high water, but owing to the awkward entrance and the difficulty of taking it with wind at S.E., thirty boats were total losses, thirty-three damaged, and stranded, and thirty-one men perished. Here, as at Wick, unbelievable and inexcusable causes added to the marine perils faced by the unfortunate men. Although the entrance was only thirty yards wide, smacks and other vessels were constantly allowed to lie close to the pierheads, and occupy two-thirds of the already narrow entrance, when it was well known that upwards of 300 boats were at sea and would be coming back into harbour before daylight. Many and many a time had the fishermen remonstrated against this dangerous practice, but *in vain*. They could clearly foresee how fatal such a state of things would be to them if caught out in a sudden on-shore gale, and, alas, they were proved right in a terrible manner on the night in question, when a steamer lay alongside the west pier and four coasting vessels along the south pier. Unfortunately many of the boats were badly handled, owing to lack of experience in the crews, who were largely composed of hired men, with little knowledge of the art of handling dipping lugsails in a gale of wind.

Altogether at Peterhead fifty-one boats were lost or seriously damaged, valued with nets at £3,820, and thirty-one men lost their lives.

At Stonehaven six boats were lost, two damaged, and nineteen men drowned, with material loss estimated at £450. Further south the fishing stations escaped, and no loss occurred in the Firth of Forth or south to Berwick.

As a result of this disaster, unparalleled in the history of the herring fishing in Scotland, 100 men were drowned, 124 boats lost or damaged, and the value of boats and nets lost amounted to £7,011, all the property of humble fishermen, who left 47 widows and 161 children totally unprovided for.

At Wick feelings ran high, and allegations were made that the harbour authorities had failed to carry out essential provisions of Statute 7 & 8 Vict., by which the harbour was regulated. One thousand and fifty pilots and fishermen signed a memorial to the Admiralty and another was sent by the Provost, Magistrates and Town Council, drawing attention to the fact that fishing and curing were carried out at Wick to a greater extent than anywhere else in Great Britain, and that on a coastline of about fifty miles no fewer than 1,200 to 1,500 open boats, manned by from six to seven thousand fishermen, afforded employment to thousands on shore.

On hearing of these serious allegations, the Admiralty took prompt action, ordering Captain John Washington, R.N., to go north and conduct inquiries at all the fishing stations concerned, and draw up a full report. This he proceeded to do, holding the first inquiry at Wick on 12th October 1848, less than two months after the disaster, a very creditable performance, considering the state of travel in those days, and a journey to the extreme north-east of Scotland.

The many witnesses let themselves go, so much so that at the end of the day of eight and a half hours, the Inspector remarked " Perhaps, at times, rather more has been said than ought to have been listened to." Fishermen stated that although the Act said stone lighthouses were to be provided, the only lights shown were miserable lanterns, which the assistant harbour-master was quick to say were "not lit by half-penny candles, but by those of four to six to the lb., which we buy by the stone." But evidence showed that when the latch of the lantern had been broken some long time before, *it was never repaired*, but a bent nail used instead. Little wonder that the light kept blowing out on such a wild night.

An emigration agent said he had been instrumental in saving life by going down the ladder at the back of the south wall, and had been told he had no right to interfere, having no interest in the harbour! His plucky action was, however, highly commended by Capt. Washington.

Then the harbour-master gave some amazing evidence. Few, if any, ropes were provided for life-saving, it being customary to go aboard any handy vessel and *cut away her running gear*, which would be replaced by the harbour authorities. Next he made the extraordinary statement that the harbour was frequently full of boats which had no right there, a remark instantly jumped on by the Inspector, "No right, is it not a public harbour and has not everyone a right to enter it on payment of usual dues?" Then came the final damning admission that the narrow entrance was partially blocked at low water by huge stones flung there during a storm in 1827, when the quay was under construction, and *never removed*, a danger to which frequent attention had been called by pilots, fishermen and others.

The engineer, next called, admitted this was the case, but he considered at the time that the trouble and cost of removing the displaced courses of masonry would be more than obtaining new stones: a few had been removed, but the others were left, "but it was now resolved to take away the rest."

One way and another it must have been a very lively meeting, relieved by the simple story of George Sinclair, a boatbuilder who was at sea fishing on the night of the disaster, who ran into harbour soon after 3 a.m., although no light was showing on the pierhead. On coming ashore he went on to the quay and saw three boats smashed against the north wall, ran and took a rope from a vessel, tied it round his waist, and went down the back of the north quay and rescued a man clinging to a mast. More could have been saved had ropes been available, as a considerable time elapsed before the remainder of the crew was drowned. This plucky conduct merited the Inspector's "It is extremely creditable to you to have thus acted, and I hope that you will have your reward. Had everybody acted with the courage and humanity of George Sinclair, there would have been a very different state of matters to represent to-day."

Other evidence showed that many of the crews of the south country boats had taken the precaution of tying the bladders from the nets round their waists, and so were able to keep afloat when their boats were wrecked.

Several of the boats, unable to make the entrance, ran for Wick Water, on which the town of Wick stands, and reached safety. Had more done so, it is highly probable that the loss of life would have been considerably reduced, but the fatal lure of the harbour seems to have been an overriding factor in the men's minds.

The inquiry at Banff brought to light that the harbour at Buckie, formed of a frame of wood, filled with excavations of rocks taken out of the basin, was erected by the local fishermen, *at the sole expense of* the Rev. Robert Shanks, Free Church Minister, Buckie. A truly Christian act.

Gilbert Manson, Fishery Officer at Banff for 33 years, said that 135 boats generally fished in the district, and 93 belonged to it. All were open boats, lugsail-rigged, except about half-a-dozen sloop-rigged, and he "could not recollect any losses in any year in the fishing season." A remarkable testimony to the skill of the local fishermen.

At Fraserburgh Captain Washington was glad to learn that there was no loss of life or property in spite of upwards of 400 boats fishing. The chief complaint of witnesses was the lack of harbour accommodation, and that 24s. was charged for dues against the 2s. to 2s. 6d. customary elsewhere for a season. Many stated that they had delivered no catches during the last five to ten years, preferring to land their fish at places offering better facilities. In spite of the fact that John Webster had built 84 boats, value £3,864, at an average price of £46 with masts and oars, or £72 complete with sails, many being half-decked, there was the same rooted objection among the fishermen to this type of boat, as everywhere else they preferred open boats.

From Peterhead, as at Wick, came the same story of lack of lights and almost unbelievable inefficiency on the part of the harbour authorities. The night of the 18th-19th August was not dark, though cloudy, being the last quarter of the moon, which had been full on the 14th; it was, therefore, possible to see the boats for a considerable distance out in the bay, making for the entrance to the harbour. Most came in from the south on the larboard tack with full sail set, dipped their lugs, and shot up into the entrance, where they found a steamer on one side and four coasters on the other, leaving only the narrowest of channels between. Once inside some of the men lost all sense of decent conduct, as John Edwards stated that one Buckie boat came in safely, and one of the crew laid hold of another to keep themselves in, when a man chopped his hand so severely that he bore the marks to that day. Two boats were endeavouring to ride out the gale in the bay; the Clerk to the Harbour Trustees offered £50 to Capt. Brand, of the steamer *Dorothy*, which was partially blocking the entrance, if he would go out to try and save the men, but met with a flat refusal. As the tide fell, the surf increased and the boats foundered, but all the crews, except two men, came ashore with bladders tied to their bodies.

Alexander Mackay, Fishery Officer for fifteen years, did not seem to have been very zealous in the execution of his duty. When asked to state how many boats went to sea and how many were lost, he replied that he had no knowledge, going on to say, "I intend to make a return when I can collect authentic material." This two months after the disaster!

Some of the boats had come in under "low lug foresail," lost way and fell to leeward, where they were smashed to pieces on the Horse Back, a reef of rocks a few hundred yards from the entrance. Others, through lack of experienced crews, were unable to dip their foresails to come about on the other tack, and tried to come in with sails aback, with the same fatal result. By gallant efforts on the part of people ashore, many of the crews were rescued and resuscitated by being placed into warm beds with children on each side of the man, who had plenty of whisky poured into him. Eleven lives were saved in this way.

An ordinary gas lamp had been lit at sunset on the pierhead, but in the excitement of the night someone climbed up the post to get a better view and accidently turned off the cock, and no one seemed to know why the light was extinguished just when it was most wanted. Several boats were deceived by a light in a cottage window, and steered straight to destruction on the rocks. About 100 boats ran into Sandford Bay, mistaking the lights there for those at Peterhead, and a good many went ashore. No lifelines were available unless ropes were taken off vessels in the harbour. Many of them were stripped of their running gear without the crews aboard being aware of the fact. Some men must sleep sound!

William Yule, for sixteen years a fisherman, said the north harbour light was "only a sham of a thing, no more use than a fish's eye stuck up on a bit of stick." Only one or two men, who knew this entrance well, dared to risk running into that shelter, more could have done so had the light been efficient, because there was a depth of 8 ft. at the entrance and more space was available inside than in the south harbour, for which the fleet made. Yule had tried the south harbour, but saw no light, so hauled on the larboard tack and lost two men overboard, after a long delay a light came on and he made port.

When another fisherman of twenty-five years' standing, William Strachan, was giving evidence that he had been delayed for two hours before he could get his boat up, owing to two ships lying right in the fairway, the Provost interrupted to say the harbour was for ships. He was promptly rebuked by the Inspector, "Yes, Provost, but also for boats, a considerable proportion of the harbour revenue is derived from these boats."

Captain Simpson and three fishermen manned a small boat and pulled about in the dangerous water at the entrance, trying to pass lines to boats coming in, but after about an hour were forced to give up, having picked up one man.

The barometer, which stood at about 30.0 or just over at 9 a.m. on the 18th

August, had fallen to 29.75 by 9 p.m., and at 9 a.m. the following morning had dropped to 29.2.

Exactly a century later, in October 1948, I had the privilege of carefully reading the questions and answers at these inquiries. They numbered thousands, and from some 300 pages of closely-printed type I made almost verbatim notes, which have enabled me to give a very full account of this astonishing state of affairs.

In his report to the Admiralty, Captain Washington found all the allegations, made at Wick and Peterhead, fully proved, and stated that the principal cause of the loss of life and property was the want of good harbours, accessible at all times, and he recommended, not the provision of a few central harbours, but a general deepening of all the existing ones along the East Coast. This would involve no considerable outlay, for, as he said, it was scarcely credible that the £2,700 a year already voted by Parliament to building harbours and piers in Scotland during the few preceding years should have given so great a stimulus to important local improvements. He suggested £10,000 annually for a few years, steadily laid out on piers and harbours, would do much to remedy the want, and assist one hundred thousand fishermen, hardy, industrious and frugal men, from one of the poorest and most unproductive districts of Scotland, continually at sea for three months together, to have the common shelter all mariners were entitled to look for in the hour of need.

He disapproved of the practice of taking so many hired men to complete the crews, finding that three out of every five of the crews in the north country boats wrecked at Peterhead were landsmen, unequal to the task of dipping sails when running in before the storm, and so hauled up for the harbour with sails aback against the mast. Hence the boats lost way and drove ashore, while the Newhaven and south country boats, ably handled, fetched up to the pierhead and were saved.

He was not in favour of making part of the bargain between curer and fishermen to consist of spirits, holding it to be a direct encouragement to excessive drinking, as was the bounty of £10 a boat, given before a single fish had been caught.

He further considered that the men should pay more attention to the state of the barometer, and not be too anxious to run for a harbour, but hold on to their nets and ride out the gale, or at least remain at sea until it was known there was sufficient water in the harbour.

Finally, he brought up the question of the form and build of boats, and whether open, decked or half-decked boats were most suitable, and told how the views of the East Coast Scots were diametrically opposed to those of Cornish fishermen, in that they maintained that none but open boats were fit for herring fishing, whereas the Englishmen as stoutly asserted that they would not go to sea in any but a decked or half-decked boat.

Mistrusting his own opinion, Captain Washington obtained the lines of the best boats around the coast, and placed them before Scottish builders and fishermen. In addition, he asked James Peake, H.M. Naval Architect at Woolwich Dockyard, to go over the plans and give his opinion.

Strongly as Captain Washington advocated improvements in the design and form of boats, still more did he urge the need for a general deepening and improving of all harbours and placing them under proper control. As he truly remarked, one could hardly expect a poor man to expend his scanty savings in building a bigger and better boat, when he well knew he might have to risk her in running for a harbour, the entrance of which was likely to be blocked by shipping, or steer for a pierhead where the light is blown out from neglect, or to risk her being dashed to pieces at the undredged entrance to a tidal harbour, or have the bottom stove in against large stones carelessly left within.

Finally he pointed out the immense importance of the herring fisheries to the economic life of Scotland.

Accurate plans of every type of fishing boat in use in the middle of the 19th century accompanied the report, and I made tracings from the originals, including small plans of the harbours so that the difficulties with which the fishermen had to contend could be more fully appreciated. Plans on pages 336-9.

Two distinct types of open boats were to be found in Scottish waters. The typical herring lugger was the Buckie boat, variously called a scaffie, scaffa, or scaith. Length of keel was 32 ft. to 33 ft., but a curved stem and a sternpost raking at 45 deg. increased the overall length to 41 ft., beam was 13 ft., and depth 4 ft. 9 in. The clinker-built hull was lightly constructed of 1½ in. larch planking with oak ribs, keel, stem and sternpost, and the boat was coated with a crude varnish. As the hull only weighed three tons, it could easily be hauled up a beach. Draught light was, for'ard 2 ft. 6 in., aft 2 ft. 9 in., but with a loaded displacement of 16 tons, the boat drew 4 ft. 3 in. for'ard, and 4 ft. 9 in. aft, a ton of ballast being carried.

The floors were flat and somewhat hollow, with the maximum beam three-fifths of length from stem, and the upper strakes aft were far more curved than those at bow, where the lines tended to be hollow. Cost of hull alone was £40, fully rigged with masts, spars and sails, £60. The mizzen mast was stepped well inboard, about one-third of length from stern, and two lugs were usually carried, but many scaffies were three-masted and the luffs of fore and main lugs were set taut by means of a spar bowline, a "wand" or "set." The normal crew was five men, and a train of nets cost from £75 to £110.

The scaffie, chiefly found along the shores of the Moray Firth and as far north as Wick, was a splendid seaboat, handy in stays, although perhaps liable to broach-to if struck by a quartering sea, but owing to the short length of keel, the running abilities were poor.

The lines of such a boat can be seen in plan 17 page 336, and the inset of the harbour emphasises the dangers of running for such a tiny shelter, surrounded by jagged reefs on all sides, except for the narrow entrance. Many of these scaffies were built by J. & W. McIntosh, of Portessie, a firm of high repute down to the last days of sail.

At many harbours in the Orkneys and Caithness and south of the Moray Firth from Whitehills in Banffshire to Berwick-on-Tweed, the second design—the fifie—was found, varying somewhat in build according to the district. Only at Fraserburgh were a few half-decked boats to be seen, the addition of a small fore-peak giving some protection for the crew, but the remainder of the hull was open.

The main difference from the scaffie was that the hull of a fifie was more powerful, but she was slow in stays owing to the long, straight keel, beam was less, and floors sharper. Both types were double-ended, and showed marked resemblance to the Viking ships of centuries before. Plan 18, page 337.

The eminent naval architect, Mr. James Peake, had little good to say about many of the designs submitted to him, and was particularly scathing about the Wick boat, with a length of 34 ft. 6 in., beam 13 ft., depth 4 ft. 9 in., built by D. Bremner at a cost of £64, ready for sea. Plan 19 page 338.

"This boat, having a form that approximates to a spheroid, is the worst that could be given to a floating body for the useful purposes of a boat. It cannot be weatherly, for the round side would divide the water laterally, or to leeward, almost as easily as the bow would for motion ahead. There is no length of body or midship form for capacity, the rising floor would render her unsafe to beach, and under the dimensions used, the least good effect has been obtained."

He disliked the lines of the famous Deal and Yarmouth luggers, and considered their high reputation as seaboats to be due more to the skill of their crews than to the build of the boats. Tolerant of the St. Ives and Penzance luggers, he approved those from the Isle of Man and Scarborough, but considered that the Newhaven fifie (plan 20 page 339) was

"only a slight improvement on the Wick boat . . . arising from the level lines being rather less rounding and thence in a degree better calculated to prevent leeway. The character the Firth of Forth boats are said to bear, of being fine seaboats, must be attributed more to skill of crews than to form of boats."

Boats from Aberdeen and Fraserburgh also failed to meet with his approval, and he considered the rake on the Buckie scaffie objectionable, although in the main the design was preferable to that of the other Scottish boats.

Having thus severely criticised the fishermen's boats, this eminent architect of naval vessels tried his hand at designing a boat of moderate speed, easy motion at sea, and capable of providing shelter and some degree of comfort to crew, as well as carrying a large catch and being suitable for beaching.

But these plans of a boat he considered suitable for the herring fishing failed to satisfy the dour old Scots builders, and the conservative fishermen.

James Leckie, boatbuilder of Leith, writing on 20th June, 1849, said:

"I beg leave to state as my opinion, that it has far too little rise in floor from keel to bilge, and also too full below in first and second waterlines forward, and rather lean aloft, also nearly the same abaft. I do not think that such a model would be at all anything likely to be a weatherly vessel. . . . The above is, from my experience as a builder of fishing boats, the only opinion I can offer.

I beg to subjoin a statement of the number and description of the boats built by me since 1829:—

| | |
|---|---|
| Large fishing boats, from 30 to 43 ft. over stems | 247 |
| Fishing yawls, from 20 to 29 ft. | 225 |
| Whale boats from 24 to 29 ft. | 34 |
| Ship and pleasure boats | 118 |
| Total number of boats | 624 |

which would reach, end on to each other, the distance of 3 miles 152 yards, $2\frac{1}{2}$ ft."

Messrs. Nisbett & Rollo, also of Leith, wrote on the 23rd June, 1849:

"The plan might be found to suit for deep-sea fishing boats very well, but it would be found very unmanageable for herring fishing boats. Being so high above the water, they would lose most of the fish in getting the nets on board, besides there would have to be a bulwark to keep the men from falling overboard, but we have no doubt that vessels or boats of this description would be far more comfortable for the fishermen than open boats, but they could not be expected to make a passage so quick as to answer a market, and also the cost of such a craft as this would far exceed the means of obtaining it, as the most part of the fishermen are not able even to procure them as they are now constructed. As to the number of boats we have built, we have been in the practice of boat building from our earliest years that we were able to work any . . . we have built 30 large boats from 34 to 37 ft. long, 94 boats of the second class, and 152 of the third class, all of which were built for the fishing, besides boats for vessels a great number of different constructions and sizes."

Messrs. Lauchlane, Rose & Son wrote on the 26th June, 1849:

"Having carefully examined the plan of a fishing boat designed by Mr. James Peake . . . we are of opinion that while a boat of that form would possess the very desirable properties of being easy at sea, of rolling easily, of drawing little water, and carrying a considerable burthen for her size, yet from the round form of her bottom, combined with her want of breadth, we fear she would prove a very dangerous boat when under sail, notwithstanding her being decked. . . We also think her masts are placed too near her extremities, and that for the purpose of beaching, she should have a round stern and sternpost similar to our Newhaven fishing boats . . . while we consider the present description of boat as being very unsafe and that almost any alteration on it would be most advisable, particularly that of adding a deck, as it is not so much the form of the Newhaven boat as the want of a deck which makes it so unsafe, yet still we think that the adoption of such a boat as that proposed by Mr. Peake is very little superior to the boat it is intended to supersede."

Mr. James Peake, commenting on the above letters, writes as follows:

"Surely after enumerating such good qualities, which are certain proofs of a good construction and not those which would arise from a round bottom, these gentlemen will see, on re-examination, that the drawing sent was for a boat with a flat and not a round bottom. As to their fear of the boat proving a dangerous one, it is only necessary to refer them to their brethren of the West of England, who have adopted a similar form, yet have no fear, and where can be found finer boats in any respect than those of the Cornish coast, which in all weathers, brave the sea of the Atlantic?"

In the face of such opposition from boat-builders, allied to the rooted objection of the fishermen themselves to any form of boat other than an open one, it was not likely that much headway would be made in persuading all concerned to change over to decked or half-decked boats.

Of all callings, few are more prejudiced in their beliefs for good or ill than fishermen, and their case was most ably put by the Hon. B. F. Primrose, Secretary to Board of Fisheries in Scotland, who wrote to Captain Washington in 14th November 1848:

". . . The Commissioners have devoted a great deal of attention and set on foot many inquiries as to the boats best adapted for the Scotch herring fisheries, but with respect to fitting out, at the expense of the Board, model boats and sending them on trial to the fisheries, the Commissioners would require a special warrant from the Treasury before they could enter upon such an undertaking. Their duties are defined by Act of Parliament, and they have no other money at their disposal than what is granted them by the Treasury to enable them to execute these duties. . . .

On the particular question of decked or undecked boats, I shall now mention the general result arrived at from inquiry among curers, fishermen, fishery officers, our naval superintendents, and I may add, from my own observation. . . . The Scotch herring fishery on the east coast is quite different from that on the west coast, my remarks therefore apply solely to the east coast. It is also totally different from the English fisheries. From the Fern (? Farne) Islands to Duncanby Head, the catching and curing departments are rigidly kept separate. A Scotch fisherman must deliver his herrings fresh to the curer within 12 hours of being caught, the English constantly rouse their fish in salt enough to keep them for a day or two, and remain that time at sea, if they cannot return to port, but fish touched with salt would not be received by the curer in Scotland, nor would it be possible to cure them for foreign markets or for the high-class home markets, unless they were delivered fresh to the curer, or completely cured on board in the Dutch mode, the latter is impracticable without reducing the produce to such a degree as to ruin our fisheries. The Dutch cure beautifully, but only a very small quantity. It is quantity and quality combined that has enabled the Scotch fisheries to take the foreign markets, open to them by moderate duties, out of the hands of the Dutch and all foreign competitors, and if prohibitory duties were done away with, Scotch herrings would obtain a continental monopoly from the low price and high excellence at which they could be supplied, but low price and high excellence can only be obtained by an immense establishment of curers being kept simultaneously engaged in preparing the herrings caught, and the fishermen who catch them being compelled to take the largest number they can, and deliver them fresh with the utmost rapidity. Providence and competition secure the quantity, the delivery fresh depends upon the sort of boat used, the exertions of the curers, and a very strict enforcement of the fishery regulations.

The Scotch herring boats lie in the harbours all day and they leave all together in the evening and return together in the morning. The men shoot their nets at sunset, haul them in at sunrise, and deliver their cargoes early in the morning. This takes place every day, and be the weather or tides what they may, the boats must go out in the evening and be back in the morning. The coast is rock-bound and precipitous, the fishermen therefore can only fish from harbours. They are very poor, constantly could not fish at all but for advances made by the curers, and have no capital to lay out on an expensive boat. The objects therefore to consider are:

1. To get a substantial boat at the smallest prime cost.
2. A boat that will yield the greatest produce and work with the fewest hands.
3. That will row easily as well as sail.
4. That will draw little water and take least room in a crowded harbour.
5. That will stow the largest quantity of fish, be capable of delivering them most expeditiously, and be washed out most easily.

The Scotch herring boat combines these qualities in a greater degree than any other boat.

In the following prices of boats the value of the nets and fishing gear is not included, as that would be the same whatever boat was used. The prices have been taken from two or three different reports:

| | |
|---|---|
| The large Yarmouth lugger, complete, costs | £400 |
| The small half-decked boat, complete, costs | £180 to £200 |
| The Cornish pilchard boat, complete, costs | £160 to £200 |
| But the Scotch boat, complete, costs only from | £60 to £70 |

... The Scotch double lug is peculiarly favourable for the uses the boat is put to. The whole of the canvas is within board, there is no gear to foul or be carried away in getting into and out of a crowded harbour, the steersman has only to measure the length of his boat and range her into her place at the first opening he sees; if her sides stand the squeeze she will get no other damage, whereas bowsprits, booms and shrouds would all be in his way, and be receiving such constant injury as to lose many days' fishing and lead to great expense in repairs. Then the herring fishing particularly requires that mast and sail shall be separate as in the lug, for the boats after their nets are shot have their masts lowered and crutched to prevent drifting, before hauling in the nets a clear area is made in the stern sheets to receive the fish, the lugs are unhooked and stowed forward; the mast, being a bare spar, lays fore and aft, and offers no impediment as the net is hauled in; it is shaken and coiled down wherever there is room, the fish by thus dropping the one on the other, strike no hard substance to knock off their scales, which unfits them for curing well, and the men being unhampered by booms and standing gear of any kind have full space for their work, and for coiling down their nets, which are of immense length and size, as each boat fishes with nearly 20,000 square yards of netting. At the last haul, if the wind be scant, or if there is none at all, they begin to row for harbour, no resistance of spars retards the boat's progress, while the enormous weight of fish, with the wet nets, gives the crew of five enough to do to get back to receive the price of good fish from the curer; they could not pull much additional weight.

A double lug is a most unhandy rig for working a boat to windward, but it has the advantages I describe for meeting the peculiarities of the Scotch fishery, and the balance appears in its favour for the produce of the fisheries, and produce must be maintained, nay somewhat increased, before there can be much hope of persuading a nation to accept of a new experiment, but it is important that the double lug should not be made more unhandy than it is, and very dangerous, which I think there would be some risk of, if decks were added to the boats.

The lugs have to be dowsed every tack, and during the operation the boat is unmanageable, having no steerage-way nor canvas to steady her. In a heavy sea her tendency is to make a stern board, while the men must be in constant movement, shifting over yards, tacks and sheets, they want as much space as they can get, and have to hold on with their legs by the thwarts; in an open boat as they stand on the floor, their weight is brought low, and they have the whole depth of the boat to save them from being canted overboard, but with a deck or half-deck boat, the space being more confined, they must occasionally stand on the deck, where a lurch of the boat is fatal if they lose this footing, and their weight renders the boats so crank, she is more liable to turn over. The same risk prevails for stepping the masts and the deck undoubtedly offers impediments for stowing away sails, coiling the nets, shovelling out the fish, and dashing water over the boat. With us, the nets are landed and dried daily, and the fisherman ought, before going home, to wash out his boat clear of fish scales fore and aft, as old scales taint the new fish. They are too careless about this, but would become doubly so if they had to work under a half-deck.

The English half-decked boats that I have seen have either been fore-and-afters, or if lug-rigged, had a jib and mizzen, which gave the boats steerage way while tacking, but our boats could not fish as they do, 800 from Wick, 300 from Fraserburgh, 400 from Peterhead, entering and leaving the harbour daily, if fitted with a bowsprit and bumpkin, still less from the smaller harbours and narrow creeks they frequent, where an exclusive herring trade is carried on with immense success. Lastly, many landsmen man the boats, who must leave them if the rig is not of the simplest kind, but whose services at the nets and handling of the fish are most valuable; they are a sort of intermediate curer, who never lose sight of what is done with the fish after it gets ashore, because they have a hand in that too, and in the general scramble for employment that attends the fishing season prove a most useful class, since they can be put to any work, and do it cheap. . . . It is a knowledge of these facts, and of the estimable importance of the fisheries to the welfare and sustenance of so poor a country as Scotland, carried on as they are in its poorest and most unproductive districts, in fact, forming the only harvest for large masses of the population, that makes the Commissioners watchful that no hasty interference on plausible premises derived from imperfect comparisons should come in to check the returns of this great source of national wealth, and hinder capital from flowing in to maintain it, but they are no less anxious to carry forward with energy and perseverance every real improvement of which it is susceptible. I trust, therefore, you will not construe the observations I have offered into an opposition to improvement, but regard them as an imperfect attempt on my part to lay before you the whole subject in all its bearings, in the hope that you will be good enough to afford the Commissioners the benefit of your advice and opinion, which must carry so much weight in directing theirs. . . . "

Some of the Buckie men went so far as to admit that a 14-in. plank run round inside the gunwale *might* be an improvement, but they emphatically did not approve of decks or half-decks, maintaining that they could not carry as many herring in such boats, stating that in one day they had landed nearly a thousand crans from ten boats, one of which had 130 cran, about 19 tons weight of fish. The first half-decked boat was not built till 1855.

The famous firm of Alexander Hall & Co., of Aberdeen, submitted a design which was undoubtedly the prototype of the boats built two decades later. Length overall was 45 ft., beam 14 ft., and depth 7 ft., with a sheer of 18 in., the floors were flat, with three rising strakes next the keel, and the hull was broader and fuller in the after body than the for'ard. Six feet from stem and sternpost were watertight bulkheads, and abaft the fore compartment was a cabin 9 ft. by 3 ft. by 6 ft. Three feet from each gunwale was an airtight compartment 3 ft. wide by 2 ft. 6 in. deep, with an open hold between, 29 ft. by 7 ft. by 3 ft., capable of being made watertight with hatches. The deck was 2 ft. 9 in. below the gunwale, with three scuttle ports a side for the oars, which were stowed in lumber irons on the gunwales, thus forming additional protection to save the crew falling overboard. But the drawback was the cost, £150 as compared with the £50 of the present boat in use at Aberdeen.

Officialdom not being prepared to do anything but talk and write about the form of the boats, it was left to the National Lifeboat Institution to step into the breach, and I first heard of their interest in a remarkable manner.

One morning in May 1949 I received a small parcel containing pieces of torn wallpaper, and wondered why on earth it had been sent, then I noticed that on the back were scraps of old newspaper. They came from Mrs. Elsie Garden, of Portessie, whose father, Mr. John Addison, went to sea in a scaffie in 1875, and she wrote that when removing some wallpaper in their old house about two years ago, she noticed the pages of newspaper and kept a few scraps out of curiosity. Luckily, they contained a vital clue, and after carefully removing any plaster still adhering, I was able to piece them together and found part of an article about an improved type of safety boat, sponsored by the National Lifeboat Institution. A date in a letter on the state of roads in some parish fixed the year as 1867. It appeared that the Committee, perturbed at the frequent loss of life through the foundering of fishing boats, decided to build a few pattern boats and place them at some of the principal fishing stations in the hands of experienced and trustworthy boatmen to whom they were lent, or let at a small percentage of their earnings, for a period of twelve months. At the end of this time they would be sold and remain in the various localities as samples from which they hoped other boats

158 *IONA*, B.K. 265 AND *BRILLIANT SUCCESS* B.K. 985, c. 1882
Note difference in design of bow in clinker and carvel build, and tack hook on chain through stem.

159 *SILVER CLOUD* L.H. 1065
Note forelug is a'monk, sheet is a'weather.

160　A RELIC OF THE 1881 DISASTER
Note skegs into which foremast lowered.

161　*COMELY*, B.F. 1560
Wrecked at the "Band" near Filey, Sunday, 19th November, 1893

162 FISHING VILLAGE OF ROSS, BERWICKSHIRE, c. 1882

163 BURNMOUTH HARBOUR, c. 1882

164 CREW OF *SUCCESS*, L.H. 890, c. 1882

165 CLEARING HERRING NETS, c. 1882

166 BARKING NETS, c. 1882
Note hand barrow on top of tub.

would be built. As they would be seen by fishermen from all parts of the coast who had assembled for the fishing, a few boats would suffice.

Small plans were reproduced of a fully-decked boat 40 ft. in length, 14 ft. beam, and 7 ft. depth, which to my eye was similar in principle to the design suggested by A. Hall, of Aberdeen, in 1848. A long central hatchway was capable of being covered with portable hatches and a watertight tarpaulin in heavy weather, while bulkheads were fitted at bow and stern. Another scrap of wallpaper carried part of a report from William Boyd of Peterhead, who said the new boat gave great satisfaction, and that John Geddes, the lifeboat coxswain, lay alongside the Lossiemouth boat in the Firth of Forth and found she was a fast sailer, having made the run from Peterhead to Granton in thirteen hours, but had not yet met such bad weather as would thoroughly test her safety powers.

Yet another fragment gave indication that the Duke of Sutherland had ordered a similar boat to be built at his expense at Wick for use at Helmsdale.

This information that the R.N.L.I. had been instrumental in urging the use of decked boats was entirely new to me, and I at once wrote to Mr. Charles Vince to see if their records threw any more light on this fascinating discovery. He most kindly made a thorough search and although many papers had been lost or destroyed, he found a mention in 1863 that the Committee contemplated introducing a boat which could be at any time made insubmergible. Another minute in 1864 conveyed the best thanks of the Committee to various officers of the Coastguard for assistance rendered in replying to various queries about fishing boats. The next reference was in 1882, when a paragraph stated that "some twelve years before, the Institution had been happily instrumental in introducing a general improvement in the form of boats on the East Coast of Scotland, by placing four samples of semi-decked boats which, when caught out in a gale far from land, could be temporarily hatched over and battened down, and rendered as safe as a decked vessel, and such boats are now in general use on that coast."

This finding of some old pieces of newspaper by Mrs. Garden produced definite proof that the chief credit for inducing the Scottish fishermen to change over from open to decked boats was due to the praiseworthy efforts of the R.N.L.I.

Meanwhile, the number of boats engaged in the herring fishing was increasing, until in 1862 1,122 boats fished out of Wick during the six weeks' season, and no less than twelve curing stations on the coast of Caithness dealt with the catches. The hired men tramped across the Highlands from the west coast to earn £3 or £4 for the fishing season with food and drink, whisky flowed like water, upwards of 500 gallons a day being consumed in Wick alone, where 22 public-houses and 23 across the river in Pulteney supplied the needs of the thousands who looked to the herring to supply their needs for the rest of the year. The smell of fish and offal on a hot August day must have been unbearable.

The Buckie boats sailed for the Caithness fishing about the 24th July, each man averaging two nets, costing £4 each. The boats were paid on the bounty system, or engaged by the curers at 10s. a barrel, with a bottle of whisky a day. Each man received 2s. at the beginning and the same amount at the end of the season. If paid by bounty, they had 5s. arrival money and 2s. a week for the Saturday pint of whisky, and 5s. departure money. The crews preferred the latter arrangement in bad seasons, but when the fishing was good, a boat might take 40 barrels a night, and then the other rate of payment was far and away higher.

In the early sixties the largest boats were only about 35 ft. long on the keel, and fully equipped with masts, sails, oars and nets cost about £200, a boat shooting about one mile of nets, each 50 yards long by 32 ft. deep, and measured by barrel, two nets going to a barrel. Fastened together by the "back rope," each net was marked by a skin bladder or buoy, made of sheep or dog skins, Buckie men breeding special dogs for the purpose, but at Fraserburgh bullock bladders were used. The boat rode to her nets by the "trail rope," and small stones fastened to the foot of the nets kept them upright in the water.

The owner provided boat, nets, buoys, ropes, etc., and engaged the crew, who were often related, and in many cases part-owners; hired men were taken on solely for the heavy work of hauling the nets, and were usually crofters who worked on their land for the rest of the year.

The boats were engaged by the curers, who bargained to take so many crans of fish, generally about 200, and they paid "arles" or binding money at the end of the season to ensure the use of the boat the following year. In addition, an agreed sum was paid over as bounty, an allowance in spirits, and the free use of ground on which to dry the nets. As the curer also provided barrels and salt, he stood at a considerable expense for some eight months before any herrings were caught. If a fisherman was trustworthy, many curers would advance him money to build a boat, thus "thirling" it to their service, and enabling them to drive a hard bargain for the catch. To do this it was sometimes necessary to borrow in turn from the buyers, and so a vicious circle was formed, of one man dependent on another, in turn dependent on a third, and a bad season might ruin all. In this case the luckless hired man came off worst, for he received no wages for his weeks of toil, if the boat-owner failed to catch enough fish to pay expenses.

A typical bargain would be £1 arles money—this was often spent at once in the public-houses, drinking to the success of the fishing—ten gallons of whisky, use of net ground, and "driving" or cartage from boat to ground and back, worth about £4, £10 to £20 as bounty, and say 12s. to 15s. a cran for all fish caught. A man known to be lucky at the fishing might get as much as £50 bounty. It can easily be seen that such an arrangement made for hundreds of boats would run into tens of thousands of pounds, with a winter and spring to pass before a single fish was caught, a gamble indeed, when one considers how chancy the herring fishing can be. At the beginning of the season a boat might bring in less than two crans, or a good night would result in ten to twelve.

In 1863 two weeks' fishing only averaged two crans a night, and the average for the season was but 79 crans, whereas the previous year's fishing at Fraserburgh was 226½ crans a boat, the highest ever known.

Barrels of early herring realised up to 45s. for export to the Continent, where the very finest salt herring made about 1s. each as a *hors d'oeuvre*, but thousands of tons of fresh fish were despatched by rail to markets inland.

With upwards of a thousand boats fishing out of Wick, the scenes ashore were animated, to say the least of it, when the boats began to come in soon after dawn. Lugger after lugger would drive into any tiny space available, drop sail, and the crew commence carrying fish to the troughs. After the curer had checked the number of crans, the fish were sprinkled with salt to enable the women to grasp them easily, otherwise they were too slippery for quick handling. When some score of baskets had been emptied, the gutters set to work, usually working in parties of five, one or two gutting, the same number carrying, and one packing. The girls, who had been lounging about joking with the men, were transformed into blood-spattered females with clothes spangled with sequins of fish scales. A bob down to grab a herring, a lightning-like movement of a razor-sharp knife, and the fish was gutted by a turn of the hand and flung back into the appropriate basket, thirty, forty, fifty fish a minute, hour after hour. The gutted fish were next plunged into a large trough, roused and mixed with salt, then the packer seized a handful and arranged them rosette fashion in a barrel, a handful of salt on each, until full with some 700 herring, the whole job of gutting, rousing and packing taking about ten minutes. The expense of curing was eight or nine shillings in addition to the price of the fish, etc., and the usual profit was 4s. a barrel.

Plate 147 shows the scene in a curing shed at Burnmouth in the early eighties.

As the fish settled down in the barrel, more were added from day to day until the cask was full and ready for branding. It was the cooper's first job each morning to examine every barrel packed the previous day, to ensure that no pickle had leaked away; if so, the fish had to be repacked. A period of fifteen days for herring to lie in salt before branding was fixed by Act of Parliament, a time considered excessive by some curers, who wanted the waiting time to be reduced to ten days.

The imagination fails to grasp the countless millions of fish cured during a season, all the way down the coast from Wick to Yarmouth, yet still the shoals persist.

The year 1873 saw 939,233 barrels cured, of these 668,008 were exported, and the Government brand, costing 4d. a barrel, was placed on 435,274.

The hemp nets of the early days had by now been largely replaced by lighter ones of cotton. I have already mentioned that the first machine for weaving cotton nets was invented in Musselburgh by James Patterson. The rights in this loom were acquired by

J. & W. Stuart, a firm established in 1812. In reply to my letter of enquiry, they most kindly offered to have a special photograph taken of one of these looms (Plate 148), and wrote that the hand looms produced at that time were still in use to-day to some extent, the output by good weavers being not much below that of automatic machines. The difficulty arises in getting labour for hand looms under present-day conditions.

Although the first decked boat had been built in Eyemouth in 1856 at a cost of £130, but little progress was made in convincing the fishermen of the advantages of this type until the late sixties, when the revival of interest was undoubtedly due to the sample boats built to the order of the R.N.L.I. By 1872 forty were registered at Berwick, and the average length had increased from 40 ft. to 44 ft., with a few up to 56 ft., and costing not less than £200 to build. The increase in cost, however, was more than paid for in improved earnings. Whereas men using open boats averaged £60 to £160 a boat at Burnmouth, in the nearby village of Coldingham the takings were from £100 to £550 per decked boat.

At Leith boats of 42 ft. to 45 ft. keel, costing from £250 to £300, were being built, and Newhaven alone had thirteen decked boats supplied within eighteen months. At many villages the open boats were cut in half, lengthened and decked over, in some instances the planks being fastened to the underside of the thwarts which ran across *over* the deck. All up the East Coast the changeover was in progress; Buckie, home of the scaffie, had some 400 on the register, with 64 new first-class boats added during the year 1872; Wick built 37 large ones, mostly fully-decked, well-finished and equipped.

Changes were also taking place ashore. The opening of railways brought new markets further afield, and fishmongers' shops superseded the hawking of fish by the wives and daughters of the fishermen. One serious consequence following the coming of the larger decked boat, able to go further to sea, was the beginning of the decline of the smaller fishing villages, and a tendency to concentrate in the larger ports. For some time past many of the boats had taken carrier pigeons to sea, which were released with an advice to the curers of the likely catch, thus enabling preparations to be made in advance to deal with it ashore.

During the seventies carvel-built replaced clench-built hulls to a great extent. Mr. Lightfoot informs me that many of the new fifies had a fairly sharp bottom, though some builders built to their own ideas and experience, varying the design of hull from full-bodied in some cases, to being as sharp as a wedge in others, the former being dry boats, the latter very wet in bad weather. The garboard strake formed a deep trough which was used to carry the stone and iron ballast. Many were of great beam, he remembers one 60 ft. long, with a 20 ft. beam and draught of 7 ft. The deck was sunk about a foot below the gunwale, and a very long, wide hatchway made the fifie almost an open boat, although the for'ard part was decked, forming the cabin.

In Wick 313 first-class and 1,180 second-class boats were registered in 1872, the majority only 24 ft. to 34 ft. length of keel. A boat of 31 ft. keel had a foremast 35 ft. 3 in. long, usually raking a little aft, but some men preferred to have it upright; the main mast was 32 ft. long, stepped just aft of midships. In the newer boats the tendency was to move this mast further aft, where it was called the mizzen, and a somewhat smaller sail was set.

The foreyard measured 16 ft. 6 in., and the fore lug was eight cloths in the head, ten in the foot, which was rounded a little, having a 4 in. gore at the tack, and a 12 in. one at the sheet; the head gores were 3 in. to 4 in. per cloth. The fore lug was made of 85 yards of No. 4 canvas, and the main, generally one cloth less, had about 3 ft. less hoist and very little peak, but in some boats both masts were the same size, and often without rake. The boat would handle well under fore lug alone. Weather bolt rope was 4 in. circumference, leech rope $2\frac{1}{4}$ in., and the sails had six reefs, 2 ft. 6 in. apart. Halyard tye was 30 ft. in length, of 4 in. rope with a knot at the end; the tye was put through the eye of an iron traveller on mast, rove through a sheave 18 in. from masthead and had a double block on end, the tackle being a luff purchase with the single block at gunwale; the halyards were $2\frac{1}{2}$ in. to $2\frac{3}{4}$ in. rope. The sheets were fast at gunwale, rove through single block at clew, and belayed to cleat.

In the sixties began the custom of going to the East Anglian Autumn fishing, some 36 boats sailing from Kirkcaldy, and 40 to 50 from Anstruther; others went north to the Shetlands and the Hebrides, fishing out of Stornoway. Whereas in 1862 12,545 boats gave employment to 41,008 fishermen, ten years later the figures were 15,232 boats and 46,178 men.

Once again I turn to those precious scraps of wallpaper sent by Mrs. Garden to learn about those far-off days. Under date Saturday, April 27th, but no year, probably 1867, is this paragraph from Fraserburgh:

"Highland fishing. Another fleet of boats, numbering fourteen to sixteen, have this week gone from the villages of Broadsea, Cairnbulg, Inverallochy and St. Combs, to the fishing stations on the islands of Lewis and the Uists. A few are to make Stornoway their headquarters, but the destination of the majority is Loch Boisdale in South Uist. Their regular engagements do not, we understand, come into operation until the 20th May, but as they have done little or nothing in the fishing at home for some time, they have preferred the chances of netting a few crans of herrings before that time."

Another torn piece reads as follows, the main substance was legible, but I had to guess at a few words, fortunately not important:

"Norway timber. Four cargoes of billet wood and staves have within these few days been discharged here from Mandal and other ports in Norway. Although arriving on chance, the timber has apparently met with ready sales at the rather high figure of £3 3s. per thousand running feet of staves, and $8\frac{1}{2}$d. per solid foot of billet wood. Hoops have also been landed in considerable quantities, but at what price we have not ascertained." This timber would be for the making of barrels.

Another most interesting item was the felling of a huge and stately fir tree in the forest of Ballachbuie, "which from the number of rings in its base, was reckoned to be at least 220 years old. Still it exhibited no signs of decay."

Finally I succeeded in deciphering the following:

"Findhorn, 26 April. A number of our herring fishing crews have last week been making active preparations for the Hebrides herring fishings, in getting their boats, nets and other fishing tackle put in order. They have this week taken their departure for the scene of action, which we understand is Barra. They have taken a good quantity of wood with them for the purpose of building houses to live in during their sojourn there. Salmon and white fishing have been very unproductive for this past week, owing to the fresh in the river and the cold weather."

On their return from these distant fishings it was frequently the custom for some of the men to combine to buy a beast at Keith market to provide meat for their families, and luckily it is possible to give some idea of what money bought in those days, as other paragraphs told:

"320 cattle, a fair turn-out, were on the ground at Torriff, but trade was dull, price for fat stock was from £3 to £2 5s. per cwt."

At such a price, one-year-olds sold at about £6 apiece, two-year-olds up to £24 and £26.

At the Braemar Spring Hogg market were over 4,000 hoggs (sic) alone, but the market was so sluggish that little business was done until late afternoon, a lot of prime hoggs was bought by the factor to the Earl of Fife at 20s., but prices declined to 17s. by 8 p.m. Black-faced "wedders" sold very stiffly, averaging 22s. to 24s. 9d., a number of lots leaving the market unsold.

It was interesting to note the use of the words "stot" and "quey" for steer and heifer, both words derived from the Icelandic *stutr* and *kviga*.

The scaffie retained her clinker build to the last, a form of construction which made a peculiar sound going through the water. The well-rounded stem, sweeping back above the waterline, reduced any possible damage to a minimum should the boat be driven over her nets. The foremast, stepped in a mastcase resting against a thwart, the "baulk," raked for'ard or aft according to fisherman's choice, and a tall, fairly high-peaked dipping lugsail was set, with narrow head and broad foot. The mizzen was stepped further inboard than in English practice, thus shortening the boom, and raked well for'ard, so that it was often almost parallel to the leech of the forelug, on it a standing lug was set. The extent of rake of stem and sternpost can be judged from a 36 ft. length of keel giving an overall length of up to 60 ft., with beam 17 ft. 6 in., and depth of hold 7 ft. The rather bluff bows, slamming into a head sea, made her slower than a fifie, but the short length of keel produced a better boat for turning to wind'ard.

When Mr. H. Oliver Hill loaned me certain documents written in the early 1930's some very faint pencil notes of names and addresses caught my eye, and drawing a bow at a venture, I wrote to some of them, hardly daring to hope that contact could still be made after a lapse of nearly fifteen years, but to my joy, every shot was a bullseye.

Mr. William McIntosh, of Buckie, replied in February, 1949, that when he was born some seventy years ago his father, grandfather, and uncle were in company, building scaffies prior to 1880 with a length of keel of about 32 ft., the stem was curved and had a 7 ft. rake off plumb, and a straight sternpost was about 10 ft. off plumb. Hulls were clinker-built, the timbers or frames being fitted after the planking was completed. For hauling in the bush or springrope attached to the nets a winch—the "ironman"—fitted with handles, stood aft of the mizzen mast.

Some two months later Mr. McIntosh, recalling my wish to contact an old fisherman with experience of these boats, sent me a cutting from the *Banffshire Advertiser*, which led to my getting into touch with Mr. John Addison. By a coincidence, a few days later came a similar paper from Mr. W. S. Cumming.

Mr. Addison, of Portessie, replied that he would be pleased to be of any assistance; he does not speak English, only broad Scots, but his daughter, Mrs. Garden, and her husband very kindly put my questions to him and noted the answers.

This interesting old fisherman went to sea in a boat called *Mowats* as a "scummer" in 1875 at the age of ten, his job to catch the fish which escaped from the nets as they were being hauled, using an iron-hooped net rather like a gigantic butterfly net. He had no pay, but received "scum money," the worth of the herring which he scummed out of the water. Strangely enough, it was always the best fish which fell out of the nets, and so they fetched a better price than the rest.

A few open boats were still in use at the time, but the majority were decked scaffies, some with three masts, which went to sea every evening, returning next morning. The boats were hired by the curers for a complement of 200 cran, and when this mark was reached they had to stop fishing. His shortest time to reach this complement was nine trips.

They fished with nets kept upright in the water by a cork rope and stones tied to the footrope, the "gales" or sides being laced together to form a "fleet" of 40 to 45 nets, the "trail end" marked with a small coloured buoy. Each net was 60 yards long, mounted on a rope several yards shorter, with lines called "ozels," costing fully mounted, 25s. The "heid back" or warp, by which the nets were connected, was supported by buoys made from sheepskins. Nets were barked before and once during season, using about one hundredweight of bark at a time.

The nets were shot on the starboard side, about half a mile from the nearest boat, when all were out the foremast was lowered back into the crutch, the mizzen removed altogether, and laid up on the foredeck, the rudder was brought inboard, and the boat lay to her nets. The fleet was hauled by hand over the stern, on both sides as tide permitted, and the nets were cleared at sea, a process known locally as "reddin' the nets."

Fifty to sixty cran would be a good haul, and the fish were sold for curing. A hired man received £7 for the eight-week season, more or less, and 1s. to 1s. 6d. per cran.

A scaffie's sails, barked once a year, were bent to the yards by "yard bands," passed round the yard, twice through the eyelets at head of sail, and fastened off on top fo spar with a "parley knot." The best point of sailing was with wind almost free, and speeds of six to seven miles an hour were common.

Although Mr. Addison spent forty years at sea before retiring through ill health, he had no experience of wrecks. He went to the Shetlands in zulus, an average passage being 24 hours, and south to East Anglia, taking about 50 hours for the trip.

He made an excellent sketch of the scaffie *Seven Brothers*, B.F.941 (Plate 149), built by W. Gardiner of Cullen for his father, who also owned *Aunt Eppie*, built by George Slater, Portessie. He himself was part-owner of two zulus, *Economy* and *Helen Morrison*.

Plate 150 was taken from a very old photo loaned me by Mr. Peter Cowie, of Buckie. It shows a laden scaffie entering Buckie harbour about 1870. The fore lug has just been dowsed, and a man is standing by the wide hatchway, holding in his hand one of the "wands." Mr. Addison drew my attention to the mizzen mast lying on the foredeck, and says it is possible she might have three masts. Mr. Garden questioned Mr. Joseph Murray, who went to sea in a three-master, and said it was the custom to remove the rudder and all three masts while fishing. The mainmast was raised first by means of three stays, and was then used to raise the other two masts, each of which was held in an iron ring on a strong thwart.

The bowlines were used when the wind was partly astern, in a light wind they made the boat go faster. The poles used for this purpose were called "wands," and were mostly utilised for pushing the boat out of and into harbour. To place the rudder back on its pintles was a bit of a job, especially if there was any sea running.

In the winter months many of the boats were hauled high up the beach, and the striking difference between the bows of a scaffie and fifie can be seen in Plate 151, taken from a photograph sent me by Mr. W. S. Cumming. He tells me the boats were often hauled up by a steam-roller, and that the bearded fellow standing by the lamp-post was one Alexander Cuthbert, a shoemaker, more intimately known as "Sandy Cuttie."

Mr. Cumming recalls the last of the scaffies sailing into Buckie harbour, and then being hauled up on the foreshore and left there until they fell to pieces, and he gave me a graphic description of the return of the fleet from down south:

"To this day I still recall the times when as a boy I used to watch the scaffies and zulus returning from the English fishing in the middle of winter, making for the harbour in very stormy weather—the breathless excitement watching them entering, wondering when and if they would be tossed up against the jetty walls, and then into the calm waters of the inner basin, truly a wonderful sight. And often have I thought of the astonishing navigation of those fishermen, men of little or no education, and of navigation only of what they learned from their forebears. How they could handle those open boats with their huge lugsails in all weathers, marvellous when you think of it. Then there was the sorrow caused in the town when any of the boats were lost—fathers, sons, brothers and uncles would all sail in the same boat and go down together. Also in the old days coming home from the English fishing, loaded up with presents for their wives and children, and carrying their earnings in hard-earned cash in the boat, for those old fishermen had no faith in banks in those days—well, fathers and sons, presents and earnings, all went to the bottom if the boat was lost."

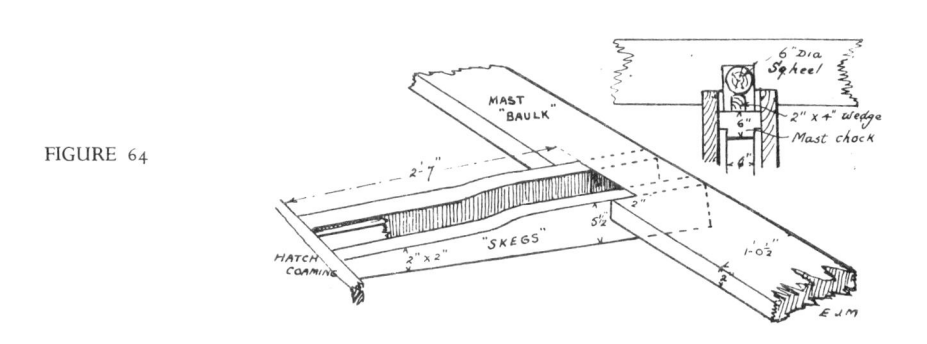

FIGURE 64

The high rocky cliffs were a constant source of danger with an off-shore wind, the fierce gusts sweeping down off them demanded the finest possible seamanship.

Unfortunately no plans of a scaffie are available, as they were built from a half model or by eye, but the lines of one of the smaller boats, known as "yawls," were taken off by the late P. J. Oke in 1936. Plans 21 pages 340-342

Although, of course, a much smaller boat than the big scaffie, there is a striking similarity between the body plan and that of the Buckie boat of 1848 (plan 17 page 336), showing that there was little change in the design in half a century.

*Gratitude*, B.C.K.252, was built in 1896 by George Innes of Portknockie, and owned by David Mair. Length of keel was 16 ft. 2½ in., length overall 25 ft. 4½ in., beam 8 ft. 6 in., inside depth 3 ft. 6 in.

The deck plan shows the wide, long hatchway, covered with 8 in. by 1 in. hatches, with two thwarts 8 in. by 2 in. and 6 in. by 2 in. below the waterways, the "baulk" 1 ft. 0½ in. by 2 in., recessed on after side to take the foremast, which is stepped on the floors in a tabernacle with 5 in. by 1 in. bridges, foreside being 3 in. thick. It lowers back into a trunk, the "skegs," which extend aft to the hatch coaming, and is kept upright with a heavy mast chock (Fig. 64). Aft is a thwart 8 in. by 1 in., resting on the after cleats; here the steersman sat with his legs in a small cockpit. Plate 152 shows the deck looking for'ard.

SCOTLAND

## SCANTLINGS

| | | |
|---|---|---|
| *Stem* | - | 6½ in. by 3 in., rakes aft 4 ft. 3¼ in. Oak. |
| *Sternpost* | - | 8½ in. by 4½ in., 6 ft. 3½ in. off plumb. Oak. |
| *Keel* | - | 6½ in. by 2½ in., with ½ in. iron. Elm. |
| *Floors* | - | 9 in. by 2 in., spacing 1 ft. 2 in. |
| *Floors, aft* | - | 10 in. deep, 3¾ in. double f. & a., by 3¼ in. |
| *Frames* | - | 1¾ in. f. & a. by 3 in., at bilge. |
| | | 2 in. f. & a. by 3 in., at deck. |
| | | Short frames to bilge between each floor and frame, 2 in. sq. |
| *Beams* | - | Forehold beam under deck, 4½ in. by 2 in., with five beams for'ard, spacing 11½ in. and 12 in., each 2 in. sq., except one on foreside of mast, 3 in. deep by 2 in. |
| *Stringers* | - | 2½ in. and 3 in. deep by 1½ in. |
| *Mast carlings* | - | 4½ in. deep o/a. by 3 in. |
| *Beams under waterways* | | 2 in. sq., spacing 1 ft. 6 in., length 2 ft. 2 in. |
| *Beam aft end of hatch* | | 4 in. deep by 2 in. |
| *Beams right aft* | - | 3 in. deep by 2 in. |
| *Hatch carlings* | - | 1 in. thick, 2½ in. wide. |
| *Deadwood aft* | - | Extends to fifth frame. |
| *Deadwood for'ard* | | Extends to fourth frame. |
| *Bulwarks on deck* | | 1¾ in. thick, by 6¾ in. |
| *Bearer on frames* | | 4 in. by 1½ in. |
| *Tiller* | - | 6 ft. 10½ in. long, 1½ in. round grip. |
| *Deck knees, three a side* | | 1 ft. by 6 in. by 2½ in. |

## PLANKING

Twelve strakes of ¾ in. larch. Lands, ⅝ in. Garboards, 5 in.
Deck planking, 5½ in. by ¾ in.

## COLOUR

Black hull, with blue top strake, white waterline, red below.

## SPARS

| | | |
|---|---|---|
| *Foremast, L.O.A.* | | 25 ft., dia. 6 in. to 4 in. |
| *Lug yard* | - | 15 ft. 8 in., dia. at strop 3½ in., ends 2 in. |
| *Jibboom* | - | 16 ft., dia. 2½ in., heel 3 in. sq. |

Thole pins just aft of first deck knee, cleats on bearer, and sheet lead below gunwale.

## SAIL PLAN

| | | |
|---|---|---|
| *Fore lug* | - | Luff: 14 ft. 5 in. |
| | | Head: 14 ft. |
| | | Leech: 22 ft. 6 in., with 2 in. roach. |
| | | Foot: 16 ft. 6 in., 8½ cloths, 5 in. round. |
| | | About 50 yards of canvas, area 280 sq. ft. |

Four lines of reef points, two lines of eyelet lacing.
Gusset at sixth cloth, 6 in. at top, 1 ft. 1 in. at foot.
Wire tye, one double block, 7 in. by 5 in. Single, 5 in. by 4 in. by 3 in., and at sheet.
Bead parrel with tye hook, 6 in. by 1 in.

*Jib* - - Luff: 16 ft. 6 in.
Leech: 12 ft. 6 in., with 4 in. roach.
Foot: 11 ft., 2½ in. belly.

*Five cloths* - Area: 70 sq. ft.

Total sail area: 350 sq. ft.

The mast was fir, spars of larch, and the iron eye-shank was bound to yard with rope binding. Tack of fore lug went to 2½ in. by 1 in. eyebolt on either bow. All timbers of oak.

Round about the 1870's the lines of the fifies were improved, and the more square-headed lugs were replaced by well-cut, higher-peaked sails, producing increased speed, as the old system of a curer taking the entire catch was giving place to auction sales on the quays, and it was a case of first come, first sold, and best price obtained.

Hulls were massively constructed, with keels of English or American elm, oak stems, sternposts and frames; planking below waterline was larch, above red, white or pitch pine, and some forty tons of undressed timber were used in the later boats, which had the cabin aft, but the custom of building with no rails persisted, and the timber-heads showed between the gunwale and the bearer inside.

The sail plan differed from the scaffies in that the fore lug was a lofty and rather narrow sail, cut less broad in the foot, and a standing lug on the mizzen, sheeting to end of an outrigger, always called in Scotland the boom, a name given to any spar projecting outboard. Both types of boat had light reeving bowsprits—jibbooms—on which a jib was set when making a passage, topsails were never set, or sails shifted, as was Cornish practice; up to nine lines of reef points were provided, and all meant for use, but it had to blow great guns before the last one was pulled down. In winter shorter spars and smaller sails were often used.

The boatbuilders of Fifeshire were renowned for the excellence of their work, with the palm awarded to the craftsmen of Anstruther and St. Monance. The rough logs were hand-sawn over open sawpits by professional sawyers, who travelled round the boat-building yards, taking on the work by contract. They were powerful men, for the task demanded great and prolonged physical effort; being their own masters, they liked an occasional few days on the spree, for many were heavy drinkers. The carpenters fashioned the keel, timbers, planks, and spars, and a boat was built without any mechanised aid whatever, the master's eye being unerring for producing that sweetness of line which made for speed and seaworthiness. Few of these men had any education in the modern sense of the word, were often completely illiterate, but that did not interfere with their craftsmanship, and the fact that a boat or ship was Anstruther-built was a sufficient guarantee of sailing ability.

One cannot help wondering if the world is not the poorer for the loss of this pride in workmanship which was so typical of past generations.

In the late '70's various attempts were made to popularise the dandy or ketch rig, and for a while the "smack" rig, as it was called, was used by the fishermen of Aberdeenshire and Banffshire, between Fraserburgh and Macduff. These fifies had a gaff mainsail and were either cutter or ketch-rigged. Handy in narrow waters, they were easier to "stay" than a lugger, but the local sailmakers were never so expert at cutting fore and aft as lug sails. The sails lasted longer, and on the whole, the design was more economical, while standing shrouds gave additional support to the foremast, but even these advantages did not outweigh the Scots love for the lugger, and after ten or fifteen years the smack rig was right out of fashion, but it spread to the Shetlands, where for a time it was very popular.

I have in my collection a very fine photograph of a brigantine and drifter leaving Yarmouth Haven in tow of an old clinker-built paddle tug (Plate 153). Just clearing the south pier is a smack-rigged fifie, with a boomless gaff mainsail hooped to the foremast and a curious rectangular topsail with a very long yard set above, and a huge balloon jib out on the bowsprit. On the mizzen is a large low-peaked standing lug sheeting to the end of a steeved-up boom, this sail is barked, but the others are not. Such a sail plan bears marked characteristics to Lowestoft practice, and I think it quite possible that this fifie is *Beautiful Star*, 31 tons, built at St. Monance 1875, owned at Lowestoft in 1885, and dandy-rigged. Or she might be *White Star*, 33 tons, built at Eyemouth 1868, owned at Gorleston and dandy-rigged; these are the only two local boats I can trace as being built in Scotland.

Efforts were also being made to improve the protection and safety of the crew by adding a fixed strake for'ard and a moveable one aft to the foot-high bulwarks, but they never caught on, and to the last they remained very low, scarcely knee-high, a source of danger in heavy weather, but Mr. Addison tells me the men got accustomed to them.

Mr. Theodore Lightfoot writes me regarding this innovation:

"A group of gentlemen, interested in the safety and well-being of the fishermen, thought out a safer type of craft, one with higher bulwarks and of a more sea-keeping model, easier to handle. The vessel had a slightly overhanging transom stern, after the usual brig or schooner style, was tubbier in build, had higher bulwarks and a wire guard rail, two feet above the bulwarks, and rigged fore and aft as a ketch, also a few as schooners. The only complaint was they were slower than the fifies, also the latter could sail two points nearer the wind."

John Gunn, of Golspie, invented a moveable rail, hinged and folding, when not in use it lay in a groove along the gunwale, and was in sections so that when hauling in bad weather, just length enough could be removed.

Like the Yorkshire fishermen, the Scots were very fond of vivid colours, and a typical scaffie in the eighties had a white, blue or green gunwale, bright varnish to the waterline, and black bottom. Registration letters and numbers were in white on a black oblong. Decks were tarred, inside the bulwarks was blue, sometimes green;

hatches, coamings, mast trunk, crutch, and heavy thwarts were dark azure blue; mast heads to just below sheave were white or blue, with blocks the same colour as the masthead. In later years many luggers had bright varnished topsides, white watercuts, and green bottoms. The watercuts extended the whole length of the boat, being wedge-shaped with the thick end fore and aft.

I am indebted to Mr. Stuart Bruce for this information.

Fifies were also gaily coloured with white or blue gunwales, black topsides, a red or yellow bend, white watercuts, and green bottoms, with all inside deck fittings, including bulwarks, blue. Blocks were usually white. For the first season sails were left white, then they were barked a rich, dark brown, almost black, colour, they were seldom tanned the warm red of the English drifters. In the early boats the names were often carved on separate boards, but about the '90's the fashion was to paint them on the hull, with various emblems and devices as scroll work. Aft, the name of the boat was on the port quarter, that of the home port on the starboard side.

In 1879 an idea was evolved of incorporating in one vessel the special advantages of scaffie and fifie, and a hull was designed with the vertical stem of the fifie and the long raking stern of the scaffie. The credit for building the first must be given to William Campbell, of Lossiemouth, who named the craft most appropriately *Nonesuch*. The deep forefoot and clean bows gave a good grip of the water for'ard, and fine weatherly ability, while aft the sternpost, raking at 45 deg., gave an overhang of 12 ft. to 14 ft. compared to the 5 ft. of the fifie. This shortening of the keel gave the handiness of the scaffie to the new model, improved deck space aft, and lengthened the waterlines, so increasing speed. The greater overall length permitted a bigger spread of canvas without long booms projecting outboard.

One can imagine the excitement when this novel design took the water, the comments of the old salts, the eagerness of designer and builder to see if their brainwave was a champion, and such it proved to be, so much so that the scaffie fell from favour, and the men of Banffshire, Morayshire, and Nairnshire discarded their old love for the new hull, which received the name of "zulu," from the conflict then proceeding between our redcoats and the dusky African warriors. Up to about 1885 the hulls were clinker-built with a keel length of about 40 ft. (Plate 154); when carvel construction was introduced length increased to 43 ft., with the "ironman" still used for hauling in the nets. When a boiler and steam capstan came in for hauling the bush-rope and hoisting the sails, the boats and gear were more easily handled, and size increased every year till keel was 62 ft., with an overall length of about 75 ft.

Spurred on by rivalry, but still sticking to the fifie, the East Coast men from Fraserburgh southwards produced magnificent craft, and in these two types the development of the lugsail reached its culmination, since the boats were far bigger than any found elsewhere around the coast. Both would handle well under fore lug alone.

CHAPTER TWELVE

## FIFIES AND ZULUS

THE improvements in the design of the fifie can clearly be seen in Plates 155 and 157. The old clinker-built hull, with deck below the thwarts, suggesting conversion from an open boat, is seen in Plate 155 of *Iona*, B.K.265, lying at low tide in Burnmouth harbour, with bladders and nets hung up to dry. Note the long sweeps resting on the starboard bow, and the rather small hatchway over the net room, with a still smaller one for'ard. This photograph was taken in 1882.

Such a boat is seen under sail in Plate 156 of 60 L.T. being rowed out of Lowestoft. The registration marks on the fore lug tell her history; first she was 62 B.K., then B.O.245, and finally was sold south to Lowestoft owners, who have chosen to fit a bonnet at the foot of the sail, typical East Anglian practice, saving the great weight of a rolled-up foot. The bowsprit is run in, and the low bulwarks will be noted. The foresail is "a'monk," by taking the tack to the foot of the mast.

A deck view of a carvel-built fifie is shown in Plate 157 of B.K.918 in Burnmouth harbour, c. 1882. The increased length of hull will be noted, the long, wide hatchway, and the crutch aft of the mizzen mast on which the foremast rested when lowered. The bowsprit is run in along the starboard coaming and the boom goes out over the port quarter, while the bladders are drying on the pole over which the nets were cleared.

The striking difference in the shape of the bows can be seen in Plate 158 of *Iona* and *Brilliant Success* lying side by side in Burnmouth, and the new fashion in displaying the registration numbers can be noted, also the chain through the stem with the tack hook to go in the cringle of the forelug. The 200-ft. cliff rises from the still waters of the harbour, with winding paths leading to the top.

The height of the foremast and the powerful sail set is shown in Plate 159 of *Silver Cloud*, L.H.1065. Here the tack is taken to the foot of the mast and the sheet is being held a'weather by the man sitting on the port quarter, whilst another of the crew is using the heavy sweep. Nets and bladders are piled up on deck, and the rope used as a downhaul for the fore lug is made fast to the fifth reef cringle.

In the eighties the newer boats measured from 44 ft. to 56 ft. on the keel, and cost varied from £150 to £300. The foremast was about 56 ft.—approximately the length of keel—and mizzen 36 ft. long. Sails were made of cotton canvas, the fore lug taking from 190 to 220 yards, the mizzen about 150 yards, the jib was of duck and contained about 50 yards. Ground gear was an anchor weighing $1\frac{1}{2}$ cwt., with 60 fathom of $\frac{5}{8}$ in. galvanised chain.

Boats carried fifty to sixty nets, each 60 yards long, 35 meshes to the yard, 18 to 20 score meshes deep, and weighing approximately 600 lb., with a total length of some 3,300 yards and a catching area of 33,000 sq. yards. Each net, made of cotton, was rigged to a manilla or tarred hemp rope—the "baulch"—in lengths of 20 fathom, with cork floats and sheepskin buoys, and stones of 3 lb. to 4 lb. weight kept the net perpendicular in the water.

A crew consisted of five or six hands, the master and owner, and four or five hired men, whose duties were to do as they were told, no particular stations being assigned them. They were generally on wages, found in board, and paid 20s. a week. It was rare to find men on the share system in those days, and bounties were given by the curers to the owner.

In the course of time the use of stones was abandoned, and the warp hung below the nets tended to keep them upright.

But even improved boats could give no guarantee that the sea would not claim its victims, and on Friday, the 14th October, 1881, occurred another of those fearful tragedies to a fishing community, still spoken of along the Berwickshire coast in hushed words as "The Disaster." The losses far exceeded those of the 1848 calamity.

From many little fishing villages 45 boats, manned by 279 men and boys, put to sea in a breathless calm, but alas, no heed was paid to the ominous fall in the glass. The lines were shot about eight miles from the shore in ideal conditions, but towards midday heavy clouds began to gather, and with the suddenness of a clap of thunder, the wind rose to hurricane force, and one of the most fearful storms within living memory swept the country from the Orkneys to the English Channel. Only 26 of the 45 boats managed to run back to Eyemouth—and many of these had lost men washed overboard —the rest were flung ashore and lifted by the waves high over the rocks (Plate 160).

Eyemouth lost half her men; out of the 189 drowned, no less than 129 belonged to the town, leaving 263 children fatherless; Burnmouth mourned 24, St. Abbs 3, the remainder coming from other villages on the Berwick and Lothian coasts. In an hour a prosperous community was ruined, and scarcely a house was without the loss of husband, son or brother.

It is more than possible that many of the boats lost were rendered unmanageable owing to crews being weakened through men washed overboard, a danger increased by the very low bulwarks. In February 1882 three men were washed off a Banffshire boat by a sea which threw three others into the open hold, leaving only one man and a boy on deck.

On Sunday, 19th November 1893, *Comely*, B.F.1560, was wrecked on the "Band" near Filey, when returning home from the East Anglian fishing (Plate 161).

What of the life in the primitive Scottish fishing villages? Thanks to some fifty photographs I had copied from albums in the National Maritime Museum, it is possible to obtain a fair idea of conditions in Ross and Burnmouth on the Berwickshire coast. Ross lies at the foot of an almost perpendicular cliff near the mouth of a small burn (Plate 162). A row of white cottages with red pantiled roofs, built on a narrow strand just above high water mark, is fully exposed to any easterly gale. There being no harbour, the boats have to be drawn up the beach, and two open and two decked can be seen, with another bottom up, and nets lie drying on the foreshore.

Adjoining and practically forming part of Ross is Burnmouth (Plate 163), with a tiny harbour improved by the building out of piers. To the eastward lie two dangerous reefs, dry at low water, which give some measure of protection in easterly winds, and rocks surround the narrow entrance. The houses face right on to the shore, with a 200-ft. cliff rising almost sheer behind. Here in the fifties were 21 large and 30 small boats, manned by 115 men and boys; ashore were two curers employing four coopers, and 40 gutters and packers, 204 were engaged in making nets, selling fish, etc., a total of 363 persons earning a fairly prosperous living from the sea.

Haddock, cod and ling were caught on long lines, the fish being sent by road to Edinburgh, while the herring season was from July to September. The men were stalwart, healthy and long-lived, when too old to go to sea they pottered around the creeks for crabs and lobsters, using small cobles which were also used for salmon fishing. Some of these can be seen in the foreground of Plate 155.

Many of my photographs show men of magnificent physique, with fine, well-cut features, and big families seem to have been the rule. Dress was blue serge trousers, with braces worn over guernseys, and a wonderful variety of headgear as can be seen in Plate 164 of the crew of *Success*, L.H.890, one of the new carvel-built fifies. At one time tall silk hats, raking well aft, were worn ashore; at sea, sealskin caps, "cheese-cutters," high soft hats, blue bonnets with tassel on top, glazed straw hats, all had their day.

One of the customs was "rapin' the nets," when whisky was sprinkled over them before the fishing, and the men took a glass (?) for luck. Some were drunken and foul-mouthed, others when smitten with a revivalist movement were addicted to psalm singing, but the majority were God-fearing, decent men. The old Scots skippers were deeply religious, and would never dream of fishing on a Sunday, remaining in port over the week-end; if delayed on the way home they carried on, but would not have the catch unloaded on the Sabbath. It was well sprinkled with salt and left until the follow-

167 FIFIE *NIGHTINGALE*
F.R. 864
Note how foreyard bends to gale, zulu beating out.

168 FIFIE *DILIGENCE* ENTERING LOWESTOFT
Note slackness in rovings, and bend in foreyard.

169  A FOREST OF MASTS AT LOWESTOFT
Kirkcaldy fifies moored in herring dock.

170  FIFIE *ONWARD*, P.D. 292

171  THE KIRKCALDY MEN ARRIVE AT LOWESTOFT
K.Y. 68 *Calceolaria*.

172 ZULUS LYING OFF YARMOUTH QUAY
   B.F. 317 *Spider*, W.K. 847 *Minnie Ha-Ha*, B.F. 1891 *Buttercup*.

173 FIFIES AND ZULUS LYING IN THE YARE, c. 1905
   Note open timber heads, no rails being fitted in Scottish luggers.

174 FIFIES AND ZULUS LEAVING LOWESTOFT
I.N.S. 323 *Jennie Dan* is a zulu, B.F. 1171, K.Y. 142 *Auricula*, and B.K. 20 *Triumph* are fifies.

175 THE HERRING FLEET STANDING OUT TO SEA
L.T. 738 *Daffodil*, 38 tons, built 1898.

ing day, when frequently the curers would not touch it, as they insisted on a 12-hour limit for being out of the sea before curing. The men would also dry their nets on the way, so that no carters and horses had to be employed on their rest-day. And was there something in their beliefs? Dunbar, just a little further along the coast, was then one of the most prosperous herring centres, but certain greedy ones broke the Sabbath and went fishing on Sundays, and the fishing declined to almost nothing, at least that is the tale of the strict Free Kirkers! A similar state of affairs happened at Stonehaven. The many superstitions would fill a book. I will give but two, to be lucky a boat had to be launched on an ebb tide, and it was unlucky to shoot nets on the port side.

As the boats came round the pierhead into Burnmouth harbour, the youngsters were there to greet their fathers, some of the little lassies shy and wide-eyed, sucking a thumb and obviously wondering what the man with the funny camera box was going to do.

Nets were cleared over a pole slung between the masts (Plate 165); only a few herring appear to have been meshed, but another photo, rather too poor to reproduce, shows a fair haul. Note how the mizzen lug is stowed up and down the mast, and the tiller well down on the rudder head; the row of cottages in the background was known as Parthenhall.

The nets were taken ashore to dry over the quay walls, or carted to drying grounds. At times they were barked by being dipped in boiling liquor in which oak bark had been steeped (Plate 166). Often one of the hand barrows seen resting on a tub was used instead of a horse-cart.

Many of the women and girls were of comely appearance, as can be seen in Plate 147, of work in a curing shed. Others were at the washtub outside their doors, pounding away at the clothes with a well-turned and very decorative "dolly," and at the same time enjoying animated conversation with the neighbours, while a young girl spreads the washing to dry on the warm rocks. One old boy, of Falstaffian girth and face covered with a bushy black beard, is mending a lobster pot, a dark-haired damsel is knitting, a hen scrattling about at her feet, while mother, with straight hair dragged back from her forehead, is sitting with her back against the cottage wall, eyes shut and mouth open, enjoying forty winks in the sunshine. At her feet lies an enormous haddock, also with mouth agape!

Other men are splicing rope, mending nets, or repairing their boats, whilst the boys, barefooted with long trousers rolled up, look on, no doubt thinking of the day when they too will have a place in dad's boat.

The still water of the tiny harbour is criss-crossed with squiggling patterns of masts, below the hulls lie perfect reflections, wives in spotless white aprons walk about with busy hands knitting as fast as they can, while some bairns paddle among the rocks and watch the old men push out the salmon cobles.

A delightful series of pictures taken some sixty or more years ago. How I wish more had been photographed when such scenes were commonplace.

The years 1870 to 1900 were the most prosperous ever known, harbours were crowded, and curing yards busy all along the coast.

In 1883 3,665 first-class fishing vessels, 15 tons and over, were registered in 21 Scottish ports, Aberdeen having 149, Banff 754, Campbelton 62, Inverness 322, Kirkcaldy 339, Kirkwall 108, Lerwick 218, Peterhead 617, and Wick 549. About a million barrels of herring were cured.

Many of the boat-builders had a history dating back far over the years, such a one being James N. Miller & Sons, of St. Monance, to whom I wrote for information. This well-known firm celebrated its bi-centenary in 1948, having been founded at Overkellie in 1747 by John Miller, the business was transferred to St. Andrews in 1768 by David, who moved to St. Monance in 1779. There the firm grew and flourished, after David came John in 1800, 46 years later his son John followed in his footsteps, to be succeeded in turn by James in 1888, until to-day the seventh generation of the Millers is at the helm, with sons to carry on this wonderful family business. A rare event indeed, and only possible because of the high standard of workmanship and integrity in business for which the name of Miller is justly famed.

One small item emphasises this standard. The chair used by Mr. Wm. P. Miller at a dinner given by the firm to its employees and friends on the 9th April 1948 had been made by his great-grandfather in 1818 at a cost of 8s. 4d., and was one of six still in use.

When David Miller started boat-building as a sideline to his business of wheelwright and joiner, the continent of Australia had yet to be explored, Napoleon was unheard of, and such modern improvements (?) as aeroplanes and the bombing of open cities, with all the attendant horrors, would have been considered the phantasmagoria of a disordered mind.

St. Monance then had a fleet of 35 boats, open from stem to stern, with cross seats or "thafts" which were spaced wider at the stern, where a short platform under carried nets and fishing gear. Length varied from 16 ft. to 40 ft., with a beam exceeding one-third of the length. A single mast, with a huge dipping lugsail, was fitted in "skegs" for'ard. Four or six oars were carried, and extensively used. Gradually design improved, and in 1850 John Miller was building boats for just under £1 a foot. An old account book shows that a 30 ft. boat cost £25, a similar one to-day would cost £950 without an engine. In 1851 five boats, ranging in length from 36 ft. to 39 ft., were built for fishermen of St. Monance, Pittenween, and Buckhaven.

In 1888 James, father of the present directors, Thos. P. and Wm. P. Miller, took over and built a large number of 50 ft. to 80 ft. sailing fifies, later building many steam drifters. At the turn of the century he developed a keen interest in the internal combustion engine, and an experimental semi-diesel two-stroke engine made by the late Prof. Peck of Edinburgh, was fitted into a 65-ft. fifie *Wave*. In 1904 the last big sailing fifie was built, but many a one driven by power followed. In the early 1920's a very successful motor capstan was designed and given the name of "fifer," being fitted to many fishing craft in Scotland and England.

To-day, after building 58 boats for war service during the years 1939-45, the firm has reverted to building fishing boats, and of 22 fishing out of Pittenween, six were built by Miller.

Great was my disappointment to learn that no half models of sailing fifies were left, but Mr. Wm. Miller kindly offered to make one up if I so wished. Judge my pleasure when one May morning a long box was delivered at my house, then the excitement of opening it to find within two old half models. A letter from Mr. W. Miller stated that he had had a search made and had come across two made by his father.

Although they carried honourable scars as befitted their age, it was possible to take off the lines. I was thrilled to handle the actual half models from which craftsmen, long dead, had taken the measurements from which so many fifies were built, each slightly different, for the design was never really standard, as befitted a trade which listened to a fisherman who knew what was wanted for his own special requirements.

I thought of the long, anxious discussions when horny fingers, sensitive to every touch, caressed the swelling curves, and keen eyes squinted along the hull, then problems were weighed up. Should the 'midships frames be a little fuller to give a better capacity than Jamie's boat, or the run a trifle finer for speed to catch an early market? The final decision that funds would run to it, and an agreement drawn up in simple language that one agreed to build, the other to buy at a certain figure.

Yes, these and many other thoughts passed through my mind as I handled the rough wood. Here were no fancy waterlines in different woods, all highly finished and varnished. Just plain, honest deal—in both senses of the word—with a lick of red paint to show up the underwater body. A working job.

The plans on pages 344-7 are of a fifie 52 ft. over stems, 17 ft. moulded breadth, with an 11 ft. 6 in. stem, and 10 ft. 9 in. sternpost, depth of hull amidships 10 ft. The half model from which I took the lines dated back to the 1860's. (Plan 23.)

The other half model, of about 1875, was a more beamy design, 58 ft. over stems, 21 ft. moulded breadth, the length of stem had increased to 14 ft. 9 in., the sternpost 12 ft. 9 in., had a slight rake of 9 in., and the forefoot was more rounded. (Plan 24.)

Both models had sharp floors with hollow garboards, a similarity shared with the early fifies.

I am deeply indebted to Mr. Wm. P. Miller for his courtesy in loaning me these interesting relics of the past.

The big fifie was in her prime from 1890 until the last was built *circa* 1904-6, a short life indeed, but the coming of the steam drifter spelt the doom of sail. Wheel-steering replaced the tiller, and the 12-h.p. Elliott & Garrood steam capstan superseded the hand-driven flywheel pattern, an inestimable boon, as the ever-increasing size of the fore lug was making it a laborious task to hoist by hand, calling for a united effort by six or seven hefty men.

By the mid-nineties a 60 ft. keel was common, with a beam of 18 ft. 6 in., and depth of hold 6 ft. 6 in., but the largest ran up to 70 ft. keel. All were carvel-built.

A typical 68 ft. keel often had a 1 ft. rake to stem, and 4 ft. rake to sternpost, a beam of 20 ft. 6 in. and depth of hold 7 ft. 6 in., displacement 56 tons, giving a carrying capacity of some 300 crans. Foremasts ranged from 55 ft. to 57 ft., 22 in. dia. to 11 in., many having an oval section, mizzens ran 45 ft. to 49 ft., 15 in. to 7 in. dia. Sails were made from cotton canvas, a forelug having an area of some 1,580 sq. ft., mizzen 1,350, big jib 800 sq. ft., but a jib was seldom set unless making a passage, the two lugs being the usual working sails.

A fleet of nets now numbered 70, each about 600 sq. yds. in area, with a warp—"bush rope"—made up of eleven coils of 120 fathom each, best manilla, and a spare set of nets was usually carried.

Such a boat cost from £800 to £1,000 to build and equip, with the fishing gear adding a further £320 to £400, a contrast to the amount expended only forty years before to fit out a boat for sea, and showing how wholeheartedly the Scots went in for the big decked boat, once they were convinced of its merits.

A fifie, with 66 ft. keel, length over stems 70 ft., was built at Fraserburgh about forty-five years ago, and cost for carpenter's work, £430; smith's work £52; steam capstan and boiler £105; suit of sails, etc., £150, a total of £737, ready for sea, but with no nets. The influence of the lofty zulu rig in ports within their environment is seen in the height of the foremast 64ft., mizzen 55 ft., and jibboom 54 ft.

Plate 167 is of *Nightingale*, F.R.864, running in, and a zulu beating out of the bay. Note the tremendous strain on the bead parrel, the fore yard bent like a bow, and the slackening of the "rovings," due to stretch. The mizzen is stowed and a lifebelt can be seen on the crutch.

Plate 168 of *Diligence*, F.R.917 again shows the power of these magnificent boats, as her stern lifts to a sea and yard bends to the gathering storm. Fenders are out and the crew for'ard are making ready to take in sail for entering Lowestoft.

When the boats were tightly packed in harbour the impression of their immense spars was that of a forest of pine trees, seen to advantage in Plate 169 of Kirkcaldy fifies in Lowestoft harbour.

I have only a small snap of one at sea with both lugs set, Plate 170 of *Onward*, P.D.292. These fifies could *sail*, as the following story tells. A 60-footer, fishing in illegal waters in the Minch, was surprised by the Fishery cruiser, and although the

Government vessel was doing 14 knots, the lugger beat her into Stornoway.

Mr. R. Stuart Bruce mentions an occasion when he was in *Earl of Zetland*, an eight-knot mail boat; the Montrose lugger *Flying Fish*, M.E.643, of Ferryden, "walked past them," and another time, when in the same steamer, "a large zulu carrying her big lug but no mizzen, sailed past the mail boat as if she had been standing still, an unforgettable picture. Occasionally the Scots boat would crack on until they sailed their foremast over the side!"

To check the way of a lugger when running into a crowded harbour, two canvas drogues—called "fly anchors"—were carried on the quarter, with a short length of rope fast to a cleat, ready for heaving overboard as the entrance was approached. Sir Henry Manwayring mentions that such a device was commonly used by fishermen in the North Sea in the days of good Queen Bess.

With improved sea-keeping abilities, the number of boats attending the English Autumn Fishing greatly increased. Whereas in 1862 only 281 fitted out in Scotland for East Anglia and the Isle of Man—until 1868 all returns for the island were made by the Scottish Fisheries Board—in 1899 no less than 679 boats sailed south, and earned nearly a quarter of a million pounds, with prices averaging 7s. a cwt., about 3½ cwt. going to a cran.

There were now three seasons for herring fishing. The winter fishing for the first three months of the year, mainly at Wick and Stornoway, and to some extent in the Firth of Forth. In May and June came the early herring fishing, followed by the great summer herring season, which lasted from July to nearly the end of the year if the boats followed the shoals to the south. Many of the big fifies and zulus went to the Kinsale fishing and to Isle of Man waters.

The Shetlands fishing fluctuated wildly. In 1857 17,860 barrels, each about 2 cwt., were cured, but in 1862 the number dropped to 3,733, rising five years later to 10,008, falling catastrophically to 1,209 the following year, only exceeding 1,800 in 1870, when 4,200 barrels were preserved. During the '70's an increasing number of boats came from the south, East Anglia, and the Isle of Man, with marked improvement to the prosperity of the fishing, by the turn of the century a season's curing being valued at £600,000, 1,024,000 barrels having been caught by 1,783 drifters, manned by some 12,500 men, but only 300 boats were local.

The cran was the standard measure, but in the few areas where counting was the custom, 128 fish made a buyer's "hundred." About 280 fresh herring went to a hundredweight, which at 8s. meant 32 fish for 10d. Prices varied enormously; in 1899 they averaged 7s. 0¼d. a cwt., in 1904 only 3s. 9d., in 1907 5s. 9d., 1912 7s. 4½d., but in 1913 the price had risen to 9s. 4½d.

The importance of the herring fishing to the economic life of Scotland can be seen from the fact that in 1910 catches realised over £2,000,000, and more than 1¾ million barrels were exported to the Continent, the best quality West Coast "maties" making £5 a barrel. Upwards of ninety thousand people were employed in the catching, gutting, packing and ancillary trades. One thousand, two hundred and fifty-seven drifters went south for the English fishing, earning £456,528; the number of steam was 706, against 500 sail and 51 motor, and average takings were £530 for steam, £134 sail, and £295 motor; the previous year sail had averaged £204 a boat. The best return in 1910 for a sailing lugger was £600, and the lowest £105.

In 1901 the first steam drifters began to make their presence known, and to show the changeover from sail to steam, I have analysed from the 1905 and 1910 *Olsen's Almanack* the number of fishing vessels over 15 tons engaged in the principal Scottish herring ports.

| Port | | 1905 | 1910 |
|---|---|---|---|
| *Aberdeen* | Sail | 71 | 44 |
| | Steam | 94 | 258 |
| | Motor | — | — |
| *Banff* | Sail | 649 | 483 |
| | Steam | 71 | 214 |
| | Motor | — | 2 |
| *Fraserburgh* | Sail | 277 | 234 |
| | Steam | 11 | 48 |
| | Motor | — | — |
| *Inverness* | Sail | 333 | 201 |
| | Steam | 11 | 78 |
| | Motor | — | 1 |
| *Kirkcaldy* | Sail | 256 | 154 |
| | Steam | 11 | 42 |
| | Motor | — | — |
| *Leith* | Sail | 122 | 112 |
| | Steam | 8 | 25 |
| | Motor | — | — |
| *Peterhead* | Sail | 191 | 74 |
| | Steam | 41 | 119 |
| | Motor | — | — |
| *Wick* | Sail | 288 | 169 |
| | Steam | 25 | 22 |
| | Motor | — | — |

To judge from these figures, many of the motor drifters must have been under 15 tons register, as after 1906 the Kelvin, Gardner and Thornycroft motors were rapidly gaining in favour. It was possible to make double the number of trips, and as one man less was needed, the extra costs and running expenses were reasonably covered.

*Maggie Jane's*, B.K.146, still fishing 1936, was one of the pioneer fifies to be fitted with an auxiliary paraffin engine of the Gardner make, and from the first one of the crew was detailed to look after the engine, being relieved of all other duties if attention to it was required. Experience soon showed that to obtain the best results such a policy was essential, and that 50 to 55 h.p. was sufficient for boats of about 40 tons, any attempts to drive them faster resulting in a great increase in working expenses, with little extra speed to compensate for the outlay.

One of the first zulus to be converted was *Prosper*, sailing out of Inverness, and fitted with a 56-h.p. Kromhout engine. The original raking sternpost was left undisturbed, and a nearly vertical propeller post was fastened to it, the keel being lengthened to support the lower end of the new post. A new iron rudder was fitted, with its head carried through the old helm port and fitted to the original steering gear. A speed of about $6\frac{1}{2}$ knots was expected, but on the trial of five hours' duration, *Prosper* attained a speed of $7\frac{3}{4}$ knots under power alone.

In the face of such results the auxiliary motor went ahead by leaps and bounds, and the 1911 Summer Herring Fishing showed the average earnings of a steam drifter to be £887, a motor auxiliary £513, and sailing lugger £281, and for the English fishing, in less settled weather, the corresponding figures were £665, £321, and £193 respectively.

When comparing these earnings with wages considered suitable after the second world war, when men have refused to sail unless guaranteed upwards of 90s. a cran, as against 30s. to 35s. in the 1920's and just over 20s. in the old days, it would be as well to realise what money bought then. I quote from advertisements in contemporary newspapers and ship chandlers' lists, *c.* 1910:

Suit of clothes made to measure from £1 12s. 6d. Trousers, 10s. Overcoats, £1 7s. 6d. Reefer jacket, best pilot cloth, 19s. 6d., and 5 per cent. discount for cash.

Oilskins, double throughout, 10s. 6d. Sou'westers, 1s. and 1s. 6d. Grain hide sea boots, 16s. 6d. a pair. Rubber thigh boots, 22s. 6d. a pair. Grey or white flannel singlets and pants, 2s. 6d. each. Navy blue jerseys, 2s. 6d. to 4s. 6d. Box calf welted boots, 8s. 11d.

Now to mention what a shilling or two would buy in the way of refreshments and amusements:

Bottled beer, 2s. 3d. a dozen. X-mild ale, 10d. a gallon, XXX ale, 1s. 8d. Stout, 1s. 4d. and 1s. 6d. a gallon. Porter, 1s. Gin, 2s. a bottle, whisky 3s. 6d. Wills' "Honeycut" tobacco, $4\frac{1}{2}$d. an oz. B.D.V. cigarettes, 10 for $2\frac{1}{2}$d. An evening at the Coliseum or any of the numerous music halls would cost from 6d. to 5s.

Cottage rents were 4s. a week; a seven-roomed house in one of the suburbs could be taken for £25 a year, and you could spend a week at a boarding house in Brighton for a guinea; a visit to Barmouth came to 4s. 6d. a day inclusive. Travelling was amazingly cheap, 11s. return fare London to Liverpool, 3s. 6d. return to Dover, 2s. 6d. to Brighton, while west to Torquay only came to 11s. return, by special excursion trains.

If emigration was thought of, numerous lines offered to convey you to Canada for £5 10s. third-class, £8 10s. cabin, and £11 saloon. To South America fares of £8 could be obtained.

Exchange rates were so stable that they were quoted in the yearly books of reference, and £1 was a golden sovereign, worth 4 dols. 84 cents, 25 francs 15 cents, in France, Belgium, Switzerland, Italy and Greece, the various national coinages circulating freely in the countries named other than their own.

Superior household coal was 19s. a ton, delivered by any coal merchant in quantities to suit customers' requirements, and different grades varied in price; slate was not charged at the rate of best household. Steam coal of the highest quality was available at any bunkering port in the world, as per sample submitted.

One item did make my mouth water—a hamper containing a loin of lamb, one chicken, and an oxtail cost 5s. 6d. for London, 5s. 9d. for country orders, or a choice hamper of fish was 6 lb. for 2s., cleaned and carriage paid, or 21 lb. for 5s.

Enough said, especially when one realises income tax was about 1s. 2d. in £1 on incomes over £3,000 a year, unearned, but those whose total incomes did not exceed £2,000 could claim to be charged at 9d. upon earned income. Super-tax at 6d. in £ was imposed on incomes exceeding £5,000. Penny post was universal, the coal did burn, and throw out a good heat, and beer would put a man half-seas over.

Were those the days?

For upwards of a decade there had been prosperity unparalleled in many a herring port, but the outbreak of war destroyed it all. The year 1913 saw only 209 luggers at the English fishing, with 100 motor and 854 steam, with earnings averaging £235, £365, and £794 respectively. However, in many instances the increased cost of a steam drifter, and the constant need to pay for coal, oil, etc., ate into takings to an alarming extent, and many a thrifty sailing skipper rued the day he went into steam; a bad season or two saw him unable to weather the storm.

I take the following from a newspaper cutting of 1910:

"A singularly low price has been fetched this week at Yarmouth for a steam drifter, the *Orcadia* of Aberdeen, which has been sold under the hammer as she lay in Southtown Dock, where she is undergoing repair at a cost of £80, to be paid by the vendor, who has also to meet the cost of her undocking and to defray the auctioneer's charges. *Orcadia* is a wooden vessel, 86 ft. long and of 19 ft. beam, built at Newcastle in 1893. The vessel, with boiler, engines, small boat and stores, including 16 tons of coal, was knocked down for £145."

But there was no denying the all-conquering advance of steam and motor power, although down to the outbreak of war many splendid fifies and zulus could be seen at Yarmouth and Lowestoft. It was, however, becoming a difficult job to man them, the younger men preferring to go in the steam drifters, even though that often meant losing their independence and part ownership of their craft.

As to the long-term results of this policy, I quote from a letter sent me by Mr. Wm. McIntosh of Buckie in February, 1949:

"The sailing boats were very profitable, say a voyage grossed £600, the expenses were just over £100; now since the steam drifters came and ousted the sailing boat, the expenses for the same trip were over £600, which included coal, oil, engineer, fireman, etc. Also along this coast since the steam drifter came hardly a private house has been built by a fisherman, previously houses were constantly being built.

The day of the sail boat is now over, and the steam drifter days are almost gone. In Cullen there was once 50 steam drifters, none now; Portknockie, I think, has four where once were 60; Findochty has six against about 60; Portessie and Portgordon the same; Buckie had over 100, now about 20. It is motor boats now, and a seine boat costs from £10,000 to £12,000. Of course, there are conditions. If the men are ex-service they have to raise £1,000, they get a grant, I think, of £5,000, and loan of £4,000 with interest. There has been a boom for seine net boats, all the yards along this coast have been full up with orders. This kind of boat does the dual purpose, herring fishing and seining according to the seasons."

Well, the days have gone when it was possible to see the imposing grandeur of a large fleet of sailing luggers making for port with a fair wind, and bowling along at ten knots and over, but luckily some record still remains in the splendid photographs I have been able to collect.

Look at the Kirkcaldy men converging on Lowestoft harbour like a flock of dark-winged seabirds, those towering sails needed *men* to handle them in a gale of wind (Plate 171). Soon in the streets would be heard the Gaelic tongue as the chaff and banter was exchanged between the newly-arrived fishermen and the braw lassies already there for the curing of the catch.

Then the picturesque sight, when the Banff zulus lay side by side in the Yare, against that background of houses and quays so reminiscent of Holland, the Town Hall surmounted by a gilded weather vane depicting one of the famous Yarmouth luggers, the gaily-coloured hulls reflected in the quiet water, with spar pens drawing fascinating patterns as the boats rock to the kiss of the tide (Plate 172).

On that sad day in November 1901 when the Caister lifeboat capsized, the river was full from the Bridge to the Point, a solid mass of drifters making an unprecedented sight. Contrast such a scene with the few rusty hulls and dingy paintwork of the steam drifters I saw in October 1946.

Plate 173 of fifies and zulus lying opposite the Nelson Monument is most valuable as it gives a good view of deck fittings. The St. Monance fifie alongside the quay has a small wheel with a stool on which the helmsman sat, a boon when long tricks were the order of the day. The companion with skylight, steam capstan, roller on aft hatch coaming, open timberheads, heavy bearer and gunwale, baulk on foreside of mast, and twin horns on stemhead to take tack cringle of fore lug, will all be noted.

The next boat is a zulu, with poop deck and hatch coamings the same height, note the crutch to starboard of mizzen mast, and the warp going down the small hatch into the "leader box." One cover is on the mast trunk, the bead parrels can clearly be seen, and the manner of stowing the lugs should be noted. Another zulu lies outside, as in the tier ahead, where two fifies have the inside berths. Note the beam of the middle one and the skin bladders on deck. This photograph must have been taken after 1904, the year in which the steam drifter *Sunbeam*, B.F.1551, was built at Port Gordon.

The well-cut lugsails can be admired in Plate 174 of a bunch of fifies and zulus crowding the narrow exit to Lowestoft harbour. K.Y.142 is *Auricula*, a fifie, as is the boat to leeward, then comes a local drifter, and just beyond is B.K.20, *Triumph*, while astern is a zulu, I.N.S.323, *Jennie Dan*, the wisps of steam are coming from the capstans and the sweeps are out.

What a noble sight these lofty fifies made as they stood out to sea (Plate 175). To wind'ard is a Banff fifie, then comes *Useful*, B.F.706, and *Daffodil*, L.T.738, of 38 tons, built 1898. Ahead the offing is dotted with the dark pyramids of sail. One very curious fact was that Scottish boats, not being built to Board of Trade requirements, seldom if ever, carried a small boat, and this feature will be noted in many of the photographs.

Finally it is most interesting to turn to Plate 176 of three fifies making sail, with a thunderstorm brewing, and mark how each skipper reacts to what it may bring in the way of wind, the boat to leeward, K.Y.2052, is all for safety, with several reefs down and tack taken to eyebolt well inboard; K.Y.1340 is hoisting a reefed sail "set a'monk," in East Anglian parlance, or with tack to eyebolt at foot of mast; but the wind'ard boat, L.H.1094, *Jessies* is boldly standing on with only one reef down, and tack set up to stemhead. Note how the rovings by which the sail is bent to yard have stretched; they should be taut as in the other luggers. One of the paddle tugs has just let go the tow from several zulus, the one to leeward has anchored as if to "wait and see."

There was a sense of power and grandeur about the Scots luggers which has never been surpassed. Built not for halcyon days, but to face the angry gales of the cold North Sea, it seemed impossible that those towering lugs could ever be manhandled on a heaving deck. Every member of the crew had to know his job thoroughly, and be able to do it on the darkest, wildest night without fumbling, and there was only the lowest of bulwarks to save a man making a false step from going overboard.

Imagine tacking in a fresh breeze with those tremendous forelugs flogging about. First they were lowered down to deck, then unhooked from the traveller, hooked on the burton, swung aft and then for'ard on the other side of the mast, unhooked and re-hooked on the traveller, and hoisted again. During this time the mast stood four-square on its reputation, being completely unstayed until the halyards were hooked to the weather side and the burton set up. Smart handling was essential, and even with the fall of the halyard taken to the capstan, it was heavy work, but hoisting by hand was back-breaking, five to ten minutes' sweating to get the sail set and drawing properly,

## SAILING DRIFTERS

for most of the old skippers were very particular about the cut and set of their sails.

When the tack of the forelug was taken to one of the eyebolts on deck, it was usual to lead the burton to the opposite side to the halyards, to give additional support to the mast. These big luggers were terribly heavy craft to row in the sweltering heat of a summer calm, then steam had the last laugh, for it was the steam drifter's certainty of delivery that brought about the downfall of sail, although in a fresh breeze a zulu making ten knots and more could romp past the plodding drifter belching out smoke like a pall.

After the first war sail was finished, and I have classified the vessels fishing in 1923 and 1936:

| Port | | 1923 | 1936 |
|---|---|---|---|
| Aberdeen | Sail | — | — |
| | Steam | 296 drifters and trawlers | 295 |
| | Motor | 8 | 2 |
| Banff | Sail | 45 (34 were in 1906 reg.) | 1 |
| | Steam | 214 | 155 |
| | Motor | 76 (42 ex sailing) | 34 (14 ex sail) |
| Fraserburgh | Sail | 9 (4 in 1906 reg.) | 1 |
| | Steam | 85 | 110 |
| | Motor | 117 (53 ex sail) | 32 (13 ex sail) |
| Inverness | Sail | 22 (13 in 1906 reg.) | — |
| | Steam | 118 | 81 |
| | Motor | 25 (13 ex sail) | 115 (1 ex sail) |
| Kirkcaldy | Sail | 6 (5 in 1906 reg.) | — |
| | Steam | 57 | 43 |
| | Motor | 19 (12 ex sail) | 24 (2 ex sail) |
| Leith | Sail | 8 (7 in 1906 reg.) | — |
| | Steam | 29 | 28 |
| | Motor | 32 (18 ex sail) | 23 (5 ex sail) |
| Peterhead | Sail | 4 (2 in 1906 reg.) | — |
| | Steam | 137 | 119 |
| | Motor | 12 (4 ex sail) | 5 |
| Wick | Sail | 10 (6 in 1906 reg.) | — |
| | Steam | 16 | 13 |
| | Motor | 34 (4 ex sail) | 21 |

Berwick had only six sail left out of 114 registered in 1906, 47 motor and 22 steam showing the preference for power, and in 1936 numbers dropped to 30 motor, four being ex-sailing fifies of 30 years before, and 11 steam.

Stornoway's 130 sail in 1906 had fallen to 24 in 1923, with 18 steam and eight motor, and in 1936 four sail still remained, I believe all big zulus, 1.1 steam and 48 motor.

The most striking fact which emerges is the total disappearance in seventeen years of the enormous fleets of sailing luggers, the rise in the number of steam drifters after the war, and then their drop in favour of motor in some ports, and, above all, the serious decline in the total number of craft fishing thirty years after sail was in its heyday.

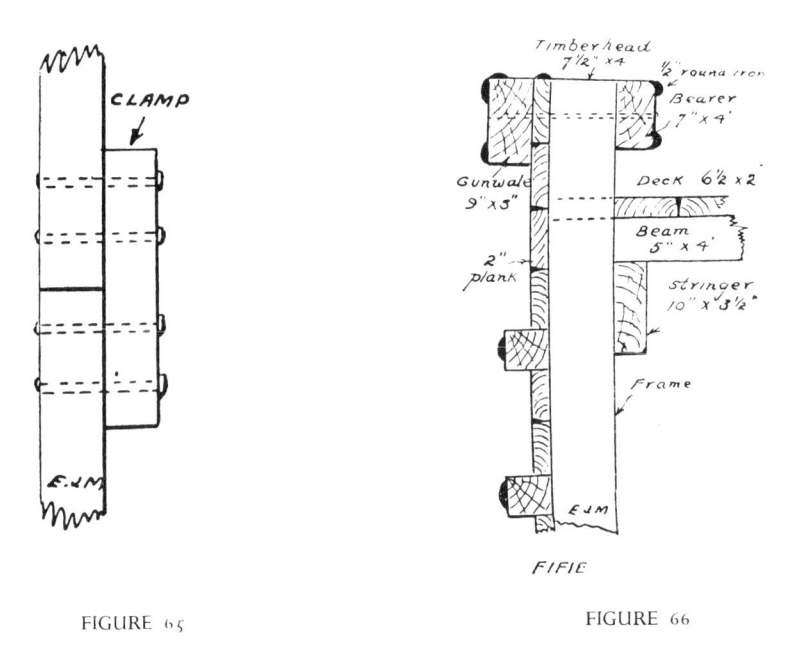

FIGURE 65

FIGURE 66

Thanks to splendid co-operation from certain sources, I can give most valuable data concerning construction and sailmaking to augment the plans prepared by the late P. J. Oke in 1936.

For fifies I learn from Messrs. J. N. Miller & Sons, of St. Monance, that hulls took from three to four months to build out in the open; keels were of oak or beech; stem, sternpost and frames of oak; beams of oak, pitchpine or larch, usually 5 in. by 4 in., spaced one to each frame, resting on the stringers.

The frames were single, butt-jointed with a clamp (Fig. 65), and bolted direct to deadwood fore and aft. Two-inch planking was fastened with galvanised patent flats, and cement was used between floors and aft framing on deadwood. As a general rule, keelsons were not fitted as standard; timberheads were carried up above the covering board, the bulwarks were an average height of 12 in., outside was the gunwale, inside the "bearer" (Fig. 66).

The three subdivisions of the hull from aft were known as the cabin, fish hold, and foreroom, ballast was stone, and no shifting ballast was carried. Seven 22-ft. sweeps were stowed on foredeck and shipped in crutches socketed in timberheads when required. Ground gear consisted of two anchors weighing 112 lbs. each, and the cable was 10 fathom of chain, and rope.

The foremast was pitchpine and lowered back into a slot known as the "skegs," mizzen mast was Norway spruce, and spars spruce. The rake of the masts varied according to individual preference, and in some districts special wedges were made to give variation of rake. No legs were required when the hull was dried out in harbour.

In my quest for information I wrote to Mr. W. Carstairs, and although unable to assist me, he gave a valued introduction to the only sailmaker he knew in the district, and Mr. Wm. Boyter, of Pittenweem, most kindly answered my questionnaire concerning sail plans of fifies.

He tells me that an apprentice served for five years, being paid 3s. a week for the first year, 4s. for second, 5s. for third, 7s. for fourth, 9s. for fifth, and 24s. when his articles were finished.

After a scale plan had been prepared, the sails were made by hand, the first cloth cut for a lugsail being the one next the weather, and known simply as "first cloth," corresponded to the "mast cloth" in Cornwall. The secret of ensuring a well-cut and setting sail was in the goring of the cloths on peak and foot, and generally speaking, there was less peak on sails in the south than the north of Scotland.

Seams were one inch wide, hand-sewn from foot to head, the weather edges of cloths and the linings, one foot wide, on weather rope and leech were always on the port side. The foot was rounded one inch in three feet, when a sail 40 ft. on the foot came back from a fishing it had stretched to 41 ft., so an allowance of 1 ft. on 40 ft. was made when making up.

A 3-in. boltrope was sewn on head, leech and foot of fore and mizzen lugs, but the weather rope of the foresail was 2½ in. wire, on the mizzen 3 in. rope. For the jibs the weather ropes were 2½ in., foot 1¾ in. The way the boltropes were sewn had a considerable influence on the set of the finished sail, as rope and canvas have different stretch factors, and it was essential that due allowance should be made for this difference.

Cringles were made of 2½ in. boltrope for the two lugs, 1¾ in. for the two jibs.

Cotton canvas, not flax, was used, bolts 24 in. wide costing 1s. 3d. per yard for No. 3, 1s. 2d. for No. 5, and 10d. for No. 10, and the quantity required for a foresail was 300 yds. of No. 3 canvas, a mizzen took 170 yds. of No. 5, large jib 150 yds. of No. 10, small jib 90 yds. of No. 10, and the "kicker" 60 yds. of No. 5.

Two men, sewing away for a nine-hour day, completed a foresail in a week, mizzen in four days, two jibs in six days, and the kicker in three days. Cost of making was 4d. per yard, plus material, so that a foresail cost 1s. 7d. a yard to make, and finished price was £30, mizzen £15, large jib £10, small jib £8, kicker £7 10s., or a total of £70 10s. for a full suit of sails.

One spare mizzen and one jib were carried and stored in the forepeak, but the lug was not kept bent to a yard. The lower lines of reefs were points, the upper eyelets and lacing, nine being a usual number.

Sails were dressed or "barked" with a mixture made in the proportion of five gallons of water to 1 lb. of cutch and ½ lb. tallow, filled in a large tank and covered. Jibs were only lightly dressed.

The lugs were bent to their yards with short lines called rovings, pulled up taut, but in the course of time, through stretching, there was often a considerable "drift"

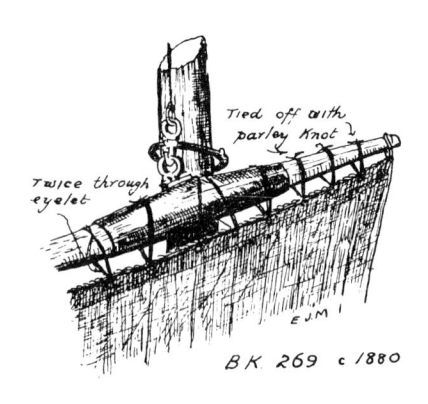

FIGURE 67

between spar and head of sail, as will be noticed in several photographs. Earings were passed through holes in the ends of yards (Fig. 67).

## RIGGING

In the smaller fifies the traveller was often an iron ring, made up in two half-hoops for ease in lowering (Fig. 67), but in the big boats bead parrels were usual. Slings were of wire rope, and all blocks were wire stropped.

Tyes were 2-in. wire, fore halyards 200 ft. long, 2¼-in. rope, mizzen halyards 150 ft.

Sheets 1¾-in. rope, with 7-in. double-sheaved wood blocks, but no special shaped hook was used, as in Cornwall.

Tack of foresail went to hook on stem, or to eyebolts between stem and mast; tack of mizzen went to hook on a length of chain round the mast.

Burton pendants were of rope. Masts and spars were varnished.

A fifie's best point of sailing was reaching, and *Families' Pride*, K.Y.625, belonging to Cellardyke, Fife, and built in 1902, was famed for her exceptional speed.

When the late Mr. P. J. Oke visited Scotland in 1936, he took off the lines of a big fifie at St. Monance, and drew up plans in pencil, but unfortunately he was killed before they were completed. I found them at the bottom of a large chest in the National Maritime Museum, and photostats were made for me. From his rough notes, etc., I have been able to complete the draughts, which had already been checked by Messrs.

J. N. Miller, who suggested various amendments as considerable alterations had been made when a motor was installed. Plans 25 pages 348-51.

*True Vine*, M.L.20, was built by Robertson Innes at St. Monance in 1905, and owned by David Mair. Length overall as measured was 71 ft. 1½ in., but the papers gave length on deck as 70 ft. 3 in., beam inside 21 ft. 6 in., depth 8 ft. Keel length was 68 ft. 3 in., and moulded depth 11 ft. 3 in. L.W.L., 69 ft. 9 in.

The deck plan shows the following features: the stemhead is sided 6 in. on foreside, 9 in. on aft side, 12 in. at deck, and moulded 1 ft. 4 in. on either side are the "horns," 1 ft. by 7 in. by 1¾ in., with chain and hook to take tack cringle of forelug. A stem knee, 11½ in. above deck and 5 in. thick, extends to first timber 2 ft. 3 in. from inside of stem, with an eyebolt 4 in. by 1¼ in., 4 in. inside.

Timberheads are 7½ in. moulded, 5 in. sided for'ard, 8 in. by 4½ in. amidships, and 8 in. by 4 in. aft, spacing varying from 10 in. to 11½ in. Inside and level with the tops of timberheads is the "bearer," 4 in. wide and 7 in. deep, with ½-in. half-round irons top and bottom, on top edge of planking is a 2-in. iron, and outside is the gunwale, 6 in. wide and 9 in. deep, with ½-in. half-round irons as shown. The total depth is 12 in. to deck (Fig. 66).

Opposite second timberheads on either side bearers are wooden cleats 3 ft. long. Between second and third timbers is a post 9½ in. high with iron socket on top, and another post is between fourth and fifth timbers.

Resting on bearers is the "baulk," 2 ft. 6 in. wide and 5 in. deep, with ringbolts on either side of the foremast, which is 22 in. sq. at deck and stepped on floors in a tabernacle with side bridges 1 ft. 3 in. long and 5 in. thick. Mast was held in position by a heavy wedge and chock immediately aft, and when lowered dropped back in a slot known as the "skegs." On bearer aft of baulk is an eyebolt, then an iron lead with sheave 8 in. by 2¼ in., with an eyebolt 5½ in. by 2 in. for the halyards on the timberhead just aft, with a 4 ft. 4 in. cleat, 4 in. deep, on inside of bearer where fall belays.

Hatches 2 ft. 3 in. sq. give access to fore room, fish hold hatch is 14 ft. 1 in. by 9 ft., with 4 in. coamings, 11 in. deep outside, with net roller on after coaming, and crutch, on which foremast rests when lowered, immediately abaft. Off-centred 1 ft. 9 in. to port is the mizzen mast, aft, the hatch over warp room.

When Mr. Oke measured up *True Vine* there was a poop deck 19 ft. 4½ in. long, but it may be that this was added when wheelhouse, etc., were fitted; beams were 10 in. wide and 4 in. deep, spacing 9 in., as most fifies had a flush deck aft with 5 in. by 4 in. beams. On deck aft were boiler and stove funnels, capstan, skylight, and scuttle, on port side of which was chock to take heel of boom.

A 10 in. by 3½ in. thwart rested on bearers; on this the helmsman sat. Many fifies had a stool instead. Opposite capstan were wooden leads 4 in. thick and 3 ft. long, on inside of bearers, and 1 ft. 6 in. for'ard of thwart were cleats 2 ft. 4 in. long, 5 in. sq.

at middle. Sternpost measures 1 ft. 5½ in. by 8 in., with stern knee extending for'ard to timberhead, 7 in. sq. and 8½ in. high. A wooden wheel, 20 in. outside dia., with 2-in. rim, 6-in. boss, 2½ in. thick, has six spokes, 4 in. by 1 in., and is connected by a worm gear (Fig. 68).

With slight variations, all these fittings can be seen on deck of fifie in Plate 173.

A scuttle 3 ft. 5½ in. long, 2 ft. 3 in. wide, with usual sliding roof, gives entry to a cabin 16 ft. 5 in. long, 3 ft. 3 in. wide aft, 11 ft. wide for'ard, containing eight bunks, 5 ft. 6 in. 6 ft. long, 2 ft. wide, and 2 ft. 2 in. deep, with lockers below. Height amidships to under cabin roof, 6 ft. 6 in.

Carlings of cabin 8½ in. sq., beams 10 in. by 4 in. deep, with beam at ladder 6 in. sq., ladder 1 ft. 6 in. by 4½ in., with steps 1 ft. by 1 in. thick. A boiler 6 ft. high,

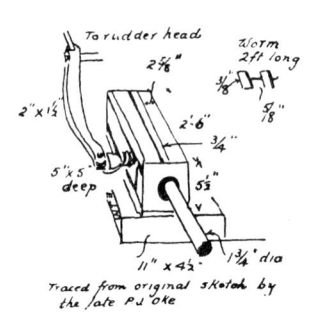

FIGURE 68

2 ft. 8 in. dia., and a stove stood against for'ard bulkhead, which divided off the warp room with the fish hold beyond, with floor boards 1 ft. by 1 in. over ballast, and a platform 2 ft. 4 in. above, side wing stanchions 6 in. sq., and spaced 3 ft. 6 in. Nets were usually stowed on the upper platform, but sometimes with the gear in foreroom, which extended to stem, the carlings of trunk 7½ in. deep by 11 in., with short beams 10 in. wide and 4 in. deep. Beams rest on stringers 10 in. deep and 3½ in. wide, fore beam being 11 in. by 4 in., others 6 in. by 5 in. wide.

At 1 ft. 6 in. below gunwale is a rubber, 4 in. deep by 3 in., faced with half-round iron, and 1 ft. below is second one of similar size.

At some time this fifie broke her back, and a keelson 10 in. deep and 1 ft. wide was bolted on top of the floors to give additional strength.

## SCANTLINGS

| | | |
|---|---|---|
| Keel | - | 12 in. by 8 in., with ⅞ in. iron. |
| Floors | - | 2 ft. 4 in. moulded, 5 in. sided, 12 in. apart. |
| Frames in hold | - | 4½ in. by 8 in. wide at bilge. |
| Timberheads | - | 5 in. by 7½ in. |
| Stem | - | To keel, 15 ft. |
| Sternpost | - | To keel, 12 ft. 8 in. |
| Hatch carlings | - | 9 in. by 3 in. deep. |
| Stringer | - | 3½ in. by 10 in. deep. |

176 AWAITING A THUNDERSTORM
K.Y. 2052 has tack to lee bow, and sail well reefed down. K.Y. 1340 has tack to foot of mast and is hoisting sail by capstan, L.H. 1094 *Jessies* has sail reefed down with tack to eye in breasthook.

177 ANSTRUTHER HARBOUR, 1936
K.Y. 18 *Mizpah* is a baldie fitted with motor. K.Y. 470 is yawl *Isabel*, note height of her mast and the wide hatches.

178 ZULU *MUIRNEAG* S.Y. 486
Note tuckle chain for mizzen tack, bead parrel, cover off hatch to warp room, heel of crutch and steam capstan.

179 ZULU *MUIRNEAG*, S.Y. 684
Note bead parrels, hitches into which mast lowers, baulk, treble block of halyards, sheet block lying on deck, crutch and mizzen thwart.

180 ZULU *PANSY*, I.N.S. 1365
   Note a few reef points are tied up to allow helmsman a clear view ahead. Fore tack is to eyebolt halfway between stem and mast, with bowline to second reef cringle.

181  A WELL CUT FORELUG
   B.F. 1094 *Blantyre*, note how yardbands have stretched, the reach in leech of sail, and perfectly straight hoist.

182 ZULU *GARLAND* ENTERING LOWESTOFT
Note white watercut, and fore sheet is a'weather.

183 FRASERBURGH HARBOUR
Note cutter rigged zulu alongside breakwater. F.R. 625 *Star of Peace*, F.R. 782 *Myosotis*.

| | |
|---|---|
| Carling inside trunk | 9½ in. deep. |
| Deck planking - | 6½ in. by 2 in. |
| Gunwale - | 5 in. wide by 9 in. deep. |
| Bearer    -       - | 4 in. wide by 7 in. deep. |

## MASTS AND SPARS

| | |
|---|---|
| Foremast -   - | 65 ft. 6 in. L.O.A., 7 ft. 9 in. below deck. Dia., 22 in. to 9 in. |
| Foreyard -   - | 31 ft. Dia., 8 in. to 4 in. |
| Bowsprit     - | 46 ft. 6 in.   Dia., 10 in. to 8 in. |
| Mizzen mast  - | 55 ft. L.O.A. 7 ft. 6 in. below deck. 15 in. dia. |
| Mizzen yard  - | 25 ft. 6 in. |
| Mizzen boom  - | 27 ft. 8 in. |

## SAIL PLAN

| | |
|---|---|
| Forelug | Head, 29 ft. |
| | Foot, 40 ft.                   Diagonals 51 ft. 3 in. and |
| | Luff, 41 ft. 6 in.                    68 ft. 9 in. |
| | Leech, 64 ft. |
| Mizzen lug  - | Head, 23 ft. |
| | Foot, 33 ft. 6 in.              Diagonals, 43 ft. and |
| | Luff, 29 ft.                            49 ft. 6 in. |
| | Leech, 50 ft. 9 in. |
| Jib    -     - | Luff, 59 ft. 6 in. |
| | Foot, 25 ft. |
| | Leech, 42 ft. 9 in. |

Lug halyards had a treble-sheaved block aloft, and a double block at gunwale, burtons had a runner and luff purchase.

The smaller fifies were known as "skiffs" in Banffshire, "baldies," in Fife, a name believed to be a corruption of Garibaldi, a popular hero of that time. Keel length varied from 23 ft. to 40 ft., and hulls were clinker or carvel-built.

One built at Peterhead in the '90's had a keel length of 37 ft., length over stems 42 ft. 6 in., beam 15 ft., depth 5 ft. Hull was clinker-built with bent timbers, fully decked with a fore cabin providing reasonable sleeping and cooking accommodation for a crew of five. Price for carpenter's work was £71, sails £30.

The lines of *Bounty*, U.L.217, were taken off by Mr. F. T. Wayne in August 1933. Plan 22 page 343.

Hull was entirely open, 23 ft. 9 in. over stems, 22 ft. keel, extreme beam 8 ft. 5 in. with a dipping lug 225 sq. ft. area, set on a mast raking aft; rake could be altered by stepping mast in alternative step.

*Bounty* was built at Gamrie Bay, Aberdeenshire, in 1880, and registered at Ullapool, Rossshire.

Mast "thaft" was 2 in. thick, with notch on aft side to take mast, which was secured by iron strap, remaining thafts were 1¾ in. thick, except after one 1½ in. thick. Frames were 2 in. sq., gunwale 2 in. by 2½ in., with holes to take thole pins, and eyebolt for halyards. Planking was ⅝ in. thick, bend inside frames 2 in. sq., extended aft to second thaft, with a stringer 4 in. by 1 in. from second to fourth thaft.

Such a boat differs but little to the fifies in use thirty years before at the time of the August disaster, 1848.

Speeds up to eight knots were common, which is not surprising considering the easy lines and big sail plan.

Plate 177 shows *Mizpah*, K.Y.18, once a sailing baldie, and now fitted with a motor, lying alongside the quay at Anstruther on 23rd March 1936. In the foreground are two "yawls," as the boats under 30 ft. keel were often called. *Isabel*, K.Y.470 is rigged with a single dipping lug, but the old baldies had a dipping lug on the foremast and a standing lug on the mizzen. The hollow garboards and sharp rise of floors will be noted.

Along the shores of the Moray Firth the zulu was popular, no less than 480 being registered at Buckie alone in 1900. Mr. William McIntosh, who commenced work in his father's yard in 1894, writes me that the price then for a 50-ft. boat was £320, but the biggest cost up to £500 for hull and spars. Lines were taken from a half model, and if boat was to be a few feet longer, an extra frame was put in amidships without altering the shape of the model. Four inches more was always allowed on the length of keel, and projected beyond the sternpost. Hulls, built under cover in a shed, were completed in about eight weeks, and wages were 5d. an hour. Oak, sawn into planks, was 2s. 6d. a cubic foot, larch 1s. 10d.

Keel was beech, stem and sternpost oak, frames—oak mostly, a few boats had larch—were bolted to apron and sternpost aft, and beams were Scotch fir. Floors were 4-in. sided, 2 ft. 6 in. moulded at throat, middle timbers 9 in. by 4 in., were bolted on fore side of floors, top timbers 8 in. by 4 in. spaced 12 in. apart, bolted at butts, with timberheads carried up. There was no cement between floors.

Hull and deck planking was larch 2 in. thick, and about 2,000 super ft. were required to plank a big zulu, fastenings being 4½ in. galvanised nails; at bilge was a thicker plank, known as the "bilge draught."

Masts were of Norwegian white wood, foremast being about 2 ft. sq. at baulk, 14 in. by 12 in. oval section some 9 ft. up, 10 in. dia. at top, and cost £15; mizzen £8, bowsprit £6, mizzen boom £1 10s. Yards were larch, costing £4 each, foreyard being about 36 ft. long, 8 in. by 7 in. at slings, tapering to 4½ in. Foremast lowered back into the "hitches," the side timbers being known as stretchers. The biggest foremast Mr. McIntosh remembers was 6 ft. 9 in. circ., or about 26 in. dia., and these immense masts stood *unsupported by any standing rigging*, the halyards and burton on the weather side being the only stays.

A keelson about 7 in. deep was fitted on top of the keel and *below* the floors, the sides being shaped to allow the garboard strakes to lie flush. Beams rested on stringers, a name also given to the timber bolted on inside of timberheads and called a bearer in a fifie. The average height of bulwarks was 14 in., the top strake, about 6 in. wide, was the "rail," below was the gunwale $7\frac{1}{2}$ in. by $4\frac{1}{2}$ in., with three rubbing strakes—the "beads"—below (Fig. 69).

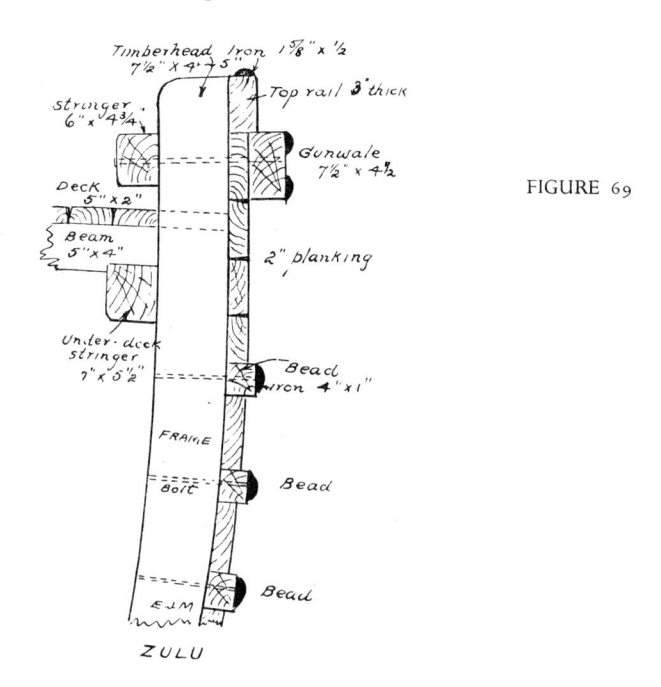

FIGURE 69

Ballast was some 30 tons of stone from the seashore, and keen skippers would make the crews shift ballast frequently to get a better trim. Legs were needed when the boat was dried out in harbour. When a tiller was used, a piece of rope prevented rudder being lost, later "locks" were used when wheel steering came in. Many zulus had small horizontal wheels, as then the helmsman could sit on the "stern stool" and steer more easily than with a vertical wheel. Carrying capacity was approximately 80 tons. Six oars, 18 ft. long, with blades 7 ft. by 5 in., were stowed on deck under the pump baulk.

Mr. W. Cormack, of Lossiemouth, gave Mr. Oke the following information concerning a typical sail plan.

Foresail -   -   333 yards of No. 2 cotton.
             Hoist, 37 ft. 2 in.
             Head, 32 ft.                    Diagonal, 47 ft. 6 in.
             Foot, 46 ft. 6 in.
             Leech, 65 ft. 6 in.

*Mizzen* -  -  220 yards of No. 5 cotton.
Hoist, 28 ft. 6 in.
Head, 24 ft. 9 in.　　　Diagonal, 45 ft. 3 in.
Foot, 36 ft. 3 in.
Leech, 58 ft. 9 in.

After stretching, the leeches will be about 1 ft. 6 in. longer, head will come out 1 ft., foot will remain about the same, while the hoist—wire rope—will not stretch.

Mr. McIntosh was good enough to give me the name of Mr. Wm. Imlach, sailmaker of Buckie, who answered my questions very fully.

To be a sailmaker a lad had to serve a five years' apprenticeship. For his first year he was paid 3s. a week, the second 4s., third 5s., fourth 6s., fifth 10s., and 18s. a week when out of his time.

When making a suit of sails a scale plan was first drawn out, and the secret of a perfect cut and set was by careful attention to the goring, as Mr. Imlach shows in Fig. 70. Seams were $1\frac{1}{4}$ in. wide, and cloths were hand-sewn from foot to head, weather edges to port, as were the linings 8 in. broad. The various sizes of boltropes used were: Foresail, $3\frac{1}{2}$ in. yacht manilla for lower part of leech, $2\frac{1}{2}$ in. for upper. Headrope $1\frac{7}{8}$ in., footrope $1\frac{1}{4}$ in. hemp, the "hoist" being $2\frac{1}{2}$ in. wire, served with spunyarn.

For the mizzen the lower part of leech was $2\frac{1}{2}$ in., upper $1\frac{1}{4}$ in. yacht manilla, headrope $1\frac{1}{4}$ in., footrope 15 thread hemp. Cringles on wire rope were iron rings.

Cotton canvas was always used, quantities required being 324 yards No. 2 for foresail, 214 yards No. 5 for mizzen, 150 yards No. 12 for jib, and time taken to make was 124 hours for foresail, 80 hours for mizzen, and 50 hours for jib.

Cost was 2s. 2d. per yard for No. 2, 1s. 9d. for No. 5, and 1s. $4\frac{1}{2}$d. for No. 12. Cost of making was extra, and a full suit came to £100.

Sails were dressed with cutch tanning, about 1 cwt. being used, jibs were only lightly dressed. Lugs were bent to their yards with "yardbands," earings through holes some 3 in. from ends of spars, but an iron bolt took the eye of the wire hoist on forelug. The slings were iron eyes, and yard was served with spunyarn in way of mast, bead parrels being used. To the ninth reef cringle a rope—the "bowline," was made fast, and used for hauling down the foresail.

The tack of foresail went to one of the "horns" on stemhead, but mizzen tack was hooked to a chain—the "tuckle chain"—at foot of mast. This can clearly be seen in Plate 178 taken on board *Muirneag*, S.Y.486, note also bead parrel, wedge on fore side of mast, crutch alongside with hatch leading to warp room, variously known as "rope box" or "leader box."

Wire tyes, spliced to hook which went into eye on yard, rove through sheaves set fore and aft in mastheads, the top blocks were wire stropped, lower ones iron stropped.

FIGURE 70

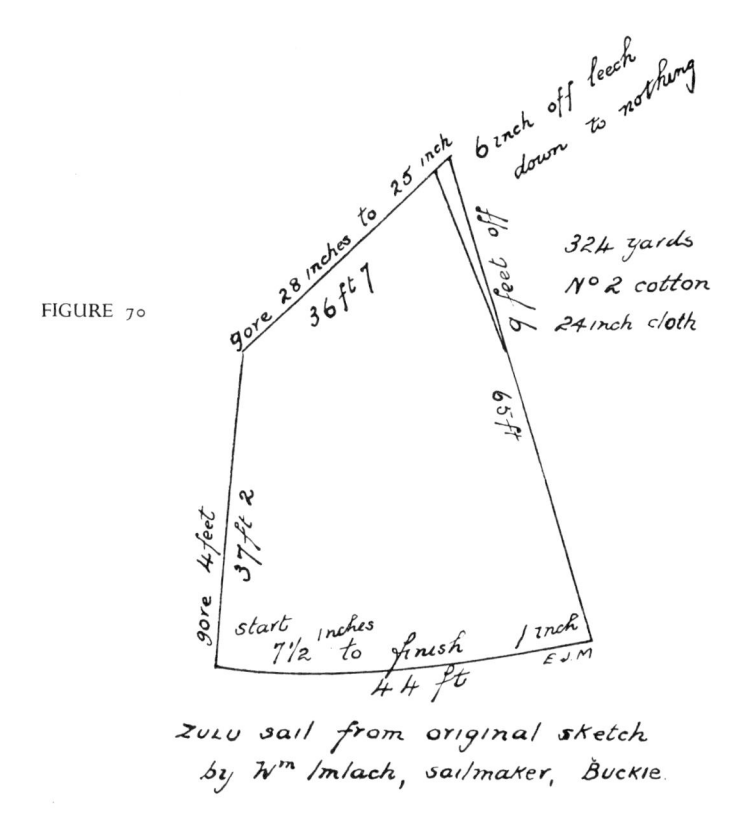

*Zulu sail from original sketch by W<sup>m</sup> Imlach, sailmaker, Buckie.*

Fore halyards were 60 fathom of 3 in. manilla, with two 15-in. treble blocks, mizzen halyards 45 fathom 2¼ in. manilla, with two 11-in. treble blocks. Plate 179 of *Muirneag* shows fore halyard hooked to eyebolt in starboard gunwale, runner purchase for burton, mizzen halyards hooked to port, and such items as open timberheads, baulks, net room hatch, crutch, poop deck, etc., will be easily indentified.

Fore sheets were 1⅞ in. manilla, and the hook which went into clew cringle had 4 ft. of 9-thread manilla for mousing the hook.

Burton pendant was wire, with runner and luff purchase, 6-in. blocks, masts and spars were oiled, with paint on tops.

Mizzen sheets had two 6-in. single blocks, as had the jib halyards. Jib outhaul was set up as a bobstay under bowsprit. The jump stay on mizzen was a runner and luff purchase, with 5-in. blocks, and was used as a backstay set up to port when required.

Plate 180 of *Pansy*, I.N.S.1365, shows the big jib set on an enormous bowsprit. A few reefs points have been tied up at the foot of the lugs to give the helmsman, sitting on his low stool, a clear view ahead in crowded waters. Note tack of foresail is taken to eyebolt halfway between stem and mast, and a curious bowline is made fast to second reef cringle.

The superb cut and set of a zulu's forelug can be seen in Plate 181, of *Blantyre*, of Findochty, B.F.1094, 62 ft. keel, 83 ft. over stems. Not a wrinkle can be seen as she sets out from Lowestoft in the wake of a fifie. See how the wire boltrope gives a perfectly straight "hoist," and the "roach" on that immense length of 65 ft. leech, and that with a vertical cut sail. It is said by yachting experts that only with cross-cut sails can a roach be given, and then battens in pockets have to be used, but those old sailmakers of fifty years ago succeeded, as many a photograph in my collection shows.

Plate 182 is *Garland*, I.N.S.425, still under sail alone in 1923, note how the foreyard has bent to the pressure of the huge foresail, which is sheeted a'weather. It is blowing pretty fresh, but she rides the seas like an eider duck.

I spotted in a postcard sent by Mrs. Garden that at least one zulu was cutter-rigged. She is lying alongside the north breakwater at Fraserburgh (Plate 183), where the herring fleet lies tightly packed. F.R.625 was *Star of Peace*, F.R.782 *Myosotis*, but unfortunately it is not possible to make out the number of this interesting zulu.

When the wind was light, these big zulus had to be rowed and poled out of harbour as can be seen in Plate 184 of *British Ensign*, B.F.1615, with one of the crew on the starboard quarter using a 36-ft. "wand"—punting on a gigantic scale! Almost smothered in the folds of the foresail, which incidentally has eleven lines of reefs, is another man using a 26-ft. sweep. The old-fashioned lute-sterned Lowestoft drifter is *Martha Ann*.

One of the largest zulus ever built was *Laverock*, B.F.787, of Hopeman, built in 1902 and measuring 59 ft. on keel, 84 ft. overall, with a beam of 20 ft. 7 in., and depth of hold 11 ft.

Mr. John Addison tells how all hands, except the skipper, who would be at the wheel, were needed to set sail, one man swigging on the "pendant" between the blocks, the rest on the fall. Plate 185 shows a scene on *Muirneag* where they are preparing to shift the foresail round the mast before hoisting on the starboard side. Note saddle on mast where it rests on the hitches, the heavy stretchers strengthened by knees, the wedge to keep mast in position, and the baulk resting on the stringer. With a fair wind, the tack was sometimes taken to an eyebolt on the bow, instead of to stemhead, and when to an eyebolt on deck—a'monk in East Anglian parlance—it was "taking the tack to the back of the back." To go about took five to ten minutes, there being little difference in time whether hoisting by hand or steam capstan. In narrow waters the sail was not lowered, the sheet was just swung round about. To sheet home in anything of a breeze took at least four men.

Provisions taken to sea included hard biscuits, potatoes, salt beef for the season, condensed milk, sugar, oat cakes, turnips, tea and tobacco; meals were eaten off sea chest.

When the nets were out, the rudder was removed and taken on board, and a zulu rode to her fleet by the bows, with foremast lowered on to crutch, but no mizzen was set as a riding sail. Nets were hauled by the stern, and fish stowed in pounds below net space and in the wings. Mr. Garden kindly drew a sketch of the way the rudder was removed and refixed (Fig. 71).

In 1936 the late Mr. P. J. Oke drew up the plans of one of the largest zulus, *Fidelity*, B.F.1479, from measurements he made on the actual boat, then converted to power. Built by William McIntosh in 1904 at Portessie, she was owned by James Smith. Length overall 78 ft. 10½ in., beam 20 ft. 4 in., inside depth 12 ft.

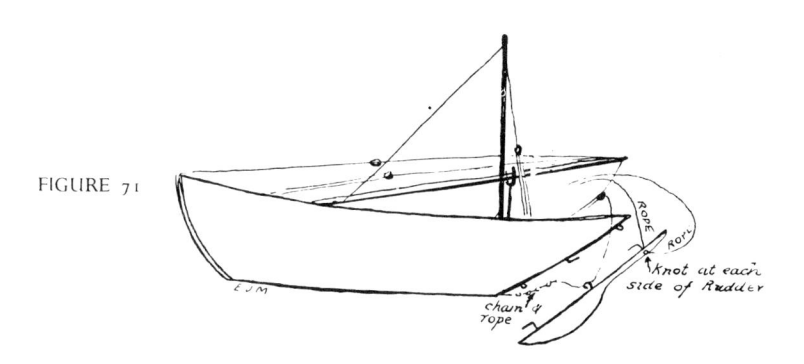

FIGURE 71

One has only to look at the lines, faired from the builder's half model, to see how easily the hull would be driven through the water by that amazing sail plan, 3,650.5 sq. ft., with summer rig. Plans 26 pages 352-4.

The first item which catches the eye is the sharp rise of floors and the rounded bilges, the long entry, and the beautiful run aft. Note also the great depth of floors, with the keelson *below*, not above as is usual practice, the second timbers bolted on fore side of floors, and open timberheads carried up above the deck, with gunwale outside and stringer inside. The straight stem and keel 10 in. below planking, give a good grip of the water for windward work, while the long, raking sternpost shortens the keel and makes the boat easy on the helm.

Below deck for'ard is the forepeak for stowage of gear, etc., then the long fish hold with a platform resting on "foot spurs," all portable, forming the "dales nest for the nets." Below were the fish pounds extending into the wings, with manholes 11 in. dia., or scudding holes in the planking, through which the fish on deck were swept. Then comes the "rope box" with F.W. tank to starboard, coal locker to port, the warp was led down through a small hatch over a short roller. Aft is the cabin with boiler and stove, and fitted with eight bunks with sliding panels, lockers, etc.

On deck the heavy bowsprit is carried to port, reeving through iron ring on bulwarks, its heel resting on the baulk in iron bitts. On centre line of deck are two eyebolts with hook to take tack cringle of forelug when required.

The baulk, 4 in. thick, 3 ft. 9 in. wide at mast, 2 ft. 4½ in. at ends, rests on the stringers, the huge foremast stands in a wooden tabernacle with side bridges 1 ft. 7 in. wide, 4 in. thick, aft is a slot in deck into which mast is lowered the stretchers 8 in. thick, 13 ft. 6 in. long, resting on 8 in. sq. carlings, taper from 2 ft. 0½ in. for'ard to 6 in. high aft. Beam at aft end is 11 in. sq., with post under 6-in. sq. to keel. Covers on top of stretchers are 2 ft. 4 in. wide, 1½ in. thick. On fore side is a cleat 15 in. long by 3 in., and another 1 ft. 5 in. by 4 in. by 3 in., is on port side aft end of stretcher.

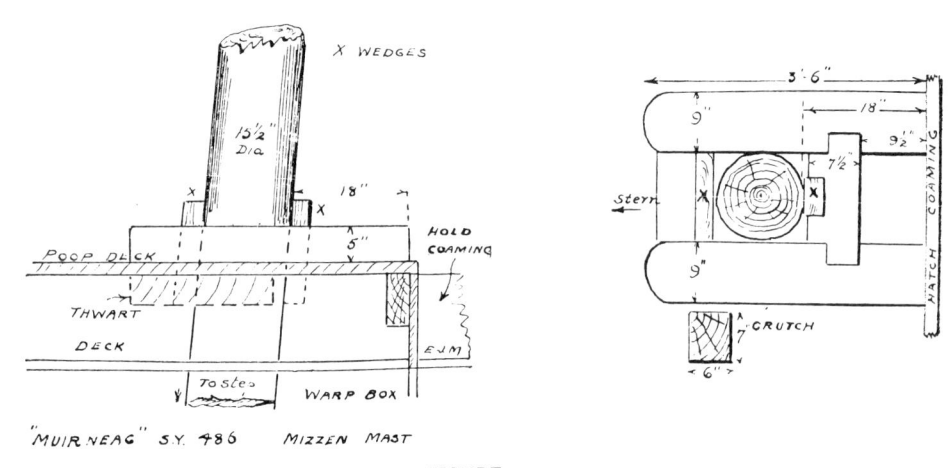

FIGURE 72

Knees, 1 ft. 9 in. long and 3 in. thick, support sides of stretchers; 8 in. out from starboard stretcher is a ringbolt through baulk with a fiddle-shaped strop 8 in. o/a., holding a 3 in. by 3½ in. single block. To starboard is hatch over chain locker, and immediately aft is the pump.

Hatch over fish hold is 8 ft. 6½ in. wide, 12 ft. 6½ in. long, with 3 in. thick coamings 12 in. deep to deck, resting on 6½ in. by 5 in. deep carlings, along fore and aft midship line is a strongback 6 in. sq., recessed to take the covers 1 ft. wide, 2 in. thick. The nine short side beams are 5 in. deep, 4 in. wide, spacing 11½ in.

Aft of hatch is the poop deck 1 ft. high, 2 in. camber, 18 ft. 8½ in. long, 8 ft. 6½ in. wide for'ard, 6 ft. 11 in. aft. Deck planking 8 in. by 1¾ in., resting on beams 7 in. by 5½ in. wide, spacing 1 ft. 6 in. The mizzen thwart 4 in. deep, 2 ft. wide amidships, 2 ft. 9 in. at ends, goes under deck and is recessed on fore side to take mizzen mast, which is supported by stretchers 9 in. wide, 5 in. thick, resting on deck, with wedges athwartships to keep mast at required rake (Fig. 72). To starboard is 7 in. by 6 in. crutch and hatch over warp room, aft is iron plate with boiler funnel, stove funnel is to starboard, then comes steam capstan and scuttle with sliding hatch, heel of mizzen boom resting on chock to port.

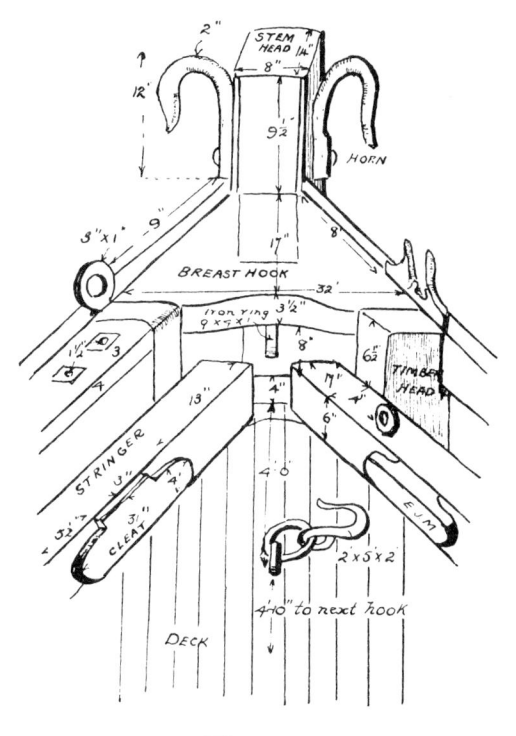

FIGURE 73

The small horizontal wheel is just for'ard of thwart 1 ft. by 3 in. thick, resting on stringers. Rudder head is under top of sternpost with chains through hawsepipes fixed to right and left-hand worm gear.

On either side of stemhead, which measures 8 in. by 14 in., $9\frac{1}{2}$ in. high, are the twin horns, 12 in. long, 6 in. wide, and 2 in. dia.; $6\frac{1}{2}$ in. below tops of timberheads is the timber known as the "stringer," 4 in. wide, 6 in. deep, with an eyebolt 17 in. from end on starboard side and 3 ft. long cleat on face; a similar cleat to port is 13 in. from for'ard end of stringer. First eyebolt on port bulwark is 9 in. from stem, on deck 4 ft. from inside of stem is first ringbolt with hook 5 in. by 2 in. by 2 in. for tack cringle; second ringbolt is 4 ft. 10 in. from first (Fig. 73). Timberheads 8 in. by 4 in. are carried up 7 in., where shown on plan, with chocks between, fitted with $1\frac{1}{2}$ in. dia. sockets at 6 and 7, 13 and 14, 15 and 16, 20 and 21 timbers; these take oar crutches. One-inch iron bolts through stringer into gunwale take tackle chains of fore sheets. Right aft, to 2 ft. 6 in. for'ard of stern thwart, the timberheads are covered with $7\frac{1}{2}$-in. by 4 in. board, with sockets for net rollers and the "cage roller pieces."

Bolted to the stringer are various cleats, fairleads and eyebolts. Heel of foremast is 10 in. fore and aft, 12 in. wide athwartships, resting in step 3 ft. by 4 ft. by $5\frac{1}{2}$ in.

thick, mizzen and crutch stepping in similar one aft. Depth of bulwarks is 17¾ in. Camber approximately 5 in.

## SCANTLINGS

| | | |
|---|---|---|
| Keel | - - | 58 ft. long, moulded 13 in., sided 8 in., with 7 in. thick keelson on top, faced to take garboard strakes |
| Stem | - - | 8 in. sided, 14 in. moulded with apron. Face 4 in. wide. |
| Sternpost | - - | 8 in. sided, moulded 7 in. at head, 1 ft. 3 in. at heel. |
| Floors | - - | 2 ft. 4½ in. deep at throat, moulded 10 in., sided 4 in. |
| Frames | - - | 4 in. sided, 7½ in. moulded, in hold moulded 9 in., sided 4 in., spacing 12 in., overlap at butts 6 in. wide, under deck 8½ in. by 4 in. |
| Beams | - - | Mostly 5 in. deep, 4 in. thick, forebeam 10 in. by 9 in. wide, netspace beams 5 in. deep, 10 in. wide, spacing 3 ft. 7 in. |
| Stringer | - - | 4 in. wide for'ard, 4¾ in. midships, 6 in. deep, bolted to timberheads. |
| Gunwale | - - | 7½ in. deep, 4½ in. wide. Three "beads" (rubbing strakes) 4 in. by 1 in. |
| Stringer | - - | 5½ in. wide, 7 in. deep. Beams rest on this stringer. |
| Stanchions | - - | 5 in. sq., one at each corner of hatch. |

## PLANKING

| | | |
|---|---|---|
| Deck | - - | 5 in. by 2 in. thick. Covering board 12½ in. wide. |
| Hull | - - | 2 in. thick. |
| Garboard | - - | 7 in. wide, then 10, 10½, 10½, 10, 10, 9, bilge, 8, 8, 8, 6, 5, 7, 7, 8, 8, up to top strake. Rubber on twelfth strake 7 in. wide, 2½ in. thick. |
| Bulwarks | - - | 3 in. thick. |
| Rudder | - - | 4½ in. thick. Five pintles. |

Name *Fidelity* on port quarter, *Portessie* on starboard, registration letters B.F.1479, 12 in. high, spacing 4 in.

Mr. Wm. McIntosh tells me *Fidelity* took about eight weeks to build, and hull and spars cost £500.

A photograph of *Masher*, B.C.K.436, *Fidelity*, B.F.1479, and *Rescue*, B.F.436, taken in 1936, when all were power-driven, shows the fine underwater lines as they lie almost dried out in Buckie harbour (Plate 186).

The foremast is colossal, a tree trunk 64 ft. long, dia. 20½ in. by 22 in. f. & a. at deck, tapering to 9 in. and raking slightly aft. On this was set a truly awe-inspiring dipping lug, bent with yardbands to a 37 ft. yard, 8 in. dia., at slings, tapering to 4 in. For summer use this sail was made from 330 yards of No. 2 cotton, and had an area of 1,575 sq. ft., six lines of reef points and three lines of eyelets for lacing are fitted with corresponding cringles in luff and leech, and *all meant for use*.

The mizzen mast measures 57 ft. overall, with dia. 15½ in.—9 in. raking for'ard, on it was set a standing lugsail with a 31 ft. yard, 7 in. dia. at slings, tapering to 4 in., and sheeting home to the end of a 30 ft. boom, dia. 10 in. to 8 in., with half its length outboard. The sail was made from 236 yards of No. 5 cotton, and had an area of

1,292.5 sq. ft. For use in moderate weather a small mizzen was made from 194 yds. of cotton.

The bowsprit was a hefty spar 52 ft. long, dia. 12 in. to 7 in., with 32 ft. 6 in. outboard. On it was set a big jib made from 180 yds. of No. 12 cotton, with area of 783 sq. ft., the small jib being made of No. 5 cotton.

## SAIL PLAN

Foresail -
- Head, 35 ft.
- Foot, 46 ft. 6 in., with 11 in. round, clew 4 ft. up.
- Hoist, 36 ft.
- Leech, 65 ft., with 12 in. roach.
- Diagonals 50 ft. and 69 ft. 8 in.
- 6 reefs, 3 ft. deep, $2\frac{1}{2}$ reefs eyelets and lacing 3 ft. and $1\frac{1}{2}$ ft. deep.

Big mizzen -
- Head, 28 ft. 6 in.
- Foot, 36 ft. 6 in., with 6 in. round, tack 3 ft. up from deck, clew 3 ft. 8 in. up.
- Hoist, 28 ft.
- Leech, 62 ft. with 14 in. roach.
- Diagonals, 47 ft. and 55 ft. 4-6 in.
- 4 reefs, 3 ft. deep, $2\frac{1}{2}$ reefs eyelets and lacing.

Small mizzen -
- Head, 26 ft. 6 in.
- Foot, 33 ft. with 6 in. round.
- Hoist, 25 ft.
- Leech, 56 ft., with 12 to 14 in. roach.
- Diagonal, 44 ft. 6 in.

Big jib -
- Luff, 58 ft.
- Foot, 38 ft. with 12 in. round.
- Leech, 42 ft. with 11 in. roach.
- Diagonal, 27 ft.
- Tack is 1 ft. 6 in., and clew 5 ft. 6 in. up.

Small jib -
- Luff, 35 ft. 2 in.
- Foot, 20 ft. with 8 in. round.
- Leech, 28 ft. 2 in. with 6 in. roach.
- Diagonal, 16 ft. 2 in.

Blocks are shown in Fig. 74, halyards have two treble blocks, fore sheets a luff purchase, one each side, fast to a tackle chain fixed to 1 in. bolts through stringer into gunwale between timber heads.

## SMALL TACKLE

Six oars, 26 ft. long, blade 12 ft. by 5 in.
Two push sticks or "wands," 36 ft. by $2\frac{3}{4}$ in. dia.
One boathook, 14 ft. by 2 in. dia.
Spar for squaring jib when running, 36 ft. by 6 in. dia.

Mr. R. Stuart Bruce tells of the bright paintwork of the zulus and recalls one

*Winsome* of Buckpool, B.C.K.119, which had inside of bulwarks, top of gunwale, and timbers white, the timberheads carried up for use as bollards were black, as were topsides, with a yellow bend, white watercuts and dark green bottom. Port letters and numbers were in white, picked out with light green, while a blue scroll with yellow surrounded the name on either bow.

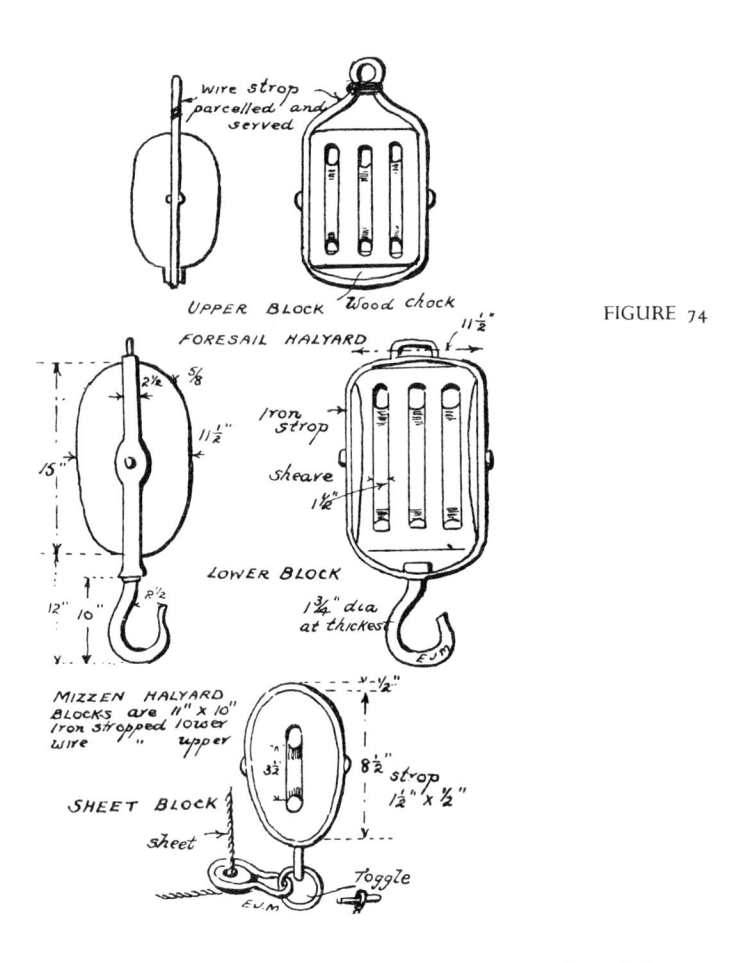

FIGURE 74

Skylight, poop deck, hatch coamings, mast trunk and thwarts were all painted oak and inside of fish hatch coaming was blue. From this it will be realised what a colourful spectacle she made at sea, foaming along with a "bone in her mouth," or reflected in the calm, green water of harbour.

The small zulus, known as "skiffs," were open except for a short foredeck affording some shelter for the crew of three or four men. Early boats were clinker-built, and in the eighties were frequently rigged with two standing lugs and a bowsprit, but the more usual rig was one mast raking well aft, fitted with a high-peaked standing lug, with its tack working on a short iron horse at foot of mast. This rig was popular on the West Coast under the name of "nabby," and the design is reputed to have been copied in the Manx "nobby."

A carvel-built zulu skiff, 30 ft. keel, length over stems 42 ft., beam 12 ft. 6 in., and depth 5 ft., cost about £100 to build, with another £35 for suit of sails.

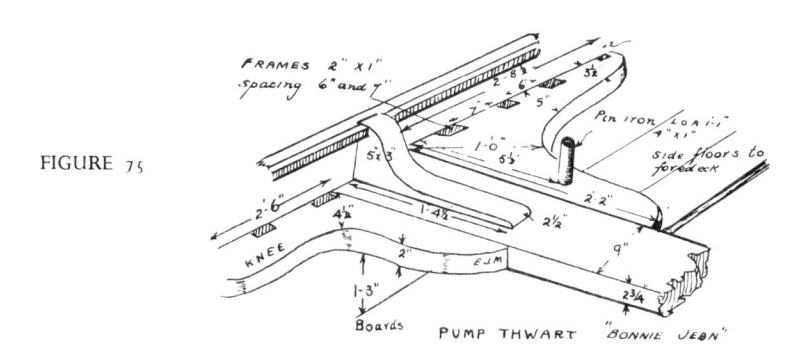

FIGURE 75

Plate 187 shows typical clinker-built skiffs at Campbeltown, 3 C.N. being named *Annie*. Generally speaking, the Loch Fyne skiffs ran somewhat smaller, being 24 ft. to 28 ft. on keel, 32 ft. to 34 ft. overall, and the lines of one, *Bonnie Jean*, T.T.177, were taken off by the late P. J. Oke, and are reproduced on pages 355-6.

Built well over fifty years ago by Henderson of Tarbert, she was owned by Robert Blake of Ardrishaig, and measured 35 ft. 1 in. overall, beam 11 ft. 1½ in., depth inside 6 ft. 3 in.

The foredeck, planked with 3 in. by 1¼ in. planks, was about 13 ft. 6 in. long, on centre line is a 4-in. sq. bitt morticed into step on floors, with iron collar on starboard side to take heel of reeving bowsprit. On deck at foot of mast is an iron horse, 1 ft. 8 in. long, 1 in. dia., 1½ in. above deck, on which the hook to take tack cringle traverses freely.

The mast is stepped in a trunk 5 ft. 8 in. overall with side pieces 6 in. deep, and secured in position by a chock 6 in. wide, 2¾ in. thick. In some boats there were three steps, the for'ard gave great rake aft, the centre more normal rake, and the after one, used when the wind was light, gave a practically upright mast. Below was cabin with two canvas cots, stove lockers, etc., with chain box to port.

Aft of bulkhead the hull was open, with three thafts resting on the stringers; the pump thaft was 9 in. by 2¾ in., kneed fore and aft (Fig. 75), steering thaft 8 in. by 2 in., with knees on for'ard side; 1 ft. 2¼ in. under fore beam is a platform for nets, swinging on fore end by iron bolt, extending to just aft of second thaft, where it rests on two 2 in. by 4 in. stanchions, boards 9 in. by 3 in. thick, below platforms is fish space (Fig. 76).

FIGURE 76

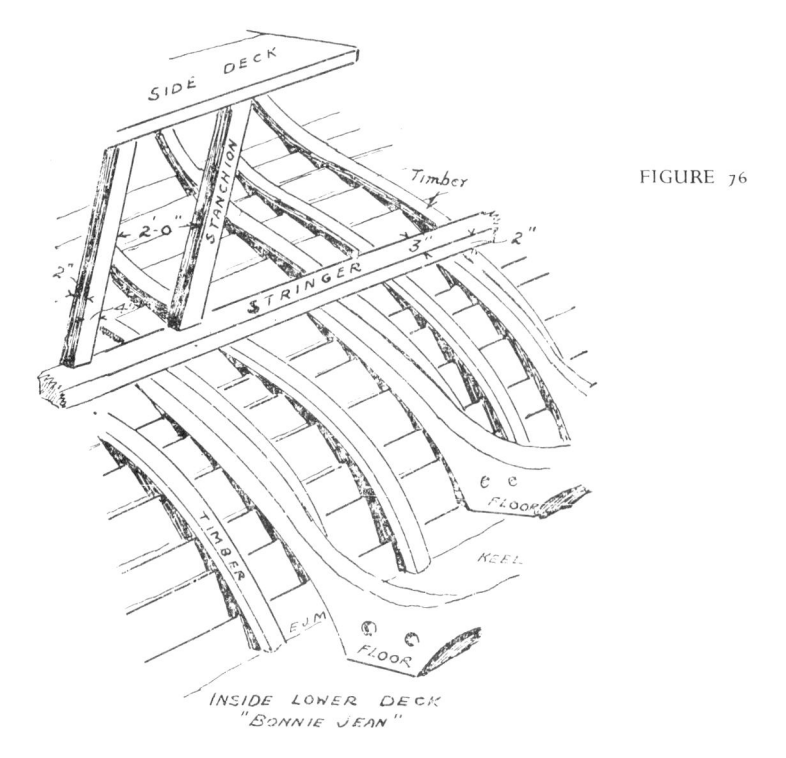

INSIDE LOWER DECK
"BONNIE JEAN"

## SCANTLINGS

| | | |
|---|---|---|
| *Keel* | - | Length 25 ft. 7$\frac{1}{2}$ in. Moulded 7 in., sided 2$\frac{1}{2}$ in. |
| *Floors* | - | On fore side of every second frame, spacing 1 ft. 1$\frac{1}{2}$ in. 10$\frac{1}{2}$ in. deep by 3 in., 2 ft. 6 in. arms tapering to 1$\frac{1}{2}$ in. deep. |
| *Frames* | - | 2 in. by 1 in., spacing 7 in. |
| *Stem* | - | Raking aft 8$\frac{1}{4}$ in., head 6$\frac{1}{2}$ in. by 4 in., with stem iron 2$\frac{1}{8}$ in. by $\frac{3}{8}$ in., carried over head, with eyebolt on top. |
| *Apron* | - | 2$\frac{1}{4}$ in. by 4 in. |
| *Sternpost* | - | Raking aft 8 ft. 3$\frac{1}{4}$ in., 2 in. wide, 3$\frac{1}{2}$ in. to rabbet at head, 6$\frac{3}{8}$ in. at heel. |
| *Gunwale* | - | 2$\frac{1}{4}$ in. by 1 in. |
| *Beams* | - | Mostly 3 in. by 2 in. deep. Aft end of trunk 5 in. sq. mast beam 8$\frac{1}{2}$ in. by 3$\frac{1}{2}$ in. deep. Slide beam 4 in. deep by 4$\frac{1}{4}$ in. |
| *Stringers* | - | Top 4 in. deep by 4$\frac{1}{4}$ in. Bottom 3 in. sq. |
| *Carlings* | - | 3 in. deep by 5$\frac{1}{4}$ in. |
| *Tiller* | - | 4 ft. 10 in. long. 2 in. dia. handgrip. |
| *Floor beams* | - | 2$\frac{1}{2}$ in. deep by 2 in., spacing 1 ft. |
| *Floor boards* | - | 8 in. by 1 in. |
| *Planking* | - | 20 planks, 1 in. thick, lands $\frac{5}{8}$ in., at bilge $\frac{7}{8}$ in. |
| *Garboard* | - | 7$\frac{1}{2}$ in. amidships, then planks vary from 6$\frac{3}{4}$ in. to 4$\frac{1}{4}$ in. Extra plank on fourth strake from top, extending from 7 ft. 6 in. on L.O.A. to 26 ft. 6 in. 1 in. to $\frac{5}{8}$ in. by 4$\frac{3}{4}$ in. |

The foremast, 35 ft. 2 in. overall, dia. 8 in. to $5\frac{1}{2}$ in., is supported by two shrouds a side, set up to chain plates, with deadeyes 3 in. dia. by 2 in., and rakes aft $2\frac{1}{5}$ in. per foot. On it is set a standing lug 447 sq. ft. in area, bent to a 24-ft. yard, dia. 6-4 in., the halyards being a luff purchase.

Bowsprit is 13 ft. 6 in. overall, 9 ft. 6 in. outboard, dia. $4\frac{1}{2}$-4 in., the big jib, 141 sq. ft. in area, is run out on an iron traveller, the outhaul being set up as a bobstay leading down under a small cleat on starboard side of stem near waterline. Cloths are 18 in. wide.

## SAIL PLAN

*Lugsail* -
- Hoist: 20 ft., wire bolt rope.
- Leech: 38 ft., with 6 in. roach.
- Head: 23 ft.
- Foot: 22 ft. 6 in., with 7 in. round.
- Diagonals: 27 ft. and 41 ft. 6 in.
- $4\frac{1}{2}$ lines of reef points, first 2 ft. deep, others 3 ft.
- Cloths: 24 in.

*Big jib* -
- Luff: 26 ft. 3 in.
- Foot: 13 ft. with 4 in. round.
- Leech: 21 ft. 3 in.
- Diagonal: 10 ft. 9 in.

*Middle jib* -
- Luff: 22 ft. 6 in.
- Foot: 9 ft. 6 in.
- Leech: 19 ft.
- Diagonal: 7 ft. 9 in.

*Small jib* -
- Luff: 14 ft. 6 in.
- Foot: 5 ft. 3 in.
- Leech: 12 ft. 3 in.
- Diagonal: 4 ft. 6 in.

Plates 188 and 189 show zulu skiffs fitted with motors.

Thanks to my correspondent, Mr. W. S. Cumming, of Edinburgh, who sent me a newspaper cutting, I am able to record the fate of the last Scots sailing drifter, *Muirneag*, S.Y.486, which was sold by public auction in March 1947 at Stornoway for £50, to be broken up into fencing posts.

This zulu was built at Buckie in 1903 and launched from the Ianstown yard of W. R. McIntosh & Sons, as she was 80 ft. long, I do not suppose she differed much from *Fidelity*, B.F.1479. She followed the fishing regularly until the outbreak of war in 1939, when she was laid up, but her 80-year-old skipper, Sandy McLeod, of Knock Point, Stornoway, took her to sea for a night in 1945.

But for long ere this many a small harbour, where once hundreds of boats lay, has been deserted, with erstwhile busy quays grass-grown and falling into decay, for the passing of sail has seen the herring industry concentrated in a few large ports. Builders' yards no longer ring to the sound of maul and mallet; curing sheds stand gaunt and silent, grim relics of the past when the gay laughter of lassies re-echoed from the rafters, and the cured herring brought prosperity to many a fisherman's home, while the boats, no longer the pride of their owners, lie rotting at every angle and ready to crumble at a touch.

Truly the passing years have brought many changes, but one thing is certain, never again shall we see the noble sight of one of these powerful luggers crashing through the seas, or hear the thunder of slatting canvas as she shoots up into the wind, and the towering lug is smartly lowered, swung round, and re-hoisted. Then leaning over majestically, she steadies on the other tack, the embodiment of grace, strength and power.

184 **ZULU** *BRITISH ENSIGN* **LEAVING LOWESTOFT**
Built by J. R. and W. McIntosh, Portessie. Note horizontal wheel, capstan, crutch, low bulwarks. Eleven reef cringles, lute sterned drifter ahead is *Martha Ann*, 28 tons, built at Kirkley Ham, 1880.

185 **ZULU MUIRNEAG. S.Y. 486**
Preparing to take forelug round mast to hoist it on starboard side.
Note men swigging on fall between blocks, size of the stretchers with covers over the hitches, wedge and saddle on aft side of huge mast, scudding hole, and the baulk resting on stringer.

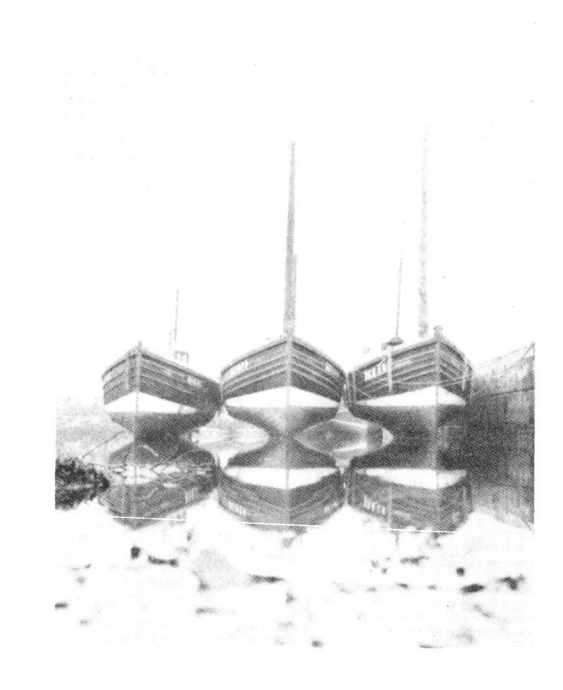

186 ZULUS DRIED OUT, BUCKIE, 1936
B.C.K. 436 *Masher*, B.F. 1479 *Fidelity*,
B.F. 436 *Rescue*.

187 ZULU SKIFFS AT CAMPBELTOWN
Note backward rake to masts, clench build, long sweeps.

188 ZULU SKIFFS AT ROSEHEARTY, *c.* 1939

189 ZUZU SKIFF AT ROSEHEARTY, *c.* 1939
  Note straight stem, raking stern post and big rudder

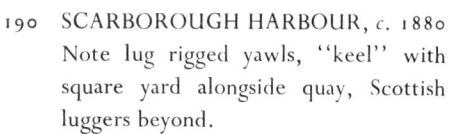

190 SCARBOROUGH HARBOUR, *c.* 1880
Note lug rigged yawls, "keel" with square yard alongside quay, Scottish luggers beyond.

191 DANDY RIGGED YAWL, SCARBOROUGH, *c.* 1880
Note high conical capstan, iron horse in front of mizzen mast.

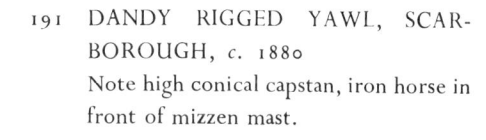

CHAPTER THIRTEEN

# YORKSHIRE COAST

To complete the story of the principal herring stations round the coast, I propose to give but passing mention to the yawls and cobles of Whitby and Scarborough, as I intend to deal with them more fully in subsequent volumes.

The big three-masted lugger—the "farm" or "five-man" boat—has been described and illustrated in Chapter Two. About 1830 she was superseded by the smaller "yawl," and during the next eighteen years only three or four were built at Scarborough, the last being *York*, built by Robert Skelton, and launched on the 14th September 1848.

Her lines were somewhat finer than those in the early boats, length overall was 63 ft. 6 in., keel 57 ft. 2 in., extreme beam 17 ft. 3 in., moulded breadth 16 ft. 11 in., depth of hold 7 ft. 2 in. Draught for'ard light was 2 ft. 8 in., loaded 5 ft., and aft 4 ft. 8 in., and 7 ft. 6 in. Hull alone weighed 17.1 tons, with a carrying capacity of 39.7 tons, or a total displacement of 56.8 tons, no less than 23 tons of ballast being needed. Her burthen of 75 16/94 tons made her one of the largest herring drifters afloat, but she was successful in every way as regards speed, capacity, and safety.

Hull was clench-built of 1 in. thick wainscot oak, copper fastened to the waterline. Timbers, inserted after planking was finished, were 5 in. broad and 5 in. thick, joggled to fit over the lands, fastenings being fir trenails, 1 in. dia., through every plank. Outside were wales 4 in. thick and 7 in. broad. Rigged with three lugs and a jib, she cost ready for sea, without fishing gear, £550, and required eight men to handle her.

Writing on the 10th October 1849, John Edmond, foreman to Robert Skelton, stated that none of these big luggers had been fishing out of Scarborough for several years, Staithes and Filey being their strongholds; boats for Staithes, built principally at Whitby, were lighter in construction and so cost less, but wore out much sooner.

He goes on to say the luggers commenced long line fishing in February, and continued until July 15th, when the herring nets were put aboard, the season lasting until November 23rd, when the boats were laid up for the winter. When line fishing, two

24-ft. cobles were carried on deck, but only one smaller one in the herring season, costing £13.

By then the mainmast in many luggers had been removed, foremast and mizzen being increased in size and larger lugs set, because the yawl, cheaper to build and worked with less expense, was rapidly ousting the old-fashioned three-master.

The first yawl, *Integrity*, had been built on speculation by Robert Skelton in 1833 at a cost of only £60, her length being 34 ft. 1 in. beam 11 ft. 0$\frac{1}{2}$ in., and depth 5 ft. 6 in. Plank was $\frac{5}{8}$ in. thick, timbers 1$\frac{1}{2}$ in. sq., steamed and bent into position after planking was completed.

John Edmonds says the idea was derived from boats frequenting the coast in the herring season from Cromer, Cley and nearby places. Size increased until 1840, when it appeared the boats had reached the most useful degree of capacity, and in that year Skelton built four of almost equal size, shape and strength, the dimensions of *Hope* being L.O.A. 47 ft. 2 in., keel 43 ft., extreme beam 15 ft. 4 in., moulded 15 ft., depth of hold 6 ft. 6 in. Hulls were clench-built of $\frac{15}{16}$ in. American oak, or 1 in. wainscot, copper fastened to the waterline, rooves often being half-pennies and pennies.

Draught light was 2 ft. 6 in. for'ard, 4 ft. aft, loaded 3 ft. 6 in. and 6 ft. Hull weight was 9.2 tons, capacity 28.8 tons, and burthen 47 45-94 tons. Rigged with fore lug and mizzen, and jib on reeving bowsprit, she cost £310 ready for sea, or £240 less than the old "five-man" lugger with one man fewer, a very considerable saving.

Yawls built for Filey ran somewhat larger, and two had round counters in place of the usual lute stern. In fifteen years Skelton built eighteen, Smith and other builders eighteen altogether, with another responsible for six. Two or three built of larch at Whitby and iron-fastened had soon gone to decay, and four had come from Flamborough, but only one was for local use. During that time only two had been lost through stress of weather, when trying to make harbour, *Jerome* and *Emulous* being lost with all hands in February 1845, a third yawl had been run down, and a fourth went on the rocks behind Scarborough pier, but both crews had been saved.

Floors at keel were 6$\frac{1}{2}$ in. deep, 5$\frac{1}{4}$ in. thick, timbers of English oak 5$\frac{1}{4}$ in. thick, 4 in. in and out, wales 3 in. thick, 6 in. broad, with keel 9 in. by 5 in.

Except for three nails to hold them in their berths, the timbers were fastened to every other plank with 1 in. dia. fir trenails.

The yawls fitted out in February for the long line fishing, and as spring advanced went off to the Dogger Bank, when they carried two 22-23 ft. cobles on deck, using them for catching small herring for bait in fine-meshed nets. In May the Scarborough boats went trawling until July, when the herring season started, finishing at Yarmouth at the end of November, when most of them were laid up for the winter.

By the '60's there were about 100 of these yawls, mostly owned and manned by Scarborough and Filey men, but for working the capstan casual labour was often picked up on the pierhead. Each boat fished with about 120 nets, every one 60 yds. long and 12 yds. deep, attached to 12 warps, each 100 fathoms long, and $7\frac{1}{2}$ in. circumference. All this length had to be hauled in by the conical capstan, which stood just for'ard of the mizzen mast, three to four men tramping round hour after hour. The nets were cleared at sea, the herring being shovelled down into the "well," as the second hatchway on deck was called. The first hatch by the foremast was over the net room, and the third, within the capstan walk, was the warp room. The coble was stowed on starboard side of deck for'ard with its stern about level with foreside of tabernacle. The warp was led in over a hawse roller on port side of stem, or through the warp roller on port bow. The foremast, stepped in a heavy wooden tabernacle, was held in position by an iron strap going right round, and lowered back into a slot in the deck—the "gantry" or "gauntry"—which was off-centred to port to allow mast to rest on mitchboard at side of deck, or against mizzen mast aft. All the rigging was hemp, necessitating the use of big blocks. The mizzen mast had a fidded topmast as in the Yarmouth boats, but sail and outrigger were to starboard, not port as in East Anglian and Cornish craft.

The cabin aft was fitted with six bunks, with a commodious one extending into the counter where the boys slept, a number of youngsters being taken to sea at an early age during the summer months to get them used to the life they would follow. If a yawl got becalmed some distance from shore, the catch would often be loaded into the coble and pulled ashore, the man on the rowing "thoft" using a pair of oars, two men on main thoft one each, and often the steersman sculled over the stern, for a ton or more of fish was no light load on a summer morning. At times the yawl was towed by the coble, with a couple of men helping her with the long sweeps.

Herring were landed by ferry boat, or direct on to the quay, and if despatched inland had to be carted a considerable distance through the streets of the now fashionable watering-place to the railway station. This was a frequent source of trouble as visitors and tradesmen objected to the smell, etc., and fishing was definitely not encouraged by the authorities of those days!

A photograph of Scarborough harbour about this time shows cobles and beach boats in the foreground, one of the luggers, listing to port as the tide falls, appears to have been doubled, but the rest are clinker-built. Alongside the pier is a bluff bow-and-sterned Yorkshire "billy-boy," with a number of brigs and schooners astern, and the masts of the Scots fifies can be seen on the other side of the quay. In the background rise the huge blocks of hotels, hydros, etc., whose guests liked fish fresh from the sea, but did not want to see it handled under their noses. Perhaps the most interesting feature is the heap of joggled timbers and lengths of planking on the foreshore. This suggests the site of one of the building berths, as most of the yawls were built on the beach just above high-water mark, and probably the square upright posts were the stocks on which they were laid down (Plate 190).

The keel was fixed in notches on top of the stocks, stem and stern post morticed in, and garboard strake fitted into the rabbet. When the planking reached above the waterline, a few floors were put in to strengthen the hull, which was now shoved down on rollers and floated round into the harbour to be finished.

I am indebted to the late Mr. E. Dade for some of this information.

This clench or clinker method of construction follows Viking tradition, so strong on the East Coast, and dating back some 2,500 years, for authentic remains of a boat of that period were discovered at Als in Denmark, the design culminating in the splendid longships which raided our shores centuries later. At Gokstad a boat was unearthed in a perfect state of preservation, having an overall length of 79 ft. 4 in., beam of 16 ft. 6 in., depth 6 ft., built of $1\frac{3}{4}$ in. planking, with frames joggled to fit over the lands, and thafts resting on stringers. I have just had the pleasure of seeing a replica sailing in my own home waters, manned by sturdy oarsmen, dressed in the traditional manner, and rowing with perfect timing.

In the 1870's the yawls followed the trend of fashion by changing over from the dipping lug to a suit of fore and aft sails, similar to that of the Yarmouth and Lowestoft boats, to which they had always borne a marked resemblance. Hemp rope gave place to wire rigging, the gaff and boom mizzen and gaff mainsail made for easier handling, although speed and some degree of picturesqueness were sacrificed (Plate 191).

A few years later many hulls were "doubled" by filling up the lands with feather-edged planks, and adding a skin of $3\frac{1}{2}$-in. American elm, thus making a smooth surface, as in carvel build. Heavy bends were fastened through frames, and iron knees within, and these strengthened hulls lasted for another thirty years or so.

Whitby and Scarborough were at the height of their fishing prosperity in the eighties when huge fleets of East Anglian, Cornish and Scottish drifters worked out of the ports. The catches were largely landed fresh for kippering, only choice fish being smoked, and every herring was counted out of the boat in the traditional manner. The Scottish fish curers and the girls for gutting and curing came south for the few weeks' season before going on to Yarmouth and Lowestoft. Square-riggers from the Baltic brought in timber for barrels and boxes, and returned with cured fish.

The herring cóbles—locally known as "splashers"—ran up to 42 ft. in length, with a beam of 13 ft. 6 in., and were half-decked for'ard, open aft with platforms below the thofts. The separate strakes of planking were gaily painted with blue, vermilion, yellow and green, the sails barked brown with tan made from the peeled bark of oak boughs—"gazel."

It is known that cobles were used on the coast in Elizabethan times, and the port of Scarborough was visited by boats from the Cinque Ports, proof of the antiquity of the herring fishery.

Scarborough harbour was awkward to take in on-shore gales, and if conditions were such that it was highly dangerous to enter, a huge bonfire of tar barrels, drift wood, etc., was lit on the pier to warn incoming drifters that it was safer for them to stay outside.

To-day the numerous smoke-houses have gone and the sailing fleets have vanished.

Such is the story of the herring, the most nutritious of fish, yet so perverse is human nature that its very cheapness causes it to be despised. Were it as highly priced and scarce as the lordly salmon, epicures would sing its praises.

To-day we are at the meeting of the tides, tossed about in broken water, the old ways have gone by the board, and the new are all uncertain. Subsidies and companies have taken the place of individual effort, but many a rope which looks sound, parts under strain. Greed and wasteful methods of fishing have seen many a prolific ground despoiled, and the vast shoals, accumulation of millions of years, are in some cases no more. Once thriving centres lie derelict, with a few old men, "bollard warmers," who can recall the glories of the past, when quays were thronged with busy men and women, and scores and hundreds of boats left on one tide and returned on another, laden with the harvest of the sea, which comes to man's hand unsown, untilled, and uncared for, yet ripe for his garnering.

It is indeed strange that the more scientific the fishing became, the more costly the taking; often expensive and elaborate methods do not yield the results of less enlightened days, when men toiled in simple faith, relying on their own judgment and an understanding of the many mysteries of the sea, knowledge handed down from father to son, each perchance adding his portion to the accumulated store of the years, trusting to ways which had stood the test of time, often unchanged through the slow centuries of our maritime history.

Discarded and almost forgotten, the sailing drifter has been flung away, yet who can say that steam and motor in the long run have solved the many problems of a fisherman's calling? Every development has to be paid for in the price of fish, whose meshing yearly costs more and more, yet in itself is free to all.

Of the splendid men who manned the sailing fleets, how do we stand to-day? Skill and knowledge of making the best use of wind and tide have given way to steam and motor power, which, while solving the problem of going anywhere, irrespective of the elements, cost far more than the harnessing of the breeze, as many an unfortunate fisherman has found to his sorrow, when savings gained in sail have been swallowed up in the hungry maw of the stokehold.

Man ever strives against the winds of adversity and the tides of destiny, now gaining a few miles to wind'ard, then maybe swept far to leeward, always trying to gain the star of achievement which seems to shine the brightest when far beyond his reach, and when attained is so often but a farthing dip instead of a wax candle, or should I say a candle compared to fluorescent lighting?

Perchance in this modern world it was inevitable to see such changes, whether these were for the ultimate good of all, posterity alone can judge. The days have gone beyond recall when those fleets of sailing drifters came in with their silvery hauls of herring, mackerel and pilchard, but I hope that the efforts I have made in these pages may enable future sail lovers to visualise times that are no more.

# PLAN SECTION
★

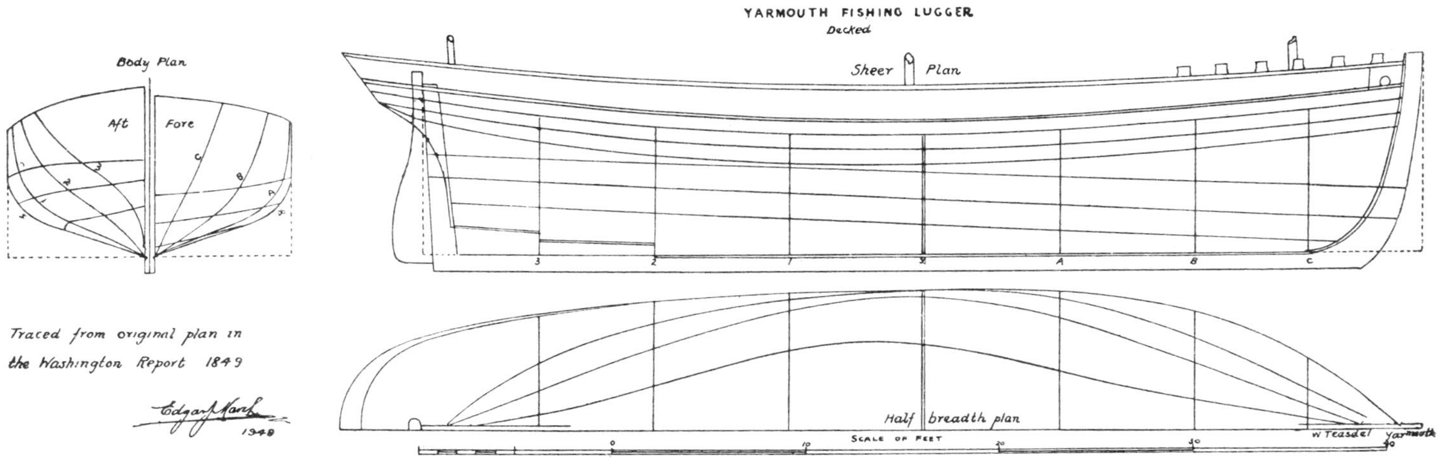

PLAN 1
3 Masted Yarmouth Lugger, c. 1848

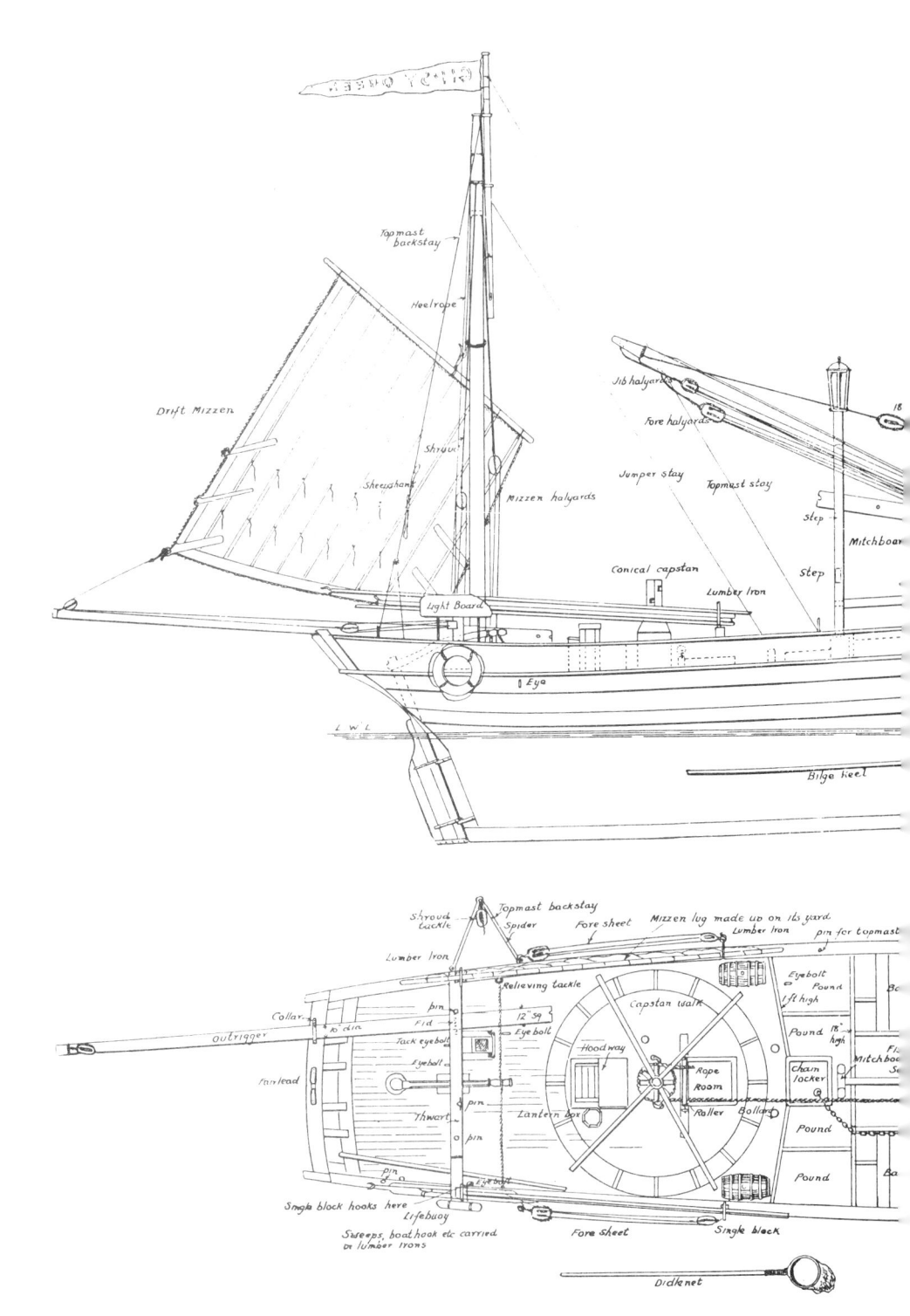

2-Mast

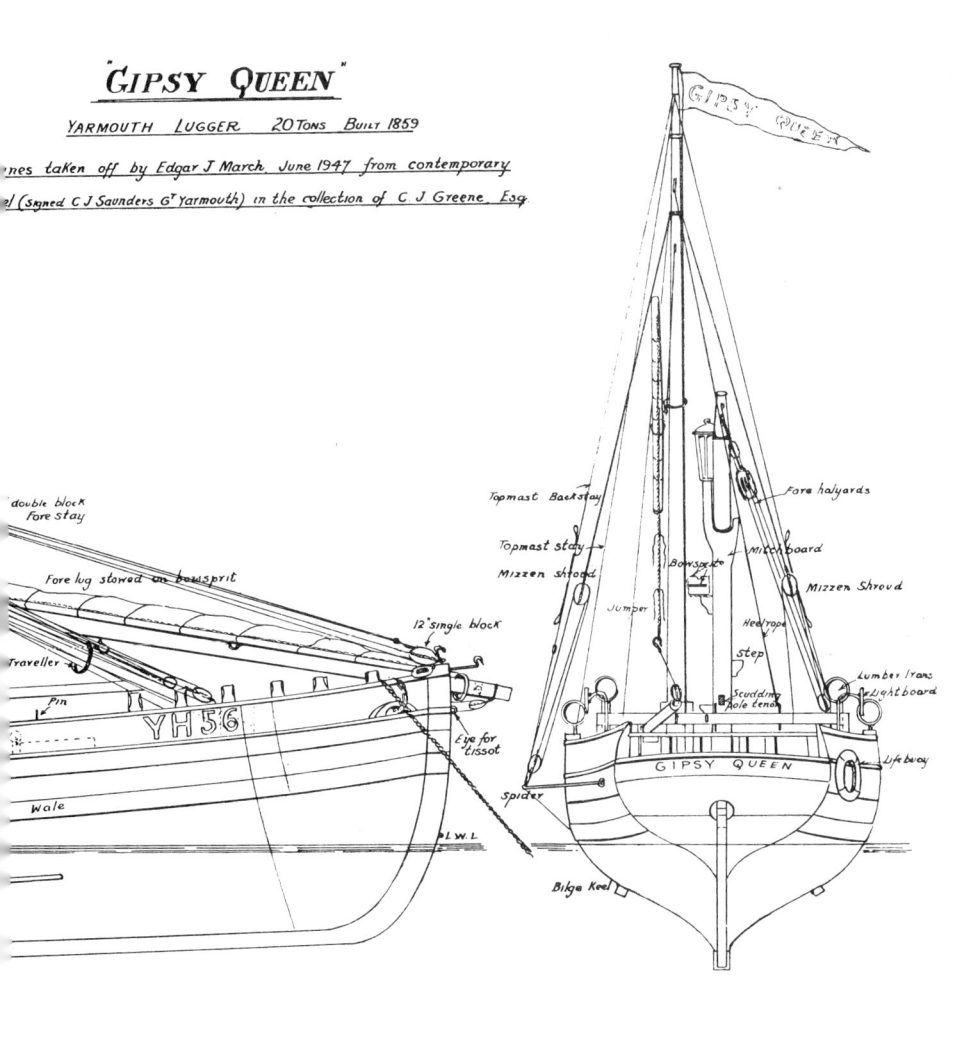

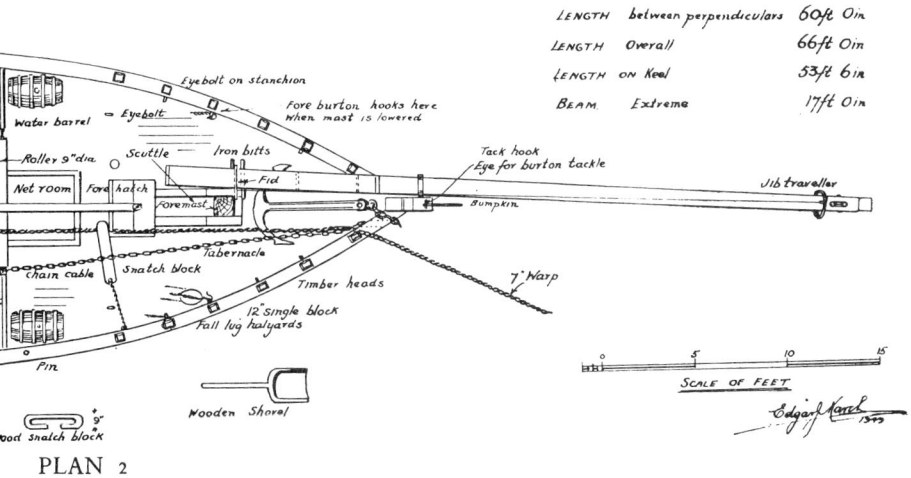

PLAN 2
…mouth Lugger, c. 1859

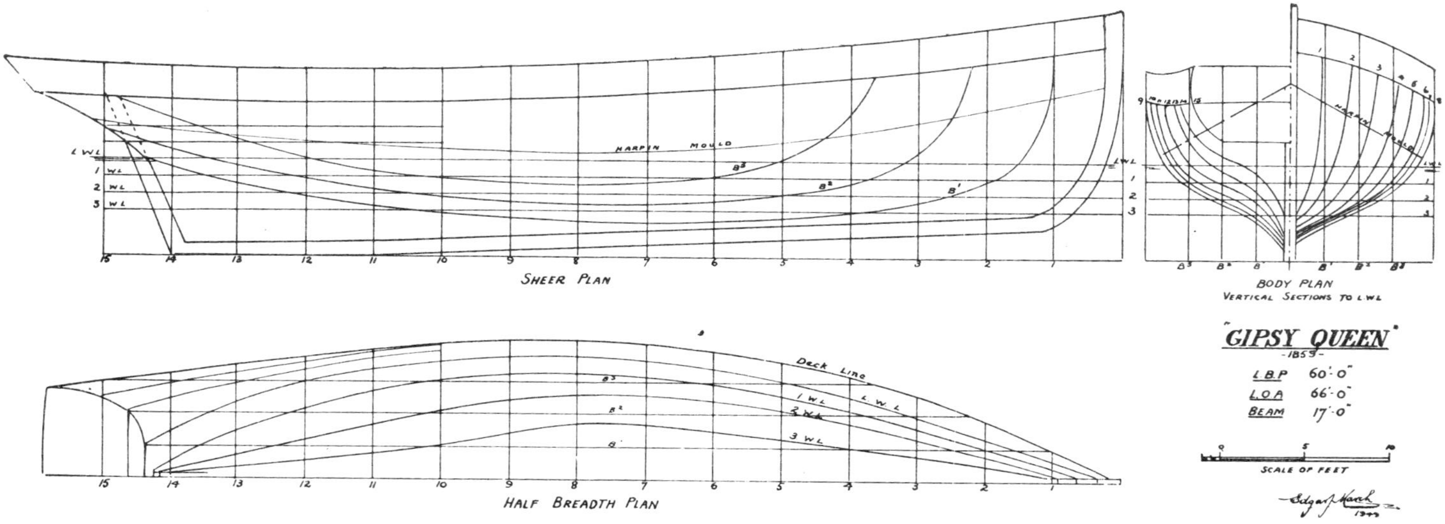

PLAN 2
2-Masted Yarmouth Lugger, c. 1859

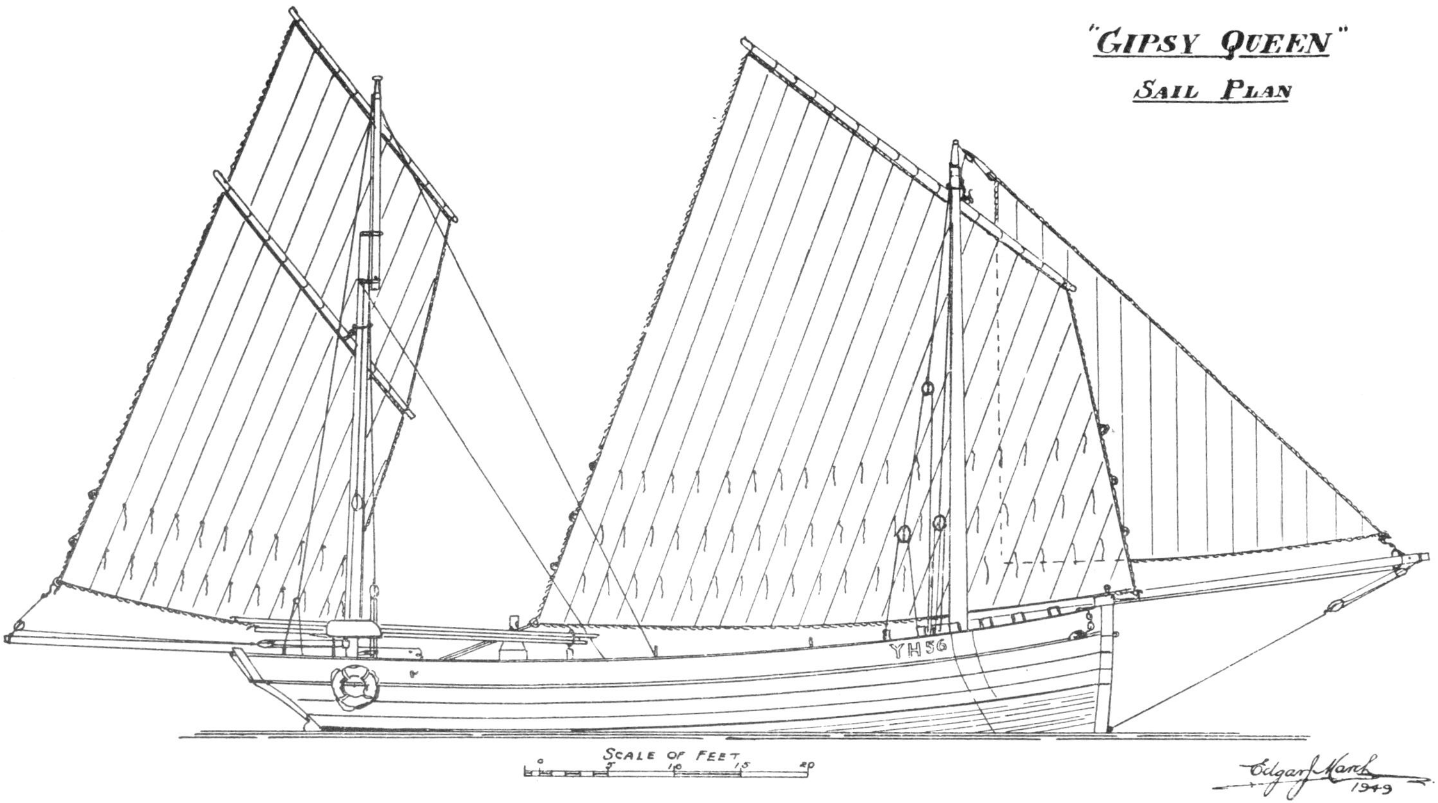

PLAN 2
2-Masted Yarmouth Lugger, c. 1859

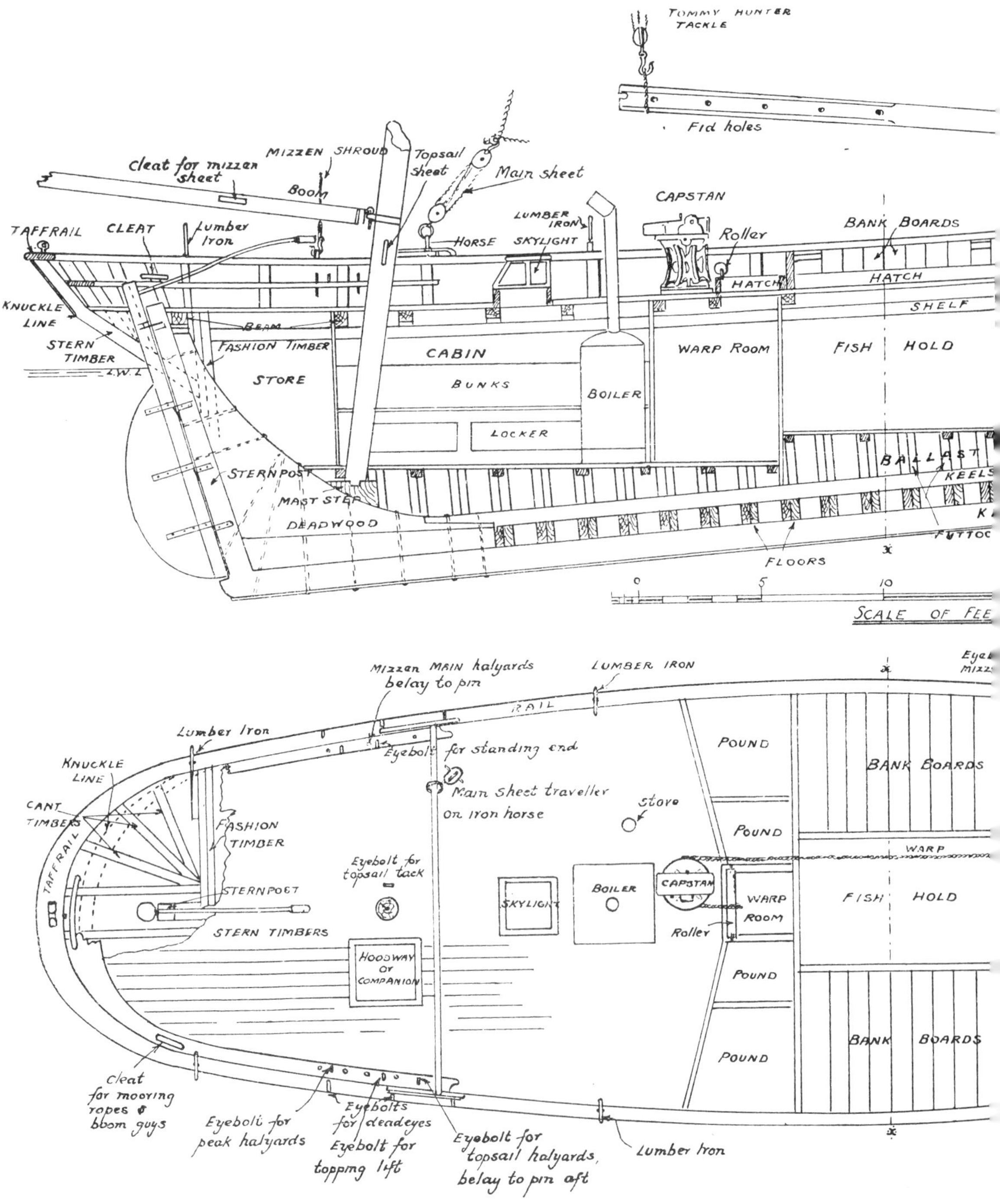
TOMMY HUNTER TACKLE
Fid holes
Cleat for mizzen sheet
MIZZEN SHROUD
Boom
Topsail sheet
Main sheet
CAPSTAN
LUMBER IRON
SKYLIGHT
HORSE
TAFFRAIL
CLEAT
Lumber Iron
Roller
BANK BOARDS
HATCH
HATCH
SHELF
KNUCKLE LINE
STERN TIMBER
L.W.L
BEAM
FASHION TIMBER
CABIN
STORE
BUNKS
BOILER
WARP ROOM
FISH HOLD
LOCKER
STERNPOST
MAST STEP
DEADWOOD
FLOORS
0
5
10
Mizzen MAIN halyards belay to pin
LUMBER IRON
RAIL
Lumber Iron
Eyebolt for standing end
KNUCKLE LINE
CANT TIMBERS
TAFFRAIL
Main sheet traveller on iron horse
Stove
FASHION TIMBER
POUND
BANK BOARDS
POUND
WARP
Eyebolt for topsail tack
STERNPOST
STERN TIMBERS
SKYLIGHT
BOILER
CAPSTAN
WARP ROOM
FISH
HOLD
Roller
HOODWAY or COMPANION
POUND
POUND
BANK BOARDS
Cleat for mooring ropes & boom guys
Eyebolt for peak halyards
Eyebolts for deadeyes
Eyebolt for topping lift
Eyebolt for topsail halyards, belay to pin aft
Lumber Iron

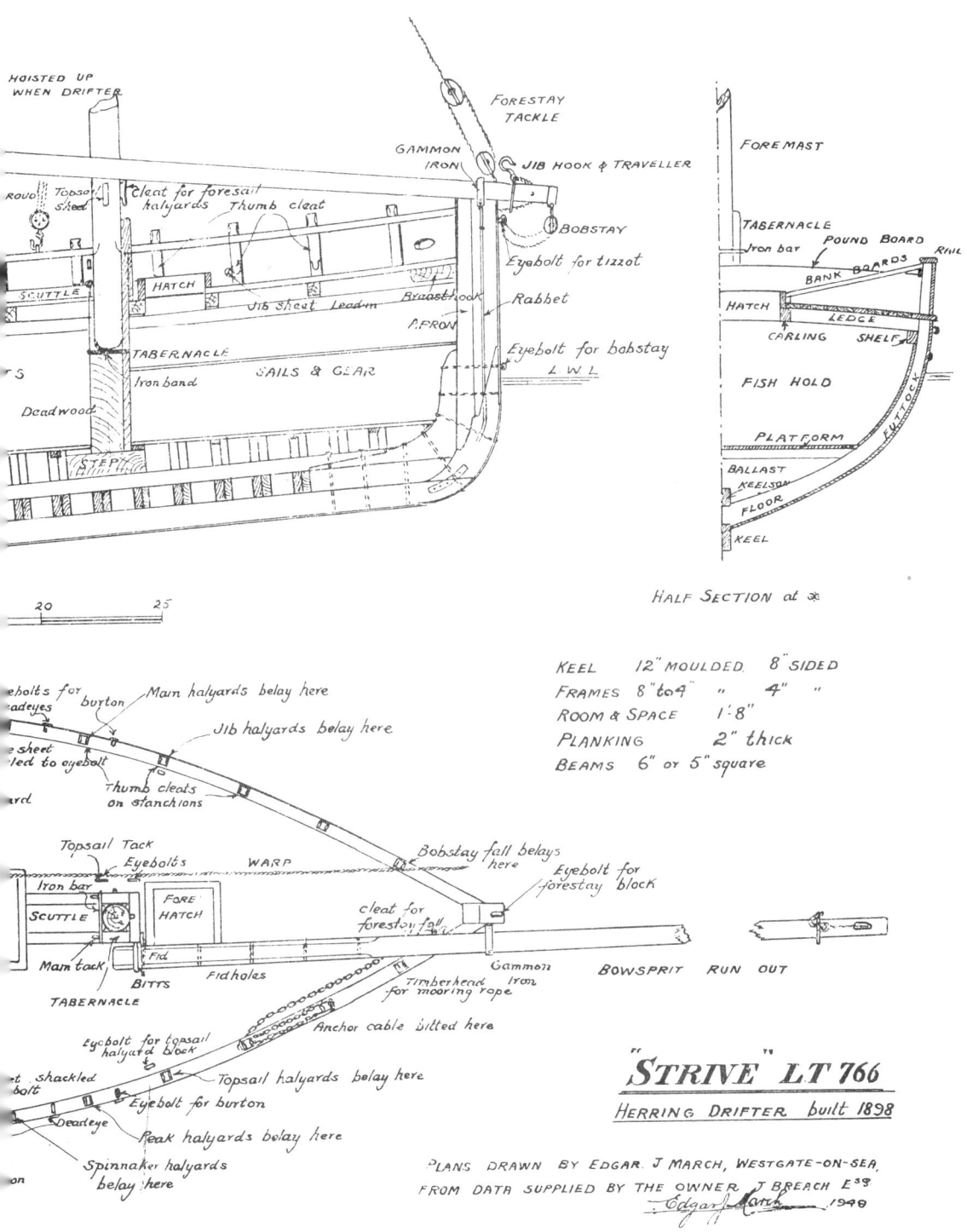

KEEL      12" MOULDED.   8" SIDED
FRAMES    8" to 9"       4"  "
ROOM & SPACE             1'·8"
PLANKING                 2" thick
BEAMS     6" or 5" square

**"STRIVE" LT 766**

HERRING DRIFTER built 1898

PLANS DRAWN BY EDGAR J MARCH, WESTGATE-ON-SEA,
FROM DATA SUPPLIED BY THE OWNER. J BREACH Esq
                                   Edgar March  1948

PLAN 3

ter, c. 1898

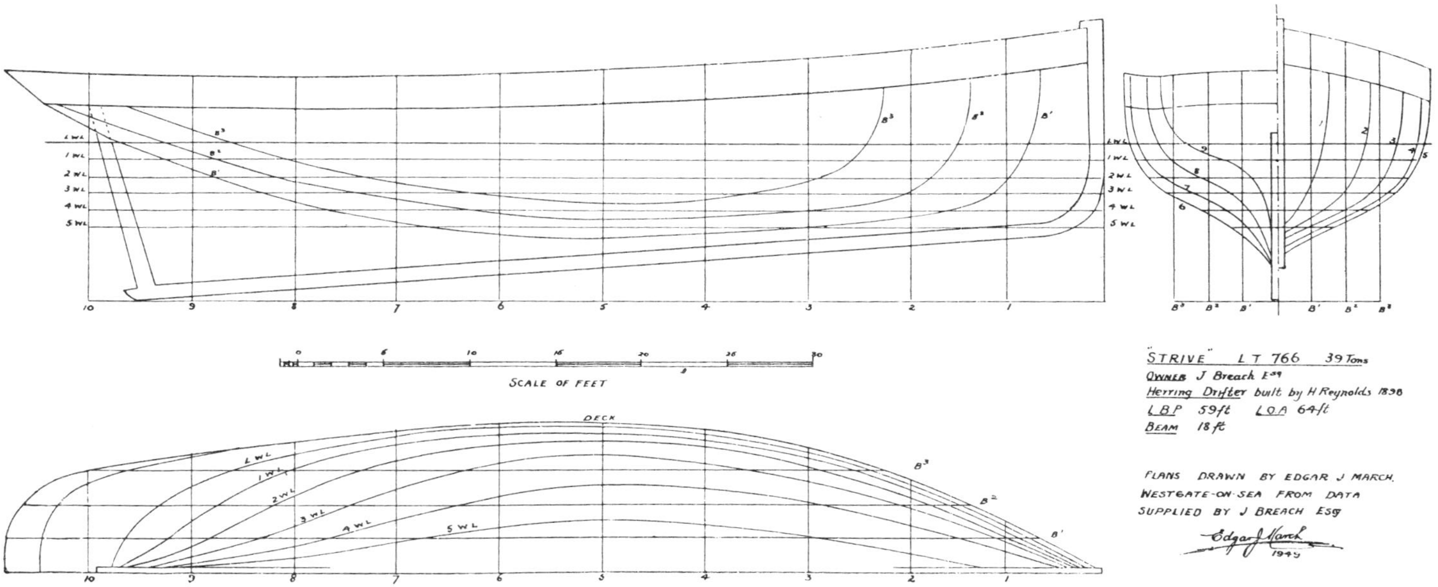

PLAN 3
Lowestoft Drifter, c. 1898

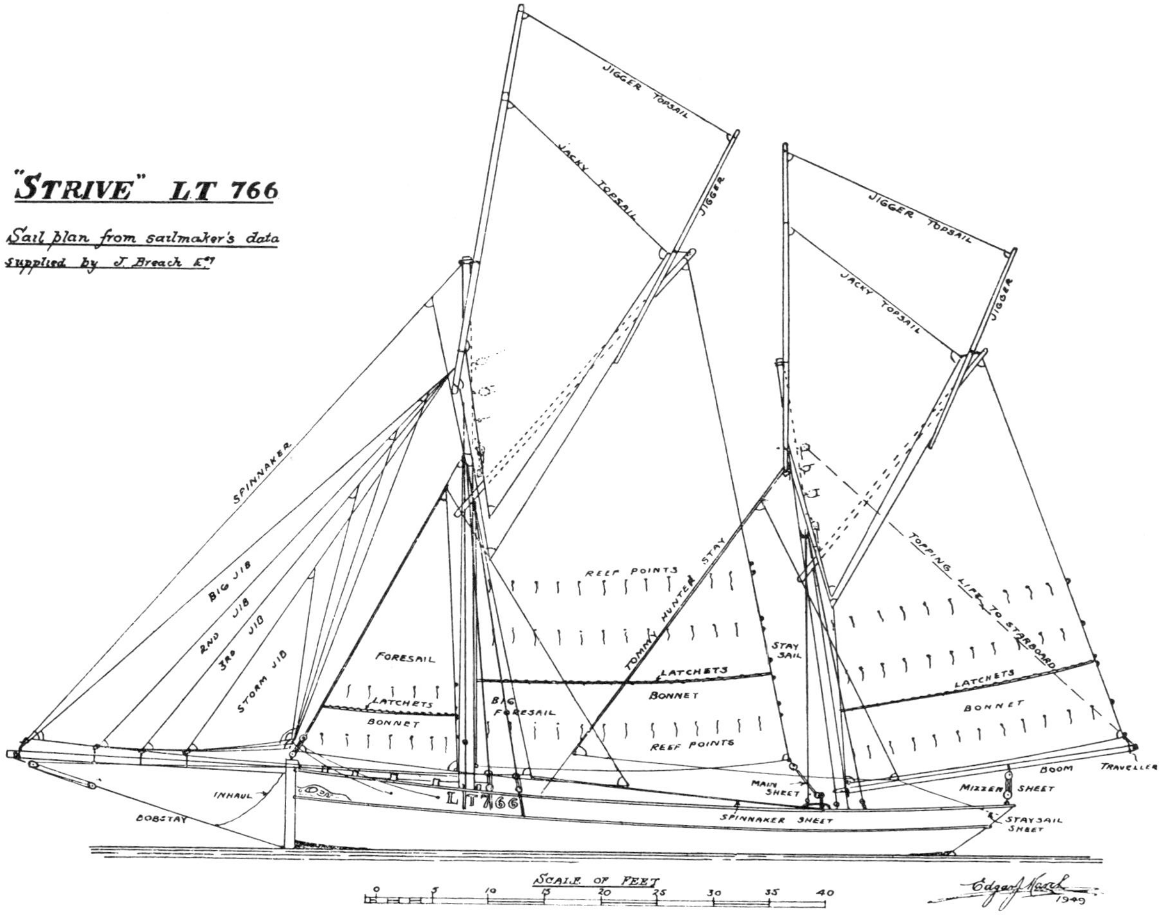

PLAN 3
Lowestoft Drifter, c. 1898

PLAN 4
French Drifter

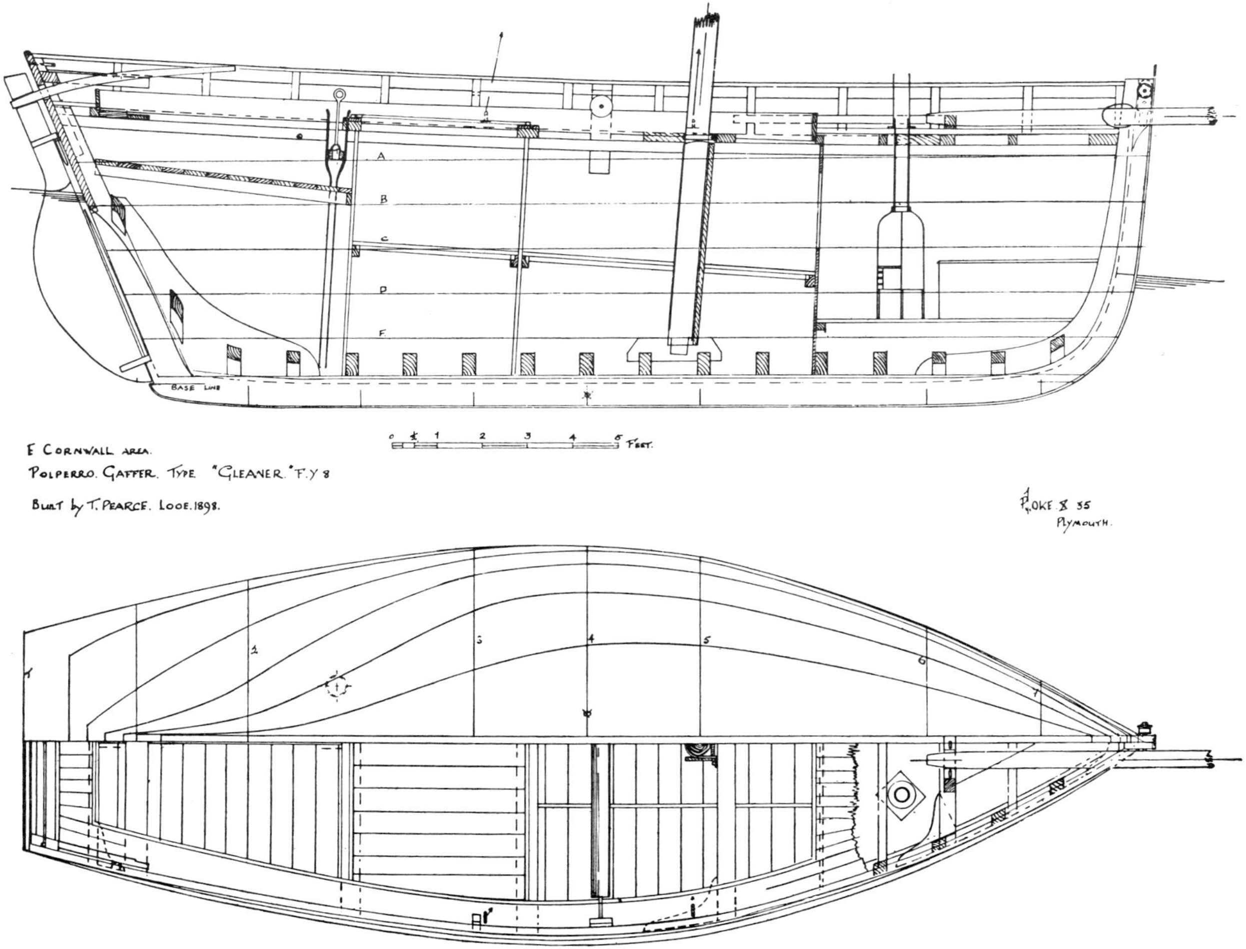

PLAN 5
Polperro Gaffer, c. 1898

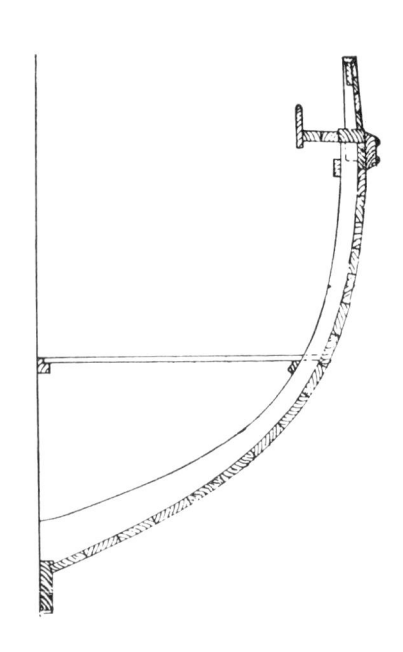

— SECTION at #4 —

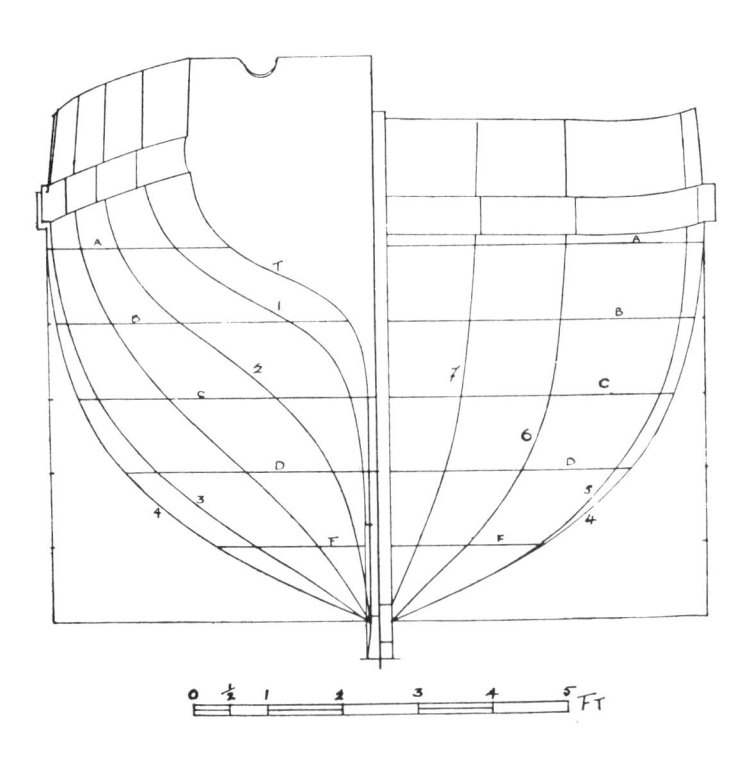

PLAN 5
Polperro Gaffer

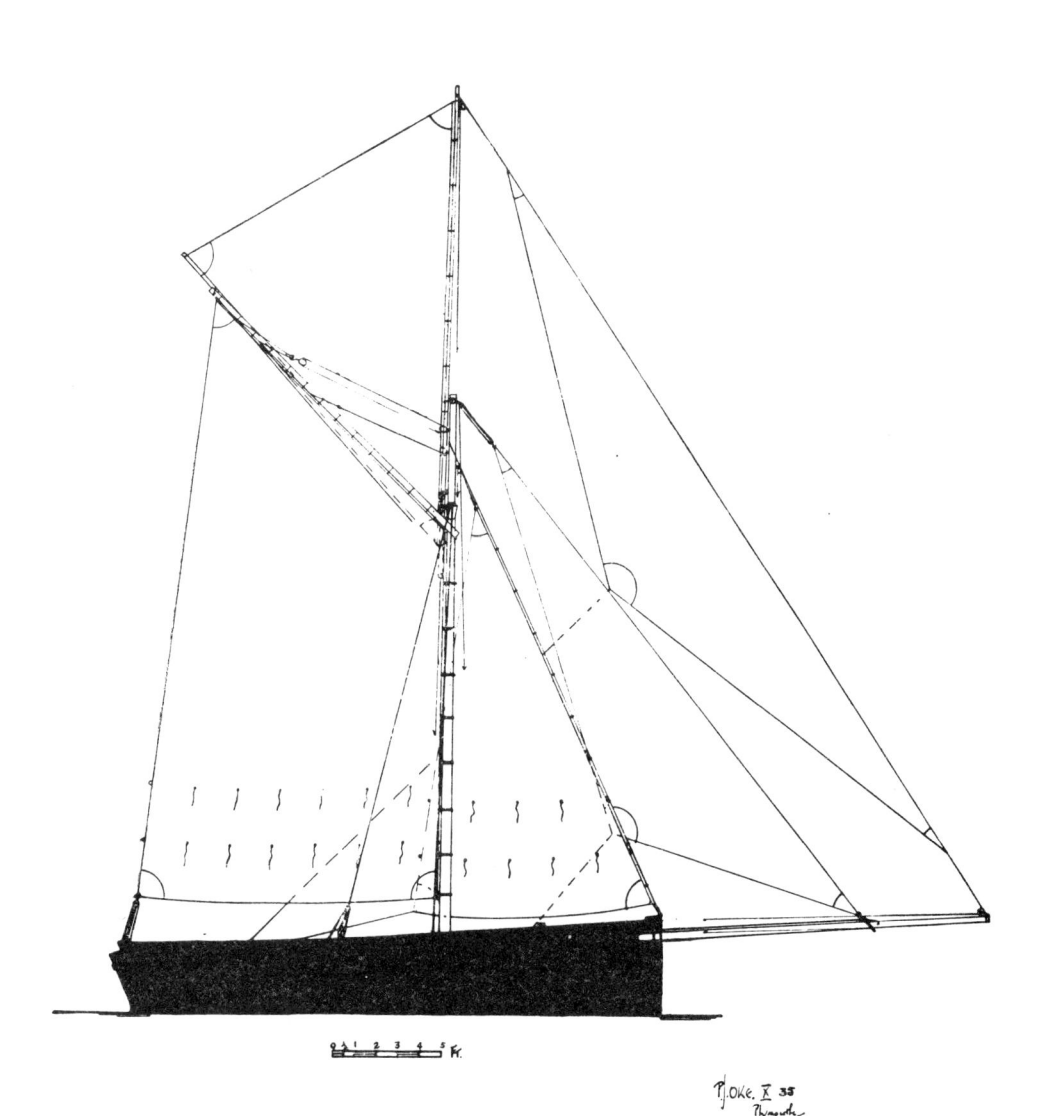

PLAN 5
Polperro Gaffer

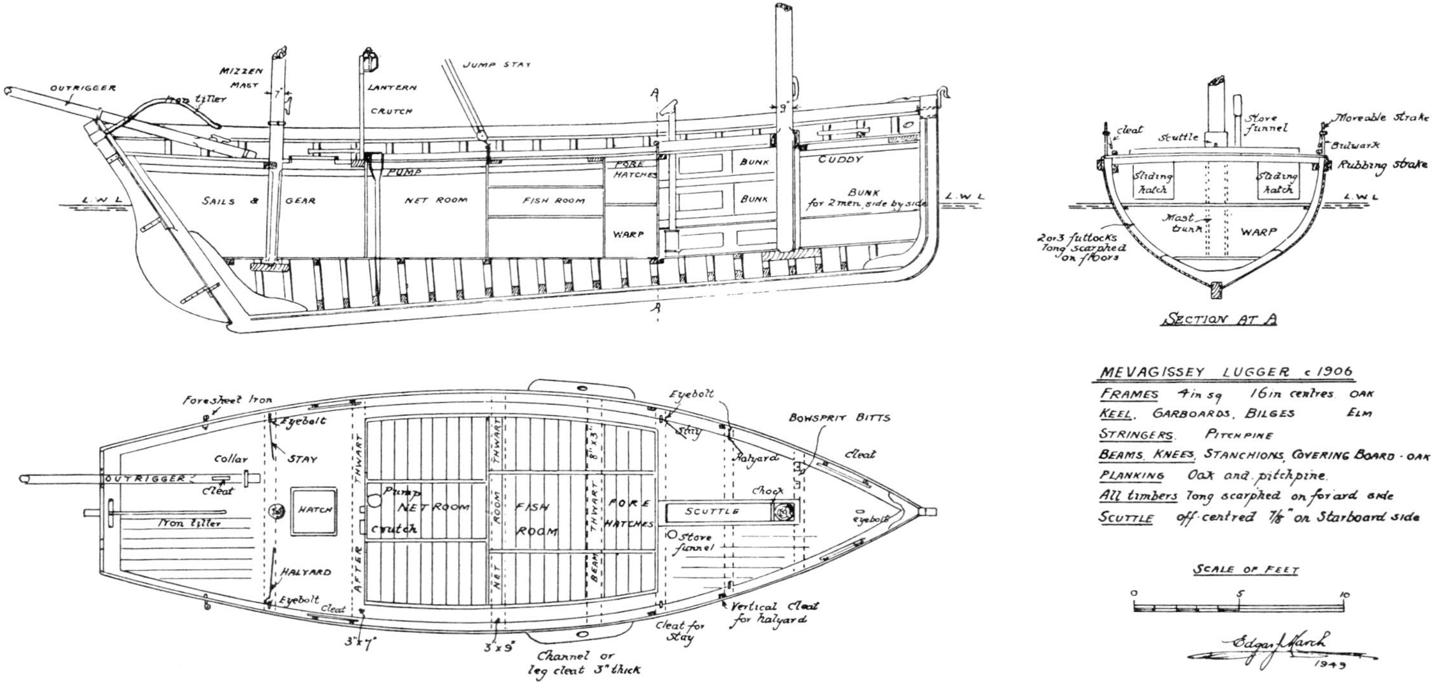

PLAN 6

Mevagissey Lugger, c. 1906

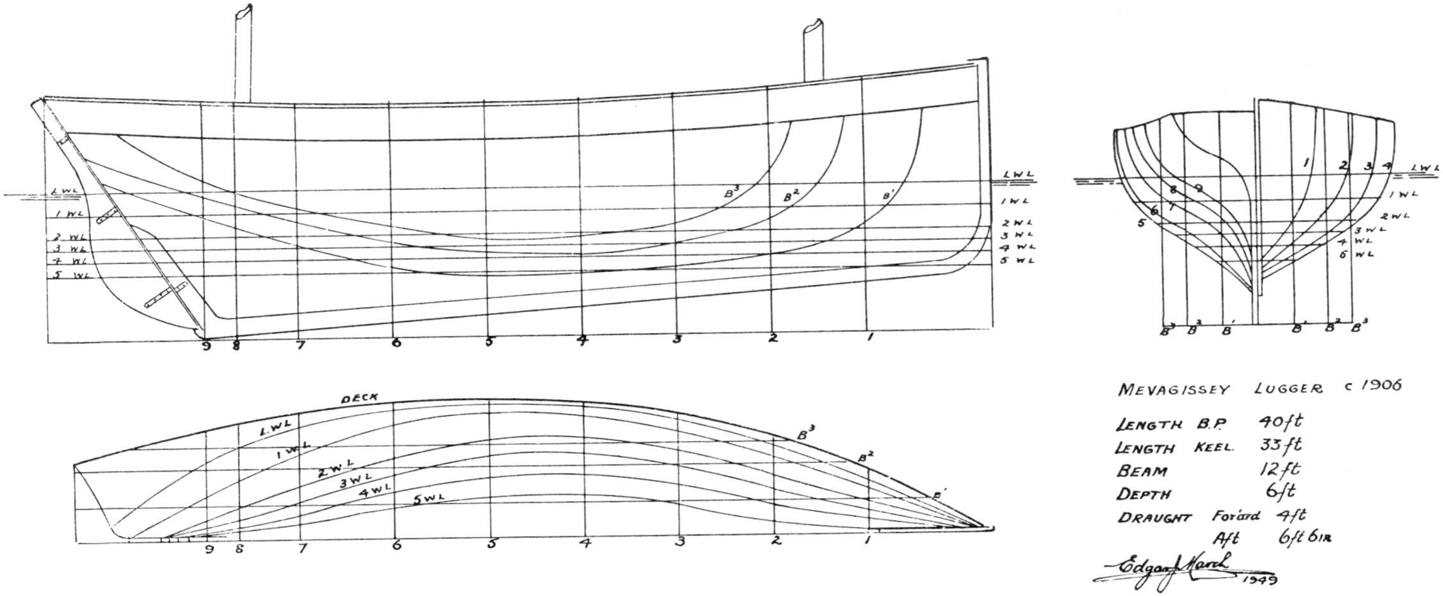

PLAN 6

Mevagissey Lugger, c. 1906

PLAN 6

Mévagissey Lugger, c. 1906

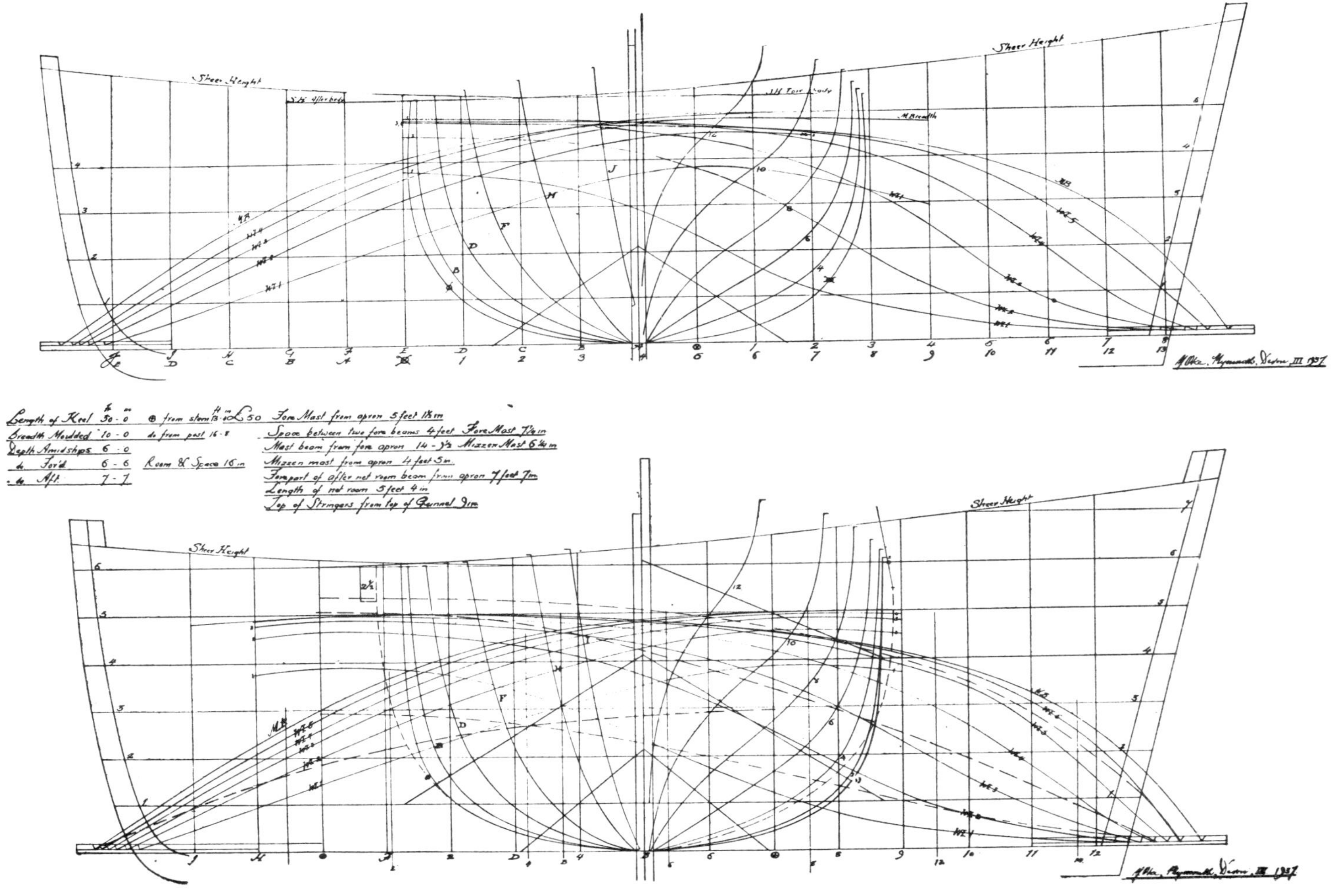

PLAN 7
West Cornish Pilchard Boats, c. 1865

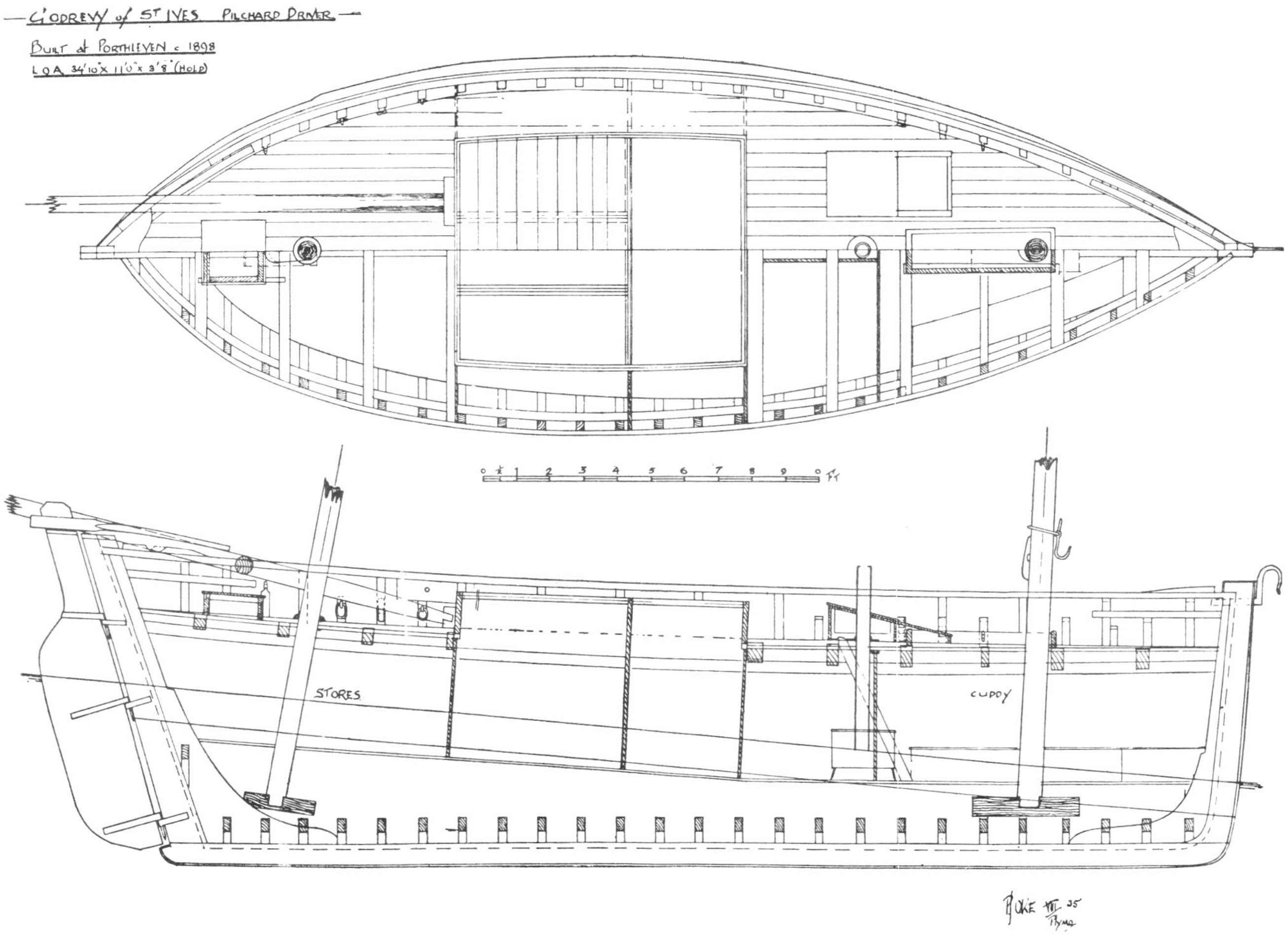

PLAN 8
St. Ives Pilchard Boat, c. 1898

PLAN 8

St. Ives Pilchard Boat, c. 1898

PLAN 8
St. Ives Pilchard Boat, c. 1898

PLAN 9

Mount's Bay Pilchard Boat, c. 1902

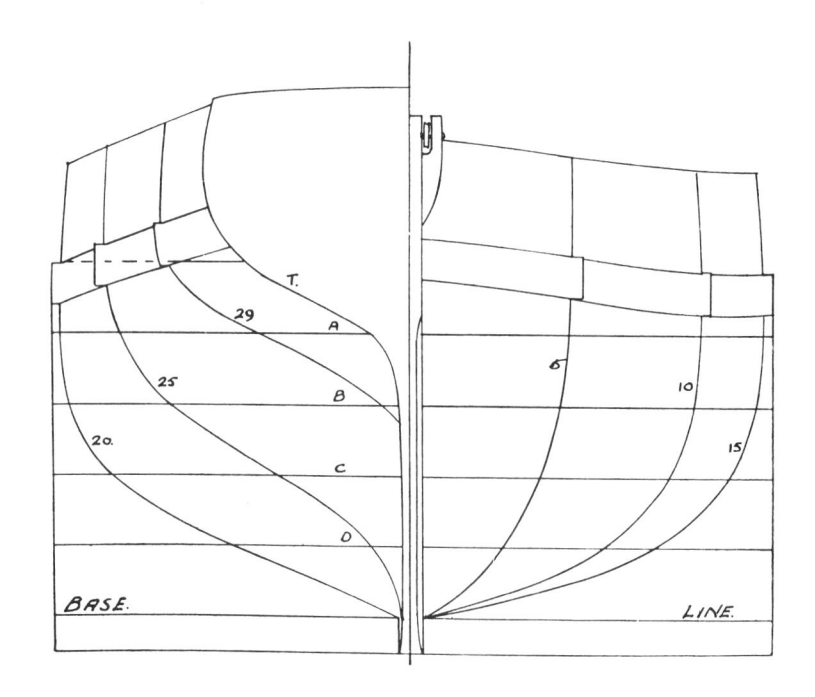

PLAN 9
Mount's Bay Pilchard Boat, c. 1902

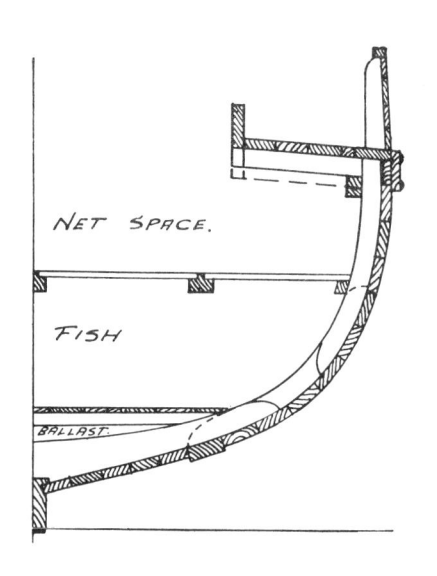

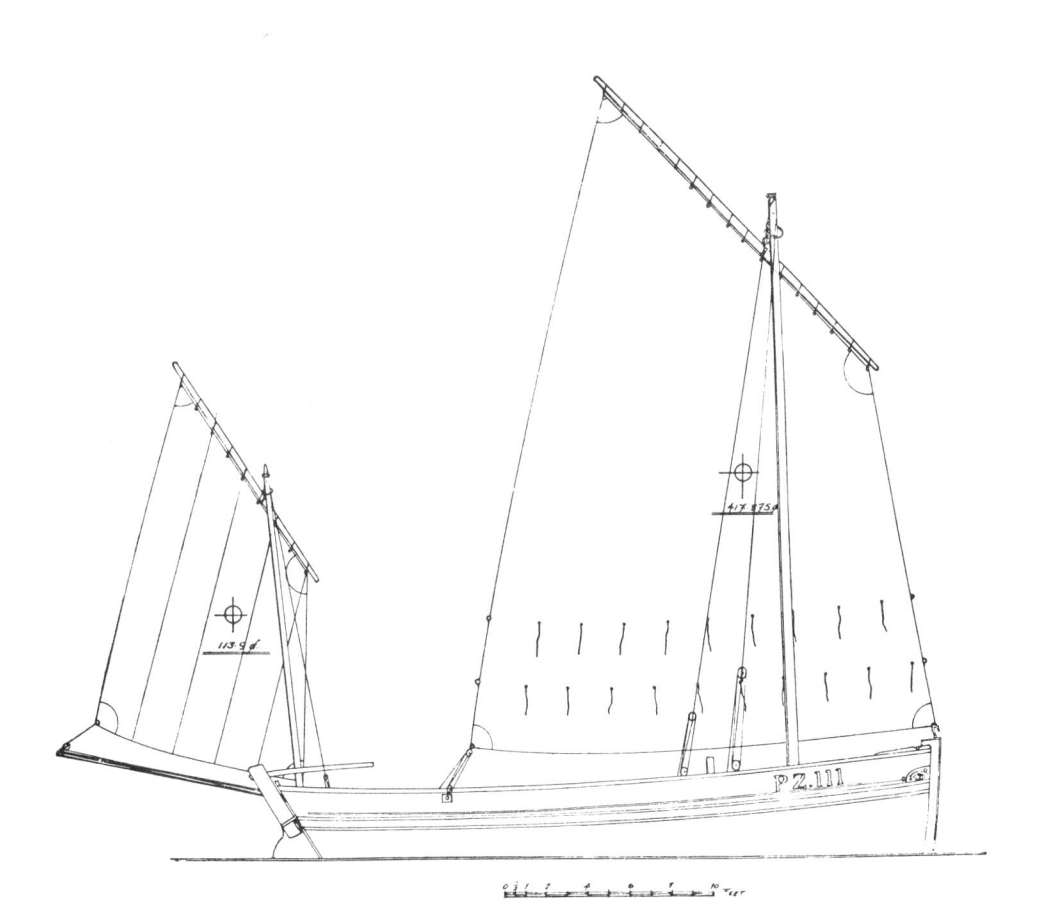

PLAN 9
Mount's Bay Pilchard Boat, c. 1902

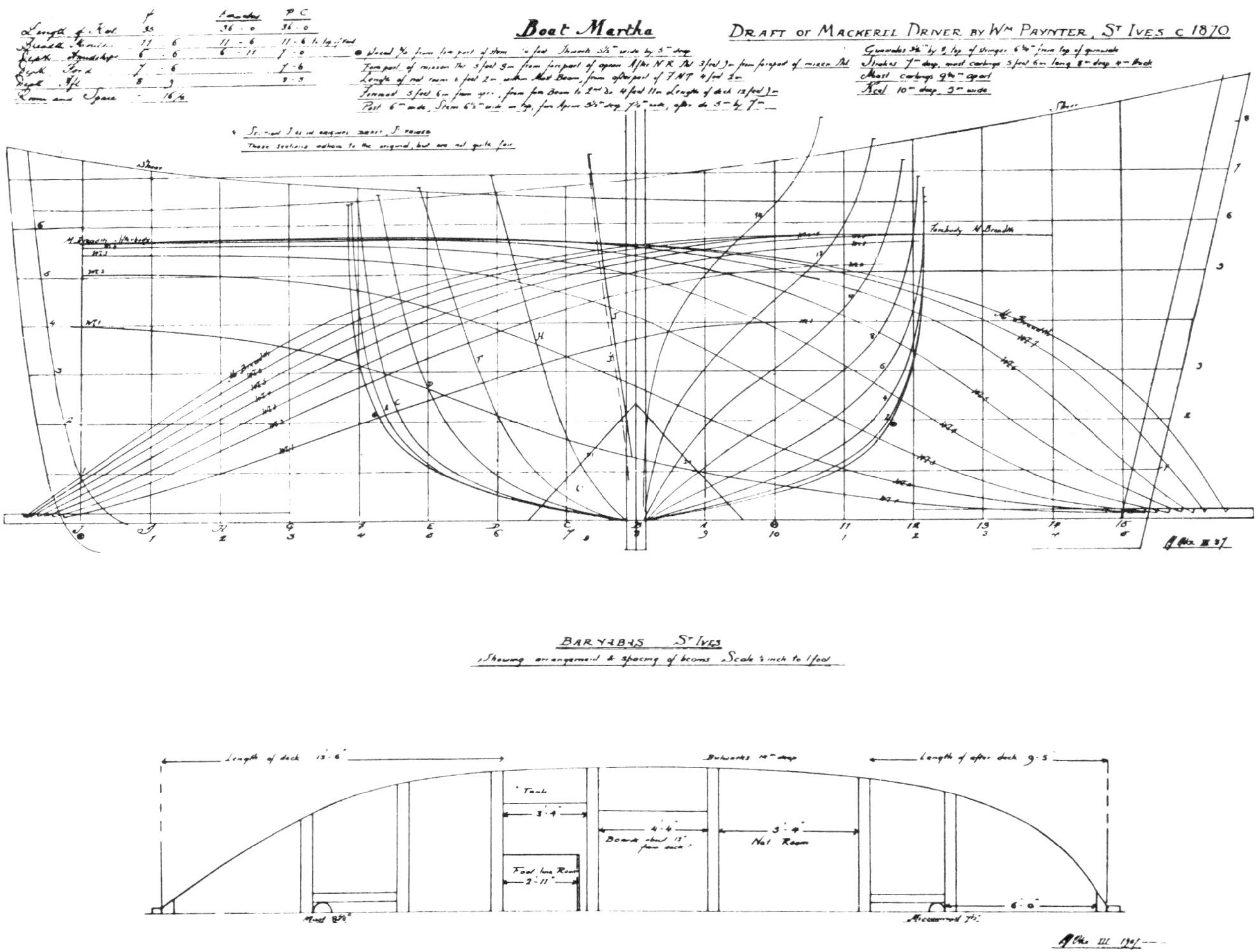

PLAN 10

St. Ives Mackerel Driver, c. 1870

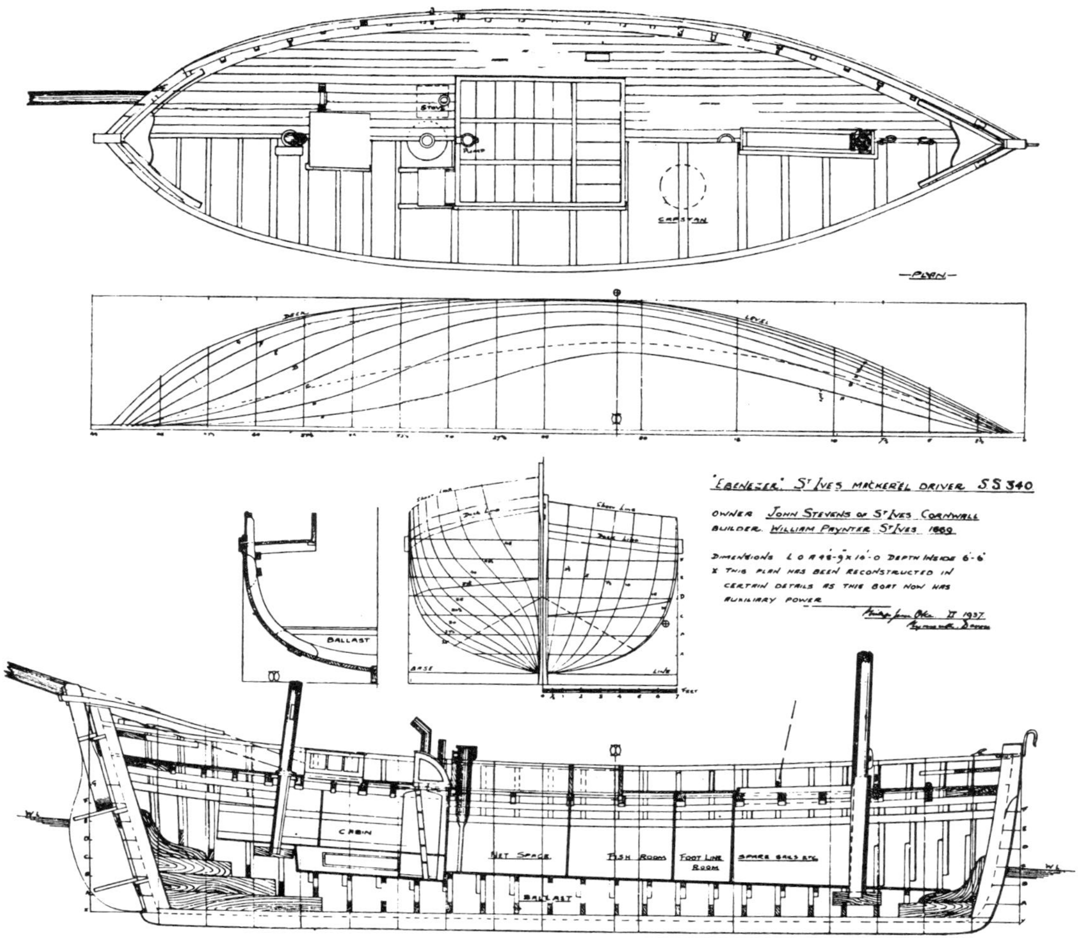

PLAN 11

St. Ives Mackerel Driver, c. 1869

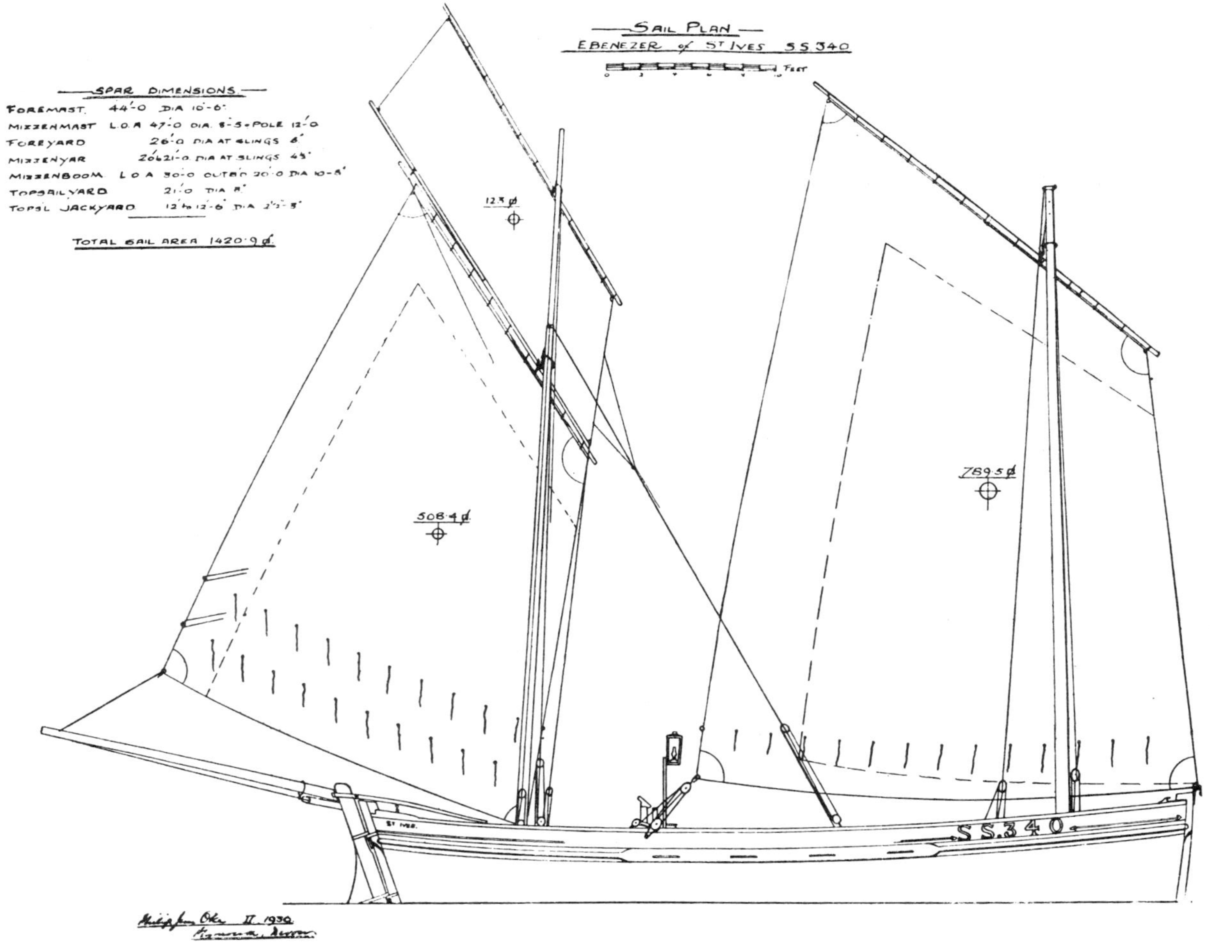

PLAN 11

St. Ives Mackerel Driver, c. 1869

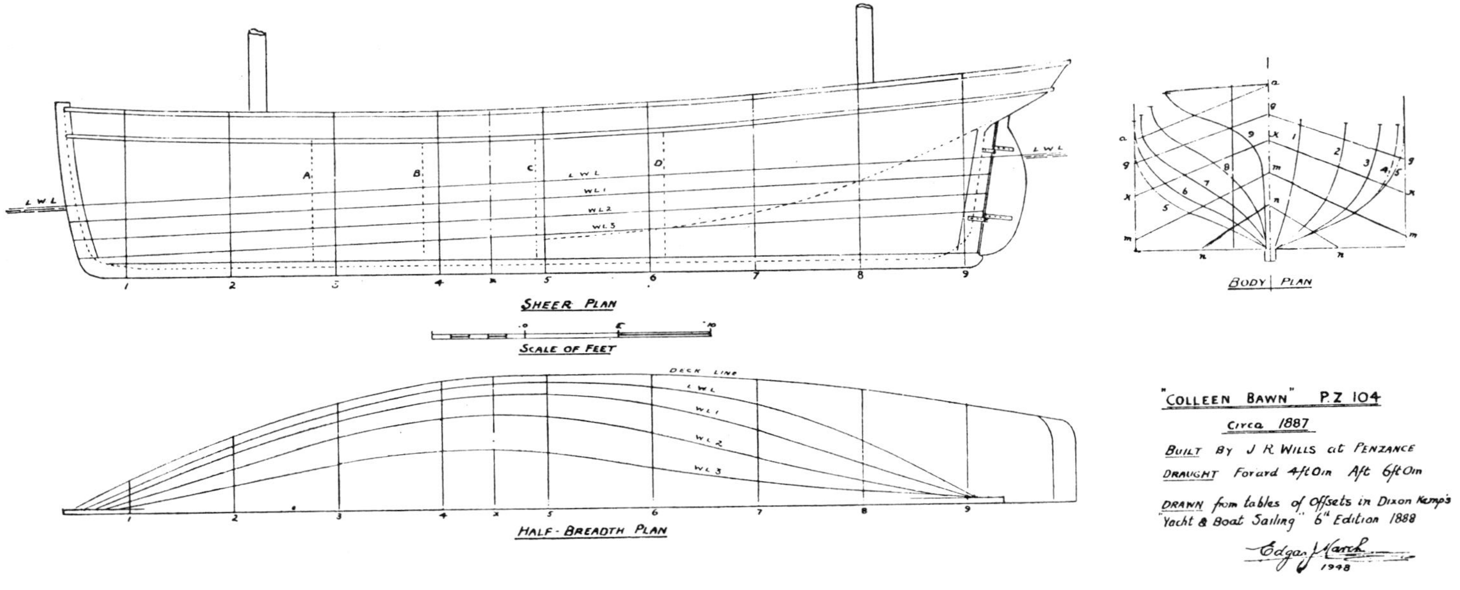

PLAN 12

Mount's Bay Counter-Sterned Mackerel Driver, c. 1887

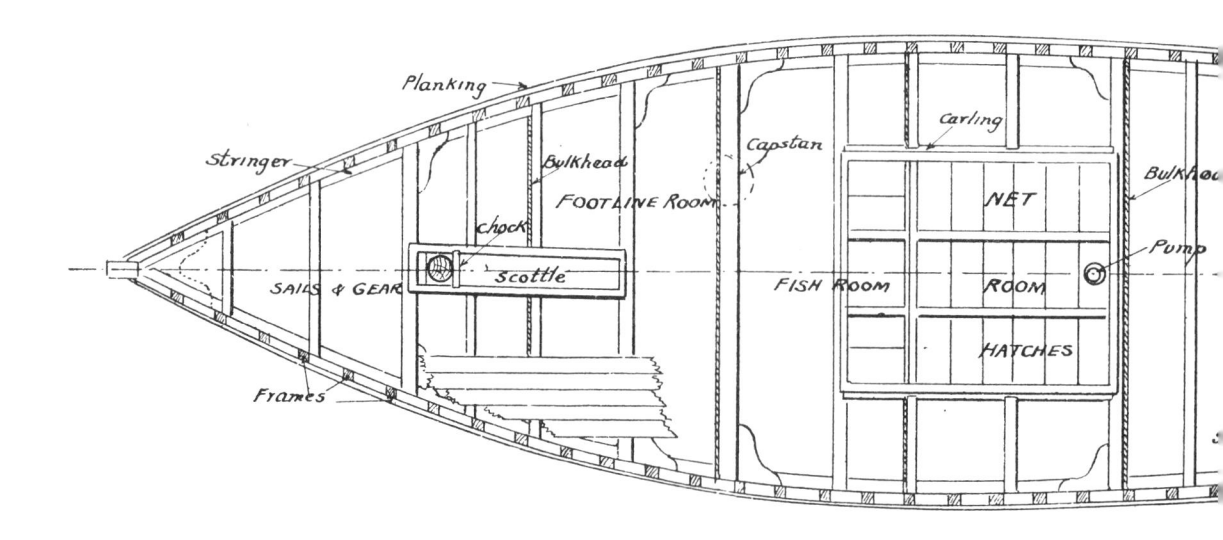

DECK FRAMING

PLAN 12

Mount's Bay Counter-Ster

324

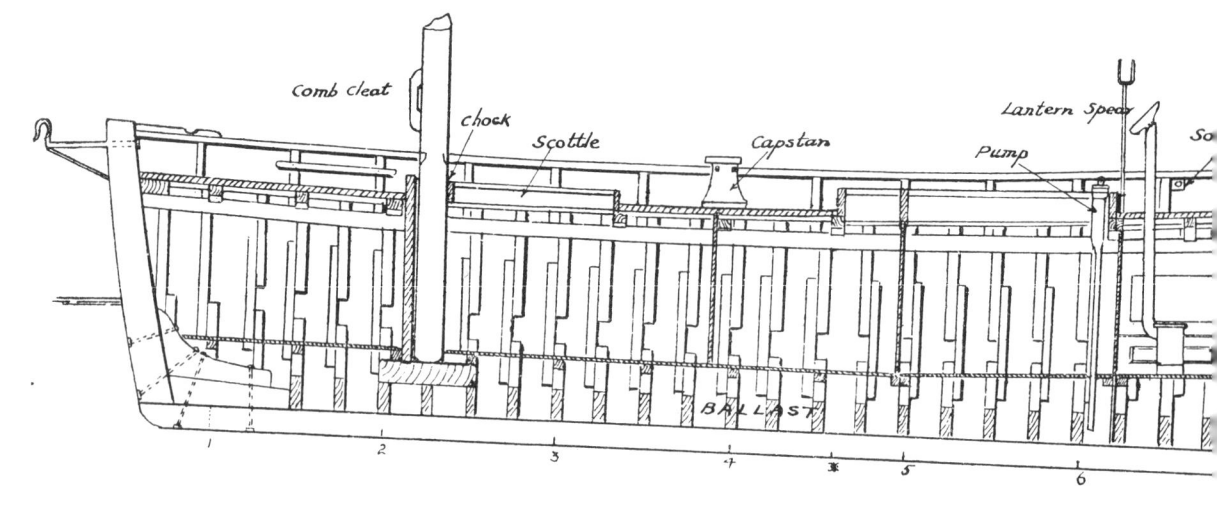

# MOUNTS BAY LUGGER
## With Counter Stern

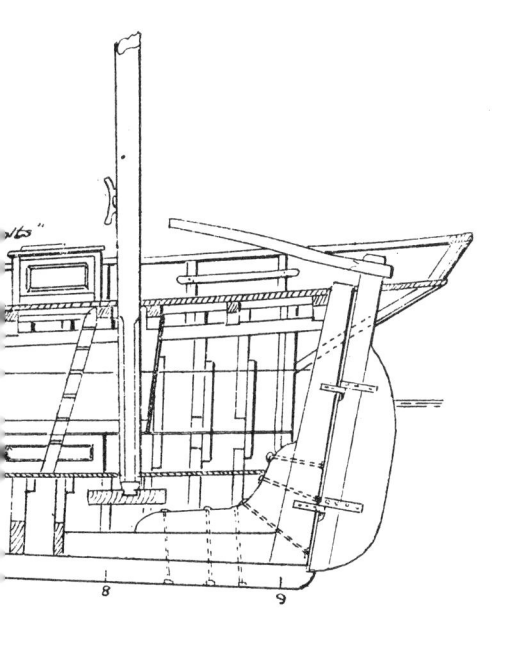

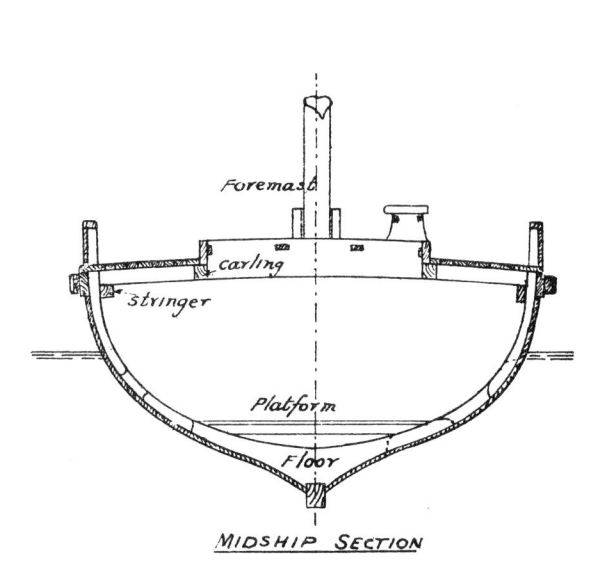

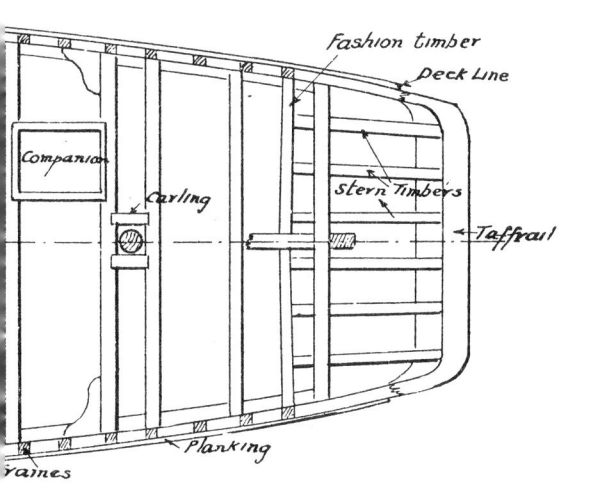

MIDSHIP SECTION

"COLLEEN BAWN"   P.Z. 104.

| | |
|---|---|
| L.B.P | 51ft 0in |
| LENGTH KEEL | 48ft 0in |
| BEAM | 14ft 10in |
| DISPLACEMENT | 36 TONS |
| BALLAST | 14 TONS |

SIZE OF TIMBERS
KEEL   9in by 6¼in
FRAMES (sided)   4in
ROOM & SPACE   1ft 5in
PLANKING   1½in

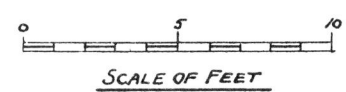

SCALE OF FEET

Edgar March
1948

Mackerel Driver, c. 1887

"COLLEEN BAWN" PZ 104

SPAR DIMENSIONS
FOREMAST  Deck to Sheave  37 ft 6 in   DIA 11 in. to 6½ in.
MIZZEN MAST      "           29 ft 0 m   DIA 10½ in. to 6½ in.
MIZZEN POLE  To halyard Sheave 8 ft 6 in  DIA 6 in. to 4 in.
OUTRIGGER      (outside)     20 ft
FOREYARD   3 ft  Dia. at slings  6 in.
MIZZEN YARD  26 ft    "    "    5 in.
MIZZEN TOPSAIL YARD  3 ft  Jenny Yard  8 ft

SAIL PLAN
FORE LUG   Luff 26 ft    Leech 46 ft
           Head 23 ft    Foot 34 ft
           Clew to weather earing 36 ft
           AREA 980 sq ft
MIZZEN LUG Luff 20 ft    Leech 41 ft
(as given by Head 24 ft   Foot 29 ft
Dixon Kemp) Clew to weather earing 36 ft
           AREA 730·9 ft
MIZZEN LUG To set as Second Forelug
           Luff 20 ft    Leech 35 ft
           Head 24 ft    Foot 28 ft

SCALE OF FEET

PLAN 12
Mount's Bay Counter-Sterned Mackerel Driver, c. 1887

PLAN 13
Mount's Bay Mackerel Driver, c. 1897

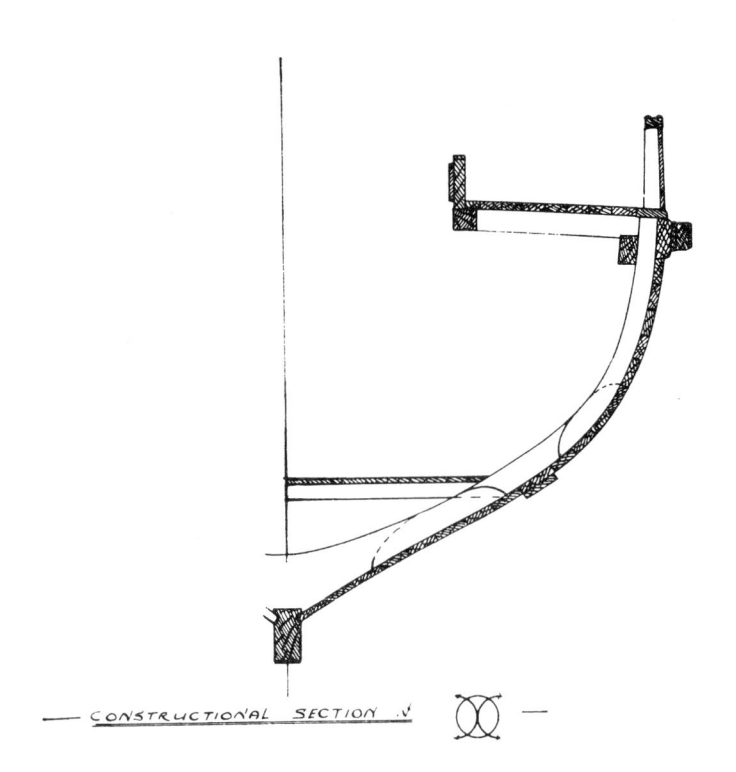

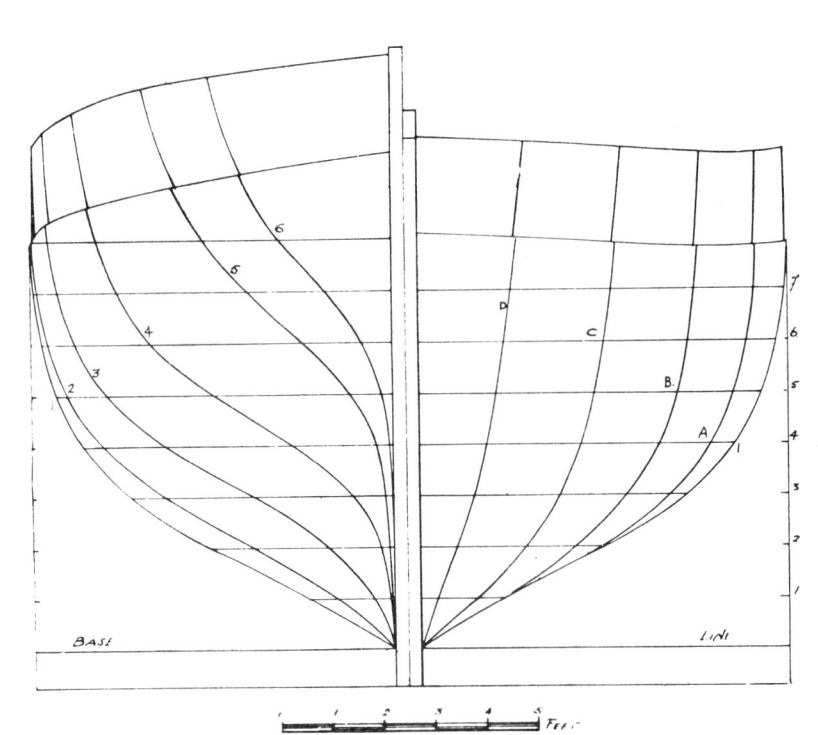

PLAN 13
Mount's Bay Mackerel Driver, c. 1897

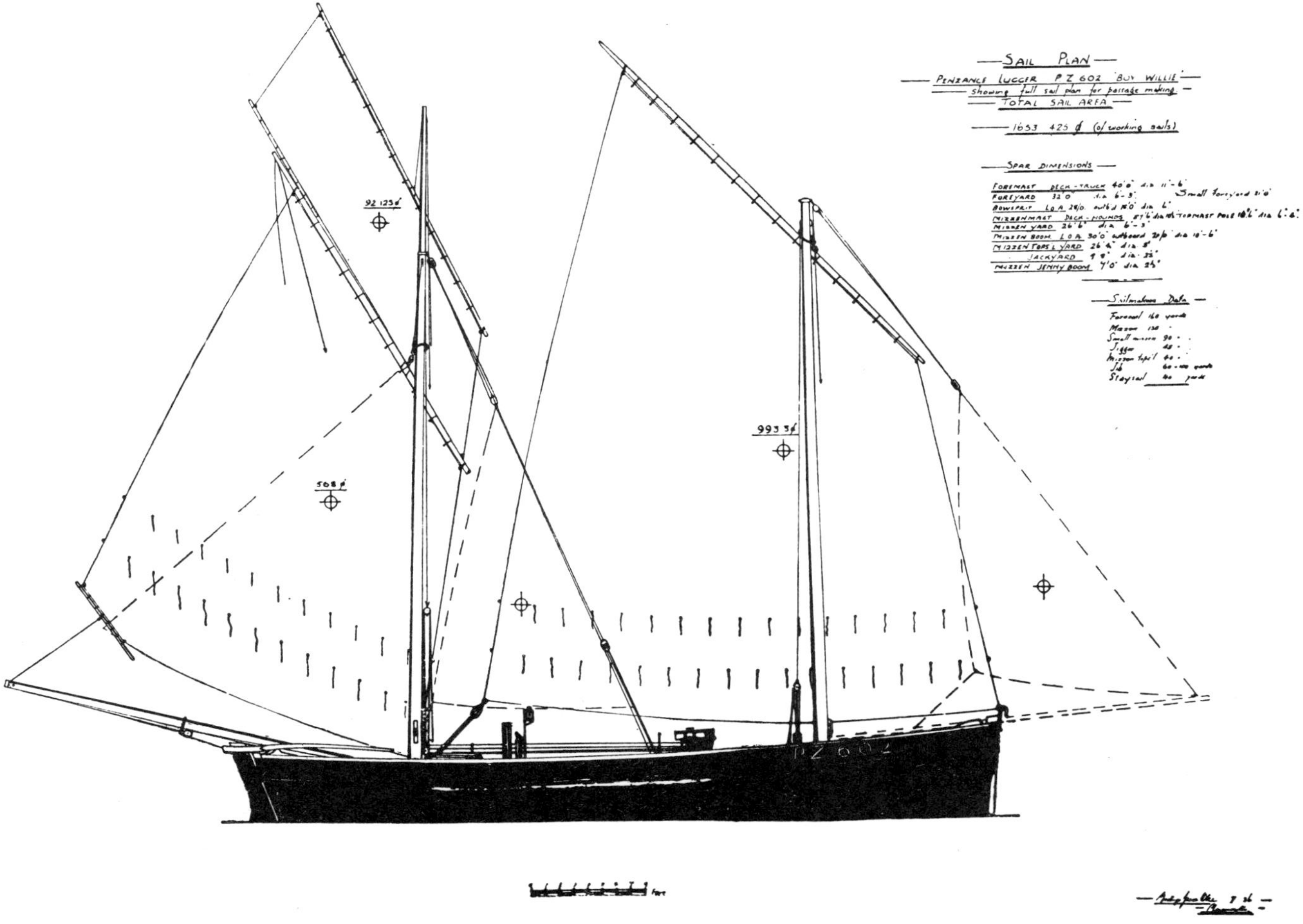

PLAN 13
Mount's Bay Mackerel Driver, c. 1897

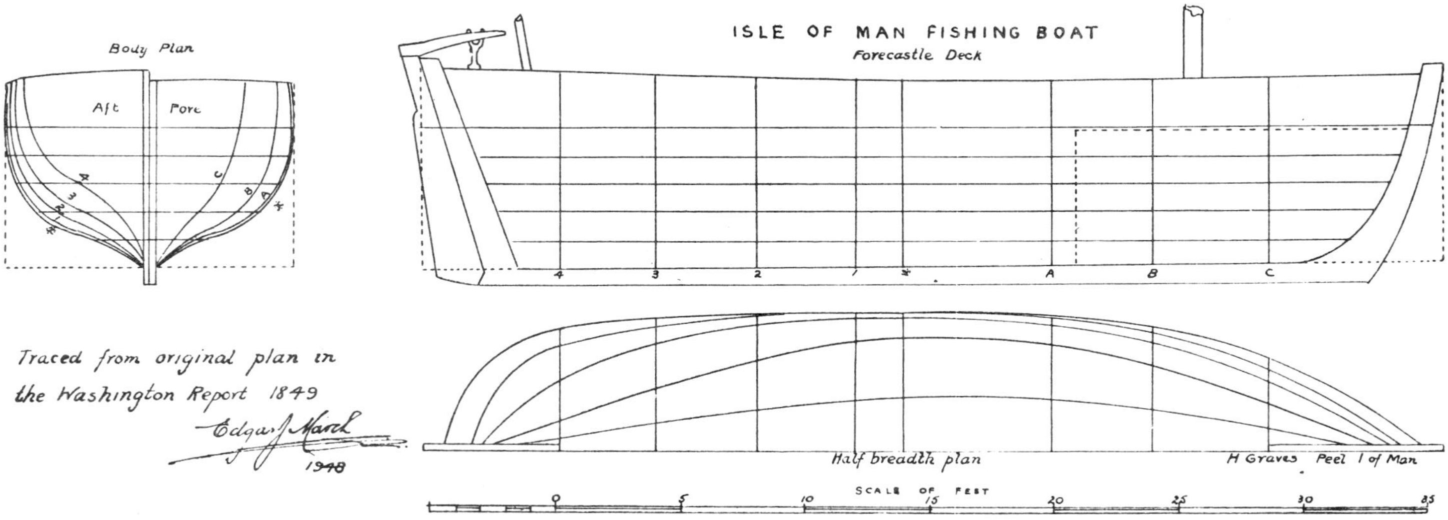

ISLE OF MAN FISHING BOAT
Forecastle Deck

Half breadth plan

SCALE OF FEET

H Graves. Peel I of Man

Body Plan
Fore
Aft

Traced from original plan in
the Washington Report 1849
Edgar March
1948

PLAN 14
Manx 'Lugger', c. 1848

PLAN 15
Manx Nickey, c. 1881

PLAN 15
Manx Nickey, c. 1881

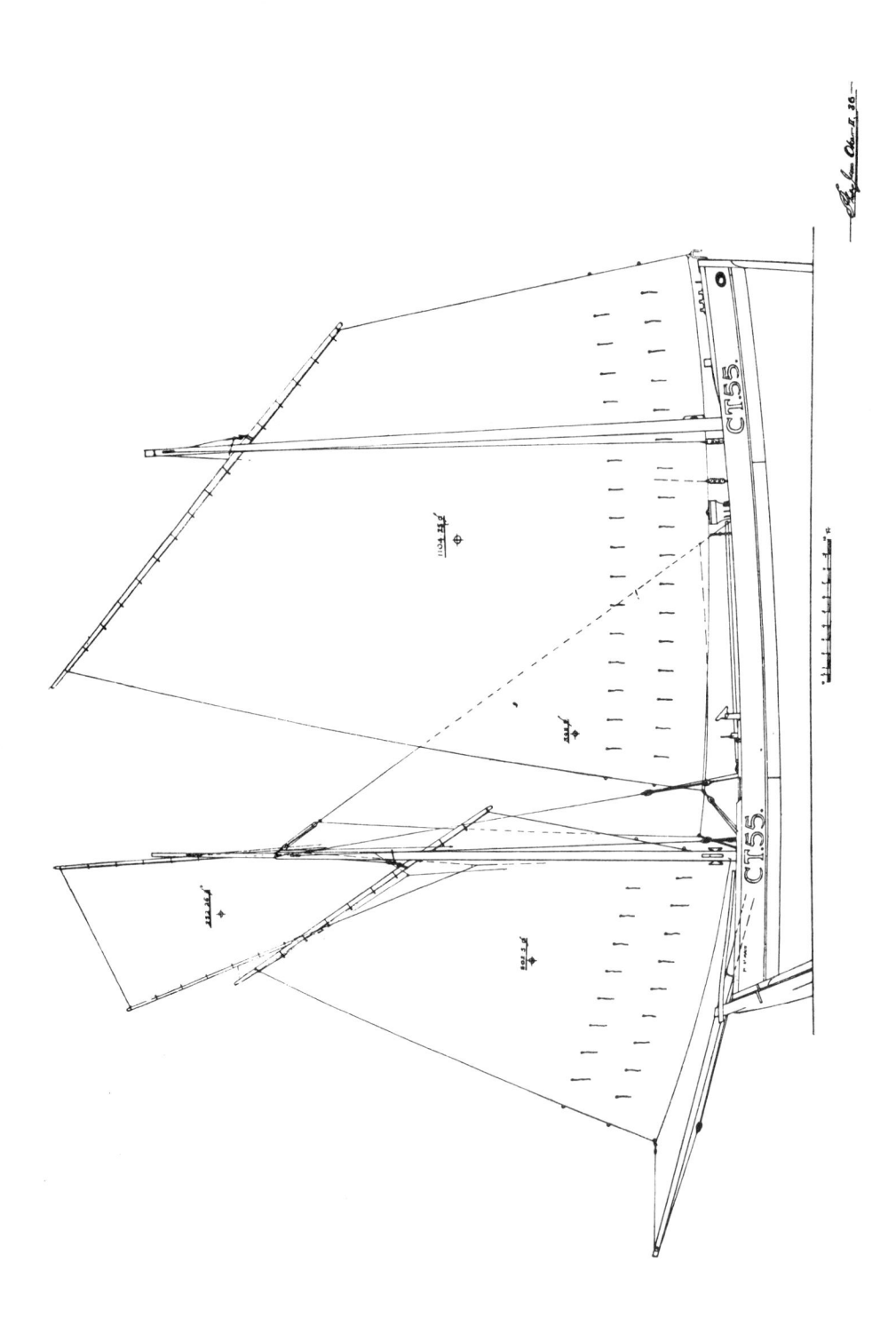

PLAN 16
Manx Nobby, c. 1901

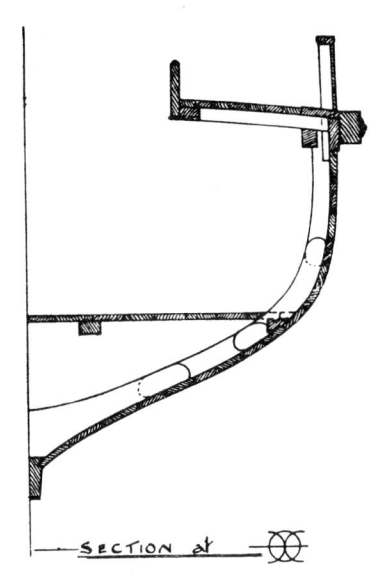

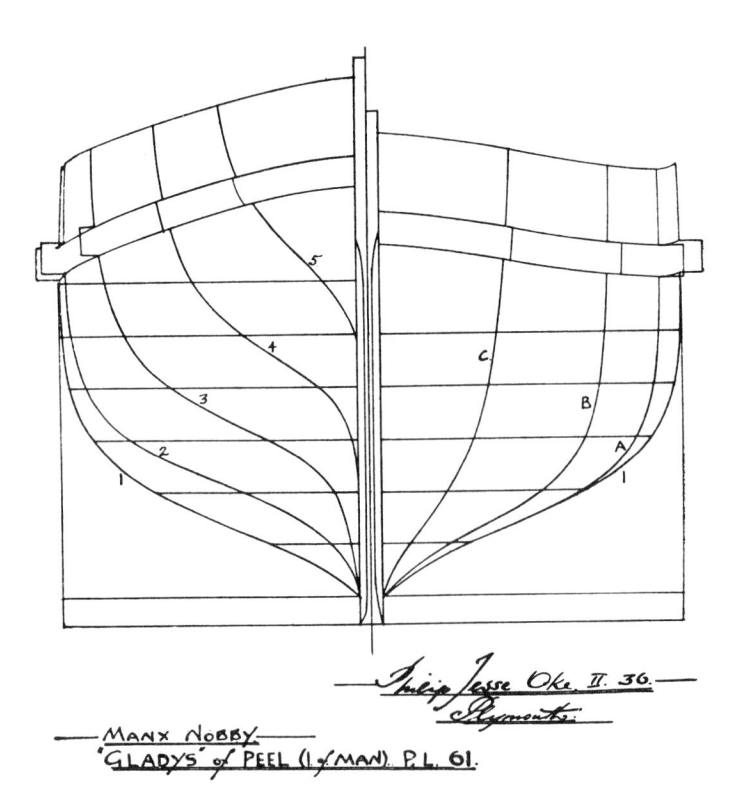

PLAN 16
Manx Nobby, c. 1901

PLAN 16
Manx Nobby, c. 1901

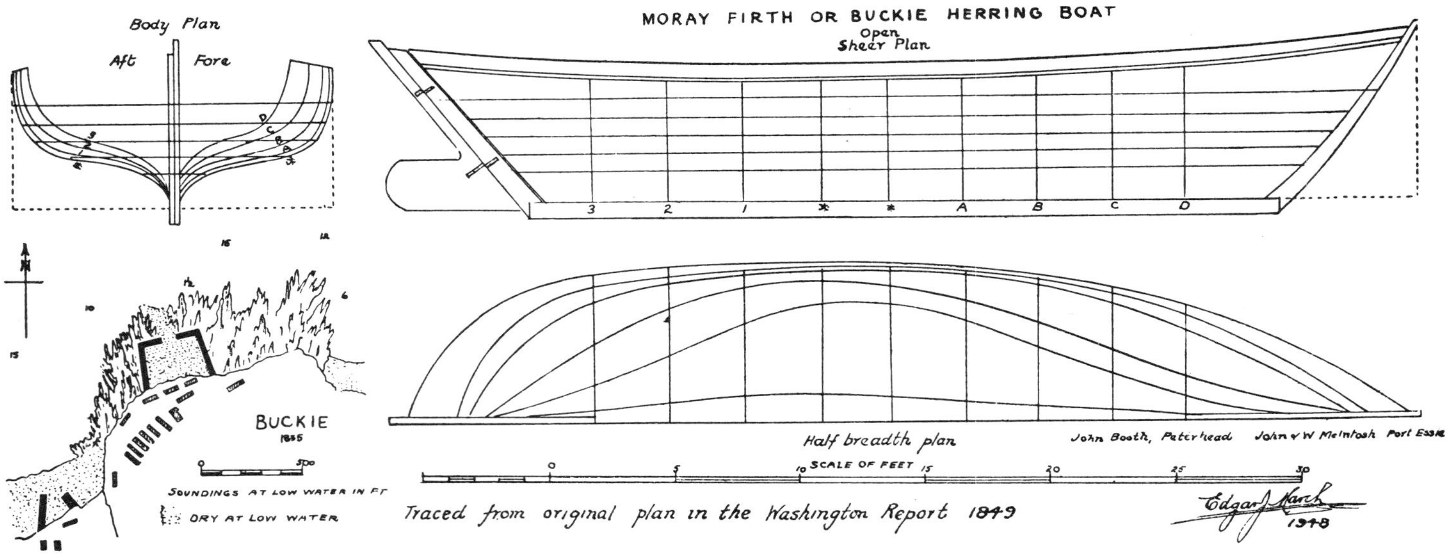

PLAN 17
Buckie Scaffie, c. 1848

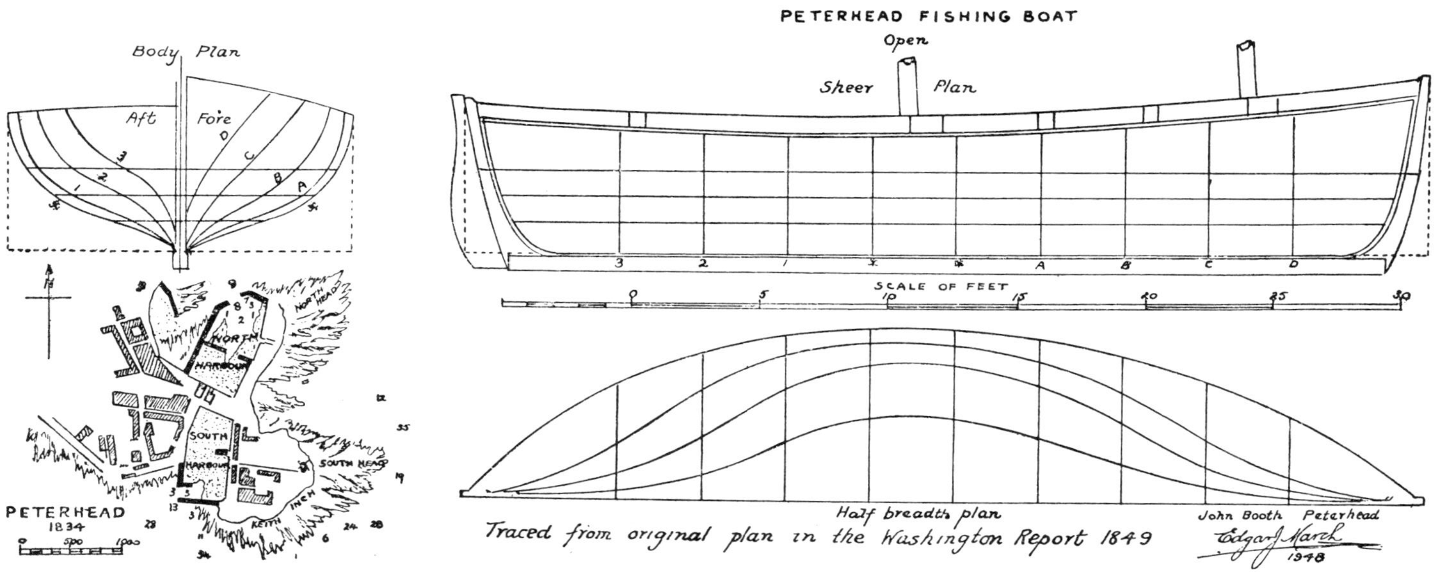

PLAN 18
Peterhead Fifie, c. 1848.

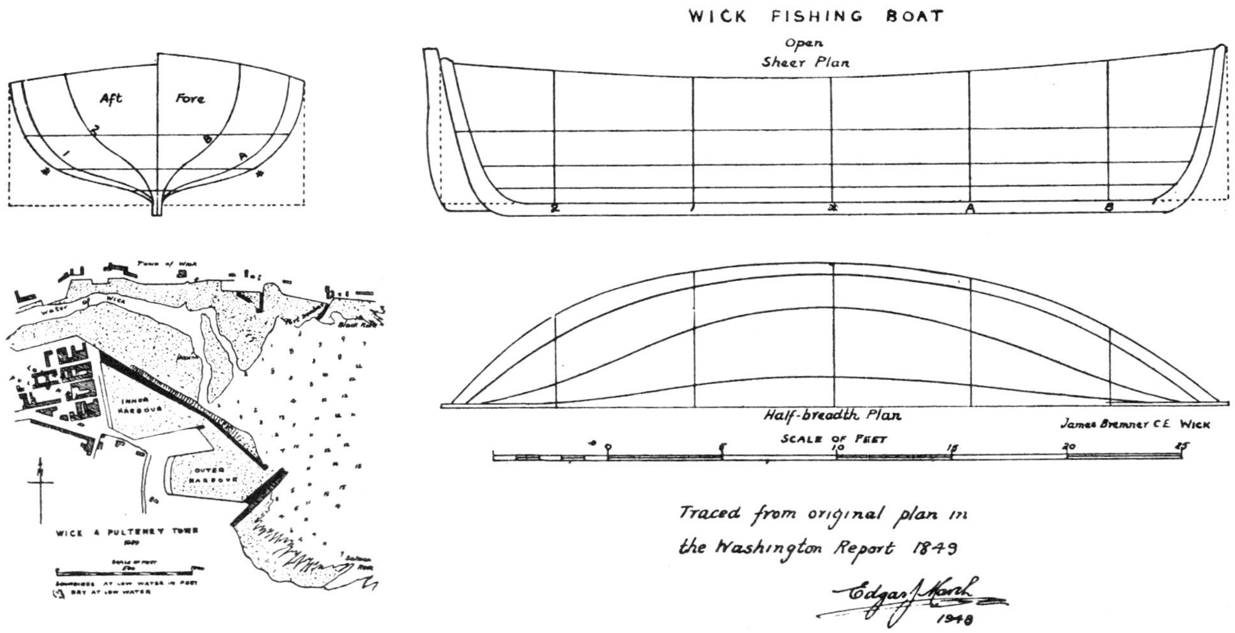

PLAN 19
Wick Boat, c. 1848

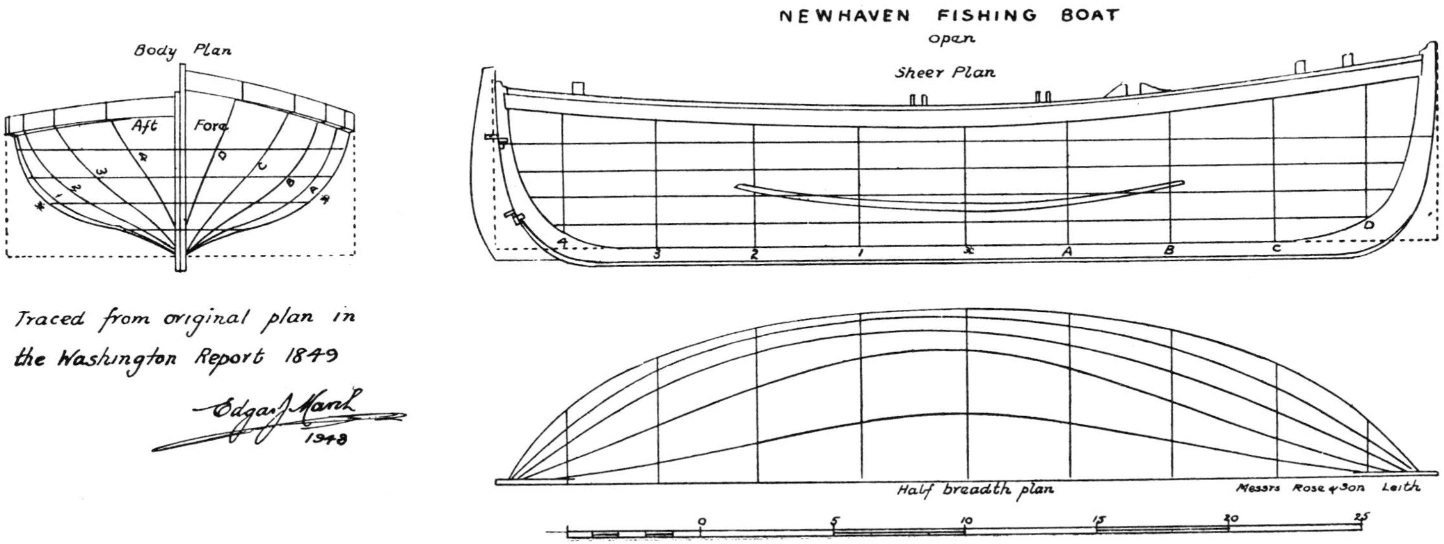

PLAN 20
Newhaven Fifie, c. 1848

PLAN 21
Scaffie Yawl, c. 1896

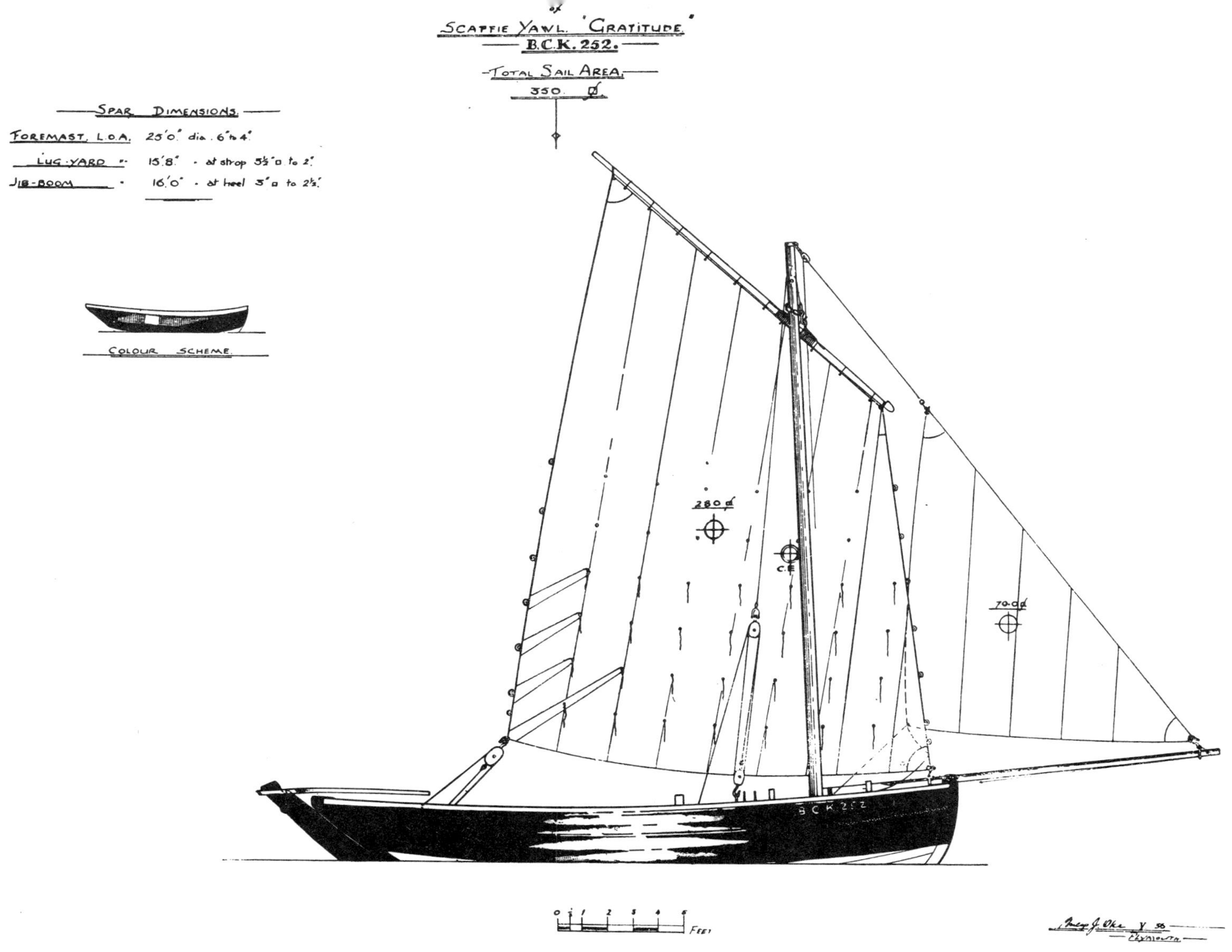

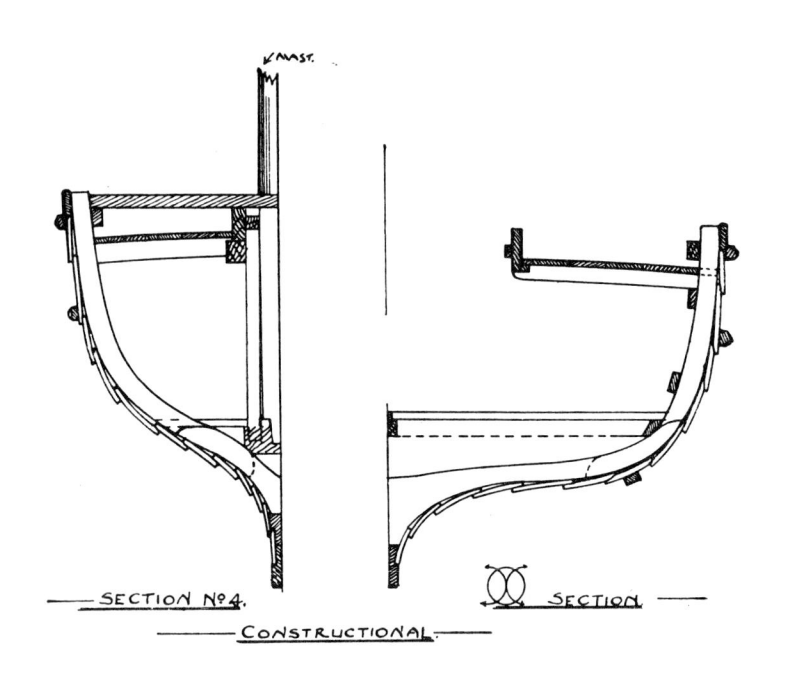

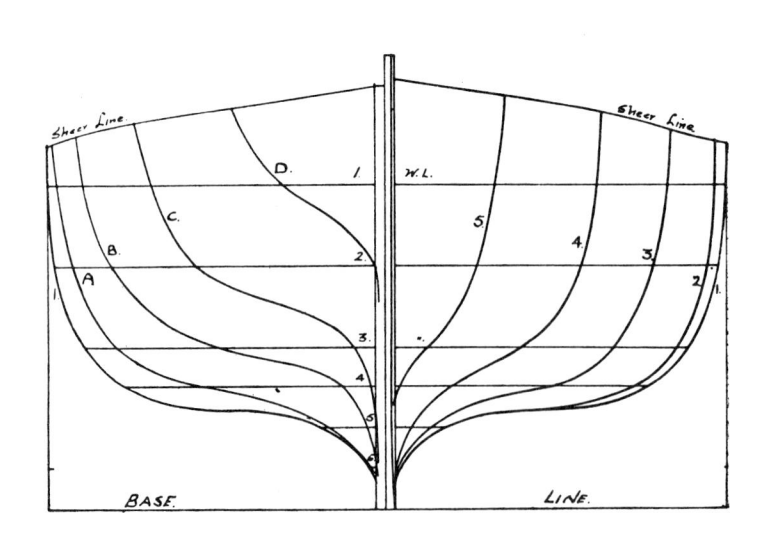

PLAN 21
Scaffie Yawl, c. 1896

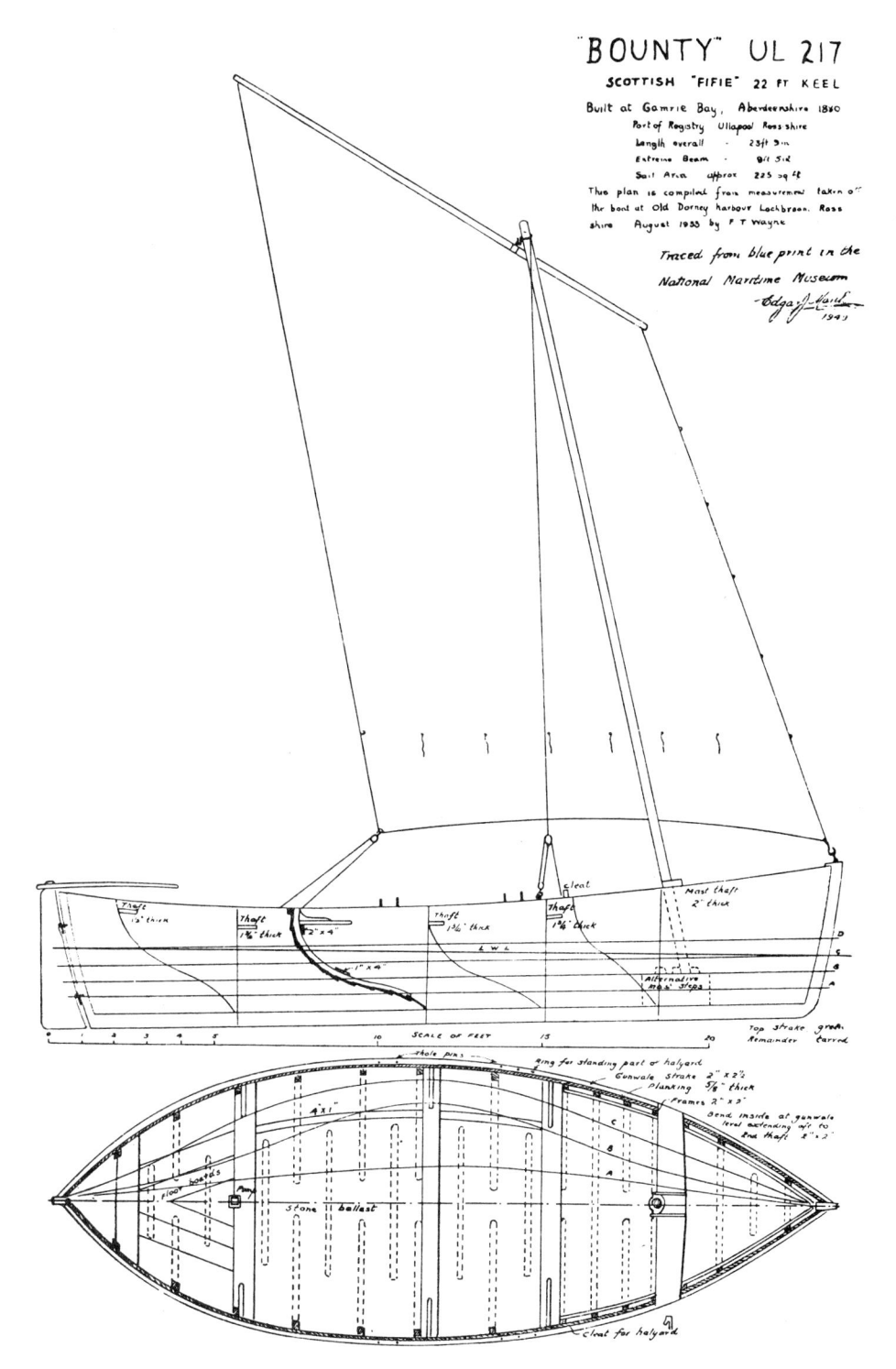

PLAN 22
Fifie Skiff, c. 1880.

343

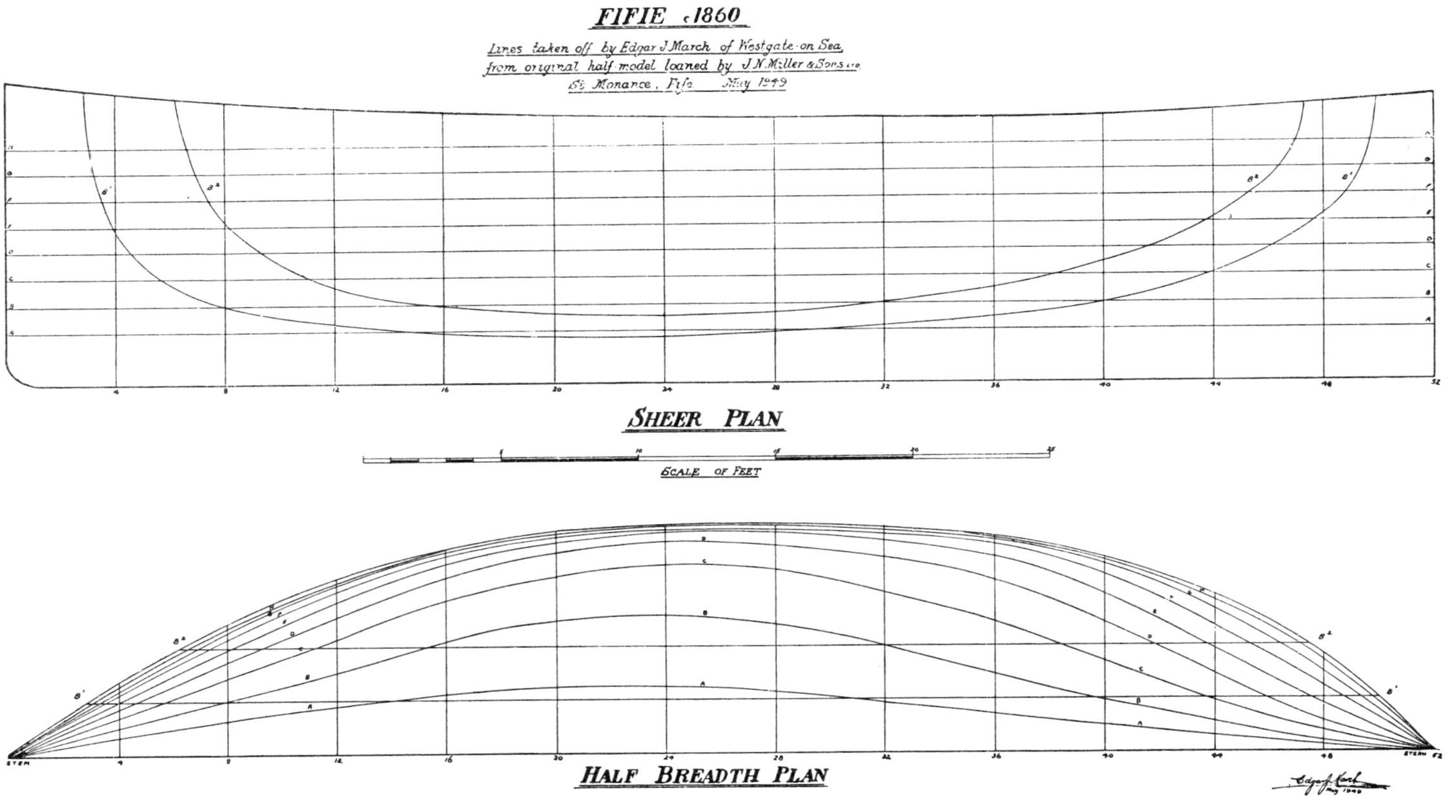

PLAN 23

St. Monance Fifie, c. 1860

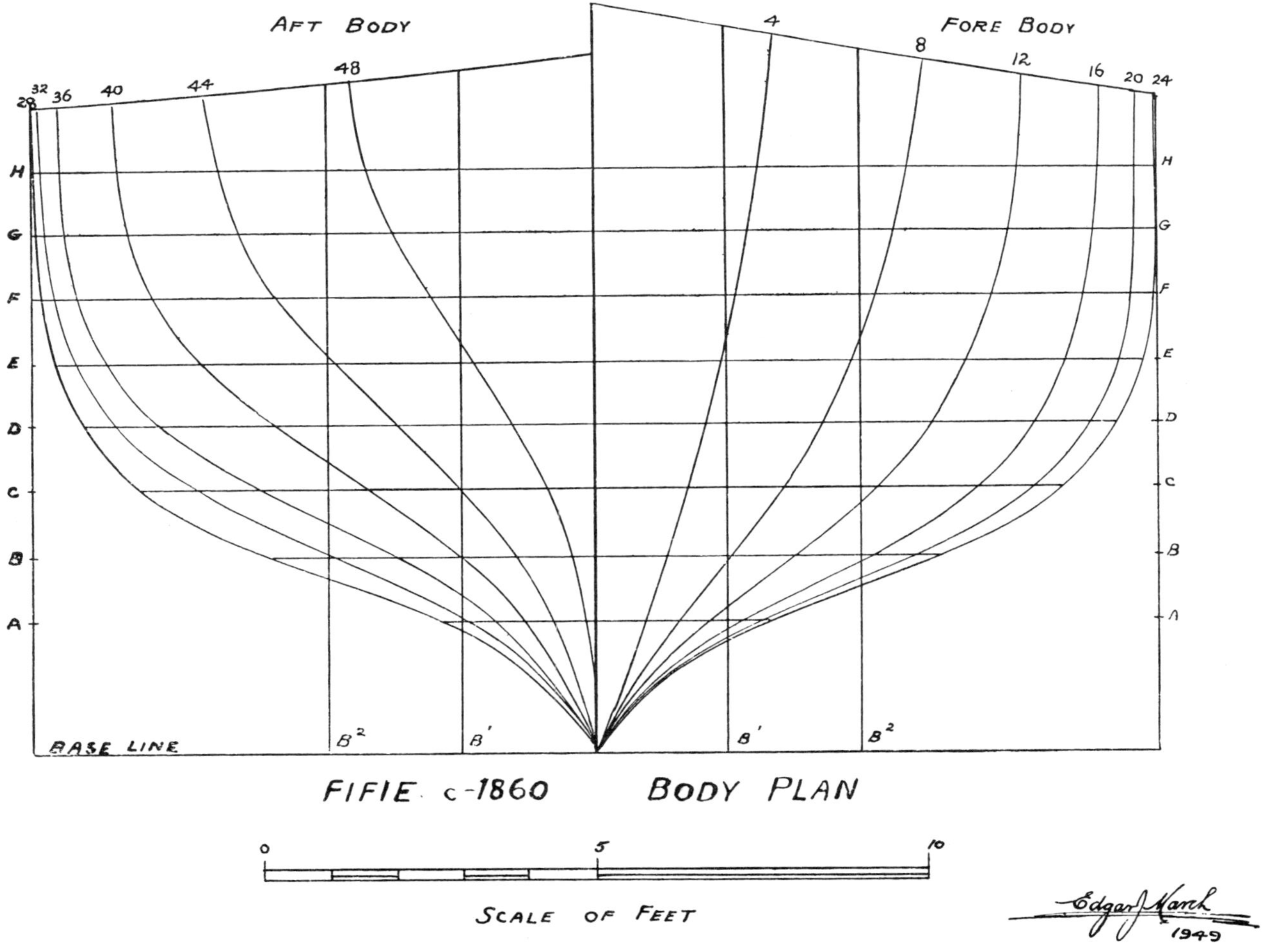

PLAN 23
St. Monance Fifie, c. 1860

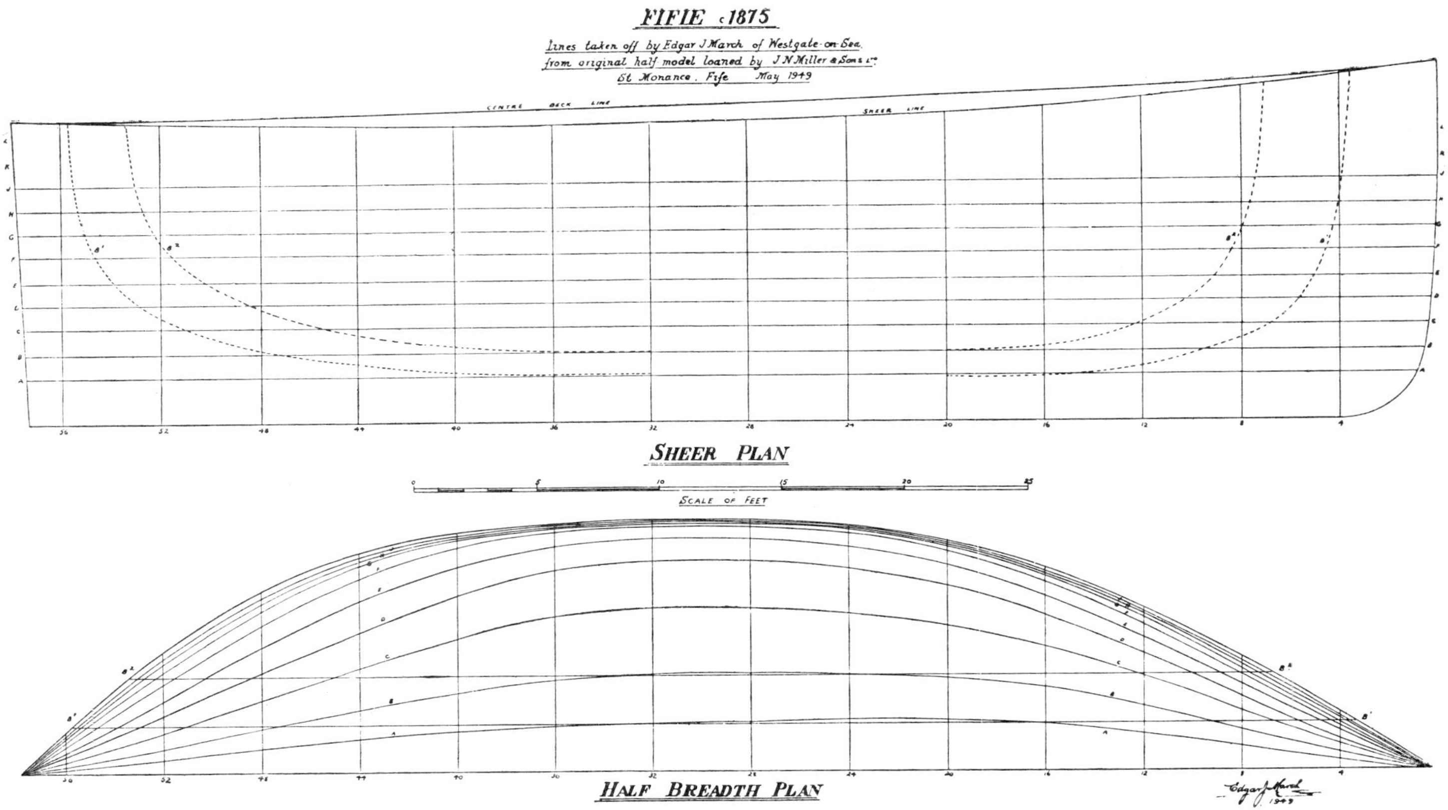

PLAN 24
St. Monance Fifie, c. 1875

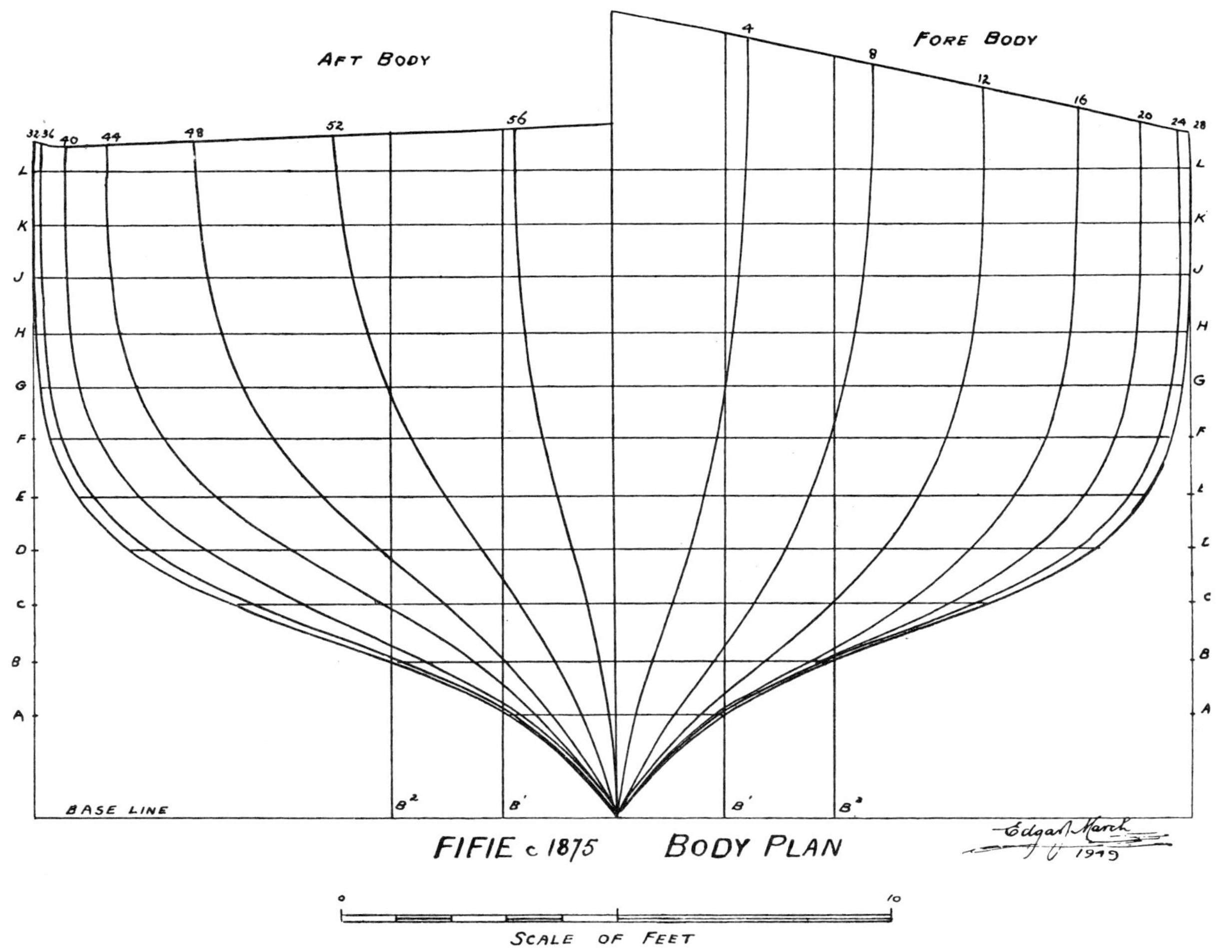

PLAN 24
St. Monance Fifie, c. 1875

"TRUE VINE" ML 20

Fifie built by Robertson Innes at
St Monance, Fife, 1905
LENGTH, over stems       71'-1½"
BEAM, inside gunwale     21'-6"
BEAM, extreme            22'-3"
DEPTH                    8'-0"
TONNAGE                  52 67

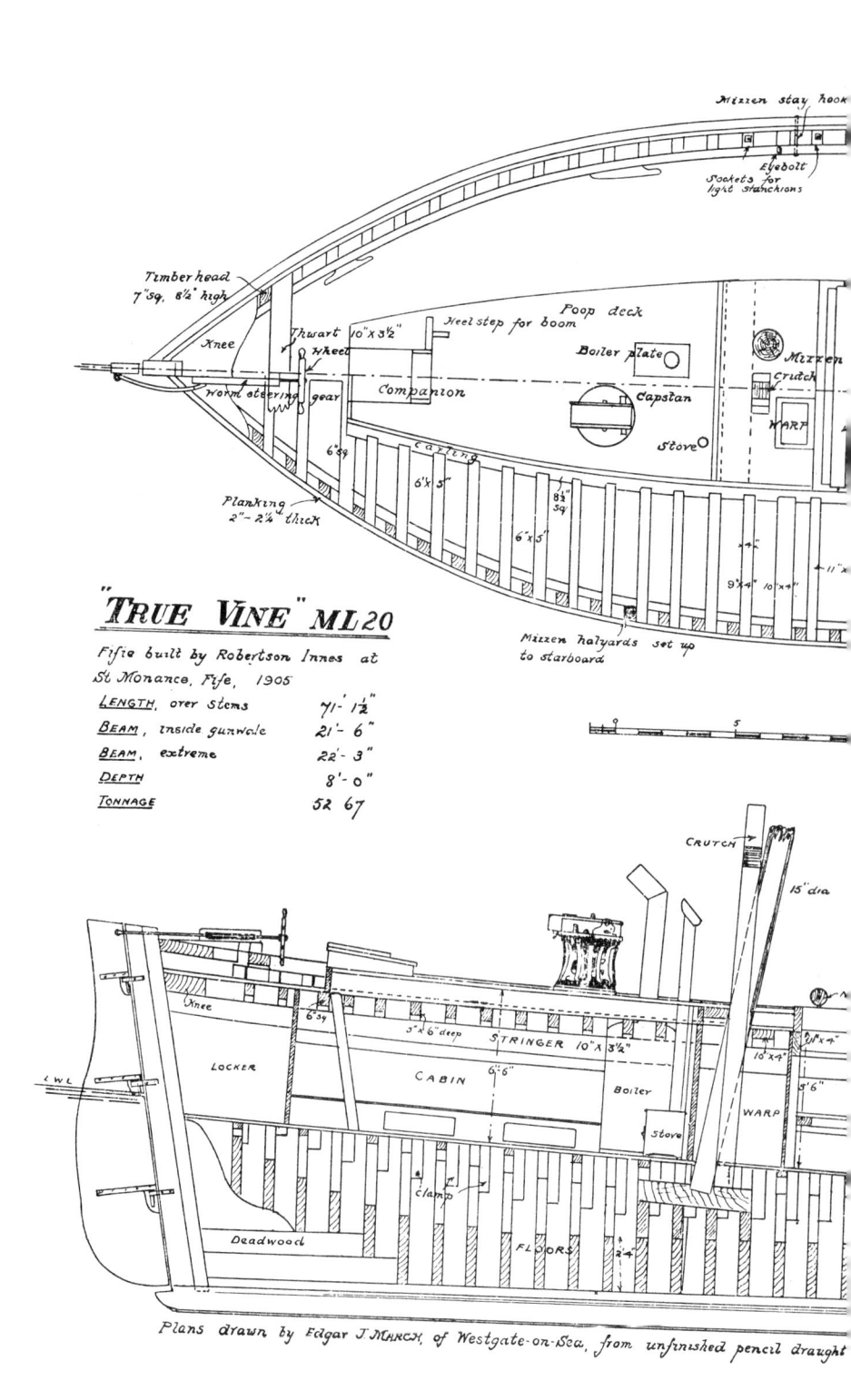

Plans drawn by Edgar J March, of Westgate-on-Sea, from unfinished pencil draught

St. Mona

PLAN 25

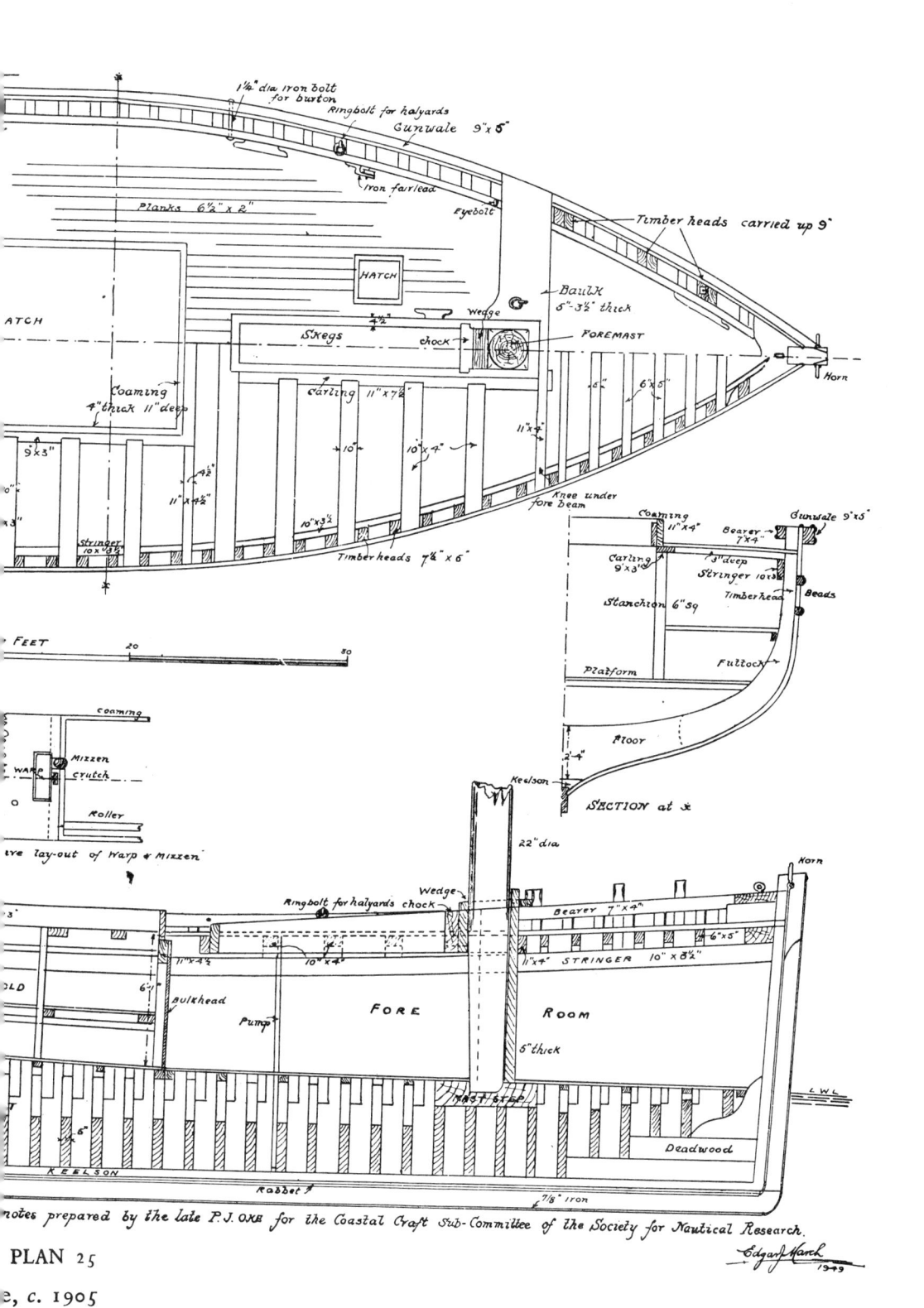

c. 1905

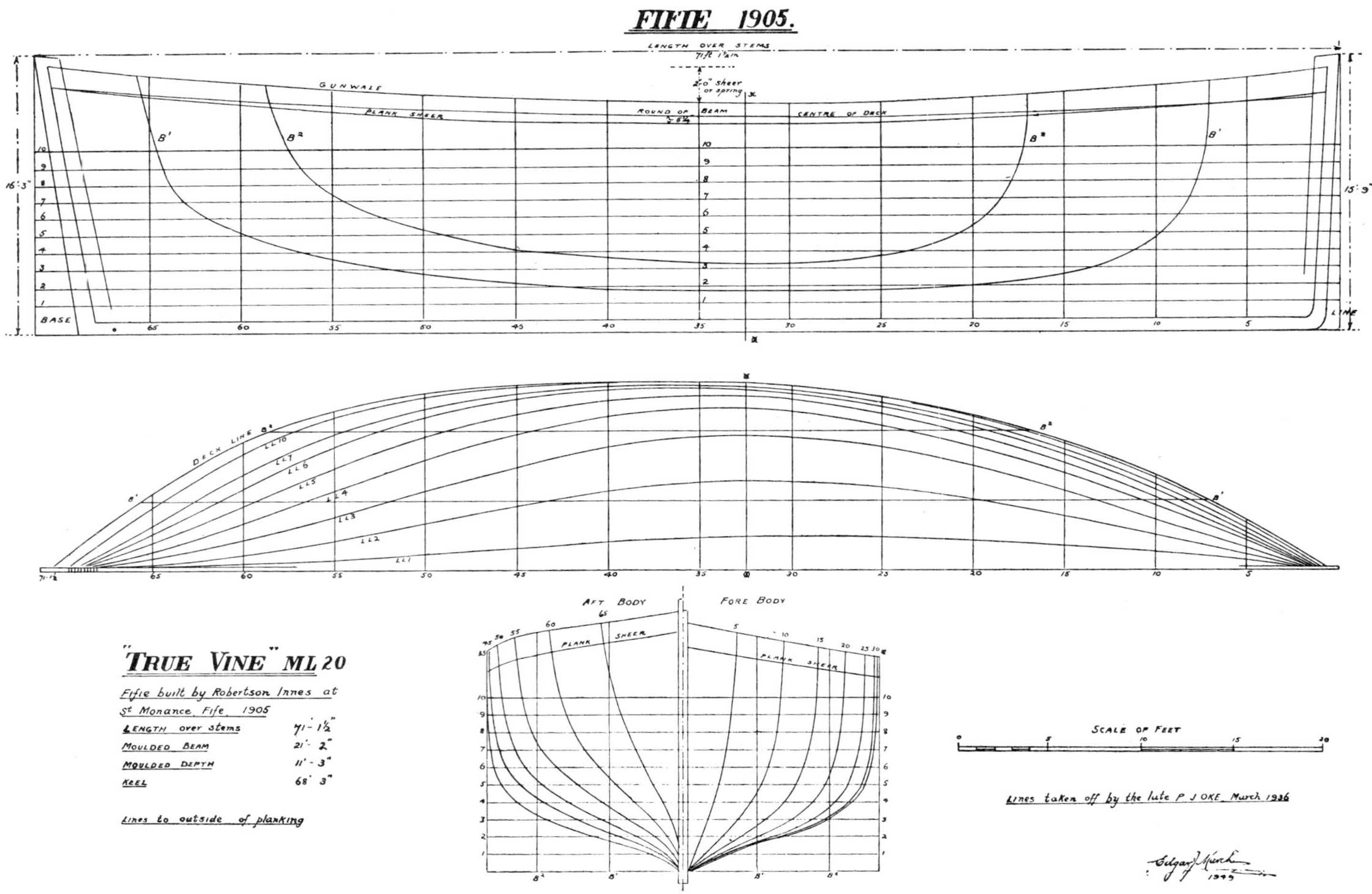

PLAN 25
St. Monance Fifie, c. 1905

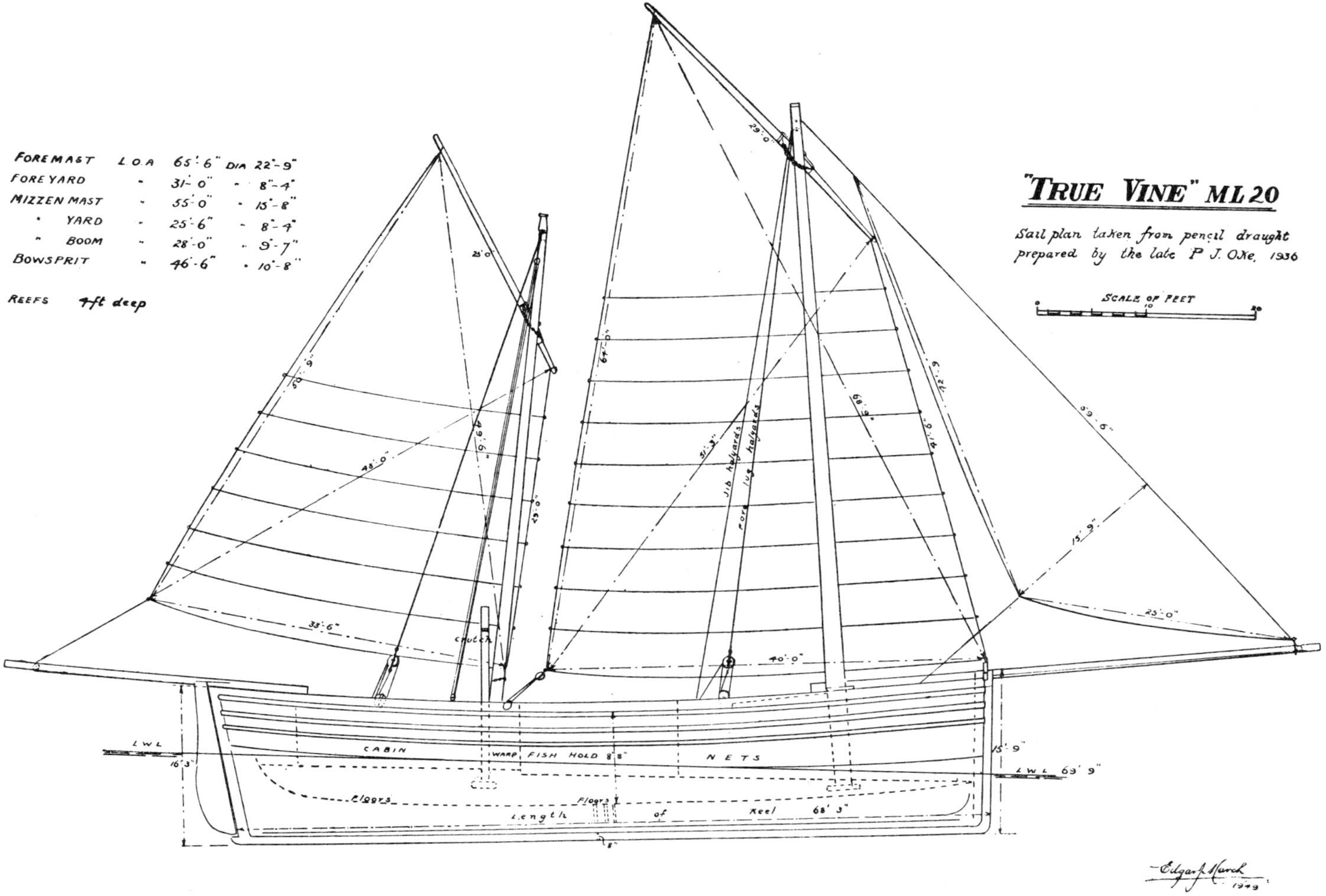

PLAN 25
St. Monance Fifie, c. 1905

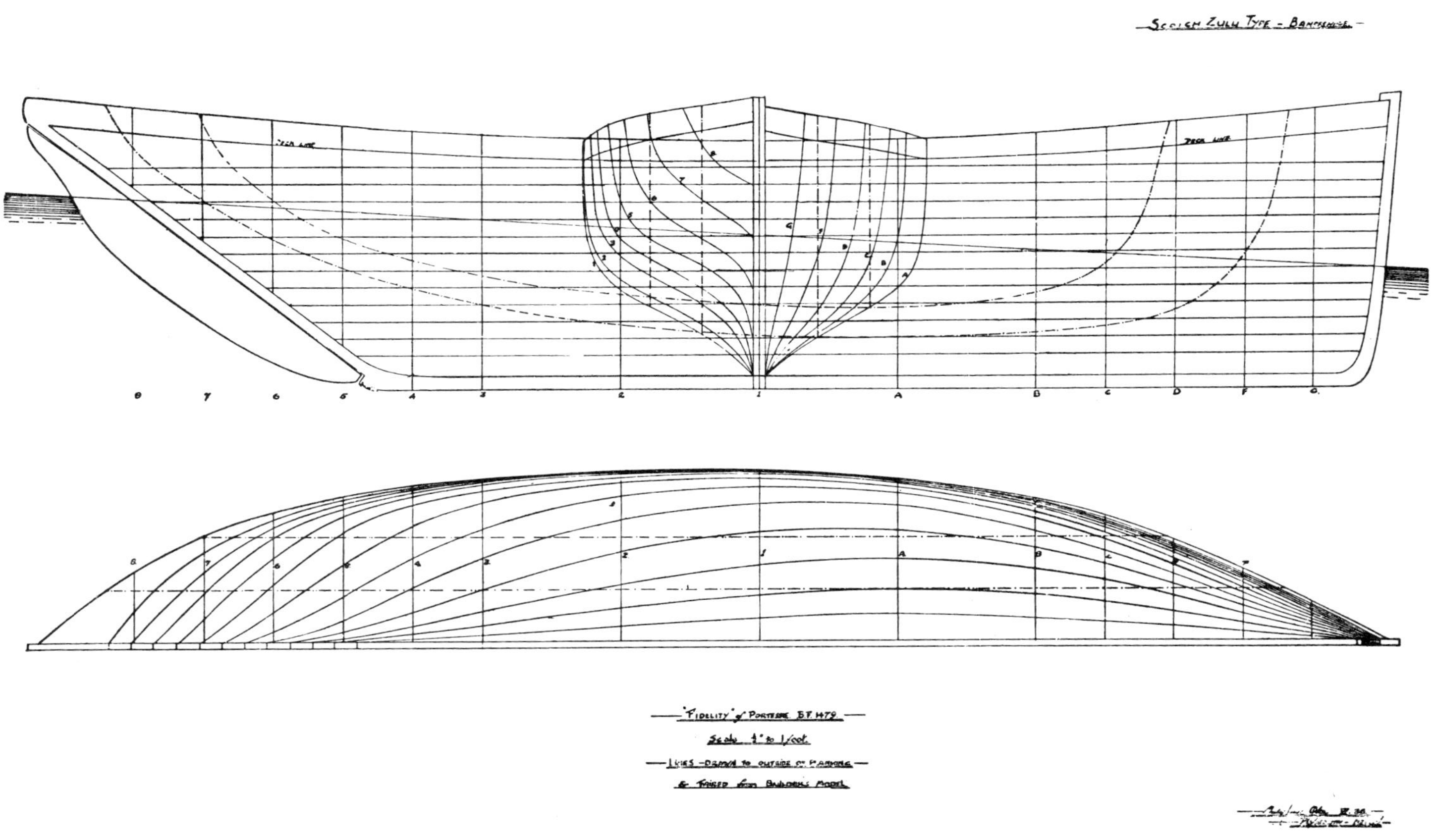

PLAN 26
Banff Zulu, c. 1904

PLAN 26
Banff Zulu, c. 1904

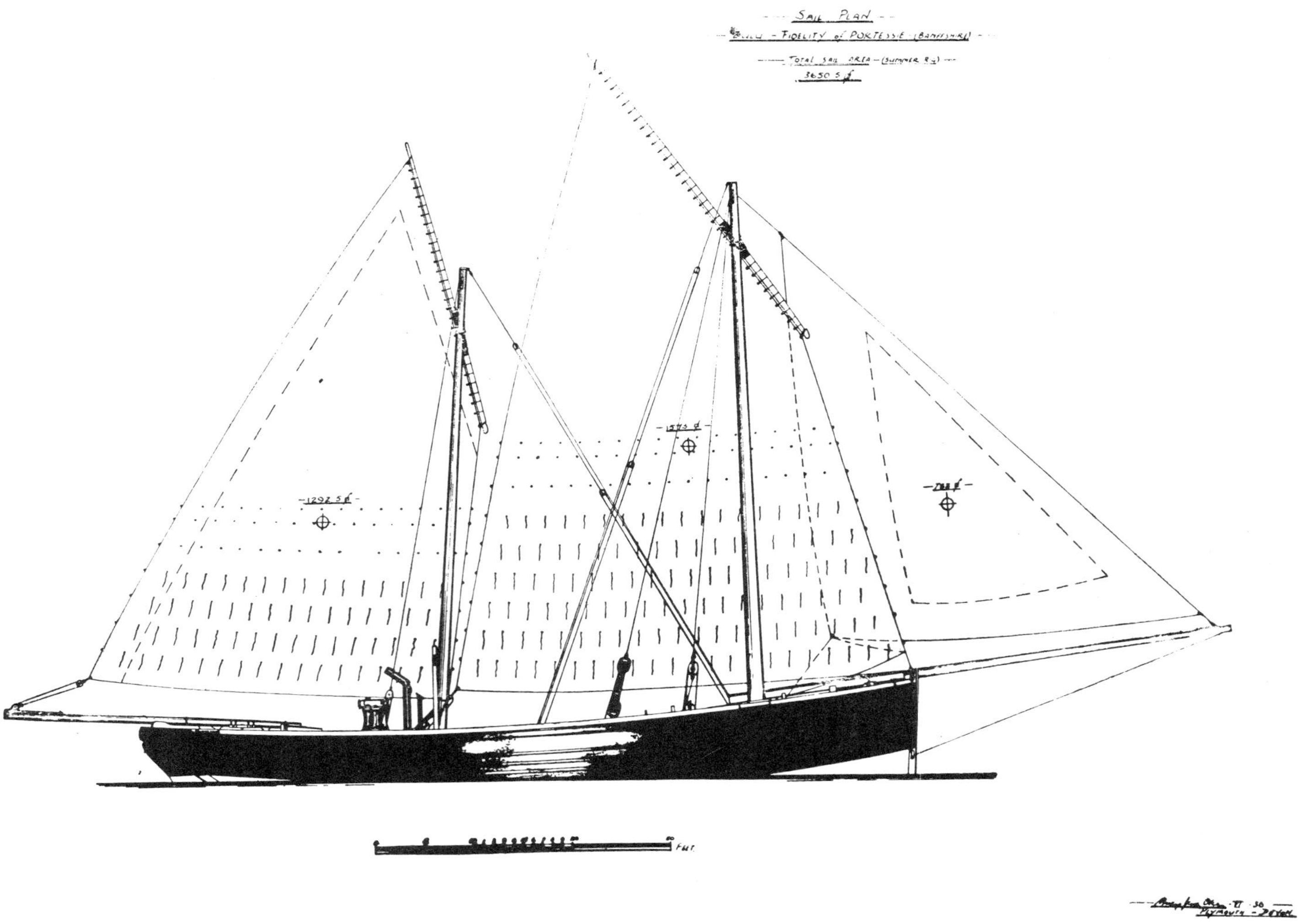

PLAN 26
Banff Zulu, c. 1904

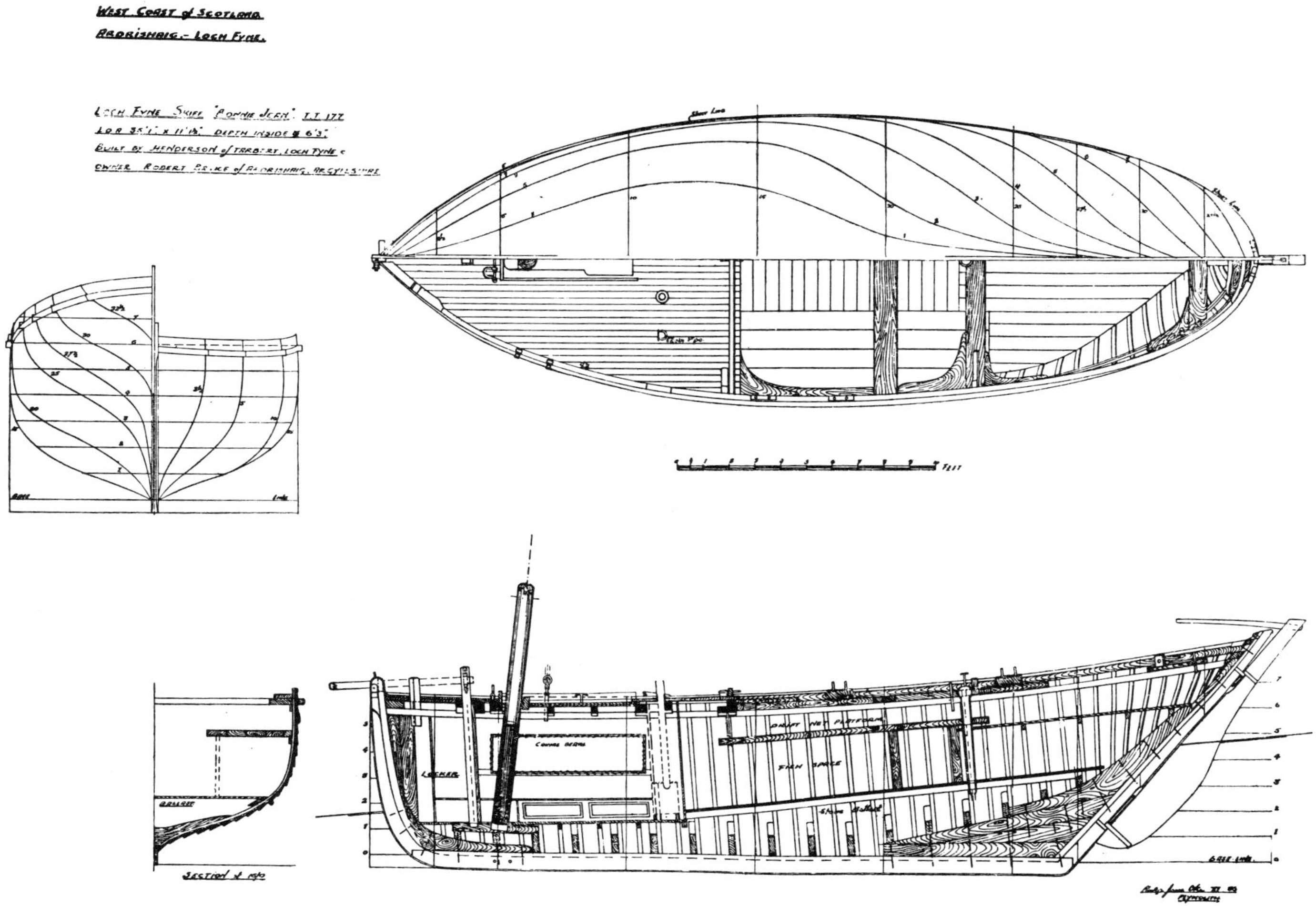

PLAN 27
Zulu Skiff, c. 1895

PLAN 27

Zulu Skiff, c. 1895

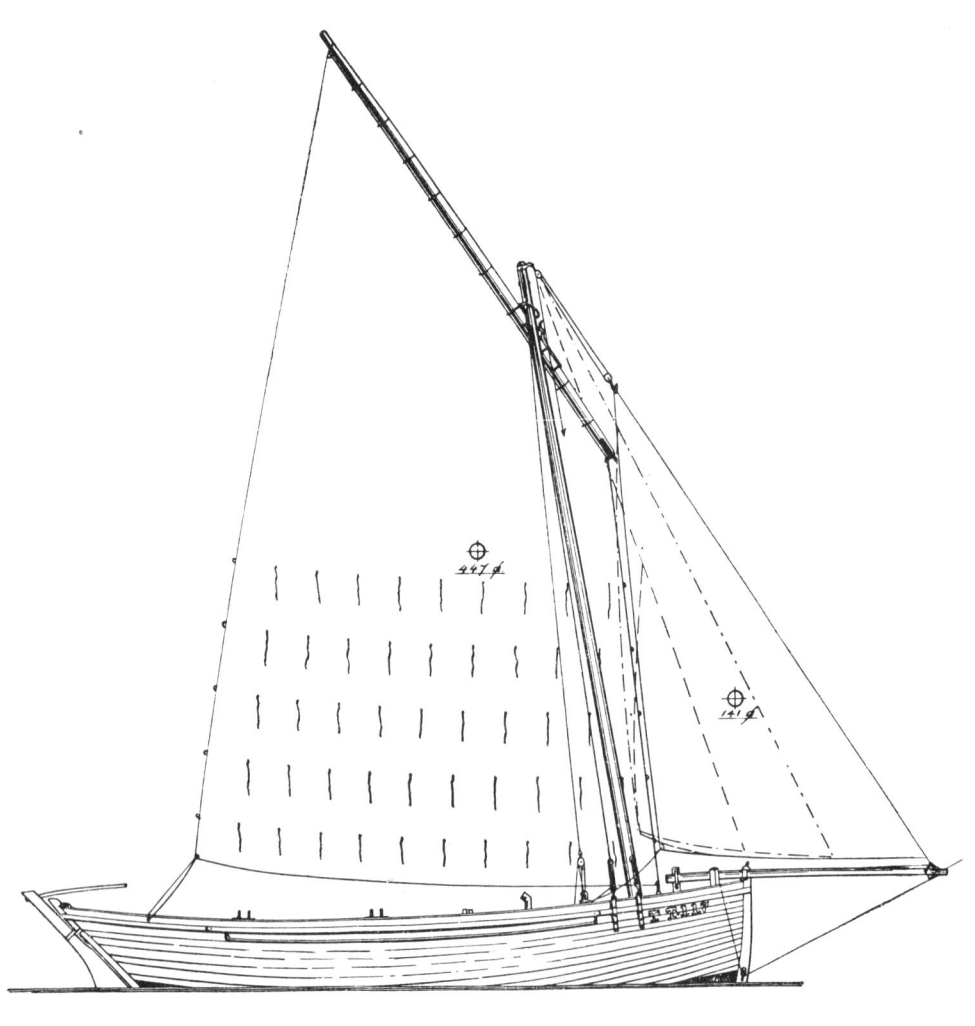

## Principal Types of Herring Drifters
### to same scale

**Yarmouth Lugger**
L.O.A 66ft

**Lowestoft Drifter**
L.O.A 64ft

**East Cornish Lugger**
L.O.A 38-40ft

**Mounts Bay "Driver"**
L.O.A 50-52ft

**Isle of Man "Nickey"**
L.O.A 52ft

**Isle of Man "Nobby"**
L.O.A 40ft

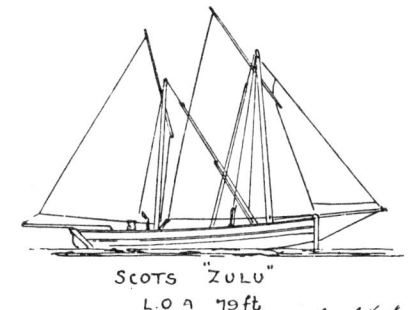

**Scots "Fifie"**
L.O.A 71ft

**Scots "Zulu"**
L.O.A 79ft

PLAN 28

# GLOSSARY

A'MONK. When the tack of the forelug is taken to the hook at foot of mast. Known as "trysailed" in Cornwall.

APRON. A timber bolted on inside of stem to strengthen and fasten it to keel. In Cornwall the inner post at stern was also called an apron (Fig. 10).

BANKBOARDS. Boards laid from fish hatch to bulwarks to prevent any catching up as nets passed over deck and rail (Plates 28 & 39).

BAULK. The heavy thwart in Scottish luggers against which the foremast rested.

BEAMS. Timbers spanning a vessel from side to side to support the deck. The moulding is the depth or perpendicular dimension, the siding is the breadth in a fore and aft direction.

BEASTERS. Men or women engaged in mending nets ashore (East Anglia).

BILGE. The round in a vessel's timbers where they begin to approach a vertical direction.

BILGE PIECES or KEELS. Planks fastened on bilge to strengthen the part which rests on the ground (Plates 7-10).

BINNS. Old word for bends or wales.

BONNET. An additional piece of canvas attached to the foot of a sail by lacings. Can be taken off in bad weather (Plates 27 & 28).

BOXING or BOX SCARPH. A method of joining two pieces of timber by letting each into the other one-half its own thickness. A usual method of uniting stem and keel (Fig. 10).

BREASTHOOKS. Strong knees bolted across inside of bow timbers to unite stem, shelf and frames.

BURTHEN. The computed number of tons that a vessel carries, or the deadweight.

BURTON. A tackle rove in a particular manner and composed of two single blocks and a hook in the bight of one of the running parts (Fig. 13). A double Spanish burton consists of two single and one double block (Fig. 14).

Also the name given to the stay set up on the windward side in a lugger and shifted over every time she goes about (Fig. 40).

BUTT. The joining endways of two timbers or planks.

CANT FRAMES. The frames at bow and stern not square to the keel.

CARLINGS. Pieces of oak fitted between beams in a fore and aft direction. Usually carry the hatch coamings.

CARVEL BUILD. A method of boat building where the planks are laid edge to edge, so presenting a smooth surface and not overlapping.

CAVIL and CAVIL RAIL. Stout pieces of timber bolted horizontally to the stanchions to which large ropes are belayed, or which carry the belaying pins (East Anglia).

CEILING. The inside planking of hull.

CLENCH BUILD. A method of boat building where the strakes of planking overlap, forming "lands". Also known as clencher, clincher, clinker and lapstrake.

CLEW. The lower after corner in a fore and aft sail (Fig. 50).

COUNTER. The projecting part of a vessel abaft the sternpost.

COVERING BOARD. The outside deck plank fitted over the timber heads. Also called the plank sheer.

CRAN. A measure containing about 1,000 herring, weighing about $3\frac{1}{2}$ cwt., $37\frac{1}{2}$ gallons.

CRUTCH. The vertical support on which a foremast rests when lowered. Also called a mitchboard, or gallows.

Also the name given to metal rowlocks (Fig. 51).

DANDY RIGGED. Originally a cutter-rigged vessel with a lug mizzen aft, set on a jigger mast. Later, fisherman's parlance for ketch rig.

DEAD RISE. The approach floor timbers make to the perpendicular.

DEAD RISING or RISING LINE. Those parts of a vessel's floor, throughout her whole length, where the floor timber is terminated upon the lower futtock.

DEADWOOD. Solid timbers bolted on top of the keel for'ard and aft to receive the heels of frames which do not cross the keel.

DEEPINGS. The various lengths of twine nets which laced together form one complete herring net (Fig. 7).

DEMERSAL. Fish swimming near the bottom of the sea.

DIPPING LUG. A quadrilateral sail bent to a yard which hooks to a traveller, set to leeward of mast with tack to stem or on weather bow. When going about the sail has to be dipped—lowered—and the yard shifted to the other side of the mast.

DOUBLING. A covering of plank, from $1\frac{1}{2}$ to 3 in. thick, fitted over original planks of old vessels and well fastened so as to give additional strength.

DRABBLER. Extra piece of sail laced to the foot of the bonnet in herring buss, removing it was equivalent to reefing sail (Fig. 1).

DRIFT. The distance between two blocks of a tackle.

EARINGS. Ropes attached to cringles in head of a sail to fasten its corners to the yard.

EYEBOLT. Round iron bolt driven into deck or timber and having an eye formed in end at least $2\frac{1}{2}$ times the diameter of the bolt.

FALL. The hauling part of a tackle.

FASHION TIMBERS. The aftermost timbers to which transoms are bolted, forming the shape of the stern.

FLOOR TIMBERS. The lowermost of the various pieces making up a "frame" and crossing the keel, into which they are often recessed. Their moulding is the depth or perpendicular dimension, their siding the thickness in a fore and aft direction.

FORE-LOCK. A flat piece of iron, driven through end of a bolt, etc., to prevent its drawing (Fig. 27).

FRAME. One of the ribs of a vessel, made up of floor timber, futtocks and top timbers. Its moulding is the thickness athwartship, i.e. between the inside and outside planking, its siding the breadth in a fore and aft direction (Fig. 42).

GARBOARD. The strake of planking next to the keel into which it is rabbetted and fastened (Figs. 9 & 10).

GORES. The angle at one or both ends of sail cloths to increase breadth or depth of a sail (Figs. 50 & 70).

GUNWALE. Originally the timber fitted inside the topstrake of planking in open or half-decked boats. In Scottish luggers the name given to the heavy timber outside topstrake (Fig. 66).

GUNTACKLE PURCHASE. A tackle composed of two single blocks.

GURRY. A hand barrow used in Cornwall, being a large open box with handles at each end.

HEEL ROPE. The rope by which a bowsprit is run in or out.

HOIST. The length of luff of a fore and aft sail. In Scottish luggers the name given to the luff or weather of a lugsail.

HOLLOW LINES. The horizontal lines of a vessel that have inflections, where they change from convex to concave.

HOODS or HOODING ENDS. The ends of planks which butt against stem and sternpost. Also called "wood ends" (Cornwall).

HOODWAY. The companion leading to cabin (East Anglia).

JENNY BOOM. The short yard at foot of mizzen lug in Cornish boats (Fig. 50).

JIGGER YARD. On foot of topsail (East Anglia).

JOGGLES. The notches cut in timbers to allow them to lie flush in the lands of planking in clench build (Fig. 12).

JUMP STAY. The fore stay on the mizzen mast (Fig. 55). Called the "Tommy Hunter" in East Anglia.

KEEL. The lowest and principal timber in a vessel, running in a fore and aft direction. Its moulding is the height in a perpendicular direction, its siding the breadth or thwartship dimension.

KEELSON. Timber lying on top of floors and through-bolted to keel. In Scottish luggers was fitted below the floors. Its moulding is the depth, its siding the breadth.

KNITTLES. Short lines used to bend the head of a sail to its yard. Also known as rovings and yardbands.

LADE-NET. A long net on an iron hoop frame attached to staff and used to pick up fish which had fallen out of nets into the water. Also known as didlenet (East Anglia), a scum net (Scotland), and a keep net in Cornwall (Fig. 2 and Plate 17).

LANDS. The overlap of planks in clench build through which the fastenings go (Fig. 11).

LAST. An old herring measure, nominally ten thousand fish, actually 13,200, weighing about two tons.

LATCHETS or LASKETS. Thin line used to lace bonnet to foot of sail, or drabbler to bonnet.

LATCHINGS. The loops on the head rope of the bonnet through which the latchets are passed.

LEECH. The lee edge of a sail (Fig. 50).

LININGS. Strengthening pieces sewn on sails where extra wear or strain is encountered.

LINTS. Narrow lengths of hand-knitted twine nets (East Anglia).

LUFF. The weather edge of a sail. Also called the weather or the hoist (Fig. 50).

LUFF PURCHASE. A tackle composed of a single and a double block, the standing part of rope being fast to the single block.

LUMBER IRONS. Rings on the quarters in which oars, spare sails, etc. are carried (East Anglia and I.o.M.). In Cornwall often called "crutches."

MAST ROPE. The rope by which a topmast is sent up or lowered. In Cornwall the name given to the short rope securing the lug halyards when yard is lowered (Fig. 26).

MAST SCUTTLE, TRUNK or BOX. The narrow slot in the deck immediately aft of foremast into which mast falls back when lowered. Known as the scuttle at Lowestoft, the lears in Yarmouth luggers, the feathers at Hastings, the scottle in Mount's Bay, the trunk or locker at St. Ives, the slides or guides in Isle of Man, the skegs or hitches in Scotland, and the gantry or gauntry in Yorkshire.

MATIES. Fat herring in the finest condition.

MILT. The soft roe of male fish.

MITCHBOARD. The vertical support with semi-circular groove at top in which a lowered foremast rests. Also known as gallows or crutch.

MOULDED or MOULDING. The depth a timber is made between its curved surfaces, the side to which the mould is applied.

ORZELS. The short lines connecting the nets to the cork rope (Figs. 7, 8 & 61). Variously known as ozels, norsolls, norsals, nossles, nozels, hauslas or hoss'ls.

PALLETS. Floats supporting the nets (East Anglia). Made of canvas or skins, in modern times are rubber bladders with a canvas covering. Also known as buffs.

PARREL. A rope used to secure the yard at the slings to the mast and rove through balls of wood—the beads or trucks—so that it hoists easily (Plate 179).

PARTNERS. Strong timbers fixed between the beams to support a mast at the deck.

PELAGIC. Fish which swim near the surface.

PENDANT. A rope to which a tackle is attached.

PLATFORM. The floor boards over the ballast, etc.

RABBET. The groove cut in keel, stem and sternpost to receive the edges or ends of outside planks (Fig. 10).

RANSACKERS. Men employed in overhauling nets (East Anglia).

RINGBOLT. An eyebolt having a ring in the eye with a diameter five times the diameter of iron of bolt. Receives hooks of tackles, etc.

RISING FLOOR. Sharp-bottomed or V-shaped.

ROACH. The curve on the foot or leech of a sail.

ROOVE. The small washer placed over a copper nail before clenching (Fig. 10).

ROUSING or ROUZING. Well mixing herring with salt.

ROVINGS. Short lines by which the head of a sail is bent to its yard (Fig. 67). So called in Scots fifies, but in zulus they are known as yardbands, possibly derived from the Norse ra-band, "ra" being a yard.

RUNNER. A rope passed through the single block on a pendant, having one end fast and a purchase on the other. A runner and luff purchase gives an eight-fold increase in power.

SCANTLING. The finished dimensions of a piece of timber.

SCUDDING. Clearing herring nets over a pole above the hatch leading to fish hold (Plate 165). Known as "reddin' the nets" in Scotland.

SCUTTLE. An opening cut through the deck, framed up similarly to a hatchway, and usually covered with a cap cover if the coamings are raised. *See also* MAST SCUTTLE.

SEIZINGS. Lines securing nets to warps (Fig. 7). Known as lanyards in Cornwall, daffins in Scotland (early days), stoppers or thows in Isle of Man.

SIDED or SIDING. The thickness of timbers between their flat surfaces, or parallel sides.

SHEETS. The ropes by which the lower after corners—clews—of sails are controlled.

SHELF. The longitudinal timber running the whole length of the hull inside the frames on which the ends of the beams rest. Also called a clamp or stringer.

SKEG. The heel or extreme after end of the keel which sometimes projects slightly abaft the sternpost (Fig. 10).

SKEGS. Scottish name for the deck slot in fifies into which a foremast lowers (Fig. 64).

SPEETS. Thin sticks, pointed at one end, thrust through gill and mouth of herring before they are hung in "loves" to smoke.

STANDING LUG. A lugsail with its tack permanently made fast to hook on the mast. Invariably set on the mizzen mast.

STEM. The foremost timber in a vessel, having an iron stemband on outer face connecting to keel (Fig. 10). Its moulding is the fore and aft dimension, its siding the thwartship dimension.

STEMSON. Heavy knee bolted on inner side of apron and upper side of keelson or deadwood.

STEP (of mast). A large timber bolted down to keelson or floors, with a mortice to receive the tenon in heel of mast.

STERNPOST. The aftermost timber connected to heel of keel by tenon and metal plates and on which the rudder is hung. Its moulding is the fore and aft dimension, its siding the thwartship dimension (Fig. 10).

STRINGERS. Strakes of heavy plank worked longitudinally for whole length of hull inside at the height of the underside of the beams and put on edgeways to serve as a shelf for beams to rest on. Also known as the shelf or clamp (Fig. 41).

The name given in Scottish zulus to the heavy timber bolted to inside faces of timberheads above deck (Fig. 69).

STROPS. The lines securing the buoys to the warp (Fig. 7). Also the rope or wire grommets round a block shell, or the iron band.

STOPPERS. Ropes securing the nets to the warp (Fig. 8).

SWIG, TO. The fall of a tackle is put under a cleat and firmly held by some of crew, another man takes hold of the fall between the blocks and puts his whole weight on it, the others taking in the slack. By swigging, that little extra can be obtained when by steady hauling the blocks cannot be moved another inch (Plate 185).

SWILLS. Double pannier-shaped baskets used at Yarmouth when landing herring.

TABERNACLE. A strong three-sided trunk, built up from keelson or floors, with aft side open. In this a mast is stepped and can be lowered back if required.

TABLING. The broad "hem" on borders of sails to which bolt ropes are sewed.

TACK. The lower fore corner of a sail (Fig. 50).

TIZZOT. A length of rope shackled to an eyebolt in stem with other end made fast to warp, so that a drifter can ride by the tizzot and save chafe on the warp (Fig. 7). Also called tizzit and tizzard.

THWART. Transverse seats in an open boat, resting on stringers. Also called thafts or thofts.

TOMMY HUNTER. A special rope strop used in Cornwall when raising the foremast (Fig. 30). The name given to the jump stay in East Anglian drifters.

TRANSOMS. The timbers lying horizontally across the sternpost and bolted to it and to the fashion timbers.

TRAVELLER. An iron ring sliding freely on a mast or spar. The lug yard is hooked to the one on the mast, the tack of a jib to the one on the bowsprit (Figs. 6 & 67).

TRENAILS. Cylindrical oak pins or bolts, 1 in. dia. and over, driven through plank and timbers as fastenings, then ends are split and wedged. An excellent fastening as wood swells in water and the weight of metal nails or bolts is saved.

TUMBLE-HOME. When the sides of a ship near the deck incline inwards.

TYE. A chain, rope or wire attached to a yard and reeving through a sheave at masthead with a tackle on lower end, the halyards (Fig. 40).

VARGORD. A long spar used to keep the luff of a lugsail taut when going to windward (Cornwall) (Figs. 19 & 20). Known as a wand in Scottish scaffies.

WALES. Thick plank on outside of hull below the gunwale or covering board, known in old days as the binns, also called bends when plank is near the load water line.

WARP. The 120-fathom lengths of 3¾ to 4 in. manilla or 7 in. hemp ropes coupled together to hold a fleet of nets. Should be laid up left-handed (Figs. 7 & 8). Variously known as footlines (Cornwall), springback (I. of M.), trail rope, bauch or baulch, and bush line in Scotland.

Also a term used when counting herring, as well as name given to the lengthwise threads in sail cloth.

WASH STRAKE. A strake of plank, fixed or movable, fitted to the gunwale of an open boat to increase the freeboard (Fig. 41).

WEATHER. The luff or weather edge of a sail (Fig. 50).

WEFT. The cross threads in sailcloth.

WHIP. A purchase consisting of one single block.

YOKE. The lower cap on a masthead.

## LIST OF PLATES

| Plate No. | Reference on page | Caption |
|---|---|---|
| Frontispiece | — | The old order changeth. |
| 1 | 16 | South coast lugger c. 1820. |
| 2 | 17 | Yorkshire 3-masted lugger c. 1800. |
| 3 | 34 | Yarmouth 3-masted lugger c. 1830. |
| 4 | 31 | Carting nets, Lowestoft. |
| 5 | 31 | Net drying ground, Lowestoft. |
| 6 | 35 | 3-masted lugger off Gorleston. |
| 7 | 39 | Lowestoft lugger c. 1870. |
| 8 | 39 | Yarmouth lugger *Dewdrop* c. 1871. |
| 9 | 40 | Lowestoft dandy *Princeps* 1884. |
| 10 | 40 | Lowestoft dandy *Princeps* 1884. |
| 11 | 41 | A Lowestoft shipyard c. 1877. |
| 12 | 41 | J. Chambers' shipyard, Lowestoft c. 1899. |
| 13 | 42 | Dressing sails, Lowestoft. |
| 14 | 42 | Lowestoft lugger *Young John* c. 1895. |
| 15 | 42 | Lowestoft lugger *Lizzie*. |
| 16 | 53 | Hauling herring nets. |
| 17 | 53 | Yarmouth lugger *Fisherman* c. 1860. |
| 18 | 54 | Yarmouth dandy *Breadwinner*. |
| 19 | 56 | *Duke of Connaught* c. 1895. |
| 20 | 56 | *James* c. 1895. |
| 21 | 56 | *Twilight* c. 1895. |
| 22 | 57 | *Young Linnet* entering Lowestoft harbour. |
| 23 | 57 | *Susie* leaving Yarmouth. |
| 24 | 57 | Caister-owned drifter entering Yarmouth. |
| 25 | 57 | *Maud* entering Yarmouth Haven. |
| 26 | 59 | *Florence May* c. 1883. |
| 27 | 59 | *Freda* c. 1884. |
| 28 | 60 | *Little Pet* c. 1884. |
| 29 | 63 | *Zealous* and drifters leaving Yarmouth. |
| 30 | 64 | *Paradox* entering Yarmouth Haven. |
| 31 | 65 | *Nell* towing down the Yare. |
| 32 | 65 | *Mizpah* c. 1895. |
| 33 | 65 | *Hildegarde* leaving Penzance. |
| 34 | 66 | *Bessie* c. 1892. |
| 35 | 66 | *Paragon*. |
| 36 | 66 | *Express* and other drifters leaving Lowestoft. |
| 37 | 73 | Sailmaker at work. |
| 38 | 74 | *Consolation* under construction. |
| 39 | 74 | *Consolation* ready for launching. |
| 40 | 77 | *Active* entering Yarmouth in gale. |

| Plate No. | Reference on page | Caption |
|---|---|---|
| 41 | 77 | *Daisy* entering Yarmouth in gale. |
| 42 | 80 | James Haylett of Caister. |
| 43 | 81 | Counting herring, *Monitor* c. 1896. |
| 44 | 82 | A big catch of mackerel. |
| 45 | 82 | The herring dock, Lowestoft. |
| 46 | 85 | Trawler and drifter ashore in entrance to Lowestoft harbour. |
| 47 | 85 | A close fit. |
| 48 | 85 | Lowestoft and Dutch drifters leaving Lowestoft. |
| 49 | 86 | Drifters leaving Lowestoft. |
| 50 | 86 | French lugger at Ramsgate. |
| 51 | 87 | Boulogne drifter entering Newlyn. |
| 52 | 87 | French drifter on launching ways. |
| 53 | 90 | Early steam drifter c. 1900. |
| 54 | 90 | *Grace Darling* entering Yarmouth. |
| 55 | 91 | Drifters packed in the Yare. |
| 56 | 92 | A curing yard, Yarmouth. |
| 57 | 92 | A cooper at work. |
| 58 | 93 | Girls rousing herring, Yarmouth. |
| 59 | 110 | Mackerel drivers leaving Penzance c. 1886. |
| 60 | 110 | Setting out for the fishing grounds c. 1880. |
| 61 | 112 | Landing mackerel at Hugh Town, c. 1880. |
| 62 | 117 | Mevagissey harbour. |
| 63 | 117 | Luggers leaving Mevagissey. |
| 64 | 117 | Polperro harbour 1931. |
| 65 | 117 | Polperro harbour 1931. |
| 66 | 118 | Drying sail, Looe. |
| 67 | 118 | Toshers at Mevagissey 1936. |
| 68 | 118 | Toshers at Mevagissey 1936. |
| 69 | 118 | *Gleaner*, looking for'ard. |
| 70 | 119 | *Gleaner*, looking aft. |
| 71 | 119 | Deck view, *Maggie*, 1935. |
| 72 | 119 | *Gleaner*, bow view. |
| 73 | 129 | Truro River oyster boat, full sail. |
| 74 | 119 | F.Y.205, full sail. |
| 75 | 120 | Mevagissey lugger, c. 1883. |
| 76 | 122 | *Foam*, c. 1894. |
| 77 | 123 | *Jane* on the hard, 1936. |
| 78 | 127 | F.Y.151, looking for'ard. |
| 79 | 127 | F.Y.151, looking aft. |
| 80 | 129 | *Ida*, c. 1908. |
| 81 | 130 | *Nellie* and the fleet leaving Mevagissey. |
| 82 | 131 | Mevagissey lugger under all sail. |
| 83 | 133 | *Swan* and the fleet putting to sea. |

| Plate No. | Reference on page | Caption |
|---|---|---|
| 84 | 133 | Unloading mackerel, Mevagissey. |
| 85 | 134 | *Edith* and *Annie* at Mevagissey, 1936. |
| 86 | 137 | Looe luggers at Brixham, c. 1880. |
| 87 | 137 | Plymouth lugger leaving Brixham, c. 1880. |
| 88 | 139 | *Godrevy* at anchor, St. Ives. |
| 89 | 140 | *Agnes* under all sail. |
| 90 | 140 | *Delhi*, fitting new stem. |
| 91 | 140 | Last sailing pilchard boat, Newlyn 1920. |
| 92 | 140 | *Delhi*, stern view, 1921. |
| 93 | 140 | Last sailing pilchard boat at sea. |
| 94 | 141 | A transom sterned pilchard driver. |
| 95 | 141 | *Veracity*, bow view. |
| 96 | 142 | Drying nets, Mount's Bay, c. 1880. |
| 97 | 145 | *Water Lily*, c. 1895. |
| 98 | 150 | *Morning Star* in Mount's Bay. |
| 99 | 151 | Model of *Morning Star* made by her builder. |
| 100 | 151 | St. Ives harbour. |
| 101 | 153 | *Temperance Star* becalmed. |
| 102 | 153 | Transom sterned mackerel driver. |
| 103 | 153 | The fleet putting to sea, c. 1885. |
| 104 | 154 | Mackerel drivers in Mount's Bay, c. 1895. |
| 105 | 154 | *St. Michael* leaving Penzance, c. 1895. |
| 106 | 156 | *Mary & Emily*, foremast lowered. |
| 107 | 156 | Breaking up a lugger, Newhaven 1945. |
| 108 | 156 | Mast covering board. |
| 109 | 156 | Scud hook and stem head. |
| 110 | 161 | Mackerel driver under all sail. |
| 111 | 161 | Outrigger, *Mary & Emily*. |
| 112 | 165 | Tacking in a light wind. |
| 113 | 167 | *Emulator*, c. 1883. |
| 114 | 169 | Luggers leaving Penzance. |
| 115 | 169 | A two mizzen breeze, *Fiona*, c. 1890. |
| 116 | 170 | Boat graveyard, Galway, 1932. |
| 117 | 171 | *Branch* at Lowestoft. |
| 118 | 173 | 49 P.Z. at Whitby, c. 1860. |
| 119 | 174 | *Lizzie Tonkin*, port side, c. 1920. |
| 120 | 174 | *Lizzie Tonkin*, bow view, c. 1920. |
| 121 | 174 | *Lizzie Tonkin*, stern view, c. 1920. |
| 122 | 174 | Newlyn harbour. |
| 123 | 176 | *Boy Willie*, starboard side, 1936. |
| 124 | 176 | *Boy Willie*, bow view. |
| 125 | 176 | *Ebenezer*, c. 1936. |
| 126 | 177 | Old harbour, Newlyn. |

| Plate No. | Reference on page | Caption |
|---|---|---|
| 127 | 177 | S.S.26 laid up at Lelant. |
| 128 | 178 | *Ebenezer* and other luggers laid up, c. 1936. |
| 129 | 185 | Model of Manx "lugger", or dandy, c. 1883. |
| 130 | 194 | *Glee Maiden* leaving Peel. |
| 131 | 195 | Model of Manx nickey, c. 1883. |
| 132 | 197 | Nickeys in Peel harbour. |
| 133 | 197 | Nickeys at Port Erin. |
| 134 | 197 | Port St. Mary harbour. |
| 135 | 203 | Fitting out, Port St. Mary. |
| 136 | 209 | Nickeys and dandies at Port Erin. |
| 137 | 210 | Model of nickey *Expert*. |
| 138 | 212 | Nobby *Lily* becalmed. |
| 139 | 212 | Nobby *Xema*. |
| 140 | 214 | Nobby *Gladys*, bow view. |
| 141 | 214 | Nobby *Gladys*, stern view. |
| 142 | 215 | *Cushag*, starboard side. |
| 143 | 215 | *Lilian*, deck view. |
| 144 | 217 | *Bonnie Jane* and *Ada*. |
| 145 | 218 | *Ada*, bow view. |
| 146 | 220 | Douglas harbour. |
| 147 | 243 | Curing shed, Burnmouth, c. 1882. |
| 148 | 244 | Early 19th century loom for net making. |
| 149 | 248 | An old fisherman's sketch of a scaffie. |
| 150 | 248 | Scaffie entering Buckie, c. 1870. |
| 151 | 248 | Scaffies and fifie hauled up, Buckie. |
| 152 | 249 | *Gratitude*, looking for'ard. |
| 153 | 252 | A smack rigged fifie, Yarmouth. |
| 154 | 253 | Clinker-built zulu. |
| 155 | 254 | Fifie *Iona*, deck view. |
| 156 | 254 | Clinker-built fifie leaving Lowestoft. |
| 157 | 254 | Fifie dried out at Burnmouth, c. 1882. |
| 158 | 254 | *Iona* and *Brilliant Success*, c. 1882. |
| 159 | 254 | *Silver Cloud* entering harbour. |
| 160 | 255 | A relic of the 1881 disaster. |
| 161 | 256 | Wreck of *Comely*, 1893. |
| 162 | 256 | Fishing village of Ross, c. 1882. |
| 163 | 256 | Burnmouth harbour, c. 1882. |
| 164 | 256 | Crew of *Success*, c. 1882. |
| 165 | 257 | Clearing the herring nets. |
| 166 | 257 | Barking nets. |
| 167 | 260 | Fifie *Nightingale* and zulu in heavy seas. |
| 168 | 260 | Fifie *Diligence* entering Lowestoft. |
| 169 | 260 | A forest of masts, Lowestoft. |

| Plate No. | Reference on page | Caption |
|---|---|---|
| 170 | 260 | Fifie *Onward* under all sail. |
| 171 | 265 | The Kirkcaldy men arrive. |
| 172 | 265 | Zulus lying off Yarmouth quay. |
| 173 | 265 | Fifies and zulus lying in the Yare. |
| 174 | 266 | Fifies and zulus leaving Lowestoft. |
| 175 | 266 | Herring fleet standing out to sea. |
| 176 | 266 | Awaiting a thunderstorm. |
| 177 | 274 | Fifie baldie and skiff. |
| 178 | 276 | Zulu *Muirneag*, tuckle chain detail. |
| 179 | 277 | Zulu *Muirneag*, deck view, looking aft. |
| 180 | 277 | Zulu *Pansy* under all sail. |
| 181 | 278 | A well-cut fore lug, *Blantyre*. |
| 182 | 278 | Zulu *Garland* in heavy seas. |
| 183 | 278 | Fraserburgh harbour. |
| 184 | 278 | Wands and sweeps, *British Ensign* leaving Lowestoft. |
| 185 | 278 | Hoisting forelug, *Muirneag*. |
| 186 | 282 | Zulus dried out, Buckie harbour. |
| 187 | 285 | Zulu skiffs at Campbeltown. |
| 188 | 287 | Zulu skiffs at Rosehearty, 1939. |
| 189 | 287 | Zulu skiff at Rosehearty, 1939. |
| 190 | 291 | Scarborough harbour, c. 1880. |
| 191 | 292 | Dandy rigged yawl, c. 1880. |

# LIST OF FIGURES
## All Sketches by Author

| Fig. No. | Reference on page | Title |
|---|---|---|
| 1 | 5 | Dutch herring buss c. 1583. |
| 2 | 6 | Dutch herring buss lying to her nets. |
| 3 | 7 | Dutch herring buss 17th century. |
| 4 | 12 | English herring buss c. 1750. |
| 5 | 13 | Hauling nets c. 1750. |
| 6 | 21 | Split ring traveller. |
| 7 | 30 | Yarmouth lugger riding to her nets. |
| 8 | 32 | Scots fifie shooting nets. |
| 9 | 36 | Garboard strake. |
| 10 | 36 | Clench built lugger on stocks. |
| 11 | 37 | Clamp. |
| 12 | 38 | Floor timbers and joggling. |
| 13 | 45 | Single Spanish burton. |
| 14 | 71 | Double Spanish burton. |
| 15 | 98 | Cornish "cok" c. 1620. |
| 16 | 98 | Pilchard boat c. 1694. |
| 17 | 98 | Pilchard boat hauling nets. |
| 18 | 99 | Cornish boats c. 1790. |
| 19 | 101 | 3 masted Cornish lugger c. 1814. |
| 20 | 102 | 3 masted Cornish lugger c. 1830. |
| 21 | 105 | Traverse board. |
| 22 | 121 | Mast rope, Mevagissey lugger. |
| 23 | 123 | Floor timbers and futtocks. |
| 24 | 125 | Cleat and bulwarks. |
| 25 | 126 | Mast covering board. |
| 26 | 128 | Mast rope and "snortner." |
| 27 | 128 | Tack hooks and bumpkin. |
| 28 | 129 | Fore sheet blocks. |
| 29 | 130 | Tack hook, mizzen mast. |
| 30 | 132 | Tommy Hunter strop. |
| 31 | 134 | Flambow. |
| 32 | 134 | Sprit rigged Pilchard driver. |
| 33 | 141 | St. Ives and Mount's Bay mid-sections. |
| 34 | 144 | Cant frames and deadwood. |
| 35 | 146 | Scud hook. |
| 36 | 146 | Fiddle block. |
| 37 | 147 | Bulwark fitting for fore sheet. |
| 38 | 147 | Masthead detail. |
| 39 | 147 | Tack hook, mizzen mast. |
| 40 | 149 | Tacking a St. Ives lugger. |
| 41 | 153 | Washstrake and gunwale details. |

| Fig. No. | Reference on page | Title |
| --- | --- | --- |
| 42 | 155 | Frames in mackerel driver. |
| 43 | 156 | Wings for shifting ballast. |
| 44 | 156 | Fore sheet block. |
| 45 | 159 | "Bremming" tools. |
| 46 | 159 | Setting out a mast. |
| 47 | 160 | Ding chain and tiller. |
| 48 | 160 | Scottle details. |
| 49 | 160 | Rope sling for yard. |
| 50 | 163 | Cutting out a lugsail. |
| 51 | 166 | Oar crutch. |
| 52 | 166 | Outrigger details. |
| 53 | 167 | Anchor bend. |
| 54 | 167 | Leads for topsail sheet. |
| 55 | 168 | Mizzen topsail details. |
| 56 | 169 | Tacking a Mount's Bay lugger. |
| 57 | 181 | Manx Scowte *c.* 1760. |
| 58 | 182 | Manx smack *c.* 1789. |
| 59 | 186 | Main sheet detail. |
| 60 | 187 | Masthead detail. |
| 61 | 191 | Detail of nets. |
| 62 | 215 | Foremast details. |
| 63 | 215 | Foreyard details. |
| 64 | 249 | Baulk and skegs. |
| 65 | 268 | Butt joint and clamp. |
| 66 | 269 | Details of gunwale, etc., in fifie. |
| 67 | 270 | Traveller and foreyard details. |
| 68 | 272 | Worm steering gear. |
| 69 | 275 | Details of gunwale, etc., in zulu. |
| 70 | 277 | Cutting out a forelug. |
| 71 | 279 | Unshipping rudder. |
| 72 | 280 | Partners for mizzen mast. |
| 73 | 281 | Stemhead details. |
| 74 | 284 | Halyard and sheet blocks. |
| 75 | 285 | Pump thwart. |
| 76 | 286 | Floors and timbers. |

## LIST OF SCALE PLANS

| Plan No. | Page No. | Reference on page | Title of Plan |
|---|---|---|---|
| 1 | 297 | 34 | 3 masted Yarmouth lugger c. 1848. Lines. |
| 2 | 298–301 | 42 | 2 masted Yarmouth lugger c. 1859. *Gipsy Queen* Lines, deck and sail plans. |
| 3 | 302–5 | 66 | Lowestoft drifter *Strive* c. 1898. Lines, deck and sail plans. |
| 4 | 306 | 86 | French drifter. Sail plan. |
| 5 | 307–9 | 118 | Polperro Gaffer *Gleaner* c. 1898. Lines, deck and sail plans. |
| 6 | 310–12 | 122 | Mevagissey Lugger c. 1906. Lines, deck and sail plan. |
| 7 | 313 | 139 | Pilchard boats c. 1865. Lines. |
| 8 | 314–16 | 139 | Pilchard Driver *Godrevy*, St. Ives c. 1898. Lines, deck and sail plan. |
| 9 | 317–19 | 140 | Pilchard Driver *Veracity* of Mount's Bay c. 1902. Lines, deck and sail plans. |
| 10 | 320 | 142 | Mackerel Driver c. 1870. Lines. |
| 11 | 321–22 | 143 | St. Ives Mackerel Driver *Ebenezer* 1869. Lines, deck and sail plans. |
| 12 | 323–26 | 154 | Mount's Bay Counter sterned Lugger *Colleen Bawn* c. 1887. Lines, deck and sail plans. |
| 13 | 327–29 | 175 | Mount's Bay Mackerel Driver *Boy Willie* c. 1897. Lines, deck and sail plans. |
| 14 | 330 | 183 | Manx "Lugger" c. 1848. Lines. |
| 15 | 331–32 | 209 | Manx Nickey *Expert* c. 1881. Lines, deck and sail plans. |
| 16 | 333–35 | 213 | Manx Nobby *Gladys* c. 1901. Lines, deck and sail plans. |
| 17 | 336 | 234 | Buckie Scaffie c. 1848. Lines. |
| 18 | 337 | 235 | Peterhead fifie c. 1848. Lines. |
| 19 | 338 | 235 | Wick boat c. 1848. Lines. |

| Plan No. | Page No. | Reference on page | Title of Plan |
|---|---|---|---|
| 20 | 339 | 235 | Newhaven fifie c. 1848. Lines. |
| 21 | 340–42 | 249 | Scaffie yawl *Gratitude* c. 1896. Lines, deck and sail plans. |
| 22 | 343 | 273 | Fifie skiff *Bounty* c. 1880. Lines and sail plan. |
| 23 | 344–45 | 259 | Fifie c. 1860. Lines from half model. |
| 24 | 346–47 | 259 | Fifie c. 1875. Lines from half model. |
| 25 | 348–51 | 271 | Fifie *True Vine* c. 1905. Lines, deck and sail plan. |
| 26 | 352–54 | 279 | Zulu *Fidelity* c. 1904. Lines, deck and sail plans. |
| 27 | 355–56 | 285 | Zulu skiff *Bonnie Jean* c. 1895. Lines, deck and sail plan. |
| 28 | 357 | 22 | Types of Herring drifters. |

Plans 1, 14, 17, 18, 19, 20, 22, were traced by Author from original plans.

Plans 2, 3, 4, 6, 12, 23, 24, 25, 28 were drawn by Author.

Plans 5, 7, 8, 9, 10, 11, 13, 15, 16, 21, 26, 27, are from photostats of original drawings prepared by the late P. J. Oke for the Coastal Craft sub-committee of the Society for Nautical Research and are reproduced by courtesy of the Director, Science Museum, South Kensington.

## INDEX

Adams, Mr. T., Shipwright, 40
Addison, Mr. John, 240, 247-8, 252, 278
Age, How to tell herring, 25
Agreement, To build, 184
A'Monk, Lugsail set, 20, 254, 266, 278
Arles, 242
Artis, Mr. A., 9, 54
Awlne, 29

Back Rope, 242
Baldies, 273-4
Baneys, 190
Bankboards, 44, 50
Barking, Nets, 28, 31, 135, 257
Barrelled Herring, 3, 7, 9, 11, 14, 93, 96, 226, 243
Baulch Rope, 255
Baulk, 246, 249, 271, 280
Beasters, 29
Billet Wood, 92, 245
Bloaters, 95
Boms, Dutch, 9, 54
Bonnet, 6, 55, 56, 57, 59, 60, 65, 254
*Bonnie Jean*, Plans of, 285-7
Bounty, Govt. Herring, 223-4
*Bounty*, Plans of skiff, 273-4
Bowline, 15, 104, 167, 248, 276, 277
Bowls, 28, 31, 32
Boyter, Mr. Wm., 269
*Boy Willie*, Plans of, 175-6
Brand, Govt., 226, 243
Breach, Mr. J., 66-73, 82, 83, 84
Breaming, 159
Breeze, Two mizzen, 169
British Fisheries Society, 224
Bruce, Mr. R. Stuart, 203, 253, 261, 283
Bryant, Mr. W., 150, 151
Buckie Harbour, Lugger entering, 248-9
Bulwarks, Low, 252, 254, 255, 266, 268, 275
Burnmouth, 244, 254, 255-7

Burton, 34, 38, 45, 46, 121, 129, 164, 266, 267, 270, 273, 274, 277
Bush Rope, 247, 260
Buss, Dutch herring, 5, 6, 7
  ,, English, 10, 11, 12, 13

Caister Lifeboat Disaster 1901, 78-80
Carrier Pigeons, Use of, 244
Carstairs, Mr. W., 269
Carvel Build, 37, 58
  ,,  ,,  , Change to, 59, 244
Capstan, First steam, 58, 59
Capstans, Types of, 56, 126, 247, 253, 259, 260
Catches, Record, 51, 52, 82, 83, 89, 200
Change from Square to Lug Rig, 15, 16
Change from Lug to Dandy Rig, 55-57, 252, 292
Clench-build, 37, 58, 234, 244, 246, 253, 254
Cobles, 289, 292
*Colleen Bawn*, Plans of Lugger, 154, 163
Company, Promotion of English Fishery, 10, 11-14
*Consolation*, First L T steam drifter, 74
Construction, Cornish lugger, 122, 144, 155-161
Construction, East Coast lugger, 35-39
  ,, , Isle of Man nickey, 209-212
  ,, , Isle of Man nobby, 213-216
  ,, , Scaffie yawl, 249-251
  ,, , Scots fifie, 268-273
  ,, , Scots Zulu, 274-284
  ,, , Scots Zulu skiff, 285-7
Converter Smacks, 39, 63
Cook's Life, A Manx, 206, 207
Cooper, Art of a, 92

377

COOPER, 225, 243
CORIN, Mr. L. J. B., 154, 170
CORK ROPE, 28
CORMACK, Mr. W., 275
CORNISH LUGGERS, Counter-sterned, 119, 153, 154
   ,,   ,, , Differences in, 97, 104, 151-2
   ,,   ,, , Historical, 97-100
   ,,   ,, , Improvements in, 109, 144, 175
CORNISH LUGGER, Sails to Australia, 104
CORNISH LUGGERS, Trips to North Sea, 106, 120, 173
CORNWALL, Living conditions, early 19th century, 110
COST OF BOATS, Cornwall, 123, 138, 150, 174, 238
  ,, ,, ,, , Isle of Man, 181, 184, 195
  ,, ,, ,, , Scotland, 231, 234, 235, 238, 240, 242, 244, 255, 258, 260, 274, 282, 285
COST OF YORKSHIRE LUGGERS, 289, 290
CRAN, Average price per, 261
  ,, , Number in a, 82
CREW, Duties of lugger, 48, 50, 52, 172, 255
CREWS, Mr. E. J., 73
CROME, Mr. R. W., 63
CRUTCHES, 99, 103, 148, 268, 271, 278, 280
CUMMING, Mr. W. S., 247, 248, 287
CURERS, Engagements by, 242-3, 247, 251
CURING HERRING, 5, 7, 8, 10, 11, 93-95, 237-8
CUSTOMS, Scottish fishermens', 225, 256

DANDY RIG, Change to, 55-57, 183
DECLINE, of Cornish fisheries, 113, 137, 177, 178
DECLINE, of Manx fishery, 221, 222
  ,, , of Scottish fishery, 262, 267-8, 287-8

DEEMSTER'S OATH, 179
DEEPINGS, 11, 28
DIAGONAL-CUT SAILS, 67
DING, chain, 159
DIPPING THE LUG, Cornish practice, 133, 148, 165, 169
DISASTERS, Scottish, 227-234, 255-6
DOLE, Herring nets, 28
DRABBLER, 6
DRESSING SAILS, 42, 224, 248, 253, 270, 276
DRIFTER, Cost of building a Lowestoft, 74
  ,, , Cost of suit of sails, Lowestoft, 69, 70
  ,, , Earnings, 84, 88, 89, 96, 261, 262-264
DRIFTERS, French, 52, 86, 87
  ,, , Last sailing, built, 74
  ,, , Local differences, 65
DRIFTER, Handling a, 62
  ,, , Outfit of a Lowestoft, 60-62
DRIFTERS, Rapid decline of sailing, 75
  ,, , Sail plan of French, 86, 87
DRIFTER, Steam, 27, 89, 90, 91, 262, 264, 265
DROGUES, 261
DUTCH FISHERY, 4, 5, 7, 8, 9, 223, 237
DUTCH WARS, 8, 9

EARNINGS, of drifters, 84, 88, 89, 96, 261, 262-264
  ,, , Scottish drifters, 261, 262, 263, 264
EAST ANGLIAN FISHERY, Scotch boats at, 245, 248, 261, 262, 263, 264
*Ebenezer*, St. Ives lugger, 143, 145-148, 178
ECHO SOUNDER, 221, 222
ELLIOTT & GARROOD, 58, 260
*Emulator*, Cornish lugger, 167, 168
ENGLISH FISHERY, 10, 11, 12
*Expert*, Plans of, 209-212

FARAGHER, Mr. F. C., 216, 217

FIDELITY, Plans of Zulu, 279-284
FIFIE, 235-6, 244, 251, 253, 254-274
,, , Construction of a, 268-273
,, , Half model of, 259
,, , Making sails for a, 269, 270
FIFIES, Smack rigged, 252
FISHER GIRLS, 93, 226, 243, 257, 292
FISHING, in Middle Ages, 2, 3
FIVE-MEN BOATS, 10, 19, 289
FLAMBOW, 134
FOGHORNS, 106
FOREMAST, Lowering and raising, 38, 45, 50, 56, 67, 102, 132, 157, 160, 238, 249, 269, 278, 291
FRESH BUYERS, Manx, 181, 182, 184

GARDEN, Mrs., 240-1, 245, 247, 278
GAUNTRY, 291
GAWNE, Mr. J., 190, 193, 196, 202, 204, 206, 218
GEORGE, Mr. Harry, 25-28, 39, 58, 64, 86
GIPSY QUEEN, Description of model, 42-48
GRATITUDE, Scaffie yawl, 249-251
GRAVEYARD, Boats', 170, 177
GROUND GEAR, Cornish lugger, 127, 149
,, ,, , Lowestoft drifter, 61
,, ,, , Scottish lugger, 255, 269
GROUPS OF FISH, 1
GUTTING, herring, 93, 225, 243
GURRY, 110, 135, 158

HAUSLAS, 190, 196
HAYLETT, Mr. J. J., 64
HAYLETT, Mr. James, 64, 77-80
HEADCORKS, 190
HERRING, age of, 25
,, , classes of, 23
,, , Desert Baltic, 3
,, , Grounds, 8, 24, 26, 27, 49, 63, 189, 225
,, , habits of, 23, 24, 26

HERRING, method of counting, 81, 84, 190, 261
,, , signs of, 24, 25
,, , smoking of, 94
HERRING SPAWN, 23, 25
,, , Trawling for, 32, 33
,, , Yarmouth fair, 3, 8
HILL, Mr. H. Oliver, 134, 157, 246
HODDY, 28
HOODWAY, 40, 42
HOSKING, Mr. R., 157, 158, 162, 163
HURRELS, 103

ICELAND, fishing, 2
IMLACH, Mr. Wm., 276

JACKY TOPSAIL, 55
JENNY, Boom, 126, 130, 162
JOGGLES, 37, 289, 291
JOSKINS, 48
JOUSTERS, 107, 135

KELLY, Miss M. J., 218-220
KINSALE FISHING, 191, 198, 199, 210, 215, 261
KIPPERS, 95, 173, 222, 292
KIRKCALDY, 245, 260, 262, 265, 267
KNITTLES, 46

LANDS, 37, 250, 286
LAST, number in a, 52
LATCHETS, 65
LAUNCH, a, 157
LIGHTFOOT, Mr. Theodore, 244, 252
LINTS, 28
LIVING, 1910 cost of, 263-4
LOOM, Pattersons, 30, 243-4
LOSSES, Cornish luggers, 114-116
,, , Manx luggers, 205
,, , Yarmouth and Lowestoft, 40, 63, 65
LOWESTOFT DRIFTERS, 59-63, 66-75
LUGGERS, Manx, 183-188
,, , construction of, 35-44

LUGGERS, Cornish, sails to Australia, 104-5
,, , Cornish open, 152
,, , fast trips by Cornish, 145, 146, 170
,, ,, ,, ,, Manx, 194, 199, 203
,, , handling, 20, 21, 165, 169
,, , Local differences in rig, 22, 39, 97, 151, 163, 251
,, , Long life of, 35, 170, 217, 222
LUGGER, need to improve design of, 21
,, , Mevagissey, 120-133
,, , Three-masted Cornish, 100-104, 106
,, , ,, ,, S. Coast, 16, 17
,, , ,, ,, Yarmouth, 34, 35
,, , ,, ,, Yorkshire, 17, 18, 19, 289
,, , Two-masted Yarmouth, 35, 42-48
LUGSAIL, Advantages of, 15, 16, 238
,, , development of, 19
,, , methods of dipping, 16, 20, 133, 148, 164-5, 169, 194-5, 266, 278
,, , Standing, 21, 104
LUMBER IRONS, 22, 44, 194
LUSITANIA, sinking of, 201
LUTE STERN, 13, 35, 56

MACKEREL DRIVER, construction of a, 144, 154-161
,, ,, , cost of, 150, 157, 158, 174
,, ,, , Cornish, 138, 141-170
MACKEREL, Prices realised, 109, 112
MACKEREL FISHERY, Scilly Isles, 112-113
MACKEREL VOYAGES, 82
MANX FISHERY, Early customs, 179-182
MANX HERRING PORTS, 196-198
MASTS, Immense size of Scottish, 274, 282

MAST MAKING, 159
MCINTOSH, Mr. William, 247, 265, 274, 279, 287
MEASE, 190
MEGAW, Mr. and Mrs. B., 179
MESH, of herring nets, 28, 29, 63, 149, 173, 190, 255
,, Mackerel nets, 62, 63, 82, 149, 171
MEVAGISSEY, Toshers, 117, 118
MILLER, Mr. Alexander, 224
MILLER & SONS, J. N., 258-9, 268, 271
MITCHBOARD, 35, 39, 44, 50
MIZPAH, fast Lowestoft drifter, 65, 84
MOLLAGS, 190
MOORE, Mr. L. W., 35, 41
MOTORS, in Scottish luggers, 259, 262-3, 267
MUIRNEAG, the last Scottish Zulu, 287

NANCE, Mr. Morton, 100, 101
NELL, best kept Yarmouth drifter, 64
NETS, Cornish, 133, 148, 149, 158, 171-174
,, , cost of herring, 28, 84, 158, 224
,, , cotton, 30, 31, 189, 190, 226, 243
,, , early mention of, 1
,, , Drift, 23, 28-31
,, , Dutch, 6, 9
,, , hauling the herring, 52, 225, 238, 247
,, , hauling mackerel, 173
,, , hemp, 28, 29, 31, 243
,, , Looe, 133
,, , Lowestoft, 83
,, , Manx, 189, 190
,, , Mevagissey, 133
,, , pilchard, 174
,, , rigging of, 28, 31, 190
,, , Scottish, 11, 30, 32, 224-226, 234, 242, 247, 255, 260
,, , shooting the herring, 49, 50, 225, 238, 247

NETS, shooting the mackerel, 172
,, , Yarmouth, 28
,, , Yorkshire, 30, 291
NEWLYN, riots, 113
NICKEYS, Manx, 192-196
NOBBY, Manx, 194, 212-218, 285
NOZELS, 28, 31

OKE, Mr. P. J., 118, 139, 140, 143, 175, 180, 209, 212, 249, 268, 270, 279, 285
ORCADIA, Auction price of, 264
OUTFIT, of drifter, 60-62

PAINTING, Cornish luggers, 134, 145, 169, 170
,, , Manx lugger, 214, 215
,, , Scottish luggers, 252-3, 284
,, , Yarmouth lugger, 43
PARADOX, fastest Yarmouth drifter, 64
PARKER, Mr. W. S., 41, 74, 86, 90
PAY, of skipper, 58, 195
PAYNTER, Mr. W., St. Ives boatbuilder, 138, 142, 143, 191
PEAKE, James, 234-7
PEEK, Mr. W., 65, 83, 84
PEZZACK, Mr. W., 106-109, 152, 156-161, 165
PILCHARDS, bulking, 110-111, 136
PILCHARD BOATS, Cornish, 98, 99, 139-141
PILCHARD BOATS, Sprit-rigged, 134
PILCHARD FISHING, 110-111, 135, 174
PINNATE, 161, 166
PLANKTON, 25
POLPERRO GAFFER, 118, 119
PRIMROSE, Letters from Hon. B. F., 223-4, 237-240
PROVISIONS, taken to sea, 181, 199, 206, 225, 278
PUNTS, prices of St. Ives, 145

RABBET, 36, 37
RAFT, 99, 103, 148
RANSACKERS, 29

REEFING, Cornish practice, 104, 128, 150, 162
REGULATION LIGHTS, 50, 57, 149
RENTS PAID WITH HERRINGS, 3
R.N.L.I., introduce prototype, 240-1, 244
ROACH, cutting a, 278
ROOVES, 37, 290
ROUSING, 11, 53, 237, 243
ROUND STERN, introduction of, 41
ROVINGS, 46, 260, 266, 270

SAILS, cutting out, 67, 162, 163, 269-270, 275-8
SAIL MAKING, Cornish, 162, 163, 164
SAIL PLAN, East Cornish lugger, 127-132
,, ,, , Fifie, 260, 269-270, 273
,, ,, , French drifter, 87
,, ,, , Lowestoft drifter, 68, 69
,, ,, , Manx luggers, 186, 187
,, ,, , Manx nickey, 193, 194, 196, 211
,, ,, , Mount's Bay driver, 154, 162-168, 176
,, ,, , Nickey, 211-212
,, ,, , Nobby, 215, 216
,, ,, , Polperro gaffer, 119
,, ,, , Scaffie, 245, 250-1
,, ,, , St. Ives lugger, 146-148
,, ,, , Yarmouth lugger, 46-48
,, ,, , Zulu, 275-8, 283
,, ,, , Zulu skiff, 287
SAW PIT, 41, 251
SCAFFIE, 234-5, 240, 244, 246-7, 252
SCOTTISH HERRING BUSS, 11
,, ,, SEASONS, 245-6, 261
SCOTTISH KINGS, restrict fishing, 4
,, LUGGERS, bright colours of, 252-3, 284
,, BOATS, number registered, 258, 262, 267
SCOWTES, Manx herring, 179, 180, 181
SCUDDING HOLES, 52, 124, 176
,; POLE, 44, 52
SCUM MONEY, 247

381

SCUTTLE, 38, 43
SEINING, 135, 136
SEIZINGS, 28, 31
SHARES, 27, 84, 88, 136, 180, 182, 188
SHETLAND FISHERY, 5, 8, 9, 12, 245, 248, 261
,, FISHING, Manx boats at, 202, 203
SHIPYARDS, Lowestoft, 40, 41, 42
SIGNS OF HERRING SHOALS, 24, 25
SMOKE HOUSES, 94
SHOOTING MACKEREL NETS, 172
SKEGS, 249, 258, 269
SMUGGLING, 15, 16, 100
SPANISH BURTON, reeving of a, 45, 71
SPEED, East Cornish lugger, 133
,, , Scottish luggers, 260-1, 270, 274
SPLASHERS, Yorkshire, 292
SPRINGBACK, 190, 199, 206
STEVENS, Mr. J., 143, 148-150
STRIVE, Plans of, 66-73
STUART, J. & W., 244
SUNDAY OBSERVANCE, 113, 180, 207, 226, 256-7
SUPERSTITIONS, 40, 180, 182, 183, 207, 257
SWILLS, 34, 53, 92
SWING ROPE, 50, 51, 190

TABERNACLE, 38, 43, 67, 102, 249, 271, 280
THREE-MASTED LUGGER, advantage of, 16
TIZZOT, 40, 73
TOP BACKS, 190
TOMMY HUNTER, 59, 65, 81, 132, 171
TRAIL ROPE, 242
TRAVELLER, Iron, 21, 46, 128, 161, 194, 270

TRAVERSE BOARD, 105, 106
TRAWLING, for herring, 32, 33
TRUE VINE, plans of, 271-3

VARGORD, 15, 99, 103, 104
VIKING INFLUENCE, 2, 38, 179, 235, 292
VINCE, Mr. Charles, 241

WANDS, 234, 248, 278, 283
WARP, 5, 28, 31, 247, 260
WASHINGTON, Capt. J., 229-234
WASHINGTON REPORT 1849, 183, 184, 229-240
WASHSTRAKES, 17, 99, 100, 152
WAYNE, Mr. F. T., 273
WICK BOAT, 235, 244-5
WHEELS, horizontal, 275, 281
WICK FISHERY, 224-6, 227-231, 241, 243
WOODHOUSE, Mr. J., 40, 80, 81

YARD BANDS, 248, 276, 282
YARMOUTH CHARTERS, 3
,, HAVEN, 53, 57, 77
,, , herring fishery, 27, 76, 81-86
,, LUGGER, 42-48, 238
YAWLER, 108-9
YORKSHIRE LUGGERS, 17, 18, 19, 289
,, YAWLS, 290-2

ZENITH, first Manx nickey, 191
ZULU, 263, 266, 274-284
,, , construction of a, 274-284
,, , design of first, 253
,, , making sails for a, 275-8
,, SKIFFS, 284-7